Architectures and Protocols for Secure Information Technology Infrastructures

Antonio Ruiz-Martínez
University of Murcia, Spain

Fernando Pereñíguez-García
University of Murcia, Spain

Rafael Marín-López
University of Murcia, Spain

A volume in the Advances in Information Security, Privacy, and Ethics (AISPE) Book Series

Managing Director:	Lindsay Johnston
Editorial Director:	Joel Gamon
Production Manager:	Jennifer Yoder
Publishing Systems Analyst:	Adrienne Freeland
Development Editor:	Monica Speca
Assistant Acquisitions Editor:	Kayla Wolfe
Typesetter:	Travis Gundrum
Cover Design:	Jason Mull

Published in the United States of America by
Information Science Reference (an imprint of IGI Global)
701 E. Chocolate Avenue
Hershey PA 17033
Tel: 717-533-8845
Fax: 717-533-8661
E-mail: cust@igi-global.com
Web site: http://www.igi-global.com

Copyright © 2014 by IGI Global. All rights reserved. No part of this publication may be reproduced, stored or distributed in any form or by any means, electronic or mechanical, including photocopying, without written permission from the publisher. Product or company names used in this set are for identification purposes only. Inclusion of the names of the products or companies does not indicate a claim of ownership by IGI Global of the trademark or registered trademark.

Library of Congress Cataloging-in-Publication Data

Architectures and protocols for secure information technology infrastructures / Antonio Ruiz Martinez, Rafael Marin-Lopez and Fernando Pereniguez Garcia, editors.
  pages cm
 Includes bibliographical references and index.
  ISBN 978-1-4666-4514-1 (hardcover) -- ISBN 978-1-4666-4515-8 (ebook) -- ISBN 978-1-4666-4516-5 (print & perpetual access) 1. Information technology--Security measures. 2. Computer networks--Security measures. I. Martinez, Antonio Ruiz, 1976-, editor of compilation. II. Marin-Lopez, Rafael, 1977-, editor of compilation. III. Garcia, Fernando Pereniguez, 1984-, editor of compilation.
 QA76.9.A25A73 2014
 005.8--dc23
                                                            2013020692

This book is published in the IGI Global book series Advances in Information Security, Privacy, and Ethics (AISPE) (ISSN: 1948-9730; eISSN: 1948-9749)

British Cataloguing in Publication Data
A Cataloguing in Publication record for this book is available from the British Library.

All work contributed to this book is new, previously-unpublished material. The views expressed in this book are those of the authors, but not necessarily of the publisher.

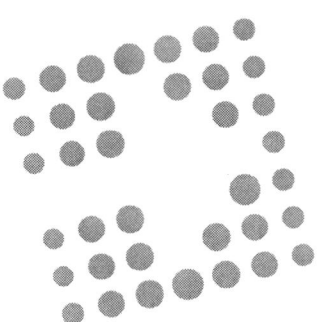

Advances in Information Security, Privacy, and Ethics (AISPE) Book Series

ISSN: 1948-9730
EISSN: 1948-9749

Mission

In the digital age, when everything from municipal power grids to individual mobile telephone locations is all available in electronic form, the implications and protection of this data has never been more important and controversial. As digital technologies become more pervasive in everyday life and the Internet is utilized in ever increasing ways by both private and public entities, the need for more research on securing, regulating, and understanding these areas is growing.

The **Advances in Information Security, Privacy, & Ethics (AISPE) Book Series** is the source for this research, as the series provides only the most cutting-edge research on how information is utilized in the digital age.

Coverage
- Access Control
- Device Fingerprinting
- Global Privacy Concerns
- Information Security Standards
- Network Security Services
- Privacy-Enhancing Technologies
- Risk Management
- Security Information Management
- Technoethics
- Tracking Cookies

IGI Global is currently accepting manuscripts for publication within this series. To submit a proposal for a volume in this series, please contact our Acquisition Editors at Acquisitions@igi-global.com or visit: http://www.igi-global.com/publish/.

The Advances in Information Security, Privacy, and Ethics (AISPE) Book Series (ISSN 1948-9730) is published by IGI Global, 701 E. Chocolate Avenue, Hershey, PA 17033-1240, USA, www.igi-global.com. This series is composed of titles available for purchase individually; each title is edited to be contextually exclusive from any other title within the series. For pricing and ordering information please visit http://www.igi-global.com/book-series/advances-information-security-privacy-ethics/37157. Postmaster: Send all address changes to above address. Copyright © 2014 IGI Global. All rights, including translation in other languages reserved by the publisher. No part of this series may be reproduced or used in any form or by any means – graphics, electronic, or mechanical, including photocopying, recording, taping, or information and retrieval systems – without written permission from the publisher, except for non commercial, educational use, including classroom teaching purposes. The views expressed in this series are those of the authors, but not necessarily of IGI Global.

Titles in this Series
For a list of additional titles in this series, please visit: www.igi-global.com

Theory and Practice of Cryptography Solutions for Secure Information Systems
Atilla Elçi (Aksaray University, Turkey) Josef Pieprzyk (Macquarie University, Australia) Alexander G. Chefranov (Eastern Mediterranean University, North Cyprus) Mehmet A. Orgun (Macquarie University, Australia) Huaxiong Wang (Nanyang Technological University, Singapore) and Rajan Shankaran (Macquarie University, Australia)
Information Science Reference • copyright 2013 • 351pp • H/C (ISBN: 9781466640306) • US $195.00 (our price)

IT Security Governance Innovations Theory and Research
Daniel Mellado (Spanish Tax Agency, Spain) Luis Enrique Sánchez (University of Castilla-La Mancha, Spain) Eduardo Fernández-Medina (University of Castilla – La Mancha, Spain) and Mario G. Piattini (University of Castilla - La Mancha, Spain)
Information Science Reference • copyright 2013 • 390pp • H/C (ISBN: 9781466620834) • US $195.00 (our price)

Threats, Countermeasures, and Advances in Applied Information Security
Manish Gupta (State University of New York at Buffalo, USA) John Walp (M&T Bank Corporation, USA) and Raj Sharman (State University of New York, USA)
Information Science Reference • copyright 2012 • 319pp • H/C (ISBN: 9781466609785) • US $195.00 (our price)

Investigating Cyber Law and Cyber Ethics Issues, Impacts and Practices
Alfreda Dudley (Towson University, USA) James Braman (Towson University, USA) and Giovanni Vincenti (Towson University, USA)
Information Science Reference • copyright 2012 • 342pp • H/C (ISBN: 9781613501320) • US $195.00 (our price)

Information Assurance and Security Ethics in Complex Systems Interdisciplinary Perspectives
Melissa Jane Dark (Purdue University, USA)
Information Science Reference • copyright 2011 • 306pp • H/C (ISBN: 9781616922450) • US $180.00 (our price)

Chaos Synchronization and Cryptography for Secure Communications Applications for Encryption
Santo Banerjee (Politecnico di Torino, Italy)
Information Science Reference • copyright 2011 • 596pp • H/C (ISBN: 9781615207374) • US $180.00 (our price)

Technoethics and the Evolving Knowledge Society Ethical Issues in Technological Design, Research, Development, and Innovation
Rocci Luppicini (University of Ottawa, Canada)
Information Science Reference • copyright 2010 • 322pp • H/C (ISBN: 9781605669526) • US $180.00 (our price)

www.igi-global.com

701 E. Chocolate Ave., Hershey, PA 17033
Order online at www.igi-global.com or call 717-533-8845 x100
To place a standing order for titles released in this series, contact: cust@igi-global.com
Mon-Fri 8:00 am - 5:00 pm (est) or fax 24 hours a day 717-533-8661

Editorial Advisory Board

Lily Chen, National *Institute of Standards and Technology (NIST), USA*
Ashutosh Dutta, *NIKSUN, USA*
Antonio Maña Gómez, *University of Málaga, Spain*
Fernando Bernal Hidalgo, *University of Murcia, Spain*
Georgios Kambourakis, *University of the Aegean, Greece*
Jong-Hyouk Lee, *TELECOM Bretagne, France*
Alejandro Pérez Mendez, *University of Murcia, Spain*
Yoshihiro Ohba, *Toshiba Corporate R&D, Japan*
Sabu M. Thampi, *Indian Institute of Information Technology and Management, India*
Alper Yegin, *Samsung Electronics, Turkey*

List of Reviewers

Tayo Arulogun, *Ladoke Akintola University of Technology, Nigeria*
Vashek Matyáš, *Masaryk University, Czech Republic*
Yuxin Meng, *City University of Hong Kong, China*
Dustin Moody, *National Institute of Standards and Technology (NIST), USA*
Meltem Sonmez Turan, *National Institute of Standards and Technology (NIST), USA*

Table of Contents

Foreword xv

Preface xvi

Acknowledgment xx

Section 1
State-of-the-Art

Chapter 1
Security and Privacy Issues in Cloud Computing 1
    Jaydip Sen, Tata Consultancy Services Ltd., India

Chapter 2
Towards a Certified Electronic Mail System 46
    Gerard Draper-Gil, University of the Balearic Islands, Spain
    Josep-Lluís Ferrer-Gomila, University of the Balearic Islands, Spain
    M. Francisca Hinarejos, University of the Balearic Islands, Spain
    Arne Tauber, Graz University of Technology, Austria

Chapter 3
Mobile IPv6: Mobility Management and Security Aspects 71
    Tayo Arulogun, Ladoke Akintola University of Technology, Nigeria
    Ahmad AlSa'deh, University of Potsdam, Germany
    Christoph Meinel, University of Potsdam, Germany

Section 2
Cryptographic Algorithms and Security Protocols

Chapter 4
A New Encryption Algorithm based on Chaotic Map for Wireless Sensor Network 103
    Ghada Zaibi, University of Sfax, Tunisia
    Fabrice Peyrard, University of Toulouse, France
    Abdennaceur Kachouri, University of Sfax, Tunisia
    Danièle Fournier-Prunaret, University of Toulouse, France
    Mounir Samet, University of Sfax, Tunisia

Chapter 5
A Polling Booth-Based Electronic Voting Scheme 124
    Md. Abdul Based, Norwegian University of Science and Technology, Norway

Chapter 6
Challenges and Solutions for DNS Security in IPv6 160
    Hosnieh Rafiee, Hasso Plattner Institute, Germany
    Martin von Löwis, Hasso Plattner Institute, Germany
    Christoph Meinel, Hasso Plattner Institute, Germany

Section 3
Malware and Intrusion Detection Systems

Chapter 7
Host–Based Intrusion Detection Systems: Architectures, Solutions, and Challenges 184
    Vít Bukač, Masaryk University, Czech Republic
    Vashek Matyáš, Masaryk University, Czech Republic

Chapter 8
Enhancing Intrusion Detection Systems Using Intelligent False Alarm Filter: Selecting the Best Machine Learning Algorithm 214
    Yuxin Meng, City University of Hong Kong, China
    Lam-For Kwok, City University of Hong Kong, China

Chapter 9
Towards Building Efficient Malware Detection Engines Using Hybrid CPU/GPU-Accelerated Approaches 237
    Ciprian Pungila, West University of Timişoara, Romania
    Viorel Negru, West University of Timişoara, Romania

Section 4
Secure Platforms and Frameworks

Chapter 10
A Mobile-Based Attribute Aggregation Architecture for User-Centric Identity Management 266
    Alexandre B. Augusto, University of Porto, Portugal
    Manuel E. Correia, University of Porto, Portugal

Chapter 11
The Austrian Identity Ecosystem: An E-Government Experience 288
    Klaus Stranacher, Graz University of Technology, Austria
    Arne Tauber, Graz University of Technology, Austria
    Thomas Zefferer, Graz University of Technology, Austria
    Bernd Zwattendorfer, Graz University of Technology, Austria

Chapter 12
Developing Secure, Unified, Multi-Device, and Multi-Domain Platforms: A Case Study from the Webinos Project 310
    Andrea Atzeni, Politecnico di Torino, Italy
    John Lyle, University of Oxford, UK
    Shamal Faily, University of Oxford, UK

Chapter 13
Securing XML with Role-Based Access Control: Case Study in Health Care 334
    Alberto De la Rosa Algarín, University of Connecticut, USA
    Steven A. Demurjian, University of Connecticut, USA
    Timoteus B. Ziminski, University of Connecticut, USA
    Yaira K. Rivera Sánchez, University of Connecticut, USA
    Robert Kuykendall, Texas State University, USA

Compilation of References 366

About the Contributors 395

Index 403

Detailed Table of Contents

Foreword xv

Preface xvi

Acknowledgment xx

Section 1
State-of-the-Art

Chapter 1
Security and Privacy Issues in Cloud Computing 1
  Jaydip Sen, Tata Consultancy Services Ltd., India

Cloud computing transforms the way Information Technology (IT) is consumed and managed, promising improved cost efficiencies, accelerated innovation, faster time-to-market, and the ability to scale applications on demand (Leighton, 2009). According to Gartner, while the hype grew exponentially during 2008 and continued since, it is clear that there is a major shift towards the cloud computing model and that the benefits may be substantial (Gartner Hype-Cycle, 2012). However, as the shape of cloud computing is emerging and developing rapidly both conceptually and in reality, the legal/contractual, economic, service quality, interoperability, security, and privacy issues still pose significant challenges. In this chapter, the authors describe various service and deployment models of cloud computing and identify major challenges. In particular, they discuss three critical challenges: regulatory, security, and privacy issues in cloud computing. Some solutions to mitigate these challenges are also proposed along with a brief presentation on the future trends in cloud computing deployment.

Chapter 2
Towards a Certified Electronic Mail System 46
  Gerard Draper-Gil, University of the Balearic Islands, Spain
  Josep-Lluís Ferrer-Gomila, University of the Balearic Islands, Spain
  M. Francisca Hinarejos, University of the Balearic Islands, Spain
  Arne Tauber, Graz University of Technology, Austria

Most of the existent certified electronic mail proposals (found in scientific papers) have been designed without considering their deployment into traditional e-mail infrastructure (e.g., Internet mail system). In fact, there is not any implementation used for commercial purposes of those proposals. On the other hand, in different countries, private companies and public administrations have developed their own applications for certified electronic mail, but these solutions are tailored to their needs and present serious drawbacks. They consider the mail providers as Trusted Third Parties (TTPs), but without being verifiable (if they cheat or fail, users cannot prove it). In most cases, users (typically recipients) cannot choose their mail provider; it is imposed, and even worse, sometimes a message is considered to have been delivered when it has been deposited in the recipient's mailbox (and perhaps, he will not be able to access it). In this chapter, the authors give a broad picture on the current state of certified e-mail, including a brief description of the current e-mail architecture and the need of certified e-mail services, and a definition of the security requirements needed for such a service. Next, they review the scientific and existent proposals. Finally, the authors give some guidelines for developing practical solutions for certified e-mail services that meet all the security requirements.

Chapter 3
Mobile IPv6: Mobility Management and Security Aspects 71
Tayo Arulogun, Ladoke Akintola University of Technology, Nigeria
Ahmad AlSa'deh, University of Potsdam, Germany
Christoph Meinel, University of Potsdam, Germany

Mobile Internet Protocol (MIP) enables a mobile node to be recognized via a single IP address while the node moves between different networks. MIP attains the connectivity to nodes everywhere without user intervention. One general improvement in Mobile IPv6 (MIPv6) compared to MIPv4 is the enhanced security. However, there are areas still susceptible to various kinds of attacks. Security approaches for the MIPv6 are still in progress and there are few unsolved concerns and problems. This chapter focuses on MIPv6 security considerations, potential threats, and possible defense mechanisms. The authors discuss and analyze in detail the MIPv6 mobility management and security approaches with respect to the efficiency and complexity and bring forward some constructive recommendations.

Section 2
Cryptographic Algorithms and Security Protocols

Chapter 4
A New Encryption Algorithm based on Chaotic Map for Wireless Sensor Network 103
Ghada Zaibi, University of Sfax, Tunisia
Fabrice Peyrard, University of Toulouse, France
Abdennaceur Kachouri, University of Sfax, Tunisia
Danièle Fournier-Prunaret, University of Toulouse, France
Mounir Samet, University of Sfax, Tunisia

A new and secure chaos-based block cipher for image encryption in wireless sensor networks is proposed. The security analysis and the performances of the proposed algorithm have been investigated. The statistical analysis includes the histograms and correlation coefficients of adjacent pixels. In the differential analysis, the authors use the Number of Pixels Change Rate (NPCR) and the Unified Changing Average (UACI) measures to demonstrate the security against differential attacks. Key sensitivity analysis and key space analysis show that the proposed cipher is secure and resistant to brute force attack. The authors demonstrate that the performance of the cipher exceeds the studied encryption algorithms as well as AES (Advanced Encryption Standard). An implementation on a real wireless sensor network testbed is realized, and the energy consumption is investigated.

Chapter 5
A Polling Booth-Based Electronic Voting Scheme 124
   Md. Abdul Based, Norwegian University of Science and Technology, Norway

A Polling booth-based Electronic Voting Scheme (PEVS) is presented in this chapter. The scheme allows only eligible voters to cast their ballots inside polling booths, and the ballots cast by the eligible voters are inalterable and non-reusable. The scheme provides vote-privacy and receipt-freeness. The scheme is modeled to fend off forced-abstention attacks, simulation attacks, or randomization attacks. Thus, the scheme is coercion-resistant. The scheme also satisfies voter verifiability, universal verifiability, and eligibility verifiability requirements. The ProVerif tool is used to formally analyze soundness, vote-privacy, receipt-freeness, and coercion-resistance of the scheme. The analysis shows that PEVS satisfies these properties. PEVS is the first electronic voting scheme (polling booth-based) that satisfies all the requirements listed above.

Chapter 6
Challenges and Solutions for DNS Security in IPv6 160
   Hosnieh Rafiee, Hasso Plattner Institute, Germany
   Martin von Löwis, Hasso Plattner Institute, Germany
   Christoph Meinel, Hasso Plattner Institute, Germany

The Domain Name System (DNS) is a necessary component of the Internet that allows hosts on the Internet to communicate with other hosts without needing to know their cryptic IP addresses. When this protocol was first introduced it did not contain robust security features because scalability was an issue. One of the useful features added to DNS was the DNS update mechanism that allowed other hosts to dynamically change DNS entries. This feature, though, exposed new vulnerabilities to DNS servers which necessitated the implementation of new security protocols. Some of the security protocols introduced to address these issues were Transaction SIGnature (TSIG) and DNS Security Extension (DNSSEC). Although, in IPv4, these mechanisms did resolve most of the security issues dealing with authentication between a node and a DNS server, they are not viable in IPv6 networks. This is because the Neighbor Discovery Protocol (NDP) introduced to organize the large IPv6 address space automatically does not support DNS authentication or have an option for secure DNS updating. In this chapter, the authors first explain the common approaches used in IPv4 to address these security issues. Then they explain the differences between the use of these approaches in IPv4 and IPv6, where the focus is on new research with regard to authentication mechanisms between hosts and DNS servers.

Section 3
Malware and Intrusion Detection Systems

Chapter 7
Host–Based Intrusion Detection Systems: Architectures, Solutions, and Challenges...................... 184
   Vít Bukač, Masaryk University, Czech Republic
   Vashek Matyáš, Masaryk University, Czech Republic

In this chapter, the reader explores both the founding ideas and the state-of-the-art research on host-based intrusion detection systems. HIDSs are categorized by their intrusion detection method. Each category is thoroughly investigated, and its limitations and benefits are discussed. Seminal research findings and ideas are presented and supplied with comments. Separate sections are devoted to the protection against tampering and to the HIDS evasion techniques that are employed by attackers. Existing research trends are highlighted, and possible future directions are suggested.

Chapter 8
Enhancing Intrusion Detection Systems Using Intelligent False Alarm Filter: Selecting the Best Machine Learning Algorithm 214
Yuxin Meng, City University of Hong Kong, China
Lam-For Kwok, City University of Hong Kong, China

Intrusion Detection Systems (IDSs) have been widely implemented in various network environments as an essential component for current Information and Communications Technologies (ICT). However, false alarms are a big problem for these systems, in which a large number of IDS alarms, especially false positives, could be generated during their detection. This issue greatly decreases the effectiveness and the efficiency of an IDS and heavily increases the burden on analyzing real alarms. To mitigate this problem, in this chapter, the authors identify and analyze the reasons for causing this problem, present a survey through reviewing some related work in the aspect of false alarm reduction, and introduce a promising solution of constructing an intelligent false alarm filter to refine false alarms for an IDS.

Chapter 9
Towards Building Efficient Malware Detection Engines Using Hybrid CPU/GPU-Accelerated Approaches 237
Ciprian Pungila, West University of Timișoara, Romania
Viorel Negru, West University of Timișoara, Romania

This chapter presents an outline of the challenges involved in constructing efficient malware detection engines using hybrid CPU/GPU-accelerated architectures and discusses how one can overcome such challenges. Starting with a general problem description for malware detection and moving on to the algorithmic background involved for solving it, the authors present a review of the existing approaches for detecting malware and discuss how such approaches may be improved through GPU-accelerated processing. They describe and discuss several hybrid hardware architectures built for detecting malicious software and outline the particular characteristics of each, separately, followed by a debate on their performance and most suitable application in real-world environments. Finally, the authors tackle the problem of performing real-time malware detection and present the most important aspects that need to be taken into account in intrusion detection systems.

Section 4
Secure Platforms and Frameworks

Chapter 10
A Mobile-Based Attribute Aggregation Architecture for User-Centric Identity Management 266
Alexandre B. Augusto, University of Porto, Portugal
Manuel E. Correia, University of Porto, Portugal

The massive growth of the Internet and its services is currently being sustained by the mercantilization of users' identities and private data. Traditional services on the Web require the user to disclose many unnecessary sensitive identity attributes like bankcards, geographic position, or even personal health records in order to provide a service. In essence, the services are presented as free and constitute a means by which the user is mercantilized, often without realizing the real value of its data to the market. In this chapter the auhors describe OFELIA (Open Federated Environment for Leveraging of Identity and Authorization), a digital identity architecture designed from the ground up to be user centric. OFELIA is an identity/authorization versatile infrastructure that does not depend upon the massive aggregation of users' identity attributes to offer a highly versatile set of identity services but relies instead on having those attributes distributed among and protected by several otherwise unrelated Attribute Authorities. Only the end user, with his smartphone, knows how to aggregate these scattered Attribute Authorities' identity attributes back into some useful identifiable and authenticated entity identity that can then be used by Internet services in a secure and interoperable way.

Chapter 11
The Austrian Identity Ecosystem: An E-Government Experience 288
    Klaus Stranacher, Graz University of Technology, Austria
    Arne Tauber, Graz University of Technology, Austria
    Thomas Zefferer, Graz University of Technology, Austria
    Bernd Zwattendorfer, Graz University of Technology, Austria

Architectures and protocols for secure information technology are crucial to satisfy security requirements of current e-government solutions. Identity plays a central role in most e-government solutions, as users typically need to be reliably identified and authenticated. User identification and authentication approaches usually rely on complex cryptographic methods and sophisticated technical solutions. Additionally, these solutions need to be backed by appropriate organizational and legal frameworks that assure the legal validity of provided identification and authentication approaches. In this chapter, the authors introduce the Austrian identity ecosystem that represents one of the main pillars of the Austrian e-government infrastructure. They discuss underlying concepts and main building blocks of this comprehensive ecosystem and show how architectures and protocols for secure information technology are employed to assure the security of user identification and authentication processes. By discussing concrete use cases, the authors illustrate the applicability of the Austrian identity ecosystem for both Austrian and foreign citizens.

Chapter 12
Developing Secure, Unified, Multi-Device, and Multi-Domain Platforms: A Case Study from the Webinos Project 310
    Andrea Atzeni, Politecnico di Torino, Italy
    John Lyle, University of Oxford, UK
    Shamal Faily, University of Oxford, UK

The need for integrated cross-platform systems is growing. Such systems can enrich the user experience, but also lead to greater security and privacy concerns than the sum of their existing components. To provide practical insights and suggest viable solutions for the development, implementation, and deployment of complex cross-domain systems, in this chapter, the authors analyse and critically discuss the security-relevant decisions made developing the Webinos security framework. Webinos is an EU-funded FP7 project, which aims to become a universal Web application platform for enabling development and usage of cross domain applications. Presently, Webinos runs on a number of different devices (e.g. mobile, tables, PC, in-car systems, etc.) and different Operating Systems (e.g. various Linux distributions, different Windows and MacOSx versions, Android 4.x, iOS). Thus, Webinos is a representative example of cross-platform framework, and even if yet at beta level, is presently one of the most mature, as a prototype has been publicly available since February 2012. Distilling the lessons learned in the development of the Webinos public specification and prototype, the authors describe how potential threats and risks are identified and mitigated, and how techniques from user-centred design are used to inform the usability of security decisions made while developing the alpha and beta versions of the platform.

Chapter 13
Securing XML with Role-Based Access Control: Case Study in Health Care 334
    Alberto De la Rosa Algarín, University of Connecticut, USA
    Steven A. Demurjian, University of Connecticut, USA
    Timoteus B. Ziminski, University of Connecticut, USA
    Yaira K. Rivera Sánchez, University of Connecticut, USA
    Robert Kuykendall, Texas State University, USA

Today's applications are often constructed by bringing together functionality from multiple systems that utilize varied technologies (e.g. application programming interfaces, Web services, cloud computing, data mining) and alternative standards (e.g. XML, RDF, OWL, JSON, etc.) for communication. Most such applications achieve interoperability via the eXtensible Markup Language (XML), the de facto document standard for information exchange in domains such as library repositories, collaborative software development, health informatics, etc. The use of a common data format facilitates exchange and interoperability across heterogeneous systems, but challenges in the aspect of security arise (e.g. sharing policies, ownership, permissions, etc.). In such situations, one key security challenge is to integrate the local security (existing systems) into a global solution for the application being constructed and deployed. In this chapter, the authors present a Role-Based Access Control (RBAC) security framework for XML, which utilizes extensions to the Unified Modeling Language (UML) to generate eXtensible Access Control Markup Language (XACML) policies that target XML schemas and instances for any application, and provides both the separation and reconciliation of local and global security policies across systems. To demonstrate the framework, they provide a case study in health care, using the XML standards Health Level Seven's (HL7) Clinical Document Architecture (CDA) and the Continuity of Care Record (CCR). These standards are utilized for the transportation of private and identifiable information between stakeholders (e.g. a hospital with an electronic health record, a clinic's electronic health record, a pharmacy system, etc.), requiring not only a high level of security but also compliance to legal entities. For this reason, it is not only necessary to secure private information, but for its application to be flexible enough so that updating security policies that affect millions of documents does not incur a large monetary or computational cost; such privacy could similarly involve large banks and credit card companies that have similar information to protect to deter identity theft. The authors demonstrate the security framework with two in-house developed applications: a mobile medication management application and a medication reconciliation application. They also detail future trends that present even more challenges in providing security at global and local levels for platforms such as Microsoft HealthVault, Harvard SMART, Open mHealth, and open electronic health record systems. These platforms utilize XML, equivalent information exchange document standards (e.g., JSON), or semantically augmented structures (e.g., RDF and OWL). Even though the primary use of these platforms is in healthcare, they present a clear picture of how diverse the information exchange process can be. As a result, they represent challenges that are domain independent, thus becoming concrete examples of future trends and issues that require a robust approach towards security.

Compilation of References 366

About the Contributors 395

Index 403

Foreword

The content of this book presents the state-of-the-art and the latest advances in some of the most important topics in the field of computer and network security. The book is focused on solutions for architectures and protocols for secure information technology infrastructures. Thus, it covers the main aspects that a researcher or an information technology consultant has to deal with when a secure information technology infrastructure has to be designed or developed. The collection of chapters included in this book is interesting not only as support material for any network security course but also as reference material for engineers and professionals. The topics covered in this book include analysis of the state-of-the art of security and privacy in cloud computing, certified electronic mail systems, and security issues in Mobile IPv6 and DNS security in IPv6 as well as new cryptographic algorithms and security protocols for encryption in wireless sensor networks and secure voting. The book also presents new solutions for dealing with malware and intrusions, new architectures for identity management and securing XML, and the results of projects and real deployed secure information technology infrastructures such as the Webinos project and the Austrian identity ecosystem. For this reason, this book is fundamental reading for those who are interested in exploring recent advances in the field of network security.

Stefanos Gritzalis
University of the Aegean, Greece

Stefanos Gritzalis *is the Deputy Head of the Dept. of Information and Communication Systems Engineering, University of the Aegean, Greece, and the Director of the Laboratory of Information and Communication Systems Security (Info-Sec-Lab). He holds a BSc in Physics, an MSc in Electronic Automation, and a PhD in Information and Communications Security from the Dept. of Informatics and Telecommunications, University of Athens, Greece. He has been involved in several national and EU funded R&D projects. His published scientific work includes 30 books or book chapters, 100 journals, and 130 international refereed conference and workshop papers. The focus of these publications is on Information and Communications Security and Privacy. His most highly cited papers have more than 1,700 citations (h-index=21). He has acted as Guest Editor in 30 journal special issues and has been involved in more than 30 international conferences and workshops as General Chair or Program Committee Chair. He has served on more than 320 Program Committees of international conferences and workshops. He is an Editor-in-Chief or Editor or Editorial Board member for 20 journals and a Reviewer for more than 50 journals. He has supervised 10 PhD dissertations. He was an elected Member of the Board (Secretary General, Treasurer) of the Greek Computer Society. His professional experience includes senior consulting and researcher positions in a number of private and public institutions. He is a Member of the Association for Computing Machinery (ACM), the Association for Information Systems (AIS), the Institute of Electrical and Electronics Engineers (IEEE), and the IEEE Communications Society "Communications and Information Security Technical Committee."*

Preface

INTRODUCTION

Information and Communications Technologies (ICT) have experienced impressive evolutions. As a consequence, they have enabled a number of technologies (laptops, smartphones, tablets, TV, etc.) with important computational power capabilities compared with devices of some years ago. These advances have made the development of applications that facilitate an important number of activities through the Internet such as communication, collaboration, learning activities, purchases, establishment of social relationships, gaming, voting, banking operations, etc., possible. Although all these possibilities are advantageous to the user, they also present a number of security risks. These risks are derived from the need to establish communications between remote entities that cannot mutually verify in a physical manner who they are. For example, some relevant security risks are concerned with verifying whether the information has not changed during its exchange or being eavesdropped upon, whether a malware is manipulating the information we are working with and that is stored in our personal computer or mobile device, whether our device is being used to attack other computers, whether the information is properly stored and secured on the server we use, etc. These potential security risks have increased since we are moving to distribute computation models where communication is essential between applications that tend to collaborate in order to achieve a common goal. To prevent and mitigate the different problems that can occur, it is necessary to provide mechanisms to guarantee important security goals such as integrity, confidentiality, identification, authentication, authorization, non-repudiation, and privacy. Thus, network security issues are one of the cornerstones of any network application, and as a consequence, research activities from both academic and industry forums need to pay attention to them...

Achieving security in any kind of networked system, application, or service requires the provision of different security mechanisms at the different levels composing a computer system: operating system, applications, storage, etc. Thus, it is required to design secure architectures protecting network communications to prevent any fraudulent access to the information exchanged (e.g. message alteration, denial of service, etc.). Additionally, the provision of means for guaranteeing the identity of the parties exchanging information is a must. In this way, it is possible to authenticate the participant entities and to control which resources they are granted access to. In general, the definition of security mechanisms involves the use of infrastructures or services provided by trusted third parties. Thus, the core elements that must be taken into account to secure any networked or distributed system, application, or service are its architecture and the protocols used to exchange the information. Currently, many cases exist where the definition of secure architectures and protocols is an issue of paramount importance. Next, we will introduce those covered by this book.

Internet Protocol version 6 (IPv6) is the most recent version of the IP protocol that is going to replace to the current version 4 (IPv4). This new version, apart from providing a larger address space, provides new or advanced features that the previous version does not cover, such as autoconfiguration, simplified processing by routers, efficient mobility, security for the network layer, and some privacy extensions. The deployment of IPv6 is being accelerated as well as its research in issues related to security, such as mobility or Domain Name System (DNS).

Another fundamental service to be secured is e-mail. Apart from providing basic features, such as confidentiality, integrity, and authentication, other more advanced features, like certified e-mail, are required. In snail (postal) mail, sometimes the sender wants proof of submission, delivery, and reception that the sender might use to show a third party in the event a dispute takes place. Certified e-mail aims to obtain the same guarantees. This is fundamental for many transactions and electronic government scenarios.

In the same way that mail has its equivalent in the electronic world, voting has its electronic version, that is, electronic voting. In this case, electronic voting is a challenging scenario for providing the same properties of traditional voting systems: only eligible voters can vote, vote-privacy, and verifiability.

Other important issues in network security from its first stages and that still constitute essential research topics are identification and access control. We must identify ourselves to prove our identity to remote systems or users. Once we have been identified, we will be able to perform a set of actions or to access a set of resources depending on a number of attributes or the role we play.

There has been an increase in the attacks that users and companies are receiving in their computers and information systems through malware or intrusions. Thus, it is required to enhance our information technology infrastructures to include systems able to detect (and in some cases react to) malware and intrusions. This problem is particularly important in mobile devices since they have more constrained resources than computers, and therefore, the security measures offered by these kinds of devices are limited, while they store an important amount of sensitive data. Therefore, it is important to define security platforms allowing the development of applications that provide the same level of security both in PC and mobile devices.

Other hot topics in security research are wireless sensor networks and cloud computing. In the former, an important research topic relies on the provision of efficient secure schemes that consume the least computational resources possible and prevent denial of service. In the later topic, the issues arise from the fact that the data is not hosted in user or organization dependencies. Thus, there are different deployment models posing different challenges related to regulation, security, and privacy.

With respect to scenarios of application where security protocols, architectures, and frameworks need to be applied, we can mention electronic government and electronic healthcare solutions. These services are being developed to provide both user and government with access to data and communication through the Internet.

The goal of this volume, *Architectures and Protocols for Secure Information Technology Infrastructures*, is to cover the topics mentioned and to provide analysis of these problems and offer security solutions for protocols, architectures, and frameworks used in Information Technology Infrastructures. Thus, this book provides an analysis of state-of-the-art indicating challenges and trends, as well as proposals of new secure algorithms and protocols. Moreover, this book presents the definition of new architectures aimed at protecting data exchanged between remote entities connected through the Internet as well as the information technology architectures needed for the provision of different kinds of secure services or applications.

BOOK ORGANIZATION

This book is organized in four sections. Section 1 provides a set of chapters analyzing the state-of-the-art for security in cloud computing, certified electronic mail, and Mobile IPv6. Section 2 presents new cryptographic algorithms and security protocols in the field of wireless sensor networks, voting, and DNS in IPv6. Section 3 introduces new systems to detect both malware and intrusions. Finally, Section 4 presents different secure platforms and frameworks for the management of identity, the definition of cross-platform solutions, and the provision of security to information technology infrastructures in different scenarios.

Section 1: State-of-the-Art

Chapter 1, "Security and Privacy Issues in Cloud Computing," provides a wide overview of different security key aspects in cloud computing. This chapter provides a detailed reference including challenges and solutions for security in this field.

Chapter 2, "Towards a Certified Electronic Mail System," analyses the current state of certified electronic mail solutions and the security requirements that they should provide. Then, it analyzes the different solutions proposed and gives some guidelines to the development of this kind of solution.

Chapter 3, "Mobile IPv6: Mobility Management and Security Aspects," analyzes the main aspects of security in the mobility protocol in IPv6.

Section 2: Cryptographic Algorithms and Security Protocols

Chapter 4, "A New Encryption Algorithm based on Chaotic Map for Wireless Sensor Network," proposes a secure chaos-based block cipher algorithm for image encryption specially conceived for wireless sensor networks. The chapter develops a complete analysis to demonstrate the security of the algorithm, the performance compared to existing algorithms, and low energy consumption.

Chapter 5, "A Polling Booth-Based Electronic Voting Scheme," presents a new voting scheme based on polling booths that improves previous work, supporting new security requirements that are verified with the ProVerif tool.

Chapter 6, "Challenges and Solutions for DNS Security in IPv6," examines the security on the service Domain Name System (DNS) in IPv6 networks. It analyzes new alternatives to improve the security of this service.

Section 3: Malware and Intrusion Detection Systems

Chapter 7, "Host-Based Intrusion Detection Systems: Architectures, Solutions, and Challenges," explores the basic ideas and state-of-the-art in host-based intrusion detection systems. The intrusion detection methods are analyzed in terms of limitations and benefits.

Chapter 8, "Enhancing Intrusion Detection Systems Using Intelligent False Alarm Filer: Selecting the Best Machine Learning Algorithm," develops a solution for filtering false alarms in intrusion detection systems. The effectiveness of the proposal is demonstrated through a use case study.

Chapter 9, "Towards Building Efficient Malware Detection Engines Using Hybrid CPU/GPU-Accelerated Approaches," outlines the challenges involved in the construction of efficient malware detection engines using hybrid CPU/GPU-accelerated architectures and presents ways to overcome these challenges.

Section 4: Secure Platforms and Frameworks

Chapter 10, "A Mobile-Based Attribute Aggregation Architecture for User-Centric Identity Management," deals with user privacy and the management of the user's identity. It details an architecture that distributes users' attributes into different unrelated Attribute Authorities.

Chapter 11, "The Austrian Identity Ecosystem: An E-Government Experience," describes a real deployment of identity management in the context of the e-government initiative promoted in Austria. It explains design decisions taken at technical, legal, and organizational levels.

Chapter 12, "Developing Secure, Unified, Multi-Device, and Multi-Domain Platforms: A Case Study from the Webinos Project," analyzes the results and the lessons learned in the Webinos project for the provision of a universal Web application platform for enabling the development and usage of cross-domain applications.

Chapter 13, "Securing XML with Role-Based Access Control: Case Study in Health Care," presents a Role-Based Access Control (RBAC) security framework for XML. This framework is evaluated by means of its application to a case study in healthcare.

Antonio Ruiz Martínez
University of Murcia, Spain

Fernando Pereñíguez García
University of Murcia, Spain

Rafael Marín-López
University of Murcia, Spain

Acknowledgment

The preparation of this book is the result of a great effort by academicians and practitioners in the area of architectures and protocols for secure information technology. The chapters in this book were written by 35 security experts coming from universities, institutes, and company research labs spanning 15 countries. We would like to thank all the contributing authors of this book for proposing new solutions and helping us to better understand how we can develop and improve secure information architectures and protocols. We greatly appreciate the effort made by the authors.

The assistance provided by the Editorial Advisory Board and the reviewers during the chapter review process has also been essential. We would like to express our most sincere gratitude to all of them. Also special thanks to IGI Global for the reception they bestowed to our proposal, the clear guidelines they offered us, and the help and support throughout the whole process. In particular, we are very grateful to the IGI Global staff including Kayla Wolfe, Jan Travers, Monica Speca, Christine Smith, and Austin DeMarco for their professional assistance and encouragement.

We also take this opportunity to record our sincere thanks to Professor Stefanos Gritzalis, one of the most well-respected researchers in the security area, for his thorough review of this book and his contribution of the book's foreword.

Finally, we would like to thank all the readers around the world who have decided to access the contents of this book. We hope that each chapter will contribute to the understanding of the different topics covered in the book, help in the development of new secure architectures and protocols, and, in the end, constitute valuable material for the book's use in teaching, practice, and research.

Antonio Ruiz Martínez
University of Murcia, Spain

Fernando Pereñíguez García
University of Murcia, Spain

Rafael Marín-López
University of Murcia, Spain

Section 1
State-of-the-Art

Chapter 1
Security and Privacy Issues in Cloud Computing

Jaydip Sen
Tata Consultancy Services Ltd., India

ABSTRACT

Cloud computing transforms the way Information Technology (IT) is consumed and managed, promising improved cost efficiencies, accelerated innovation, faster time-to-market, and the ability to scale applications on demand (Leighton, 2009). According to Gartner, while the hype grew exponentially during 2008 and continued since, it is clear that there is a major shift towards the cloud computing model and that the benefits may be substantial (Gartner Hype-Cycle, 2012). However, as the shape of cloud computing is emerging and developing rapidly both conceptually and in reality, the legal/contractual, economic, service quality, interoperability, security, and privacy issues still pose significant challenges. In this chapter, the authors describe various service and deployment models of cloud computing and identify major challenges. In particular, they discuss three critical challenges: regulatory, security, and privacy issues in cloud computing. Some solutions to mitigate these challenges are also proposed along with a brief presentation on the future trends in cloud computing deployment.

INTRODUCTION

As per the definition provided by the National Institute for Standards and Technology (NIST) (Badger et al., 2011), "*cloud computing* is a model for enabling convenient, on-demand network access to a shared pool of configurable computing resources (e.g., networks, servers, storage, applications, and services) that can be rapidly provisioned and released with minimal management effort or service provider interaction." It represents a paradigm shift in information technology many of us are likely to see in our lifetime. While the customers are excited by the opportunities to reduce the capital costs, and the chance to divest themselves of infrastructure management and

DOI: 10.4018/978-1-4666-4514-1.ch001

focus on core competencies, and above all the agility offered by the on-demand provisioning of computing, there are issues and challenges which need to be addressed before a ubiquitous adoption may happen.

Cloud computing refers to both the applications delivered as services over the Internet and the hardware and systems software in the datacenters that provide those services. There are four basic cloud delivery models, as outlined by NIST (Badger et al., 2011), based on who provides the cloud services. The agencies may employ one model or a combination of different models for efficient and optimized delivery of applications and business services. These four delivery models are: 1) *Private cloud* in which cloud services are provided solely for an organization and are managed by the organization or a third party. These services may exist off-site. (2) *Public cloud* in which cloud services are available to the public and owned by an organization selling the cloud services, for example, Amazon cloud service. (3) *Community cloud* in which cloud services are shared by several organizations for supporting a specific community that has shared concerns (e.g., mission, security requirements, policy, and compliance considerations). These services may be managed by the organizations or a third party and may exist off-site. A special case of community cloud is the Government or G-Cloud. This type of cloud computing is provided by one or more agencies (service provider role), for use by all, or most, government agencies (user role). (4) *Hybrid cloud* which is a composition of different cloud computing infrastructure (public, private or community). An example for hybrid cloud is the data stored in private cloud of a travel agency that is manipulated by a program running in the public cloud.

From the perspective of service delivery, NIST has identified three basic types of cloud service offerings. These models are: (1) *Software as a Service* (SaaS) which offers renting application functionality from a service provider rather than buying, installing and running software by the user. (2) *Platform as a Service* (PaaS) which provides a platform in the cloud, upon which applications can be developed and executed. (3) *Infrastructure as a Service* (IaaS) in which the vendors offer computing power and storage space on demand.

From a hardware point of view, three aspects are new in the paradigm of cloud computing (Armbrust et al., 2009). These aspects of cloud computing are: (1) The illusion of infinite computing resources available on demand, thereby eliminating the need for cloud computing users to plan far ahead for provisioning. (2) The elimination of an up-front commitment by cloud users, thereby allowing companies to start small and increase hardware resources only when there is an increase in their needs. (3) The ability to pay for use of computing resources on a short-term basis as needed and release them when the resources are not needed, thereby rewarding conservation by *letting machines and storage go when they are no longer useful*. In a nutshell, cloud computing has enabled operations of large-scale data centers which has led to significant decrease in operational costs of those data centers. On the consumer side, there are some obvious benefits provided by cloud computing. A painful reality of running IT services is the fact that in most of the times, peak demand is significantly higher than the average demand. The resultant massive over-provisioning that the companies usually do is extremely capital-intensive and wasteful. Cloud computing has allowed and will allow even more seamless scaling of resources as the demand changes.

In spite of the several advantages that cloud computing brings along with it, there are several concerns and issues which need to be solved before ubiquitous adoption of this computing paradigm happens. First, in cloud computing, the user may not have the kind of control over his/her data or the performance of his/her applications that he/she may need, or the ability to audit or change the processes and policies under which he/she must work. Different parts of an application might be in different place in the cloud that can have an adverse impact on the performance of the application. Complying with regulations may be difficult especially when talking about cross-border issues – it should also be noted that regulations still need to be developed to take all aspects of cloud computing into account. It is quite natural that monitoring and maintenance is not as simple a task as compared to what it is for PCs sitting in the Intranet. Second, the cloud customers may risk losing data by having them locked into proprietary formats and may lose control over their data since the tools for monitoring who is using them or who can view them are not always provided to the customers. Data loss is, therefore, a potentially real risk in some specific deployments. Third, it may not be easy to tailor *Service-Level Agreements* (SLAs) to the specific needs of a business. Compensation for downtime may be inadequate and SLAs are unlikely to cover the concomitant damages. It is sensible to balance the cost of guaranteeing internal uptime against the advantages of opting for the cloud. Fourth, leveraging cost advantages may not always be possible always. From the perspective of the organizations, having little or no capital investment may actually have tax disadvantages. Finally, the standards are immature and insufficient for handling the rapidly changing and evolving technologies of cloud computing. Therefore, one cannot just move applications to the cloud and expect them to run efficiently. Finally, there are latency and performance issues since the Internet connections and the network links may add to latency or may put constraint on the available bandwidth.

ARCHITECTURE OF CLOUD COMPUTING

In this section, we present a top-level architecture of cloud computing that depicts various cloud service delivery models. Cloud computing enhances collaboration, agility, scale, availability and provides the potential for cost reduction through optimized and efficient computing. More specifically, cloud describes the use of a collection of distributed services, applications, information and infrastructure comprised of pools of compute, network, information and storage resources (CSA Security Guidance, 2009). These components can be rapidly orchestrated, provisioned, implemented, and decommissioned using an on-demand utility-like model of allocation and consumption. Cloud services are most often, but not always, utilized in conjunction with an enabled by virtualization technologies to provide dynamic integration, provisioning, orchestration, mobility and scale.

While the very definition of cloud suggests the decoupling of resources from the physical affinity to and location of the infrastructure that delivers them, many descriptions of cloud go to one extreme or another by either exaggerating or artificially limiting the many attributes of cloud. This is often purposely done in an attempt to inflate or marginalize its scope. Some examples include the suggestions that for a service to be cloud-based, that the Internet must be used as a transport, a Web browser must be used as an access modality or that the resources are always shared in a multi-tenant environment outside of the "perimeter." What is missing in these definitions is context.

From an architectural perspective, given this abstracted evolution of technology, there is much confusion surrounding how cloud is both similar and different from existing models and how these similarities and differences might impact the organizational, operational, and technological approaches to cloud adoption as it relates to traditional network and information security practices. There are those who say cloud is a novel sea-change and technical revolution while other suggests it is a natural evolution and coalescence of technology, economy and culture. The real truth is somewhere in between.

There are many models available today which attempt to address cloud from the perspective of academicians, architects, engineers, developers, managers and even consumers. The architecture that we will focus on this chapter is specifically tailored to the unique perspectives of IT network deployment and service delivery.

Cloud services are based upon five principal characteristics that demonstrate their relation to, and differences from, traditional computing approaches (CSA Security Guidance, 2009). These characteristics are: (1) abstraction of infrastructure, (2) resource democratization, (3) service oriented architecture, (4) elasticity/dynamism, (5) utility model of consumption and allocation.

Abstraction of Infrastructure: The computation, network, and storage infrastructure resources are abstracted from the application and information resources as a function of service delivery. Where and by what physical resource that data is processed, transmitted, and stored on becomes largely opaque from the perspective of an application or services' ability to deliver it. Infrastructure resources are generally pooled in order to deliver service regardless of the tenancy model employed – shared or dedicated. This abstraction is generally provided by means of high levels of virtualization at the chipset and operating system levels or enabled at the higher levels by heavily customized file systems, operating systems or communication protocols.

Resource Democratization: The abstraction of infrastructure yields the notion of resource democratization—whether infrastructure, applications, or information—and provides the capability for pooled resources to be made available and accessible to anyone or anything authorized to utilize them using standardized methods for doing so.

Service-Oriented Architecture: As the abstraction of infrastructure from application and information yields well-defined and loosely-coupled resource democratization, the notion of utilizing these components in whole or part, alone or with integration, provides a services oriented architecture where resources may be accessed and utilized in a standard way. In this model, the focus is on the delivery of service and not the management of infrastructure.

Elasticity/Dynamism: The on-demand model of cloud provisioning coupled with high levels of automation, virtualization, and ubiquitous, reliable and high-speed connectivity provides for the capability to rapidly expand or contract resource allocation to service definition and requirements using a self-service model that scales to as-needed capacity. Since resources are pooled, better utilization and service levels can be achieved.

Utility Model of Consumption and Allocation: The abstracted, democratized, service-oriented, and elastic nature of cloud combined with tight automation, orchestration, provisioning and self-service then allows for dynamic allocation of resources based on any number of governing input parameters. Given the visibility at an atomic level, the consumption of resources can then be used to provide a metered utility-cost and usage model. This facilitates greater cost efficacies and scale as well as manageable and predictive costs.

Cloud Service Delivery Models

Three archetypal models and the derivative combinations thereof generally describe cloud service delivery. The three individual models are often referred to as the "SPI MODEL," where "SPI" refers to Software, Platform, and Infrastructure (as a service) respectively (CSA Security Guidance, 2009).

Software as a Service (SaaS): The capability provided to the consumer is to use the provider's applications running on a cloud infrastructure and accessible from various client devices through a thin client interface such as Web browser. In other words, in this model, a complete application is offered to the customer as a service on demand. A single instance of the service runs on the cloud and multiple end users are services. On the customers' side, there is no need for upfront investment in servers or software licenses, while for the provider, the costs are lowered, since only a single application needs to be hosted and maintained. In summary, in this model, the customers do not manage or control the underlying cloud infrastructure, network, servers, operating systems, storage, or even individual application capabilities, with the possible exception of limited user-specific application configuration settings. Currently, SaaS is offered by companies such as Google, Salesforce, Microsoft, Zoho, etc.

Platform as a Service (PaaS): In this model, a layer of software or development environment is encapsulated and offered as a service, upon which other higher levels of service are built. The customer has the freedom to build his own applications, which run on the provider's infrastructure. Hence, a capability is provided to the customer to deploy onto the cloud infrastructure customer-created applications using programming languages and tools supported by the provider (e.g., Java, Python, .Net etc.). Although the customer does not manage or control the underlying cloud infrastructure, network, servers, operating systems, or storage, but he/she has the control over the deployed applications and possibly over the application hosting environment configurations. To meet manageability and scalability requirements of the applications, PaaS providers offer a predefined combination of operating systems and application servers, such as LAMP (Linux, Apache, MySql and PHP) platform, restricted J2EE, Ruby etc. Some examples of PaaS are: Google's App Engine, Force.com, etc.

Infrastructure as a Service (IaaS): This model provides basic storage and computing capabilities as standardized services over the network. Servers, storage systems, networking equipment, data center space etc. are pooled and made available to handle workloads. The capability provided to the customer is to rent processing, storage, networks, and other fundamental computing resources where the customer is able to deploy and run arbitrary software, which can include operating systems and applications. The customer does not manage or control the underlying cloud infrastructure but has the control over operating systems, storage, deployed applications, and possibly select networking components (e.g., firewalls, load balancers, etc.). Some examples of IaaS are: Amazon, GoGrid, 3 Tera, etc.

Understanding the relationship and dependencies between these models is critical. IaaS is the foundation of all cloud services with PaaS building upon IaaS, and SaaS—in turn—building upon PaaS. An architecture of cloud layer model is depicted in Figure 1.

Cloud Service Deployment and Consumption Models

Regardless of the delivery model utilized (SaaS, PaaS, IaaS) there are four primary ways in which cloud services are deployed (CSA Security Guidance, 2009). Cloud integrators can play a vital role in determining the right cloud path for a specific organization.

Public Cloud: Public clouds are provided by a designated service provider and may offer either a single-tenant (dedicated) or multi-tenant (shared) operating environment with all the benefits and functionality of elasticity and the accountability/utility model of cloud. The physical infrastructure is generally owned by and managed by the designated service provider and located within the provider's data centers (off-premises). All customers share the same infrastructure pool with limited configuration, security protections, and availability variances. One of the advantages of a public cloud is that they may be larger than an enterprise cloud, and hence they provide the ability to scale seamlessly on demand.

Private Cloud: Private clouds are provided by an organization or their designated services and offer a single-tenant (dedicated) operating environment with all the benefits and functionality of elasticity and accountability/utility model of cloud. The private clouds aim to address concerns

Figure 1. An architecture of the layer model of cloud computing

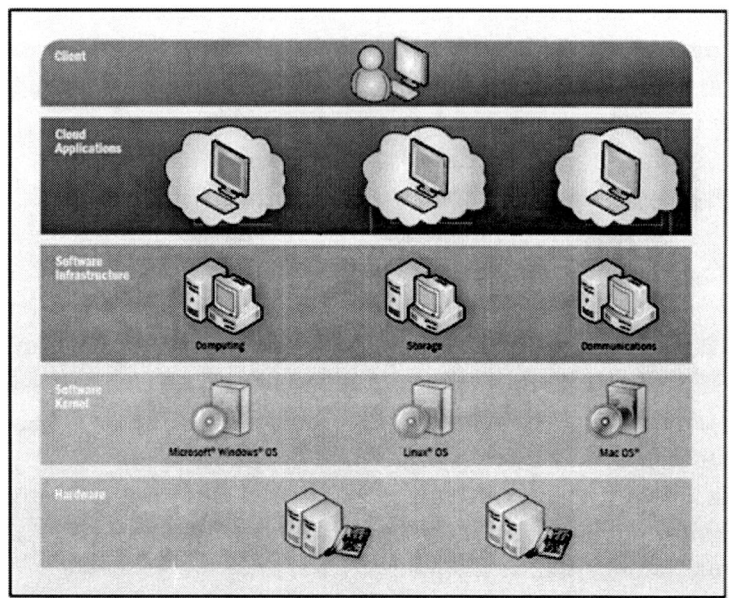

on data security and offer greater control, which is typically lacking in a public cloud. There are two variants of private clouds: (1) on-premise private clouds and (2) externally hosted private clouds. The on-premise private clouds, also known as internal clouds are hosted within one's own data center. This model provides a more standardized process and protection, but is limited in aspects of size and scalability. IT departments would also need to incur the capital and operational costs for the physical resources. This is best suited for applications, which require complete control and configurability of the infrastructure and security. As the name implies, the externally hosted private clouds are hosted externally with a cloud provider.

Hybrid Cloud: Hybrid clouds are a combination of public and private cloud offerings that allow for transitive information exchange and possibly application compatibility and portability across disparate cloud service offerings and providers utilizing standard or proprietary methodologies regardless of ownership or location. With a hybrid cloud, service providers can utilize third party cloud providers in a full or partial manner, thereby increasing the flexibility of computing. The hybrid cloud model is capable of providing on-demand, externally provisioned scale. The ability to augment a private cloud with the resources of a public cloud can be used to manage any unexpected surges in workload.

Managed Cloud: Managed clouds are provided by a designated service provider and may offer either a single-tenant (dedicated) or multi-tenant (shared) operating environment with all the benefits and functionality of elasticity and the accountability/utility model of cloud. The physical infrastructure is owned by and/or physically located in the organizations' data centers with an extension of management and security control planes controlled by the designated service provider.

The notion of public, private, managed and hybrid when describing cloud services really denotes the attribution of management and the availability of service to specific consumers of the services. Table 1 summarizes various features of the four cloud deployment models.

Table 1. Summary of the various features of cloud deployment models

Deployment Model	Managed By	Infrastructure Owned By	Infrastructure Located At	Accessible and Consumed By
Public	Third party provider	Third party provider	Off-premise	Untrusted
Private	Organization	Organization	On-premise Off-premise	Trusted
	Third party provider	Third party provider	On-premise Off-premise	
Managed	Third party provider	Third party provider	On-premise	Trusted or Untrusted
Hybrid	Both organization and third party provider	Both organization and third party provider	Both on-premise and off-premise	Trusted or Untrusted

When assessing the impact a particular cloud service may have on one's security posture and overall security architecture, it is necessary to classify the assets/resource/service within the context of not only its location but also its criticality and business impact as it relates to management and security. This means that an appropriate level of risk assessment is performed prior to entrusting it to the vagaries of the cloud (CSA Security Guidance, 2009). In addition, it is important to understand various tradeoffs between the various cloud service models:

- Generally, SaaS provides a large amount of integrated features built directly into the offering with the least amount of extensibility and in general a high level of security (or at least a responsibility for security on the part of the service provider).
- PaaS offers less integrated features since it is designed to enable developers to build their own applications on top of the platform, and it is, therefore, more extensible than SaaS by nature. However, this extensibility features trade-offs on security features and capabilities.
- IaaS provides few, if any, application-like features, and provides for enormous extensibility but generally less security capabilities and functionalities beyond protecting the infrastructure itself, since it expects operating systems, applications and contents to be managed and secured by the customers.

In summary, from security perspective, in the three service models of cloud computing, the lower down the stack the cloud service provider stops, the more security capabilities and management the customer is responsible for implementing and managing themselves.

CLOUD COMPUTING SECURITY AND PRIVACY ISSUES

This section addresses the core theme of this chapter, i.e., the security and privacy-related challenges in cloud computing. There are numerous security issues for cloud computing as it encompasses many technologies including networks, databases, operating systems, virtualization, resource scheduling, transaction management, load balancing, concurrency control and memory management. Therefore, security issues for many of these systems and technologies are applicable to cloud computing. For example, the network that interconnects the systems in a cloud has to be secure. Furthermore, virtualization paradigm in cloud computing leads to several security concerns. For example, mapping the virtual machines to the physical machines has to be carried out securely. Data security involves encrypting the data as well as ensuring that appropriate policies are enforced for data sharing. In addition, resource allocation and memory management algorithms have to be secure. Finally, data mining techniques may be applicable for malware detection in the clouds – an approach which is usually adopted in *Intrusion Detection Systems* (IDSs) (Sen & Sengupta, 2005; Sen et al., 2006b, 2008; Sen, 2010a, 2010b, 2010c).

As shown in Figure 2, there are six specific areas of the cloud computing environment where equipment and software require substantial security attention (Trusted Computing Group's White Paper, 2010). These six areas are: (1) security of data at rest, (2) security of data in transit, (3) authentication of users/applications/ processes, (4) robust separation between data belonging to different customers, (5) cloud legal and regulatory issues, and (6) incident response.

For securing data at rest, cryptographic encryption mechanisms are certainly the best options. The hard drive manufacturers are now shipping self-encrypting drives that implement trusted storage standards of the trusted computing group (Trusted Computing Group's White Paper, 2010). These self-encrypting drives build encryption hardware into the drive, providing automated encryption with minimal cost or performance impact. Although software encryption can also be used for protecting data, it makes the process slower and less secure since it may be possible for an adversary to steal the encryption key from the machine without being detected.

Encryption is the best option for securing data in transit as well. In addition, authentication and integrity protection mechanisms ensure that data only goes where the customer wants it to go and it is not modified in transit.

Strong authentication is a mandatory requirement for any cloud deployment. User authentication is the primary basis for access control. In the cloud environment, authentication and access control are more important than ever since the cloud and all of its data are accessible to anyone over the Internet. The *Trusted Computing Group's* (TCG's) IF-MAP standard allows for real-time communication between a cloud service provider and the customer about authorized users and other security issues. When a user's access privilege is revoked or reassigned, the customer's identity management system can notify the cloud provider in real-time so that the user's cloud access can be modified or revoked within a very short span of time.

Figure 2. Areas for security concerns in cloud computing: (1) data at rest, (2) data in transit, (3) authentication, (4) separation between customers, (5) cloud legal and regulatory issues, and (6) incident response

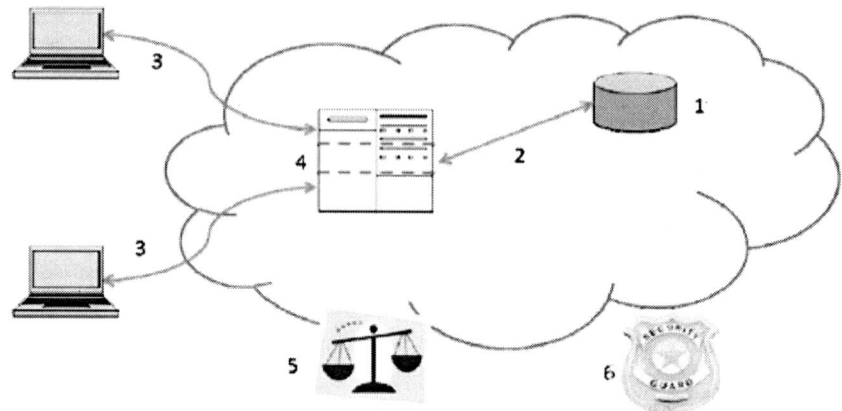

One of the more obvious cloud concerns is separation between a cloud provider's users (who may be competing companies or even hackers) to avoid inadvertent or intentional access to sensitive information. Typically a cloud provider would use *Virtual Machines* (VMs) and a hypervisor to separate customers. Technologies are currently available that can provide significant security improvements for VMs and virtual network separation. In addition, the *Trusted Platform Module* (TPM) can provide hardware-based verification of hypervisor and VM integrity and thereby ensure strong network separation and security.

Legal and regulatory issues are extremely important in cloud computing that have security implications. To verify that a cloud provider has strong policies and practices that address legal and regulatory issues, each customer must have its legal and regulatory experts inspect cloud provider's policies and practices to ensure their adequacy. The issues to be considered in this regard include data security and export compliance, auditing, data retention and destruction, and legal discovery. In the areas of data retention and deletion, trusted storage and trusted platform module access techniques can play a key role in limiting access to sensitive and critical data.

As part of expecting the unexpected, customers need to plan for the possibility of cloud provider security breaches or user misbehavior. An automated response of at least automated notification is the best solution for this purpose. The IF-MAP (Metadata Access protocol) of the *Trusted Computing Group* (TCG) specification enables the integration of different security systems and provides real-time notifications of incidents and of user misbehavior.

Threat Vectors: What to Worry About in Security

How does the landscape of threats to security and privacy change as organizations shift to cloud-based systems, storage and applications? New vectors are introduced, and old ones can be exploited in new ways. In the following, we briefly discuss some of the threats, highlighting what is genuinely different and new in a world of cloud hosting, what threats are similar to the dominant model of local applications and in-house IT management but will manifest in different ways.

Before categorizing new threats, it is important to acknowledge that the structure of many cloud architectures can mitigate or negate some current security threats. If data are kept in the cloud, for example, then a lost or stolen laptop is much less likely to put sensitive information at risk. Standardized interfaces could make security management easier (ENISA, 2009), while the scale of a provider hosting many parties can generate more information for better threat monitoring. Centralized security management and monitoring can be more effective than local efforts by IT professionals with limited security experience.

Still, moving critical systems and data to a network-accessible framework introduces new classes of vulnerabilities in and of itself, by creating new surfaces to attack and new interfaces to exploit. When those network resources are built on systems, platforms and applications shared with others, another set of threat vectors is introduced. The control mechanisms itself can be attacked, breaking down isolation between users, potentially allowing another user to access data or resources. Even without direct access, a providers' other clients can learn valuable transaction data about an organization (Ristenpart et al., 2009). The shared architecture also puts a cloud user at risk from other cloud users if their bad behavior draws attention from either law enforcement or media, leading to hardware seizure or bad publicity (Molnar & Schechter, 2010).

Some threat vectors are not new to cloud, but have somewhat different dynamics. In classic IT architecture, PCs inside the organization may be at risk of compromise through a host of attack vectors exploiting local applications such as browses or documents viewers. If less data is stored locally, the data is immediately at risk, but now the attacker could compromise credentials to gain access to the user's cloud privileges. A compromise to an entire Gmail database probably began with a compromised PC (Zetter, 2010). Similarly, in an attack on the Twitter management team in 2009, a compromised email password led to exposure of a wide range of other important documents in other cloud infrastructures (Lowensohn & McCarthy, 2009). Shared authentication tokens can lead to brittle defenses.

Organizations must be careful to safeguard data as they move it around their organization, even without the benefit of cloud computing. When they no longer need data, it must be properly deleted, or else risk leaking sensitive data to the outside (Garfinkel & Shelat, 2003). When relying on a cloud service to handle data, appropriate care must be made to arrange for appropriate security management practices, such as encryption and appropriate deletion.

Similarly, all organizations are vulnerable to an insider attack from a trusted insider, but moving things to the cloud can raise the costs of misplaced trust. A cloud system with a well thought out identity interface and a clear access control system can restrict access and foster accountability. However, a unified data system with more people accessing more different types of data through more applications can actually make it harder to appropriately limit access and detect misuse (Sinclair & Smith, 2008).

Security Issues in Cloud Computing

Security in the cloud is achieved, in part, through third party controls and assurance much like in traditional outsourcing arrangements. But since there is no common cloud computing security standard, there are additional challenges associated with this. Many cloud vendors implement their own proprietary standards and security technologies, and implement differing security models, which need to be evaluated on their own merits. In a vendor cloud model, it is ultimately down to adopting customer organizations to ensure that security in the cloud meets their own security polices through requirements gathering, provider risk assessments, due diligence, and assurance activities (CPNI Security Briefing, 2010).

Thus, the security challenges faced by organizations wishing to use cloud services are not radically different from those dependent on their own in-house managed enterprises. The same internal and external threats are present and require risk mitigation or risk acceptance. In the following, we examine the information security challenges that adopting organizations will need to consider, either through assurance activities on the vendor or public cloud providers or directly, through designing and implementing security control in a privately owned cloud. In particular, we examine the following issues:

- The threats against information assets residing in cloud computing environments.
- The types of attackers and their capability of attacking the cloud.
- The security risks associated with the cloud, and where relevant considerations of attacks and countermeasures.
- Emerging cloud security risks.
- Some example cloud security incidents.

Cloud Security Threats

The threats to information assets residing in the cloud can vary according to the cloud delivery models used by cloud user organizations. There are several types of security threats to which cloud computing is vulnerable. Table 2 provides an overview of the threats for cloud customers categorized according to the *Confidentiality, Integrity,* and *Availability* (CIA) security model and their relevance to each of the cloud service delivery model.

Table 2. A list of cloud security threats

Confidentiality	Threat Description
Insider User Threats: • Malicious cloud provider user • Malicious cloud customer user • Malicious third party user (Supporting either the cloud provider or customer organizations)	The threat of insiders accessing customer data held within the cloud is greater as each of the delivery models can introduce the need for multiple internal users: SaaS: Cloud customer and provider administrators PaaS: Application developers and test environment managers IaaS: Third party platform consultants
External Attacker Threats: • Remote software attack of cloud infrastructure • Remote software attack of cloud applications • Remote hardware attack against the cloud • Remote software and hardware attack against cloud user organizations' endpoint software and hardware • Social engineering of cloud provider users, and cloud customer users.	The threat from external attackers may be perceived to apply more to public Internet facing clouds, however all types of cloud delivery models are affected by external attackers, particularly in private clouds where user endpoints can be targeted. Cloud providers with large data stores holding credit card details, personal information and sensitive government or intellectual property, will be subjected to attacks from groups, with significant resources, attempting to retrieve data. This includes the threat of hardware attack, social engineering and supply chain attacks by dedicated attackers.
Data Leakage: • Failure of security access rights across multiple domains • Failure of electronic and physical transport systems for cloud data and backups	A threat from widespread data leakage amongst many, potentially competitor organizations, using the same cloud provider could be caused by human error or faulty hardware that will lead to information compromise.
Integrity	
Data Segregation: • Incorrectly defined security perimeters • Incorrect configuration of virtual machines and hypervisors	The integrity of data within complex cloud hosting environments such as SaaS configured to share computing resource amongst customers could provide a threat against data integrity if system resources are effectively segregated.
User Access: • Poor identity and access management procedures	Implementation of poor access control procedures creates many threat opportunities, for example that disgruntled ex-employees of cloud provider organizations maintain remote access to administer customer cloud services, and can cause intentional damage to their data sources.
Data Quality: • Introduction of faulty application or infrastructure components	The threat of impact of data quality is increased as cloud providers host many customers' data. The introduction of a faulty or misconfigured component required by another cloud user could potentially impact the integrity of data for other cloud users sharing infrastructure.
Availability	
Change Management: • Customer penetration testing impacting other cloud customers • Infrastructure changes upon cloud provider, customer and third party systems impacting cloud customers	As the cloud provider has increasing responsibility for change management within all cloud delivery models, there is a threat that changes could introduce negative effects. These could be caused by software or hardware changes to existing cloud services.
Denial of Service Threat: • Network bandwidth distributed denial of service • Network DNS denial of service • Application and data denial of service	The threat of denial of service against available cloud computing resource is generally an external threat against public cloud services. However, the threat can impact all cloud service models as external and internal threat agents could introduce application or hardware components that cause a denial of service.
Physical Disruption: • Disruption of cloud provider IT services through physical access • Disruption of cloud customer IT services through physical access • Disruption of third party WAN providers services	The threat of disruption to cloud services caused by physical access is different between large cloud service providers and their customers. These providers should be experienced in securing large data center facilities and have considered resilience among other availability strategies. There is a threat that cloud user infrastructure can be physically disrupted more easily whether by insiders or externally where less secure office environments or remote working is standard practice.
Exploiting Weak Recovery Procedures: • Invocation of inadequate disaster recovery or business continuity processes	The threat of inadequate recovery and incident management procedures being initiated is heightened when cloud users consider recovery of their own in house systems in parallel with those managed by third party cloud service providers. If these procedures are not tested then the impact upon recovery time may be significant.

Types of Attackers in Cloud Computing

Many of the security threats and challenges in cloud computing will be familiar to organizations managing in house infrastructure and those involved in traditional outsourcing models. Each of the cloud computing service delivery models' threats result from the attackers that can be divided into two groups as depicted in Table 3.

Although internal and external attackers can be clearly differentiated, their capability to execute successful attacks is what differentiates them as a threat to customers and vendors alike.

In the cloud environment, attackers can be categorized into four types: random, weak, strong, and substantial (CPNI Security Briefing, 2010). Each of these categories is based on ability to instigate a successful attack, rather than on the type of threat they present (i.e., criminal, espionage, or terrorism):

Table 3. A list of attacks on cloud computing environments

Internal Attackers	An internal attacker has the following characteristics: • Is employed by the cloud service provider, customer or other third party provider organization supporting the operation of a cloud service • May have existing authorized access to cloud services, customer data or supporting infrastructure and applications, depending on their organizational role • Uses existing privileges to gain further access or support third parties in executing attacks against the confidentiality integrity and availability of information within the cloud service.
External Attackers	An external attacker has the following characteristics: • Is not employed by the cloud service provider, customer or other third party provider organization supporting the operation of a cloud service • Has no authorized access to cloud services, customer data or supporting infrastructure and applications • Exploits technical, operational, process and social engineering vulnerabilities to attack a cloud service provider, customer or third party supporting organization to gain further access to propagate attacks against the confidentiality, integrity and availability of information within the cloud service.

- **Random:** The most common type of attacker uses simple tools and techniques. The attacker may randomly scan the Internet trying to find vulnerable components. They will deploy well known tools or techniques that should be easily detected.
- **Weak:** Semi-skilled attackers targeting specific servers/cloud providers by customizing existing publicly available tools or specific targets. Their methods are more advanced as they attempt to customize their attacks using available exploit tools.
- **Strong:** Organized, well-financed and skilled groups of attackers with an internal hierarchy specializing in targeting particular applications and users of the cloud. Generally this group will be an organized crime group specializing in large scale attacks.
- **Substantial:** Motivated, strong attackers not easily detected by the organizations they attack, or even by the relevant law enforcement and investigative organizations specializing in eCrime or cyber security. Mitigating this threat requires greater intelligence on attacks and specialist resources in response to detection of an incident or threat.

Cloud Security Risks

The security risks associated with each cloud delivery model vary and are dependent on a wide range of factors including the sensitivity of information assets, cloud architectures, and security control involved in a particular cloud environment. In the following, we discuss these risks in a general context, except where a specific reference to the cloud delivery model is made. Table 4 summarizes the security risks relevant in the cloud computing paradigm.

Security and Privacy Issues in Cloud Computing

Table 4. A list of security risks in cloud computing

Risk	Description
Privileged user access	Cloud providers generally have unlimited access to user data, controls are needed to address the risk of privileged user access leading to compromised customer data.
Data location and segregation	Customers may not know where their data is being stored and there may be a risk of data being stored alongside other customers' information.
Data disposal	Cloud data deletion and disposal is a risk, particularly where hardware is dynamically issued to customers based on their needs. The risk of data not being deleted from data stores, backups and physical media during de-commissioning is enhanced within the cloud.
e-investigations and Protective monitoring	The ability for cloud customers to invoke their own electronic investigations procedures within the cloud can be limited by the delivery model in use, and the access and complexity of the cloud architecture. Customers cannot effectively deploy monitoring systems on infrastructure they do not own; they must rely on the systems in use by the cloud service provider to support investigations.
Assuring cloud security	Customers cannot easily assure the security of systems that they do not directly control without using SLAs and having the right to audit security controls within their agreements.

Privileged User Access

Once data is stored in the cloud, the provider has access to that data and also controls access to that data by other entities (including other users of the cloud and other third party suppliers). Maintaining confidentiality of data in the cloud and limiting privileged user access can be achieved by at least one of two approaches by the data owner: first, encryption of the data prior to entry into the cloud to separate the ability to store the data from the ability to make use of it; and second, legally enforcing the requirements of the cloud provider through contractual obligations and assurance mechanisms to ensure that confidentiality of the data is maintained to required standards. The cloud provider must have demonstrable security access control policies and technical solutions in place that prevent privilege escalation by standard users, enable auditing of user actions, and support the segregation of duties principle for privileged users in order to prevent and detect malicious insider activity.

Encryption of data prior to entry into the cloud poses two challenges. For encryption of data to be effective means of maintaining data confidentiality, decryption keys must be segregated securely from the cloud environment to ensure that only an authorized party can decrypt data. This could be achieved by storing keys on segregated systems in house or by storing keys with a second provider.

An additional challenge around encryption in the cloud is to prevent manipulations of encrypted data such that plain text, or any other meaningful data, can be recovered and be used to break the cipher. This constraint in encryption technology means that cloud providers must not be granted unlimited ability to store and archive encrypted data. If the cloud user organization permits the cloud service provider to handle unencrypted data, then the cloud service provider must provide assurance that the data will be protected from unauthorized access, both internally and externally. Within the cloud, the generation and use of cryptographic keys for each cloud customer could be used to provide another level of protection above and beyond data segregation controls. However, providers need robust key management processes in place and the challenge for customers then becomes gaining assurances over that process.

A strong or substantial attacker could exploit weak encryption policies, and privileged cloud provider management access, to recover customer data using a complex software or hardware attack on user endpoint devices, or cloud infrastructure devices. This attack may involve long-term compromise of the cloud provider supply chain, or social engineering of a particular cloud customer user.

The use of encryption technology may also be subject to limitations or specific requirements depending on the jurisdiction in which the cloud provider will be storing cloud customers' data. For example, in some countries, the use of encryption technologies may be restricted based upon the type of encryption or its purpose of operation. Cloud customers should review whether the application of encryption as mandated by the local jurisdiction of the cloud provider is acceptable and does not enhance risk to their data. For example, in the UK, the Regulatory Investigatory Powers Act (RIPA) can impose a legal obligation to disclose encryption keys to enable access to data by security and law enforcement agencies. Cloud customers should ensure that they understand their obligations within all of the jurisdictions used by the cloud provider, and have policies and procedures in place to deal with specific external enquiries with respect to encrypted data.

Data Location and Segregation

Data location and data segregation are of particular importance in the cloud, given the disparate physical location of data and shared computing resources. Cloud users may be under statutory, regulatory, or contractual obligations to ensure that data is held, processed and managed in a certain way. There are a number of associated security risks in this situation:

- The cloud provider being required to disclose data (and potentially decryption keys) or hand over physical media to a third party or statutory authority.
- Development of liabilities to pay tax to local authorities as a result of processing sales or other transactions within their jurisdictions.
- Environmental hazards such as earthquakes, flooding, and extreme weather affecting the security of customer data, and
- Macro-economic hazards such as hyper-inflation or deep recession affecting the providers' services and personnel conditions.

Central storage arrangements in cloud computing also provide attackers with a far richer target of information. In a single attack, attackers could potentially gain access to confidential information belonging to several customer organizations. If adequate segregation of data is not applied many customers may find themselves suffering a security breach due to an incident that should have been limited to a single customer.

Virtualization is one of a number of enabling technologies of cloud computing that itself is a run-time method of segregation for processing data. Many of the security concerns and issues associated with virtualization are relevant in cloud computing, regardless of whether or not the cloud service provider employs virtualization technologies. Security of data depends on having adequate security controls in each of the layers of the virtualized environment. In addition, secure deletion of memory and storage must be used to prevent data loss in a multi-tenant environment where systems are reused.

The hypervisor layer between the hardware and virtual machine / guest OS has privileged access to layers above. It also has a great deal of control over hardware, and increasingly so, as hardware manufacturers implement hypervisor functions directly into chipsets and CPUs. Cloud users, therefore, need to assess cloud service providers' use and operation of virtualization technologies and whether the risk profile can be tolerated.

Data Disposal

Cloud services that offer data storage typically provide either guarantees or service-level objectives around high availability of that data. Cloud providers achieve this by keeping multiple copies of the data. Where the cloud customer has a requirement to delete data, cloud-based storage may be inappropriate for that data at all points in its lifecycle.

Depending on the type of data hosted in the cloud, customers may require providers to delete data in accordance with industry standards. Unless the cloud architecture specifically limits the media on which data may be stored and the data owner can mandate use of media sanitization techniques on that media in line with the required standards, customers may need to preclude their data from being transmitted in the cloud.

e-Investigations and Protective Monitoring

Implementing protective monitoring in the cloud presents challenges for both cloud customers and providers given the disparate location of physical data and the high number of providers involved. While cloud enabling technologies are designed to place a security perimeter between the cloud service systems and the cloud users, vulnerabilities in this layer of security cannot be ruled out altogether. There is a risk of insider threats and attacks on the cloud and this is likely to require expertise in e-investigations and protective monitoring.

Effective protective monitoring of cloud-based information assets is likely to require integration between monitoring tools employed by the cloud provider as well as tools employed by the cloud user. Tracing actions back to accountable users and administrators in the cloud may require an integrated or federated (mutual trust) identity management and associated logging system which permits unambiguous identification of all authorized individual with access to the cloud resources.

Managing identity and access in the cloud for an enterprise is likely to require integration with a pre-existing identity management system. Federating the cloud customer's identity management system with the cloud provider's identity and access management system is one solution.

Protective monitoring of the cloud will, in certain cases, depend on cloud customers' ability to trace actions back to all authorized identities in both cloud and customer IT environment. This is likely to require a federated identity management approach which encompasses the cloud users as well as the cloud service provider.

The technology supporting federated identity management is currently in its very early stages, with several competing standards vying for dominance in a landscape of numerous proprietary identity management technologies.

Access to accurate information is, of course, vital in investigating incidents. Having access to data within protective monitoring logging systems, and the ability to carry out forensic investigations on computing devices and other infrastructure within a cloud environment may be difficult for cloud customers pursuing an investigation. Therefore, customers should address this issue within their contractual agreements with providers, and understand how their provider implements protective monitoring within their cloud environment. Customers placing specific requirements within a contract relating to investigations will need to consider how their investigation team integrates with their equivalent investigations team within the cloud provider organization. This is of particular importance where investigations are taking place on multi-tenant systems and providers have a responsibility to protect other customers' data. Generally, collecting digital evidence within the cloud should be the responsibility of the cloud service provider, and it should be handed over as part of the chain of custody of evidence to the customer for their own investigation process. Should customers request more direct access to specific data devices that are part of a shared customer infrastructure, then the provider may choose to change the architecture of that customer's service which may substantially increase the costs to the customer and may impact the original business case for choosing cloud services.

Assessing the Security of a Third Party Cloud Provider

One of the most significant challenges for vendor cloud customers in particular is assurance over the security controls of their cloud provider (CPNI Security Briefing, 2010). This is exacerbated by the fact that there is currently no common industry cloud computing security standard from which customers can benchmark their providers. Customers are primarily concerned with the following issues:

- **Defining Security Requirements:** The customers' information security requirements are derived from the organization's own policy, legal and regulatory obligations, and may carry through from other contracts or SLAs that the company has with its customers.
- **Due Diligence on Cloud Service Providers:** Prospective cloud customers should undertake proper due-diligence on providers before entering into a formal relationship. Detailed due-diligence investigations can provide an unbiased and valuable insight into a providers' past track record, including its financial status, legal action taken against the organization and its commercial reputation. Certification schemes such as ISO27001 also provide customers with some assurances that a cloud provider has taken certain steps in its management of information security risks.
- **Managing Cloud Supplier Risks:** The outsourcing of key services to the cloud may require customer organizations to seek new and more mature approaches to risk management and accountability. While cloud computing means that services are outsourced, the risk remains with the customer and it is therefore in the customer's interest to ensure that risks are appropriately managed according to their risk appetite. Effective risk management also requires maturity both in vendor relationship management processes and operational security processes.

Classification of Security Issues in Cloud Computing

The security issues in cloud computing can be categorized into the following three broad classes:

- Traditional security concerns
- Availability issues
- Third party data control-related issues

In the following, we discuss these three classes of security issues and also highlight some additional security vulnerabilities in cloud computing.

Traditional Security Issues

These security issues involve computer and network intrusions or attacks that will be made possible or at least easier by moving to the cloud. Cloud providers respond to these concerns by arguing that their security measures and processes are more mature and tested than those of the average company. Another argument, made by the Jericho Forum (Don't Cloud Vision) is: "It could be easier to lock down information if it's administered by a third party rather than in-house, if companies are worried about insider threats... In addition, it may be easier to enforce security via contracts with online services providers than via internal controls."

Concerns in this category include the following:

VM-level Attacks: Potential vulnerabilities in the hypervisor or VM technology used by cloud vendors are a potential problem in multi-tenant architectures. Vulnerabilities have appeared in VMWare (Security Tracker: VMWare Shared

Folder Bug), Xen (Xen Vulnerability), and Microsoft's Virtual PC and Virtual Server (Microsoft Security Bulletin MS07-049). Vendors such as Third Brigade mitigate potential VM-level vulnerabilities through monitoring and firewalls.

Cloud Service Providers' Vulnerabilities: These could be at platform-level, such as an SQL-injection or cross-site scripting vulnerability. For instance, there have been a couple of recent Google Docs vulnerabilities (Microsoft Security Bulletin MS07-049). IBM has repositioned its Rational AppScan tool, which scans for vulnerabilities in Web services as a cloud security service (IBM Blue Cloud Initiative).

Phishing Cloud Provider: Phishers and other social engineers have a new attack vector (Salesforce.com Warns Customers).

Expanded Network Attack Surface: The cloud user must protect the infrastructure used to connect and interact with the cloud, a task complicated by the cloud being outside the firewall in many cases. For instance, an example of how the cloud might attack the machine connecting to it has been shown in (Security Evaluation of Grid).

Authentication and Authorization: The enterprise authentication and authorization framework does not naturally extend into the cloud. How does a company mend its existing framework to include cloud resources? Furthermore, how does an enterprise merge cloud security data (if available) with its own security metrics and policies?

Forensics in the Cloud: CLOIDIFIN project (Biggs & Vidalis, 2009) summarizes the difficulty of cloud forensic investigations: "Traditional digital forensic methodologies permit investigators to seize equipment and perform detailed analysis on the media and data recovered. The likelihood, therefore, of the data being removed, overwritten, deleted, or destroyed by the perpetrator in this case is low. More closely linked to a cloud-computing environment would be businesses that own and maintain their own multi-server type infrastructure, though this would be on a far smaller scale in comparison. However, the scale of the cloud and the rate at which data is overwritten is of concern."

Availability

These concerns center on critical applications and data being available. Well-publicized incidents of cloud outages include Gmail's one-day outage in mid-October 2008 (Extended Gmail Outage), Amazon S3's over seven-hour downtime on July 20, 2008 (Amazon S3 Availability Event, 2008), and FlexiScale's 18-hour outage on October 31, 2008 (Flexiscale Outage). Maintaining the uptime, preventing denial of service attacks (especially at the single-points-of-failure) and ensuring robustness of computational integrity (i.e. the cloud provider is faithfully running an application and giving valid results) are some of the major issues in this category of threats.

Third Party Data Control

The legal implications of data and applications being held by a third party are complex and not well understood. There is also a potential lack of control and transparency when a third party holds the data. Part of the hype of cloud computing is that the cloud can be implementation-independent, but in reality, regulatory compliance requires transparency into the cloud. Various security and data privacy issues are prompting some companies to build clouds to avoid these issues and yet retain some of the benefits of cloud computing. However, the following concerns need to be addressed properly.

Due Diligence: If served a subpoena or other legal action, can a cloud user compel the cloud provider to respond in the required time-frame? A related question is the provability of deletion, relevant to an enterprise's retention policy: How can a cloud user be guaranteed that data has been deleted by the cloud provider?

Auditability: Audit difficulty is another side effect of the lack of control in the cloud. Is there sufficient transparency in the operations of the cloud provider for auditing purposes? Currently, this transparency is provided by documentation and manual audits. Performing an on-site audit in a distributed and dynamic multi-tenant computing environment spread all over the globe is a major challenge. Certain regulations will require data and operations to remain in certain geographic locations.

Contractual Obligations: One problem with using another company's infrastructure besides the uncertain alignment of interests is that there might be surprising legal implications. For instance, a passage from Amazon's terms of use is as follows: "Non-assertion" during and after the term of the agreement, with respect to any of the services that you elect to use, you will not assert nor will you authorize, assist, or encourage any third party to assert, against us or any of our customers, end users, vendors, business partners (including third party sellers on Websites operated by or on behalf of us), licensors, sub-licensees, or transferees, any patent infringement or other intellectual property infringement claim with respect to such Services." This could be interpreted that after one uses E2C, one cannot file infringement claims against Amazon. It is not clear whether this non-assert would be upheld by the courts, but any uncertainty is bad for business.

Cloud Provider Espionage: The worry of theft of company propriety information by the cloud provider.

Transitive Nature of Contracts: Another possible concern is that the contracted cloud provider might itself use sub-contractors, over whom the cloud user either has no control or very less control. However, the sub-contractor must be trusted. For example, the online storage service called "Linkup" uses an online storage company called Nirvanix (Loss of Customer Spurs Closure of LinkUp) for its cloud service. Another example is Carbonite (Latest Cloud Storage Hiccups), which is using its hardware providers for faulty equipment causing loss of customer data.

Emerging Cloud Security Threats

In the following, we discuss some additional security threats that are relevant in cloud computing and are being detected and researched by academia, security organization and both cloud service providers and the cloud customers.

Side Channel Attacks: An emerging concern for cloud delivery models using virtualization platforms is the risk of side channel attacks causing data leakage across co-resident virtual machine instances. This risk is evolving, though currently it is considered to be in its infancy, as the virtual machine technologies mature. However, it is possible that attackers who fail to compromise endpoints or penetrate cloud infrastructure from outside the cloud perimeter, may consider this technique - acting as a rogue customer within a shared cloud infrastructure to access other customers' data.

Denial of Service Attacks: Availability is a primary concern to cloud customers and as such it is equally of concern to the service providers who must design solutions to mitigate this threat. Traditionally, denial of service (DoS) has been associated with network layer distributed attacks flooding infrastructure with excessive traffic in order to cause critical components to fail or to consume all available hardware resources (Sen et al., 2006a; Sen, 2011a, 2011b). Within a multi-tenant cloud infrastructure, there are more specific threats associated with DoS. Some of these threats are: (a) Shared resource consumption – attacks that deprive other customers of system resources such as thread execution time, memory, storage requests and network interfaces can cause a targeted DoS, (b) Virtual machine and hypervisor exploitation – attacks that exploit vulnerabilities in the underlying hypervisor, or operating system hosting a virtual machine instance will allow attackers to cause targeted outages or instability. Attacks using these methods are designed to circumvent traditionally well-defined cloud architecture that has concentrated on securing against external network-based DoS attacks.

Social Networking Attacks: With the increased popularity of business and personal social networking sites the risk of advanced social engineering attack is increased. Cloud computing systems are targeted due to their large customer data stores. The complex set of relationships between cloud providers, customers, suppliers and vendors means that many employees of these organizations will be listed on social networking sites and be connected to each other. Attackers can setup identities to gain trust, and use online information to determine relationships and roles of staff to prepare their attacks. A combination of technical attack and social engineering attacks can be deployed against a target user by taking advantage of the people they know and the online social network they use.

Mobile Device Attacks: The use of smart phones has increased and cloud connectivity is now no longer limited to laptop or desktop computing devices. Attacks are now emerging that are targeted for mobile devices and rely on features traditionally associated with laptops and desktops, including: (1) rich Application Programming Interfaces (APIs) that support network communications and background services, (2) always on wireless Internet access, and (3) large local data storage capabilities. As mobile devices now have these equivalent features, Internet-based spyware, worms or even physical attacks may be more likely to occur against mobile devices, as they are potentially less risky targets to an attacker that wishes to remain undetected. This is generally supported by the fact that most mobile devices do not have the equivalent security features enabled, or in some cases the security features may not be available. For example, mature antimalware, antivirus or full disk encryption technologies are not widespread on currently available smart phones.

Insider and Organized Crime Threat: Cloud providers will store a range of different data types, including credit card and other financial and personal data. All of this data may be aggregated from multiple customers and therefore be extremely valuable to criminals. There is a risk that insiders are deliberately used to gain access to customer data and probe systems in order to assist any external attackers that require additional information in order to execute complex Internet-based attacks. Cloud customers should ensure that service providers are aware of this threat and have rigorous identity validation and security vetting procedures built into their recruitment process.

Cheap Data and Data Analysis: The advent of cloud computing has created enormous data sets that can be monetized by applications such as advertising. Google, for example, leverages its cloud infrastructure to collect and analyze consumer data for its advertising network. Collection and analysis of data is now possible cheaply, even for companies lacking Google's resources. The availability of data and cheap data mining techniques have high impact on the privacy of user data. The attackers have massive, centralized databases available for analysis and also the raw computing power to mine these databases. Because of privacy concerns, enterprises running clouds for collecting data are increasingly finding the requirement of anonymizing their data. EPIC called for Gmail, Google Docs, Google Calendar, and the company's other Web applications to shut down until appropriate privacy guards were in place (FTC Questions Cloud Computing Security). Google and Yahoo!, because of pressure from privacy advocates, now have an 18 months retention policy for their search data, after which they are to be anonymized by removing some identifiers of those data such as IP addresses and cookie information. The anonymized data is retained though, to support the continual testing of their algorithms. Another reason to anonymize data is to share with other parties for supporting research (AOL Incident, 2007) or to subcontract out data mining on the data (Netflix Prize). More sophisticated tools will be required for robust anonymization as increasing deployment of cloud applications takes place.

Cost-effective Defense of Availability: Availability also needs to be considered in the context of an adversary whose goals are simply to sabotage activities. Increasingly, such adversaries are becoming realistic as political conflict is taken onto the Web, and as the recent cyber attacks on Lithuania confirm (Lithuania Weathers Cyber Attack). The damages are not only related to the losses of productivity but they degrade the trust in the infrastructure and make the backup processes more costly.

Increased Authentication Demands: The development of cloud computing may, in the extreme, allow the use of thin clients on the client side. Rather than purchasing a license and installing a software on the client side, users will authenticate in order to be able to use a cloud application. There are some advantages in such a model, such as making software piracy more difficult and making centralized monitoring more convenient. It may also help prevent the spread of sensitive data on untrustworthy clients. This architecture also supports enhanced mobility of users, but demands more robust authentication protocols. Moreover, the movement towards increased hosting of data and applications in the cloud and lesser reliance on specific user machines is likely to increase the threat of phishing and theft of access credentials.

Mash-up Authorization: As adoption of cloud computing grows, more services performing mashups of data will be witnessed. This development has potential security implications, both in terms of data leaks, and in terms of the number of sources a data user may have to pull data from. This, in turn, places requirements on how access is authorized. A centralized access control mechanism may not be a feasible proposition in such deployment scenarios. One example in this area is provided by Facebook. Facebook users upload both sensitive and non-sensitive data. This data is used by Facebook to present the data to other users, and this data is also utilized by third party applications. Since these applications are typically not verified by Facebook, malicious applications running in Facebook's cloud can potentially steal sensitive data (Facebook Users Suffer Viral Surge, 2009).

SOME PROPOSITIONS FOR SECURITY IN CLOUD COMPUTING

In this section, we discuss some novel security approaches that may be utilized in cloud computing deployments. The core issue is that with the advent of the cloud, the cloud provider also has some control of the cloud users' data. In this section, some propositions have been made in such a way that the current capabilities of the cloud are not curtailed while limiting the cloud providers' control on data and enabling all cloud users to benefit from the cloud.

Information-centric Security: In order for enterprises to extend control of data in the cloud, it may be worthwhile to take an approach of protecting data from within. This approach is known as information-centric security. This self-protection technique requires intelligence be put in the data itself. Data needs to be self-describing and defending, regardless of its environment. When accessed, data consults its policy and attempts to recreate a secure environment that is verified as trustworthy using the framework of *Trusted Computing* (TC).

High-assurance Remote Server Attestation: At present, lack of transparency is discouraging businesses from moving their data to the cloud. Data owners wish to audit how their data is being handled at the cloud, and in particular, ensure that their data is not being abused or leaked, or at least have an unalterable audit trail when it does happen. Currently, customers must be satisfied with cloud providers using manual auditing procedures like SAS-70. A promising approach to address this problem is based on *trusted computing*. In a trusted computing environment, a trusted monitor is installed at the cloud server that can monitor or audit the operations of the cloud server. The trusted monitor can provide *proof of compliance* to the data owner, guaranteeing that certain access policies have not been violated. To ensure integrity of the monitor, trusted computing also allows secure bootstrapping of this monitor to run beside (and securely isolated from) the operating system and applications. The monitor can enforce access control policies and perform monitoring/auditing tasks. To produce a proof of compliance, the code of the monitor is signed, as well as a *statement of compliance* produced by the monitor. When the data owner receives this proof of compliance, it can verify that the correct monitor code is run, and that the cloud server has complied with access control policies.

Privacy-enhanced Business Intelligence: A different approach for retaining control of data is to require the encryption of all cloud data. The problem in this approach is that encryption limits data use. In particular, searching and indexing the data becomes problematic, if not impossible. For example, if data is stored in clear-text form, one can efficiently search for a document by specifying a keyword. This is impossible to do with traditional, randomized encryption schemes. The state-of-the-art cryptographic mechanisms may offer new tools to solve these problems. Cryptographers have invented versatile encryption schemes that allow for operations and computations on the cipher-texts. For example, *searchable encryption* (also referred to as *predicate encryption*) (Song et al., 2000) allows the data owner to compute a capability from his secret key. A capability encodes a search query, and the cloud can use this capability to decide which documents match the search query. The cloud can use this capability to decide which documents match the search query, without learning any additional information. Other cryptographic primitives such as *homomorphic encryption* (Gentry, 2009) and *Private Information Retrieval* (PIR) (Chor et al., 1998) perform computations on encrypted source data without decrypting them. As these cryptographic techniques mature, they may open up new possibilities and directions for research, development, and deployment of cloud security protocols and algorithms.

While in many cases more research is needed to make these cryptographic tools sufficiently practical for the cloud, they present the best opportunity for a clear differentiator for cloud computing since these mechanisms can enable cloud users to benefit from one another's data in a controlled manner. In particular, even encrypted data can enable anomaly detection that is valuable from a business intelligence standpoint. Apart from ensuring privacy, applied cryptography also offers tools to address other security problems related to cloud computing. For example, in *proofs of retrievability* (Shacham & Waters, 2008), the storage server can show a compact proof that it is correctly storing all of the client's data.

Table 5 summarizes some important security issues in cloud computing and their possible defense mechanisms.

Table 5. Cloud computing threats and suggested defense mechanisms for these threats

Security Threats	Possible Defense Mechanisms
Spoofing identity	Authentication Protect secrets Don't store secrets
Tampering with data	Authorization Hashes Message authentication codes Digital signatures Tamper-resistant protocols
Repudiation	Digital signatures Time-stamps Audit trails
Information disclosure	Authorization Privacy-enhanced protocols Encryption Protect secrets Don't store secrets
Denial of Service (DoS)	Authentication Authorization Filtering Throttling Quality of service (QoS)
Elevation of privilege	Run with least privilege

STANDARDIZATION ACTIVITIES IN CLOUD COMPUTING

This section presents a discussion on the various activities being undertaken by different Standard Development Organizations (SDOs) in the world in the domain of cloud application and service deployments particularly with regards to security and privacy issues. For each Standard Development Organization (SDO), we identify the focus on cloud computing related works particularly with regard to security and privacy issues.

NIST Cloud Standards

NIST is a key organization in defining various standards for cloud computing. With regard to security and privacy aspects of cloud computing NIST has released standard guidelines for public clouds (Badger et al., 2011). The primary focus of the report issued by NIST is to provide an overview of public cloud computing and the security and privacy considerations involved. It discusses the threats, technology risks, and safeguards surrounding public cloud environments, and their suitable defense mechanisms. The report observes that "since the cloud computing has grown out of an amalgamation of technologies, including *Service-Oriented Architecture* (SOA), virtualization, Web2.0, and utility computing, many of the security and privacy issues involved in cloud computing can be viewed as known problems cast in a new setting" (Badger et al., 2011). However, public cloud computing manifests itself as a thought-provoking paradigm shift from conventional computing to an open deperimeterized organizational infrastructure – at the extreme, displacing applications form one organization's infrastructure to the infrastructure of another organization, where the applications of potential adversaries may also operate. The security and privacy issues which are identified by NIST to be relevant in cloud computing are: (1) governance, (2) compliance, (3) trust, (4) hardware and software architecture, (5) identity and access management, (6) software isolation, (7) data protection, (8) availability, and (9) incident response.

Governance implies control and oversight by the organization over policies, procedures, and standards for application development and information technology service acquisition, as well as the design, implementation, testing, use, and monitoring of deployed or engaged services.

Compliance refers to an organization's responsibility to operate in agreement with established laws, regulations, standards, and specifications. Various types of security and privacy laws and regulation exist within different countries at the national, state, and local levels, making compliance a potentially complicated issue for cloud computing.

Trust is a critical issue in cloud computing since an organization relinquishes direct control over many aspects of security and privacy, and in doing so, confers a high level of trust onto the cloud provider. At the same time, federal agencies have a responsibility to protect information and information systems commensurate with the risk and magnitude of the harm resulting from unauthorized access, use, disclosure, disruption, modification, or destruction, regardless of whether the information is collected or maintained by or on behalf of the agency. In addition, the organization's ownership rights over the data must be firmly established in the service contract to enable a basis for trust and privacy of data.

The architecture of the software and hardware used to deliver cloud services can vary significantly among public cloud providers for any specific service model. Many cloud-based applications require a client side to initiate and obtain services. However, many of the simplified interfaces and service abstractions on the client, server, and network belie the inherent underlying complexity that affects security and privacy. Therefore, the NIST report recommends that it is important to understand the technologies the cloud provider uses to provision services and the implications the technical control involved have on security and privacy of the system throughout its lifecycle. With such information, the underlying system architecture of a cloud can be decomposed and mapped to a framework of security and privacy controls that can be used to access and manage risk. The hypervisor or virtual machine monitor is an additional layer of software between an operating system and hardware platform that is used to operate multi-tenant virtual machines and is common to IaaS clouds. Compared with traditional, non-virtualized implementation, the addition of hypervisor cause an increase in the attack surface in cloud computing, i.e., there are additional methods (e.g. application programming interfaces), channels (e.g., sockets), and data items (e.g., input strings) an attacker can use to cause damage to the system. The report of NIST recommends that care should be taken to provision security for the virtualized environments in which the images of various applications run. It also recommends the use of virtual firewalls to isolate groups of virtual machines from other hosted groups, such as production systems from development systems or development systems from other cloud-resident systems. Another aspect of security that is critical in cloud computing is the client-side protection. Since the services from different cloud providers, as well as cloud-based applications developed by the organization, can impose stringent demands on the client-side, which may have implications for security and privacy that need to be taken into account for system design. Likewise, the Web browsers, which are key elements for many cloud computing services and various plug-ins and extensions available for them are notorious for their security problems. The growing availability and use of social media, personal Webmail, and other publicly available sites also have associated risks that a concern, since they increasingly serve as avenues for social engineering attacks that can negatively impact the security of the browser, its underlying platform, and cloud services accessed. Since data sensitivity and privacy of information have become increasingly an area of concern for organizations in the paradigm of cloud computing, preventing unauthorized access to information resources in the cloud is a critical requirement. The NIST report recommends the use of identity federation as one solution to the complicated authentication requirements in cloud computing. Identity federation allows an organization and a cloud provider to trust and share digital identities and attributes across both domains, and to provide a means for single sign-on. For such federation to succeed, identity and access management transactions must be interpreted carefully and unambiguously and protected against attacks. There are several ways in which an identity federation can be accomplished such as with the *Security Assertion Markup Language* (SAML) standard or the OpenID standard (Badger et al., 2011). A growing number of cloud providers support the SAML standard and use it to administer users and authenticate them before providing access to application and data. SAML request and response messages are typically mapped over SOAP, which relies on the eXtensible Markup Language (XML) for its format. SOAP messages are digitally signed. In a public cloud, for instance, once a user has established a public key certificate with the service, the private key can be used to sign SOAP requests. However, SOAP message security validation is complicated and must be carried out carefully to prevent attacks. XML wrapping attacks have been successfully demonstrated against a public IaaS cloud (Gajek et al., 2009; Gruschka & Iacono, 2009). XML wrapping involves manipulation of SOAP messages. A new element (i.e., the wrapper) is introduced into the SOAP security header: the original message body is then moved under the wrapper and replaced by a bogus body containing an operation defined by the attacker (Gajek et al., 2009; Gruschka & Iacono, 2009). The original body can still be referenced and its signature verified, but the operation in the replacement body is executed instead. Since SAML alone is not sufficient to provide cloud-based identity and access management services, the NIST report recommends the use of eXtensible Access Control Markup Language (XACML) by a cloud provider to control access to cloud resources. XACML focuses on the mechanism for arriving at authorization decisions, which complements SAML's focus on the means for transferring authentication and authorization decisions between cooperating entities.

Since multi-tenancy in IaaS cloud computing environments is typically done by multiplexing the execution of virtual machines from potentially different consumers on the same physical server, applications deployed on guest virtual machines remain susceptible to attack and compromise, much the same as their non-virtualized counterparts (Badger et al., 2011). However, regardless of the service model and multi-tenant software architecture used, the computations of different consumers must be able to be carried out in isolation from one another, mainly through the use of logical separation mechanisms. This becomes an especially challenging proposition since multi-tenancy in virtual machine-based cloud infrastructures, together with the subtleties in the way physical resources are shared between guest virtual machine, can give rise to new sources of threat. The most serious threat is that malicious code can escape the confines of its virtual machine and interfere with the hypervisor or other guest virtual machines. Live migration, the ability to transition a virtual machine between hypervisors on different host computers without halting the guest operating system, and other features provided by virtual machine monitor environments to facilitate systems management, also increase software size and complexity and potentially add other areas to target in an attack.

Since the data stored in a public cloud typically resides in a shared environment co-located with data from other customers, the NIST report strongly recommends that access to the data should be controlled and the data should be kept secure (Badger et al., 2011). These requirements are also applicable for the data that is migrated within or between clouds. In addition, data can take many forms in the cloud. For example, for cloud-based application development, data may include the application programs, scripts, and configuration settings, along with the development tools. For developed applications, it includes records and other contents created or used by the applications, including deallocated objects, as well as account information about the users of the applications.

The NIST report recommends two methods for keeping data away from unauthorized users: (1) access controls, and (2) encryption. Access controls are typically identity-based, which makes authentication of the user's identity an important issue in cloud computing. However, lacking physical control over the storage of information, encryption is the only way to ensure that it is truly protected. In addition, data must be secured while at rest, in transit, and in use, and access to the data must be controlled. The standards for communication protocols and public key certificates allow data transfers to be protected using cryptography and can usually be implemented with equal effort in SaaS, PaaS, and IaaS environments (Badger et al., 2011). The NIST report observes that the security of a system that employs cryptography depends on the proper control of central keys and key management component. Currently, the responsibility for cryptographic key management falls mainly on the cloud consumer. Key generation and storage is usually performed outside the cloud using hardware security modules, which do not scale well to the cloud paradigm. NIST is currently undertaking the Cryptographic Key Management Project for identifying scalable and usable cryptographic key management and exchange strategies for use by government, which would help to alleviate the problem eventually (Cryptographic Key Management Project). NIST also recommends that before proceeding in cloud environments where the cloud provider provides facilities for key management, the organization must fully understand and weigh the risks involved in the processes defined by the cloud provider for the key management lifecycle (Badger et al., 2011). Hence, the cryptographic operations performed in the cloud become part of the key management process and, therefore should be managed and audited by the organization.

In a public cloud, data from one consumer is physically collocated (e.g., in an IaaS data store) or commingled (e.g., in a SaaS database) with the data of other consumers, which can complicate matters. Hence, NIST recommends that sufficient measures should be taken to ensure that data sanitization should be performed appropriately throughout the system lifecycle.

The NIST report also observes that availability of services is a critical requirement for cloud service providers. Denial of service attacks, equipment outages, and natural disasters are all threats to availability. In most of these cases, the downtime is unplanned and can adversely affect the mission of the organization. Despite employing architectures designed for high service reliability and availability, cloud computing services can and do experience outages and performance slowdowns (Leavitt, 2009). NIST recommends that the level of availability of a cloud service and its capabilities for data backup and disaster recovery need to be addressed in the organization's contingency and continuity planning to ensure the recovery and restoration of disrupted cloud services and operations, using alternate services, equipment, and locations, if required.

NIST report points out the fact that a cloud service provider's role is vital in performing incident response activities, including incident verification, attack analysis, containment, data collection and preservation, problem remediation, and service restoration. Each layer in a cloud application stack, including the application, operating system, network, and database, generates event logs, as do other cloud components, such as load balancers and intrusion detection systems; many such event sources and the means of accessing them are under the control of the cloud service provider. The report also observes that availability of relevant data from event monitoring is essential for timely detection of security incidents. However, the cloud customers are often confronted with extremely limited capabilities for detection of incidents in public cloud environments and the service providers have insufficient access to event sources and vulnerability information, inadequate interfaces for accessing and processing event data automatically, and do not have the capability to add detection points within the cloud infrastructure, and have difficulty in directing third-party reported abuses and incidents effectively back to the correct customer or the cloud provider for handling. The report also observes that an incident should be handled in a way that limits damage and minimizes recovery time and costs. Hence, collaboration between the cloud consumer and provider in recognizing and responding to an incident is vital to security and privacy in cloud computing.

In summary, the NIST report on security and privacy issues in public cloud computing provides an overview of the public cloud and describes the threats, technology risks, and safeguards that are surrounding the public cloud environment. It also provides detailed guidelines for the service providers and the consumers to handle various security and privacy issues in cloud computing.

Cloud Security Alliance (CSA)

This non-profit organization provides security guidance for critical areas of focus in cloud computing (CSA Homepage). The alliance covers key issues and provides advice for both cloud computing customers and providers within various strategic domains. CSA has published a report on cloud computing that outlines the areas of concern and guidance for organizations adopting cloud computing with an objective to provide the security practitioners with a comprehensive roadmap for being proactive in developing positive and secure relationships with cloud providers. The CSA guide on cloud computing deals with fifteen broad domains of cloud computing: (1) cloud computing architectural framework, (2) governance and enterprise risk management, (3) legal aspects of cloud computing, (4) electronic discovery, (5) compliance and audit, (6) information lifecycle management, (7) portability and interoperability issues, (8) traditional security, business continuity and disaster recovery, (9) data center operations, (10) incident response, notification and remediation, (11) application security, (12) encryption and key management, (13) identity and access management, (14) storage, and (15) virtualization.

From security perspective, the CSA report recommends that a portion of the cost savings obtained by cloud computing services must be invested into the increased scrutiny of the security capabilities of the provider and ongoing detailed audits to ensure requirements are continuously met. It also recommends the following: (1) the service providers should have regular third party risk assessment and these should be made available to the customers, (2) the cloud provider's key risk and performance indicators must be understood clearly and methods must be designed to monitor and measure these indicators from the perspective of the customers, (3) the onus should be on the customer to perform due diligence of a cloud provider for usage in mission critical business functions or hosting regulated personally identifiable information, (4) the cloud providers should adopt as a security baseline the most stringent requirements of any customer, (5) centralization of data implies the risk of insider threats from within the cloud provider is a significant concern, (6) any data classified as private for the purpose of data breach regulations should always be encrypted to reduce the consequences of a breach incident and the customer should stipulate encryption requirements (algorithm, key length and key management at a minimum) contractually, (7) IaaS, PaaS and SaaS create differing trust boundaries for the software development lifecycle, which must be accounted for during the development, testing and production deployment of applications, (8) securing inter-host communications must be the rule, there can be no assumption of a secure channel between hosts, whether existing in a common data center or even on the same hardware platform, (9) application providers who are not controlling backend systems should assure that data is encrypted when being stored on the backend, (10) segregate the key management from the cloud provider hosting the data, creating a chain of separation. This protects both the cloud provider and customer from conflict when being compelled to provide data due to a legal mandate.

Distributed Management Task Force (DMTF)

DMTF develops standards for interoperable IT management solutions (DMTF Homepage). From this perspective, DMTF is working on several topics like (1) open virtualization format (OVF) that formats for packaging and distributing software to run over virtual machines (2) Open Cloud Standards Incubator, for interactions between cloud environments by developing cloud resource management protocols. The activity was moved to Cloud Management Working Group (CMWG) and (3) Cloud Audit Data Federation (CADF) working group that develops solutions that allows sharing of audit information / logs.

For security issues in cloud computing, DMTF have established a partnership with CSA to promote standards for cloud security as part of DMTF Open Cloud Standard Incubator. The Open Cloud Standard Incubator group is charged with first formulating a series of management protocols, packaging formats and security tools to foster interoperability between cloud, followed by specifications that will foster cloud service portability and cross-cloud management consistency.

Storage Networking Industry Association (SNIA)

SNIA has created the Cloud Storage Technical Work Group for the purpose of developing SNIA architecture related to system implementations of cloud storage technology (SNIA Homepage). It is promoting cloud storage as a new delivery model that provides elastic, on-demand storage billed only for what is used. The initiative, known as the Cloud Data Management Interface (CDMI), lets the customer to tag his/her data with special metadata (data system metadata) that the cloud storage provider what data services to provide that data (backup, archive, encryption, etc.). These data services all add value to the data the customer stores in the cloud and by the implementation of the standard interface of CDMI, the customer can freely move his/her data from one cloud vendor to another without experiencing any pain of recoding to different interfaces.

SNIA is also involved in storage network security related activities. Although storage network security is a new subject, it is rapidly gaining in importance in the minds of both users and product developers. The increase is born of a general realization of the increasing importance and value of the information held in on-line systems, and of the separation of processing and storage functions enabled by the development of Storage Area Networks (SANs). SINA's mission is "to ensure that storage networks become efficient, complete, and trusted solutions across the IT community." However, to achieve this goal, SNIA will have to develop new standards and technologies in storage network security. While storage network security seeks to learn from the application of similar techniques to communications security in general and to network security in particular, it has some unique requirements that will necessitate the development of new and specialized techniques. Currently, the development of such techniques is in its infancy.

Open Grid Forum (OGF)

OGF's Open Cloud Computing Interface (OCCI) (OCCI Homepage) group creates practical solutions to interface with cloud infrastructures exposed as a service. The focus is on a solution which covers the provisioning, monitoring and definition of cloud infrastructure services.

The Open Cloud Computing Interface comprises a set of open community-led specifications delivered through the Open Grid Forum. OCCI is a protocol and API for all kinds of management tasks. OCCI was originally initiated to create a remote management API for IaaS model based Services, allowing for the development of interoperable tools for common tasks including deployment, autonomic scaling and monitoring. It has since evolved into a flexible API with a strong focus on integration, portability, interoperability and innovation while still offering a high degree of extensibility. The current release of the Open Cloud Computing Interface is suitable to serve many other models in addition to IaaS, including e.g., PaaS and SaaS. The security group of OGF is concerned with technical and operational security issues in the grid and cloud environments, including authentication, authorization, privacy, confidentiality, auditing, firewalls, trust establishment, policy establishment, and dynamics, scalability and management aspects of these issues. The purpose of the Certificate Authority Operations (CAOPS) working group is to develop and standardize a framework for cross-grid authentication.

Open Cloud Consortium (OCC)

OCC (OCC Homepage) is a member-driven organization that: (1) supports development of standards, (2) supports development of benchmarks, (3) supports reference implementations of cloud computing, preferably open source, and (4) sponsors workshops and other events related to cloud computing. OCC has four working groups: (1) large data clouds working group, (2) open cloud test-bed working group, (3) standard cloud performance measurement (SCPM) working group, and (4) information sharing and security working group. The SCPM working group is responsible for establishing benchmarks appropriate for four use cases: (1) moving an application between two clouds, (2) obtaining burst instances from multiple cloud service providers for a private/public hybrid application, (3) moving a large data cloud application to another large data cloud storage service, and (4) moving a large data cloud application to another large data cloud computing service.

Organization for the Advancement of Structured Information Standards (OASIS)

OASIS is a not-for-profit, international consortium that drives the development, convergence, and adoption of e-business standards (OASIS Homepage). The consortium produces more Web services standards than any other organization along with standards for security, e-business, and standardization efforts in the public sector and application-specific markets. In cloud computing domain, OASIS has the following technical committees, each having its clearly defined objectives and goals.

1. **Advanced Message Queuing Protocol (AMQP) TC:** It defines a ubiquitous, secure, reliable and open ended Internet protocol for handling business messaging.
2. **Cloud Application Management for Platforms (CAMP) TC:** It is responsible for standardizing cloud PaaS management API.
3. **Cloud Authorization (CloudAuthZ) TC:** It focuses on enabling contextual attributes and entitlements to be delivered to Policy Enforcement Points in real-time.
4. **Identity in the Cloud TC:** It is involved in developing profiles of open standards for identity deployment, provisioning and management in cloud computing.
5. **Open Data Protocol (OData) TC:** Its goal is to simplify data sharing across disparate applications in enterprise, cloud and mobile devices.
6. **Privacy Management Reference Model (PMRM) TC:** It is responsible for providing a guideline for developing operational solutions to privacy issues.
7. **SOA Reference Model TC:** It is involved in developing a core reference model to guide and foster the creation of specific Service-Oriented Architecture (SOA).
8. **Topology and Orchestration Specification for Cloud Applications (TOSCA) TC:** It is responsible for enhancing the portability of cloud applications and services.
9. **Transformational Government Framework TC:** It is advancing an overall framework for using IT to improve delivery of public services.

TM Forum

TM Forum (TM Forum Homepage)—an association that includes technology vendors such as HP and IBM, as well as more than 750 of the world's largest service providers in the communications, media, and cloud service markets—has delivered what it calls the industry's first set of *enterprise-grade external compute Infrastructure as a Service (IaaS) requirements*. Put together by the association's Enterprise Cloud Leadership Council (ECLC), the document includes guidelines for technology; requirements for external private clouds in commercial, technical, and operational terms; the business case for external private clouds; and sample use cases. It also details how business and technical agreements between enterprise customers and cloud service providers should be defined and managed to maximize benefits for both parties.

Focused on enabling best-in-class IT for service providers in the communications, media, defense and cloud service market, TM Forum created ECLC in 2009 to provide a forum for enterprise cloud users to share requirements and drive the development of best practices and standards that will remove the barriers to development and adoption of cloud services. Its list of members includes Deutsche Bank, Boeing, ING, Dassault Systems, and Northrop-Grumman.

Incorporating the input from the top cloud innovators and thought leaders, this document of TM Forum intends to create a way forward for the industry that separates out the vital needs from the minor and secondary requirements. Based on end users' experience and requirements the document is intended to assist cloud service providers and technology suppliers to determine customer demands, drive direction on standards and best practices, and remove barriers to adoption. The vendors need to map their product and service offerings against those requirements.

The cloud services initiative of TM Forum, therefore, intends to deliver the following:

- An ecosystem of enterprise customers, cloud service providers and technology suppliers that enable the commercialization of this major business opportunity.
- Business guidance including benchmarks and service quality metrics.
- Technical agreements in collaboration with other industry groups.

With a particular focus on developing standards in cloud computing, the Enterprise Cloud Leadership Council (ECLC) of the TM Forum has the following programs in its agenda of activities:

- Defining Service Level Agreements (SLAs) for cloud services
- Data-as-a-Service (DBaaS) reference architecture
- Cloud API requirements
- Business process and information frameworks for cloud
- Secure virtual private cloud reference architecture
- Standard service definitions/SKUs (Taxonomy of services)
- Cloud SDO liaisons
- eTOM and ITIL; how to combine them in a cloud context?
- Cloud service provider benchmarking and metrics
- Billing engine, client billing and partner revenue sharing for cloud services
- Common definition of commercial terms (business contract language)

The TM Forum has created a Cloud Services Initiative with the purpose to define a range of common approaches, processes, metrics and other key service enablers (TM Forum Homepage).

International Telecommunication Union (ITU)

The International Telecommunications Union-Telecommunications Standards Group (ITU-T) (ITU-T Homepage) has formed a focus group on cloud computing (FG Cloud) to further ITU-T TSAG (Telecommunication Standardization Advisory Group) agreement at its meeting in Geneva during 8-11 February 2010. The focus group, established in accordance with Recommendation ITU-T A.7, from the standardization viewpoints and within the competencies of ITU-T contributes to telecommunication aspects, i.e., the transport via telecommunications networks, security aspects of telecommunications, service requirements, etc., in order to support services/applications of cloud computing making use of telecommunication networks, specifically in the following activities:

- Identify the potential impacts on standard development and priorities for standards needed to promote and facilitate telecommunication/ICT support for cloud computing
- Investigate the need for future study items for fixed and mobile network in the scope of ITU-T
- Analyze which components would benefit most from interoperability and standardization
- Familiarize ITU-T and standardization communities with emerging attributes and challenges of telecommunication/ICT support for cloud computing
- Analyze the rate of change for cloud computing attributes, functions and features for the purpose of assessing the appropriate timing of standardization of telecommunication/ICT in support of cloud computing

The focus group on cloud computing in ITU-T collaborates with worldwide cloud computing communities (e.g., research institutions, laboratories, forums, and academia) including other SDOs and consortia. The group has also identified its specific tasks and deliverables in cloud computing standards development activities. The identified deliverables are: (1) identification of the benefits of cloud computing from telecommunication/ICT perspectives, (2) gap analysis of ITU-T standards for telecommunication/ICT to support cloud computing, (3) collection and summarization of vision and value propositions of cloud computing with a focus on telecommunication/ICT aspects, (4) leveraging expertise within the ITU-T in building telecom networks to take advantage of cloud concepts and capabilities, (5) analysis of telecommunication/ICT networking requirements functions and capabilities to support cloud computing services/applications (for both fixed and mobile devices), (6) use case of services and reference models for telecommunication/ICT to support cloud computing, (7) designing the roadmap to guide further development of relevant ITU-T recommendations.

The European Telecommunications Standards Institute (ETSI)

ETSI (ETSI Homepage) Technical Committee (TC) GRID, now known as TC CLOUD, has been formed to address issues associated with the convergence between IT (Information Technology) and Telecommunications. The focus is on scenarios where connectivity goes beyond the local network. This includes not only grid computing but also the emerging commercial trend towards cloud computing which places particular emphasis on ubiquitous network access to scalable computing and storage resources. Since TC CLOUD has particular interest in interoperable solutions in situations which involve contributions from both the IT and Telecom industries, the emphasis is on the Infrastructure as a Service (IaaS) delivery model.

The focus of the ETSI TC Cloud is on the following issues: (1) to complement progress being made elsewhere with a networking perspective and a more formal approach to standards and test specifications, (2) introduce new requirements into networking (e.g., next-generation networks) standards to support new kinds of application such as grid and cloud, (3) achieving the desired level of interoperability needed in next-generation networks, grids and clouds, (4) collaborate with other SDOs in developing standards in cloud computing.

Object Management Group (OMG)

OMG is an international, open membership, not-for-profit computer industry standards consortium. OMG Task Forces (TFs) develop enterprise integration standards for a wide range of industries. In cloud computing standardization, OMG's focus

Security and Privacy Issues in Cloud Computing

is on modeling deployment of applications and services on clouds for portability, interoperability and reuse (OMG Homepage). The standardization activities in cloud computing in OMG are mainly focused on the following broad areas:

- **Meta-element Association:** For defining *distributed and non-deterministic computing* from the cloud and SOA perspective.
- **Governance:** There is a services governance domain and a cloud governance domain. The key is how to integrate these two points of view for governing *distributed and non-deterministic computing*.
- **SLAs:** Developing SLAs for services delivered over the cloud
- **SOA, Events, and Agents:** Defining communication among and within clouds between services enabled in these clouds.

Association for Retail Technology Standards (ARTS)

ARTS (ARTS Homepage) is an international membership organization dedicated to reducing the costs of technology through standards. ARTS has been delivering application standards exclusively to the retail industry. ARTS released a white paper on cloud computing in 2009 that offers unbiased guidance for achieving maximum results from this relatively new technology. The version 1.0 of the whitepaper represents a significant update to the draft version released in October 2009. The document seeks to identify the characteristics of cloud computing that makes it compelling for retailers, and attempts to highlight areas in which a cloud-based solution offers strong benefits to retailers. It also discusses the key obstacles to adopting cloud-based solutions, including reliability, availability, and security. It also covers issues relating to portability, manageability, and interoperability.

Institute of Electrical and Electronics Engineers (IEEE)

Hoping to propel cloud computing to new heights, the IEEE (IEEE Homepage) has launched a design guide and a standard for interoperable cloud services. According to IEEE, these two initiatives are by far the first ever attempt by any formal standards body to address the issues hounding cloud services. In order to enable transfer of customer data from one provider to another in a seamless standardized manner, the IEEE P2301 draft guide is being designed to provide an intuitive roadmap for application portability, management, and interoperability interfaces, as well as for file formats and operating conventions. The standard is expected to be completed in 2014 and will help vendors, service providers, and consumers involved in every aspects of procuring, developing, building, and using cloud computing.

In addition, IEEE is involved in preparation of another draft standard – IEEE P2302 draft standard for intercloud interoperability and federation. There is a growing demand from the consumers for the same kinds of global roaming, portability, and interoperability capabilities for storage and computing as with voice and text messaging. To meet this requirement, IEEE P2302 is defining the topology, protocols, functionality, and governance required for cloud-to-cloud interoperability. The term "intercloud" refers to an interconnected mesh of clouds that depends on open standards for their operation. "Federation" allows users to move their data across internal and external clouds and access services running on other clouds according to the business and application requirements. The IEEE P2302 working group is also focusing on building a system among cloud product and service providers that would be transparent to users. The group plans to address transparent interoperability and federation in much the same way that standards do for the global telephony systems and the Internet.

Alliance for Telecommunications Industry Solutions (ATIS)

ATIS (ATIS Homepage) is the leading technical planning and standards development organization committed to the rapid development of global, market-driven standards for the information, entertainment and communications industry. ATIS' Cloud Services Forum (CSF) facilitates the adoption and advancement of cloud services from a network and IT perspective. Its primary focus is on the basic APIs in the control plane layer of the network rather than on the services on the network. Drawing upon business use cases that leverage cloud services' potential, CSF addresses industry priorities and develops implementable solutions for this evolving marketplace. CSF is working to ensure that services are quickly put into operation to facilitate the delivery of interoperable, secure, and managed services. Current priorities of CSF include content distribution network interconnection, cloud services framework, inter-carrier tele-presence, virtual desktop, virtual private network, and development of a cloud services checklist for onboarding. The current initiatives of CSF include the following activities:

- Develop video service specifications as a component of a unified communications framework (e.g., telepresence, mobility etc.).
- Advance a Trusted Information Exchange (TIE) solution to address the directory, routing, privacy, and accessibility.
- Progress the next phase of Content Distribution Network-Interconnection (CDN-I) – building on initial use cases to address more complicated models and additional content types. CSF currently leads the market in standardization aspects of CDN-I for content delivery, for example Multicast.
- Define virtual desktop functional requirements to take advantage of cloud resources to reduce management costs and support ay-device, any-network access to desktops by end-users.

Internet Engineering Task Force (IETF)

IETF (IETF Homepage) has established the Cloud OPS WG (working group on cloud computing and maintenance) which is currently discussing cloud resource management and monitoring, and Cloud-APS-BOF which has focused on cloud applications. There are several existing working groups within the IETF that are also working in the technical areas that could be useful to cloud computing activities. Among these working groups are Decade working group within IETF application area, nfsv4 working group within TSV application area, and netconf working group within OPS application area. Similarly, IRTF (Internet Research Task Force) has been working on the technical issues related to cloud computing as part of P2PRG working group and VNRG research group. While the above working groups have been in existence for some time, in the last year, there has been some renewed effort to focus on providing cloud services. Currently, there is an effort underway in the form of *birds of feather* (BOF) to discuss various contributions related to cloud computing. Most of the work being discussed as part of this effort would hopefully be very useful to the service providers.

EMERGING TRENDS IN SECURITY AND PRIVACY IN CLOUD COMPUTING

Cloud computing environments are multidomain environments in which each domain can use different security, privacy, and trust requirements and potentially employ various mechanisms, interfaces, and semantics. Such domain could represent individually enabled services or other infrastructural or application components. Service-oriented architectures are naturally relevant technology to facilitate such multidomain formation through service composition and orchestration. It is important to leverage existing research on multidomain policy integration and the secure service composition to build a comprehensive policy-based management framework in cloud computing environments (Takabi et al., 2010). In the following, we identify some critical security and privacy issues in cloud computing that need immediate attention for ubiquitous adoption of this technology.

Authentication and Identity Management: By using cloud services, user can easily access their personal information and make it available to various services across the Internet. An Identity Management (IDM) mechanism can help authenticate users and services based on credentials and characteristics (Bertino et al., 2009). A key issue concerning IDM in cloud is interoperability drawbacks that could result from using different identity tokens and identity negotiation protocols. Existing password-based authentication has an inherited limitation and poses significant risks. An IDM system should be able to protect private and sensitive information related to users and processes. However, multi-tenant cloud environments can affect the privacy of identity information and isn't yet well understood. In addition, the multi-jurisdiction issue can complicate protection measures (Bruening & Treacy, 2009). While users interact with a front-end service, this service might need to ensure that their identity is protected from other services with which it interacts (Bertino et al., 2009; Ko et al., 2009). In multi-tenant cloud environments, providers must segregate customer identity and authentication information. Authentication and IDM components should also be easily integrated with other security components. Design and development of robust authentication and identity management protocols is, therefore, a critical requirement for cloud computing.

Access Control and Accounting: Heterogeneity and diversity of services, as well as the domains' diverse access requirements in cloud computing environments, demand fine-grained access control policies. In particular, access control services should be flexible enough to capture dynamic, context, or attribute-or credential-based access requirements and to enforce the principle of least privilege. Such access control services might need to integrate privacy-protection requirements expressed through complex rules. It's important that access control system employed in clouds is easily managed and its privilege distribution is administered efficiently. It should also be ensured that the cloud delivery models provide generic access control interfaces for proper interoperability, which demands a policy-neutral access control specification and enforcement framework that can be used to address cross-domain access issues (Joshi et al., 2004). Utilizing a privacy-aware framework for access control and accounting services that is easily amenable to compliance checking is therefore a crucial requirement which needs immediate attention from the researches.

Trust Management and Policy Integration: Although multiple service providers coexist in cloud and collaborate to provide various services, they might have different security approaches and privacy mechanisms. Hence, we must address heterogeneity among their policies (ENISA, 2009; Blaze et al., 2009; Zhang & Joshi, 2009). Cloud service providers might need to compose multiple services to enable bigger application services. Therefore, mechanisms are necessary to ensure that such a dynamic collaboration is handled securely and that security breaches are effectively monitored during the interoperation process. Existing work has shown that even though individual domain policies are verified, security violations can easily occur during integration (Zhang & Joshi, 2009). Hence, providers should carefully manage access control policies to ensure that policy integration doesn't lead to any security breaches. In cloud computing, the interactions between different service domains driven by service requirements can be dynamic, transient, and intensive. Thus, a trust framework should be developed to allow for efficiently capturing a generic set of parameters required for establishing trust and to manage evolving trust and interaction/sharing requirements (Zhang & Joshi, 2009; Shin & Ahn, 2005). In addition cloud's policy integration tasks should be able to address challenges such as semantic heterogeneity, secure interoperability, and policy evolution management. Since the customers' behavior can evolve rapidly, there is a need for integrated, trust-based, secure interoperation framework that helps establish, negotiate, and maintain trust to adaptively support policy integration. Design of efficient trust management frameworks for wireless and peer-to-peer networks is a widely researched problem (Sen, 2006c; Sen et al., 2007; Sen, 2010d, 2010e, 2010f, 2010g, 2011c). However, there is an urgent need for developing robust and reliable trust models for cloud computing environments. This will be a particularly challenging issue to address due to various interoperability issues and global deployments of cloud service delivery models.

Secure Service Management: In cloud computing environments, cloud service providers and service integrators compose services for their customers. The service integrator provides a platform that lets independent service providers orchestrate and interwork services and cooperatively provide additional services that meet customers' protection requirements. Although many cloud service providers use the Web Services Description Language (WSDL), the traditional WSDL can't fully meet the requirements of cloud computing services description. In clouds, issues such as quality of service, price, and SLAs are critical in service search and composition. These issues must be addressed to describe services and introduce their features, find the best interoperable options, integrate them without violating the service owner's policies, and ensure that SLAs are satisfied (Takabi et al., 2010). In essence, an automatic and systematic service provisioning and composition framework that considers security and privacy issues is crucial and needs urgent attention.

Privacy and Data Protection: Privacy is a core issue in many challenges in cloud computing including the need to protect identity information, policy components during integration, and transaction histories. Many organizations are not comfortable in storing their data and applications on systems that reside outside their on-premise data centers (Chen et al., 2010). By migrating workloads to a shared infrastructure, customers' private information faces increased risk of potential unauthorized access and exposure. Cloud service providers must assure their customers and provide a high degree of transparency into their operations and privacy assurance. Privacy-protection mechanisms must be embedded in all cloud security solutions. In a related issue, it is becoming important to know who created a piece of data, who modified it and how, and so on. Provenance information could be used for various purposes such as traceback, auditing, and history-based access control. Balancing between data provenance and privacy is a significant challenge in clouds where physical perimeters are abandoned. This is also a critical research challenge.

Organizational Security Management: Existing security management and information security life-cycle models significantly change when enterprises adopt cloud computing. In particular, shared governance can become a significant issue if not addressed properly. Despite the potential benefits of using clouds, it might mean less coordination among different communities of interest within client organizations. Dependence on external entities can also raise fears about timely response to security incidents and implementing systematic business continuity and disaster recovery plans. Similarly, risk and cost-benefit issues will need to involve external parties. Customers consequently need to consider newer risks introduced by a perimeter-less environment, such as data leakage within multi-tenant clouds and resiliency issues such as their provider's economic instability and local disasters. Similarly, the possibility of an insider threat is significantly extended when outsourcing data and processes to clouds. Within multi-tenant environments, one tenant could be a highly targeted attack victim, which could significantly affect the other tenant. Existing life-cycle models, risk analysis and management processes, penetration testing, and service attestation must be reevaluated to ensure that clients can enjoy the potential benefits of clouds (Takabi et al., 2010).

The information security area has faced significant problems in establishing appropriate security metrics for consistent and realistic measurements that help risk assessment. We must reevaluate best practices and develop standards to ensure the deployment and adoption of secure clouds. These issues necessitate a well-structured cyber insurance industry, but the global nature of cloud computing makes this prospect extremely complex. As well as trends specific to the cloud, general IT industry trends will also drive the change in cloud computing services and approach to future services, architectures and innovations (CPNI Security Briefing, 2010). Some of these trends are as follows:

Increasing use of Mobile Devices: Laptop sales have overtaken desktops over the last few years and the trend will continue as an increasing range of mobile devices such as notebooks, PDAs and mobile phones incorporate many of the features found on a desktop-based PC only about ten years ago, including Internet access and custom application functionality.

Hardware Capability Improvements: The inevitable improvements in processor speed and increased memory capacities across IT infrastructure will mean that the cloud will be able to support more complex environments with improved performance capabilities as standard.

Tackling Complexity: Despite the efforts of multiple technology vendors, this challenge of complexity remains unresolved. IT architectures continue to be difficult to implement, under-utilized and expensive to operate. The massive scale of cloud computing only strengthens the need for self-monitoring, self-healing and self-configuring IT systems comprising heterogeneous storage, servers, applications, networks and other system elements.

Legislation and Security: As larger companies consider the cloud computing model, vendors and providers will respond, but within the terms set out by their potential customers. As there are still many issues with respect to data privacy and transfer of data across international borders, the cloud service providers need to continue to invest time and effort in order to meet the necessary laws required to operate within some of the business areas of their major customers.

CONCLUSION

Today, cloud computing is being defined and talked about across the ICT industry under different contexts and with different definitions attached to it. The core point is that cloud computing means having a server firm that can host the services for users connected to it by the network. Technology has moved in this direction because of the advancement in computing, communication, and networking technologies. Fast and reliable connectivity is a must for the existence of cloud computing.

Cloud computing is clearly one of the most enticing technology areas of the current times due, at least in part to its cost-efficiency and flexibility. However, despite the surge in activity and interest, there are significant, persistent concerns about cloud computing that are impeding the momentum and will eventually compromise the vision of cloud computing as a new IT procurement model. Despite the trumpeted business and technical advantages of cloud computing, many potential cloud users have yet to join the cloud, and those major corporations that are cloud users are for the most part putting only their less sensitive data in the cloud. Lack of control is transparency in the cloud implementation – somewhat contrary to the original promise of cloud computing in which cloud implementation is not relevant. Transparency is needed for regulatory reasons and to ease concern over the potential for data breaches. Because of today's perceived lack of control, larger companies are testing the waters with smaller projects and less sensitive data. In short, the potential of the cloud is not yet being realized.

When thinking about solutions to cloud computing's adoption problem, it is important to realize that many of the issues are essentially old problems in a new setting, although they may be more acute (Chow et al., 2009). For example, corporate partnerships and offshore outsourcing involve similar trust and regulatory issues. Similarly, open source software enables IT department to quickly build and deploy applications, but at the cost of control and governance. Similarly, virtual machine attacks and Web service vulnerabilities existed long before cloud computing became fashionable. Indeed, this very overlap is reason for optimism; many of these cloud computing roadblocks have long been studied and the foundations for solutions exist. For the enhancement of technology, and hence healthy growth of global economy, it is extremely important to iron out any issues that can cause road-blocks in this new paradigm of computing.

REFERENCES

Alliance for Telecommunications Industry Solutions. (n.d.). *Homepage*. Retrieved from http://www.atis.org

Amazon S3 Availability Event. (2008). Retrieved from http://status.aws.amazon.com/s3-20080720.html

AOL Apologizes for Release of User Search Data. (2006). Retrieved from news.cnet.com/2010-1030_3-6102793.html

Armbrust, M., Fox, A., Griffith, R., Joseph, A. D., Katz, R. H., & Konwinsky, A. … Zaharia, M. (2009). *Above the clouds: A Berkeley view of cloud computing* (Technical Report No. UCB/EECS-2009-28). Berkeley, CA: University of California at Berkeley. Retrieved from http://www.eecs.berkeley.edu/Pubs/TechRpts/2009/EECS-2009-28.pdf

Association for Retail Technology Standards (ARTS). (n.d.). *Homepage*. Retrieved from http://www.nrf-arts.org

Badger, L., Grance, T., Patt-Corner, R., & Voas, J. (2011). *Draft cloud computing synopsis and recommendations* (Special Publication 800-146). National Institute of Standards and Technology (NIST). US Department of Commerce. Retrieved from http://csrc.nist.gov/publications/drafts/800-146/Draft-NIST-SP800-146.pdf

Bertion, E., Paci, F., & Ferrini, R. (2009, March). Privacy-preserving digital identity management for cloud computing. *IEEE Computer Society Data Engineering Bulletin*, 1-4.

Biggs & Vidalis. (2009). Cloud computing: The impact on digital forensic investigations. In *Proceedings of the 7th International Conference for Internet Technology and Secured Transactions (ICITST'09)*. London, UK: ICITST.

Blaze, M., Kannan, S., Lee, I., Sokolsky, O., Smith, J. M., Keromytis, A. D., & Lee, W. (2009). Dynamic trust management. *IEEE Computer*, *42*(2), 44–52. doi:10.1109/MC.2009.51

Bruening, P. J., & Treacy, B. C. (2009). *Cloud computing: Privacy, security challenges*. Washington, DC: Bureau of National Affairs.

Center for the Protection of Natural Infrastructure (CPNI). (2010). *Information security briefing on cloud computing, 01/2010*. Retrieved from http://www.cpni.gov.uk/Documents/Publications/2010/2010007-ISB_cloud_computing.pdf

Chen, Y., Paxson, V., & Katz, R. H. (2010). *What's new about cloud computing security?* (Technical Report UCB/EECS-2010-5). Berkeley, CA: EECS Department, University of California, Berkeley. Retrieved from http://www.eecs.berkeley.edu/Pubs/TechRpts/2010/EECS-2010-5.html

Chor, B., Kushilevitz, E., Goldreich, O., & Sudan, M. (1998). Private information retrieval. *Journal of the ACM, 45*(9), 965–981. doi:10.1145/293347.293350.

Chow, R., Golle, P., Jakobsson, M., Shi, E., Staddon, J., Masuoka, R., & Molina, J. (2009). Controlling data in the cloud: Outsourcing computation without outsourcing control. In *Proceedings of the ACM Workshop on Cloud Computing Security (CCSW'09)*, (pp. 85-90). Chicago, IL: ACM Press.

Cloud Security Alliance. (n.d.). *Homepage*. Retrieved from https://cloudsecurityalliance.org

Cloud Security Alliance (CSA). (2009). Security guidance for critical areas of focus in cloud computing. *CSA*. Retrieved from https://cloudsecurityalliance.org/csaguide.pdf

CNet. (2009). *FTC questions cloud computing security*. Retrieved from http://news.cnet.com/8301-13578_3-10198577-38.html?part=rss&subj=news&tag=2547-1_3-0-20

Cryptographic Key Management Project. (n.d.). *Website*. Retrieved from http://csrc.nist.gov/groups/ST/key_mgmt/

Distributed Management Task Force. (n.d.). *Homepage*. Retrieved from http://www.dmtf.org

Don't Cloud Your Vision. (n.d.). Retrieved from http://www.ft.com/cms/s/0/303680a6-bf51-11dd-ae63-0000779fd18c.html?nclick_check=1

European Network and Information Security Agency (ENISA). (2009). *Cloud computing: Benefits, risks and recommendations for information security*. Geneva, Switzerland: ENISA.

European Telecommunication Standards Institute. (n.d.). *Homepage*. Retrieved from http://www.etsi.org

Flexiscale Suffers 18-Hour Outage. (2008). Retrieved from http://www.thewhir.com/web-hosting-news/flexiscale-suffers-18-hour-outage

Forum, T. M. (n.d.). *Homepage*. Retrieved from http://www.tmforum.org

Gajek, S., Jensen, M., Liao, L., & Schwenk, J. (2009). Analysis of signature wrapping attacks and countermeasures. In *Proceedings of the IEEE International Conference on Web Services*, (pp. 575-582). Los Angeles, CA: IEEE.

Garfinkel, S., & Shelat, A. (2003). Remembrance of data passed: A study of disk sanitization practices. *IEEE Security and Privacy, 1*(1), 17–27. doi:10.1109/MSECP.2003.1176992.

Gartner Hype-Cycle. (2012). *Cloud computing and big data*. Retrieved from http://www.gartner.com/technology/research/hype-cycles/

Gentry, C. (2009). Fully homomorphic encryption using ideal lattices. In *Proceedings of the 41st Annual ACM Symposium on Theory of Computing (STOC'09)*, (pp. 169-178). Bethesda, MD: ACM.

Gruschka, N., & Iacono, L. L. (2009). Vulnerable cloud: SOAP message security validation revisited. In *Proceedings of IEEE International Conference on Web Services (ICWS'09)*, (pp. 625-631). Los Angeles, CA: IEEE.

IBM Blue Cloud Initiative Advances Enterprise Cloud Computing. (n.d.). Retrieved from http://www-03.ibm.com/press/us/en/pressrelease/26642.wss

Institute of Electrical and Electronics Engineers (IEEE). (n.d.). *Homepage.* Retrieved from http://www.ieee.org

International Telecommunication Union – Telecommunication Standardization Sector (ITU-T). (n.d.). *Homepage.* Retrieved form http://www.itu.int/ITU-T

Internet Engineering Task Force. (n.d.). *Homepage.* Retrieved from http://www.ietf org

Joshi, J. B. D., Bhatti, R., Bertino, E., & Ghafoor, A. (2004). Access control language for multi-domain environments. *IEEE Internet Computing, 8*(6), 40–50. doi:10.1109/MIC.2004.53.

Ko, M., Ahn, G.-J., & Shehab, M. (2009). Privacy-enhanced user-centric identity management. In *Proceedings of IEEE International Conference on Communications,* (pp. 998-1002). Dresden, Germany: IEEE.

Latest Cloud Storage Hiccups Prompts Data Security Questions. (n.d.). Retrieved from http://www.computerworld.com/action/article.do?command=viewArticleBasic&articleId=9130682&source=NLT_PM

Leavitt, N. (2009). Is cloud computing really ready for prime time? *IEEE Computer, 42*(1), 15–20. doi:10.1109/MC.2009.20.

Leighon, T. (2009). Akamai and cloud computing: A perspective from the edge of the cloud (White Paper). *Akamai Technologies.* Retrieved from http://www.essextec.com/assets/cloud/akamai/cloud-computing-perspective-wp.pdf

Lowensohn, J., & McCarthy, C. (2009). *Lessons from Twitter's security breach.* Retrieved from http://news.cnet.com/8301-17939_109-10287558-2.html

Molnar, D., & Schechter, S. (2010). Self hosting vs. cloud hosting: Accounting for the security impact of hosting in the cloud. In *Proceedings of the Workshop on the Economics of Information Security.* Retrieved from http://weis2010.econinfosec.org/papers/session5/weis2010_schechter.pdf

Netflix Prize. (n.d.). Retrieved from http://www.netflixprize.com/

Network World. (2008). *Loss of customer data spurs closure of online storage service the linkup.* Retrieved from http://www.networkworld.com/news/2008/081108-linkup-failure.html?page=1

News, B. B. C. (2009). *Facebook users suffer viral surge.* Retrieved from http://news.bbc.co.uk/2/hi/technology/7918839.stm

Object Management Group. (n.d.). *Homepage.* Retrieved from http://www.omg.org

Open Cloud Computing Interface. (n.d.). *Homepage.* Retrieved from http://occi-wg.org

Open Cloud Consortium. (n.d.). *Homepage.* Retrieved from http://opencloudconsortium.org

Organization for the Advancement of Structured Information Standards. (n.d.). *Homepage.* Retrieved from http://www.oasis-open.org

Post, W. (2008). *Lithuania weathers cyber attack, braces for round 2.* Retrieved from http://blog.washingtonpost.com/securityfix/2008/07/lithuania_weathers_cyber_attac_1.html

Ristenpart, T., Tromer, E., Shacham, H., & Savage, S. (2009). Hey, you, get off of my cloud: Exploring information leakage in third-party compute clouds. In *Proceedings of the 16th ACM Conference on Computer and Communications Security (CCS'09),* (pp. 199-212). Chicago: ACM Press.

Security Bulletin, M. MS07-049. (2007). *Vulnerability in virtual PC and virtual server could allow elevation of privilege (937986).* Retrieved from http://www.microsoft.com/technet/security/bulletin/ms07-049.mspx

Security Evaluation of Grid Environments. (n.d.). Retrieved from http://www.slideworld.com/slideshows.aspx/Security-Evaluation-of-Grid-Environments-ppt-217556

Sen, J. (2010a). An agent-based intrusion detection system for local area networks. *International Journal of Communication Networks and Information Security, 2*(2), 128–140.

Sen, J. (2010b). An intrusion detection architecture for clustered wireless ad hoc networks. In *Proceedings of the 2nd IEEE International Conference on Intelligence in Communication Systems and Networks (CICSyN'10)*, (pp. 202-207). Liverpool, UK: CICsyN.

Sen, J. (2010c). A robust and fault-tolerant distributed intrusion detection system. In *Proceedings of the 1st International Conference on Parallel, Distributed and Grid Computing (PDGC'10)*, (pp. 123-128). Waknaghat, India: PDGC.

Sen, J. (2010d). A distributed trust management framework for detecting malicious packet dropping nodes in a mobile ad hoc network. *International Journal of Network Security and its Applications, 2*(4), 92-104.

Sen, J. (2010e). A distributed trust and reputation framework for mobile ad hoc networks. In *Proceedings of the 1st International Workshop on Trust Management in Peer-to-Peer Systems (IWT-MP2PS)*, (pp. 538-547). Chennai, India: Springer.

Sen, J. (2010f). A trust-based robust and efficient searching scheme for peer-to-peer networks. In *Proceedings of the 12th International Conference on Information and Communication Security (ICICS)* (LNCS), (vol. 6476, pp. 77-91). Barcelona, Spain: Springer.

Sen, J. (2010g). Reputation- and trust-based systems for wireless self-organizing networks. In *Security of Self-Organizing Networks: MANET, WSN, WMN, VANET* (pp. 91–122). Boca Raton, FL: CRC Press. doi:10.1201/EBK1439819197-7.

Sen, J. (2011a). A robust mechanism for defending distributed denial of service attacks on web servers. *International Journal of Network Security and its Applications, 3*(2), 162-179.

Sen, J. (2011b). A novel mechanism for detection of distributed denial of service attacks. In *Proceedings of the 1st International Conference on Computer Science and Information Technology (CCSIT'11)*, (pp. 247-257). Springer.

Sen, J. (2011c). A secure and efficient searching for trusted nodes in peer-to-peer network. In *Proceedings of the 4th International Conference on Computational Intelligence in Security for Information Systems (CISIS'11)* (LNCS), (vol. 6694, pp. 101-109). Berlin: Springer.

Sen, J., Chowdhury, P. R., & Sengupta, I. (2006c). A distributed trust mechanism for mobile ad hoc networks. In *Proceedings of the International Symposium on Ad Hoc and Ubiquitous Computing (ISAHUC'06)*, (pp. 62-67). Surathkal, India: ISAHUC.

Sen, J., Chowdhury, P. R., & Sengupta, I. (2007). A distributed trust establishment scheme for mobile ad hoc networks. In *Proceedings of the International Conference on Computation: Theory and Applications (ICCTA'07)*, (pp. 51-57). Kolkata, India: ICCTA.

Sen, J., & Sengupta, I. (2005). Autonomous agent-based distributed fault-tolerant intrusion detection system. In *Proceedings of the 2nd International Conference on Distributed Computing and Internet Technology (ICDCIT'05)* (LNCS), (vol. 3186, pp. 125-131). Bhubaneswar, India: Springer.

Sen, J., Sengupta, I., & Chowdhury, P. R. (2006a). A mechanism for detection and prevention of distributed denial of service attacks. In *Proceedings of the 8th International Conference on Distributed Computing and Networking (ICDCN'06)* (LNCS), (vol. 4308, pp. 139-144). Berlin: Springer.

Sen, J., Sengupta, I., & Chowdhury, P. R. (2006b). An architecture of a distributed intrusion detection system using cooperating agents. In *Proceedings of the International Conference on Computing and Informatics (ICOCI'06)*, (pp. 1-6). Kuala Lumpur, Malaysia: ICOCI.

Sen, J., Ukil, A., Bera, D., & Pal, A. (2008). A distributed intrusion detection system for wireless ad hoc networks. In *Proceedings of the 16th IEEE International Conference on Networking (ICON'08)*, (pp. 1-5). New Delhi, India: IEEE.

Shacham, H., & Waters, B. (2008). Compact proofs of retrievability. In *Proceedings of the 14th International Conference on the Theory and Application of Cryptology and Information Security: (ASIACRYPT'08)* (LNCS), (vol. 5350, pp. 90-107). Melbourne, Australia: Springer.

Shin, D., & Ahn, G.-J. (2005). Role-based privilege and trust management. *Computer Systems Science and Engineering Journal, 20*(6), 401–410.

Sinclair, S., & Smith, S. W. (2008). Preventive directions for insider threat mitigation using access control. In Stolfo, S., Bellovin, S. M., Hershkop, S., Keromytis, A. D., Sinclair, S., & Smith, W. (Eds.), *Insider Attack and Cyber Security: Beyond the Hacker*. London: Springer. doi:10.1007/978-0-387-77322-3_10.

Song, D., Wagner, D., & Perrig, A. (2000). Practical techniques for searches on encrypted data. In *Proceedings of the IEEE Symposium on Research in Security and Privacy*, (pp. 44-55). Oakland, CA: IEEE.

Storage Networking Industry Association. (n.d.). *Homepage*. Retrieved from http://www.snia.org

Takabi, H., Joshi, J. B. D., & Ahn, G.-J. (2010). Security and privacy challenges in cloud computing environments. *IEEE Security and Privacy, 8*(6), 24–31. doi:10.1109/MSP.2010.186.

Tracker, S. (n.d.). *VMWare shared folder bug lets local users on the guest OS gain elevated privileges on the host OS*. Security Tracker ID: 1019493. Retrieved from http://securitytracker.com/id/1019493

Trusted Computing Group (TCG). (2010). *Cloud computing and security- A natural match*. Retrieved from http://www.trustedcomputinggroup.org

World, C. (2008). *Extended gmail outage hits apps admins*. Retrieved from http://www.computerworld.com/s/article/9117322/Extended_Gmail_outage_hits_Apps_admins

World, P. C. (2007). *Salesforce.com warns customers of phishing scam*. Retrieved from http://www.pcworld.com/businesscenter/article/139353/article.html

Xen Vulnerability. (n.d.). Retrieved from http://secunia.com/advisories/26986/

Zetter, K. (2010). Google hackers targeted source code of more than 30 companies. *Wired Threat Level*. Retrieved from http://www.wired.com/threatlevel/2010/01/google-hack-attack/

Zhang, Y., & Joshi, J. (2009). Access control and trust management for emerging multidomain environments. In Upadhyay, S., & Rao, R. O. (Eds.), *Annals of Emerging Research in Information Assurance, Security and Privacy Services* (pp. 421–452). Dublin, Ireland: Emerald Group Publishing.

ADDITIONAL READING

Barham, P., Dragovic, B., Fraser, K., Hand, S., Harris, T., & Ho, A. ... Warfield, A. (2003). *Xen and the art of virtualization* (Technical Report). Cambridge, UK: University of Cambridge. Retrieved from www.cl.cam.ac.uk/research/srg/netos/papers/2003-xensosp.pdf

Bhattacherjee, B., Abe, N., Goldman, K., Zadrozny, B., Chillakuru, V. R., Del Caprio, M., & Apte, C. (2006). Using secure coprocessors for privacy preserving collaborative data mining and analysis. In *Proceedings of the 2nd International Workshop on Data Management on New Hardware (DaMoN'06)*. Chicago, IL: ACM Press.

Boneh, D., & Waters, B. (2007). Conjunctive, subset, and range queries on encrypted data. In *Proceedings of the 4th Conference on Theory of Cryptography (TCC'07)*, (pp. 530-534). TCC.

Brandic, I., Music, D., Leitner, P., & Dustdar, S. (2009). VieSLAF framework: Enabling adaptive and versatile SLA-management. In *Proceedings of the 6th International Workshop on Grid Economics and Business Models (GECON'09)*, (pp. 60-73). Delft, The Netherlands: GECON.

Cavoukian, A. (2008). *Privacy in the clouds: A white paper on privacy and digital identity: Implications for the internet.* Retrieved from http://www.ipc.on.ca/images/resources/privacy-intheclouds.pdf

Chappel, D. (2008). *Introducing the azure services platform.* Retrieved from http://download.microsoft.com

Chong, F., Carraro, G., & Wolter, R. (2006). *Multi-tenant data architecture.* Retrieved from http://msdn.microsoft.com/en-us/library/aa479086.aspx

Creeger, M. (2009). Cloud computing: An overview. *ACM Queue-. Distributed Computing, 7*(5), 2.

DeCandia, G., Hastorun, D., Jampani, M., Kakulapati, G., Lakshman, A., & Pilchin, A. ... Vogels, W. (2007). Dynamo: Amazon's highly available key-value store. In *Proceedings of the 21st ACM SIGOPS Symposium on Operating Systems Principles (SOSP'07)*, (pp. 205-220). Stevenson, WA: SOSP.

Desisto, R. P., Plummer, D. C., & Smith, D. M. (2008). *Tutorial for understanding the relationship between cloud computing and SaaS.* Stamford, CT: Gartner.

Emig, C., Brandt, F., Kreuzer, S., & Abeck, S. (2007). Identity as a service- Towards a service-oriented identity management architecture. In *Proceedings of the 13th Open European Summer School and IFIP TC6.6 Conference on Dependable and Adaptable Network and Services (EUNICE'07)*, (pp. 1-8). Twente, The Netherlands: EUNICE.

Everett, C. (2009). Cloud computing- A question of trust. *Computer Fraud & Security*, (6): 5–7. doi:10.1016/S1361-3723(09)70071-5.

Gellman, R. (2009). *Privacy in the clouds: Risks to privacy and confidentiality from cloud computing.* World Privacy Forum (WPF) Report. Retrieved from http://www.worldprivacyforum.org/cloudprivacy.html

Golden, B. (2009). *Capex vs. opex: Most people miss the point about cloud economics.* Retrieved from http://www.cio.com/article/484429/Capex_vs._Opex_Most_People_Miss_the_point_About_Cloud_Economic

Heritage, T. (2009). Hosted informatics: Bringing cloud computing down to earth with bottom-line benefits for pharma. *Next Generation Pharmaceutical*, (17).

Itani, W., Kayssi, A., & Chehab, A. (2009). Privacy as a service: Privacy-aware data storage and processing in cloud computing architectures. In *Proceedings of the 8th IEEE International Conference on Dependable, Automatic and Secure Computing (DASC'09)*, (pp. 711-716). Chengdu, China: DASC.

Kaufman, L. M. (2009). Data security in the world of cloud computing. *IEEE Security & Privacy, 7*(4), 61–64. doi:10.1109/MSP.2009.87.

Messmer, E. (2009). Gartner on cloud security: Our nightmare scenario is here now. *Network World* Retrieved from http://www.networkworld.com/news/2009/102109-gartner-cloud-security.html

Open Cloud Manifesto. (n.d.). Retrieved from http://www.opencloudmanifesto.org/Open%20Cloud%20Manifesto.pdf

Pearson, S. (2009). Taking account of privacy when designing cloud computing services. In *Proceedings of the ICSE Workshop on Software Engineering Challenges of Cloud Computing (CLOUD'09)*, (pp. 44-52). Vancouver, Canada: ICSE.

Pearson, S., & Charlesworth, A. (2009). Accountability as a way forward for privacy protection in the cloud. In *Proceedings of the 1st International Conference on Cloud Computing (CloudCom'09)*, (pp. 131-144). Beijing, China: CloudCom.

Petry, A. (2007). *Design and implementation of a xen-based execution environment*. (Diploma Thesis). Technische Universitat Kaiserslautern, Kaiserslautern, Germany.

Price, M. (2008). The paradox of security in virtual environments. *IEEE Computer, 41*(11), 22–38. doi:10.1109/MC.2008.472.

RightScale Inc. (2009). *RightScale cloud management features*. Retrieved from http://www.rightscale.com/products/cloud-management.php

Rochwerger, R., Caceres, J., Montero, R. S., Breitgand, D., Elmroth, E., & Galls, A. et al. (2009, September). The reservoir model and architecture for open federated cloud computing. *IBM Systems Journal*.

Schubert, L., Kipp, A., & Wesner, S. (2009). Above the clouds: From grids to service-oriented operating systems. In Tselentis, G. et al. (Eds.), *Towards the Future Internet - A European Research Perspective* (pp. 238–249). Amsterdam: IOS Press.

Sims, K. (2009). *IBM blue cloud initiative advances enterprise cloud computing*. Retrieved from http://www-03.ibm.com/press/us/en/pressrelease/26642.wss

Sotomayor, B., Montero, R. S., Llorente, I. M., & Foster, I. (2009). Virtual infrastructure management in private and hybrid cloud. *IEEE Internet Computing, 13*(5), 14–22. doi:10.1109/MIC.2009.119.

TechRepublic. (2013). *Cloud computing security: Making virtual machines cloud ready*. Retrieved from http://www.techrepublic.com/whitepapers/cloud-computing-security-making-virtual-machines-cloud-ready/1728295

Vaquero, L. M., Rodero-Merino, L., Caceres, J., & Linder, M. (2009). A break in the clouds: Towards a cloud definition. *ACM SIGCOMM Computer Communication Review, 39*(1), 50–55. doi:10.1145/1496091.1496100.

Vouk, M. A. (2008). Cloud computing – Issues, research and implementations. In *Proceedings of the 30th International Conference on Information Technology Interfaces (ITI'08)*, (pp. 31-40). Cavtat, Croatia: ITI.

Vozmediano, R. M., Montero, R. S., & Llorente, I. M. (2011). Multi-cloud deployment of computing clusters for loosely-coupled MTC applications. *IEEE Transactions on Parallel and Distributed Systems, 22*(6), 924–930. doi:10.1109/TPDS.2010.186.

Zimory Gmb, H. (2009). *Zimory distributed cloud – Whitepaper*. Retrieved from http://www.zimory.de/index.php?eID=tx_nawsecuredl&u=0&file=fileadmin/user_upload/pdf/Distributed_Clouds_Whitepaper.pdf&t=1359027268&hash=93c5f42f8c91817a746f7b8cff55fbdc68ae7379

KEY TERMS AND DEFINITIONS

Advanced Message Queuing Protocol (AMQP): AMQP is an open standard application layer protocol for message-oriented middleware. The defining features of AMQP are message orientation, queuing, routing, reliability, and security. It defines a ubiquitous, secure, reliable, and open ended Internet protocol for handling business messaging.

Cloud Computing: As per the definition provided by the National Institute for Standards and Technology (NIST), USA, Cloud Computing is defined as "a model for enabling convenient, on-demand network access to a shared pool of configurable computing resources (e.g., networks, servers, storage, applications, and services) that can be rapidly provisioned and released with minimal management effort or service provider interaction."

Homomorphic Encryption: Homomorphic Encryption is a form of encryption that allows specific types of computations to be carried out on ciphertext and obtain an output that is the result of operations performed on the plaintext. For example, one person could add two encrypted numbers and then another person could decrypt the result, without either of them being able to find the value of the individual numbers. The homomorphic property of various cryptosystems can be used to create secure voting systems, collision-resistant hash functions, private information retrieval schemes and enable widespread use of cloud computing by ensuring the confidentiality of processed data.

Hybrid Cloud: The Hybrid Clouds are a combination of public and private cloud offerings that allow for transitive information exchange and possibly application compatibility and portability across disparate cloud service offerings. They utilize standard or proprietary methodologies regardless of the ownership or the location. With a hybrid cloud, the service providers can utilize third party cloud providers in a full or partial manner, thereby increasing the flexibility of computing.

Hypervisor: A hypervisor, also called a virtual machine manager, is a program that allows multiple operating systems to share a single hardware host. Each operating system appears to have the host's processor, memory, and other resources all to itself. However, the hypervisor is actually controlling the host processor and resources, allocating what are needed to each operating system in turn and making sure that the guest operating systems (i.e., the virtual machines) cannot disrupt each other.

Identity Management: Identity Management is the task of controlling information about users on computing machines. Such information includes information that authenticates the identity of a user, information that describes information and actions they are authorized to access and/or perform. It also includes the management of descriptive information about the user and how and by whom the information can be accessed and modified. Managed entities typically include hardware and network resources and even applications.

Infrastructure as a Service (Iaas): This cloud service delivery model provides basic storage and computing capabilities as standardized services over the network. Servers, storage systems, networking equipment, data center space etc. are pooled and made available to handle workloads. The capability provided to the customer is to rent processing, storage, networks, and other fundamental computing resources where the customer is able to deploy and run arbitrary software, which can include operating systems and applications. The customer does not manage or control the underlying cloud infrastructure but has the control over operating systems, storage, deployed applications, and possibly select networking components (e.g., firewalls, load balancers etc.). Some examples of IaaS are: Amazon, GoGrid, 3 Tera, etc.

Platform as a Service (PaaS): In this cloud service model, a layer of software or development environment is encapsulated and offered as a service, upon which the higher levels of services are built. The customer has the freedom to build his own applications, which run on the provider's infrastructure. Hence, a capability is provided to the customer to deploy onto the cloud infrastructure customer-created applications using programming languages and tools supported by the provider (e.g., Java, Python, .Net, etc.). Although the customer does not manage or control the underlying cloud infrastructure, network, servers, operating systems, or storage, but he/she has the control over the deployed applications and possibly over the application hosting environment configurations. Some examples of PaaS are: Google's App Engine, Force.com, etc.

Private Cloud: The Private Clouds are provided by an organization or its designated services that offers a single-tenant (dedicated) operating environment with all the benefits and functionality of elasticity and accountability/utility model of cloud. The private clouds aim to address concerns on data security and offer greater control, which is typically lacking in a public cloud.

Public Cloud: The Public Clouds are provided by a designated service provider and may offer either a single-tenant (dedicated) or multi-tenant (shared) operating environment with all the benefits and functionality of elasticity and the accountability/utility model of cloud. The physical infrastructure is generally owned by and managed by the designated service provider and located within the provider's data centers (off-premises). All customers share the same infrastructure pool with limited configuration, security protections, and availability variances.

Security Assertion Markup Language (SAML): It is a standard for exchanging authentication and authorization data between security domains. Essentially the standard is based on an XML (eXtended Markup Language)-based protocol that uses security tokens containing assertions to pass information about a principal (usually an end user) between an SAML authority, that is an identity provider, and a Web service, that is a service provider. SAML 2.0 standard enables Web-based authentication and authorization scenarios including Single Sign-On (SSO).

Side Channel Attack: A side channel attack is any attack based on information gained from the physical implementation of a system; e.g., timing information, power consumption, electromagnetic leaks or even sound can provide an extra source of information that can be exploited to access or damage the system. Since these attacks are non-invasive, passive and they can generally be performed using relatively cheap equipment, they pose a serious threat to the security of most cryptographic hardware devices.

Software as a Service (SaaS): In this cloud service delivery model, the capability provided to the consumer is to use the provider's applications running on a cloud infrastructure and accessible from various client devices through a thin client interface such as Web browser. A complete application is offered to the customer as a service on demand. On the customers' side, there is no need for upfront investment in servers or software licenses, while for the provider, the costs are lowered, since only a single application needs to be hosted and maintained. Currently, SaaS is offered by companies such as Google, Salesforce, Microsoft, Zoho, etc.

Trusted Platform Module (TPM): The Trusted Platform Module (TPM) is a component on a computing machine that is specifically designed to enhance platform security above-and-beyond the capabilities of security software by providing a protected space for key operations and other critical security-related tasks. Using both hardware and software modules, TPM protects encryption and signature keys at their most vulnerable stages-operations when the keys are being used unencrypted in plain-text form.

Virtual Machine (VM): A Virtual Machine (VM) is a software implementation of a computing environment in which an operating system or a program can be installed and run. It typically emulates a physical computing environment, but requests for CPU time slot, memory,, hard disk, network and other resources are managed by a virtualization layer which translates these requests to the underlying physical hardware. VMs are created within a virtualization platform that runs on top of a client or server operating system. This operating system is known as the host operating system. The virtualization layer can be used to create many individual, isolated VM environments.

Web Services Description Language (WSDL): WSDL is an XML format describing network services as a set of endpoints operations on messages containing either document-oriented or procedure-oriented information. The operations and messages are described abstractly and then bound to a concrete network protocol and message format to define an endpoint. Related endpoints are combined into abstract endpoints 9services). WSDL is extensible to allow description of endpoints and their messages regardless of what message formats or network protocols are used to communicate.

Chapter 2
Towards a Certified Electronic Mail System

Gerard Draper-Gil
University of the Balearic Islands, Spain

M. Francisca Hinarejos
University of the Balearic Islands, Spain

Josep-Lluís Ferrer-Gomila
University of the Balearic Islands, Spain

Arne Tauber
Graz University of Technology, Austria

ABSTRACT

Most of the existent certified electronic mail proposals (found in scientific papers) have been designed without considering their deployment into traditional e-mail infrastructure (e.g., Internet mail system). In fact, there is not any implementation used for commercial purposes of those proposals. On the other hand, in different countries, private companies and public administrations have developed their own applications for certified electronic mail, but these solutions are tailored to their needs and present serious drawbacks. They consider the mail providers as Trusted Third Parties (TTPs), but without being verifiable (if they cheat or fail, users cannot prove it). In most cases, users (typically recipients) cannot choose their mail provider; it is imposed, and even worse, sometimes a message is considered to have been delivered when it has been deposited in the recipient's mailbox (and perhaps, he will not be able to access it). In this chapter, the authors give a broad picture on the current state of certified e-mail, including a brief description of the current e-mail architecture and the need of certified e-mail services, and a definition of the security requirements needed for such a service. Next, they review the scientific and existent proposals. Finally, the authors give some guidelines for developing practical solutions for certified e-mail services that meet all the security requirements.

INTRODUCTION

More than 200 billion e-mails are sent each day. Without doubt, e-mail is a core service of Internet. In the early days of Internet e-mail, only text messages (ASCII-7 bits) could be sent among users. That was a serious restriction and drawback. Users wanted to send video, audio, enriched text, files, etc., inserted or attached to e-mails. For this reason, Internet e-mail was enhanced in 1992 with

DOI: 10.4018/978-1-4666-4514-1.ch002

MIME (Multipurpose Internet Mail Extensions). A second problem to be solved was the lack of security, and in 1998 S/MIME (Secure/MIME) was proposed to provide confidentiality, integrity, authentication, and proof of e-mail origin (a sender cannot deny having sent a message).

But in the paper world, people are accustomed to sending valuable documents in a secure and reliable way. This includes documents like deeds, contracts, bids, subpoenas, summons, notifications, etc. Regular mail has no security provisions and senders rely on the assumption of a correct and successful delivery. This is where registered mail and certified mail come into play. Registered mail is a useful vehicle in the postal world for secure mail delivery by providing extended tracking possibilities. The certified mail service provides the sender additional proofs of submission, delivery and reception. In the same way, it is necessary to provide a similar service in the electronic world.

Probably for that reason, Internet e-mail was enhanced providing to users some kind of receipt (MDNs, Message Disposition Notification, and DSNs, Delivery Status Notifications). These are useful services but with a poor evidential quality: users can decide not to send these receipts (or once sent, they can deny having done it).

Due to the previous gap, the research community has provided many protocols for secure messaging over the last two decades. They have been published as fair non-repudiation protocols or certified electronic mail protocols. The aim was to design security extensions for asynchronous communications providing similar added value as traditional certified mail does in the postal world. The term Certified Electronic Mail (CEM) is used when applying fair non-repudiation protocols in the context of electronic mailing systems, for example Internet e-mail. In a nutshell, the certified e-mail service is to ensure that if a recipient receives an e-mail (usually with a proof of origin), the sender receives an acknowledgment (not rejectable by the recipient).

Fair exchange basically means that each party gets its expected items (in certified e-mail, a message for a proof of receipt), or none party is in an advantageous situation. But how is this fair exchange ensured? In traditional postal systems, the postal service acts as Trusted Third Party (TTP) and ensures the fair exchange of a delivery for a signed receipt.

First approaches for certified e-mail proposed protocols without TTP. However, these protocols were not practical. Either they required a high amount of communicational and computational power or they ensured fairness only with a certain probability. These conditions are not desired in practice. Moreover, some protocols assumed equal computational power of participants, which is unrealistic, e.g., a single user vs. a large corporation. Protocols with TTP differ in the extent of the TTP's involvement: inline TTP, online TTP and offline TTP. Inline TTPs act as a proxy between sender and recipient, being involved in every protocol step. Meanwhile, online TTPs are involved in each protocol run, but not in every step. Finally, in the optimistic approaches the TTP is only involved if a dispute arises, which is expected to be an exceptional case (see Figure 1). First practical certified e-mail approaches used inline TTPs. However, these kinds of protocols require the users to put a great amount of trust in the TTP. Moreover, since the TTP participates in each protocol step, it supposes a great workload for the TTP and it may become a bottleneck. The research community worked towards better approaches by increasing efficiency and reducing the amount of trust in TTPs proposing online TTP protocols. Newer approaches make use of offline TTPs, which are only involved if a dispute arises. Therefore, they are called optimistic. Some additional properties, apart from fairness, have to be met (timeliness, verifiability of the TTP, non-repudiation, etc.), in order the solutions to be useful.

Most existing certified e-mail protocols require a direct interaction between the sender and the recipient. However, in asynchronous protocols

Figure 1. Trusted third parties configurations

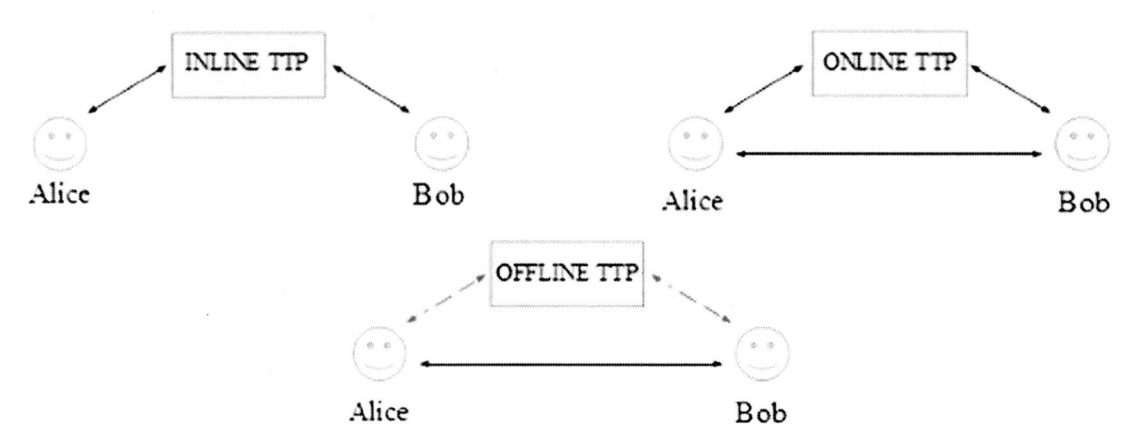

like e-mail, such a direct interaction is not desired. This circumstance has been taken into account by some protocols, which use so-called semi-trusted transfer agents to decouple the sender from the recipient. Most proposed approaches use a single transfer agent, which does not fully reflect the e-mail communication infrastructure. Probably this disconnection between proposals and e-mail infrastructure has made that no real implementation of those technical solutions can be found. But, in recent years, some organizations (especially public administrations) have demanded a certified electronic mail service. So, in different countries we find certified email services, many times with a limited scope, and without a standard guaranteeing the interoperability among different certified email services in different countries. Obviously, it is not a desirable situation, and for this reason some additional work is necessary, and in this chapter we provide some guidelines to be taken into account.

We will sketch how optimistic CEM protocols can be designed where both sender and recipient can choose their own semi-trusted transfer agent. In this way the CEM protocol can be more easily deployed on the Internet, for example by extending existing mail providers to semi-trusted transfer agents. By using an optimistic approach, less trust is needed in those transfer agents. By using SMTP (Simple Mail Transfer Protocol) as underlying transport protocol of the certified e-mail protocol, existing systems remain untouched and the protocol can be seamlessly integrated into the existing infrastructure. This is not only user-friendly, but it also saves a lot of infrastructural investments.

INTERNET E-MAIL

In this section we give a brief introduction to Internet e-mail and its general mail handling architecture. We further introduce the main e-mail security mechanisms provided by the Internet community to ensure the basic security features of integrity (a message cannot be modified), confidentiality (the content is protected from eavesdropping) and authenticity (the message's originator is who he says he is).

The Internet e-mail technology dates back to the early 1970s where it was used for communications in the Advanced Research Projects Agency Network (ARPANET), a network funded by the Defense Advanced Research Projects Agency (DARPA) of the US Department of Defense. At that time, e-mail messages were carried over the File Transfer Protocol (FTP). Later, when the ARPANET was replaced by the Internet protocol suite named TCP/IP (Transmission Control Protocol/Internet Protocol), transferring e-mail over FTP was replaced by using the Simple Mail Transfer

Figure 2. General e-mail architecture

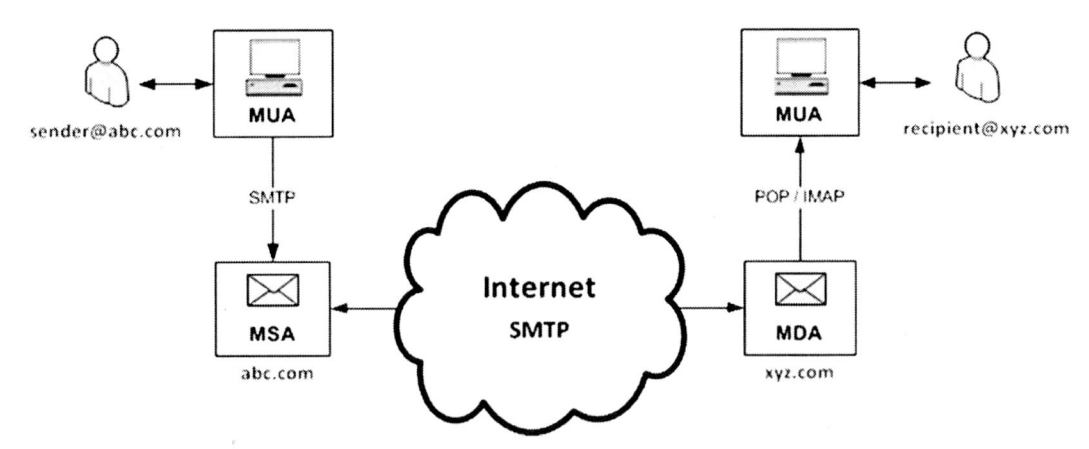

Protocol (SMTP, RFC821) in 1982. E-mail was designed as a simple text-based communication system. By default, e-mail had no security provisions. This applies to the basic security features of integrity, confidentiality and authenticity, but also the non-repudiation and fair exchange as provided by traditional postal certified mail.

Due to the lack of evidence, several receipting mechanisms have been proposed by the community and are regularly used in e-mail communications. We discuss these mechanisms and explain why their evidential quality does not meet the requirements of fair exchange.

General E-Mail Handling Architecture

Figure 2 illustrates the typical e-mail architecture with its main actors. E-mail was designed as an asynchronous service, where messages are delivered through intermediary agents. This allows the e-mail to operate in a fire-and-forget basis, i.e., senders and recipients do not need to be simultaneously online to send and receive messages. Intermediary e-mail servers are in charge of relaying the messages from the sender to the recipient's server, which stores them into a mailbox for the later retrieval by the recipient. The typical steps for delivering an e-mail message from a sender to a recipient having the address recipient@xyz.com are as follows:

1. The sender composes the message with her Mail User Agent (MUA). Besides plain text, Multipurpose Internet Mail Extensions (MIME, RFC2045) are the default format to enrich e-mails with formatted text (e.g. HTML), images, videos, etc. Figure 3 shows an e-mail message, which is formatted as a MIME message. It has two parts. The first part represents the e-mail body. The second part represents the message signature. MIME supports an arbitrary number of parts, e.g. to carry attachments.

2. By using the SMTP protocol, the sender's MUA submits the message to her Mail Sender Agent (MSA), which is usually operated by the sender's Internet provider.

3. The MSA resolves the address of the recipient's Mail Delivery Agent (MDA) by looking up the Mail eXchange (MX) record in the Domain Name System (DNS) entry of the recipient's e-mail domain address part, which is the part following the "@" sign, i.e. "xyz.com". The part preceding the "@" is called the local part, which usually identifies the recipient's mailbox at the MDA.

4. Due to the heterogeneous Internet architecture, the transmission of the e-mail message from the MSA to the MDA is not necessarily made through a direct connection, but rather somehow routed through several untrusted

intermediary servers and networks. The protocol used for the transmission is SMTP.
5. After having received the message, the MDA stores it into the recipient's mailbox, which is identified by the local part of the recipient's e-mail address.
6. By using the Post Office Protocol (POP3) (RFC1939) or the Internet Message Access protocol (IMAP) (RFC3501), the recipient's MUA can fetch the message from his MDA mailbox.

Basic e-Mail Security Mechanisms

Pure e-mail without any extensions has no security provisions. It can be compared to sending a postcard, which lacks confidentiality, authenticity, integrity and non-repudiation, i.e., a sender can deny having sent a message (non-repudiation of origin) and a recipient can deny having received it (non-repudiation of receipt). The Internet community has addressed the lack of e-mail security with two proposals: Secure MIME (S/MIME) and Pretty Good Privacy (PGP).

S/MIME (see example in Figure 3) is an Internet Engineering Task Force (IETF) standard specified in RFC5751 to send and receive secure MIME data. S/MIME supports two content types: one for digital signatures (the terms electronic signatures and digital signatures are used indistinctly) and one for data encryption. S/MIME signatures ensure authenticity, data integrity and non-repudiation with proof of origin, while S/MIME encryption provides confidentiality. An S/MIME signed message has two MIME parts: the first part holds the MIME headers and the message content. The second part holds the signature plus any additional information to verify the signature. An S/MIME encrypted message is structured similarly, the first part holds the necessary information to decrypt the message, and the second part holds the encrypted data. S/MIME is based on the Cryptographic Message Syntax standard (CMS), specified in RFC5652, and makes use of X.509 certificates as defined in the IETF's Public Key Infrastructure Exchange (PKIX) and Certificate Revocation List (CRL) profile, specified in RFC5280.

Figure 3. S/MIME message example

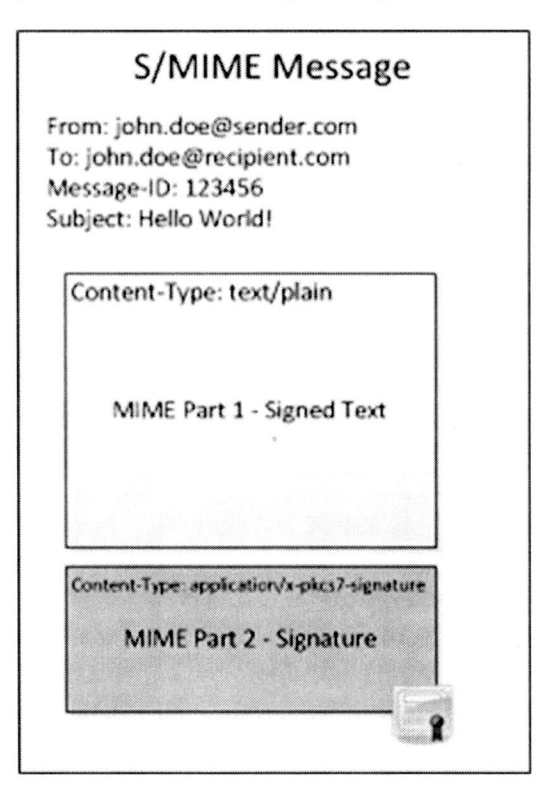

An alternative to S/MIME is OpenPGP, which is a signature and encryption standard based on PGP and it is specified in RFC4880. OpenPGP uses the PGP/MIME method for signatures and encryption (superseding the outdated PGP/INLINE method), allowing signing and encrypting all file attachments. As S/MIME, OpenPGP provides authenticity, data integrity and non-repudiation via digital signature, and confidentiality via encryption. It further provides compression diminishing the overall message size (compression is applied after signature and before encryption). To provide compatibility between systems, raw data (streams of octets) is encoded in blocks of 7 bits with radix-64 conversion. Instead of using the PKIX and the CRL for managing public keys, OpenPGP uses a decentralized system called "Web of Trust" in which users can digitally sign other user's certificates asserting their validity.

Receipting Mechanisms

Even if e-mail security enhancements like S/MIME or PGP provide the basic security features (integrity, authenticity, confidentiality and a proof of e-mail origin), lack of reception evidence still remains. Senders do not know whether the intended recipient has read or even received a message. The Internet community has tried to address this gap with four receipting mechanisms, namely Message Disposition Notifications (MDNs), Delivery Status Notifications (DSNs), SMTP service extension for message tracking and S/MIME receipts. We introduce these mechanisms in the following sections. However, from a security point of view, they still do not solve the lack of evidence. This is subsequently discussed.

Message Disposition Notification

MDNs are receipting or acknowledgment mechanisms for the e-mail protocol and are specified in RFC3798 for POP3 and in RFC5303 for IMAP. MDNs are requested by the sender's MUA by including a "Disposition-Notification-To" header in the message. The purpose of MDN is to report the final delivery status (success or failure) of messages. Most e-mail clients already implement the MDN mechanism. These e-mail clients usually offer several ways to customize the acknowledgment behavior, for example by providing "Ignore," "Ask," "Reject," and "Always Send" options for the receiver. The recipient's MUA returns the MDN report back to the sender by using a MIME container message. This container has at least two parts. The first part contains a human-readable description of the report. The second part contains a machine-readable version for automated processing by e-mail clients. If the original message has to be returned along with the report, it can be included in a third MIME part.

MDN does not have any security provisions to ensure the integrity and authenticity of reports. To provide these security mechanisms, the Internet community has published a secure MDN mechanism known as Applicability Statement (AS). MDN is used as basic receipting mechanism in the three AS standards, which specify the secure Peer-to-Peer (P2P) exchange of structured business data for Electronic Data Interchange (EDI), eXtensible Markup Language (XML), or other data structures. The first standard (AS1) describes the transport using SMTP and is specified in RFC3335. The second one (AS2) describes the HyperText Transfer Protocol (HTTP) transport and is specified in RFC4130. The third one (AS3) describes the FTP transport and is specified in RFC4823. In contrast to the standard MDN, the secure AS requires the recipient's environment to provide an adapter for processing MDN requests before forwarding the message to the recipient's inbox. Furthermore, the returning MDN must be signed and must contain a hash value over the original message.

Delivery Status Notification

DSN is an SMTP service, which allows the sender or the MSA to request a report on the delivery status of a message. A DSN error report message is also called Non-Delivery Report (NDR) or "bounce message." DSN success reports have to be explicitly requested by the sender, whereas DSN error reports are automatically returned to the sender. DSN is specified by the following IETF standards tracks:

- **RFC3461:** SMTP Service Extension for Delivery Status Notifications.
- **RFC3462:** The Multipart/Report Content Type for the Reporting of Mail System Administrative Messages.
- **RFC3463:** Enhanced Mail System Status Codes.
- **RFC3464:** An Extensible Message Format for Delivery Status Notifications.
- **RFC5337:** Internationalized Delivery Status and Disposition Notifications.

In contrast to NDR, which is widely implemented as de-facto e-mail "bouncing" mechanism to report a failed delivery attempt, the functionality to request a DSN status report is not supported and implemented by all mail servers.

SMTP Service Extension for Message Tracking

RFC3888 describes active and passive tracking mechanisms on the basis of DSN or MDN. DSN and MDN are the standard way for tracking e-mail messages. However, mail servers may not have implemented these standards or recipients may have MDN disabled. There may be cases where DSN or MDN do not provide any tracking information. In this particular case the IETF has published specifications for a last additional mechanism to determine the message status. The SMTP service extension for message tracking is specified by the following standards tracks:

- **RFC3885:** SMTP Service Extension for Message Tracking.
- **RFC3886:** An Extensible Message Format for Message Tracking Responses.
- **RFC3887:** Message Tracking Query Protocol.

S/MIME Receipts

Another receipting standard are S/MIME-signed receipts as defined in RFC2634. The standard aims to provide the sender a proof of delivery and to demonstrate the sender that the recipient was able to verify the S/MIME signature of the original message. The concept of signed receipts is as follows:

1. The sender creates a signed S/MIME message, which includes an attribute indicating that a signed receipt is requested. This is achieved by adding the "receiptRequest" attribute to the "signedAttributes" field of the S/MIME signature.
2. The sender sends the final message to the intended recipient.
3. The recipient receives the message, validates the signature and checks if there is any request for a signed receipt.
4. The recipient creates a signed receipt. A signed receipt is an abstract syntax notation one (ASN.1) "signedData" object.
5. The recipient returns the signed receipt to the sender.
6. The sender receives the message and validates if it contains a signed receipt. This validation requires particular data of the original message. Therefore, the sender has to keep a copy of these data either by extracting it from the original message or by preserving the whole original message.

Security Considerations

We have briefly reviewed the four receipting mechanisms MDN, DSN, SMTP service extension for message tracking and S/MIME signed receipts. Even if these mechanisms provide added value to the standard e-mail protocol, the evidential security level of e-mail increases only partially. In fact, none of them can prevent the recipient from configuring the receiving environment in such a way that MDN, DSN, S/MIME receipt requests, or SMTP tracking requests are completely ignored. All the discussed mechanisms act on the assumption of fairly acting infrastructural entities, meaning that all entities including the recipient actually return the expected receipt or status notification.

Furthermore, none of the mentioned mechanisms, except S/MIME receipts, uses any cryptographic technologies to ensure message tracking or receipting. Even if S/MIME ensures confidentiality, authenticity and integrity, it still lacks mechanisms to ensure the fair and non-repudiable exchange of a message for a receipt.

These mechanisms require infrastructural changes and this means they have to be deployed along the message delivery path. For example, mail servers need to be updated to process DSNs, and MUAs are required to understand MDN requests. Even if all infrastructural components would be able to process the mentioned mechanisms, the open and heterogeneous nature of the Internet and the lack of appropriate cryptographic technologies still allow to spoof messages and to deny the participation in a message exchange.

CERTIFIED ELECTRONIC MAIL

Even with the receipting mechanisms specified by the IETF standards tracks, e-mail has no electronic counterpart to traditional postal certified mail. In the last two decades, the research community has tried to fill this gap by proposing and publishing a number of non-repudiation protocols for secure, reliable and evidential messaging meeting the requirements for certified mail. Interestingly, there is no consensus among researchers on the security properties a Certified Electronic Mail (CEM) protocol has to fulfill and what services it has to provide. By looking at regular mail delivery, certified mail must be:

1. **Fair:** Due to physical presence of postal employees, a delivery is only handed over to the recipient if and only if a receipt is signed in exchange. Therefore, the postal service acts as Trusted Third Party (TTP) to ensure that the exchange of a delivery for a receipt between the sender and the recipient is fair.
2. **Non-repudiable:** The recipient has to sign a receipt, which is returned to the sender. With this signature the recipient will not be able to deny having received a certain delivery. This is more stringent if the delivery is restricted and the recipient's identity is verified with an official document, for example a driver's license, passport or identity card.

Postal certified mail delivery can thus be defined as the fair exchange of a message for a signed receipt. Zhou and Gollmann (1996) follow this approach and define CEM as the fair exchange of a message for a Non-Repudiation of Receipt (NRR) evidence. NRR evidence is usually linked to the message content, whereas postal certified mail only acknowledges a message envelope. In contrast to Zhou and Gollmann (1996), not all researchers follow this definition. Ferrer-Gomila et al. (2010) start their definition of CEM as a service, which provides exchange of a message plus a Non-Repudiation of Origin (NRO) evidence for an NRR evidence. The NRO evidence certifies the sender's authenticity and ensures that the sender cannot deny having participated in a communication. This is not the case for regular mail delivery, where the sender's identity is not usually verified by the postal service.

However, it is commonly accepted that CEM protocols are a subset of the Fair Exchange protocols' family. In a fair exchange every party involved has an element that wants to deliver in exchange of another element, but no one wants to give his part unless he obtains assurance he will get the items expected from the other parties. In the case of CEM, sender and recipient exchange a message and a proof of origin for a proof of message receipt. Therefore, a CEM protocol must comply with the fair exchange security requirements, stated by Asokan et al. (1998a) and later reviewed by Zhou et al. (2000): effectiveness (only for optimistic solutions), fairness, timeliness, non-repudiation and verifiability of the TTP.

Here, we describe and discuss these requirements focusing on core CEM security requirements. Many CEM protocols have been designed with the aim to increase efficiency by reducing the amount of computation and communication power and to avoid the involvement of Trusted Third Parties (TTPs). However, these protocols and their properties are often questionable whether they are actually convenient and practicable when being deployed in real environments and under real conditions. Ferrer-Gomila et al. (2010) recently published a work summarizing definitions, properties, and requirements related to CEM.

We now review the following CEM security requirements in more detail:

- Effectiveness
- Fairness
- Timeliness
- Non-repudiation
- Verifiability of TTP
- Confidentiality
- Non Selective receipt
- No-author based selective receipt

Effectiveness

A protocol meets the effectiveness requirement if the TTP does not intervene when all participants behave honestly.

This property is related to the extent of the TTP's involvement in the protocol, which is often used to classify the CEM proposals (see *State of The Art* section). Protocols which meet the effectiveness requirement are called optimistic. From a research viewpoint optimistic approaches are the most efficient ones and require less trust in TTPs.

Fairness

Fairness is a core property and makes a CEM protocol useful. Consider the scenario where an e-mail sender signals the intention for the exchange of a message for a receipt. The recipient confirms that with a receipt and a malicious sender in the end does not send the message. Or the sender transmits the message to the recipient and a malicious recipient does not acknowledge with a receipt. Such scenarios lead to a disadvantageous position for one entity and possibly to a dispute. However, cheating parties may not be the only reason for a dispute. Other factors may also lead to disadvantageous situations for one or more entities. Consider for example a network failure during the transmission of a receipt from the recipient to the sender. This is what fairness should prevent.

A protocol meets the fairness requirement if upon the finalization of an execution, all honest participants get what they expect, or none of them get it.

Timeliness

This property is of practical relevance. Without this property entities would not be able to stop the protocol execution. For example, if recipients deny signing a receipt, senders would eventually have to wait endlessly for the receipt and the protocol would never terminate. In practice this is a non-acceptable circumstance.

A protocol fulfills the timeliness requirement if honest entities can stop the protocol execution in a finite amount of time while keeping fairness.

Non-Repudiation Services

A communication between different entities may lead to a dispute. Senders may claim not having submitted or sent a message. They may also claim not being the originator of a message. Recipients, on the other side, may claim not having received, read, retrieved or downloaded a message. Even TTPs may cheat and deny the execution of particular operations or services. This is why non-repudiation is a core property of CEM protocols. It ensures that none of the involved parties can cheat denying their participation in a message exchange. A CEM protocol must comply with the following non-repudiation services:

- **Non-Repudiation of Origin (NRO):** A protocol provides non-repudiation of origin if it gives evidence against the false denial of having originated the message. It is addressed to the recipient. The non-repudiation token generated by the NRO service is called Evidence Of Origin (EOO).

- **Non-Repudiation of Receipt (NRR):** A protocol provides non-repudiation of receipt if it gives evidence against the false denial of having received the message. It is addressed to the sender. The non-repudiation token generated by the NRR service is called Evidence Of Receipt (EOR). The NRR service can be compared with a signed receipt used by postal certified mail. There are different approaches to implement an NRR service. Some protocols require the recipient to simply acknowledge the reception of a message envelope as done in postal systems. Some CEM protocols, however, require the recipient to acknowledge the reception of the message content (Ferrer-Gomila et al., 2010).

Usually both NRO and NRR services are provided on an end-to-end basis where the evidence are created by the sender and recipient without the intervention of a third party. In case an intermediary (MSA or MDA) is involved in the communication flow, two more non-repudiation services can be useful, as stated by Onieva et al. (2009b):

- **Non-Repudiation of Submission (NRS):** A protocol provides non-repudiation of submission if it gives evidence against the false denial of having submitted the message. This service only attests that a sender submitted a particular message to a certain MSA. It cannot be used to draw any conclusions on the remaining delivery process. The resulting non-repudiation token is called Evidence Of Submission (EOS).
- **Non-Repudiation of Delivery (NRD):** A protocol provides non-repudiation of delivery if it gives evidence against the false denial of having delivered the message. This service only attests that an MTA has delivered a particular message into the recipient's mailbox for later retrieval. It cannot be used to draw any conclusions on the remaining delivery process. This means the service does not give evidence if the recipient actually received, read or downloaded the message. The resulting non-repudiation token is called Evidence Of Delivery (EOD).

Verifiability of TTP

TTPs may misbehave like in the real world and may thus not be totally trusted. Therefore, the TTP has to generate enough evidence to verify its correct intervention.

A protocol meets the verifiability of TTP requirement if, in case the TTP misbehaves, no honest participant lose fairness. Moreover, those participants are able to prove the TTP's misbehaviour.

Confidentiality

Confidentiality does not appear on the list of mandatory security requirements (Ferrer-Gomila et al., 2010; Zhou, et al., 2000), but it is desirable in order to keep the privacy of the communications between sender and receiver.

A protocol meets the confidentiality requirement if the content of the messages exchanged is only available to those who participated in the exchange (senders and recipients). Neither the TTP nor the intermediaries must have access to them.

Non-Selective Receipt

In the context of the NRR service, many protocols prevent a so-called selective receipt. This means that if the recipient knows the message content before the receipt is generated, the recipient can refuse to sign the receipt. Consider the situation where a person is in debt and receives a certified mail, he may guess the content of the delivery beforehand and thus refuse its acceptance. As confidentiality, it is not mandatory for generic fair exchange, but it is desirable in the particular case of CEM protocols.

A protocol meets the non-selective receipt requirement if the recipient is not allowed to choose whether receive the message or not, according to its content.

No-Author-Based Selective Receipt

Another type of selective receipt is author-based selective receipt. As example, consider the situation where a person receives a certified mail from the traffic authorities, he may suspect it contains a fine and thus refuse its acceptance to avoid or delay its payment. This problem was first addressed by Kremer and Markowitch (2001) presenting two CEM protocols taking this property into account. Again, it is not mandatory, but it is desirable in the case of CEM protocols.

A protocol meets the no-author based selective receipt if a recipient is not allowed to choose whether receive a message or not, according the sender's identity.

STATE OF THE ART

Governments, postal services, and private businesses are putting custom certified mail systems into operation on the Internet. Governmental systems are usually based on specific legislation, have well defined policies and are usually supervised by regulatory authorities. They are thus often called "de iure" systems. Private sector systems are normally not based on legal regulations but rather on contractual basis or agreement between the service provider and its customers. Tauber (2011) has assessed and evaluated dominant certified mail systems and standards with respect to their security properties. Interestingly, all systems in operation are using inline TTPs, whereas the research community is focusing on optimistic approaches. This has a simple reason: even though optimistic approaches are more efficient and require less trust in TTPs, high interactions between the sender and recipient, as well as changes in the sending and receiving environment (e.g. e-mail client plug-ins) make them harder to deploy in practice.

The objective of this section is to give an overview on the existing work related to CEM systems. The remainder of this section is organized as follows. In the *Scientific Work* section we will review the efforts done by the research community, and the *Existing Solutions* subsection will present the most relevant solutions in place. Finally, the *CEM Standards* subsection will present the Registered Electronic Mail (REM) standard of the European Telecommunications Standards Institute (ETSI), created to provide interoperability between the existing solutions.

Scientific Work

The scientific community is working since the late 1980s on secure protocols for the fair exchange family, including protocols for certified e-mail applications. Remember that one of the core properties of fair exchange protocols is fairness. Initially, two different research lines appeared to address fairness: protocols relying on Trusted Third Parties (TTP) (Kremer, et al., 2002; Onieva, et al., 2009) and protocols without TTP (Even, et al., 1985; Ben-Or, et al., 1990; Okamoto & Ohta, 1994; Markowitch & Roggeman, 1999). The latter ones require either a high communication bandwidth or the assumption of equal computational power of participants, which is not realistic in practice, so the majority of scientific proposals tend to use TTPs.

The vast majority of proposals for certified e-mail protocols assume that senders and recipients can communicate directly, without intermediaries. Among them we find proposals with online TTP (Deng, et al., 1996; Schneier & Riordan, 1998;

Abadi, et al., 2002; Permpoontanalarp & Kanokkanjanapong, 2008; Liu, et al., 2010; Imamoto & Sakurai, 2002), and optimistic ones (Kremer & Markowitch, 2001; Imamoto & Sakurai, 2002; Ferrer-Gomila, et al., 2000; Monteiro & Dahab, 2002; Wang, et al., 2005; Mut, et al., 2000; Ferrer-Gomila, et al., 2002; Ateniese & Nita-Rotaru, 2002; Lopez, et al., 2004; Nenadic, et al., 2004; Zhou, 2004; Ma, et al., 2006; Oppliger & Stadlin, 2004; Wang, et al., 2007; Liang, et al., 2008; Cederquist, et al., 2007; Hwang & Lai, 2008; Wang, et al., 2009; Gao, et al., 2010; Wang, et al., 2011).

Schneier and Riordan (1998) proposed a protocol where the keys to decipher the messages are published in publicly available forums, which requires them to be totally trusted. Abadi *et al.* (2002) approach does not require a Public-Key Infrastructure (PKI), and no software installation is required on the recipient's side. Permpoontanalarp and Kanokkanjanapong (2008) solution is based on Abadi *et al.* (2002) protocol, and they further enhance it adding protection to Denial of Service attacks, and measures to penalize the selective receipt of messages, to the point where recipients cannot receive messages anymore. The authors refer to this property as undeniable fairness.

Ferrer-Gomila *et al.* (2000) presented an efficient certified e-mail protocol requiring only three steps to deliver a certified e-mail. Their proposal was reviewed by Monteiro and Dahab (2002), who proposed a fix. But in a later paper, Wang *et al.* (2005) exposed some weaknesses and security flaws that could affect both proposals (Ferrer-Gomila, et al., 2000; Monteiro & Dahab, 2002). Mut *et al.* (2000) presented an optimistic protocol which uses a group of TTPs, where the resolution decisions are made by majority vote of the TTPs. Kremer and Markowitch (2001) major contribution is the definition of a new property for certified e-mail: no-author based selective receipt. In order to meet this new property, their proposal requires a TTP to provide anonymity to the sender, and it is not entirely optimistic.

Imamoto and Sakurai (2002) solution with online TTP has the particularity that is the receiver who chooses the TTP.

Ateniese and Nita-Rotaru (2002) and Nenadic *et al.* (2004) proposed optimistic protocols with transparent TTP. Their solutions are based on different forms of Verifiable and Recoverable Encrypted Signatures (VRES) Ateniese, G. (1999), Asokan *et al.* (2002). Ma *et al.* (2006) showed that Nenadic *et al.* (2004) protocol does not meet fairness, and proposed a fix. But later, Hwang and Lai (2008) reviewed Ma *et al.* (2006) protocol, exposing some weaknesses, and presented a solution. Wang *et al.* (2007) use Convertible Signatures to obtain TTP transparency in their optimistic certified e-mail protocol.

Ferrer-Gomila *et al.* (2002), Lopez *et al.* (2004), and Zhou (2004) proposed optimistic multi-party protocols. In a multi-party CEM protocol, we have a sender and a set of recipients. Ferrer-Gomila *et al.* (2002) proposed a protocol where the sender could notify a set of recipients (the same message to each recipient), but only those who acknowledged the reception of the message could have access to its content. Lopez *et al.* (2004) proposal is an extension of Micali S. (2003) two-party fair exchange protocol, allowing a sender to deliver the same certified message to several recipients. Zhou, J. (2004) exposed some security flaws in Ferrer-Gomila *et al.* (2002)'s multi-party certified e-mail protocol, and proposed an improved version fixing the weaknesses detected.

Oppliger and Stadlin (2004) proposed a certified mail system for the Internet based on an online TTP, which uses dual signatures to cryptographically link keys to the corresponding certified mail messages. Liang *et al.* (2008) based their optimistic protocol in the use of bilinear pairing (Boneh et al., 2003). Cederquist *et al.* (2007) proposed a certified e-mail protocol using key-chains (Lamport, L. (1981)). A key-chain is a sequence of keys where are the result of executing a hash function on the previous key. Later, Liu *et al.* (2010) presented an enhanced version of Cederquist *et al.* (2007) protocol, which solves a security flaw and adds TTP transparency using a VRES scheme (Zhang et al., 2003). Wang *et al.* (2009) and Wang *et al.* (2011) proposals are based on signcryption (Zheng, 1997).

Even though there are many interesting proposals for certified e-mail, most of them do not meet the TTP's verifiability requirement. Moreover, the assumption of direct communication between sender and receiver does not fit with the general e-mail architecture (see Figure 2), where senders and recipients communicate through intermediaries asynchronously. Therefore, we cannot consider them as useful solutions for certified e-mail, as we have defined it (see *Introduction* section).

There are, though, some proposals for certified e-mail that assume sender and recipient communicate through some kind of intermediary (Zhou & Gollmann, 1996; Bahreman & Tygar, 1994; Ateniese et al., 2001; Park & Cho, 2004; Liu et al., 2008), either a TTP, a trusted agent or a semi-trusted one. The term semi-trusted was first introduced by Franklin and Reiter (1997), referring to a TTP that can misbehave but not collude with other entities. These solutions are more interesting from a practical point of view because their architecture resembles to the general e-mail one (see Figure 2). Following we will describe these proposals and we will explain why they are not proper solutions for the certified e-mail service.

Bahreman and Tygar (1994) proposed 2 different certified e-mail protocols, one with inline TTP (B-CEM) and the other one without TTP (S-CEM). In the B-CEM proposal, the sender uses an inline TTP, the Postmaster, to deliver certified e-mails. It generates non-repudiation of origin, submission, and receipt evidence, but fails to meet the non-selective receipt, verifiability of the TTP, and confidentiality requirements. Moreover, fairness depends on the assumption that the TTP cannot misbehave and there are no network failures. Even though the authors recommend that messages exchanged should be MIME compliant, it cannot be easily deployed on the existent Internet e-mail architecture where senders and recipients can be registered in different mail providers, and these mail providers are not TTPs. The S-CEM proposal, assumes that senders and recipients have equal computational power, which is unrealistic.

Zhou and Gollmann (1996) proposed a protocol where a certified e-mail is delivered through a set of delivery agents. The protocol provides evidence of submission, delivery, and receipt, but fairness is not addressed. It relies on the honest behavior of users and delivery agents.

With their TRICERT protocol, Ateniese *et al.* (2001) proposed an optimistic protocol, which makes use of an offline TTP and a unique semi-trusted postal agent, which acts as a proxy between the sender and the recipient to ensure a fair exchange. However, from a trust point of view, the protocol is more beneficial for the sender since she can choose the postal agent. Further, by looking at the decentralized Internet e-mail system this approach cannot be easily deployed on top of the existing architecture for e-mail. Senders and recipients are usually registered with different mail providers, thus a protocol with two postal agents is required. Park and Cho (2004) enhanced the TRICERT protocol adding a delivery deadline to avoid indefinite delays on the e-mail delivery. Neither Ateniese *et al.* (2001) or Park and Cho (2004) solutions meet the verifiability of TTP requirement, thus in case of dispute, fairness relies on the TTP's good will.

Liu *et al.* (2008) presented an optimistic CEM protocol based on the current e-mail infrastructure. Their approach is the most practical, using Mail User Agents (MUA) as client applications and Mail Transfer Agents (MTA) as intermediaries (each participant chooses his own). However, to solve recovery protocol requests from the sender's MTA, the TTP requires contacting the recipient, which is not practical. As Ateniese *et al.* (2001), Liu *et al.* (2008) assume that the TTP and the sender's MTA are trusted entities, i.e., they cannot cheat. But at the same time, when the sender's MTA receives

Towards a Certified Electronic Mail System

a new message, she uses a Time Stamp Server to certify the time of delivery. Moreover, the protocol does not provide the necessary non-repudiation services. In particular, it lacks the non-repudiation of submission and the non-repudiation of delivery.

Existing Solutions

The Austrian Document Delivery System (DDS) is the certified e-mail system for the public sector of Austria (Figure 4). Its policies and requirements are laid down by the "Service of Documents Act." It was put into operation on the Internet in 2004. The technical specifications are maintained by the Austrian Federal Chancellery. In the Austrian DDS architecture we can find the following entities:

- **Senders:** All public bodies can register as a sender.
- **Delivery Agents:** They act as inline TTP between senders and recipients. They provide an MTA for senders and an MS for recipients. Delivery agents must be accredited by the Austrian Federal Chancellery.
- **Recipients:** All natural and legal persons can register with one or more delivery agents.
- **Central Lookup Service (CLS):** A lookup service that holds the address data for all recipients registered with a delivery agent. It is operated by the Austrian Federal Chancellery.

In order to send and receive certified e-mails, the senders must register with the CLS, and the recipients must do it with one or more delivery agents. The senders have to provide an X.509 SSL client certificate for registration. This certificate must have a particular X.509 Object Identifier (OID) extension, called the Austrian e-Government OID, which certifies that the authenticating party belongs to a public body. Registration with delivery agents is based on the Austrian citizen card, the national eID, which is legally equivalent to standard ID documents. The CLS is a directory holding the data of all registered recipients, providing the list of delivery agents with which a recipient is registered. Delivery agents bind a

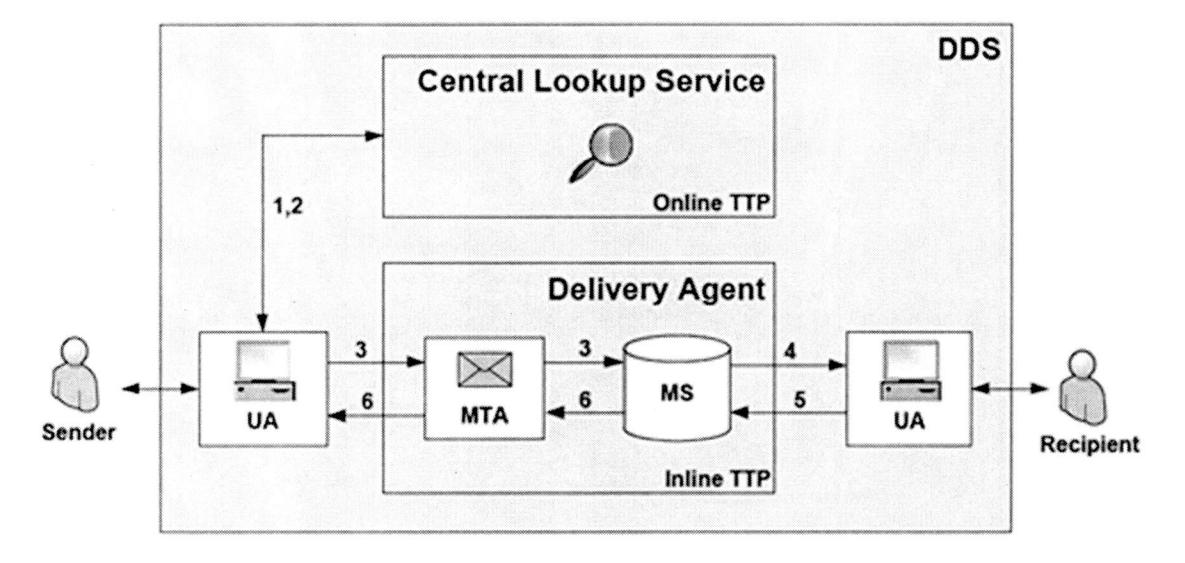

Figure 4. Austrian DDS architecture

recipient's electronic mailbox to his national ID number, and senders cannot determine a recipient's list of delivery agents using his national ID, therefore they have to query the CLS.

The *Posta Elettronica Certificata* (PEC) is the Italian certified e-mail system for the public and private sector (Figure 5). The legal basis for the PEC is laid down by the presidential decree °68. A decree of 6th May 2009 provided the basis for the allocation of free PEC mailboxes for all Italian citizens. With law °2, which was enacted on 28th January 2009, the registration of a PEC mailbox was rendered compulsory for all companies, freelancers and public administrations. The decree °266 of 2th November 2005 provides the basic technical rules of all aspects of the PEC system. Its annex provides the detailed technical specifications for all PEC communications.

The system is layered on top of the Internet e-mail architecture and operates according to the e-mail standard specified in the RFC2822. The PEC system uses the so-called PEC providers as inline TTPs between senders and recipients, to assure the messages are delivered. In contrast to the Austrian DDS, senders and recipients must register an account with a PEC provider. Therefore we can have up to two providers (inline TTPs) involved in the delivery of one message, the sender's and the recipient's provider. The PEC specifications define three main services that a provider has to implement: Access Point (AP), Reception Point (RP), and Delivery Point (DP). The AP provides an MTA to forward submitted messages to other MTAs. The RP and DP can be seen as two logical units of the recipient's MTA, where the RP accepts the message from the sender's MTA and the DP stores the message into the recipient's MS.

The De-Mail system is the project of the German government for providing a reliable, evidential and legally binding communication infrastructure to the public and private sector (Figure 6). The "De-Mail-law" enacted on 2th May 2011 defines the organizational and legal regulations for the provision of De-Mail services. The technical specifications are published and maintained by the Federal Office for Information Security. Like the

Italian PEC system it is layered on top of the existing e-mail, and it uses a provider as inline TTP. To obtain an electronic mailbox, senders and recipients must register with a provider using an official ID document or the national eID. Once registered, each user will receive an e-mail address

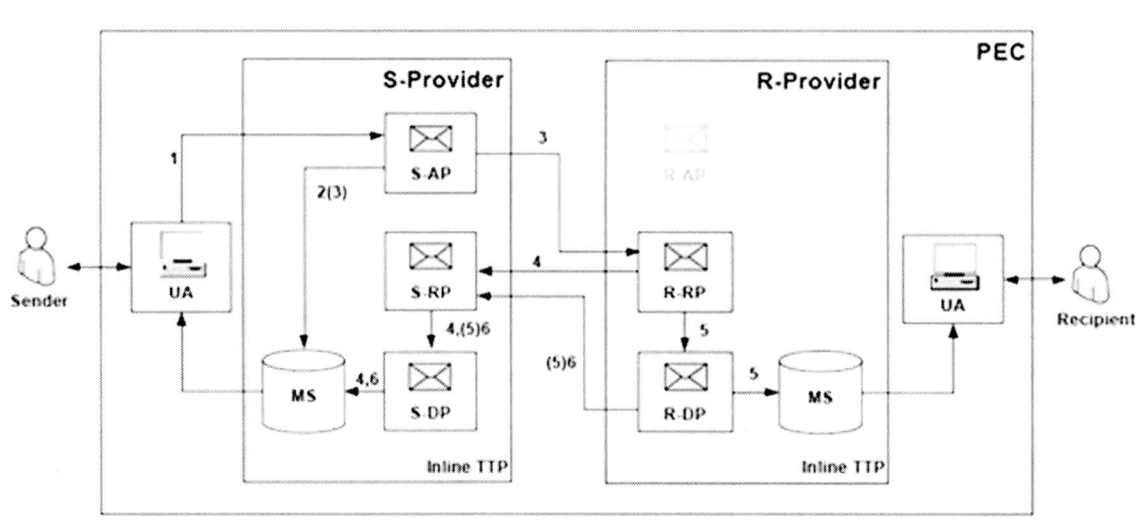

Figure 5. Italian PEC architecture

Towards a Certified Electronic Mail System

Figure 6. German de-mail architecture

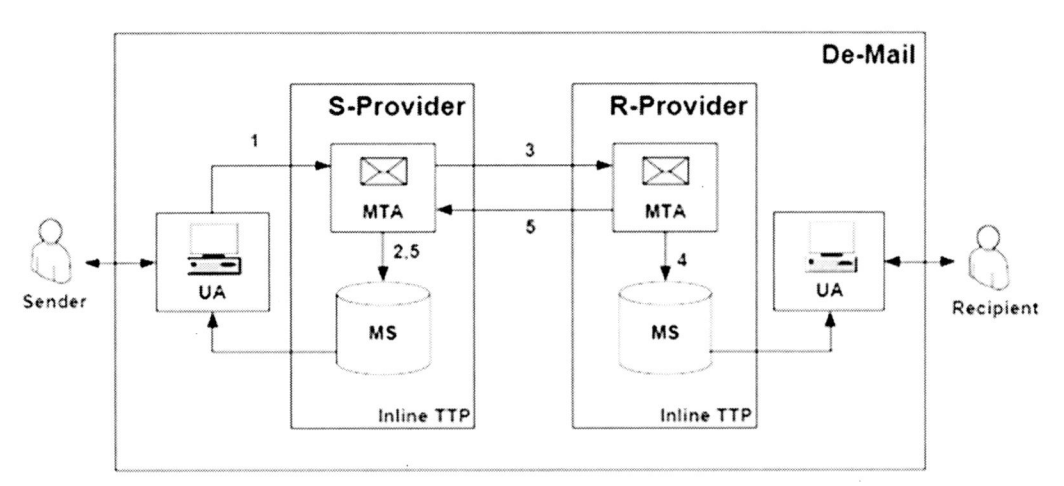

with this format: givenname.familyname.number@providername.de-mail.de.

Moja.posta.si is a private business certified e-mail service operated by the Slovenian Post (Figure 7). It is aimed to be used by the public and private sector. Slovenia does not have a dedicated law for certified e-mail, therefore the system is based on a contractual agreement between the operator (Moja.posta.si) and its customers (senders and recipients).

The Moja.posta.si is operated on a single Web Server acting as inline TTP between senders and recipients. Besides browser-based UA access, the system provides a Web Service interface for business access to enable the automated submission and retrieval of messages. In contrast to the other systems, Moja.posta.si allows the recipients to be addressed in multiple ways: either with the official Slovenian tax number or with the recipient's "@moja.posta.si" mailbox account address.

Figure 7. Slovenian moja.posta architecture

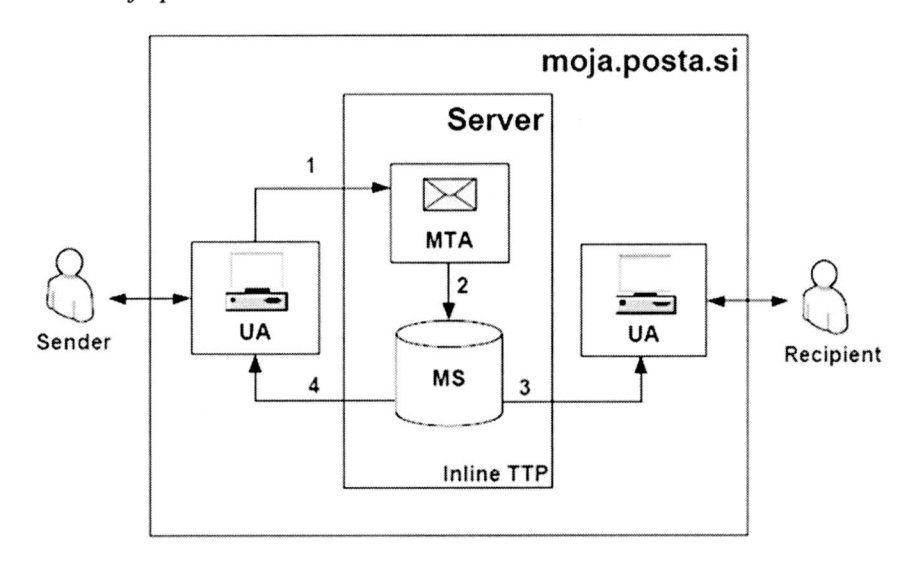

These four certified e-mail systems are examples of the solutions that government and private businesses have implemented. In Tauber's thesis (Tauber, 2012) we can find a more detailed analysis on these systems and other solutions.

CEM Standards

The current CEM solutions in place (see *Existing Solutions* section) apply only to their own country, its domain. It is not possible for senders and recipients from different countries to exchange certified messages. Therefore, in 2008, the European Telecommunications Standards Institute (ETSI) published the first version of the Registered Electronic Mail (REM) standard TS 102 640 (ETSI TS 102 640-1, 640-2, 640-3, 640-4, 640-5). REM is intended to be an evidence standard to establish interoperability between different CEM domains operating under different policies.

In Figure 8 we have depicted the REM architecture. A single REM system is called REM Management Domain (REM-MD) and acts as inline TTP between senders and recipients. A REM-MD consists of at least three components: and MTA, an MS and an EP. REM supports two basic styles of operation: Store and Forward (S&F) and Store and Notify (S&N). Under the S&F style, messages are directly forwarded to the recipient (or the recipient's REM-MD MS), whereas the S&N style means that the recipient is only notified and must retrieve the message from the sender's REM-MD MS.

A REM-MD envelope is defined as a MIME message encapsulating both REM dispatches and REM evidence. A REM dispatch holds the delivery content as payload. REM evidence are well-structured containers holding all evidence-related data like IDs, evidence event, etc. To ease interoperability between different REM-MDs, the standard maps REM evidence to basic messaging-related events like submission/acceptance/rejection by REM-MD (classifiable as NRS), relay to remote REM-MD, delivery/non-delivery to recipient (classifiable as NRD) or retrieval/non-retrieval/download/non-download (classifiable as NRR). To ease interoperability and cross-border mutual recognition evidence, signatures should be either AdES (Advanced Electronic Signature) or QES (Qualified Electronic Signature).

In the Table 1, we can find a comparison between the four existent solutions (explained in the previous section) and the REM standard.

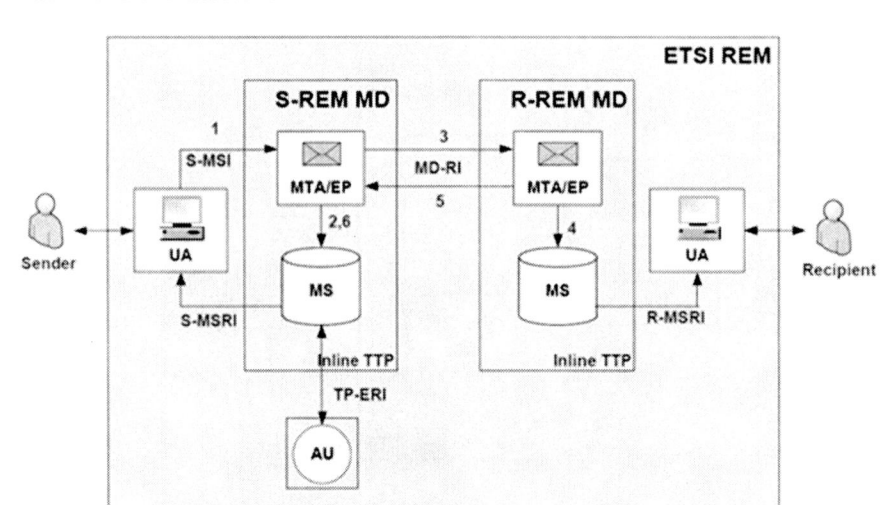

Figure 8. REM standard architecture

Table 1. Existent CEM and standards comparison

	DDS	PEC	De-Mail	Si-Moja	REM
Effectiveness	-	-	-	-	-
Fairness	√	√	√	√	√
Timeliness	√	√	√	√	√
Verifiability of TTP	-	-	-	-	-
Non-Repudiation:					
NRO	√	√	√	√	√
NRS	-	√	√	-	√
NRD	-	√	√	-	√
NRR	√	-	-	√	√
Confidentiality	√	√	√	√	√
Non-Selective Receipt	√	√	√	√	-
No-Author Based Selective Receipt	-	-	-	-	-
Architecture:					
Single MTA	√	-	-	√	-
Multiple MTA	-	√	√	-	√
TTP:					
Inline	√	√	√	√	√
Online	-	-	-	-	-
Offline	-	-	-	-	-
MTA:					
Untrusted	-	-	-	-	-
Semi-Trusted	-	-	-	-	-
Trusted	√	√	√	√	√
Message Protocol:					
SOAP	√	-	-	√	-
E-mail (SMTP)	-	√	√	-	√
√ yes; - no					

GUIDELINES FOR A PRACTICAL CERTIFIED E-MAIL PROTOCOL

As we have seen in the previous section, most of the scientific approaches require a direct interaction between the sender and the recipient with several steps. In asynchronous communication systems, like e-mail, such a high interaction between the sender and the recipient is neither desirable nor practical. Therefore, some approaches have adopted the model of semi-trusted Mail Transfer Agents (MTAs), which act as a proxy (like a mail server) between the sender and the recipient to guarantee fairness. But these approaches either fail to meet some of the requirements needed or do not fully reflect the current Internet e-mail architecture: they use the same MTA for senders and recipients. On the other hand, solutions developed by governments and private companies present serious drawbacks. They consider the MTAs as TTPs, but without being verifiable, i.e., if they misbehave users cannot prove it. In most cases, users (typically recipients of certified mail) cannot choose their mail provider (it is imposed).

And even worse, sometimes a certified mail is considered to have been delivered when it has been deposited in the recipient's mailbox (and perhaps, he will not be able to access to it).

In this section, we will give some guidelines to follow when developing new practical CEM solutions.

Protocol Architecture

One of the keys to the success of a CEM system proposal will be its feasibility. Thus, the CEM services should be integrated in the current e-mail architecture. For a protocol to be easily integrated with the current e-mail infrastructure, it will have to share its architecture, i.e., it must foresee the participation of intermediaries, the MTAs. Moreover, as traditional e-mail offers no security features, users do not need to trust the MTAs: they are not trusted entities, TTPs. Therefore, CEM protocols should also assume that the MTAs are untrusted.

Also related to the protocol architecture is its data flow. The traditional e-mail is an asynchronous service, where the operations of sending and receiving messages are always initiated by the users. Senders deliver messages using the SMTP protocol, and recipients receive messages as response to a POP3 or IMAP request. Ideally, a CEM protocol should be able to use the SMTP protocol, to send certified messages, and either POP3, IMAP, or a specific protocol to fetch them.

As guidelines regarding the protocol architecture, research efforts should be focused on protocols following the traditional e-mail architecture, and the protocol data flow should follow an e-mail-like approach regarding sending and receiving messages (SMTP, POP3, and IMAP). In addition, MTAs should be treated as untrusted entities (they could cheat and collude).

If we look at Table 1, only the Italian PEC, the German De-Mail and the standard REM follow the guideline about the protocol architecture, but all of them treat the MTAs as trusted entities. Moreover, the MTAs behave as inline TTPs.

Trusted Third Parties

Practical fair exchange protocols require the involvement of a TTP in order to assure fairness (see *Certified Electronic Mail* section). Solutions with inline TTP are the option chosen by government and private initiatives (see *Existing Solutions* section), while offline or optimistic are the Scientifics' community one (see *Scientific Work* section). As benefits, an inline TTP protocol can be designed in a way that it does not require any modification on the sender's side, only on the MTA's side. This facilitates its adoption by users, but at the same time, it imposes a high level of trust on the TTP, and not all users would be willing to do it. Moreover, it imposes serious restrictions to the entities willing to act as MTA: they must comply with all requirements needed to become a TTP.

Optimistic solutions, on the other hand, are more efficient: the TTP only intervenes in case of dispute (due to a participant's misbehaviour or a network failure), and it is expected to be an exceptional case. Compared with the inline approach, an optimistic solution requires the modification of the MUA in order to support the protocol, which can difficult its adoption by users, but at the same time it eases its adoption by MTAs: they are not required to become a TTP. Moreover, if we compare the inline and offline TTP approaches with the traditional e-mail where messages are delivered through untrusted MTAs and in case of dispute users can complain to an external arbiter (e.g., a judge), the offline solutions are closer.

In addition to the TTP's involvement, we must also define its level of interaction with the participants. As we said in the previous section (*Protocol Architecture* section), the operations of sending and receiving messages are always initiated by the users; in other words, they do not operate as a service, waiting to receive incoming requests. Therefore, we must apply the same rule here, when solving claims. The TTP must be able to contact the MTAs to solve a request, but never the MUAs. Finally, TTPs can misbehave or fail in real deployments. Thus, to keep fairness, we must assure we can prove the TTP's failure or misbehaviour. That is what verifiability of TTP's requirement assures us.

As guidelines regarding TTPs, research efforts should be devoted to optimistic solutions with verifiable TTP. Additionally, this TTP should resolve disputes without contacting the MUAs (it can contact the MTAs though).

As we can see in Table 1, none of the existent solutions neither the REM standard use offline TTP, all of them use inline TTPs. Moreover, none of them is verifiable.

Security Requirements

We have stated that effectiveness (mandatory requirement for optimistic protocols) and verifiability of TTP are required in order to design a practical protocol. Fairness and timeliness are core properties of fair exchange, therefore they are needed. Confidentiality is not an essential property, strictly speaking it does not have direct relation to fair exchange, but thinking on the user experience of a possible CEM protocol implementation, if not mandatory, it should be optional but offered to users. Finally, we have the non-repudiation and non-selective receipt requirements which we will further explain in the next paragraphs.

The sole purpose of sending a certified mail is to obtain evidence that the recipient has received the message, i.e., Evidence of Receipt (EOR). Therefore, Non-Repudiation of Receipt (NRR) is required. In some protocol proposals, Non-Repudiation of Origin (NRO) is not seen as needed; some mail certified delivery services do not offer NRO. But as part of the fair exchange family, a CEM protocol must comply with the NRO requirement; otherwise a sender could always deny having sent a message, breaking fairness. Non-Repudiation of Submission (NRS) and Non-Repudiation of Delivery (NRD) are consequence of the use of intermediaries (Onieva et al., 2009b). Someone could argue that, since the MTAs should be untrusted, it makes no sense to ask them to generate evidence. But from a practical point of view, even though they are untrusted, it is in their best benefit to act honestly in order to satisfy their customers. Therefore, the protocol must also comply with the NRS and NRD requirements, in order to provide the MTAs with evidence to prove their honest behavior.

Non-selective receipt and no-author based selective receipt are not mandatory for generic fair exchange. But when we focus on CEM protocols, where knowing the content or the source of a message may give an advantage to the recipient (he may decide to refuse it), both are desirable requirements. Approaches like the one proposed by Permpoontanalarp and Kanokkanjanapong (2008) may be a good option to address non-selective receipt without adding complexity to the protocol. No-author based selective receipt, though, requires the use of another TTP (a pseudo-anonym service) to be able to send messages as anonymous user.

As guidelines regarding security requirements, research efforts must focus on protocols that comply with: effectiveness, fairness, non-repudiation (NRO, NRD, NRS, and NRR), timeliness and verifiability of TTP. Confidentiality, non-selective receipt and no-author based selective receipt are desirable but optional requirements.

As Table 1 shows, none of the existent solutions neither the standard REM meet the effectiveness requirement; they all use a non-verifiable inline TTP. The REM standard is the only one meeting all the necessary non-repudiation services requirement (NRO, NRS, NRD, and NRR). Moreover, none of the solutions seems to address the no-author based selective receipt.

CONCLUSION

Internet e-mail is continuously replacing traditional paper-based communications. To meet the requirements of an evidential document exchange, governments, postal services, and private businesses have made available a number of CEM proposals with implementations on the Internet. They all guarantee the fair and non-repudiable delivery of electronic documents. However, these systems are tailored to custom needs and do not seamlessly integrate into the existing Internet e-mail architecture. To ensure an easy deployment and supervision of the fair exchange, all existing CEM systems rely on inline TTPs. This requires a high trust in TTPs and it is not efficient.

In this chapter, we have provided guidelines for the design and development of practical CEM protocols. This means that CEM protocols should seamlessly integrate into the existing e-mail architecture, since users usually may want to use their accustomed communication channels. A CEM protocol should thus rely and be based on SMTP for sending messages and POP3 and IMAP for receiving messages. It is also recommended to use an optimistic approach with verifiable TTPs to ensure an efficient protocol, which does require minimum trust in TTPs. By relying on the traditional e-mail architecture with intermediary transfer agents, the MTAs should also comply with the NRS and NRD requirements to prove their correct behavior. Practical also means that a protocol has to meet the timeliness requirement. Even though confidentiality increases the overall security, it is not considered as a requirement for a fair and non-repudiable exchange. Finally, to ensure a fair exchange, a practical CEM protocol should provide NRO evidence and guarantee non-selective receipt as well as no-author based selective receipt.

REFERENCES

Abadi, M., Glew, N., Horne, B., & Pinkas, B. (2002). Certified email with a light on-line trusted third party: Design and implementation. In *Proceedings of the 11th international World Wide Web conference* (pp. 387-395). ACM Press.

Asokan, N., Shoup, V., & Waidner, M. (1998a). Asynchronous protocols for optimistic fair exchange. In *Proceedings of the IEEE Symposium on Security and Privacy,* (pp. 86-99). Washington, DC: IEEE Computer Society.

Asokan, N., Shoup, V., & Waidner, M. (1998b). Optimistic fair exchange of digital signatures. In *Proceedings of Advances in Cryptology - Eurocrypt'98* (*Vol. 1403,* pp. 591–606). Berlin: Springer. doi:10.1007/BFb0054156.

Ateniese, G. (1999). Efficient verifiable encryption (and fair exchange) of digital signatures. In *Proceedings of the 6th ACM Conference on Computer and Communications Security* (pp. 138-146). New York: ACM Press.

Ateniese, G., de Medeiros, B., & Goodrich, M. T. (2001). TRICERT: A distributed certified e-mail scheme. In *Proceedings of ISOC 2001 Network and Distributed System Security Symposium (NDSS'01).* NDSS.

Ateniese, G., & Nita-Rotaru, C. (2002). Stateless-recipient certified e-mail system based on verifiable encryption. In *Proceedings of the Cryptographer's Track at the RSA Conference on Topics in Cryptology* (pp. 182-199). London, UK: Springer-Verlag.

Bahreman, A., & Tygar, J. (1994). Certified electronic mail. In *Proceedings of Network and Distributed System Security Conference* (pp. 3-19). Pittsburgh, PA: Carnegie Mellon University.

Ben-Or, M., Goldreich, O., Micali, S., & Rivest, R. (1990). A fair protocol for signing contracts. *IEEE Transactions on Information Theory, 36*(1), 40–46. doi:10.1109/18.50372.

Boneh, D., Gentry, C., Lynn, B., & Shacham, H. (2003). Aggregate and verifiably encrypted signatures from bilinear maps. In *Proceedings of the 22nd International Conference on Theory and Applications of Cryptographic Techniques* (pp. 416-432). Berlin: Springer-Verlag.

Cederquist, J., Dashti, M. T., & Mauw, S. (2007). A certified email protocol using key chains. In *Proceedings of the 21st International Conference on Advanced Information Networking and Applications Workshops*, (vol. 1, pp. 525-530). Washington, DC: IEEE Computer Society.

Deng, R., Gong, L., Lazar, A., & Wang, W. (1996). Practical protocols for certified electronic mail. *Journal of Network and Systems Management*, 4(3), 279–297. doi:10.1007/BF02139147.

ETSI TS 102 640-1. (n.d.). *Electronic signatures and infrastructures (ESI), registered electronic mail (REM), part 1: Architecture* (Tech. Rep.). Paris: Sophia Antipolis Cedex.

ETSI TS 102 640-2. (n.d.). *Electronic signatures and infrastructures (ESI), registered electronic mail (REM), part 2: Data requirements, formats and signatures for REM* (Tech. Rep.). Paris: Sophia Antipolis Cedex.

ETSI TS 102 640-3. (n.d.). *Electronic signatures and infrastructures (ESI), registered electronic mail (REM), part 3: Information security policy requirements for REM management domains* (Tech. Rep.). Paris: Sophia Antipolis Cedex.

ETSI TS 102 640-4. (n.d.). *Electronic signatures and infrastructures (ESI), registered electronic mail (REM), part 4: REM-md conformance profiles* (Tech. Rep.). Paris: Sophia Antipolis Cedex.

ETSI TS 102 640-5. (n.d.). *Electronic signatures and infrastructures (ESI), registered electronic mail (REM), part 5: REM-md interoperability profiles* (Tech. Rep.). Paris: Sophia Antipolis Cedex.

Even, S., Goldreich, O., & Lempel, A. (1985). A randomized protocol for signing contracts. *Communications of the ACM*, 28, 637–647. doi:10.1145/3812.3818.

Ferrer-Gomila, J. L., Payeras-Capella, M., & Huguet i Rotger, L. (2000). An efficient protocol for certified electronic mail. In *Proceedings of the Third International Workshop on Information Security* (pp. 237-248). London, UK: Springer-Verlag.

Ferrer-Gomila, J. L., Payeras-Capella, M., & Huguet i Rotger, L. (2002). A realistic protocol for multi-party certified electronic mail. In *Proceedings of the 5th International Conference on Information Security* (pp. 210-219). London, UK: Springer-Verlag.

Ferrer-Gomilla, J. L., Onieva, J. A., Payeras, M., & Lopez, J. (2010). Certified electronic mail: Properties revisited. *Computers & Security*, 29, 167–179. doi:10.1016/j.cose.2009.06.009.

Franklin, M. K., & Reiter, M. K. (1997). Fair exchange with a semi-trusted third party (extended abstract). In *Proceedings of the 4th ACM Conference on Computer and Communications Security* (pp. 1-5). New York, NY: ACM.

Gao, Y.-X., Peng, D.-Y., & Yan, L.-L. (2010). Design and formal analysis of a new fair multi-party certified mail protocol. In *Proceedings of the 2010 International Conference on Machine Learning and Cybernetics (ICMLC)*, (pp. 3101-3106). IEEE Computer Society.

Hwang, R.-J., & Lai, C.-H. (2008). Efficient and secure protocol in fair certified e-mail delivery. *WSEAS Transactions on Information Science and Applications*, 5(9), 1385–1394.

Imamoto, K., & Sakurai, K. (2002). A certified e-mail system with receiver's selective usage of delivery authority. In *Proceedings of the Third International Conference on Cryptology: Progress in Cryptology* (pp. 326-338). London, UK: Springer-Verlag.

Kremer, S., & Markowitch, O. (2001). Selective receipt in certified e-mail. In *Proceedings of Progress in Cryptology Indocrypt 2001* (Vol. 2247, pp. 136–148). Berlin: Springer. doi:10.1007/3-540-45311-3_14.

Kremer, S., Markowitch, O., & Zhou, J. (2002). An intensive survey of fair non-repudiation protocols. *Computer Communications, 25*, 1606–1621. doi:10.1016/S0140-3664(02)00049-X.

Lamport, L. (1981). Password authentication with insecure communication. *Communications of the ACM, 24*(11), 770–772. doi:10.1145/358790.358797.

Liang, X., Cao, Z., Lu, R., & Qin, L. (2008). Efficient and secure protocol in fair document exchange. *Computer Standards & Interfaces, 30*(3), 167–176. doi:10.1016/j.csi.2007.08.003.

Liu, D., Qing, S., Li, P., & Yuan, C. (2008). A practical certified e-mail system with temporal authentication based on transparent TSS. In *Proceedings of the 2008 Ninth ACIS International Conference on Software Engineering, Artificial Intelligence, Networking, and Parallel/Distributed Computing* (pp. 285-290). Washington, DC: IEEE Computer Society.

Liu, Z., Pang, J., & Zhang, C. (2010). Extending a key-chain based certified email protocol with transparent TTP. In *Proceedings of the 2010 IEEE/IFIP International Conference on Embedded and Ubiquitous Computing* (pp. 630-636). Washington, DC: IEEE Computer Society.

Lopez, J., Onieva, J. A., & Zhou, J. (2004). Enhancing certified email service for timeliness and multicast. In *Proceedings of 2004 International Network Conference* (pp. 327-335). Plymouth, UK: University of Plymouth.

Ma, C., Li, S., Chen, K., & Liu, S. (2006). Analysis and improvement of fair certified e-mail delivery protocol. *Computer Standards & Interfaces, 28*(4), 467–474. doi:10.1016/j.csi.2005.03.002.

Markowitch, O., & Roggeman, Y. (1999). Probabilistic non-repudiation without trusted third party. In *Proceedings of the 2nd Conference on Security in Communication Networks*. IEEE.

Micali, S. (2003). Simple and fast optimistic protocols for fair electronic exchange. In *Proceedings of the Twenty Second Annual Symposium on Principles of Distributed Computing* (pp. 12–19). New York, NY: ACM.

Monteiro, J. R. M., & Dahab, R. (2002). An attack on a protocol for certified delivery. In *Proceedings of the 5th International Conference on Information Security* (pp. 428-436). London, UK: Springer-Verlag.

Mut Puigserver, M., Ferrer Gomila, J., & Huguet i Rotger, L. (2000). Certified electronic mail protocol resistant to a minority of malicious third parties. In *Proceedings of the Nineteenth Annual Joint Conference of the IEEE Computer and Communications Societies* (pp. 1401-1405). IEEE.

Nenadic, A., Zhang, N., & Barton, S. (2004). Fair certified e-mail delivery. In *Proceedings of the 2004 ACM Symposium on Applied Computing* (pp. 391-396). New York, NY: ACM.

Okamoto, T., & Ohta, K. (1994). How to simultaneously exchange secrets by general assumptions. In *Proceedings of the 2nd ACM Conference on Computer and Communications Security* (pp. 184 - 192). New York, NY: ACM.

Onieva, J. A., Lopez, J., & Zhou, J. (2009). *Secure multi-party non-repudiation protocols and applications* (Vol. 43). London: Springer Publishing Company, Incorporated. doi:10.1007/978-0-387-75630-1.

Onieva, J. A., Zhou, J., & Lopez, J. (2009b). Multiparty nonrepudiation: A survey. *ACM Computing Surveys, 41*(1), 5:1-5:43.

Oppliger, R., & Stadlin, P. (2004). A certified mail system (CMS) for the internet. *Computer Communications, 27*(13), 1229–1235. doi:10.1016/j.comcom.2004.04.006.

Park, Y., & Cho, Y. (2004). Fair certified e-mail protocols with delivery deadline agreement. In *Proceedings of Computational Science and its Applications - ICCSA 2004* (Vol. 3043, pp. 978–987). Berlin: Springer. doi:10.1007/978-3-540-24707-4_110.

Permpoontanalarp, Y., & Kanokkanjanapong, J. (2008). Dynamic undeniable fair certified email with DDOS protection. In *Proceedings of the 22nd International Conference on Advanced Information Networking and Applications* (pp. 763-770). Washington, DC: IEEE Computer Society.

Schneier, B., & Riordan, J. (1998). A certified e-mail protocol. In *Proceedings of the 14th Annual Computer Security Applications Conference* (pp. 347-352). Washington, DC: IEEE Computer Society.

Tauber, A. (2011). A survey of certified mail systems provided on the Internet. *Computers & Security, 30*(6-7), 464–485. doi:10.1016/j.cose.2011.05.001.

Tauber, A. (2012). *Cross-border certified electronic mailing.* (Thesis). Graz University of Technology, Graz, Austria.

Wang, C., Lan, C., Niu, S., & Cao, X. (2011). An id-based certified e-mail protocol suitable for wireless mobile environments. In *Proceedings of the 2011 Fourth International Symposium on Parallel Architectures, Algorithms and Programming* (pp. 146-150). Washington, DC: IEEE Computer Society.

Wang, C., Yang, X., Lan, C., & Cao, X. (2009). An efficient identity-based certified e-mail protocol. In *Proceedings of the 2009 Fifth International Conference on Intelligent Information Hiding and Multimedia Signal Processing* (pp. 1197-1200). Washington, DC: IEEE Computer Society.

Wang, G., Bao, F., & Zhou, J. (2005). On the security of a certified e-mail scheme. In *Proceedings of Progress in Cryptology - Indocrypt 2004* (Vol. 3348, pp. 48–60). Berlin: Springer. doi:10.1007/978-3-540-30556-9_5.

Wang, H., Ou, Y., Ling, J., Xu, X., & Guo, H. (2007). A new certified email protocol. In *Proceedings of the 18th International Conference on Database and Expert Systems Applications* (pp. 683-687). Washington, DC: IEEE Computer Society.

Zhang, F., Safavi-Naini, R., & Susilo, W. (2003). Efficient verifiably encrypted signature and partially blind signature from bilinear pairings. In *Proceedings of Progress in Cryptology - Indocrypt 2003* (Vol. 2904, pp. 191–204). Berlin: Springer. doi:10.1007/978-3-540-24582-7_14.

Zheng, Y. (1997). Digital signcryption or how to achieve cost (signature & encryption) << cost(signature) + cost(encryption). In *Proceedings of the 17th Annual International Cryptology Conference on Advances in Cryptology* (pp. 165-179). London, UK: Springer-Verlag.

Zhou, J. (2004). On the security of a multi-party certified email protocol. [). Berlin: Springer.]. *Proceedings of Information and Communications Security, 3269,* 277–280.

Zhou, J., Deng, R., & Bao, F. (2000). Some remarks on a fair exchange protocol. [). Berlin: Springer.]. *Proceedings of Public Key Cryptography, 1751,* 46–57. doi:10.1007/978-3-540-46588-1_4.

Zhou, J., & Gollmann, D. (1996). Certified electronic mail. In *Proceedings of Computer Security ESORICS 96* (Vol. 1146, pp. 160–171). Berlin: Springer. doi:10.1007/3-540-61770-1_35.

KEY TERMS AND DEFINITIONS

Certified Electronic Mail (CEM): A fair exchange in which the items to be exchanged are a message from the sender for an evidence of its reception from the recipient.

Evidence: A digital message proving that some event has occurred: a message has been sent, delivered, received, etc. Typically, these messages are generated applying cryptographic techniques like digital signatures.

Fair Exchange: An exchange of items/information between different participants where all honest participants receive what they expect, and whatever dishonest participants do, the latter cannot gain any advantage over the honest ones; neither during the exchange nor after it.

Internet E-Mail: A service that allows users to send digital messages through Internet to one or more recipients.

Mail Transfer Agent: An entity that offers e-mail services to its subscribers.

Mail User Agent: An end-user application to send and receive e-mails.

Optimistic Fair Exchange Protocol: A fair exchange in which, if every participant follows the protocol specifications, the TTP does not intervene.

Trusted Third Party (TTP): An external entity that ensures an exchange remains fair, either participating in it or solving disputes related to it.

Chapter 3
Mobile IPv6:
Mobility Management and Security Aspects

Tayo Arulogun
Ladoke Akintola University of Technology, Nigeria

Ahmad AlSa'deh
University of Potsdam, Germany

Christoph Meinel
University of Potsdam, Germany

ABSTRACT

Mobile Internet Protocol (MIP) enables a mobile node to be recognized via a single IP address while the node moves between different networks. MIP attains the connectivity to nodes everywhere without user intervention. One general improvement in Mobile IPv6 (MIPv6) compared to MIPv4 is the enhanced security. However, there are areas still susceptible to various kinds of attacks. Security approaches for the MIPv6 are still in progress and there are few unsolved concerns and problems. This chapter focuses on MIPv6 security considerations, potential threats, and possible defense mechanisms. The authors discuss and analyze in detail the MIPv6 mobility management and security approaches with respect to the efficiency and complexity and bring forward some constructive recommendations.

INTRODUCTION

Mobile devices will undoubtedly dominate the population of the future Internet due to reduced cost, enhanced portability, increased capabilities, pervasive computing, etc. This dominance of mobile devices has made researches in mobility and security of IPv6 to be a hot area.

MIPv6 allows Mobile Nodes (MN) to move within the Internet while maintaining reachability without disruption to active sessions, using a permanent Home Address (HoA). MIPv6 was designed to serve as the basic mobility management method in the IP-based wireless networks (Perkins, Johnson, & Arkko, 2011) but some shortcomings, such as prolonged handover latency and security vulnerabilities which reduce the quality of users experience and trust. Research in MIPv6 is very active due to these shortcomings and more importantly due to the current Internet architecture being insecure and originally designed to be relatively static.

The theme of this chapter is to bring to focus the current and anticipated positions of security solutions in MIPv6 and to project what can be done further to enhance the security in this important domain. Through this chapter, we set the following objectives to be achieved: (1) to identify and analyze the anatomy of MIPv6 protocol and its mode of operations, (2) to review with purpose to bring out security designs and implementations in MIPv6, and (3) to gather and bring to the focus of the readers new suggestions or modifications to MIPv6. We conclude with the summary and findings presented in the chapter.

MIPV6 DESIGN

MIPv6 is network-layer mobility protocol-based on IPv6 and standardized by the Internet Engineering Task Force (IETF) via the Request for Comments (RFC) number 6275. Its design was based on the MIPv4 and offers more enhancements as summarized in (Perkins et al., 2011). One of the main differences between MIPv4 and MIPv6 is that, in the latter, MN can perform mobility signaling directly with mobile and non-mobile Correspondent Nodes (CN) (Aura & Roe, 2006). The architecture of MIPv6, Figure 1(a), allows MN to move within the Internet while maintaining reachability without noticeable disruption to active sessions, using a permanent Home Address (HoA) and Care of Address (CoA) for communication with a CN. MIPv6 operates using multiple IPv6 extension headers: the *Mobility Option Header*, the *Destination Option Header*, the *Type 2 Routing Header (RH2)* and Internet Control Message Protocol for IPv6 (ICMPv6) messages for signaling. These headers are used to send packets to and from the MN at its CoA, to CN as if HoA is the source and the destination of these packets respectively. When a MN moves away from its home location to a foreign network, it registers with its HA. To register, the MN sends a packet from its CoA to the HA with the *Destination Option Header* containing the HoA of the MN and a *Mobility Option Header* with a *Type 5 Binding Update (BU)* message. HA confirms this BU by sending a packet to the CoA of the MN that contains an *RH2* that lists the HoA of the MN and contains a *Mobility Option Header* with a *Type 6 Binding Acknowledgment* (BA) message. The MIPv6 mobility can be blue printed via *Transparent* mode or *Route Optimization* (RO) mode as shown in Figure 1(a).

In *Transparent* mode, HA is a router at the home network, acts as the MN's trusted agent and link to the CoA. The HA intercepts packets sent by CN to the HoA and forwards them to the CoA over IPv6 tunnel. When the mobile wants to send packets to CN, it sends them to the HA over the reverse tunnel. The HA decapsulates the packets and forwards them to the CN. When MN moves to a new location, it tells HA its new CoA by sending a BU message. The BU message causes the HA to update the IP-in-IP tunnel in such a way that the tunneled packets are routed to and from the new CoA. The binding update and the subsequent BA are authenticated using a preconfigured IP security (IPsec) security association between the MN and the HA.

In Figure 1(b), RO uses the BU and BA messages. When MN changes its current address, it sends BUs to its CN to notify about its new location. The BU contains the MN's HoA and CoA. CN acknowledges the BU with a BA and stores the location information in the binding cache, which is the routing table that describes how packets destined to HoA should be sent to the CoA. RO protocol eliminates the triangle routing between the MN, HA and the CN that is inherent in the transparent route mode. This enables a more efficient routing of data to and from the MN and

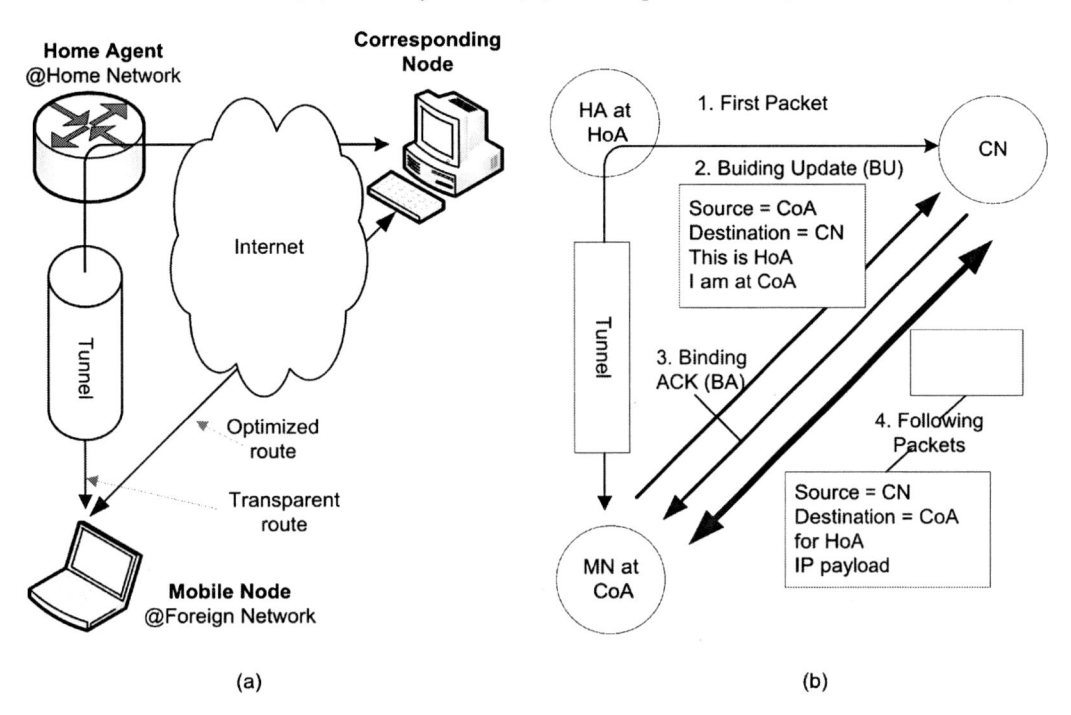

Figure 1. MIPv6 architecture: (a) mobility route, (b) route optimization (Aura & Roe, 2006)

the removal of possible congestion at the home network because MN may communicate with several CN.

Unauthorized binding update protocol implemented as described in RO would create BU spoofing, security vulnerability that could lead to session hijacking, Denial of Service (DoS) and packet flooding attacks (Bombing Attack). Unauthorized location information updates make it possible for an attacker to steal address to deceive CN about the MN's location and, thus, redirect packets intended for MN to an erroneous destination. The simple and unauthorized BU procedure was based on the need to make MIPv6 simpler, efficient and transparent to higher level protocols. The risk of this vulnerability is reduced with the Stateless Address Auto-configuration (Thomson, Narten, & Jinmei, 2007) based on Privacy Extension (Narten, Draves, & Krishnan, 2007) or Cryptographically Generated Address (CGA) (Aura, 2005) because the attacker needs to know both MN and CN IP addresses. Moreover RO is optional and can be disabled by either the MN or the CN.

The Return-Routability protocol (RR) was proposed to secure binding updates from MNs to CNs.

The Return-Routability (RR) Protocol

Return-Routability (RR) protocol was design and standardized to authorize a BU for RO. RR protocol enables the CN to verify that the MN is indeed reachable at its claimed CoA, as well as at its HoA (Perkins et al., 2011). Successful usage of RR implies that there is indeed a node at each of the claimed addresses and CN can accept BU from MN and direct MN's data traffic to its claimed CoA. This is done by testing whether packets addressed to the two claimed addresses are routed to the MN. The MN can pass the test only if it is able to supply proof that it received certain data sent by CN to the claimed addresses. These data from CN are combined by the MN into a binding management key (K_{bm}) (Perkins et al., 2011).

RR procedure consists of Home Test (HoT) and Care-of Test (CoT) with the signaling flows from the three nodes. The MN sends a Home Test Init (HoTI), Care-of Test Init (CoTI) simultaneously to CN to start HoT, and CoT. The CN replies to both messages independently by sending a HoT and a CoT via different routes. The HoT has a nonce index and a Home keygen token. A Home keygen token is generated by CN with its node key (K_{cn}), known only by the CN. A CoT has a nonce index and a care-of keygen token. A Care-of keygen token is generated with K_{cn}. A Home keygen token and a care-of keygen token are calculated by the following formulas respectively.

Home keygen token = hash (K_{cn} | HoA | nonce | 0)

Care-of keygen token = hash (K_{cn} | CoA | nonce | 1)

The Home keygen token received by the MN is used for proving that the MN is indeed at the HoA. And Care-of keygen token received by the MN is used for proving that the MN is indeed at the CoA. Each nonce index allows CN to easily find the nonce which was used during generation of keygen token. The MN which has a Home keygen token and a Care-of keygen token can create a binding management key (K_{bm}) to substantiate that the MN stays at the HoA and CoA concurrently.

K_{bm} = hash (Home keygen token | Care-of keygen token)

The tunnel between the MN and the HA is protected by IPsec's Encapsulated Security Payload (ESP), which makes it impossible for the outsiders to learn the contents of a HoT. Therefore RR is secure from malicious attacks. The RR procedure was designed with the objective to provide a level of security that compares to that of today's non-mobile Internet (Nikander, Arkko, Aura, Montenegro, & Nordmark, 2005).

Prior to MN receiving the first packet from CN at CoA in the MIPv6 mobility blueprint, two other processes must precede the BU process namely Movement Detection (MD); and Address Con-figuration (AC). The process of transferring the connection of a MN from one point of attachment in the Internet to another one is called handover in wireless communication systems. The period during which the MN loses the connectivity with its current network link until the time it receives the first packet after connecting to the new network link is known as handover latency. During a handover, the MN may experience connectivity interruption due to long handover latency. Further discussion will continue on the key processes in the mobility blueprint: MD, AC, BU and BU authentication, security goals and requirements of MIPv6 design.

Movement Detection

The movement detection process detects the movement of a MN from the current connected router and eventual connection to an appropriate new access router via router discovery process. Router discovery process is the method that allows MN to automatically discover the identity of local routers on the current link, and learn important details of the routers. MIPv6 uses Neighbor Discovery for IPv6 (Narten, Nordmark, Simpson, & Soliman, 2007) for router discovery process as specified in (Perkins et al., 2011). IPv6 nodes on the same link can discover each other's presence, determine each other's link-layer addresses, find routers, and maintain reachability information about the paths to active neighbors with Neighbor Discovery for IPv6 specifications.

Neighbor Discovery for IPv6 (Narten et al., 2007) and Stateless Address Auto-Configuration (SLAAC) for IPv6 (Thomson et al., 2007) are collectively called Neighbor Discovery Protocol (NDP). NDP is used for router, address prefix and parameter discoveries, address auto-configuration, address resolution, Duplicate Address Detection (DAD), Neighbor Unreachability Detection (NUD), next-hop determination and redirect. NDP defines the following additional ICMPv6 messages (Conta, Deering, & Gupta, 2006) so as to perform its functionalities:

1. **Router Solicitation (RS), type 133:** RS is sent by IPv6 host to discover the default router and to learn network information, such as prefixes and Domain Name Server (DNS) address.
2. **Router Advertisement (RA), type 134:** The router that receives a RS message sends back a RA message (solicited router advertisement). Also, RA is sent by IPv6 routers periodically (unsolicited multicast router advertisements).
3. **Neighbor Solicitation (NS), type 135:** NS is used to resolve the neighbor nodes IPv6 address to its Media Access Control (MAC) address or to verify if the node is still reachable.
4. **Neighbor Advertisement (NA), type 136:** NA is a response to NS. NA message include the MAC address of the node.
5. **Redirect message, type 137:** Used by router to inform other nodes of a better first-hop toward a destination.

Generically, MN movement detection in MIPv6-based mobility uses *Neighbor Unreachability Detection* to detect when the default router is no longer bi-directionally reachable, in which case the mobile node must discover a new default router usually on a new link (Perkins et al., 2011) using RS and RA messages.

Address Configuration

Address Configuration (AC) is the method employed by MN in acquiring a CoA using SLAAC in conjunction with network prefix advertised by the new access router and the confirmation of the CoA uniqueness using DAD procedure. AC also relies on NDP ICMPv6 messages for effective implementation. MIPv6 supports both stateful and stateless address autoconfiguration, such as address configuration with Dynamic Host Configuration Protocol for IPv6 (DHCPv6) (Droms et al., 2003) server and SLAAC mechanisms respectively. With SLAAC of NDP, hosts on a link can automatically configure link-local addresses for themselves. Global network addresses can be obtained by combining the interface identifier part with address prefixes advertised by routers located in the network segment (Thomson, Narten, & Jinmei, 2007).

SLAAC is the preferred address configuration method for MN because of its lightweight address configuration that supports plug-and-play IP connectivity as compared to DHCPv6. SLAAC generates the address by combining two pieces of information: the network prefix, obtained from the routers located in the network segment to which MN is attached and link-local address obtained by appending an interface identifier to the link-local prefix (FE80::/10). The interface identifier could be obtained from the MN's network interface. Also, the interface identifier can be generated by Privacy Extension (Narten, Draves & Krishnan, 2007) mechanism to make it more difficult for eavesdroppers and other information collectors or by using Cryptographically Generated Addresses (CGA) (Aura, 2005) to make it more secure. Using CGA ensures IP address authentication for MN. Before assigning the new link-local address to its interface, MN must verify that the address is unique. This is accomplished by sending an NS message targeted to the new address. If reply is received then the address is a duplicate and the process is terminated after three failed attempts. When no reply is received to the NS message, the MN now has a valid CoA for mobility activities. The likelihood of this process being terminated due to failed DAD procedure is very small unless the MN is under attack from malicious node. This attack is basic to MIPv6 as inherited from IPv6 and SEcure Neighbor Discovery (SEND) (Arkko, Kempf, Zill, & Nikander, 2005) was proposed to counteract the attack.

Security Goal and Requirements of MIPv6 Design

The security goal in designing MIPv6 was simply to make it, at least, as secure as IPv6 with minimal signaling among the communicating nodes (Aura & Roe, 2006). To achieve this goal, the following design and security assumptions were made by MIPv6 working group for the architecture and security design of MIPv6.

MIPv6 Design Assumptions

The MIPv6 design relies heavily on the following assumptions:

1. The routing prefixes available to a MN are determined by its current location, and therefore the MN must change its IP address as it moves.
2. The routing infrastructures deliver packets to their intended destinations as identified by the destination address.
3. The design of MIPv6 is to follow the end-to-end principle, to duly notice the differences in trust relationships between the nodes, and not to make the security any worse than IPv4 is today.
4. The end-to-end principle is applied by restricting mobility related state primarily to the HA, and CN.

MIPv6 Security Assumptions

The following MIPv6 security assumptions were made:

1. Pre-established security association between a MN and HA: MN and HA know each other, and can thus have a pre-established strong security association to reliably authenticate exchanged messages between them using IPsec's ESP to set up a secure tunnel between MN and HA.
2. No pre-established security association between MN and a random CN: It is expected that MIPv6 will be used on a global basis between nodes belonging to different administrative domains, hence building a global Public Key Infrastructure (PKI) to authenticate any MN and random CN would be very complex and demanding task. It may be possible to have global PKI or its semblance in the nearest future.

With these goals and assumptions, infrastructure-less security protocols, such as RR and SEND were specified and further standardized for MIPv6 (Perkins et al., 2011) along with traditional security protocol such as IPsec (Arkko, Devarapall, & Dupont, 2004; Devarapalli & Dupont, 2007) and Internet Key Exchange (IKE) (Kaufman, Hoffman, Nir, & Eronen, 2010). These security protocols are discussed under Security threats and counteract proposals of this chapter. The stated goal of MIPv6 using the design and security assumptions were achieved with the final MIPv6 standard specification. However, standard MIPv6 still surfer from some mobility and security issues, such as long handover latency in homogeneous and heterogeneous networks, DoS, Address stealing, etc. These issues are not only peculiar to MIPv6 alone but to IPv6 and MIPv4.

There have been various suggestions, and some IETF standardized alternative mobility management solutions engineered for MIPv6 with couple of security management protocols and algorithms. We will discuss it in more details in the next section.

MIPV6 MOBILITY MANAGEMENTS AND SECURITY ISSUES

A number of extensions and security suggestions for enhancing the mobility management and security of MIPv6 are discussed in the following sections.

MIPv6 Mobility Management

Mobility management is the planning and control of transparent MN movement from its home network to foreign networks with the aim of optimizing the handover latencies by reducing signaling overhead, reducing packet loss, and reducing location updates, for efficient and effectiveness IP-based communication with any CN in the Internet. Maintaining connections during movement is the basic necessity that has given rise to MIPv6. MIPv6 provides the optimal packet routing but requires high signaling cost and long handover latency. Due to this inadequacy, IETF currently standardized four enhancements to MIPv6 namely: Hierarchical MIPv6 (HMIPv6) (Soliman, Castelluccia, ElMalki & Bellier, 2008), Fast Handovers for MIPv6 (FMIPv6) (Koodli, 2009), Proxy MIPv6 (PMIPv6) (Gundavelli, Leung, Devarapalli, Chowdhury, & Patil, 2008), and Proxy-Based Fast Handovers for Mobile IPv6 (PFMIPv6) (Yokota, Chowdhury, Koodli, Pati, & Xia, 2010).

MIPv6, HMIPv6 and FMIPv6 are host-based mobility management protocols while PMIPv6 and PFMIPv6 are network-based mobility management protocol. Host-based mobility management rely mainly on MN for the mobility related signaling while Network-based mobility management do not require MN's participation in any mobility-related signaling.

HMIPv6 (Soliman et al., 2008) allows MN to signal its local handovers to a Mobility Anchor Point (MAP) located somewhere nearby the MN. In this way, HMIPv6 avoids high latency signaling to the MN's HA and CN. FMIPv6 (Koodli, 2009) aims at reducing handover latencies by proactively executing the configuration of the MN interface for the link to the target access router while the MN is still connected to the link on the current serving access router. FMIPv6 also exploit packets forwarding by the serving access router to the target access router during the critical phase of the handover and buffering of these packets at the target access router until the MN attaches to it. PMIPv6 (Gundavelli et al., 2008) extends MIPv6 with improved signaling and mobility supports to nodes that do not have MIPv6 functionality. PFMIPv6 (Yokota et al., 2010) combines the features of FMIPv6 and PMIPv6 for mobility enhancement.

Hierarchical MIPv6 (HMIPv6)

HMIPv6 introduces a new MIPv6 node known as Mobility Anchor Point (MAP) that provides mobility management on behalf of MN. MAP could be located at any level in a hierarchical network of routers, including the Access Router (AR). The MAP limits the amount of MIPv6 signaling outside the local domain. The architecture of HMIPv6 is shown in Figure 2. When MN enters a MAP domain, it will receive RAs containing information on one or more local MAPs.

The On-Link CoA (LCoA), in Figure 2, is configured on the MN's interface based on the prefix advertised by the current link default router. This is equivalent to the CoA of MIPv6, and Regional CoA (RCoA) is analogous to the HoA in the case of MIPv6. A local BU is sent by the MN to the MAP to create a mapping between an address on the MAP's subnet called RCoA and LCoA (Soliman et al., 2008). This is because the RCoA remains the same when a MN moves within the domain of the MAP, but the LCoA changes and hence a BU is required to be sent to MAP. HA and CN only receives BU when MN moves to another MAP domain hence, MN creates a new RCoA and new LCoA binding in the new MAP domain. Acting as a local HA, the MAP will receive all packets on behalf of the MN it is serving and will encapsulate and forward them directly to the MN's current address. If MN changes its current address within a local MAP domain (LCoA), it only needs to register the new address with the MAP. Hence, only the RCoA needs to be registered with correspondent nodes and the HA. The RCoA does not change as long

Figure 2. HMIPv6 architecture

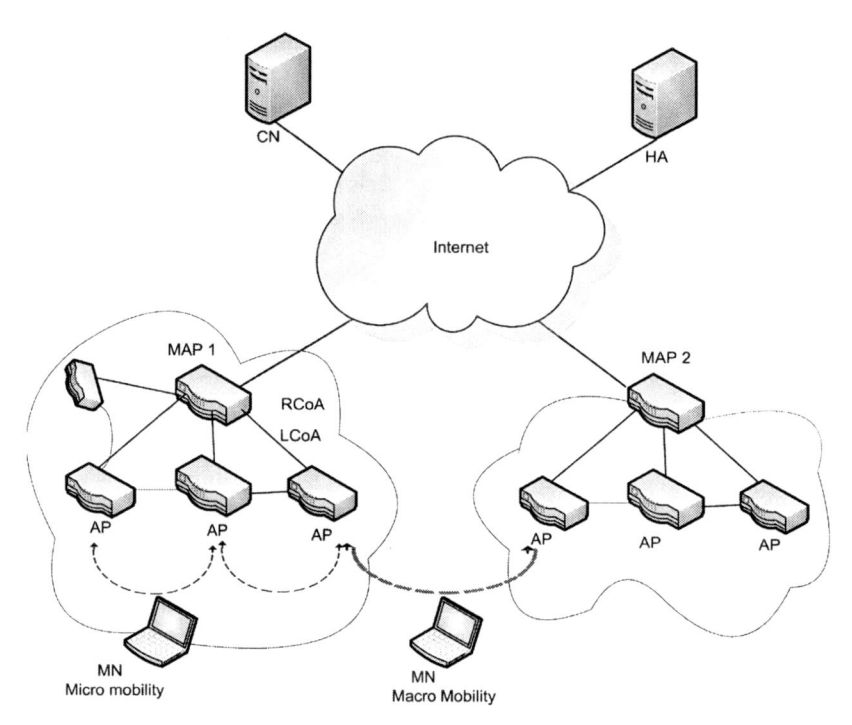

as the MN moves within a MAP domain. In HMIPv6, MN hides its LCoA from its CN and its HA by using its RCoA in the source field of the packets that it sends. As a result, the location tracking of MN by its CN, HA or adversaries is difficult because only RCoA is known and not its LCoA. The rest of the mobility procedure remains the same as in MIPv6 with RO being utilized.

Fast Handover for MIPv6 (FMIPv6)

Fast handover mobility management for Mobile IPv6 was proposed to reduce the handover latency by initiating and executing some of the time-consuming handover processes such as Router Discovery, Address Configuration, and Duplicate Address Detection while MN is still present on the current link with the help of timely generated link Layer-trigger (Koodli, 2009). The architecture of FMIPv6 is shown in Figure 3(a). A MN in its home network has address know as Previous CoA (PCoA) and is connected to the access router known as the Previous Access Router (PAR). On moving to the new network, it connects with a New Access Router (NAR) and acquires a New CoA (NCoA) and packet destined to MN from CN during the movement are tunneled by PAR to NAR. FMIPv6 uses Router Solicitation for Proxy Advertisement (RtSolPr) and Proxy Router Advertisement (PrRtAdv) for fast handover as shown in Figure 3(b) to obtain details of suitable NAR. There are three modes of initiating FMIPv6 namely; predictive, reactive and network modes.

Predictive Handovers

In predictive mode, the MN anticipates a change of network link and initiates handover by sending an RtSolPr message to the PAR to indicate that it wants to perform a fast handover. PAR sends this message to NAR, if it has not the details of NAR. The PAR replies MN with a PrRtAdv that provides the MN with tuple about the new link for accelerated movement detection. The received

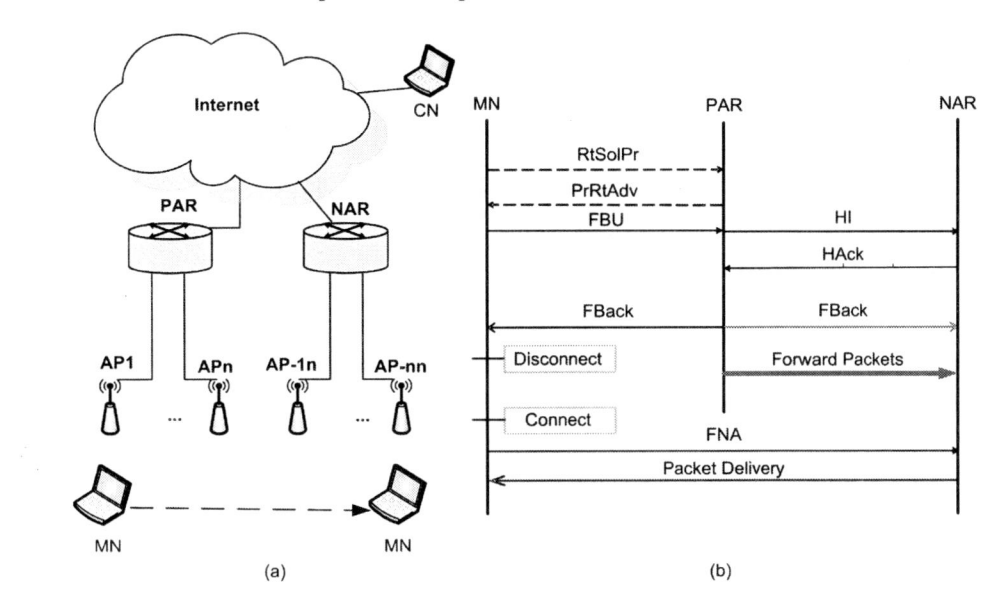

Figure 3. FMIPv6 structure and operation sequence

tuple (access point ID (AP-ID), AR-Info) contains an AR's layer two (L2) and IP addresses, and the prefix valid on the interface to which the Access Point (identified by AP-ID) is attached. This is the tuple that the MN would receive when it moves to a new access point with AP-ID. MN also forms an NCoA while it is still connected to PAR. MN sends a Fast Binding Update (FBU) to the PAR using this NCoA and receives a Fast Binding Acknowledgement (FBack) to indicate success. A tunnel between the PCoA and the NCoA is created when PAR sends a Handover Initiation (HI) message to NAR and it replies with a Handover Acknowledgement (HAck). After the tunneling phase is over, packet forwarding starts. PAR begins tunneling packets arriving for PCoA to NCoA. The tunnel remains active until the MN completes the Binding Update with its CN. Forwarding support for PCoA is provided through a reverse tunnel between the MN and the PAR since CN's have to be updated with a Binding Cache entry that has the NCoA. MN sends a Fast Neighbor Advertisement (FNA), to start the packet flow from NAR to itself.

Network Initiated Handover

If the PAR detects low link quality on MN link or topologically better NAR or believe that MN should move to better link served by another NAR, it will send an unsolicited PrRtAdv to the MN containing the information with which the MN can connect to the new network. Apart from the absence of the initial RtSolPr message, the message exchanges are the same as in Figure 3(b). MN must only be able to connect to the network specified in the PrRtAdv message by configuring a CoA for itself and issuing a FBU to the PAR.

Reactive Handover

Reactive handover mode is used when a node suddenly loses its connection with its current PAR or current Access Point (AP) during the fast handover procedure. Therefore, MN does not get an FBack for the FBU from the PAR, or the MN could not send the FBU to the PAR before the movement. Once the MN is in NAR's link, a FBU is sent and is usually encapsulated in the FNA. The NAR forwards the FBU to the PAR and the PAR starts the tunneling packets destined for PCoA to NCoA after receiving the FBU. Packets may be lost in FMIPv6 Reactive handover mode depending on the interval between the MN moving and the PAR receiving the FBU.

Proxy MIPv6 (PMIPv6)

PMIPv6 is a network-based mobility protocol that aims to keep MN with or without MIPv6 functionality unaware of the process of mobility (Gundavelli et al., 2008). MN involvement is removed completely in PMIPv6 mobility management by involving a network node called Mobility Access Gateway (MAG) and a HA known as Local Mobility Anchor (LMA) in the signaling process creating a Proxy Mobile IPv6 Domain (Gundavelli et al., 2008). LMA in PMIPv6 domain serves as an anchor point for the MN possible home addresses and manages MN's binding state. MAG is an access router that tracks the MN's movement to and from the access link and informs the LMA regarding this movement. LMA has an address configured on its interface known as the LMA Address (LMAA). It is the endpoint of the bi-directional tunnel between it and the MAG. Proxy CoA (PCoA) forms the other end of this bi-directional tunnel. This address is configured on the outer interface of the MAG and this serves as the CoA of the MN and is used in the binding cache entry for the MN. A prefix advertised by the MAG in the PMIPv6 domain for MN is known as the Mobile Node-Home Network Prefix (MN-HNP). The MN always configures its address from this prefix that is anchored at the LMA. The address used by the MN for communication is the Mobile Node Home Address (MN-HoA). The LMA is aware of the MN-HNP and not the exact MN-HoA that is configured on the MN. The MN can use this address at all attachment points in the PMIPv6 domain (Gundavelli et al., 2008). PMIPv6 stands a good chance as the mobility management protocol of choice for use in next generation IP-based heterogeneous networks.

Proxy-Based Fast-Handovers for MIPv6 (PFMIPv6)

The fundamental performance of PMIPv6 in terms of handover latency and packet loss is considered not any different from that of basic MIPv6 (Yokota et al., 2010). PFMIPv6 protocol is designed to adapt FMIPv6 effectively in PMIPv6 by optimizing the associated data and control flow during handover which significantly improve the required handover latency and signaling cost of the mobility management protocol.

Other Proposed Mobility Management Extensions

While the experimentation and standardization of the four Mobility Management Extensions; HMIPv6, FMIPv6, PMIPv6, and PFMIPv6 were ongoing there, were a number of proposals on the extension of MIPv6. Most of these proposals suggest enhancements to optimize the operations and security while others try to amalgamate some of these mobility management protocols.

Jung, Soliman, Koh and Lee (2005), proposed Fast Handover for Hierarchical MIPv6 (F-HMIPv6) that optimally combines HMIPv6 and FMIPv6 using the structures of HMIPv6 and the FMIPv6 signaling messages for handover support with the aim of shortening the handover latency in ARs within the same MAP domain. Yoo, Tolentino, Park, Chang and Kim (2009), proposed a scheme for Efficient Fast Hierarchical Mobile IPv6 (ESFMHIPv6) to overcome ineffectiveness of the simple combination of FMIPv6 and HMIPv6 using dual buffer for storing beacon message and control factor for assigning a beacon message time interval to supporting a fast handover effectively. Ryu and Mun (2005) proposed a Tentative and Early Binding Update (TEBU) scheme for FMIPv6 that ensures that NCoA is registered to HA before layer 2 trigger signal with possible 21% lower handover latency than FMIPv6. Ryu and Mun (2007) further proposed an enhancement to TEBU scheme to include implementation of RR procedure before layer 2 trigger signal. Na, Ryu, Lee, and Mun (2010), proposed enhance route optimization in PMIPv6 with reduced signaling cost using the prediction algorithm in PFMIPv6 protocol. Choi, Kim, Lee, Min, and Han (2011) proposed a Smart Buffering scheme for enhanced handover in PMIPv6 to prevent packet loss by proactively buffering packets that will be lost in current serving MAG. It proposes network-side handover prediction mechanism, and an MAG discovery mechanism to achieve the buffering.

Shih, Kuo, Huang, and Chen (2011) proposed the combination of F-HMIPv6 and PFMIPv6 protocols to provide seamless handover scheme for PMIPv6 in hierarchical architecture with the introduction of two new messages called Local Proxy Binding Update and Local Proxy Binding Acknowledge where Local Proxy Binding is sent to the MAP rather than the HA during handover. Simulation results showed that this proposed scheme avoided packet loss during a handover and ensure ordered packet sequence while the handover latency is effectively reduced by up to 23% and 22% compared with PMIPv6 and FHMIPv6 in predictive and reactive modes respectively. Most of the above described proposals introduce more signaling load, or security threats or implementation and interoperability challenges.

A summary of six MIPv6-based Mobility Management extensions based on analysis of various mobility schemes is shown in Table 1. It is based on Key infrastructure used, Optimization for movement detection/address configuration, Signaling load, Packet loss, Handover performance and location privacy of MN. Most of the mobility management protocols are either optimized for Movement Detection (MD) or Address Configuration (AC) and in some cases such as MIPv6, HMIPv6 and FHMIPv6 that are optimized for both AC and MD operation as shown in Table 1 so as to improve the overall handover performance. In terms of total signaling load, MIPv6 still has the minimum mobility signaling load between MN, key infrastructure such as HA, MAP, LMA, MAG, etc; and CN when compared to other protocols. Nevertheless, MIPv6 with its very good signaling load comes at high latency that increases the signaling cost resulting in high packet loss as compared to other protocols.

Other Special Mobility Management Protocol

There are some special mobility management protocols, such as Network Mobility (NEMO) Basic Support Protocol and Mobile Ad-Hoc Network

Table 1. Summary of mobility management extensions

Mobility Protocol	Class	Address of MN	Key Infrastructure	Optimized for MD/AC	Signaling Load	Reduced Packet Loss	Overall Handover Latency
MIPv6	Host	CoA; HoA	HA	MD; AC	Very Good	Poor	Fair
H MIPv6	Host	LCoA	HA; MAP	MD; AC	Good+	Good	Good
F MIPv6	Host	CoA	HA; AR	AC	Fair	Very good*	Good
P MIPv6	Network	HoA	LMA; MAG	AC	Good	Fair	Fair+
PFMIPv6	Network	LCoA	HA; AR	AC	Good	Very good	Very good
F-HMIPv6**	Host	LCoA	HA; AR; MAP	MD; AC	Good	Good	Very good

* Packet loss will be higher in reactive mode.** FHMIPv6 is IETF draft,+ Slight improvement

(MANET). NEMO basic support is described briefly because of its importance and its similarity to MIPv6 mobility management.

Network Mobility (NEMO) Basic Support Protocol

NEMO basic support is a special extension of MIPv6 with the main goal of supporting mobility of a whole network as against an MN that allows session continuity for every node in the Mobile Network as the network moves. It enables Mobile Networks to attach to different points in the Internet with the reachability of every node in the Mobile Network. The nodes can be static or mobile node and are called Mobile Network Node (MNN). The Mobile Router (MR), which connects the network to the Internet, runs the NEMO basic support protocol with its Home Agent. The protocol is designed so that network mobility is transparent to the nodes inside the Mobile Network (Devarapalli, Wakikawa, Petrescu, & Thubert, 2005). NEMO has adopted the methods used for host mobility support in Mobile IP and has extended them in the simplest way possible to achieve its goals (Ernst, 2007). NEMO is designed as in Figure 4 such that each MR has a HA, and use bi-directional tunneling between the MR and HA to preserve session continuity while the MR moves. The MR acquires a CoA at its attachment point much like what is done for mobile hosts. There are NEMO basic supports variants, such as PMIPv6 and MIPv6 based NEMO management.

POTENTIAL SOURCES OF SECURITY CONCERNS IN MIPV6

Security concerns and possible threats are not usually unanticipated in a new protocol design and more particularly in its implementation. There is no exception to MIPv6 with the following five categories of sources of security and privacy concerns; Binding Updates to Home Agents, Binding Updates to Correspondent Nodes, Dynamic Home Agent Address Discovery, Mobile Prefix Discovery, and Payload Packets (Perkins

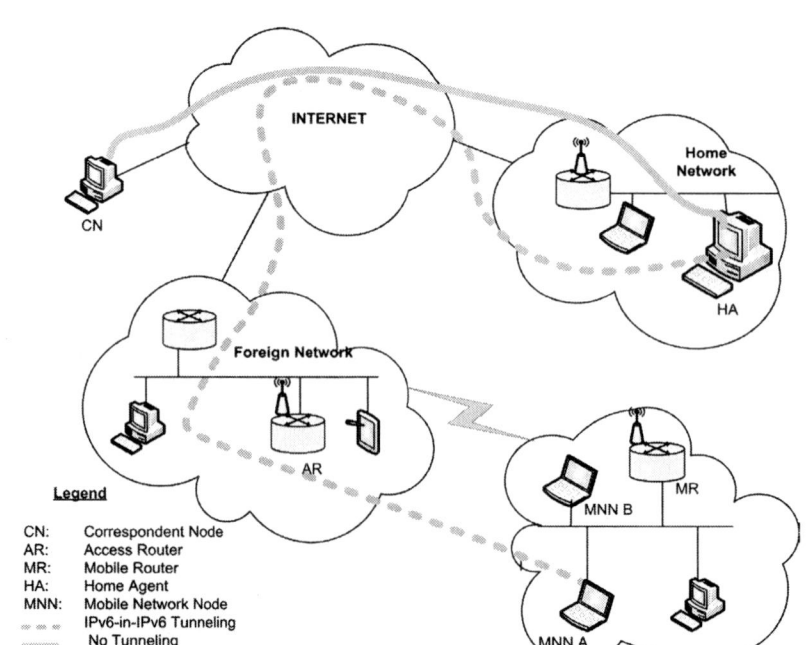

Figure 4. Architecture of NEMO basic support protocol

et al., 2011). These security issues could lead to security threats, such as connection interception attack, connection redirect attack, replay attack, reflection attack, forced non-optimized routing of packets, ICMPv6 message based attacks, etc. These security issues, threat and mitigation methods are discussed in more details as follows:

1. **Binding Updates to Home Agents:** To prevent an attacker from spoofing the BU from MN to HA, the MN and the HA MUST use an IPsec Security Association (SA) to protect the integrity and authenticity of the Binding Updates and Acknowledgements (Perkins et al., 2011). Both the mobile nodes and the home agents must support the Encapsulating Security Payload (ESP) header in transport mode and MUST use a non-null payload authentication algorithm to provide data origin authentication, connectionless integrity, and optional anti-replay protection. AH protocol of IPsec is also useful to secure MN-HA route.

2. **Binding Updates to Correspondent Nodes:** The links between CN-MN and CN-HA are vulnerable to attacks, hence the integrity and authenticity of the Binding Update messages to CN needs to be protected by using a keyed-hash algorithm rather than infrastructure based method due to absence of prior mutual relationship of MN to CN unlike as existed between HA to MN. The following are the components of binding update messages to CN that may need protective handling; Node Keys, Nonces, Cookies and Tokens, Cryptographic Functions, Authorizing Binding Management Messages, Updating Node Keys and Nonces, Handling Interruptions to Return Routability.

3. **Dynamic Home Agent Address Discovery:** Dynamic Home Agent Address Discovery (DHAAD), allows a MN to discover the address of a preferred HA on the home link. Dynamic home agent address discovery has been designed for use in deployments where security is not needed (Perkins et al., 2011) because the procedure involves Anycast address and it is not possible to establish IPsec security association with Anycast address. Another possible reason for absence of security in DHAAD is that there is the assumed trust relationship between MN and HA. However, DHAAD could suffer from security threats because the trust relationship may not be there, hence the signaling is neither authenticated nor its integrity protected and prone to attack from malicious host on the home link.

4. **Mobile Prefix Discovery:** The HA can send an unsolicited ICMPv6 prefix reply message to the MN when network renumbering event occurs or the MN send an ICMPv6 prefix solicitation message to the HA for the same event. The reply message contain subnet prefix for the MN home link. An attacker can spoof the unsolicited mobile prefix reply message, causing MN to update its home subnet prefix to that of the attacker. An attacker could also eavesdrop to the ICMPv6 prefix reply message to discover topology of the home network, which could be used for future attacks.

5. **Payload Packets:** Mobile IPv6 introduces the Home Address destination option and a new routing header type 2, and uses tunneling headers in the payload packets. The Home Address destination option could be used to direct response traffic toward a node whose IP address appears in the option. In this case, ingress filtering would not be effective against the fake "return address". The protocol must protect against potential new threats involving the use of these mechanisms in payload packets using Home Address destination option. Payload packets exchanges with MN are also exposed to similar threats as that of regular IPv6 traffic.

MIPv6 Security Threats

The following security threats are possible from the earlier discussed sources of MIPv6 security concerns such as connection interception attack, connection redirect attack, replay attack, reflection attack, forced non-optimized routing of packets, ICMPv6 message attacks.

Connection Interception and Redirect Attack

An attacker could determine the MN's home address through MIPv6 mobile prefix solicitation and reply DHAAD, or through the home address option in payload packets. At some point in an ongoing session between an MN and a CN, the attacker can send a BU to the CN using the acquired HoA and a malicious CoA with purpose of tampering with the CN binding cache. The CN would believe that the MN has moved to a new CoA. CN updates the entry for the MN in its binding cache. The packet stream for the ongoing session from the CN to the MN is now diverted to the specified malicious CoA. This attack is known as Traffic Redirection. If the CoA specified is the address of the attacker, then this attack is known as Traffic Hijacking. It is also possible for the attacker to send a BU to the MN, supposedly from the CN, and hence insert himself as a man in the middle (MitM) for traffic between the two. The attacker in MitM must be located in the same link as the MN or the CN.

Replay Attack

Replay attacks are possible for route optimization as with any signaling protocol. An attacker can record authenticated or non-authenticated Binding Update messages, and resend it when the MN has moved to a different CoA, thereby disrupting the ongoing MN's traffic with CN. The attacker can record BU only if the attacker is on the same link with MN.

Inducing Unnecessary Binding Updates

An attacker can induce the MN to initiate binding update protocols with a large number of CN at the same time. If the correspondent addresses are real addresses of existing IP nodes, then most instances of the binding update protocol might even complete successfully. The entries created in the Binding Cache are correct but useless. In this way, the attacker can induce the MN to execute the binding update protocol unnecessarily, which can drain the mobile's resources, thereby causing DoS. A CN can also be attacked in a similar way by using it as target node. The attacker sends spoofed IP packets to a large number of mobiles, with the target node's address as the source address. These mobiles will initiate the binding update protocol with the target node. Again, most of the binding update protocol executions will complete successfully. By inducing a large number of unnecessary binding updates, the attacker is able to consume the target node's resources (Nikander et al., 2005).

Forced Non-Optimized Routing of Packets

A variant of the Inducing Unnecessary Binding Updates attack is Forced Non-optimized Routing of Packets. The attacker can prevent a CN from using route optimization by filling its Binding Cache with unnecessary entries so that most entries for real mobiles are dropped. Any successful DoS attack against a MN or CN can also prevent the processing of binding updates. The target of this DoS attack may respond by stopping route optimization for all or some communication. Obviously, an attacker can exploit this fallback mechanism and force the target to use the less efficient home agent-based routing. The attacker only needs to mount a noticeable DoS attack against the MN or CN so as to default to non-optimized routing.

Flooding Attack

By sending spoofed binding updates, an attacker could redirect data traffic to an arbitrary IP address. This could be used to overburden an arbitrary Internet address with an excessive volume of packets. The attacker could also target a network by redirecting the data to one or more IP addresses within the network. There are two main variations of flooding: basic flooding and return-to-home flooding. In basic flooding, the attacker starts the download of heavy data stream from CN which is a server, after performing TCP handshake it sends a forge BU involving victim address as CoA. Once the BU is accepted by CN a huge amount of unsolicited data traffic are transmitted to the victim to degrade its performance as well as to waste its bandwidth. Thus while the BU is authenticated, the MN (attacker) is not at the claimed CoA. The attacker also sends spoofed acknowledgement for the ongoing communication to CN to ensure that the data flood to the victim's node continues. In return-to-home flooding, a variation of the basic flooding attack would target the HoA or the home network instead of the CoA or a visited network. The attacker would claim to be MN with the HoA equal to the target address. While claiming to be away from home, the attacker would start downloading a data stream. The attacker would then send a binding update cancellation from the Binding Cache or just allow the cache entry to expire. Either would redirect the data stream to the home network. As when flooding a CoA in basic flooding, the attacker can keep the stream alive and even increase the data rate by spoofing acknowledgements as in basic flooding.

Rogue HA

It is possible for an attacker on the same subnet as the HA of MN to pretend to be the HA while the MN is in foreign network; intercepts the BUs from the MN and its destined traffic which originates from other CNs. Camouflaging the HA's identity can lead to drastic effects, which open the door for various MitM attacks, and DoS attacks with spoofed addresses or Home Agent Address Discovery messages.

Space-Time Shift Attack

This attack is possible in MIPv6, if an attacker can eavesdrop the return routability state of the network at the time when the HoT and CoT messages were sent out, thereby having access to the binding cache entry and K_{bm}. It after that moves to a safer place and starts an attack from there or the attacker waits for a better point in time to start attack.

Security Threats Counteract Proposals

The identified MIPv6 security threats and the possible counteract methods are described in Table 2. Some threats' severity such as traffic redirection, traffic hijacking are classified as moderate because the effect of the threat will affect the target only. If the threat affects the whole network, then it is classified as high severity. A very high threat severity is one that can affect any node in the Internet, open more threats or affects the whole Internet. Some of the counteract methods will not eradicate the threats but will mitigate the effect because the threat is still possible and the threat can reduce performance such as QoS. For example, basic flooding attack is still possible but the attacker is also affected by his attack based on the counteract methods.

A number of security solutions are specified for MIPv6 in RFC6275 (Perkins et al. 2011), RFC4877 (Devarapalli & Dupont, 2007) and RFC3971 (Arkko et al., 2005) for securing MIPv6 signals to make it secure as the regular IPv6 protocol. Perkins et al. (2011) specifies the use of RR procedure for securing BU/BA between MN and CN while (Arkko et al., 2005) specifies SEND for securing address configuration of MN. IPsec with IKEv2 was specified for establishing security association to secure traffics on MN-HA route,

Table 2. MIPv6 security threats and counteracts methods

Threat	Severity	Target	Counteract Methods	Solution Type	Comment
Traffic Redirection	Moderate	MN	Securing ICMPv6 message type 144-147.	Mitigation	
Traffic Hijacking	Moderate	MN; CN	Same as above. Authenticate BU from MN-AH, MN-CN routes.	Eradication on MN-HA route; Mitigation on MN-CN route	
Man-in-the-Middle	High	MN; CN; HA	Same as above. Security Association between MN and HA using IPsec.	Mitigation	DoS is possible
Replay attacks	Moderate	MN; CN	Sequence number for BU freshness, time stamping, Nonces.	Eradication	
Inducing Unnecessary Binding Updates	High	MN; CN	Selective BU processing, disable route optimization	Mitigation	QoS degrades
Forced Non-optimized Routing of Packets	High	MN; CN	Same as above	Mitigation	QoS degrades
Basic Flooding	Very High	Any node in the Internet	Verification of CoA location, TCP reset	Mitigation	Attacker is also affected
Return-to-Home Flooding	Very High	MN at HoA, HA, any home network nodes	Verification of CoA and HoA locations, TCP reset	Mitigation	Attacker is also affected
Rogue HA	Very High	MN, CN	Securing ICMPv6 message with SEND, DNSsec	Mitigation	DoS, MitM
Space-time shift attacks	Moderate	MN, CN	Refreshing CoA registration regularly	Eradication	

HA prefix discovery procedure as described in RFC4877. No security association was specified for DHAAD procedure. CN-MN route was not recommended for IPsec based security because there is presently no way to globally manage the required pre-shared keys in IPsec security association or Public Key Infrastructure (PKI) to validate authenticity of various CNs and MNs. Protection of payload routing mechanism for home address destination option and type 2 routing header against misuse is also important.

Secure Neighbor Discovery (SEND)

Neighbor Discovery Protocol (NDP) (Narten et al., 2007; Thomson et al., 2007) introduces security vulnerabilities in router discovery, prefix discovery, and address auto-configuration mechanisms that could affect the IPv6 network address resolution, Duplicate Address Detection (DAD), Router Advertisement (RA), and address configuration. SEcure Neighbor Discovery (SEND) (Arkko et al., 2005) protocol is a response to security vulnerabilities in NDP; these vulnerabilities are documented in IPv6 Neighbor Discovery (ND) Trust Models and Threats (Nikander, Kempf, & Nordmark, 2004). Proof of address ownership, message protection and router authorization mechanism were the three enhancement features recommended by SEND to secure NDP. To realize these enhancements, SEND comes with four new options and two new ICMPv6 discovery messages. The options are *CGA*, *RSA Signature*, *Timestamp*, and *Nonce* while the ICMPv6 messages are *Certificate Path Solicitation* and *Certificate Path Advertisement* for the router authorization mechanism. The options and the messages are described as follows:

1. **CGA Option:** A public-private key pair is generated by all nodes in order to claim an address. CGA option carries the public key and the associated parameters to enable the receiver of ND messages to validate the proper binding between the owner's public key and the CGA.
2. **RSA Signature Option:** This option is used to protect all ND messages relating to Neighbor and Router discovery. The message which is sent from CGA address is signed with the address owner private key and attached the public key to the sent packet to enable the receiver to verify the identity of the sender. This signature prevents an attacker from spoofing NDP messages.
3. **Nonce Option:** This option is used to protect messages from replay attacks, and to ensure that an advertisement is a fresh response to a solicitation which is sent earlier by the node.
4. **Timestamp Option:** This option is used to protect the unsolicited advertisements (periodic RA and Redirect messages) from replay attacks.
5. **ICMPv6 Discovery Messages:**
   a. **Certificate Path Solicitation (CPS):** Is sent by hosts during the Authorization Delegation Discovery (ADD) process to request a certification path between a router and one of the host's trust anchors.
   b. **Certificate Path Advertisement (CPA):** Is sent in reply to the CPS message and contains the router certificate.

SEND protocol uses an ADD process to validate and authorize IPv6 routers to act as default gateways, and specifies the IPv6 prefixes that a router is authorized to announce on the link (Arkko et al., 2005). ADD relies on an electronic certificate issued by a trusted third party called Trust Anchor (TA). A TA is an entity that the node trusts to authorize routers to act as routers. A trust anchor configuration consists of a public key and some associated parameters (Arkko et al., 2005).

Before any MN can accept a router as its default router, the MN must be configured with a TA(s) that can certify the router via certificate paths. The MN requests the router to provide its X.509 certificate path to a TA which is preconfigured on the node using ICMPv6 discovery message. Any router that could not provide the path to TA should not be trusted by nodes as the default router. SEND can be used to secure the local network of MN against attacks targeted at MN and the default HA using the various SEND options and ICMPv6 messages. Specifically, it can protect against router solicitation and advertisement attack, replay attack, duplicate address detection attack, neighbor solicitation and advertisement spoofing attack. SEND options could also be used to protect DHAAD messages between MN and HAs in the home network, if the trust relationship of MN and HA no longer assured.

HA-MN route require IPsec security because of established trust relationship between HA and MN. The HoTi and HoT messages require a non-NULL authentication algorithm and non-NULL encryption algorithm, with ESP protocol in tunnel mode. The binding updates and acknowledgement messages transmitted between the MN and HA require a non-NULL authentication algorithm and ESP protocol in transport mode.

IP Security (IPsec)

IPsec is IP layer security framework consisting suite of protocols, standards, and algorithms designed to protect the traffic at the IP level and all upper layer protocols. It enables data flow protection services between host-to-host, host-to-network or network-to-network arrangements. The security services provided by IPsec can be classified into three categories namely; confidentiality, authentication with anti-replay feature and integrity. Confidentiality means no one could eavesdrop on the data communication; Integrity denotes the data is not tampered with; Authentication denotes confirmation of the identity of the data source.

IPsec as specified in Security Architecture for the Internet Protocol (Kent & Seo, 2005) consist of suite of protocols, standards, and algorithms that provide security services to the Internet communications at the IP layer that include: Security Protocols-Authentication Header (AH) and Encapsulating Security Payload (ESP), Security Associations (SAs), Cryptographic algorithms for authentication and encryption, Internet Key Exchange (IKE). HA-MN route require IPsec security because of established trust relationship between HA and MN. The HoTi and HoT messages of the RR procedure require a non-NULL authentication algorithm and non-NULL encryption algorithm, with ESP protocol in tunnel mode. The binding updates and acknowledgement messages transmitted between the MN and HA require a non-NULL authentication algorithm and ESP protocol in transport mode.

The architecture of IPsec is shown in Figure 5, consisting of AH, ESP, Security Association Database (SAD), Security Policy Database (SPD), Peer Authentication Database (PAD) and IKE in relation to the Internet Protocol stack. Security Association is a one-way agreement between two communicating peers that specifies the IPsec protections to be provided to their communications, such as cryptographic algorithms, and secret keys to be applied, as well as the specific types of traffic to be protected. SAD is repository of SAs while PAD stores information necessary to conduct remote peer authentication of identities. SPD is an ordered database that expresses the security protection policies to be afforded to inbound and outbound traffics. The three general classes of traffic policies are traffics to be discarded, traffics to be allowed without IPsec protection and traffics that requires IPsec protection.

Figure 5. IPsec architecture

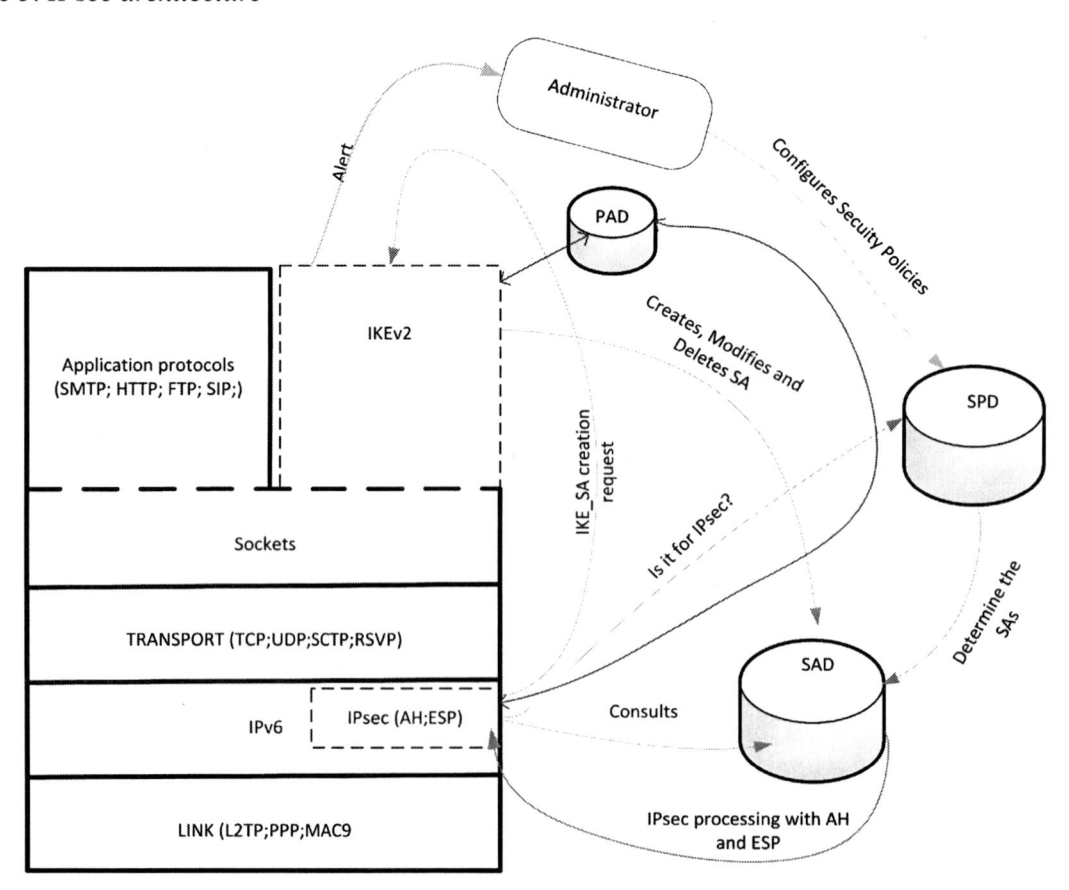

When an IP packet needs to be transmitted securely, SPD is consulted to determine if such packet is privileged to use IPsec, to be dropped or allowed without IPsec. For a privileged packet, the SA for the traffic is located in SAD and then IPsec processing with AH, ESP can start. If automated keying is to be used for IPsec processing, then IKE security association (IKE_SA) is initialized with SAs stored in SAD and IPsec processing can start.

IPsec specified in (Kent & Seo, 2005) is IPsec$_{v3}$ and obsoletes IPsec$_{v2}$. IPsec$_{v2}$, and IPsec$_{v1}$ are described in Kent and Atkinson (1998) and Atkinson (1995), respectively. The interrelationship among RFC documents that specifies the protocols, standards, and mandatory algorithms in IPsec suite is shown in Figure 6(a) with four levels.

Level one of Figure 6(a) shows the main IPsec architecture document (RFC 4301) that broadly covers the general concepts, security requirements, definitions, and mechanisms defining IPsec technology. On the next level, are ESP Protocol document (Kent, 2005b) and AH Protocol document (Kent, 2005a) that cover the packet format and general issues regarding the respective protocols. The third level consists of encryption algorithm document set specified in (Glenn & Kent, 1998; Frankel, Glenn, & Kelly, 2003; Manral, 2007). It is the set of documents describing how various encryption algorithms are used for ESP. Still on level three is the Combined Algorithm (Housley, 2005; Viega & McGrew, 2005; Manral, 2007) document set. The set of documents suggests how various combined mode algorithms are used to provide both encryption and integrity protection for ESP. The integrity protection algorithm document set (Madson & Glenn, 1998a, b; Frankel & Herbert, 2003; Manral, 2007), is the set of documents describing how various integrity protection algorithms are used for both ESP and AH. The last level shows the Key Management documents (Schiller, 2005; Eronen, Tschofenig & Sheffer, 2010), describing the IETF Standards Internet Key Exchange (IKE) protocol and cryptographic algorithms for IKE.

Figure 6. IPsec: (a) documents interrelationships, (b) cryptographic algorithms

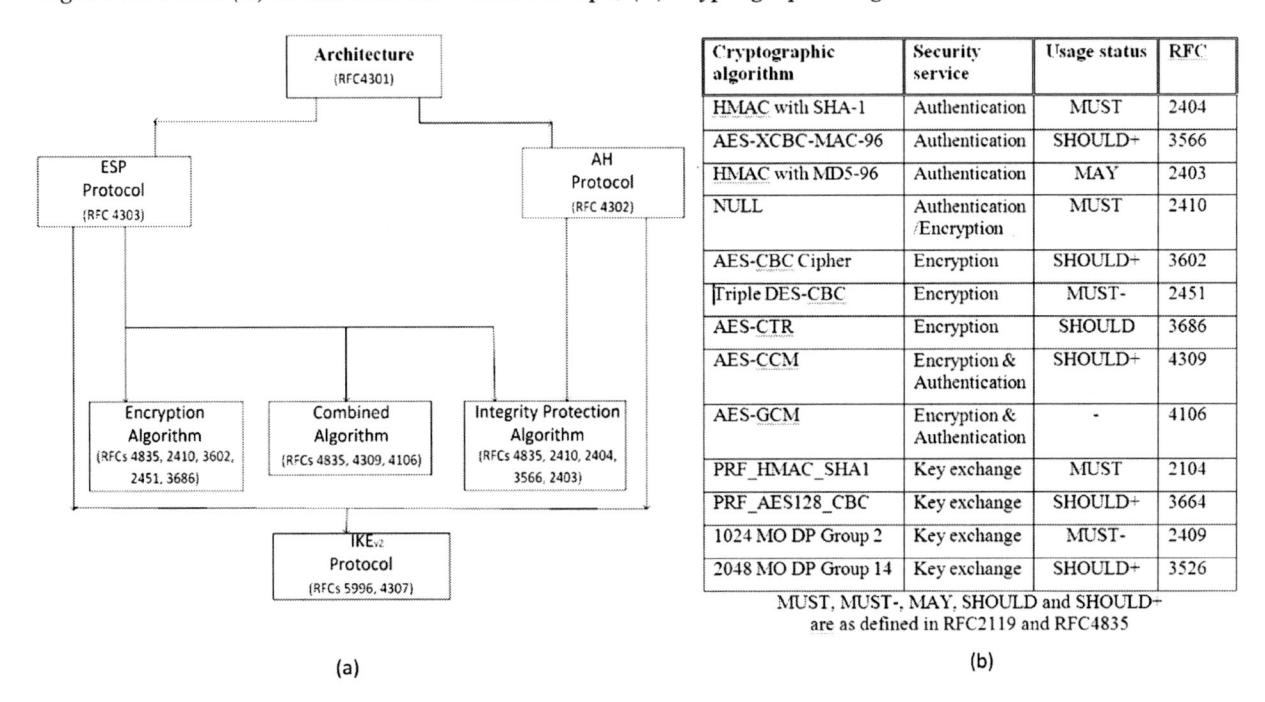

Cryptographic algorithm	Security service	Usage status	RFC
HMAC with SHA-1	Authentication	MUST	2404
AES-XCBC-MAC-96	Authentication	SHOULD+	3566
HMAC with MD5-96	Authentication	MAY	2403
NULL	Authentication /Encryption	MUST	2410
AES-CBC Cipher	Encryption	SHOULD+	3602
Triple DES-CBC	Encryption	MUST-	2451
AES-CTR	Encryption	SHOULD	3686
AES-CCM	Encryption & Authentication	SHOULD+	4309
AES-GCM	Encryption & Authentication	-	4106
PRF_HMAC_SHA1	Key exchange	MUST	2104
PRF_AES128_CBC	Key exchange	SHOULD+	3664
1024 MO DP Group 2	Key exchange	MUST-	2409
2048 MO DP Group 14	Key exchange	SHOULD+	3526

MUST, MUST-, MAY, SHOULD and SHOULD- are as defined in RFC2119 and RFC4835

(a)   (b)

Security Protocols

IPsec consists of two security protocols for authentication and encryption of communication between communicating hosts namely Authentication Header and Encapsulating Security Payload protocols.

Authentication Header

Authentication Header (AH) provides authentication and integrity protection, for IP packets with optional anti-replay protection against unauthorized retransmission of packets. AH protocol protects the packet's source address, destination address, and data from being modified along the route, the sender and receiver are authenticated with no data's confidentiality protection. This simply means that AH ensures users know whom they are communicating with, know if the communicated data is changed in transit but will not be sure if it is copied or eavesdropped while in transit due to absence of data encryption. The AH format consists of the following fields; *Next Header*, *Payload length*, *Reserved*, *Security Parameter Index (SPI)*, *Sequence Number*, and *Integrity Check Value (ICV)* (Kent, 2005a). Kent (2005a) provides more detail about AH format fields' description. AH guarantees authentication and integrity with the calculation of ICV over the packet's non changing contents, using a cryptographic algorithm, such as hash-based message authentication code (HMAC) with SHA-1 Algorithm (Madson & Glenn, 1998b), AES-XCBC-MAC-96 Algorithm (Frankel & Herbert, 2003), HMAC with MD5-96 Algorithm (Madson & Glenn, 1998a), NULL Encryption Algorithm (Glenn & Kent, 1998). A shared secret key employed by the cryptographic algorithm known to both ends, allows the recipient to compute the ICV value of the received packet. If the recipient gets the same ICV value, the sender has effectively authenticated itself to the receiver and validates the integrity of the received packet. The replay protection is achieved using the sequence number field in the AH structure.

The AH protocol operates in Transport Mode or Tunnel Mode. With Transport Mode, the AH header is inserted between the IP header and the upper layer headers. An attacker can learn the source and destination of packet, because IPsec in Transport mode does not shield the information in the IP header. In Tunnel Mode, the entire packet is encrypted, including its IP header, the AH header goes at the front of this and a new IP header is added in front of the AH header. Tunnel mode prevents an attacker from knowing the source and destination of packet. Transport Mode is for host-to-host communication while Tunnel Mode is for host-to-gateway and gateway-to-gateway communication.

Encapsulating Security Payload

Encapsulating Security Payload (ESP) can also operate in Transport or Tunnel Modes like AH protocol. ESP provides authentication, integrity, and confidentiality security protection against data tampering and message content protection that is absent in HA protocol using encryption algorithms (Kent, 2005b). Data encryption transforms a readable message into an unreadable format to hide the message content. The reverse process, called decryption, transforms the message content from an unreadable format to a readable message. Encryption-decryption allows only the sender and the authenticated receiver to read the data. The following encryption algorithms are currently recommended for use in ESP; NULL Encryption Algorithm (Kent & Atkinson, 1998), AES-CBC Cipher Algorithm (Frankel et al., 2003), Triple DES-CBC Algorithm (Pereira & Adams, 1998), furthermore, algorithms recommended for AH can be used for integrity protection service by ESP. ESP also support combined encryption and integrity algorithms that may provide significant efficiency and throughput advantages such as AES-CCM Algorithm (Housley, 2005) and AES-GCM Algorithm (Viega & McGrew, 2005). ESP authentication and integrity services are only for the payload and not for the IP header. AH and ESP can be used together to secure the IP header and the packet payload, when additional protections are needed.

IPsec Security Association

The Security Association (SA) provides the method used by IPsec to track all the particulars concerning a given IPsec communication session. It provides logical relationships between two or more IPsec enabled systems that express what security services and related parameters to be used to communicate securely among them. The systems must agree on security protocol identifier (50 for ESP and 51 for AH) that are required along with other parameters, such as cryptographic algorithm, key, duration and SPI to be used for inbound and outbound connections. The SPI is a unique value identifying the SA and differentiating it from other SAs linked to the same destination address. Security Association Database (SAD) keeps all records of SA information including type of encryption or authentication algorithms, key lengths, and key lifetimes negotiated with each IPsec enabled system. There is an SA for each traffic direction. If a traffic stream in one direction uses both AH and ESP, two separate SA will be needed for that destination. SAs can be negotiated manually for small deployments with the creation of SPD. Automatically, SAs can be created with the use of IKE protocol.

IPsec Cryptographic Algorithms for Authentication and Encryption

Algorithms used by IPsec security protocols can be classified into authentication and encryption algorithms. Encryption is performed using symmetric key encryption algorithms. Symmetric key algorithm means that a single key is used to encrypt as well as decrypt data by the sender and the receiver respectively. This key is created during IKE's exchange. IPsec uses hash algorithms to compute Message Authentication Codes (MAC) for authentication and integrity check. The sender calculates the MAC of the message (M) using hash cryptographic function and attaching this hash to the end of the message. When the receiver gets the message, it again calculates a new MAC on the message and compares the hash it received and the new calculated MAC. If they are the same, the data was not tampered with in transit. There are several cryptographic algorithms available for use by IPsec, while new ones are coming up; some are no longer secured for IPsec use. Manral (2007) specifies a set of cryptographic algorithms that could be used in IPsec implementation and those that could not be used. A summary of these mandatory, recommended and optional algorithms with Request For Comment (RFC) numbers is shown in Figure 6(b). The usage status, MUST, MUST-, MAY, SHOULD are as defined in RFC2119 while SHOULD+ is defined in RFC4835.

Internet Key Exchange (IKE)

IKE is a protocol that provides automated keying utility services for the establishment of IPsec connection among systems. It provides authentication of the IPsec peers, establishment of keys for cryptographic algorithms, initiation and management of SAs in accordance with policies in the SPD. Creation of IPsec SA using IKE_{v2} consists of three message exchanges: IKE_SA_INIT, IKE_AUTH and CREATE_CHILD_SA exchanges as shown in Figure 7. Each message exchange between the two hosts always consists of a request and a response message pair for each exchange. The first pair of messages known as "IKE_SA_INIT" negotiates cryptographic algorithms, exchange nonces, and do a Diffie-Hellman (DH) exchange. The initiator sends its supported cryptographic algorithms, nonce and initial value for DH key exchange while the responder must send its choice of cryptographic algorithm, nonce, initial value for DH key and possibly an optional request for digital certificate based authentication (CERTREQ). With the first exchange completed, both parties can generate master secret key, encryption and authentication keys based on initial DH values using DH algorithm.

The second pair of messages "IKE_AUTH" authenticates the previous messages, exchange identities, traffic selectors and certificates, and establish the IKE_SA. Parts of these messages are encrypted and integrity protected with keys established through the IKE_SA_INIT exchange, so the identities of the initiator and the responder are hidden from eavesdroppers and all fields in all the messages are authenticated. The host can chose among Pre-shared secret based authentication, certificate-based authentication or Extensible Authentication Protocol (EAP)-based authentication. In certificate-based authentication, the initiator sends its signed certificate to the responder while the responder sends its signed certificate in returned. EAP-based authentication uses any of already established authentication methods such as authentication, authorization and accounting (AAA) servers (Aboba, Simon, &Eronen, 2008). No further authentication is needed if pre-shared secret is the choice and is the preferred mode in small scale environments.

Figure 7. IKE message exchanges

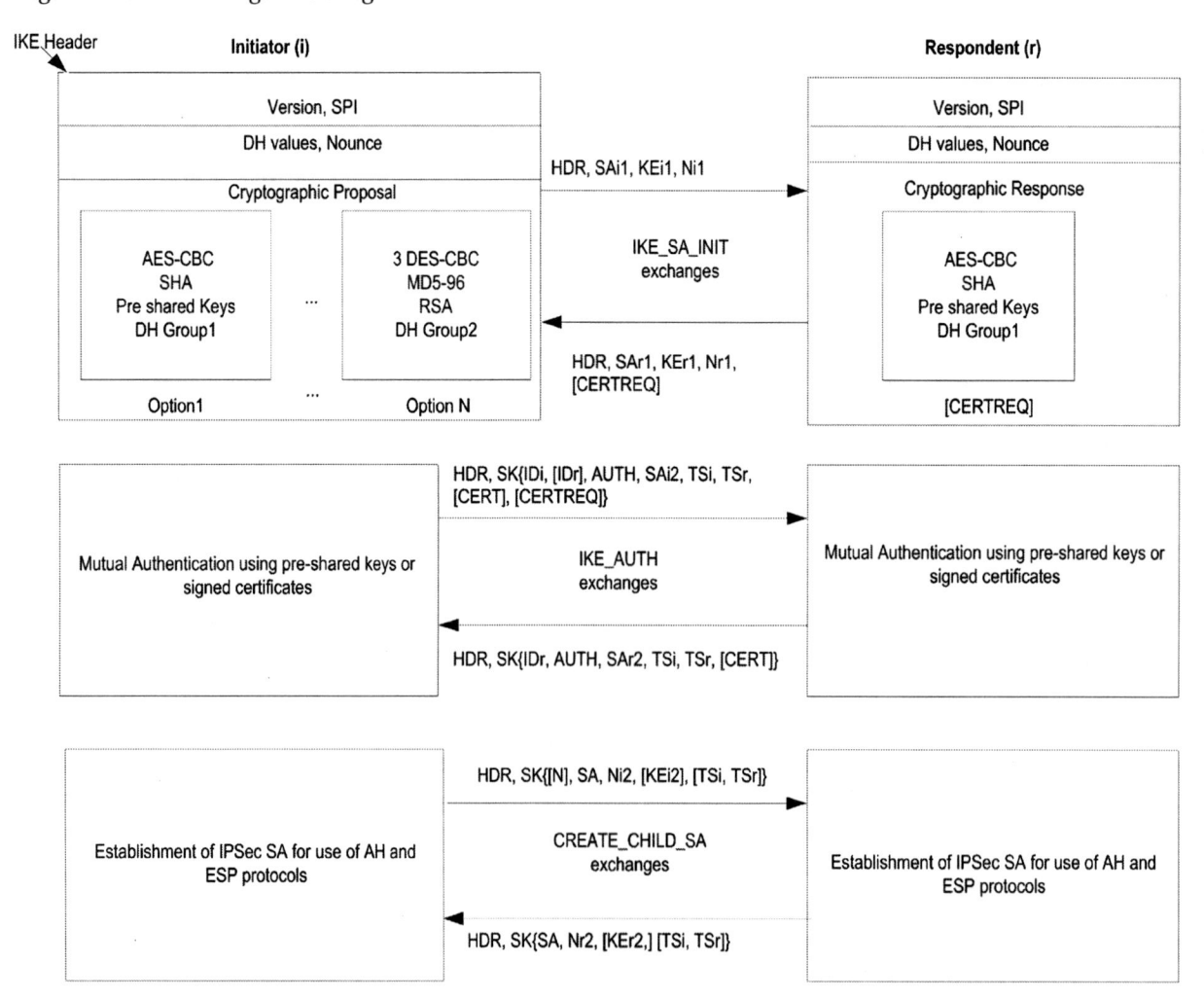

The CREATE_CHILD_SA is the next exchange from the initiator to the responder. The initiator sends some proposals for parameters, such as traffic selector, session key of the cryptographic algorithms which will be used for AH or ESP, the responder answers with the chosen parameters to accept the secured connection. These parameters are stored in SAD for IPsec services. This CREATE_CHILD_SA is known as IPsec SA. An established IKE SA may be used to create many IPsec SAs by including a new nonce (N) in the CREATE_CHILD_SA exchange to indicate new IPsec SA.

Securing MIPv6 Route Optimization with RR Procedure

The RR procedure overview was discussed earlier in MIPv6 Design section. RR procedure ensures that CN verifies that the MN is able to receive messages at the HoA and CoA. These verifications alleviate a number of security threats, such as flooding attacks. The procedure also eliminates the replay attack with the nonces in the computation of K_{bm}. Traffic Redirection and Traffic Hijacking attacks are mitigated by RR procedure by limiting the number of potential attackers that could spoof BU to redirect or hijack an ongoing session because the attacker must be on the route of the hijacked connection. This mitigation level is better than when every node on the Internet could be an attacker compared to few nodes on the CN-AH route. RR protocol could verify reachability of authorized nodes on CN-HA route but not address ownership and therefore could not provide totally strong security solutions to IPv6 based security threats. It was not the goal of RR to protect against attacks that were already possible before the introduction of IP mobility (Perkins et al., 2011).

Several proposals for securing BU exist such as the Early Binding Updates (EBU) protocol (Vogt, Bless, Doll, & Kuefner, 2004), Child-Proof Authentication for MIPv6 (O'Shea & Roe, 2001), Applying Cryptographically Generated Addresses to Optimize MIPv6 (Haddad, Madour, Arkko, & Dupont, 2004), Certificate-based Binding Update (CBU) protocol (Deng, Zhou, & Bao, 2002), Hierarchical Certificate-based Binding Update (HCBU) protocol (Ren et al., 2006) and many other related proposals. Most of these protocols based on CGA are computationally intensive while others are infrastructure based protocol.

Securing MIPv6 with Firewall

Firewalls are an integral aspect of a majority of IP networks that provide some security services against security threats and vulnerabilities to data networks. Firewalls are not aware of MIPv6 protocol details, will probably interfere with the smooth operation of the protocol. Therefore, smooth running of MIPv6 and security threat mitigation using firewall depend on proper implementation and configuration of firewall filtering rules. Firewall filtering rules are based on the following parameters, source IP address, destination IP address, protocol type, and source port number, destination port number to allow a traffic packet or to drop the packet.

To allow smooth operation of MIPv6 in a network, the following MIPv6 messages should be allowed by the firewall at the network perimeter (Davies & Mohacsi, 2007):

- Type 2 routing header based packets (IPv6 header type 43), Destination option header with home address option for all MN originated packets (type 201).
- Mobility headers messages (type 1-6) used by MN and HA for binding updates and acknowledgement; and RR procedure.
- ICMPv6 message type 144, 145 (HAAD request/reply).

- ICMPv6 message type 146, 147 (Mobile prefix solicitation/advertisement reply).
- ESP and AH headers are allowed according to the security policy.
- While Type 0 routing header based packets, expired binding life time packets should be dropped.

FUTURE RESEARCH DIRECTIONS

It is evident that huge and successful researches have gone into the mobility management and security concerns in MIPv6 in recent time. These concerns were not seen as weakness of MIPv6 but motivation for enhancement as evidenced in huge research output in this filed, however more research still need to be done in the following areas; Securing MN-CN route, Layer 2 handover latency enhancement, mobility of MN in Heterogeneous networks, flat MIPv6 architecture that do away with some entities such as AH, MAP, MAG, etc., authentication, authorization and accounting of MN in visited foreign network domains.

More importantly, the research into securing MN-CN route with infrastructure based security such as IPsec has been a challenge due to complexity of developing and managing global PKI to handle automatic keying needed for this form of security. HCBU protocol (Ren et al., 2006) could be a promising proposal in this regard using hierarchical PKI and possible extension to cover heterogeneous networks. This is possible due to the ongoing current standardization of Resource PKI (RPKI) framework designed to secure the Internet's routing infrastructure for Border Gateway Protocol (BGP) (Kent, Kong, Seo, & Watro, 2012).

Research into performance of mobility and multihoming management of MN in heterogeneous networks such as WiFi, General Packet Radio Services (GPRS), CDMA, LTE, WiMax, etc. is a promising area due to increasing acceptance of IP based mobility in these heterogeneous networks and an increasing proportion of mobile devices are outfitted with more than one radio access technology.

CONCLUSION

Mobility and security concerns are very important to this generation of telecommuting users due to rapid reduction in price, increase processing power, and portability of computing devices. MIPv6 has shown a remarkable potential to be the preference in mobility management of computing devices used insecure, ubiquitous mobile computing and general communication services. This chapter has presented the design and operation of MIPV6, pointing out the design and security assumptions leading to the use infrastructure less RR and SEND protocol on one hand and traditional infrastructure based IPsec protocol suite on the other hand. Management of mobility of MN in relation to CN was discussed based on IETF standardized mobility management protocols such as HMIPv6, FMIPv6, PMIPv6, FPMIPv6 and other promising proposal such as F-HMIPv6 with a summary of their performances with respect to handover latency. The standardized mobility management protocols have relative ease of implementation, security threats similar to MIPv6 and interoperability with existing Internetworking platforms than other proposed mobility management scheme for MIPv6. Sources of security concerns, security threats, and security threat counter proposals were discussed with detail explanation of the security protocols for eradicating these threats. Security wise, MIPv6 is not as vulnerable as being portrait, as most of the identified vulnerabilities have been researched with positive results and are already taken care of in the design and the implementation.

REFERENCES

Aboba, B., Simon, D., & Eronen, P. (2008). *Extensible authentication protocol (EAP) key management framework*. Internet Engineering Task Force (IETF), Request for Comments: 5247. Retrieved from http://tools.ietf.org/html/rfc5247

Arkko, J., Devarapalli, V., & Dupont, F. (2004). *Using IPsec to protect mobile IPv6 signaling between mobile nodes and home agents*. Internet Engineering Task Force (IETF), Request for Comments: 3776. Retrieved from http://tools.ietf.org/html/rfc3776

Arkko, J., Kempf, J., Zill, B., & Nikander, P. (2005). *Secure neighbor discovery (SEND)*. Internet Engineering Task Force (IETF), Request for Comments: 3971. Retrieved from http://tools.ietf.org/html/rfc3971

Atkinson, R. (1995). *Security architecture for the internet protocol*. Internet Engineering Task Force (IETF), Request for Comments: 1825. Retrieved from http://tools.ietf.org/html/rfc1825

Aura, T. (2005). *Cryptographically generated addresses (CGA)*. Internet Engineering Task Force (IETF), Request for Comments: 3972. Retrieved from http://tools.ietf.org/html/rfc3972

Aura, T., & Roe, M. (2006). Designing the mobile IPv6 security protocol. *Annales des Télécommunications*, *61*(3-4), 332–356. doi:10.1007/BF03219911.

Choi, H.-Y., Kim, K.-R., Lee, H.-B., Min, S.-G., & Han, Y.-H. (2011). Smart buffering for seamless handover in proxy mobile IPv6. *Wireless Communication and Mobile Computing*, *11*(4), 491–499. doi:10.1002/wcm.843.

Conta, A., Deering, S., & Gupta, M. (2006). *Internet control message protocol (ICMPv6) for the internet protocol version 6 (IPv6) specification*. Internet Engineering Task Force (IETF), Request for Comments: 4443. Retrieved from http://tools.ietf.org/html/rfc4443

Davies, E., & Mohacsi, J. (2007). *Recommendations for filtering ICMPv6 messages in firewalls*. Internet Engineering Task Force (IETF), Request for Comments: 4890. Retrieved from http://tools.ietf.org/html/rfc4890

Deng, R. H., Zhou, J., & Bao, F. (2002). Defending against redirect attacks in mobile IP. In *Proceedings of the 9th ACM Conference on Computer and Communications Security*, (pp. 59–67). New York, NY: ACM.

Devarapalli, V., & Dupont, F. (2007). *Mobile IPv6 operation with IKEv2 and the revised IPsec architecture*. Internet Engineering Task Force (IETF), Request for Comments: 4877. Retrieved from http://tools.ietf.org/html/rfc4877

Devarapalli, V., Wakikawa, R., Petrescu, A., & Thubert, P. (2005). *Network mobility (NEMO) basic support protocol*. Internet Engineering Task Force (IETF), Request for Comments: 3963. Retrieved from http://tools.ietf.org/html/rfc3963

Droms, R., Bound, E. J., Volz, B., Lemon, T., Perkins, C., & Carney, M. (2003). *Dynamic host configuration protocol for IPv6 (DHCPv6)*. Internet Engineering Task Force (IETF), Request for Comments: 3315. Retrieved from http://tools.ietf.org/html/rfc3315

Ernst, T. (2007). *Network mobility support goals and requirements*. Internet Engineering Task Force (IETF), Request for Comments: 4886. Retrieved from http://tools.ietf.org/html/rfc4886

Eronen, P., Tschofenig, H., & Sheffer, Y. (2010). *An extension for EAP-only authentication in IKEv2*. Internet Engineering Task Force (IETF), Request for Comments: 5998. Retrieved from http://tools.ietf.org/html/rfc5998

Frankel, S., Glenn, R., & Kelly, S. (2003). *The AES-CBC cipher algorithm and its use with IPsec*. Internet Engineering Task Force (IETF), Request for Comments: 3602. Retrieved from http://tools.ietf.org/html/rfc3602

Frankel, S., & Herbert, H. (2003). *The AES-XCBC-MAC-96 algorithm and its use with IPsec*. Internet Engineering Task Force (IETF), Request for Comments: 3566. Retrieved from http://tools.ietf.org/html/rfc3566

Glenn, R., & Kent, S. (1998). *The NULL encryption algorithm and its use with IPsec*. Internet Engineering Task Force (IETF), Request for Comments: 2410. Retrieved from http://tools.ietf.org/html/rfc2410

Gundavelli, S., Leung, K., Devarapalli, V., Chowdhury, K., & Patil, B. (2008). *Proxy mobile IPv6*. Internet Engineering Task Force (IETF), Request for Comments: 5213. Retrieved from http://tools.ietf.org/html/rfc5213

Haddad, W., Madour, L., Arkko, J., & Dupont, J. (2004). *Applying cryptographically generated addresses to optimize MIPv6 (CGA-OMIPv6)*. Expired Internet Engineering Task Force (IETF) Internet draft. Retrieved from http://tools.ietf.org/html/draft-haddad-mip6-cga-omipv6-04

Housley, R. (2005). *Using advanced encryption standard (AES) CCM mode with IPsec encapsulating security payload (ESP)*. Internet Engineering Task Force (IETF), Request for Comments: 4309. Retrieved from http://tools.ietf.org/html/rfc4309

Jung, H., Soliman, H., Koh, S., & Lee, J. Y. (2005). *Fast handover for hierarchical MIPv6 (F-HMIPv6)*. Expired Internet Engineering Task Force (IETF) Internet draft. Retrieved from http://tools.ietf.org/html/draft-jung-mobopts-fhmipv6-00

Kaufman, C., Hoffman, P., Nir, Y., & Eronen, P. (2010). *Internet key exchange protocol version 2 (IKEv2)*. Internet Engineering Task Force (IETF), Request for Comments: 5996. Retrieved from http://tools.ietf.org/html/rfc5996

Kent, S. (2005a). *IP authentication header*. Internet Engineering Task Force (IETF), Request for Comments: 4302. Retrieved from http://tools.ietf.org/html/rfc4302

Kent, S. (2005b). *IP encapsulating security payload (ESP)*. Internet Engineering Task Force (IETF), Request for Comments: 4303. Retrieved from http://tools.ietf.org/html/rfc4303

Kent, S., & Atkinson, R. (1998). *Security architecture for the internet protocol*. Internet Engineering Task Force (IETF), Request for Comments: 2401. Retrieved from http://tools.ietf.org/html/rfc2401

Kent, S., Kong, D., Seo, K., & Watro, R. (2012). *Certificate policy (CP) for the resource public key infrastructure (RPKI)*. Internet Engineering Task Force (IETF), Request for Comments: 6484. Retrieved from http://tools.ietf.org/html/rfc6484

Kent, S., & Seo, K. (2005). *Security architecture for the internet protocol*. Internet Engineering Task Force (IETF), Request for Comments: 4301. Retrieved from http://tools.ietf.org/html/rfc4301

Koodli, R. (2009). *Mobile IPv6 fast handovers*. Internet Engineering Task Force (IETF), Request for Comments: 5568. Retrieved from http://tools.ietf.org/html/rfc5568

Madson, C., & Glenn, R. (1998a). *The use of HMAC-MD5-96 within ESP and AH*. Internet Engineering Task Force (IETF) Request for Comments: 2403. Retrieved from http://tools.ietf.org/html/rfc2403

Madson, C., & Glenn, R. (1998b). *The use of HMAC-SHA-1-96 within ESP and AH*. Internet Engineering Task Force (IETF) Request for Comments: 2404. Retrieved from http://tools.ietf.org/html/rfc2404

Manral, V. (2007). *Cryptographic algorithm implementation requirements for encapsulating security payload (ESP) and authentication header (AH)*. Internet Engineering Task Force (IETF) Request for Comments: 4835. Retrieved from http://tools.ietf.org/html/rfc4835

Na, J., Ryu, S., Lee, K., & Mun, Y. (2010). Enhanced PMIPv6 route optimization handover using PFMIPv6. *IEICE Transactions on Communications. E (Norwalk, Conn.), 93-B*(11), 3144–3147.

Narten, T., Draves, R., & Krishnan, S. (2007). *Privacy extensions for stateless address autoconfiguration in IPv6, RFC 4941*. Internet Engineering Task Force (IETF). Retrieved from http://tools.ietf.org/html/rfc4941

Narten, T., Nordmark, E., Simpson, W., & Soliman, H. (2007). *Neighbor discovery for IP version 6 (IPv6)*. IETF Request for Comments: 4861. Retrieved from http://tools.ietf.org/html/rfc4861

Nikander, P., Arkko, J., Aura, T., Montenegro, G., & Nordmark, E. (2005). *Mobile IP version 6 route optimization security design background*. Internet Engineering Task Force (IETF), Request for Comments: 4225, Dec. 2005. Retrieved from http://tools.ietf.org/html/rfc4225

Nikander, P., Kempf, J., & Nordmark, E. (2004). *IPv6 neighbor discovery (ND) trust models and threats*. Internet Engineering Task Force (IETF) Request for Comments: 3756. Retrieved from http://tools.ietf.org/html/rfc3756

O'Shea, G., & Roe, M. (2001). Child-proof authentication for MIPv6 (CAM). *SIGCOMM Computer Communications Review, 31*(2), 4–8. doi:10.1145/505666.505668.

Pereira, R., & Adams, R. (1998). *The ESP CBC-mode cipher algorithms*. Internet Engineering Task Force (IETF) Request for Comments: 2451. Retrieved from http://tools.ietf.org/html/rfc2451

Perkins, C., Johnson, D., & Arkko, J. (2011). *Mobility support in IPv6*. Internet Engineering Task Force (IETF), Request for Comments: 6275. Retrieved from http://tools.ietf.org/html/rfc6275

Ren, K., Lou, W., Zeng, K., Bao, F., Zhou, J., & Deng, R. H. (2006). Routing optimization security in mobile IPv6. *Computer Networks, 50*(13), 2401–2419. doi:10.1016/j.comnet.2005.09.019.

Ryu, S., & Mun, Y. (2005). The tentative and early binding update for mobile IPv6 fast handover. In *Proceedings of the First International Conference on Mobile Ad-Hoc and Sensor Networks*, (pp. 825–835). Berlin: Springer-Verlag.

Ryu, S., & Mun, Y. (2007). A scheme to enhance TEBU scheme of fast handovers for mobile IPv6. In *Proceedings of the 3rd International Conference on Embedded Software and Systems*, (pp. 773–782). Berlin: Springer-Verlag.

Schiller, J. (2005). *Cryptographic algorithms for use in the internet key exchange version 2 (IKEv2)*. IETF Request for Comments: 4307. Retrieved from http://tools.ietf.org/html/rfc4307

Shih, C.-H., Kuo, J.-L., Huang, C.-H., & Chen, Y.-C. (2011). A proxy-based fast handover scheme for hierarchical mobile IPv6. In *Proceedings of the 5th International Conference on Ubiquitous Information Management and Communication*, (pp. 21:1–21:10). New York, NY: ACM.

Soliman, H., Castelluccia, C., ElMalki, K., & Bellier, L. (2008). *Hierarchical mobile IPv6 (HMIPv6) mobility management*. Internet Engineering Task Force (IETF), Request for Comments: 5380. Retrieved from http://tools.ietf.org/html/rfc5380

Thomson, S., Narten, T., & Jinmei, T. (2007). *IPv6 stateless address autoconfiguration*. RFC 4862. Internet Engineering Task Force (IETF). Retrieved from http://tools.ietf.org/html/rfc4862

Viega, J., & McGrew, D. (2005). *The use of galois/counter mode (GCM) in IPsec encapsulating security payload (ESP)*. IETF Request for Comments: 4106. Retrieved from http://tools.ietf.org/html/rfc4106

Vogt, C., Bless, R., Doll, M., & Kuefner, T. (2004). *Early binding updates for mobile IPv6*. Expired Internet Engineering Task Force (IETF) Internet draft. Retrieved from http://tools.ietf.org/html/draft-vogt-mip6-early-binding-updates-00

Yokota, H., Chowdhury, K., Koodli, R., Patil, B., & Xia, F. (2010). *Fast handovers for proxy mobile IPv6*. Internet Engineering Task Force (IETF), Request for Comments: 5949. Retrieved from http://tools.ietf.org/html/rfc5949

Yoo, H., Tolentino, R. S., Park, B., Chang, B. Y., & Kim, S.-H. (2009). ES-FHMIPv6: An efficient scheme for fast handover over HMIPv6 networks. *International Journal of Future Generation Communication and Networking*, 2(2), 11–24.

ADDITIONAL READING

Bernardos, C. J., Soto, I., & Calderón, M. (2007). IPv6 network mobility. *The Internet Protocol*, 10(2), 16–27.

Elgoarany, K., & Eltoweissy, M. (2007). Security in mobile IPv6: A survey. *Elsevier Information Security Technical Report*, 12, 32–43. doi:10.1016/j.istr.2007.02.002.

Faigl, Z., Lindskog, S., & Brunstrom, A. (2010). Performance evaluation of IKEv2 authentication methods in next generation wireless networks. *Security Communications Networks*, 3, 83–98. doi: doi:10.1002/sec.114.

Hogg, S., & Vyncke, E. (2008). *IPv6 security*. Indianapolis, IN: Cisco Press.

Kim, H., & Kim, Y. (2006). An early binding fast handover for high-speed mobile nodes on MIPv6 over connectionless packet radio link. In *Proceedings of the Seventh International Conference on Software Engineering, Artificial Intelligence, Networking, and Parallel/Distributed Computing* (pp. 237–242). Las Vegas, NV: IEEE Computer. doi:10.1109/SNPD-SAWN.2006.17

Park, J. T., & Chun, M. N. (2011). Extension of hierarchical mobility management with multicasting tunnels in heterogeneous wireless networks. In *Proceedings of the 5th International Conference on Ubiquitous Information Management and Communication*. Seoul, Korea: ACM. doi:10.1145/1968613.1968640

Sousa, B. M., Pentikousis, K., & Curado, M. (2011). Multihoming management for future networks. *Mobile Network Application Journal*, 16(4), 505–517. doi:10.1007/s11036-011-0323-5.

Wei, A., Wei, G., & Dupeyrat, G. (2009). Improving mobile IPv6 handover and authentication in wireless network with E-HCF. *International Journal of Network Management, 19*(6), 479–489. doi:10.1002/nem.723.

You, Y. H., & Sakurai, K. (2011). Enhancing SVO logic for mobile IPv6 security protocols. *Journal of Wireless Mobile Networks, Ubiquitous Computing, and Dependable Applications, 2*, 26–52.

Zhou, H., Zhang, H., Qin, Y., Wang, H., & Chao, H. C. (2010). A proxy mobile IPv6 based global mobility management architecture and protocol. *Mobile Networks and Applications, 15*, 530–542. doi:10.1007/s11036-009-0185-2.

KEY TERMS AND DEFINITIONS

Handover Latency: Is the time interval between an MN detaching from its current network to when it first receive packets in the new attached network.

HMIPv6: Is an extension to MIPv6 that support mobility of IPv6 based host device with enhanced performance than basic MIPv6.

IKEv2: Internet Key Exchange version two is an application layer abstraction that provides automatic keying services used by IPsec security protocols.

IPsec: Is an inbuilt set of security protocol in IPv6 for securing communication between two communicating parties to prevent security attacks.

MIPv6: Is the mobility management protocol designed for IPv6 based devices that are capable of moving from one network to the other transparently in the Internet without disruption to ongoing communication.

PMIPv6: Is an extension to MIPv6 that support mobility of IPv6 based host device. This support is provided by the network rather than the host device itself as contrasted from MIPv6 and HMIPv6 that are host-based support.

Route Optimization: Is the removal of triangular routing of packets from a correspondent mobile device destined to a mobile device that has roamed to a foreign network by its home network router known as home agent.

SEND: Is a security protocol that is used to secure automatic address configuration procedures of hosts and routers in a network against address spoofing related attacks.

APPENDIX

List of Abbreviations

- **AC:** Address Configuration
- **ADD:** Authorization Delegation Discovery
- **AH:** Authentication Header
- **AP:** Access Point
- **AP-ID:** Access Point ID
- **AR:** Access Router
- **AR:** Access Router
- **AR:** Access Router
- **BA:** Binding Acknowledgment message
- **BU:** Binding Update message
- **CGA:** Cryptographically Generated Addresses
- **CN:** Correspondent Node
- **CoA:** Care of Address
- **CoT:** Care-of Test message
- **DAD:** Duplicate Address Detection
- **DHAAD:** Dynamic Home Agent Address Discovery
- **DHCPv6:** Dynamic Host Configuration Protocol for IPv6
- **DoS:** Denial of Service
- **EAP:** Extensible Authentication Protocol
- **ESP:** Encapsulated Security Payload
- **FBack:** Fast Binding Acknowledgement
- **FBU:** Fast Binding Update ()
- **F-HMIPv6:** Fast Handovers for Hierarchical MIPv6
- **FMIPv6:** Fast Handover MIPv6
- **FPMIPv6:** Fast Handovers for Proxy MIPv6
- **HA:** Home Agent
- **HMAC:** Hash-Based Message Authentication Code
- **HMIPv6:** Hierarchical MIPv6
- **HoA:** Home Address
- **HoT:** Home Test message
- **ICMPv6:** Internet Control Message Protocol for IPv6
- **ICV:** Integrity Check Value
- **IDi; IDr:** Identification of the initiator; Identification of the responder
- **IKE:** Internet Key Exchange ()
- **IKE_SA:** IKE security association
- **IPsec:** IP security
- **Kbm:** Binding management key
- **Kcn:** Node Key
- **KE:** Diffie-Hellman values Key Exchange

- **LCoA:** On-Link CoA
- **LMA:** Local Mobility Anchor
- **LTE:** Long Time Evolution
- **MAG:** Mobility Access Gateway
- **MAP:** Mobility Anchor Point
- **MD:** Movement Detection
- **MIPv6:** Mobile IPv6
- **MN:** Mobile Node
- **MR:** Mobile Router
- **N:** Negotiation of new IPsec SA
- **NAR:** New Access Router
- **NCoA:** New CoA
- **NDP:** Neighbor Discovery Protocol
- **NEMO:** Network Mobility
- **Ni; Nr:** Nonce of initiator; Nonce of responder
- **Nonce:** Random value for freshness
- **PAD:** Peer Authentication Database
- **PAR:** Previous Access Router
- **PCoA:** Previous CoA
- **PCoA:** Proxy CoA
- **PFMIPv6:** Proxy-Based Fast Handovers for Mobile IPv6
- **PKI:** Public Key Infrastructure
- **PMIPv6:** Proxy MIPv6
- **PrRtAdv:** Proxy Router Advertisement
- **RA:** Router Advertisement
- **RCoA:** Regional CoA
- **RO:** Route Optimization
- **RR:** Return Routability Protocol
- **RS:** Router Solicitation
- **RtSolPr:** Router Solicitation for Proxy Advertisement
- **SA:** Security Association proposal; SAi2 and SAr2 are negotiations of IPSec SA algorithms.
- **SAD:** Security Association Database
- **SEND:** SEcure Neighbor Discovery
- **SK{}:** Encrypted payload
- **SLAAC:** Stateless Address Auto-configuration
- **SPD:** Security Policy Database
- **SPI:** Security Parameter Index
- **TA:** Trust Anchor
- **TSi; TSr:** Traffic Selector of the initiator; Traffic Selector of the responder
- **WiFi:** Wireless Fidelity (IEEE 802.11x)
- **WiMax:** Worldwide Interoperability for Microwave Access

Section 2
Cryptographic Algorithms and Security Protocols

Chapter 4
A New Encryption Algorithm based on Chaotic Map for Wireless Sensor Network

Ghada Zaibi
University of Sfax, Tunisia

Abdennaceur Kachouri
University of Sfax, Tunisia

Fabrice Peyrard
University of Toulouse, France

Danièle Fournier-Prunaret
University of Toulouse, France

Mounir Samet
University of Sfax, Tunisia

ABSTRACT

A new and secure chaos-based block cipher for image encryption in wireless sensor networks is proposed. The security analysis and the performances of the proposed algorithm have been investigated. The statistical analysis includes the histograms and correlation coefficients of adjacent pixels. In the differential analysis, the authors use the Number of Pixels Change Rate (NPCR) and the Unified Changing Average (UACI) measures to demonstrate the security against differential attacks. Key sensitivity analysis and key space analysis show that the proposed cipher is secure and resistant to brute force attack. The authors demonstrate that the performance of the cipher exceeds the studied encryption algorithms as well as AES (Advanced Encryption Standard). An implementation on a real wireless sensor network testbed is realized, and the energy consumption is investigated.

INTRODUCTION

The unprecedented development of information technology and miniaturization has accelerated the growth and the spread of the Wireless Sensor Networks (WSN).

A wireless sensor network is a network of active tiny nodes that collect data from environment through a sensor unit, treat the information, and forward it via the processing and transmission units.

DOI: 10.4018/978-1-4666-4514-1.ch004

These tiny and smart devices are invading our daily life and give rise to many applications of wireless sensor network. Ranging from military applications to agriculture, transport, environment, etc., the security of collected and transmitted information has become imperative but also critical (Kavitha & Sridharan, 2010).

Concerns of data security in a WSN are facing sensors with a reduced volume, a limited storage space and especially limited battery power. The design of an encryption algorithm must meet these restrictions, creating a compromise between security on one hand and the speed and energy consumption on the other.

The type of information collected by wireless sensors may be temperature, luminosity, or image in some specific applications.

Multimedia data especially image contain often private or confidential information or even financial interests. For example, smartphone security threats can be countered by biometric identification. Access to the smartphones will be limited to owners who are identified by their identity image.

The exchanges of these data are secured by techniques that guarantee the integrity, confidentiality, and authenticity. Image encryption is a widely studied discipline and chaotic dynamics is a potential rival of conventional cryptosystems.

In fact, according to (Socek, Li, Magliveras, & Furht, 2005) and (Furht, Socek, & Eskicioglu, 2004), the conventional encryption algorithms such as DES (Data Encryption Standard) or AES are not adequate to image and video encryption. Their main argument was the real-time speed reduced by these algorithms.

The author in (Lian, 2009) shows that images encrypted with the AES algorithm are still intelligible. Thereby, the author questions the reliability of AES.

Several studies suggest improving or replacing these algorithms with chaotic ciphers (Socek et al., 2005; Furht et al., 2004; Lian, 2009; Mansour, Chalhoub, & Bakhache, 2012; Zaibi, Peyrard, Kachouri, Fournier-Prunaret, & Samet, 2010).

Chaos theory is part of the most recent and advanced contemporary research fields. It is defined as a study of nonlinear and complex dynamical systems. These complex systems are expressed by recurrences and mathematical algorithms. Furthermore, they are dynamic, variable and some of these systems show no periodic behaviour.

Chaos is having a growing interest in secure communications due to many attractive properties like the sensitivity to initial conditions and parameters variations as well as the random-like behavior of chaotic sequences.

The main purpose of this chapter is proposing a low-power and secure chaos based cryptosystem suitable for wireless sensor network.

In the first section, we give first a brief state of the art of different chaotic cryptosystems and some existing chaotic ciphers for wireless sensor networks. The second part presents image encryption algorithms based on chaos and the AES algorithm. Then we detail our contribution, in the second section. Our algorithm focused on the confusion and diffusion properties as well as the simplicity of the used operations. A security analysis and a comparison with AES and chaotic ciphers are depicted.

The last section describes in the first subsection the wireless sensor networks and their application areas. The second subsection is a brief overview of the existing and the used simulators, the simulation process with the chosen simulators as well as the implementation of our proposal on a real Wireless Sensor Network testbed equipped with 16-bit microcontrollers. We exhibit also the operation mode of the chosen platform. Finally, a study on energy consumption of the proposed and investigated ciphers is exposed in both simulation and experimental tests.

OVERVIEW OF CHAOS-BASED CRYPTOGRAPHY

From the ancient Greek to the early twentieth century, the chaos was considered as an uncontrollable and even useless system. It was related to the disorder and the unpredictable phenomena, in spite of demonstrating the determinism in seemingly random aspects. The chaos theory may start with some common philosophical thoughts, which believe that chaos is a source of life or of the "ordered universe" (Stavroulakis, 2006). However, trying to create order from chaos is not as simple as it seems and is not evident. These difficulties and unsolved questions have prompted the scientists to dig deeper to find the answers. A famous anecdote about Edward Lorenz (a well-known meteorologist) says that he discovered accidentally in 1961 the extreme sensitivity to initial conditions of some equations or nonlinear system of equations used for weather forecast. It is obviously the basis of deterministic chaos. In fact, chaos theory influences the explanation of many phenomena and finds application in various areas such as:

- **Economy:** Forecast of economic cycles, trade flows and financial markets
- **Weather:** Weather Forecast
- **Health:** Prediction of epileptic seizures
- **Social Science:** behavior of social systems
- **Encryption of Information**

Definition and Properties

Many definitions can be given to the chaos. Chaos in its linguistic form means the general confusion of elements, material, before the world creation. It is the absolute disorder. Another definition considers chaos as one of the intriguing system of the deterministic nonlinear dynamics. Dynamic systems are systems that vary over time, for example: the pendulum or the solar system. There is a state space or phase space that contains all possible state of the system and its evolution law describes the future when the present is given. A geometric figure of the phase space, showing the behavior of a chaotic system, is the attractor. An attractor can be defined as an asymptotic limit of any initial condition solutions localized in a non-zero volume field or a basin of attraction. The complex trajectories in the phase space which attract the chaotic system solutions are then called attractors. The attractor may be strange, with fractal structure, fixed point or limit cycle. The Lorenz attractor and the Chua's double scroll attractor are among the first example of strange attractors mentioned in the history of chaos. We will give more details about them later.

Many attractive characteristics of the chaotic signals can define their randomness and their useful aspect in cryptography, such as:

- The wide-band spectrum as white noise.
- The auto-and cross correlations are similar to those of random signals.
- The long-term unpredictability, which can explain the nonexistence of periodic orbits, fixed points or quasi-periodic solutions for systems in long-term.
- Determinism, that is, a deterministic dynamical system is a system that evolves according to a pre-established law, completely determined when its initial conditions are known.
- The high sensitivity to initial conditions and system parameters (secret key).
- The ergodicity, that is, most orbits lead to the same distribution.

Chaotic Generators and Chaotic Cryptosystems

There are several systems, which are used to generate the chaotic signals. These systems are classified into two categories: continuous chaotic systems and discrete time chaotic systems.

Among the most famous continuous chaotic systems, we cite the Lorenz attractor. The Lorenz attractor is published in 1963, and it is generated by the following formula (Equation 1):

$$\begin{cases} \dot{x} = -\sigma x + \sigma y \\ \dot{y} = \rho x - y - xz \\ \dot{z} = -\beta z + xy \end{cases} \quad (1)$$

The parameters σ, β and ρ are strictly positive reals. The chaos is obtained for the following values:

$$\sigma > \beta + 1;\ \rho > 0 \text{ and } \rho > \frac{\sigma(\sigma + \beta + 3)}{\sigma - \beta - 1}.$$

Another continuous chaotic system is Chua's system which describes Chua's circuit. It is given by Equation 2:

$$f(x) = \begin{cases} \dot{x} = p(-x + y - f(x)) \\ \phantom{\dot{x}} = p(-x + y - (m_o x + \frac{(m_1 - m_o)(|x+1| - |x-1|)}{2})) \\ \dot{y} = x - y + z \\ \dot{z} = -qy \end{cases} \quad (2)$$

where $f(x)$ is the nonlinear characteristic of the Chua's diode, with m_0 and m_1 are negative constants. The double scroll attractor can be obtained by chosen these values: $p = 10$, $m_0 = -0.7$, $m_1 = -1.3$ and $q = 15$.

The second category of chaos generators is the discrete time chaotic systems such as the logistic map given by Equation 3 and the one dimensional Piecewise Linear Chaotic Map (PWLCM) described in Equation 4.

$$x_{n+1} = r.x_n.(1 - x_n) \quad (3)$$

with $x_n \in [0,1]$ and $r \in [0,4]$, the chaotic behavior is found for $r > 3.6$.

$$X(t+1) = F_r(X(t)) = \begin{cases} X(t)/p & 0 \leq X(t) < p \\ (X(t) - p)/(0.5 - p) & p \leq X(t) < 0.5 \\ (1 - X(t) - p)/(0.5 - p) & 0.5 \leq X(t) < 1 - p \\ (1 - X(t))/p & 1 - p \leq X(t) \leq 1 \end{cases} \quad (4)$$

where p is the parameter control, $p \in [0,1]$.

The PWLCM map is generally chosen for its continuous interval parameters. In other words, the chaos is found for all the values, not like the logistic map, where the user may find some periodic windows even for the interval mentioned above (Alvarez & Li, 2006).

To design a chaotic cryptosystem, there exist two approaches: analog and digital.

Analog cryptosystems are based on the synchronization between two chaotic systems in a noisy environment (Pecorra & Carrol, 1990).

Digital chaotic cryptosystems are designed for digital computers where one or more chaotic sequences are implemented (Alvarez & Li, 2006). They can be classified into two main categories: chaotic stream cryptosystems and chaotic block cryptosystems (Masuda & Aihara, 2002).

For the stream cipher, in the general case, the message is encrypted bit by bit, with an XOR applied at the output of a Pseudorandom Number Generator (PRNG) based on a chaotic map (Alvarez & Li, 2006). The use of discrete dynamical chaotic systems dates back to 1989 when Matthews presented a one dimensional map with chaotic behavior. This map is the source of the pseudo-random numbers sequence used to design a one time pad in order to encrypt the information (Alvarez, Montoya, Romera, & Pastor, 1999; Pareek, Patidar, & Sud, 2003).

Compared to the ordinary pseudorandom number generators, chaos is easier and cheaper to be built on embedded systems (Zhou, Yu, & Ye, 2006).

The output of the chaotic PRNG is the stream key that is used to hide the message (using an XOR).

In literature, there exist two main algorithms for generating chaotic pseudo-random numbers (Li, 2003). The first one is based on the extraction of bits partially or completely from the chaotic orbits. An example called CCS-PRBG (Coupled Chaotic Systems Based PRBG) where two chaotic systems are used. The second deals with the division of the phase space into m subspaces (for example $m = 2^n$ parts) and assign each part to an integer between 0 and m-1 and generating the pseudo-random number $i \in \{0, ..., m-1\}$ where the chaotic orbit corresponds to the ith sub-space.

The chaotic bloc ciphers encrypt data blocks of different length depending on the used algorithm. The chaotic transformation properties and the algorithm design and implementation process determine the security level of such an algorithm (Masuda, & Aihara, 2002). Many chaotic block cipher proposed in literature are based on Feistel architecture (Jakimoski, & Kocarev, 2001; Xiang, 2007), where the chaotic map are used to generate the subkeys or the substitution tables (S-Box).

Like the conventional block cryptographic systems, the chaotic block ciphers are chosen to secure the transmitted information in wireless sensor networks.

Chaotic Block Ciphers for Wireless Sensor Network

Chaotic cryptosystems oriented for sensor networks are not very numerous but challenge well-known ciphers such as Rivest's Cipher 5 called RC5 (Rivest, 1995), RC6 (Rivest, Robshaw, & Yiqun Lisa Yin, 1998), and AES. An example of such cryptosystems was proposed by Chen (Chen, Zhong, & Wu, 2008), it is essentially based on a function f given by the following 8-bit chaotic map claimed by the authors:

$$y = (x << 2) - ((x^2)) >> 6 - 1; \qquad (5)$$

where x and y are 8 bits unsigned integers. The operators "<<" and ">>" are respectively right bit shifting and left bit shifting.

Its chaotic characteristics have not been checked in the original article. The four bits to the right (R) of the 8-bit block are considered a half byte; it is extended to form an entire byte (this procedure of extension was not explained in the original article). The XOR operation is applied to the resulting byte and the secret key. The supposed chaotic map is then iterated and having as input vectors (input) the result of the previous Xor operation. The Feistel structure is adopted for four laps only, which does not comply with the Feistel structure restrictions and makes the algorithm accessible to attacks. The weakness of this algorithm was proved and it has been cryptanalysis through the differential attack (Yang, Xiao, Xiang, 2011).

Another algorithm based on chaotic maps is developed by Fang et al in (Fang, Liu, Zhao, 2008).

The original logistic map is a continuous function on the interval [0, 1], while the sensor network is a digital communication system. For any used digital system, the function in use is not continuous and the inputs and the control parameters have limited points of the variation interval; which generates a result that is not really chaotic because the ergodicity will not be maintained over the entire interval [0, 1]. Thus, the authors, proposed to expand the variation range of the previous map, and the logistic map will become the modified logistic map given by Equation 6:

$$x_{n+1} = \mu x_n \left(N - x_n / m \right) / N; \qquad (6)$$

where $x \in [0, mN]$, $N = 2^K$ and $m = 2^k$; K and k are both integers.

Since m and N are powers of 2, the process in the microcontroller will be based on binary operations, and the output is also binary.

This equation requires only multiplication, addition, shift but also division operations.

When mN tends to infinity, the sequence is ergodic, and more the number mN is large more the sequence becomes chaotic.

The authors propose a chaotic system formed by the association of two maps: logistics and "Tent map" called N-Logistic-Tent. Compared to the original maps, these suites have a larger range of data.

Another advantage is the larger size of the key which is expanded from (x_i, λ) to $(x_i, y_i, \mu, \beta, m, N)$.

Equation 7 represents the modified logistic map and Equation 8 is N-tent map.

$$x_{n+1} = \mu x_n (N - x_n / m) / N - y_n / 2; \quad (7)$$

where $x \in [0, mN]$ and $\mu \in [0, 4]$;

$$y_{n+1} = \beta (N - |N - y_n|) \quad (8)$$

where $y \in [0, 2N]$, $\beta \in \{1, 2\}$,

The diversification key or "seed key" of this algorithm is the set $(x_i, y_i, \mu, \beta, m, N)$. A preamble is used to synchronize between transmitter and receiver. The encryption is performed using the XOR operation, as well as the decryption function.

Studied Image Encryption Algorithms

In this subsection we will present three different algorithms that are used to encrypt information and images. The security of the following algorithms will be examined and compared to our proposal in the third section.

ECKBA Algorithm

The first chaos-based algorithm that we studied is called Enhanced Chaotic Key-Based Algorithm: ECKBA (Socek et al., 2005; Awad, El Assad, & Carragata, 2008; Abd El-Wahed, Mesbah, & Shoukry, 2008; Noura, El Assad, Vladeanu & Caragata, 2011; Philip & Das, 2011). It is given by Figure 1. It encrypts an image I, using a network of Substitution-Permutation (SP) controlled by the piecewise linear function (PWLCM).

A substitution-permutation network is a principal cryptosystem design which allows good mixing properties suggested by Shannon (1949) and considered among its simplest implementation. It consists on several round of S-Box ensuring substitution linked by P permutations. A different key is used in each round to encrypt the input block of bits. Those keys are generated from the seed key. Many well-known ciphers have substitution-permutation network architecture like Serpent cipher (Heys & Adams, 1999).

The idea of the ECKBA cipher is inspired from the original algorithm CKBA (Chaotic Key-Based Algorithm) proposed by Yen and Guo (2000). The authors improved the original algorithm by increasing the key length, changing the 1D-Logistic map by the 1D-Piecewise linear chaotic map and adding a pseudo-random generator based on the PWLCM to generate the permutation box. Another improvement of the original proposal is adding another operation of addition modulo the maximum pixel intensity in order to construct stronger S-Boxes.

Therefore, ECKBA algorithm makes r rounds of the network SP on each pixel. The $(i+1)$ iteration of the chaotic function is controlled by the previously encrypted block C_i.

Figure 1. ECKBA algorithm flowchart

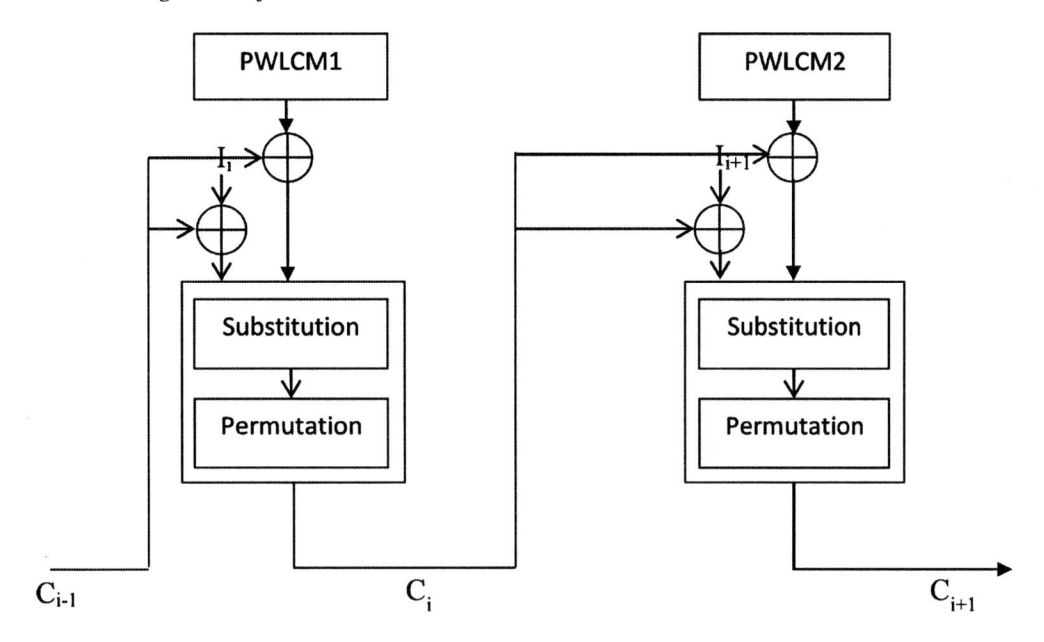

This algorithm implements the encryption mode CBC (Cipher Block Chaining): an XOR is applied between the pixel I_i and the encrypted pixel C_{i-1}. Two pseudorandom chaotic sequences are used in the substitution step. The S-Box and its inverse are constructed by Equations 9 and 10:

$$sigma_r(u,v) = \begin{cases} u \oplus v, & \text{if r is even;} \\ u+v \mod 256, & \text{if r is od,} \end{cases} \quad (9)$$

$$sigma_r^{-1}(u,v) = \begin{cases} u \oplus v, & \text{if r is even;} \\ u-v \mod 256, & \text{if r is od,} \end{cases} \quad (10)$$

The P-box is obtained from the lexicographic permutation operation. This permutation is applied to each bit of each block (pixels) with the permutation index $i \in [0:8![$. For example, if we choose $i = 17331$, then the permutation result of the byte $O = [b_1, b_2, b_3, b_4, b_5, b_6, b_7, b_8]$ is equal to $[b_4, b_5, b_1, b_6, b_2, b_7, b_8, b_3]$.

Chaotic Block Cipher Based on Two PWLCM

The second algorithm is presented in (Mansour et al., 2012) where two PieceWise Linear Chaotic Maps (PWLCM) are used to obtain two pseudo-random numbers x_i and $y_j \in [0,1]$. The results (last k bits) are disturbed by two Linear FeedBack Shift Registers (LFSR) with two seeds (initial conditions). The perturbation is applied after a chosen iteration number. The authors applied then an XOR between the two obtained disturbed sequences; in order to have more random-like behavior. Encryption is performed by an XOR between the disturbed output and the input. The previous steps are applied on each two bytes input. Therefore, to encrypt 128 bytes the process is repeated 64 times. The authors chose to convert the output of each LFSR from decimal to integer to simplify the processing operation. They just multiply the output by 10^6 and change the type to integer value. The initial key includes the initial values of the two chaotic maps as well as their parameters.

AES Algorithm

The third algorithm is Rijndael well-known as AES algorithm. Rijndael is a block cipher adopted as the new Advanced Standard Encryption (AES) selected by NIST in 2001 to replace DES. It uses 128, 192 or 256 bits keys to encrypt and decrypt fix data length (128 bits). The input data can be considered as a 4 × 4 array of bytes called the state. Each element of the state is composed of eight bits represented in the finites Galois Field $GF(2^n)$ (Ebrahimi, Leprévost, & Warusfel, 2006).

After an initial Round Key addition, the state array is transformed by executing a round function, consisting of the four main transformations: SubBytes, ShiftRows, Mix-Columns, and AddRoundKey. The round function is run iteratively 10, 12, or 14 times (it depends on the key length). The last round differs by not applying Mix-Columns.

Regarding the existing wireless sensor network standards, the most widely used standard for these networks is IEEE802.15.4. This standard, implemented in many sensors transceivers, offers the service to conserve the integrity and the confidentiality of the transmitted packets using the AES algorithm.

PROPOSED ALGORITHM

Admittedly, the security of images is an important issue at the transmission process, but the speed and resources consumption remain a challenge especially for wireless sensor network.

Two principal properties of good ciphers are diffusion and confusion. The diffusion is often performed by swapping blocks or binary permutations (Schneier, 1996). Many conventional algorithms implement permutation technique like DES, AES, RC4, etc. We use a simple left cyclic permutation of pixels block to ensure diffusion. Confusion is achieved through a chaotic map. The choice of the chaotic map must take into account the limited power and accuracy in the sensor node. Floating-point operations cannot be totally managed. For this reason, we selected the following discretized Lorenz map where the variables and the parameters are integers. This chaotic map, given by Equation 11, has three integers inputs (xk, yk, and zk). It was used to conceive a Pseudorandom Number Generator (PRNG) and an enhanced version a chaotic stream cipher (Silva, Crespo & Nunes, 2009, 2010). In order to avoid short cycle problems, the discretized Lorenz map is perturbed, via a linear feedback shift register as it shown in Equation 12.

$$\begin{cases} x_{k+1} = x_k + \sigma(y_k - x_k)\Delta t \\ y_{k+1} = y_k + [x_k(\rho - z_k) - y_k]\Delta t \\ z_{k+1} = z_k + [x_k y_k - ^2 z_k]\Delta t \end{cases} \quad (11)$$

$$\begin{cases} y_{k+1} = y_{k+1} \oplus LFSR_i \\ z_{k+1} = z_{k+1} \oplus LFSR_i \\ \Delta t = \Delta t \oplus x_{k+1} \end{cases} \quad (12)$$

Complex chaotic systems involve the use of floating point arithmetic, which affects the speed of the algorithm and its hardware and software achievability. The fixed-point arithmetic and simple chaotic systems are recommended to increase the speed of encryption and to ensure the simple hardware and software design. However, fixed-point numbers may be truncated or rounded in a loss of information.

Since chaotic systems are deterministic, there are tools of chaos theory to discern the chaos. When an intruder found some information about the orbits of the chaotic systems, it can use this information to reduce the complexity of finding the secure key. With the use of several chaotic systems or several dimensions, cryptanalysis of chaos is more difficult since the output is determined by many mixed chaotic orbits.

The implementation of chaotic algorithms on computers or microcontrollers confronts inconvenient limitation which is the finite precision of the represented numbers. This finite precision creates a major problem which is the occurrence of short cycles and convergence to a fixed point. Short cycle problems are one of the most serious problems that prevented the progression of chaotic cryptography from theory to practice (Tao, Ruili, & Yixun, 1998).

Tao in (Tao et al., n.d.) suggests injecting a disturbance to the system to enhance its cryptographic properties. The changes will affect the orbit value, the parameters or both at once. This disturbance leads to a larger cycle length.

The disturbance can be achieved using an LFSR or a Linear Congruential genrators (Tao et al., n.d.; Bose & Pathak, 2006).

The perturbation is chosen according to the following principles:

- It must have a long controllable cycle length and a uniform distribution.
- It must not degrade the statistical properties of chaotic dynamics; the amplitude of the interfering signal must be much less than that of the chaotic signal. We define the signal to noise ratio SNR by Equation 13:

$$SNR = 10 \log_{10} \left(\frac{\max\ imum\ magnitude\ of\ chaotic\ signal}{\max\ imum\ magnitude\ of\ perturbing\ signal} \right)$$
(13)

The SNR should be greater than 1.

- The perturbation time must be small compared to the total execution time of the system.

The disturbance generator LFSR produce sequences having the following advantages:

- A definite length of the cycles $(2^L - 1)$ (L is the degree).
- A uniform distribution.
- An easy implementation.
- A maximum controllable signal amplitude given by $2^p (2^L - 1)$ when it is used in a system with P-precision (number of bits).

Disruption is triggered at $t=0$ with a period Δ. It is applied by an XOR with the chaotic signal with $t = k\Delta$, and $k = 0, 1, 2, \ldots$

$$x_{t+1,i} = \begin{cases} \left[F(x_t)\right]_i & 1 \leq i \leq P - L \\ \left[F(x_t)\right]_i \oplus a_{k+P+1-i} & P - L + 1 \leq i \leq P \end{cases}$$
(14)

$\left[F(x_t)\right]_i$ represents the ith bit of $F(x_t)$. When $t \neq k\Delta$ in each interval Δ, no disturbance occurs, then $x_{t+1} = F(x_t)$.

In our case, we used an m-LFSR ensuring $2^{128} - 1$ cycle length. The primitive polynomial of the used LFSR is: $x^{128} + x^7 + x^2 + x + 1$.

Plaintext is encrypted by block of 3 bytes. The block size can also be a multiple of three, since the variable size can be extended to more than one byte using unsigned integers.

Our proposed block cipher with CBC mode is designed to be simple and secure to fit the wireless sensor network requirements.

The six principal steps of our Image Cipher Algorithm based on Lorenz (ICAL) are:

Step 1: A whitening step: we applied an XOR between portions of the input block and a part of the key to increase the attacks complexity.

$$\begin{cases} x_0 = x_0 \oplus Input(i); \\ y_0 = y_0 \oplus Input(i+7); \\ z_0 = z_0 \oplus Input(i+15); \end{cases}$$
(15)

The set $\{x_0, y_0, z_0\}$ is the initial conditions of the discretized Lorenz map.

Step 2: A diffusion step: the lexicographic permutation (Socek et al.) consumes lots of memory resources in the case of "lookup table" and seem to add extra execution time if the permutation of the bits is done progressively. Left cyclic permutation of the pixels seems more adequate.

Step 3: We apply the CBC mode by an XOR between a swapped pixel block and a pixels block previously encrypted.

$$\begin{cases} C_p(i) = C(i-1) \oplus shiftedpixel(i), \\ C_p(i+1) = C(i) \oplus shiftedpixel(i+1), \\ C_p(i+2) = C(i+1) \oplus shiftedpixel(i+2); \end{cases} \quad (16)$$

The advantage of using CBC mode is to prevent transmitted message redundancy detection. However, sequential decryption is its most important drawback.

Step 4: Iterate the discretized Lorenz map. Each iteration generates three variables x_k, y_k and z_k. Apply an Xor between the previous step result and the outputs of Lorenz system.

$$\begin{cases} C(i) = C_p(i) \oplus (x_k \oplus y_k), \\ C(i+1) = C_p(i+1) \oplus (x_k \oplus z_k), \\ C(i+2) = C_p(i+2) \oplus z_k; \end{cases} \quad (17)$$

Step 5: An XOR is applied between portions of the key and the encrypted byte C.

$$\begin{cases} C(i) = \Delta t \oplus C(i); \\ C(i+1) = x_0 \oplus C(i+1); \\ C(i+2) = z_0 \oplus C(i+2); \end{cases} \quad (18)$$

Step 6: Repeat the steps 1 and 5 until all the input blocks are encrypted.

Steps 1 and 5 are a form of the "key whitening," defined by applying an XOR between elements of the key with the input, and another XOR between another key with the output (Schneier, 1996).

The key whitening was used for the first time in the DES-X algorithm developed by RSA, and then this technique spreads to several other algorithms such as FEAL (Fast Data Encipherment Algorithm) cipher where the same key is used for input and output. The "whitening" requires the cryptanalyst to guess at least one of the whitening operation's input in addition to the key. It is not vulnerable to MITM attack and it increases the security of the algorithm in question (Schneier, 1996) (see Figure 2).

SECURITY ANALYSIS

A good image encryption algorithm must produce an encrypted image with a very low pixels correlation. The simple visual inspection is insufficient to judge the quality of an image encryption. To evaluate the efficiency of our proposed cipher and compare it to previous studied algorithms, we performed a series of analysis.

Statistical Analysis

Statistical analysis can decipher several encryption algorithms as mentioned by Shannon (1949). In this section, we will study the encrypted images histograms and the correlation of adjacent pixels.

Histogram Analysis

An histogram is the distribution of the pixel intensity values. It represents the number of pixels for each intensity value. Figure 3 shows that the distribution of pixels of the encrypted image by

A New Encryption Algorithm based on Chaotic Map for Wireless Sensor Network

Figure 2. Proposed algorithm ICAL

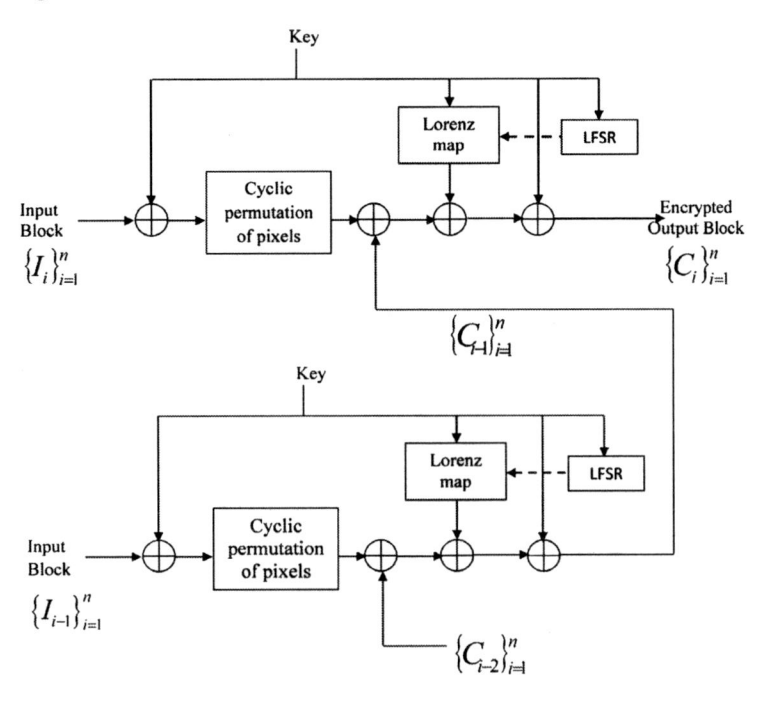

ICAL is uniform and considerably different from that of the original image.

Correlation Coefficient

The correlation coefficient allows the evaluation of the encryption quality. If two pixels are correlated, the correlation coefficient will be close to 1 or -1. A value close to 0 indicates that the two pixels are uncorrelated and unpredictable.

The correlation coefficient is obtained by Equation 19:

$$r_{xy} = \frac{\text{cov}(x,y)}{\sqrt{D(x)}\sqrt{D(y)}} \qquad (19)$$

We calculated the correlation between adjacent pixels for lena image encrypted with ECKBA algorithm, ICAL, (Mansour et al., 2012) algorithm and AES. Table 1 regroups the correlation coefficient

Figure 3. Histograms of the original lena image and the encrypted image by ICAL

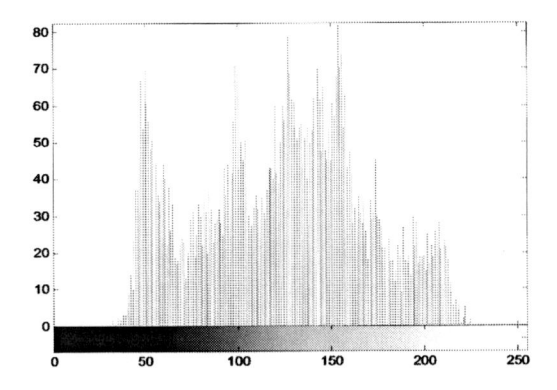

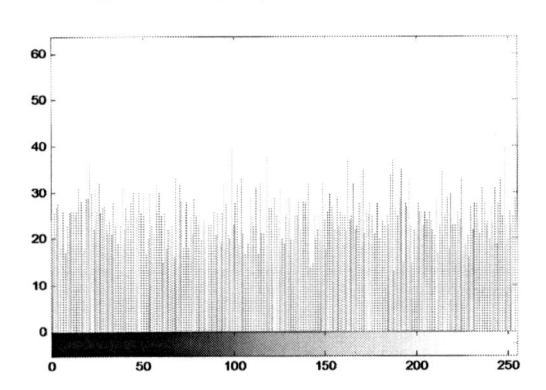

of N pairs of adjacent pixels of the encrypted image in horizontal, vertical and diagonal directions. It shows that ICAL produced lower horizontal and vertical correlation coefficient values than AES (Mansour et al., 2012) algorithm and ECKBA. The diagonal correlation coefficient of ECKBA is slightly lower than the other tested algorithms. We conclude that our proposal reduces the correlation between adjacent pixels and has similar statistical performances compared to AES, ECKBA and (Mansour et al., 2012) algorithm.

Key Space and Key Sensitivity Analysis

The key space of an encryption/decryption algorithm is the total of different keys which can be used in the process of encryption / decryption. It should be large enough (greater than 128 bits) to ensure that a brute force attack is not feasible (Patidar, Pareek, Purohit, & Sud, 2011).

The initial key of ICAL is about 144 bits which includes the initial conditions (x_k, y_k, z_k), the initial integration step of the Lorenz map and the initial seed of LFSR. The number of operations to retrieve the key is about $2^{144} = 2.2301 \times 10^{43}$. The size of the initial key is larger than ECKBA and AES keys (128-bit each one). Mansour et al. (2012) propose a 96-bits key which is smaller than ICAL key. Brute force attack is then infeasible.

We can expand the key space of ICAL by adding the parameters of the discretized Lorenz map, but a study of the lyapunov exponent should be done to calculate the parameter interval which maintain the chaotic aspect of the Lorenz map and minimize the short cycle occurring.

Furthermore, any reliable cipher must be extremely sensitive to minor changes of the secret key to ensure, to some extent, the security against brute force attacks.

A cryptosystem key sensitivity can be observed by two different methods:

- The encrypted image should be very sensitive to the secret key (i.e., if an image is encrypted with two slightly different keys, then the two encrypted images must be completely independent (low correlation)).
- The encrypted image cannot be decrypted correctly if the secret key is slightly changed at the decryption phase.

Table 2 gathers the correlation coefficients calculated for the Lena image encrypted with slightly different key pairs of the studied algorithms.

Encrypted images with ICAL have the lowest correlation coefficient (-0.0008) which means that our proposed algorithm is extremely sensitive to the secret key and robust against exhaustive key search.

Differential Analysis

A desirable property of good cryptosystems is the high sensitivity to small changes in the original image. An opponent can make a slight modification (e.g., one pixel) of the encrypted image and observes the result change. Then, he may be able to find a significant relationship between the original image and the encrypted one. However, if a minor modification in the original image can produce a significant change in the encrypted image, then the differential attack becomes useless.

Table 1. Correlation between adjacent pixels

I. Algorithms	II. Correlation between Adjacent Pixels		
	Horizontal	Vertical	Diagonal
ECKBA	0,0760	0,0227	-0,0012
ICAL	-0,0172	-0,0029	-0,0018
(Mansour et al., 2012)	0,0479	-0,0414	-0,0416
AES	0,0237	-0,0139	-0,0162

Table 2. Correlation coefficient for single-bit different encryption keys

Algorithms	Key pairs	Correlation
ECKBA	Key1 = (132CC12DFB03D6403DFD240); Key2 = (132CC12DFB03D6403DFD241);	-0.0082
(Mansour et al., 2012)	Key1 = (x_0=0.95031;y_0=0.567217;p_1=0.372134;p_2=0.292134) Key2 = (x_0=0.95031005; y_0=0.567217; p_1=0.372134 ; p_2=0.292134)	0.0352
ICAL	Key1 = (x_0=3589; y_0=47542; z_0=32294;Δ=1 ;$LFSR_0$=44257) Key2 = (x_0=3588; y_0=47542; z_0=32294;Δ=1 ;$LFSR_0$=44257)	-0.0008
AES	Key1 = (000102030405060708090a0b0c0d0e0f); Key2 = (000102030405060708090a0b0c0d0e0e);	0.0049

The resistance to differential attacks can be investigated by two common measures; NPCR (Number of Pixels Change Rate), and UACI (Unified Changing Average) defined as:

$$NPCR = \frac{\sum_{i=0}^{M-1}\sum_{j=0}^{N-1} D(i,j)}{M \times N} \times 100 \quad (20)$$

$$UACI = \frac{1}{M \times N}\sum_{i=0}^{M-1}\sum_{j=0}^{N-1} \frac{|I_1(i,j) - I_2(i,j)|}{255} \times 100 \quad (21)$$

where M and N are the width and height of the image.

$I_1(i,j)$ and $I_2(i,j)$ are the pixel values at the (i,j) position of the two encrypted images. The plain-images differ with only one single-bit. I_1 and I_2 are sometimes used as the original image and the encrypted image.

$D(i,j)$ is a matrix of the same size as I_1 and I_2 and defined as:

$$D(i,j) = \begin{cases} 1 & if\ I_1(i,j) \neq I_2(i,j) \\ 0 & else \end{cases} \quad (22)$$

The NPCR measures the different pixels number percentage between two images relative to the total pixels number while the UACI measures the average intensity of differences between the two images.

A high NPCR / UACI score means a strong resistance to differential attacks.

Table 3 shows that ICAL has higher NPCR value than the other studied ciphers. The UACI calculated values of these studied ciphers are lower than those of ICAL except for the AES algorithm.

Table 4 gathered, on the other hand, the NPCR and UACI between two encrypted images with one different pixel of the plain-image. We can notice that ICAL has the best NPCR/UACI. Therefore, it is more sensitive to plain-image and more resistant to differential attacks. We can also conclude that AES and (Mansour et al., 2012) ciphers are indifferent to minor change in the plain-image. The modification of one pixel only affects its corresponding encrypted pixel and not the other pixels in the encrypted image.

Table 3. NPCR And UACI between plain and encrypted image

Algorithms	NPCR (%)	UACI (%)
ECKBA	99,5625	13,4146
(Mansour et al., 2012)	99,5937	13,0731
ICAL	99,7187	28,1804
AES	99,5781	28,2150

Table 4. NPCR and UACI between two encrypted image with one different pixel

Algorithms	NPCR (%)	UACI (%)
ECKBA	100	15,9849
(Mansour et al., 2012)	0,0156	0,0059
ICAL	100	50,3355
AES	0,25	0,0800

Performance Analysis

The encryption speed is an important issue to evaluate the cipher performance. It depends on the processor in use, the operating system, the memory, and the programming language.

Firstly, we have simulated these algorithms using MATLAB in order to quantify the computational complexity of each code. We perform simulations taking as an input to encrypt a gray scale image (80 × 80).

Table 5 contains the execution time ratio (ICAL as reference) required for each algorithm to encrypt the gray scale image.

By using MATLAB to calculate the time execution ratio, we were able to realize that ICAL has the lowest complexity and it meets the known cryptographic criteria. In fact, it is lighter and more suitable for sensor networks. We also excluded ECKBA algorithm regarding the high ratio compared with ICAL.

Performance analysis simulated with MATLAB is also an indicator of energy consumption during the code implementation on the sensor nodes. Moreover, these obtained results encourage us to implement ICAL in a real wireless sensor network testbed.

IMPLEMENTATION ON WIRELESS SENSOR NETWORK

The recent advance in wireless communications and microelectronics has led to the development of a new technology of low power and low cost multifunctional wireless sensors. These sensors are equipped with embedded processors that allow them to perform simple operations and transmit partially treated data. These properties have attracted more attention to the need for Wireless Sensor Network (WSN) and extend the application domains to many high-end applications. A wireless sensor network consists of a large number of sensor nodes which condense in the medium to explore. The node positions are not fixed, which allowed deployment flexibility especially in an abrupt and dangerous environment.

In this section we will enumerate first some applications of the wireless sensor networks, and then we will present the used wireless sensor network simulators and we will give a detailed explanation on how to use the SensLab platform to perform experiments and measures. The final subsection will expose the energy consumption of our proposed algorithm by simulations and when implemented on SensLab sensors. The results are compared to the energy consumption of the standard AES algorithm with 128 bits key length.

Wireless Sensor Network Applications

Sensor networks have a wide spectrum of applications ranging from military to everyday life.

- **Military Applications:** Wireless sensor networks are a promising technology for military applications owing to some spe-

Table 5. Execution time ratio of the simulated algorithms

Algorithms	Execution Time Ratio
ICAL	1
(Mansour et al., 2012)	2.046
AES	5.88
ECKBA	139.242

cific characteristics such as rapid deployment, self-organization and graceful degradation. These networks have generally a defensive role. In fact, they monitor enemy or friendly forces. They gather information about their states, their equipment and their geo-localizations. In wartime, they monitor the battlefield, detect and foresee nuclear (WATS project: identify nuclear devices by detection of neutrons and gamma rays [Gosnell, et al., 1997]), biological (JBREWS project [Brown, 1999]), or chemical terrorist attacks. The data sent by the sensor nodes in this case are of great strategic and security importance and must be hidden and not spotted by the enemy.

- **Medical Applications:** The wireless sensor networks can be applied to the local or remote monitoring of patients. They can record and sometimes send their vital signs such as temperature, blood glucose level, blood pressure or heartbeat, to the attending physicians. They can help disabled patients by detecting their falls, their movements or schedule their medication.
- **Environment Monitoring:** Wireless sensor network could be widely used to detect and predict flood, dams collapse, landslides, earthquake, forest devastating fire, volcano eruption, or even invasive Tsunami. They could prevent damages and warn the authorities about an incoming disaster.
- **Ecological Protection:** Sensors can be deployed to track species in danger of extinction or to improve research on animals and birds. Notable research projects were conducted on seabirds by the universities of California and Berkeley using wireless motes (Iyengar, 2011).
- **Home Automation:** It boils down to the concept of smart home where sensors are embedded in appliances or inside the house. These sensors can detect the presence of the owner and automatically launch his corresponding program (brightness, television, shutters...). In case of burglary they can also trigger an alarm system linked to the owner or to the police.

Simulators and Experimental Testbed

Simulation and practice are two essential phases of cipher design. The simulation could estimate the performances of a given cipher with expectable accuracy which depends on the operating system, the calculator precision and frequency as well as the simulator's models. In the other hand, the real experiments could validate or reject simulated results and prove the efficiency or the failure of an encryption algorithm.

WSIM and Wsnet Simulators

Many simulation tools have been developed for sensor networks such as Tossim, Atemu, Avrora and WSIM / Wsnet simulators. These simulators differ in their development language (NESC for Tossim, and Java for Avrora) and the type of the supported microcontroller. For example, Avrora and Atemu are emulators processors used in AVR processors of the MICA2 sensors. We chose to use WSIM / Wsnet for two reasons: First, because they support MSP430 microcontrollers integrated on WSN430 SensLab nodes, and second because the codes are written in C, which offers more flexibility and compatibility with other programming languages.

WSIM and Wsnet are two complementary integrated simulation tools. WSIM is a system emulator for microcontrollers based platforms. It supports cycle accuracy level for platform simulation. It can perform a complete simulation of hardware event and give the developer an accurate timing analysis of the simulated software. An accurate estimation of timing, memory usage and power can be obtained during simulation.

Moreover, WSIM may be used in standalone mode, for debugging code when there is not a radio device used. Wsnet is an event simulator of sensor networks. It includes realistic models of sensor nodes used in WSIM.

We chose to run our codes on a WSIM platform of MSP430 microcontroller MSP430f1611 with 16 bits and Ti CC1100 Radio chipset.

The developed codes on these simulators are directly portable and executable on the SensLab nodes without modification.

SensLab Platform

Admittedly, the simulation is an important step to code debugging, to estimate and to optimize the cipher performances but, it remains limited and suffers from several drawbacks such as assumptions and approximations which sometimes hinder accuracy. Then we need to validate our algorithm using a real wireless sensor network platform.

To achieve real experiments, there are many wireless sensor network testbeds such as Motelab testbed (developed by Harvard university in 2005), Twist testbed (developed at Berlin university in 2006), Indriya testbed (developed at Singapore university in 2009), etc…The major drawback for all the existing testbeds is the limited number of available sensors, so they are not classified as large scale platforms. We decided to achieve our experiments on a platform called SensLab.

SensLab is an open large scale platform. It has 1024 nodes deployed at four sites namely: Rennes, Lilles, Strasbourg and Grenoble.

SensLab node has three modules: a gateway and two wsn430 nodes powered by a battery and a DC power supply.

- **Open Node:** The user has access to this node and he can program it. All Applications are running on this node.
- **Control Node:** The user does not have access to this node. However, it can record useful information such as signal quality, energy consumption and then set the power supply type (AC or battery).
- **Gateway:** It helps to reprogram, control, power and connect the open node and the control node with the server. The connection is established by their IP addresses.

Additional elements can be added such as a GPS or an accelerometer.

Each Wsn430 node is equipped with:

- A Ti-f1611 MSP430 16-bit microcontroller with a frequency equal to 8MHz. It has 10KB of RAM and 48 KB of ROM. The included devices are: two USART modules with SPI, I2C and UART interfaces; a watchdog; DMA; ADC / DAC converter with 12 bit resolution. It can be programmed via JTAG or BSL.
- Three physical sensors: acoustic (omnidirectional microphone KECG1540), brightness (Taos TSL2550) and temperature (Maxim DS1722).
- A radio interface Ti CC2420 (2.4 GHz) or CC1101 (868MHz).
- An external flash memory ST M25P80 (1MB).
- A battery Varta Polyflex (Chaballier, 2008).

Energy Consumption

A wireless sensor has low power computing devices, low storage memory and especially low energy resources (Anastasi, Conti, Francesco & Passarella, 2009; Li, Ling, Znati, Wu, 2006; Kaps & Sunar, 2006).

Energy consumption is very critical since nodes placed in nature include limited battery lifetime and replacing them is not evident, hence we need to focus on this aspect in order to extend the battery lifetime.

We tested our algorithm ICAL by using WSIM and Wsnet. We encrypt and decrypt the data on the same node and on different nodes as well. With Esimu we evaluate the number of cycles and the energy consumed in joules for each function of our code.

Esimu is a complete energy model of system based on non-intrusive measurements.

This model is designed to be integrated into cycle accurate and fast simulation tools in order to give a feedback on energy consumption of the embedded systems software programming. The given estimation is independent from the compilation tools or software components such as the network protocols or the operating systems (Fournel, Fraboulet, & Feautrier, 2007).

The assessments take into account the whole system consumption including peripherals. Esimu is then an energy consumption simulator for embedded system platforms, such as the nodes of the sensor network.

Experiences of the developers on a complex ARM9 platform show that the model estimations engender an error less than 10% compared to the consumption of a real system, whereas for a WSN430 platform the error rate is less than 5% which are sufficiently precise and acceptable for the design of source code. In our case, we used Esimu to estimate the energy consumed from the execution traces of WSIM.

The energy consumed in Joule for encrypting and decrypting a block of 16 bytes is 3.7756×10^{-5} J for the encryption function and 3.7767×10^{-5} J for the decryption function. The two functions have almost the same value and the total energy consumed by our proposal ICAL is 7.5523×10^{-5} J.

The second algorithm that we simulate is the AES algorithm. The energy consumption of all the AES function is given as Table 6.

Despite the use of an optimized AES version which is based on look-up-tables (instead of constructing the S-Box and its inverse), the total simulated energy consumption is 8.07×10^{-5} J.

Table 6. Energy consumption of the different AES functions

AES functions	Energy consumption (10^{-6} J)
Encryption function	0.993
Mixsubcolumn function (subbyte+mixcolumn)	15.283
Shiftrow Function	6.62
Decryption function	1.082
Invmixsubcolumn	23.816
Invshiftrow function	6.62
Key establishment function	16.4
Add round Key function	7.774

The second phase is to achieve the real experiments. For this purpose, we implement our encryption algorithm and an optimized AES version (using the lookuptable) on real wireless sensor network testbed called SensLab.

We measure the energy consumption for 16 bytes encrypted test vector (Table 7). We find that AES consumes $1.618 \cdot 10^{-4}$ J and our proposed cipher consumes $8.97 \cdot 10^{-5}$ J.

These results verify the simulation values and show that our proposed algorithm preserves the energy and it can be implemented on the real sensor nodes without affecting their performances. This reduced consumption is due to the good choice of the chaotic map and the simplicity of the basic functions of our algorithm. Optimization and reduction in numbers of instructions is considered by adopting a non-sequential and parallel programming code.

The obtained results confirm the performances analysis in the previous section and demonstrate

Table 7. Energy consumption of AES and ICAL tested on SensLab

Algorithms	Energy consumption (10^{-4} J)
AES	1.618
ICAL	0.897

that our proposed cipher ICAL has the best performance and it is suitable to wireless sensor network security.

CONCLUSION

Security in wireless sensor network is becoming an important issue since the wireless sensors are being employed in many critical domains. If the gathered information is an image, more attention should be paid to the execution time and the energy consumption as well as reliability. Indeed, some studies proved the flaws of conventional encryption algorithms such as DES and AES for image and video encryption. Due to their extreme sensitivity to initial conditions and their random-like behavior, chaotic dynamics seem to be a good alternative to enhance the performance or replace these algorithms.

In this chapter, we proposed a new image encryption algorithm dedicated to wireless sensor network. ICAL is a simple and effective algorithm in CBC mode that applies the techniques of diffusion, confusion and whitening.

We have demonstrated by statistical, differential, key space and key sensitivity security analysis that ICAL is reliable and can withstand conventional cryptanalysis techniques. We compared its performances with AES algorithm and other ciphers based on chaotic dynamics. ICAL has the lowest correlation between adjacent pixels and it has the best NPCR/UACI ratio. We also noticed its extreme sensitivity to the secret key.

We simulated our chaotic dynamic cipher with Wsim/Wsnet simulators and then we implemented it on a real sensor nodes platform (SensLab) equipped with Ti MSP430f1611 microcontroller. The measured energy consumption (simulation and experimental result) is better than an optimized version of AES algorithm that we also implemented.

We can conclude that ICAL, with its good performance, is suitable for the security of wireless sensor network.

The future work will focus on optimizing the speed of the encryption/decryption process by using parallel programming. The key size of ICAL could be extended and more security analysis could be done.

REFERENCES

Abd El-Wahed, M., Mesbah, S., & Shoukry, A. (2008). Efficiency and security of some image encryption algorithms. In *Proceedings of the World Congress on Engineering* (Vol. 1, pp. 561-564). IEEE.

Alvarez, G., & Li, S. (2006). Some basic cryptographic requirements for chaos-based cryptosystems. *International Journal of Bifurcation and Chaos in Applied Sciences and Engineering*, *16*(8), 2129–2151. doi:10.1142/S0218127406015970.

Alvarez, G., Montoya, F., Romera, M., & Pastor, G. (1999). Chaotic cryptosystems. In L. D. Sanson (Ed.), *Proceedings of the 33rd Annual International Carnahan Conference on Security Technology*, (pp. 332–338). IEEE.

Anastasi, G., Conti, M., Francesco, M. D., & Passarella, A. (2009). Energy conservation in wireless sensor networks: A survey. *Ad Hoc Networks*, *7*(3), 537–568. doi:10.1016/j.adhoc.2008.06.003.

Awad, A., El Assad, S., & Carragata, D. (2008). *A robust cryptosystem based chaos for secure data*. Paper presented at IEEE, ISIVC Conference on Image/Video Communications over Fixed and Mobile Networks. Bilbao, Spain.

Bose, R., & Pathak, S. (2006). A novel compression and encryption scheme using variable model arithmetic coding and coupled chaotic system. *Transactions on Circuits and Systems*, *53*(4).

Brown, M. J. (1999). *Users guide developed for the JBREWS project* (Technical Report LA-UR-99-4676). Los Alamos, CA: Los Alamos National Laboratory of California University.

Chaballier, C. (2008). *SensLab D1.1a: SensLAB node hardware*. Retrieved from www.senslab.info

Chen, S., Zhong, X. X., & Wu, Z. Z. (2008). Block chaos cipher for wireless sensor network. *Science in China Series F – Information Science, 51*, 1055–1063. doi:10.1007/s11432-008-0102-5.

Ebrahimi, T., Leprévost, F., & Warusfel, B. (2006). *Cryptographie et sécurité des systèmes et réseaux: Sous la direction de Touradj Ebrahimi, Franck Leprévost, Bertrand Warusfel*. Paris: Hermès Science.

Fang, Q., Liu, Y., & Zhao, X. (2008). A chaos-based secure cluster protocol for wireless sensor networks. *International Journal of the Institute of Information Theory and Automation Kybernetika, 44*(4), 522–533.

Fournel, N., Fraboulet, A., & Feautrier, P. (2007). eSimu: A fast and accurate energy consumption simulator for real embedded system. In *Proceedings of WOWMOM: IEEE International Symposium on a World of Wireless Mobile and Multimedia Networks*. IEEE.

Furht, B., Socek, D., & Eskicioglu, A. M. (2004). Fundamentals of multimedia encryption techniques. In Furht, B., & Kirovski, D. (Eds.), *Multimedia Security Handbook*. Boca Raton, FL: CRC Press. doi:10.1201/9781420038262.

Gosnell, T. B., Hall, J. M., Ham, C. L., Knapp, D. A., Koenig, Z. M., & Luke, S. J. ... Wolford, J.K. (1997). *Gamma-ray identification of nuclear weapon materials* (Technical Report DE97053424). Livermore, CA: Lawrence Livermore National Lab.

Heys, H., & Adams, C. (Eds.). (1999). *Proceedings of Selected Areas in Cryptography: 6th Annual International Workshop*. Berlin: Springer.

Iyengar, S. S. (2011). *Fundamentals of sensor network programming: Applications and technology*. Oxford, UK: Wiley-Blackwell.

Jakimoski, G., & Kocarev, L. (2001). Chaos and cryptography: Block encryption ciphers based on chaotic maps. *IEEE Transactions on Circuits and Systems: Fundamental Theory and Applications, 48*(2), 163–169. doi:10.1109/81.904880.

Kaps, J. P., & Sunar, B. (2006). Energy comparison of AES and SHA-1 for ubiquitous computing. *Lecture Notes in Computer Science, 4097*, 372–380. doi:10.1007/11807964_38.

Kavitha, T., & Sridharan, D. (2010). Security vulnerabilities in wireless sensor networks: A survey. Journal of Information Assurance and Security, (5), 31-44.

Li, G., Ling, H., Znati, T., & Wu, W. (2006). A robust on-demand path-key establishment framework via random key predistribution for wireless sensor network. *EURASIP Journal on Wireless Communications and Networking, 2*, 1–10. doi:10.1155/WCN/2006/91304.

Li, S. (2003). *Analyses and new designs of digital chaotic ciphers*. (Ph. D. Dissertation). Xi'an Jiaotong University, Shaanxi, China.

Lian, S. (2009). A block cipher based on chaotic neural networks. *Neurocomputing, 72*, 1296–1301. doi:10.1016/j.neucom.2008.11.005.

Mansour, I., Chalhoub, G., & Bakhache, B. (2012). *Evaluation of a fast symmetric cryptographic algorithm based on the chaos theory for wireless sensor networks*. Paper presented at MWNS International Symposium on Mobile Wireless Network Security. New York, NY.

Masuda, N., & Aihara, K. (2002). Cryptosystems with discretized chaotic maps. *IEEE Transactions on Circuits and Systems, 49*, 28–40. doi:10.1109/81.974872.

Noura, H., El Assad, S., Vladeanu, C., & Caragata, D. (2011). *An efficient and secure SPN cryptosystem based on chaotic control parameters*. Paper presented at the 6th International Conference on Internet Technology and Secured Transactions. Abu Dhabi, UAE.

Pareek, N. K., Patidar, V., & Sud, K. K. (2003). Discrete chaotic cryptography using external key. *Physics Letters. [Part A], 309*, 75–82. doi:10.1016/S0375-9601(03)00122-1.

Patidar, V., Pareek, N. K., Purohit, G., & Sud, K. K. (2011). A robust and secure chaotic standard map based pseudorandom permutation-substitution scheme for image encryption. *Optics Communications, 284*, 4331–4339. doi:10.1016/j.optcom.2011.05.028.

Pecorra, L., & Carrol, T. (1990). Synchronization in chaotic systems. *Physical Review Letters, 64*(8), 821–824. doi:10.1103/PhysRevLett.64.821 PMID:10042089.

Philip, M., & Das, A. (2011). Survey: Image encryption using chaotic cryptography schemes. *International Journal of Computers and Applications*, (1): 1–4.

Rivest, R., Robshaw, M., & Yiqun Lisa Yin, R. S. (1998). *The RC6 block cipher, v1.1*. Retrieved from http://theory.lcs.mit.edu/~rivest/

Rivest, R. L. (1995). The RC5 encryption algorithm. In *Proceedings of Fast Software Encryption (LNCS)* (pp. 86–96). Berlin: Springer. doi:10.1007/3-540-60590-8_7.

Schneier, B. (1996). *Applied cryptography: Protocols, algorithms, and source code in C (cloth)* (2nd ed.). New York: John Wiley & Sons, Inc..

Shannon, C. E. (1949). Communication theory of secrecy system. *The Bell System Technical Journal, 28*, 656–715.

Silva, R. M., Crespo, R. G., & Nunes, M. S. (2009). LoBa128, a lorenz based PRNG for wireless sensor networks. *International Journal of Communication Networks and Distributed Systems, 3*(4), 301–318. doi:10.1504/IJCNDS.2009.027596.

Silva, R. M., Crespo, R. G., & Nunes, M. S. (2010). Enhanced chaotic stream cipher for WSNs. In *Proceedings of the IEEE International Conference on Availability, Reliability and Security*, (pp. 210-215). IEEE.

Socek, D., Li, S., Magliveras, S. S., & Furht, B. (2005). Enhanced 1-D chaotic key based algorithm for image encryption. In *Proceedings of the IEEE Security and Privacy for Emerging Areas in Communications Networks* (pp. 406-407). IEEE.

Stavroulakis, P. (2006). *Chaos applications in telecommunications*. Boca Raton, FL: CRC.

Tao, S., Ruili, W., & Yixun, Y. (1998). Perturbance-based algorithm to expand cycle length of chaotic key stream. *Electronics Letters, 34*(9), 873–874. doi:10.1049/el:19980680.

Xiang, T. (2007). A novel symmetrical cryptosystem based on discretized two-dimensional chaotic map. *Physics Letters. [Part A], 364*(3-4), 252–258. doi:10.1016/j.physleta.2006.12.020.

Yang, J., Xiao, D., & Xiang, T. (2011). Cryptanalysis of a chaos block cipher for wireless sensor network. *Communications in Nonlinear Science and Numerical Simulation, 16*, 844–850. doi:10.1016/j.cnsns.2010.05.005.

Yen, J. C., & Guo, J. I. (2000). A new chaotic key-based design for image encryption and decryption. In *Proceedings of 2000 IEEE International Conference on Circuits and Systems* (ISACS 2000), (vol. 4, pp. 49–52). IEEE.

Zaibi, G., Peyrard, F., Kachouri, A., Fournier-Prunaret, D., & Samet, M. (2010). A new design of dynamic S-box based on two chaotic maps. In *Proceedings of the ACS/IEEE International Conference on Computer Systems and Applications - AICCSA 2010*(AICCSA '10). IEEE Computer Society.

Zhou, T., Yu, M., & Ye, Y. (2006). A robust high-speed chaos-based truly random number generator for embedded cryptosystems. In *Proceeding of Circuits and Systems*. IEEE. doi:10.1109/MWSCAS.2006.381785.

KEY TERMS AND DEFINITIONS

Chaotic Signals: Chaotic signals are generated by nonlinear dynamic systems. They are extreme sensitive to initial conditions and have random-like behavior. The chaos is used to encrypt information.

Encryption: Encryption is the fact of scrambling and encoding information in order to protect it from intruder. Only the legal user can decrypt and read the information.

Energy Consumption: The energy consumption is the amount of power consumed from the battery to execute a program or a code.

Implementation: Implementation is the carrying out of a design or a program, properly, in its target environment.

Information Security: Securing the data is protecting it from alteration and illegal use. Encryption algorithms can ensure the security of information.

SensLab Platform: SensLab is a real wireless sensor testbed, deployed in four sites in France. It offers 1024 different nodes to fulfill experiments via distant communication.

Wireless Sensor Network: The wireless sensor network is composed of tiny nodes with reduced battery power and restricted resources. Sensors gather the information from the insecure field and then communication devices transmit the data.

Chapter 5
A Polling Booth-Based Electronic Voting Scheme

Md. Abdul Based
Norwegian University of Science and Technology, Norway

ABSTRACT

A Polling booth-based Electronic Voting Scheme (PEVS) is presented in this chapter. The scheme allows only eligible voters to cast their ballots inside polling booths, and the ballots cast by the eligible voters are inalterable and non-reusable. The scheme provides vote-privacy and receipt-freeness. The scheme is modeled to fend off forced-abstention attacks, simulation attacks, or randomization attacks. Thus, the scheme is coercion-resistant. The scheme also satisfies voter verifiability, universal verifiability, and eligibility verifiability requirements. The ProVerif tool is used to formally analyze soundness, vote-privacy, receipt-freeness, and coercion-resistance of the scheme. The analysis shows that PEVS satisfies these properties. PEVS is the first electronic voting scheme (polling booth-based) that satisfies all the requirements listed above.

INTRODUCTION

Trusted election processes and outcomes are fundamental requirements to democratic societies. Government leaders must be elected in a proper way so that they can truly represent people's opinion and therefore, people can trust them. One possible solution could be a secure electronic voting scheme to reduce election problems and irregularities, especially in the countries where voting is a prominent issue.

The complex requirements of a secure electronic voting (e-voting) scheme include among others, the eligibility of the voter (Backes, Hritcu, & Maffei, 2008), inalterability and non-reusability of the ballot (Backes, Hritcu, & Maffei, 2008),

DOI: 10.4018/978-1-4666-4514-1.ch005

vote-privacy (Delaune, Kremer, & Ryan, 2008), receipt-freeness (Delaune, Kremer, & Ryan, 2008), coercion-resistance (Juels, Catalano, & Jakobsson, 2005), and verifiability (Delaune, Kremer, & Ryan, 2008).

Eligibility means only the legitimate voters are allowed to cast their ballots. *Inalterability* ensures that the ballot cast by an eligible voter should not be altered and *non-reusability* ensures that each voter should be allowed to cast a ballot only once. Backes et al. (Backes, Hritcu, & Maffei, 2008) summarize these properties under the notion soundness of an election scheme.

According to Delaune et al. (Delaune, Kremer, & Ryan, 2008), vote-privacy, receipt-freeness, and coercion-resistance are the privacy requirements of a secure e-voting scheme. The property vote-privacy states that it is not possible to reveal for which candidate the voter casts the ballot, receipt-freeness means a voter cannot convince the coercer how the ballot was cast, and coercion-resistance means a coercer should not be able to force a voter to abstain from voting or to cast a ballot for a particular candidate or in a particular way (Juels, Catalano, & Jakobsson, 2005).

Verifiability means voter verifiability and universal verifiability. If the voter can verify that the ballot has been counted properly then the scheme is called voter verifiable and when any observer can verify that the published tally is the outcome of the cast ballots then the scheme is called universally verifiable. Delaune et al. (Delaune, Kremer, & Ryan, 2008) introduced a third aspect of verifiability; eligibility verifiability. Eligibility verifiability means the ballot in the tally is cast by an eligible voter and there is at most one ballot for each voter.

There are two categories of e-voting in terms of control of people and terminals. These are remote e-voting and polling booth based e-voting. A voter can cast a ballot from any place in a remote e-voting scheme. There is no cryptographic way to defend a voter from physical coercion in such voting. In the second category, a voter casts the ballot inside a polling booth (also known as election booth). Cryptographic mechanisms are then used inside the booth to achieve receipt-freeness and coercion-resistance. Since remote e-voting cannot achieve coercion-resistance, we choose polling booth based e-voting and name our scheme Polling booth-based Electronic Voting Scheme (PEVS). A preliminary version of PEVS is published in (Based, Tsay, & Mjølsnes, 2012) without the detail of the formal analysis of PEVS. However, this chapter describes PEVS in detail and provides the detail of the formal analysis of PEVS.

Figure 1 shows the basic diagram of PEVS. In PEVS the voter can generate any number of key pairs using the voter computer inside the polling booth. Each pair consists of a private key and a corresponding public key. The registrar signs the public keys in a blind signature scheme to ensure that there is no link between the voter and the keys. This satisfies the vote-privacy requirement. The voter computer inside the booth performs the cryptographic tasks to construct the ballot using one of these keys. So, the voter cannot prove to anyone how the ballot is cast and this satisfies the receipt-freeness requirement.

In a forced-abstention attack the attacker coerces a voter by demanding that the voter refrains from voting (Juels, Catalano, & Jakobsson, 2002). PEVS is modeled to fend off this attack by allowing the voter to cast the ballot using one key pair and the voter gives the coercer the number of unused key pairs requested by the coercer before the voter enters the polling booth. In a simulation attack the attacker coerces a voter by demanding that the voter divulges the private keys so that the attacker can simulate the voter on his behalf (Juels, Catalano, & Jakobsson, 2002) and in a randomization attack the attacker coerces a voter by demanding that the voter submits randomly composed balloting material to nullify the choice with a large probability (Juels, Catalano, & Jakobsson, 2002). In PEVS the coercer cannot perform these attacks

Figure 1. PEVS: VC = voter computer, R = registrar, BA = ballot acquirer, BB = bulletin board, and CS = counting server (Based, Tsay, & Mjølsnes, 2012)

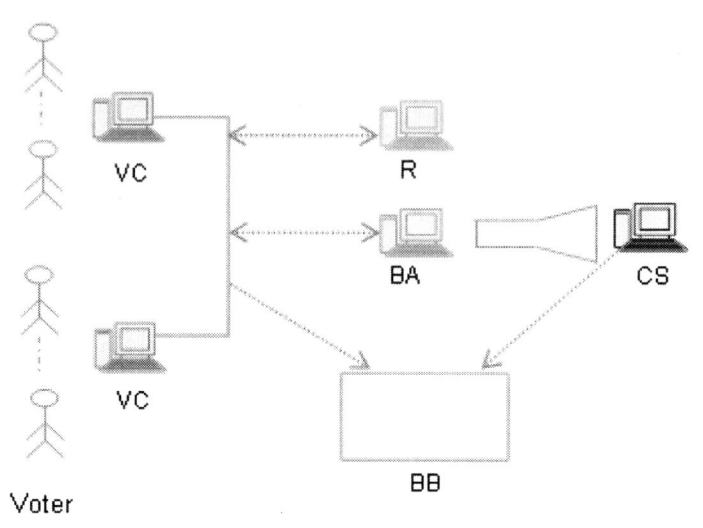

since the voter casts the ballot with the fresh keys only inside the booth. Thus PEVS is coercion-resistant. For the detail of these attacks we refer to Backes, Hritcu, and Maffei (2008) and Juels, Catalano, & Jakobsson (2002).

PEVS uses a bulletin board, the content of the bulletin board is public and anyone can verify it. On the bulletin board, the voters can verify the keys signed and published by the counting servers. This indicates that their ballots have been counted since the keys were associated with the ballots by the voters using the voter computer. Thus, PEVS satisfies the voter verifiability requirement. The counting servers also publish the ballots and the tally on the bulletin board. Any observer can verify that the tally corresponds to the published ballots and this satisfies the universal verifiability requirement. The keys published on the bulletin board are signed by the registrar. The registrar only signs the keys of the eligible voters. By allowing the observers to verify the signature of the registrar on these keys, PEVS achieves the eligibility verifiability requirement.

With the ProVerif tool (Blanchet, 2001; Blanchet, Cheval, Allamigeon, & Smyth, 2012), we formally analyze vote-privacy, receipt-freeness, and coercion-resistance of PEVS. We also verify soundness of PEVS with ProVerif. We believe that PEVS is the first polling booth based e-voting scheme that satisfies all these required properties.

In the following sections, we first provide the background information and related works. Then we present our voting scheme as a message sequence diagram followed by the security analysis of the scheme. The conclusions and future plans are presented towards the end of this chapter.

BACKGROUND AND RELATED WORK

Though there is not much software available that can be purchased or downloaded for running e-voting, there are many countries that have already introduced e-voting in their areas. For example, the United Kingdom in 2002 and 2003, and the Dutch government in 2004, and the French government in 2007 ran e-voting. However, the first country that introduced Internet voting is Estonia for elections in March 2007 (The Internet Rights Forum, 2003; European University Institute, 2007). For the municipal and regional elections of 2011, the Norwegian Ministry of Local Government and Regional Development (KRD) ran an electronic voting pilot project (E-valg 2011 Project) (Gjøsteen, 2010). Flaws are found in both voting schemes in Estonia (European University Institute, 2007) and Norway (Cortier & Wiedling, 2012).

Nielsen et al. (Nielsen, Andersen, & Nielson, 1996) and Delaune et al. (Delaune, Kremer, & Ryan, 2008) analyze the 'FOO92' protocol (Fujioka, Okamoto, & Ohta, 1992) (which is based on a blind signature scheme) and show that the protocol is not receipt-free. PEVS is receipt-free, and also uses a blind signature technique in order to get signed keys for the voter from the registrar.

Benaloh and Tuinstra introduce receipt-freeness in (Benaloh & Tuinstra, 1994), and receipt-freeness in mix-net based voting protocols is presented in (Lee, Boyd, Dawson, Kim, Yang, & Yoo, 2004). Formal definitions of vote-privacy, receipt-freeness and coercion-resistance applied to different voting schemes (Fujioka, Okamoto, & Ohta, 1992; Lee, Boyd, Dawson, Kim, Yang, & Yoo, 2004; Okamoto, 1996) are provided by Delaune et al. in (Delaune, Kremer, & Ryan, 2008). However, the definition of coercion-resistance (Delaune, Kremer, & Ryan, 2008) is not suitable for automatic verification. A voting scheme with an aim to be coercion-resistant is published in (Okamoto, 1996). A flaw was found in (Okamoto, 1996) due to the lack of formal definitions and proofs of receipt-freeness and coercion-resistance in (Benaloh & Tuinstra, 1994). Helios (Adida, 2008) is a Web-based open-audit voting scheme and provides verifiability. Ryan et al. (Ryan & Teague, 2009) show that Helios is not receipt free.

Clarkson et al. implement a remote electronic voting system in (Clarkson, Chong, & Myers, 2008). This system is called Civitas and is based on the voting scheme published by Juels et al. (Juels, Catalano, & Jakobsson, 2002; Juels, Catalano, & Jakobsson, 2005). If the coercer is able to see how the voter is casting the ballot, a remote voting scheme can never be completely coercion-resistant. In addition, the paper-based voting schemes are not coercion-resistant if there are options for postal voting. Civitas shows some sort of coercion-resistance under the assumption that all the talliers are honest. In Civitas a voter is allowed to cheat the coercer with fake credentials and then any ballot cast by the coercer with the fake credentials are silently dropped by the counting servers. Compared to Civitas, PEVS uses polling booths, which are controlled environments where physical coercion is not possible. Also, PEVS requires only a threshold number of counting servers to act honestly.

A formal definition of coercion-resistance that can be used for automatic verification for remote electronic voting schemes is provided by Backes et al. (Backes, Hritcu, & Maffei, 2008). We adopt their definition of coercion-resistance to polling booth based voting schemes and verify coercion-resistance of PEVS. Furthermore, we analyze vote-privacy and receipt-freeness using the definitions in (Delaune, Kremer, & Ryan, 2008). Regarding the ballot construction in a secret sharing scheme and counting of ballots, we refer to (Based & Mjølsnes, 2009; Based & Mjølsnes, 2010; Schoenmakers, 1999). For the verification of ballots by the counting servers, we refer to the non-interactive zero-knowledge protocol (Based & Mjølsnes, 2009; Based & Mjølsnes, 2010).

The VoteBox (Sandler, Derr, & Wallach, 2008) and the scheme in (Benaloh, 2006) are two verifiable electronic voting schemes. These two schemes are not yet formally analyzed and coercion-resistance is not addressed explicitly. In the current form (The voter sees the VoteBox page for voting and can verify the vote later), VoteBox is not immune to forced-abstention attacks. In the Benaloh scheme (Benaloh, 2006), the voter swipes the magnetic-stripe card through a reader to record the encrypted ballot together with the voter's name. The voter then can leave the poll with the magnetic-stripe card and later confirm (if desired) that the encrypted ballot is properly associated with the voter's name on the published set of the encrypted ballots which will be used to verify the tally. Since voter's name is associated with the encrypted ballots, this scheme cannot be immune to forced-abstention attacks. An Internet voting scheme is presented in (Based & Mjølsnes, 2011). However, the scheme is also not formally analyzed and not immune to forced-abstention attacks. A paper-based voting system is presented in [Rivest, R. L. (2006)].

Bingo Voting [Bohli, J. M., Mueller-Quade, J., & Roehrich, S. (2007)] scheme is a local e-voting protocol and is designed for remote electronic voting. Since the design is for remote voting, this scheme does not protect against over-the-shoulder attacks (The coercer can watch or influence a voter in an over-the-shoulder attack). The Mental Voting Booths (Dossogne & Lafitte, 2012) scheme does not protect the voter from an attacker denying him access to a computer or rendering his ballots void by entering random values as input to the voting system. Thus, this scheme is not immune to randomization attacks.

The voting protocols in (Backes, Hritcu, & Maffei, 2008; Delaune, Kremer, & Ryan, 2008; Kremer & Ryan, 2005) are analyzed using (variants of) the applied pi calculus (Abad & Fournet, 2001) with the advantage that the analyses can be conducted automatically with the ProVerif (Blanchet, 2001; Blanchet, Cheval, Allamigeon, & Smyth, 2012) tool. We also take this advantage and apply ProVerif to automatically verify soundness, vote-privacy, receipt-freeness, and coercion-resistance properties of PEVS.

THE POLLING BOOTH-BASED ELECTRONIC VOTING SCHEME (PEVS)

The message sequence diagram of the Polling booth-based Electronic Voting Scheme (PEVS) is shown in Figure 2. There are Voters (V), Voter Computers (VC), a Ballot Acquirer (BA), a Registrar (R), a Bulletin Board (BB), and a set of Counting Servers (CS) in PEVS. We assume that there are polling booths in which the voters cast their ballots and the polling booths are controlled by the election officials or independent authorities. Though PEVS allows multiple voters to cast their ballots in the same polling booth, only one voter is allowed inside the booth at a specific time. That is, a voter is not allowed to interact with other voters or the attackers inside a booth.

We present the voter and the voter computer as a single entity in Figure 2. The underlying assumption is that all operations of the voter (for example, encryption, decryption, and digital signature) will be performed by the voter computer. In addition, the voter communicates with other parties using the voter computer. The honest parties of PEVS are: the registrar, the voter computer, and a threshold number of counting servers. The voter and the counting servers communicate with the bulletin board over the Internet. We also assume that the counting servers perform the same role though these servers are different parties and the communication between them is done over authenticated and encrypted channels. Other communications between different parties are done over the Internet.

The notations used in PEVS are: K is a public key, K^{-1} is the private key of K, K' is the blinded copy of K. $\{m\}_{K^{-1}}$ is the signature of the message m under the key K^{-1}. $[m]_K$ is the encryption of the plain text m under the key K.

In practice, voter authentication can be done by using a smartcard with local biometric identification (fingerprint) technology. For example, the voter first inserts the smartcard into a smartcard reader and supplies his fingerprint by the fingerprint scanner on the smartcard. The smartcard verifies the fingerprint of the voter, the Web server then authenticates the smartcard and the voter gets access to the voting protocol.

Inside the booth the voter can generate an unbounded number of keys according to the request of the coercer in a forced-abstention attack. That is, if the coercer requests n key pairs from the voter, then the voter typically generates $n+1$ key pairs.

Figure 2. The message sequence diagram of PEVS: V = voter, VC = voter computer, R = registrar, BA = ballot acquirer, CS = counting server, and BB = bulletin board

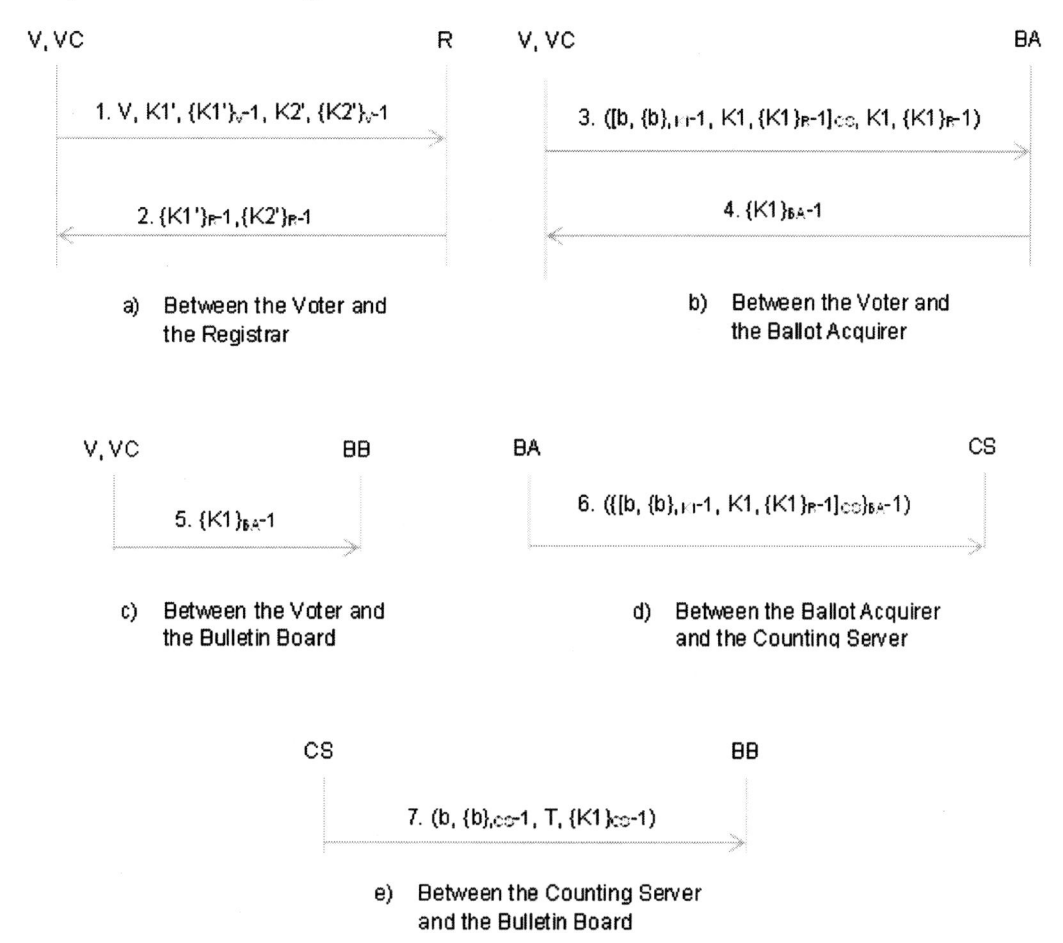

V, VC → R

1. V, K1', {K1'}$_{V^{-1}}$, K2', {K2'}$_{V^{-1}}$

2. {K1'}$_{R^{-1}}$, {K2'}$_{R^{-1}}$

a) Between the Voter and the Registrar

V, VC → BA

3. ([b, {b}$_{K1^{-1}}$, K1, {K1}$_{R^{-1}}$]$_{CS}$, K1, {K1}$_{R^{-1}}$)

4. {K1}$_{BA^{-1}}$

b) Between the Voter and the Ballot Acquirer

V, VC → BB

5. {K1}$_{BA^{-1}}$

c) Between the Voter and the Bulletin Board

BA → CS

6. ({[b, {b}$_{K1^{-1}}$, K1, {K1}$_{R^{-1}}$]$_{CS}$}$_{BA^{-1}}$)

d) Between the Ballot Acquirer and the Counting Server

CS → BB

7. (b, {b}$_{CS^{-1}}$, T, {K1}$_{CS^{-1}}$)

e) Between the Counting Server and the Bulletin Board

For simplicity, we use two key pairs in describing PEVS. The voter generates two fresh key pairs ($K1$, $K1^{-1}$ and $K2$, $K2^{-1}$) using the Voter Computer (VC). As shown in Figure 2a, the voter sends (V, $K1'$, $\{K1'\}_V^{-1}$, $K2'$, $\{K2'\}_V^{-1}$) to the registrar using the VC. Here, $K1'$ is the blinded copy of $K1$ and $K2'$ is the blinded copy of $K2$, V is the public key of the voter. The blinded keys ($K1'$ and $K2'$) are signed with the private key of the voter V^{-1}.

The registrar verifies the signature of the voter after receiving the message (V, $K1'$, $\{K1'\}_V^{-1}$, $K2'$, $\{K2'\}_V^{-1}$) since the registrar has a list of public keys of the eligible voters. Then the registrar signs the blinded keys ($K1'$, $K2'$) with the private key R^{-1} and sends the signatures to the voter. As shown in Figure 2a, the message sent from the registrar to the voter is ($\{K1'\}_R^{-1}$, $\{K2'\}_R^{-1}$). After receiving this message, the voter verifies the signature of the registrar, then unblinds the message and gets two signed public keys ($\{K1\}_R^{-1}$, $\{K2\}_R^{-1}$). One of these keys is used by the voter for voting and the other key is used to fend off forced-abstention attacks.

The voter computer generates the ballot b from the vote of the voter for a particular candidate. The detail of the ballot construction is presented in the next sub-section. As shown in Figure 2b, the voter sends ($[b, \{b\}_{K1}^{-1}, K1, \{K1\}_R^{-1}]_{CS}$, $K1$, $\{K1\}_R^{-1}$) to the ballot acquirer using the voter computer. Here, the voter signs the ballot b using the VC with the private key $K1^{-1}$, adds $K1$ and the signature $\{K1\}_R^{-1}$ to the ballot, and encrypts the message with the public key of the Counting

Servers (CS). Then the VC adds the key $K1$ and the signature $\{K1\}_R^{-1}$ again with this message. In order to fend off forced-abstention attacks, the voter can use $\{K2\}_R^{-1}$ in this particular case. Since the voter computer and the registrar are assumed to act honestly, the voter computer will construct only one ballot for each voter, and the registrar will decline the initiation of the protocol by the same voter to generate more than one ballot since the registrar maintains the list of the public keys of the eligible voters.

In Figure 2b, the ballot acquirer receives $([b, \{b\}_{K1}^{-1}, K1, \{K1\}_R^{-1}]_{CS}, K1, \{K1\}_R^{-1})$, then parses the message and verifies the signature of the registrar on the key $K1$. The ballot acquirer verifies the freshness of the key $K1$ since it also maintains a list of the keys. After the verification, the ballot acquirer signs the key and sends the signature on this key $\{K1\}_{BA}^{-1}$ to the voter (Shown in Figure 2b). The voter publishes it on the bulletin board (Shown in Figure 2c) using the voter computer.

In Figure 2d, the ballot acquirer sends $(\{[b, \{b\}_{K1}^{-1}, K1, \{K1\}_R^{-1}]_{CS}\}_{BA}^{-1})$ to the counting servers. Here, the ballot acquirer signs the encrypted message $([b, \{b\}_{K1}^{-1}, K1, \{K1\}_R^{-1}]_{CS}])$ received from the voter with its private key BA^{-1}, and sends it to the counting servers. In PEVS the counting servers only accept ballots signed by the ballot acquirer.

In Figure 2d, each of the counting servers receives $(\{[b, \{b\}_{K1}^{-1}, K1, \{K1\}_R^{-1}]_{CS}\}_{BA}^{-1})$, then decrypts the message, and verifies the signature of the registrar on the key $(\{K1\}_R^{-1})$ and the signature of the voter on the ballot $(\{b\}_{K1}^{-1})$. After the verification of the signatures, a threshold number of honest counting servers jointly sign and publish the ballots, then count the ballots and publish the tally. In addition, the threshold number of counting servers also signs the key $K1$ and publishes the signature $\{K1\}_{CS}^{-1}$ on the bulletin board (BB). As shown in Figure 2e, the message sent by the counting servers to the BB is $(b, \{b\}_{CS}^{-1}, T, \{K1\}_{CS}^{-1})$. In this message, T is the tally of the counted ballots.

In PEVS the ballot is sent as encrypted shares, so the dishonest counting servers do not get complete information about the individual ballot. However, the threshold number of counting servers together reaches a result that they agree upon. The ballot verification can be done by the counting servers using the non-interactive zero knowledge protocol presented in (Based & Mjølsnes, 2009; Based & Mjølsnes, 2010).

Anyone can observe the content of the bulletin board (since the content of the bulletin board is public). The ballot acquirer sends the signature on the key $K1$ ($\{K1\}_{BA}^{-1}$) to the voter (Shown in Figure 2b). This signature ensures that the ballot acquirer has received the ballot sent by that voter. In Figure 2c, we see that this signature is published on the bulletin board by the voter using the voter computer. The counting servers also publish on the bulletin board (Figure 2e) the signature $\{K1\}_{CS}^{-1}$ on the key $K1$ signed by these servers and the voter can easily verify this. The dishonest counting servers cannot cheat with this signature without detection since the threshold number of counting servers publishes the same signature. The other signature ($\{K2\}_R^{-1}$ on the key $K2$) is normally not used for voting and not published on the bulletin board. The voter uses this in order to fend off the forced-abstention attacks whenever needed. In that case, the voter casts the ballot using the signature $\{K1\}_R^{-1}$ and gives the coercer the signature $\{K2\}_R^{-1}$ or vice-versa.

Any observer or voter can verify that the number of signatures published on the bulletin board by the counting servers is equal to or less than the number of signatures published on the bulletin board by the voters using the voter computer. This is because some invalid ballots may be discarded by the counting servers after ballot verification. The list of the discarded ballots can be maintained by the counting servers for future claims. The valid ballots are published on the bulletin board, so the observer can verify that the tally is the outcome of the ballots published on the bulletin

A Polling Booth-Based Electronic Voting Scheme

board. Furthermore, the observers can verify the signature of the registrar on the published keys on the bulletin board to achieve eligibility verifiability. Thus, PEVS satisfies voter verifiability, universal verifiability, and eligibility verifiability.

Ballot Construction

The public values are $((e, g_1, n_1), (e, g_2, n_2), ..., (e, g_j, n_j))$. Here, j is the number of counting servers, e is a prime number agreed by all the counting servers. Let g_j be an element in Z^*n_j such that e divides the order of g_j, and $n_j = p_j.q_j$. Here, p_j and q_j values are chosen by counting server j such that e divides $(p_j - 1)$, but does not divide $(q_j - 1)$. The p_j and q_j values are private to counting server j. The value of e must be larger than the total number of eligible voters.

The Voter Computer (VC) picks the random values $(r_{11}, r_{21}, ..., r_{j1})$ which are elements of Z^*n_1, $(r_{12}, r_{22}, ..., r_{j2})$ which are elements of Z^*n_2, and similarly $(r_{1j}, r_{2j}, ..., r_{jj})$ which are elements of Z^*n_j.

Then the VC generates the random string $R = (r_1, r_2, ..., r_j)$, where

$$r_1 = \sum_{i=1}^{j} r_{i1} (\mod e)$$
$$r_2 = \sum_{i=1}^{j} r_{i2} (\mod e)$$
$$...$$
$$r_j = \sum_{i=1}^{j} r_{ij} (\mod e)$$

The VC uses these random values to compute the ballot $B = (b_1, b_2, ..., b_j)$, such that

$$b_1 = (g_1^{r11} (\mod n_1), g_2^{r12} (\mod n_2), ..., g_j^{r1j} (\mod n_j))$$
$$b_2 = (g_1^{r21} (\mod n_1), g_2^{r22} (\mod n_2), ..., g_j^{r2j} (\mod n_j))$$
$$...$$
$$b_j = (g_1^{rj1} (\mod n_1), g_2^{rj2} (\mod n_2), ..., g_j^{rjj} (\mod n_j))$$

Here, a ballot is sent as secret shares to j counting servers. The random values are chosen such that a vote $V = (v_1, v_2, ..., v_j)$, where

$$v_1 = \sum_{i=1}^{j} r_{1i} (\mod e)$$
$$v_2 = \sum_{i=1}^{j} r_{2i} (\mod e)$$
$$...$$
$$v_j = \sum_{i=1}^{j} r_{ji} (\mod e)$$

Ballot Counting

The counting servers receive ballots $(B_1, B_2, ..., B_p)$ from p voters where $B_1 = (b_{11}, b_{12}, ..., b_{1j})$ sent by voter 1, $B_2 = (b_{21}, b_{22}, ..., b_{2j})$ sent by voter 2, and so on.

The net ballot is

$$B_p = \sum_{i=1}^{p} b_{i1}, \sum_{i=1}^{p} b_{i2}, ..., \sum_{i=1}^{p} b_{ij} (\mod e).$$

The total vote for candidate 1 is

$$\sum_{l=1}^{p} \left(\sum_{i=1}^{j} r_{1i}[l] \right) (\mod e).$$

The total vote for candidate 2 is,

$$\sum_{l=1}^{p} \left(\sum_{i=1}^{j} r_{2i}[l] \right) (\mod e).$$

and so on.

To compute this tally, the counting servers should publish the sub-tallies. For example, to compute the value of $\sum_{i=1}^{j} r_{1i}$, r_{11} should be published by the first counting server (CS1), r_{12} should be published by second counting server (CS2), and so on.

The sub tallies that should be published by server 1 is

$$\left(\sum_{l=1}^{p} b_{i1}[1], \sum_{l=1}^{p} b_{i2}[1], ..., \sum_{l=1}^{p} b_{ij}[1] \right).$$

By server 2 is

$$\left(\sum_{l=1}^{p} b_{i1}[2], \sum_{l=1}^{p} b_{i2}[2], \cdots, \sum_{l=1}^{p} b_{ij}[2]\right),$$

and similarly, by server j is

$$\left(\sum_{l=1}^{p} b_{i1}[j], \sum_{l=1}^{p} b_{i2}[j], \cdots, \sum_{l=1}^{p} b_{ij}[j]\right).$$

The counting servers can compute these sub-tallies because they know the factorization of n_i ($i = 1$ to j). After all the servers publish their own sub-tallies, the total tally will be computed. In a threshold homomorphic scheme, when at least the threshold number of servers publishes the sub-tallies, then the total tally can be computed. Using the properties of homomorphic cryptosystems the counting servers can add all encrypted ballots before decryption.

SECURITY ANALYSIS OF PEVS

For the formal analysis of PEVS, we have used the ProVerif tool (Blanchet, 2001; Blanchet, Cheval, Allamigeon, & Smyth, 2012). The ProVerif is an automatic cryptographic protocol verifier tool developed by Blanchet et al. (Blanchet, 2001; Blanchet, Cheval, Allamigeon, & Smyth, 2012) and can prove properties of security protocols with respect to the so-called *Dolev-Yao* model. This tool supports a wide range of cryptographic primitives including asymmetric encryption, digital signatures, blind signatures, and non-interactive zero-knowledge proofs.

Overview of ProVerif

The input language of ProVerif is a variant of the applied pi-calculus, which is a formal language introduced in (Abad & Fournet, 2001) for reasoning about concurrent processes. In ProVerif, terms are built from *names a, b, c, m, n,.., variables x, y, z,...* and a set Σ of *function symbols* that are applied to terms. Cryptographic primitives are typically represented by function symbols (each with an arity) and the equivalences that hold on terms are described by an *equational theory E*. In addition, a function symbol with arity *0* is a constant and the function symbols are divided in *constructors f* and *destructors g* which are related via equations in *E*. We write $M =_E N$ for equality modulo (the equations in) E for two terms M, N, and $M_1/x_1, ..., M_l/x_l$ denotes the substitution of $x_1,..., x_l$ by, respectively, $M_1, ..., M_l$.

ProVerif's language is strongly typed; any term n has one of the (user-defined) types t, written n:t. We refer to (Blanchet, 2001; Blanchet, Cheval, Allamigeon, & Smyth, 2012) and to the ProVerif user manual that ships with the tool for details on Proverif and its language.

In ProVerif, processes are built according to the grammar in Figure 3 (where u is a meta variable that may represent a name or a variable). In Figure 3, the null process does nothing, $P|Q$ represents the parallel execution of P and Q, while $!P$ behaves like an unbounded number of concurrently running copies of P. And the name restriction new n: t; P generates a fresh name n of type t and behaves like P, the process $out(u, N)$; P sends out term N on channel u and then behaves like P, while $in(u, x:t)$; P receives a term of type t on channel u before it behaves like P. The conditional process if $M = N$ then P else Q behaves like P in case $M =_E N$, otherwise it behaves like Q, and let $x = M$ in P behaves like $P\{M/x\}$.

Figure 3. ProVerif process grammar (Based, Tsay, & Mjølsnes, 2012)

$P, Q ::=$	plain processes
$\bar{0}$	null process
$P \mid Q$	parallel composition
$!P$	replication
new $n : t ; P$	name restriction
in $(u, x : t) ; P$	message input
out $(u, N) ; P$	message output
if $M = N$ then P else Q	conditional
let $x = M$ in P	term evaluation

The sets of free names, bound names, free variables and bound variables of R are denoted by $fn(R)$, $bn(R)$, $fv(R)$, and $bv(R)$ respectively, where R is an extended process or a term. If fv(A) = Ø, then an extended process A is *closed*.

A *context* C[.] is a process with a hole, and an *evaluation context* is a context where the hole is not under a replication, a conditional, an input or an output. If C[A] is closed, then context C[.] *closes* process A. In order to capture relationships between events correspondence assertions [Woo, T. Y. C., & Lam, S. S. (1993)] are used in ProVerif.

In ProVerif, the operational semantics is defined by *structural equivalence* ($\equiv$), *internal reduction* ($\rightarrow$), and *observational equivalence* ($\approx$). Here, structural equivalence is an equivalence relation that defines when syntactically different processes represent identical processes, e.g., it is $(P|Q)|\bar{O} \equiv P|(Q|\bar{O}) \equiv P|Q \equiv Q|P$, and P| new $a; Q \equiv$ new $a;(P|Q)$ if $a \in fn(P)$ is not true. And internal reduction determines the ways a process progresses, e.g., $out(c, M); P \mid in(c, x); Q \rightarrow P \mid Q\{M/x\}$ describes how the message M is sent and received on channel c, and let $x = D$ in P else Q $\rightarrow P\{M/x\}$ if D evaluates to M.

The attacker cannot control the free variables and these variables are declared as private. We declare type *pkey* as public key and *skey* as private key for asymmetric encryption. We declare type *sskey* as private signing key and *spkey* as public signing key for digital signatures.

Modeling PEVS

We follow the general definition of (Delaune, Kremer, & Ryan, 2008) in order to formalize PEVS in the language of ProVerif. The cryptographic primitives used in PEVS are: a public-key encryption scheme, a digital signature scheme, and a blind digital signature scheme consisting of a digital signature and a blinding scheme. These primitives are modeled by the equational theory in Box 1.

The types that are used for modeling PEVS with this theory are defined in Process 1. We formalize processes for PEVS's honest voter (Process 2), and registrar, ballot acquirer and counting server (Process 4) in ProVerif's language. The election process, given in Process 5, consists of executing all these processes in parallel. Without loss of generality, we consider the case where the coercer in a forced-abstention attack asks for at most one key from the coerced honest voter. That is, the voter generates only two key pairs in the polling booth (recall that in an actual implementation the voter can generate as many keys in the polling booth as the voter wishes). We model the set of counting servers as a single process; in our formal analysis we do not focus on the secure multiparty computations for ballot counting.

Soundness of PEVS

Eligibility means only the legitimate voters are allowed to cast their ballots in a voting scheme. The ballot cast by an eligible voter should not be altered; this property is known as *inalterability*. Furthermore, every voter should be allowed to vote only once. This property is called *non-reusability*. Backes et al. (Backes, Hritcu, & Maffei, 2008) summarize these properties under the notion *soundness* of an election scheme. We use the correspondence assertions techniques (Blanchet, Cheval, Allamigeon, & Smyth, 2012; Woo & Lam, 1993) presented in (Backes, Hritcu, & Maffei, 2008) to verify soundness of PEVS using the ProVerif tool.

In order to reason about correspondence assertions we annotate four events. These events are: Voterkey(key), CvoterKey(key), Beginvote(key,ballot), and Endvote(ballot);

Box 1.

```
       adec(aenc(m, pk (k)), k) = m
     checksign(sign(m, k), spk(k)) = m
  checksignkey(signkey(m, k), spk(k))  = m
unblind(sign(blind(m, r), k), r)  = sign(m, k)
```

VoterKey(key) marks the start of the blind signature scheme for signed key generation of an honest voter, Cvoterkey(key) marks the start of the blind signature scheme for signed key generation of a corrupted voter, Beginvote(key,ballot) records the start of the voting phase for an honest voter who casts the ballot with the key, while corrupted voters cast ballots without asserting any event. And Endvote(ballot) indicates the start of tallying by the counting servers. For simplicity, we have used two key pairs by the voter in the description and in the formal analysis of PEVS.

The eligibility of the voter and the inalterability of the ballot are modeled by requiring that every counted ballot matches a ballot cast by an eligible voter. We model non-reusability by requiring that the matching between the events Endvote(ballot) and Beginvote(key,ballot) is injective (Backes, Hritcu, & Maffei, 2008). In addition, each Beginvote(key,ballot) event is preceded by a distinct Voterkey(key) and the event Voterkey(key) and Cvoterkey(key) depend on distinct keys. In PEVS only the eligible voters get their keys signed by the registrar and the signed keys are used for voting by the eligible voters.

In order to analyze the soundness property, we annotate Process 1, Process 2, Process 3, Process 4, and Process 5 (see Figures 10 through 14 in Appendix A). The analysis succeeds and the result shows that PEVS guarantees soundness for an unbounded number of honest voters and corrupted participants. Nonce handshakes (Backes, Hritcu, & Maffei, 2008) are used in ProVerif to send certain messages only once.

Process 1 shows the free variables, events, types, and functions used in ProVerif. Process 2 models the activities of an honest voter. In this process, the voter enters the polling booth, generates fresh key pairs, blinds the public keys, sends the blinded keys to the registrar, and gets signed keys from the registrar after unblinding them. The voter then casts the ballot using the fresh signed keys. We assume that the first key pair is normally used for voting though the voter can use any of the key pair. In Process 2, the event Voterkey(key) marks the start of the blind signature scheme for signed key generation of the voter and the event Beginvote(key,ballot) records the start of the voting phase for the voter.

Figure 4. Soundness of PEVS

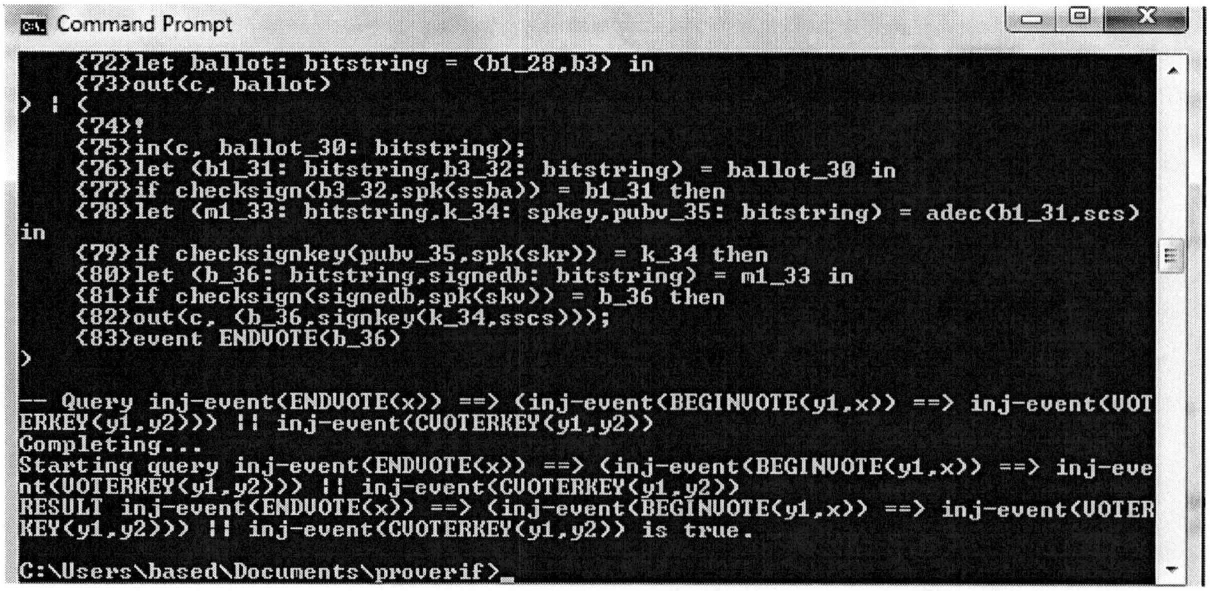

Figure 5. ProVerif query

```
query x:bitstring,y1:spkey,y2:spkey; inj-event(Endvote(x))==>((inj-
event(Beginvote(y1,x))==>inj-event(Voterkey(y1,y2))) | inj-event(Cvoterkey(y1,y2))).
```

Process 3 shows the corrupted voter. In this process, the event Cvoterkey(key) marks the key generation phase of the corrupted voter and the corrupted voters cast ballots without asserting any event.

Process 4 shows the registrar, the ballot acquirer, and the counting server of PEVS in ProVerif. In this process, the event Endvote(ballot) in the counting server process (CountingServer) indicates the tallying by the counting server. The main process is shown in Process 5 and the result is shown in Figure 4. The query in Figure 5 is executed in ProVerif to verify soundness of PEVS:

Vote-Privacy

Definition 1: Vote-privacy (Delaune, Kremer, & Ryan, 2008). A voting scheme respects vote-privacy if

$$S\left[Voter_A\left\{a/v\right\} \mid Voter_B\left\{b/v\right\}\right]$$
$$\approx S\left[Voter_A\left\{b/v\right\} \mid Voter_B\left\{a/v\right\}\right]$$

for all possible ballots *a* and *b*.

Here, S is an evaluation context, for further detail we refer to (Delaune, Kremer, & Ryan, 2008). If an intruder cannot detect when arbitrary honest voters $Voter_A$ and $Voter_B$ swap their ballots, then in general the intruder cannot know anything about how $Voter_A$ and $Voter_B$ cast their ballots (see Figures 15 and 16 in Appendix A).

We verify that PEVS satisfies the vote-privacy property given in Definition 1. The declarations of channels, free variables, events, types, and functions are same as in Process 1 with the addition of two free variables for representing the ballots of $Voter_A$ and $Voter_B$. These two variables are *b1*

and *b2*, where *b1* is the ballot of $Voter_A$ and *b2* is the ballot for $Voter_B$. $Voter_A$ and $Voter_B$ are modeled in Process 6 and Process 7 respectively. The public values are same in both processes and the differences are only in the private values. The modified process for the registrar, ballot acquirer and counting server is shown in process 8 (Figure 17). Process 9 (Figure 18) shows the main process for verifying vote-privacy and the result is shown in Figure 6.

Receipt-Freeness

The property receipt-freeness says that a voter does not obtain any information (receipt) which can be used later to prove to another party how the ballot was cast. In order to sell the vote, the voter may voluntarily reveal additional information to the coercer. The receipt-freeness property does not allow the voter to convince the coercer with such a proof that the ballot was cast in a particular way. We follow the following formal definition of receipt-freeness (Delaune, Kremer, & Ryan, 2008):

Definition 2: Receipt-freeness (Delaune, Kremer, & Ryan, 2008). A voting scheme is receipt-free if there exists a closed plain process *V'* such that

- $V'^{\setminus out(c1)} \approx Voter_A\left\{a/v\right\}$, and
- $S\left[Voter_A\left\{c/v\right\}^{c1} \mid Voter_B\left\{a/v\right\}\right] \approx S\left[V' \mid Voter_B\left\{c/v\right\}\right]$

for all possible ballots *a* and *c*.

The context *S* in the second equivalence includes the honest authorities. In the process *V'*, the voter $Voter_A$ casts the ballot for candidate *a* but communicates with the coercer on channel

Figure 6. Vote-privacy

```
    (86)if checksign(signedb,spk(skv1)) = b then
    (87)out(c, (b,signkey(k_16,sscs)));
    (88)if checksign(signedb,spk(skv2)) = b then
    (89)out(c, (b,signkey(k_16,sscs)))
)

-- Observational equivalence
Termination warning: v_346 <> v_347 && attacker2(v_345,v_346) && attacker2(v_345
,v_347) -> bad
Selecting 0
Termination warning: v_349 <> v_350 && attacker2(v_349,v_348) && attacker2(v_350
,v_348) -> bad
Selecting 0
Completing...
Termination warning: v_346 <> v_347 && attacker2(v_345,v_346) && attacker2(v_345
,v_347) -> bad
Selecting 0
Termination warning: v_349 <> v_350 && attacker2(v_349,v_348) && attacker2(v_350
,v_348) -> bad
Selecting 0
200 rules inserted. The rule base contains 190 rules. 104 rules in the queue.
400 rules inserted. The rule base contains 297 rules. 44 rules in the queue.
RESULT Observational equivalence is true (bad not derivable).

C:\Users\based\Documents\proverif>
```

$c1$ to convince that the ballot is cast for candidate c. The process $V'^{out(c1)}$ behaves similarly as the process V' but hides the outputs on channel $c1$. The coercer cannot learn whether the ballot is cast for candidate a or for candidate c since the ballot is constructed by the voter computer inside the polling booth. The voter process $Voter_A\{c/v\}^{c1}$ communicates with the coercer on channel $c1$ and cooperates with the coercer to cast a ballot for candidate c.

We verify that PEVS satisfies the receipt-freeness property given in Definition 2 with the ProVerif tool. The first equivalence can be seen informally by considering V' (Figure 19 in Appendix A) without the instructions "out(c1,...)", and comparing it with $Voter_A\{a/v\}$ visually (Delaune, Kremer, & Ryan, 2008). Note that these two processes are same. The process for $Voter_A\{a/v\}$ is equal to Process 2.

For the second bullet point, Process 11 (Figure 20 Appendix A) models $Voter_A\{c/v\}^{c1}$, and V' is shown in Process 10. The process for $Voter_B$ is also equal to Process 2. We declare bc as the ballot for V' and bd as the ballot for $Voter_A\{c/v\}^{c1}$. The modified process for the registrar, ballot acquirer, and counting server is shown in process 12 (Figure 21 Appendix A). The declarations of channels, free variables, events, types, and functions are the same as in Process 1 with the addition of the private channel $c1$. The $c1$ channel is used by the coerced voter to publish the secret values to the coercer. The main process for receipt-freeness is shown in Process 13 (Figure 22 Appendix A) and the result is shown in Figure 7.

Coercion-Resistance

Backes et al. define coercion-resistance of remote electronic voting schemes that is suitable for automated verification in (Backes, Hritcu, & Maffei, 2008). Backes et al. automatically verify that the protocol by Juels et al. (Juels, Catalano, & Jakobsson, 2002) satisfies their notion of coercion-resistance. The protocol by Juels et al. allows the voter to provide fake credentials to the coercer, the coercer may later either casts a ballot using these fake credentials or just abstains from voting. That is, in particular, the protocol allows voting

A Polling Booth-Based Electronic Voting Scheme

Figure 7. Receipt-freeness

```
(113)if checksign(signedb,spk(skvc)) = b_51 then
(114)out(c, (b_51,signkey(k_49,sscs)))
)
-- Observational equivalence
Termination warning: v_380 <> v_381 && attacker2(v_379,v_380) && attacker2(v_379
,v_381) -> bad
Selecting 0
Termination warning: v_383 <> v_384 && attacker2(v_383,v_382) && attacker2(v_384
,v_382) -> bad
Selecting 0
Completing...
Termination warning: v_380 <> v_381 && attacker2(v_379,v_380) && attacker2(v_379
,v_381) -> bad
Selecting 0
Termination warning: v_383 <> v_384 && attacker2(v_383,v_382) && attacker2(v_384
,v_382) -> bad
Selecting 0
200 rules inserted. The rule base contains 185 rules. 159 rules in the queue.
400 rules inserted. The rule base contains 357 rules. 55 rules in the queue.
600 rules inserted. The rule base contains 435 rules. 29 rules in the queue.
800 rules inserted. The rule base contains 621 rules. 53 rules in the queue.
RESULT Observational equivalence is true (bad not derivable).

C:\Users\based\Documents\proverif>
```

with fake credentials. The ballots cast with the fake credentials are silently dropped by the talliers. This is modeled in ProVerif by Backes et al. (Backes, Hritcu, & Maffei, 2008) using an extractor process. The extractor behaves according to the behavior of the coercer. That is, when the coercer abstains from voting (with fake credentials), then the extractor does nothing. And when the coercer casts a ballot with the fake credentials then the extractor adjusts the tally by removing the ballot cast by the coercer.

Compared to the protocol in (Juels, Catalano, & Jakobsson, 2002), the voters in PEVS cast their ballots inside a polling booth and this limits the capacity of the coercer to cast a ballot using the fake key. Inside the booth, the voters freshly generate the keys and give the alternative keys to the coercer based on the type of attack that needs to be fended off.

The voter casts the ballot with one key pair and gives the second key pair to the coercer to defend against forced-abstention attacks. The voter gives the coercer the key pair used for casting the ballot to fend off randomization attacks or simulation attacks. Now, even though the coercer has the keys, the coercer cannot cast any ballot with these keys since fresh keys generated inside the booth are needed to cast a ballot each time.

We derive from (Backes, Hritcu, & Maffei, 2008) the following definition of coercion-resistance for polling booth based voting schemes. Note that the definition of (Delaune, Kremer, & Ryan, 2008) is not suitable for automatic verification since it quantifies over an infinite set of contexts.

Definition 3: Coercion-resistance. A polling booth based voting scheme is coercion-resistant if

- $S\left[Voter_A^{coerced(c1)} \mid Voter_B\{a/v\}\right] \approx S\left[Voter_A^{cheat(c1)}\{a/v\} \mid Voter_B^{abs}\right]$, and
- $S\left[Voter_A^{coerced(c1,c2)}\{?/v\} \mid E\{a/v\}^{(c2)}\right] \approx S\left[Voter_A^{cheat(c1,c2)}\{a/v\} \mid E\{?/v\}^{(c2)}\right]$

We consider the first bullet point, on both sides the number of messages exchanged is equal and the ballot of $Voter_A$ is compensated by the additional voter $Voter_B$ and observational equivalence holds. A coerced voter is modeled in the process

$Voter_A^{coerced(c1)}$. This voter gets the signed keys from the registrar and gives the coercer the keys on the channel $c1$. This voter can give any key pair to the coercer and does not cast any ballot. The process $Voter_A^{cheat(c1)}\{a/v\}$ on the right hand side models the behaviour of a voter who casts a ballot using one key pair and gives the coercer the other key pair on the channel c1 trying to convince the coercer that the ballot was cast as requested. This is because it is not possible for the coercer to distinguish which key pair was used by the voter to cast the ballot. The behaviour of a voter who just abstains from voting is modeled in the process $Voter_B^{abs}$.

Now let us consider the second bullet point, the number of messages exchanged on both sides is equal and the ballot of the coerced voter $Voter_A$ is compensated by the extractor process E. Here, the extractor process E behaves according to the behaviour of the coerced voter. The coerced voter $Voter_A^{coerced(c1,c2)}\{?/v\}$ on the left hand side, may cast *any* ballot for a particular candidate according to the choice of the coercer. The coerced voter then publishes this ballot to the extractor on channel $c2$ and to the coercer on channel $c1$. Then the extractor $E\{a/v\}^{(c2)}$ casts the ballot according to the choice of the coerced voter. The $Voter_A^{cheat(c1,c2)}\{a/v\}$ on the right hand side, models the behaviour of a voter who casts a ballot according to his own choice and tries to convince the coercer that the ballot was cast as the coercer wanted. This voter then publishes the ballot to the extractor as the coercer wanted on channel $c2$ and the extractor process $E\{?/v\}^{(c2)}$ then casts the ballot accordingly.

We assume that the extractor is honest and there is a communication between the extractor and the counting servers so that the tally does not include the ballot cast by the coerced voter (on the left side) and by the extractor (on the right side). However, the threshold number of counting servers publishes the keys on the bulletin board that the coercer will try to find and counts only the valid ballots. So, the dishonest counting servers will not be able to leak any information to the coercer. In comparison to the extractor defined in (Backes, Hritcu, & Maffei, 2008), this extractor does not only extract/discard unwanted ballots from the tally, but also casts ballots if needed by a coerced voter. Note that the definition of (Backes, Hritcu, & Maffei, 2008) cannot be applied to polling booth based voting schemes where coercers cannot cast ballots with fake keys and the definition of coercion-resistance in (Delaune, Kremer, & Ryan, 2008) applies to polling both based voting schemes is not suitable for automatic verification.

We verify that PEVS satisfies the coercion-resistance property given in Definition 3 with the ProVerif tool. The declarations of channels, free variables, events, types, and functions are the same as in Process 1 with the addition of the private channels $c1$ and $c2$, where, the $c1$ channel is used by the coerced voter to publish the secret values to the coercer and $c2$ channel is used for the communication between the coerced voter and the extractor. We declare bc as the ballot for V'. The modified process for the registrar, ballot acquirer, and counting server is shown in process 14 (Figure 23 in Appendix A).

We consider the first bullet point, Process 15 (Figure 24 in Appendix A) models $Voter_A^{coerced(c1)}$. The process $Voter_B\{a/v\}$ is the same as Process 2. The process $Voter_A^{cheat(c1)}\{a/v\}$ is the same as Process 10. The process $Voter_B^{abs}$ is similar to the process $Vote_A^{coerced(c1)}$ without the communication with the coercer on channel $c1$. The voter in $Voter_A^{cheat(c1)}\{a/v\}$ gives the key pair to the coercer on $c1$ after voting to obstruct simulation attacks and randomization attacks. The key pair is freshly generated, so the attacker cannot mount such attacks using this key pair. Furthermore, the coercer cannot detect which key pair was used to cast the ballots by the voter. Process 16 (Figure 25 in Appendix A) shows the main process for coercion-resistance (first bullet point) and the result is shown in Figure 8.

Figure 8. Coercion-resistance

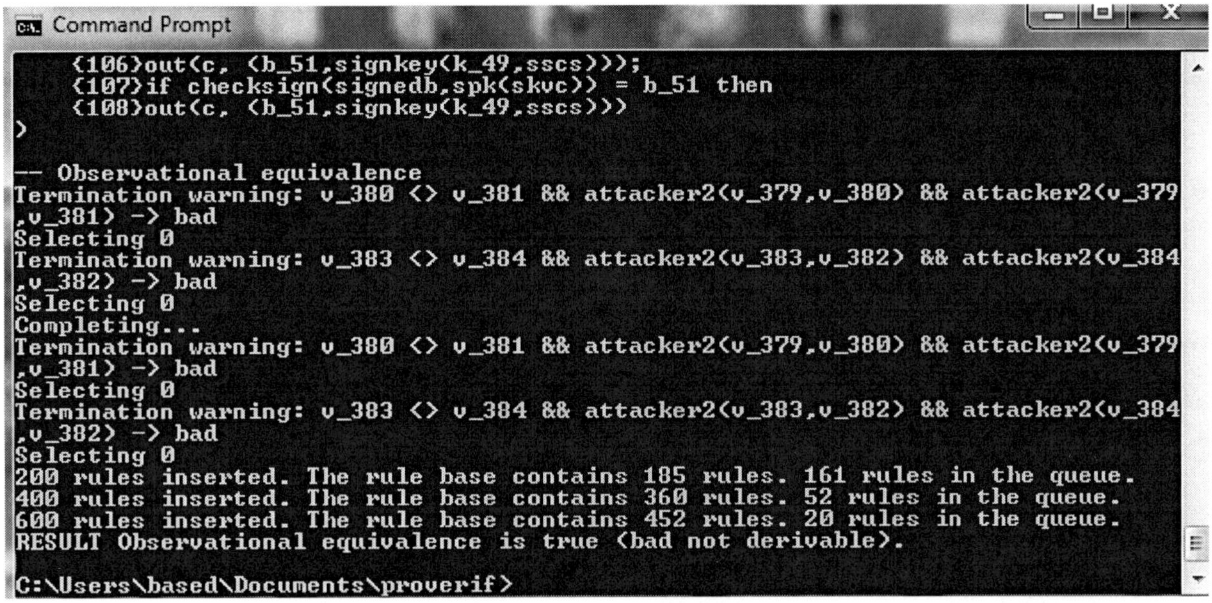
Command Prompt
{106}out(c, (b_51,signkey(k_49,sscs)));
{107}if checksign(signedb,spk(skvc)) = b_51 then
{108}out(c, (b_51,signkey(k_49,sscs)))
>
-- Observational equivalence
Termination warning: v_380 <> v_381 && attacker2(v_379,v_380) && attacker2(v_379,v_381) -> bad
Selecting 0
Termination warning: v_383 <> v_384 && attacker2(v_383,v_382) && attacker2(v_384,v_382) -> bad
Selecting 0
Completing...
Termination warning: v_380 <> v_381 && attacker2(v_379,v_380) && attacker2(v_379,v_381) -> bad
Selecting 0
Termination warning: v_383 <> v_384 && attacker2(v_383,v_382) && attacker2(v_384,v_382) -> bad
Selecting 0
200 rules inserted. The rule base contains 185 rules. 161 rules in the queue.
400 rules inserted. The rule base contains 360 rules. 52 rules in the queue.
600 rules inserted. The rule base contains 452 rules. 20 rules in the queue.
RESULT Observational equivalence is true (bad not derivable).
C:\Users\based\Documents\proverif>

Now we consider the second bullet point, Process 17 (Figure 26 in Appendix A) models $Voter_A^{coerced(c1,c2)}\{?/v\}$ and Process 18 (Figure 27 in Appendix A) models the extractor. In Process 17, the voter casts the ballot according to the choice of the coercer, and then publishes it on channel *c1* to the coercer and on channel *c2* to the extractor. On channel *c2*, the extractor receives the ballot and then casts the ballot accordingly. The $Voter_A^{cheat(c1,c2)}\{a/v\}$ process is similar to Pro-

Figure 9. Coercion-resistance (second bullet point)

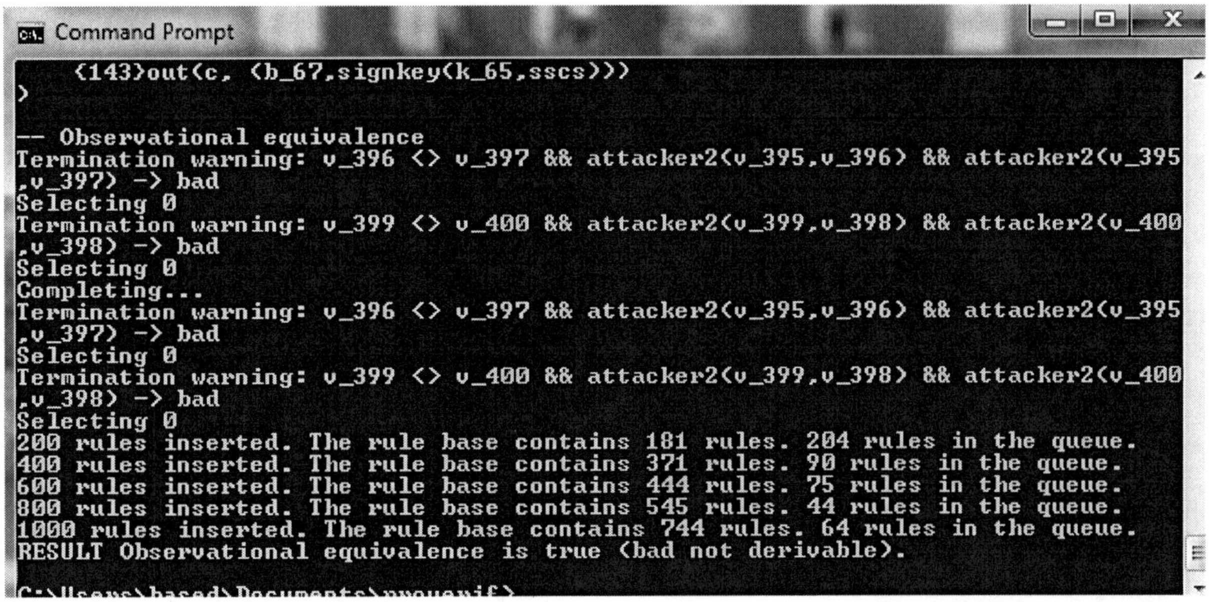
Command Prompt
{143}out(c, (b_67,signkey(k_65,sscs)))
>
-- Observational equivalence
Termination warning: v_396 <> v_397 && attacker2(v_395,v_396) && attacker2(v_395,v_397) -> bad
Selecting 0
Termination warning: v_399 <> v_400 && attacker2(v_399,v_398) && attacker2(v_400,v_398) -> bad
Selecting 0
Completing...
Termination warning: v_396 <> v_397 && attacker2(v_395,v_396) && attacker2(v_395,v_397) -> bad
Selecting 0
Termination warning: v_399 <> v_400 && attacker2(v_399,v_398) && attacker2(v_400,v_398) -> bad
Selecting 0
200 rules inserted. The rule base contains 181 rules. 204 rules in the queue.
400 rules inserted. The rule base contains 371 rules. 90 rules in the queue.
600 rules inserted. The rule base contains 444 rules. 75 rules in the queue.
800 rules inserted. The rule base contains 545 rules. 44 rules in the queue.
1000 rules inserted. The rule base contains 744 rules. 64 rules in the queue.
RESULT Observational equivalence is true (bad not derivable).

cess 10 with the addition that the voter publishes the ballot on channel $c2$ to the extractor so that the extractor can cast the ballot as the coercer wanted. We declare bc as the ballot for V', be for the extractor, and bcc for $Voter_A^{coerced(c1,c2)}\{?/v\}$. The modified process for the registrar, ballot acquirer, and counting server is shown in process 19 (Figure 28 in Appendix A). Process 20 (Figure 29 in Appendix A) models the process for coercion-resistance (second bullet point) and the result is shown in Figure 9.

CONCLUSION AND FUTURE WORK

A polling booth based electronic voting scheme has been presented in this chapter. The ProVerif tool is used to formally verify that PEVS satisfies soundness, vote-privacy, receipt-freeness, and coercion-resistance. We have also shown that a voter can verify that the ballot cast by that voter is counted and that the scheme is also universally verifiable and eligibility verifiable. Automated verification of these (voter verifiability, universal verifiability, and eligibility verifiability) properties will be done in future. Moreover, we are planning to implement PEVS and we also intend to verify by hand that PEVS satisfies the notion of coercion-resistance given in Delaune, Kremer, and Ryan (2008).

REFERENCES

Abadi, M., & Fournet, C. (2001). Mobile values, new names, and secure communication. In *Proceedings of the 28th ACM SIGPLAN-SIGACT Symposium on Principles of Programming Languages (POPL'01)*, (pp. 104-115). ACM Press.

Adida, B. (2008). Helios: Web-based open-audit voting. In *Proceedings of the Seventeenth Usenix Security Symposium*, (pp. 335-348). USENIX Association.

Backes, M., Hritcu, C., & Maffei, M. (2008). Automated verification of remote electronic voting protocols in the applied pi-calculus. In *Proceedings of the 21st IEEE Computer Security Foundations Symposium*, (pp. 195-209). Washington, DC: IEEE.

Based, M. A., & Mjølsnes, S. F. (2009). A non-interactive zero knowledge proof protocol in an internet voting scheme. In *Proceedings of the 2nd Norwegian Information Security Conference (NISK 2009)*, (pp. 148-160). Tapir Akademisk Forlag.

Based, M. A., & Mjølsnes, S. F. (2010). Universally composable NIZK protocol in an internet voting scheme. In Cuellar, J. et al. (Eds.), *STM 2010 (LNCS)* (Vol. 6710, pp. 147–162). Berlin: Springer-Verlag.

Based, M. A., & Mjølsnes, S. F. (2011). A secure internet voting scheme. In Xiang, Y. et al. (Eds.), *ICA3PP (LNCS)* (Vol. 7017, pp. 141–152). Berlin: Springer.

Based, M. A., Tsay, J. K., & Mjølsnes, S. F. (2012). PEVS: A secure electronic voting scheme using polling booths. In Xiang, Y. et al. (Eds.), *ICDKE 2012 (Co-located with NSS 2012) (LNCS)* (Vol. 7696, pp. 189–205). Berlin: Springer-Verlag. doi:10.1007/978-3-642-34679-8_18.

Benaloh, J. (2006). Simple verifiable elections. In *Proceedings of the USENIX/ACCURATE Electronic Voting Technology Workshop*. USENIX/ACCURATE.

Benaloh, J., & Tuinstra, D. (1994). Receipt-free secret-ballot elections (extended abstract). In *Proceedings of the 26th Annual Symposium on Theory of Computing (STOC'94)*, (pp. 544-553). ACM Press.

Blanchet, B. (2001). An efficient cryptographic protocol verifier based on prolog rules. In *Proceedings of the 14th IEEE Computer Security Foundations Workshop (CSFW)*, (pp. 82-96). IEEE Computer Society Press.

Blanchet, B., Cheval, V., Allamigeon, X., & Smyth, B. (2012). *ProVerif: Cryptographic protocol verifier in the formal model*. Retrieved from http://www.proverif.ens.fr/

Bohli, J. M., Mueller-Quade, J., & Roehrich, S. (2007). *Bingo voting: Secure and coercion-free voting using a trusted random number generator*. Retrieved from http://eprint.iacr.org/2007/162

Clarkson, M. R., Chong, S., & Myers, A. C. (2008). Civitas: Toward a secure voting system. In *Proceedings of the 2008 IEEE Symposium on Security and Privacy*, (pp. 354-368). Washington, DC: IEEE Computer Society.

Cortier, V., & Wiedling, C. (2012). *A formal analysis of the Norwegian e-voting protocol*. Paper presented at ETAPS 2012. Tallinn, Estonia.

Cortier, V., & Wiedling, C. (2012). *A formal analysis of the Norwegian e-voting protocol*. Paper presented at ETAPS 2012. Tallinn, Estonia.

Delaune, S., Kremer, S., & Ryan, M. D. (2008). *Verifying privacy-type properties of electronic voting protocols* (Research Report LSV-08-01). Paris: Laboratorie Specification et Verification, ENS Cachan.

Dossogne, J., & Lafitte, F. (2012). Mental voting booths. In Laud, P. (Ed.), *NordSec 2011 (LNCS)* (*Vol. 7161*, pp. 82–97). Berlin: Springer-Verlag.

European University Institute. (2007). *Internet voting in the March 2007 parliamentary elections in Estonia*. Robert Schuman Center for Advanced Studies, Report for the Council of Europe.

Fujioka, A., Okamoto, T., & Ohta, K. (1992). A practical secret voting scheme for large scale elections. In Seberry, J., & Zheng, Y. (Eds.), *Advances in Cryptology - AUSCRYPT '92 (LNCS)* (*Vol. 718*, pp. 244–251). Berlin: Springer. doi:10.1007/3-540-57220-1_66.

Gjøsteen, K. (2010). *Analysis of an internet voting protocol*. Cryptology ePrint Archive, Report 2010/380.

Juels, A., Catalano, D., & Jakobsson, M. (2002). *Coercion-resistant electronic elections*. Cryptology ePrint Archive. *Report, 2002*(165), 2002.

Juels, A., Catalano, D., & Jakobsson, M. (2005). Coercion-resistant electronic elections. In *Proceedings of the 2005 ACM Workshop on Privacy in the Electronic Society*, (pp. 61-70). New York, NY: ACM.

Kremer, S., & Ryan, M. (2005). Analysis of an electronic voting protocol in the applied pi calculus. In *Programming Languages and Systems (LNCS)*. Berlin: Springer. doi:10.1007/978-3-540-31987-0_14.

Lee, B., Boyd, C., Dawson, E., Kim, K., Yang, J., & Yoo, S. (2004). Providing receipt-freeness in mixnet-based voting protocols. In *Proceedings of Information Security and Cryptology (ICISC'03) (LNCS)*, (vol. 2971, pp. 245-258). Berlin: Springer.

Nielsen, C. R., Andersen, E. H., & Nielson, H. R. (1996). Static analysis of a voting protocol. In *Proceedings of the IFIP World Conference in IT Tools*, (pp. 21-30). IFIP.

Okamoto, T. (1996). An electronic voting scheme. In N. Terashima, et al. (Ed.), *IFIP World Congress*, (pp. 21-30). London: Chapman & Hall Publications.

Rivest, R. L. (2006). *The threeballot voting system*. Retrieved from http://people.csail.mit.edu/rivest/Rivest-TheThreeBallotVotingSystem.pdf

Ryan, P. Y. A., & Teague, V. (2009). Pretty good democracy. In *Proceedings of the 17th International Workshop on Security Protocols* (LNCS). Cambridge, UK: Springer.

Sandler, D., Derr, K., & Wallach, D. S. (2008). Votebox: A tamper-evident, verifiable electronic voting system. In *Proceedings of the 17th Conference on Security Symposium (SS'08)*, (pp. 349-364). Berkeley, CA: USENIX Association.

Schoenmakers, B. (1999). A simple publicly verifiable secret sharing scheme and its application to electronic voting. In *Advances in Cryptology-CRYPTO'99 (LNCS)* (*Vol. 1966*, pp. 148–164). Berlin: Springer-Verlag. doi:10.1007/3-540-48405-1_10.

The Internet Rights Forum. (2003). Retrieved from http://www.forumInternet.org/telechargement/documents/reco-evote-en-20030926.pdf

Woo, T. Y. C., & Lam, S. S. (1993). A semantic model for authentication protocols. In *Proceedings IEEE Symposium on Research in Security and Privacy*, (pp. 178-194). Oakland, CA: IEEE.

KEY TERMS AND DEFINITIONS

Coercion-Resistance: Coercion-resistance means a coercer should not be able to force a voter to abstain from voting or to cast the ballot for a particular candidate or in a particular way (Juels, Catalano, & Jakobsson, 2002).

Eligibility: Eligibility ensures that only the legitimate voters are allowed to cast their ballots.

Forced-Abstention Attack: In a forced-abstention attack the attacker coerces a voter by demanding that the voter refrains from voting (Juels, Catalano, & Jakobsson, 2002).

Inalterability: Inalterability means the ballot cast by the eligible voters should not be altered.

Non-Reusability: Non-reusability ensures that each voter should be allowed to vote only once.

Randomization Attack: In a randomization attack, the attacker coerces a voter by demanding that the voter submits randomly composed balloting material to nullify his choice with a large probability (Juels, Catalano, & Jakobsson, 2002).

Receipt-Freeness: Receipt-freeness means a voter cannot convince the coercer how the ballot was cast.

Simulation Attack: In a simulation attack, the attacker coerces a voter by demanding that the voter divulges his private keys so that the attacker can simulate the voter on his behalf (Juels, Catalano, & Jakobsson, 2002).

Soundness: Soundness means the eligibility of the voter, and the inalterability and non-reusability of the ballot.

Vote-Privacy: The property vote-privacy states that it is not possible to reveal for which candidate the voter casts the ballot.

APPENDIX

Figure 10. Process 1: Declaration

```
free c:channel. (*public channel*)

type spkey. (*public key for signature verification*)
type sskey. (*private key for signature*)
type skey. (*private key for decryption*)
type pkey. (*public key for encryption*)
type nonce. type rand.

fun pk(skey):pkey. fun aenc(bitstring,pkey):bitstring.
reduc forall m:bitstring, k:skey; adec(aenc(m,pk(k)),k) =m.

fun spk(sskey):spkey. fun sign(bitstring,sskey):bitstring.
reduc forall m:bitstring, k: sskey; checksign(sign(m,k),spk(k))=m.

fun signkey(spkey,sskey):bitstring.
reduc forall m:spkey, k: sskey; checksignkey(signkey(m,k),spk(k))=m.

fun blind(spkey,rand):spkey.
reduc forall m:spkey, k:sskey, r:rand; unblind(signkey(blind(m,r),k),r)=signkey(m,k).

free b:bitstring. (*b is ballot*)
free n1:bitstring. free n2:bitstring.

event Endvote(bitstring).
event Beginvote(spkey,bitstring).
event Voterkey(spkey,spkey).
event Cvoterkey(spkey,spkey).
```

Figure 11. Process 2: Voter Process

```
let  Voter(skv1:sskey,pkr:spkey,pcs:pkey,pkba:spkey)
   =
   new r1:rand; new r2:rand; new nv:nonce;
   new sv1:sskey; (*private key of k1*)
   let k1=spk(sv1) in (*the voting key*)
   let blindedkey1=blind(k1,r1) in
   new sv2:sskey;
   let k2=spk(sv2) in   let blindedkey2=blind(k2,r2) in

   event Voterkey(k1,k2);

   out(c,(n1,nv,blindedkey1,signkey(blindedkey1,skv1),blindedkey2,signkey(blindedkey2,skv1)));

   in(c,(=n2,=nv,m1:bitstring,m2:bitstring));
   let key1=checksignkey(m1,pkr) in
   let key2=checksignkey(m2,pkr) in

   if key1=blindedkey1 then let signedkey1=unblind(m1,r1) in
   if key2=blindedkey2 then let signedkey2=unblind(m2,r2) in

   let msg1=(b,sign(b,sv1)) in (*b is ballot*)
   let b1=(aenc((msg1,k1,signedkey1),pcs),k1,signedkey1) in

   event Beginvote(k1,b);

   out(c,b1);

   in(c,signedkey:bitstring);
   if checksignkey(signedkey,pkba)=k1 then out(c,signedkey).
```

Figure 12. Process 3: Corrupted Voter

```
let  CorruptedVoter(skv2:sskey,pkr:spkey,pcs:pkey,pkba:spkey)
    =
    new r1:rand; new r2:rand; new nv:nonce;
    new sv1:sskey; let k1=spk(sv1) in let blindedkey1=blind(k1,r1) in
    new sv2:sskey; let k2=spk(sv2) in let blindedkey2=blind(k2,r2) in
    event Cvoterkey(k1,k2);
    out(c, (n1,nv,blindedkey1,signkey(blindedkey1,skv2),blindedkey2,signkey(blindedkey2,skv2)));
    in(c,(=n2,=nv,m1:bitstring,m2:bitstring));

    let key1=checksignkey(m1,pkr) in
    let key2=checksignkey(m2,pkr) in

    if key1=blindedkey1 then let signedkey1=unblind(m1,r1) in
    if key2=blindedkey2 then let signedkey2=unblind(m2,r2) in

    out(c, ((k1,signedkey1),(k2,signedkey2))).
```

Figure 13. Process 4: Registrar, Ballot Acquirer, and Counting Server

```
let Registrar(skr:sskey,pkv1:spkey,pkv2:spkey)
    =
    in(c,(nv:nonce,m1:bitstring,m2:bitstring,m3:bitstring,m4:bitstring));
    checksign(m2,pkv1)=m1 then
    if checksign(m4,pkv1)=m3 then
    out(c,(nv,sign(m1,skr),sign(m3,skr)));

    in(c,(nv:nonce,m1:bitstring,m2:bitstring,m3:bitstring,m4:bitstring));
    if checksign(m2,pkv2)=m1 then
    if checksign(m4,pkv2)=m3 then
    out(c,(nv,sign(m1,skr),sign(m3,skr))).

let  BallotAcquirer(pkr:spkey,sba:skey,ssba:sskey)
    =
    in(c,b2:bitstring);
    let (b1:bitstring,k:spkey,pubv:bitstring) = b2 in

    if checksignkey(pubv,pkr)=k then
    out(c,signkey(k,ssba));
    let b3=sign(b1,ssba) in
    let ballot=(b1,b3) in
    out(c,ballot).

let  CountingServer(scs:skey,sscs:sskey,pkba:spkey,pkr:spkey)
    =
    in(c,ballot:bitstring);

    let (b1:bitstring,b3:bitstring)=ballot in
    if checksign(b3,pkba)=b1 then
    let (m1:bitstring,k:spkey,pubv:bitstring)=adec(b1,scs) in
    if checksignkey(pubv,pkr)=k then
    let (b:bitstring,signedb:bitstring) = m1 in
    if checksign(signedb,k)=b then
    out(c,(b,signkey(k,sscs)));

    event Endvote(b).
```

A Polling Booth-Based Electronic Voting Scheme

Figure 14. Process 5: The Main Process

```
process
    new skr:sskey;   let pkr=spk(skr) in
    new sba:skey;    let pba=pk(sba) in
    new scs:skey;    let pcs=pk(scs) in
    new skv1:sskey;  let pkv1=spk(skv1) in
    new skv2:sskey;  let pkv2=spk(skv2) in
    new ssba:sskey;  let pkba=spk(ssba) in
    new sscs:sskey;  let pkcs=spk(sscs) in
    out(c,(pkcs,pkba,pcs,pba,pkr,pkv1,pkv2));

((!Voter(skv1,pkr,pcs,pkba))| (!CorruptedVoter(skv2,pkr,pcs,pkba))  |  (!Registrar(skr,pkv1,pkv2))|
(!BallotAcquirer(pkr,sba,ssba))  |  (!CountingServer(scs,sscs,pkba,pkr)))
```

Figure 15. Process 6: Voter$_A$

```
let VoterA(skv1:sskey,pkr:spkey,pcs:pkey,pkba:spkey,ballot1:bitstring)
    =
    new nv1:nonce; new r11:rand;   new r21:rand;
    new sv11:sskey; let k11=spk(sv11) in
    let blindedkey11=blind(k11,r11) in
    new sv21:sskey; let k21=spk(sv21) in
    let blindedkey21=blind(k21,r21) in

    out(c,(n1,nv1,blindedkey11,signkey(blindedkey11,skv1),blindedkey21,signkey(blindedkey21,skv1)));

    in(c,(=n2,=nv1,m11:bitstring,m21:bitstring));

    let key11=checksignkey(m11,pkr) in
    let key21=checksignkey(m21,pkr) in

    if key11=blindedkey11 then let signedkey11=unblind(m11,r11) in
    if key21=blindedkey21 then let signedkey21=unblind(m21,r21) in
    let msg11=(b1,sign(b1,sv11)) in
    let b11=(aenc((msg11,k11,signedkey11),pcs),k11,signedkey11) in
    out(c,b11);

    in(c,signedkey:bitstring);
    if checksignkey(signedkey,pkba)=k11 then out(c,signedkey).
```

Figure 16. Process 7: Voter$_B$

```
let VoterB(skv2:sskey,pkr:spkey,pcs:pkey,pkba:spkey,ballot2:bitstring)
    =
    new nv2:nonce;new r12:rand; new r22:rand;
    new sv12:sskey; let k12=spk(sv12) in
    let blindedkey12=blind(k12,r12) in
    new sv22:sskey; let k22=spk(sv22) in
    let blindedkey22=blind(k22,r22) in

    out(c,(n1,nv2,blindedkey12,signkey(blindedkey12,skv2),blindedkey22,signkey(blindedkey22,skv2)));

    in(channelVR,(=n2,=nv2,m12:bitstring,m22:bitstring));

    let key12=checksignkey(m12,pkr) in
    let key22=checksignkey(m22,pkr) in

    if key12=blindedkey12 then let signedkey12=unblind(m12,r12) in
    if key22=blindedkey22 then let signedkey22=unblind(m22,r22) in

    let msg12=(b2,sign(b2,sv12)) in
    let b12=(aenc((msg12,k12,signedkey12),pcs),k12,signedkey12) in
    out(c,b12);

    in(c,signedkey:bitstring);
    if checksignkey(signedkey,pkba)=k12 then out(c,signedkey).
```

A Polling Booth-Based Electronic Voting Scheme

Figure 17. Process 8: Registrar, Ballot Acquirer, and Counting Server for Vote-Privacy

```
let Registrar(skr:sskey,pkv1:spkey,pkv2:spkey)
    =
    in(c,(=n1,nv:nonce,m1:bitstring,m2:bitstring,m3:bitstring,m4:bitstring));
    if checksign(m2,pkv1)=m1 then
    if checksign(m4,pkv1)=m3 then
    out(c,(n2,nv,sign(m1,skr),sign(m3,skr)));

    in(c,(=n1,nv:nonce,m1:bitstring,m2:bitstring,m3:bitstring,m4:bitstring));
    if checksign(m2,pkv2)=m1 then
    if checksign(m4,pkv2)=m3 then
    out(c,(n2,nv,sign(m1,skr),sign(m3,skr))).

let BallotAcquirer(pkr:spkey,sba:skey,ssba:sskey)
    =
    in(c,b22:bitstring); let (b11:bitstring,k:spkey,pubv:bitstring) = b22 in
    if checksignkey(pubv,pkr)=k then out(c,signkey(k,ssba));

    let b3=sign(b11,ssba) in let ballot=(b11,b3) in out(c,ballot).

let CountingServer(scs:skey,sscs:sskey,pkba:spkey,pkr:spkey)
    =
    in(c,ballot:bitstring); let (b1:bitstring,b3:bitstring)=ballot in
    if checksign(b3,pkba)=b1 then
    let (m1:bitstring,k:spkey,pubv:bitstring) = adec(b1,scs) in
    if checksignkey(pubv,pkr)=k then
    let (b:bitstring,signedb:bitstring) = m1 in
    if checksign(signedb,k)=b then
    out(c,(b,signkey(k,sscs))).
```

Figure 18. Process 9: The Process for Verifying Vote-Privacy

```
process
    new skr:sskey;  let pkr=spk(skr) in new sba:skey; let pba=pk(sba) in
    new scs:skey; let pcs=pk(scs) in new skv:sskey; let pkv=spk(skv) in
    new skv1:sskey; let pkv1=spk(skv1) in  new skv2:sskey; let pkv2=spk(skv2) in
    new ssba:sskey; let pkba=spk(ssba) in new sscs:sskey; let pkcs=spk(sscs) in
    out(c,(pkcs,pkba,pkv2,pkv1,pcs,pba,pkr))

    let ballot1=choice[b1,b2] in let ballot2=choice[b2,b1] in

(!VoterA(skv1,pkr,pcs,pkba,ballot1))  |  (!VoterB(skv2,pkr,pcs,pkba,ballot2))  |
(!Registrar(skr,pkv1,pkv2))|(!BallotAcquirer(pkr,sba,ssba))  |  (!CountingServer(scs,sscs,pkba,pkr))
```

Figure 19. Process 10: V'

```
let CorruptedVoter(skvc:sskey,pkr:spkey,pcs:pkey,pkba:spkey)
    =
    new nv:nonce;   new r1:rand;  new r2:rand;
    new sv1:sskey; new sv2:sskey;

    let k1=spk(sv1) in let blindedkey1=blind(k1,r1) in
    let k2=spk(sv2) in let blindedkey2=blind(k2,r2) in
    out(c, (n1,nv,blindedkey1,signkey(blindedkey1,skvc),blindedkey2,signkey(blindedkey2,skvc)));

    in(c,(=n2,=nv,m1:bitstring,m2:bitstring));

    let key1=checksignkey(m1,pkr) in
    let key2=checksignkey(m2,pkr) in

    if key1=blindedkey1 then let signedkey1=unblind(m1,r1) in
    if key2=blindedkey2 then let signedkey2=unblind(m2,r2) in


    let msgc=(bc,choice[(sign(bc,sv1)),sign(bc,sv2)]) in
    let b1c=(aenc((msgc,choice[(k1,signedkey1),(k2,signedkey2)]),pcs),choice[(k1,signedkey1),(k2,signedkey2)]) in

    out(c,b1c); out(c1,b1c);

    in(c,signedkey:bitstring);
    if checksignkey(signedkey,pkba)=k1 then out(c,signedkey);
    if checksignkey(signedkey,pkba)=k2 then out(c,signedkey).
```

Figure 20. Process 11: Voter$_A$ {c/v}^{c1}

```
let DishonestVoter(skvd:sskey,pkr:spkey,pcs:pkey,pkba:spkey)
    =
    new nv:nonce; new r1:rand; new r2:rand;
    new sv1:sskey; new sv2:sskey;
    let k1=spk(sv1) in let blindedkey1=blind(k1,r1) in
    let k2=spk(sv2) in let blindedkey2=blind(k2,r2) in
    out(c,(n1,nv,blindedkey1,signkey(blindedkey1,skvd),blindedkey2,signkey(blindedkey2,skvd)));

    in(c,(=n2,=nv,m1:bitstring,m2:bitstring));
    let key1=checksignkey(m1,pkr) in
    let key2=checksignkey(m2,pkr) in

    if key1=blindedkey1 then let signedkey1=unblind(m1,r1) in
    if key2=blindedkey2 then let signedkey2=unblind(m2,r2) in

    let msgd=(bd,sign(bd,sv1)) in
    let bld=(aenc((msgd,k1,signedkey1),pcs),k1,signedkey1) in
    out(c,bld); out(c1,bld);

    in(c,signedkey:bitstring);
    if checksignkey(signedkey,pkba)=k1 then out(c,signedkey).
```

Figure 21. Process 12: Registrar, Ballot Acquirer, and Counting Server for Receipt-Freeness

```
let Registrar(skr:sskey,pkv:spkey,pkvd:spkey,pkvc:spkey)
    =
    in(c, (=n1,nv:nonce,m1:bitstring,m2:bitstring,m3:bitstring,m4:bitstring));
    if checksign(m2,pkv)=m1 then
    if checksign(m4,pkv)=m3 then
    out(c, (n2,nv,sign(m1,skr),sign(m3,skr)));

    in(c, (=n1,nv:nonce,m1:bitstring,m2:bitstring,m3:bitstring,m4:bitstring));
    if checksign(m2,pkvd)=m1 then
    if checksign(m4,pkvd)=m3 then
    out(c, (n2,nv,sign(m1,skr),sign(m3,skr)));

    in(c, (=n1,nv:nonce,m1:bitstring,m2:bitstring,m3:bitstring,m4:bitstring));
    if checksign(m2,pkvc)=m1 then
    if checksign(m4,pkvc)=m3 then
    out(c, (n2,nv,sign(m1,skr),sign(m3,skr))).

let BallotAcquirer(pkr:spkey,sba:skey,ssba:sskey)
    =
    in(c,b2:bitstring); let (b1:bitstring,k:spkey,pubv:bitstring) = b2 in
    if checksignkey(pubv,pkr)=k then out(c,signkey(k,ssba));

    let b3=sign(b1,ssba) in   let ballot=(b1,b3) in out(c,ballot).

let CountingServer(scs:skey,sscs:sskey,pkba:spkey,pkr:spkey)
    =
    in(c,ballot:bitstring); let (b1:bitstring,b3:bitstring)=ballot in
    if checksign(b3,pkba)=b1 then
    let (m1:bitstring,k:spkey,pubv:bitstring) = adec(b1,scs) in
    if checksignkey(pubv,pkr)=k then
    let (b:bitstring,signedb:bitstring) = m1 in
    if checksign(signedb,k)=b then
    out(c, (b,signkey(k,sscs))).
```

Figure 22. Process 13: Receipt-Freeness

```
process
    new skr:sskey; let pkr=spk(skr) in new sba:skey; let pba=pk(sba) in
    new scs:skey;  let pcs=pk(scs) in new skv:sskey; let pkv=spk(skv) in
    new skvd:sskey; let pkvd=spk(skvd) in new skvc:sskey; let pkvc=spk(skvc) in
    new ssba:sskey; let pkba=spk(ssba) in new sscs:sskey; let pkcs=spk(sscs) in
    out(c,(pkcs,pkba,pkv,pkvd,pkvc,pcs,pba,pkr));

    (!Voter(skv,pkr,pcs,pkba)) | (!DishonestVoter(skvd,pkr,pcs,pkba)) |
    (!CorruptedVoter(skvc,pkr,pcs,pkba)) | (!Registrar(skr,pkv,pkvd,pkvc)) |
    (!BallotAcquirer(pkr,sba,ssba))  | !(CountingServer(scs,sscs,pkba,pkr))
```

Figure 23. Process 14: Registrar, Ballot Acquirer, and Counting Server for Coercion-Resistance

```
let Registrar(skr:sskey,pkv:spkey,pkvc:spkey,pkvcc:spkey)
    =
    in(c,(=n1,nv:nonce,m1:bitstring,m2:bitstring,m3:bitstring,m4:bitstring));
    if checksign(m2,pkv)=m1 then
    if checksign(m4,pkv)=m3 then
    out(c,(n2,nv,sign(m1,skr),sign(m3,skr)));

    in(c,(=n1,nv:nonce,m1:bitstring,m2:bitstring,m3:bitstring,m4:bitstring));
    if checksign(m2,pkvc)=m1 then
    if checksign(m4,pkvc)=m3 then
    out(c,(n2,nv,sign(m1,skr),sign(m3,skr)));

    in(c,(=n1,nv:nonce,m1:bitstring,m2:bitstring,m3:bitstring,m4:bitstring));
    if checksign(m2,pkvcc)=m1 then
    if checksign(m4,pkvcc)=m3 then
    out(c,(n2,nv,sign(m1,skr),sign(m3,skr))).

let BallotAcquirer(pkr:spkey,sba:skey,ssba:sskey)
    =
    in(c,b2:bitstring); let (b1:bitstring,k:spkey,pubv:bitstring) = b2 in
    if checksignkey(pubv,pkr)=k then out(c,signkey(k,ssba));

    let b3=sign(b1,ssba) in   let ballot=(b1,b3) in out(c,ballot).

let CountingServer(scs:skey,sscs:sskey,pkba:spkey,pkr:spkey)
    =
    in(c,ballot:bitstring); let (b1:bitstring,b3:bitstring)=ballot in
    if checksign(b3,pkba)=b1 then
    let (m1:bitstring,k:spkey,pubv:bitstring) = adec(b1,scs) in
    if checksignkey(pubv,pkr)=k then
    let (b:bitstring,signedb:bitstring) = m1 in
    if checksign(signedb,k)=b then out(c,(b,signkey(k,sscs))).
```

A Polling Booth-Based Electronic Voting Scheme

Figure 24. Process 15: Voter$_A^{coerced(c1)}$

```
let CoercedVoter(skvcc:sskey,pkr:spkey,pcs:pkey,pkba:spkey)
   =
   new nv:nonce;  new r1:rand;  new r2:rand;
   new sv1:sskey; new sv2:sskey;

   let k1=spk(sv1) in let blindedkey1=blind(k1,r1) in
   let k2=spk(sv2) in let blindedkey2=blind(k2,r2) in

   out(c,(n1,nv,blindedkey1,signkey(blindedkey1,skvcc),blindedkey2,signkey(blindedkey2,skvcc)));

   in(c,(=n2,=nv,m1:bitstring,m2:bitstring));

   let key1=checksignkey(m1,pkr) in
   let key2=checksignkey(m2,pkr) in

   if key1=blindedkey1 then let signedkey1=unblind(m1,r1) in
   if key2=blindedkey2 then let signedkey2=unblind(m2,r2) in

   out(c1,(choice[(k1,signedkey1),(k2,signedkey2)])).
```

Figure 25. Process 16: Coercion-Resistance

```
process
    new skr:sskey;   let pkr=spk(skr) in new sba:skey; let pba=pk(sba) in
    new scs:skey;  let pcs=pk(scs) in new skv:sskey; let pkv=spk(skv) in
    new ssba:sskey;  let pkba=spk(ssba) in new sscs:sskey; let pkcs=spk(sscs) in
    new skvcc:sskey; let pkvcc=spk(skvcc) in new skvc:sskey; let pkvc=spk(skvc) in
    out(c,(pkcs,pkba,pkv,pkvc,pkvcc,pcs,pba,pkr));

       (!Voter(skv,pkr,pcs,pkba))  |  (!CoercedVoter(skvcc,pkr,pcs,pkba))  |
       (!CorruptedVoter(skvc,pkr,pcs,pkba))  |  (!Registrar(skr,pkv,pkvc,pkvcc))  |
       (!BallotAcquirer(pkr,sba,ssba))   |(!CountingServer(scs,sscs,pkba,pkr))
```

Figure 26. Process 17: $Voter_A^{coerced(c1,c2)}\ \{?/v\}$

```
let CoercedVoter(skvcc:sskey,pkr:spkey,pcs:pkey,pkba:spkey)
 =
  new nv:nonce;   new r1:rand;   new r2:rand;
  new sv1:sskey; new sv2:sskey;

  let k1=spk(sv1) in let blindedkey1=blind(k1,r1) in
  let k2=spk(sv2) in let blindedkey2=blind(k2,r2) in

  out(c,(n1,nv,blindedkey1,signkey(blindedkey1,skvcc),blindedkey2,signkey(blindedkey2,skvcc)));

  in(c,(=n2,=nv,m1:bitstring,m2:bitstring));

  let key1=checksignkey(m1,pkr) in
  let key2=checksignkey(m2,pkr) in

  if key1=blindedkey1 then let signedkey1=unblind(m1,r1) in
  if key2=blindedkey2 then let signedkey2=unblind(m2,r2) in

  let msgcc=(bcc,choice[(sign(bcc,sv1)),sign(bcc,sv2)]) in
  let b1cc=(aenc((msgcc,choice[(k1,signedkey1),(k2,signedkey2)]),pcs),choice[(k1,signedkey1),(k2,signedkey2)]) in

  out(c,b1cc); out(c1,b1cc); out(c2,b1cc);

  in(c,signedkey:bitstring);
  if checksignkey(signedkey,pkba)=k1 then out(c,signedkey);
  if checksignkey(signedkey,pkba)=k2 then out(c,signedkey).
```

A Polling Booth-Based Electronic Voting Scheme

Figure 27. Process 18: The Extractor

```
let Extractor(skve:sskey,pkr:spkey,pcs:pkey,pkba:spkey)
    =
    new nv:nonce;  new r1:rand; new r2:rand; new sv1:sskey; new sv2:sskey;
    let k1=spk(sv1) in let blindedkey1=blind(k1,r1) in
    let k2=spk(sv2) in let blindedkey2=blind(k2,r2) in

    out(c,(n1,nv,blindedkey1,signkey(blindedkey1,skve),blindedkey2,signkey(blindedkey2,skve)));

    in(c,(=n2,=nv,m1:bitstring,m2:bitstring));

    let key1=checksignkey(m1,pkr) in
    let key2=checksignkey(m2,pkr) in

    if key1=blindedkey1 then let signedkey1=unblind(m1,r1) in
    if key2=blindedkey2 then let signedkey2=unblind(m2,r2) in

    in(c2,be:bitstring);

    let msge=(be,choice[(sign(be,sv1)),sign(be,sv2)]) in
    let ble=(aenc((msge,choice[(k1,signedkey1),(k2,signedkey2)]),pcs),
    choice[(k1,signedkey1),(k2,signedkey2)]) in out(c,ble);

    in(c,signedkey:bitstring);
    if checksignkey(signedkey,pkba)=k1 then out(c,signedkey);
    if checksignkey(signedkey,pkba)=k2 then out(c,signedkey).
```

Figure 28. Process 19: Registrar, Ballot Acquirer, and Counting Server for Coercion-Resistance (Second Bullet Point)

```
let Registrar(skr:sskey,pkv:spkey,pkvc:spkey,pkvcc:spkey,pkve:spkey)
    =
    in(c,(=n1,nv:nonce,m1:bitstring,m2:bitstring,m3:bitstring,m4:bitstring));
    if checksign(m2,pkv)=m1 then
    if checksign(m4,pkv)=m3 then
    out(c,(n2,nv,sign(m1,skr),sign(m3,skr)));

    in(c,(=n1,nv:nonce,m1:bitstring,m2:bitstring,m3:bitstring,m4:bitstring));
    if checksign(m2,pkvc)=m1 then
    if checksign(m4,pkvc)=m3 then
    out(c,(n2,nv,sign(m1,skr),sign(m3,skr)));

    in(c,(=n1,nv:nonce,m1:bitstring,m2:bitstring,m3:bitstring,m4:bitstring));
    if checksign(m2,pkvcc)=m1 then
    if checksign(m4,pkvcc)=m3 then
    out(c,(n2,nv,sign(m1,skr),sign(m3,skr)));

    in(c,(=n1,nv:nonce,m1:bitstring,m2:bitstring,m3:bitstring,m4:bitstring));
    if checksign(m2,pkve)=m1 then
    if checksign(m4,pkve)=m3 then
    out(c,(n2,nv,sign(m1,skr),sign(m3,skr))).

let BallotAcquirer(pkr:sskey,sba:skey,ssba:sskey)
    =
    in(c,b2:bitstring); let (b1:bitstring,k:spkey,pubv:bitstring) = b2 in
    if checksignkey(pubv,pkr)=k then out(c,signkey(k,ssba));

    let b3=sign(b1,ssba) in   let ballot=(b1,b3) in out(c,ballot).

let  CountingServer(scs:skey,sscs:sskey,pkba:spkey,pkr:spkey)
    =
    in(c,ballot:bitstring); let (b1:bitstring,b3:bitstring)=ballot in
    if checksign(b3,pkba)=b1 then
    let (m1:bitstring,k:spkey,pubv:bitstring) = adec(b1,scs) in
    if checksignkey(pubv,pkr)=k then
    let (b:bitstring,signedb:bitstring) = m1 in
    if checksign(signedb,k)=b then out(c,(b,signkey(k,sscs))).
```

Figure 29. Process 20: Coercion-Resistance (Second Bullet Point)

```
process
    new skr:sskey; let pkr=spk(skr) in new sba:skey; let pba=pk(sba) in
    new scs:skey; let pcs=pk(scs) in new skv:sskey; let pkv=spk(skv) in
    new ssba:sskey; let pkba=spk(ssba) in new sscs:sskey; let pkcs=spk(sscs) in
    new skvc:sskey; let pkvc=spk(skvc) in new skve:sskey; let pkve=spk(skve) in
    new skvcc:sskey; let pkvcc=spk(skvcc) in
    out(c,(pkcs,pkba,pkv,pkve,pkvc,pkvcc,pcs,pba,pkr));

    (!Voter(skv,pkr,pcs,pkba)) | (!CoercedVoter(skvcc,pkr,pcs,pkba)) |
    (!Extractor(skve,pkr,pcs,pkba)) | (!CorruptedVoter(skvc,pkr,pcs,pkba)) |
    (!Registrar(skr,pkv,pkvc,pkvcc,pkve))|(!BallotAcquirer(pkr,sba,ssba))| (!CountingServer(scs,sscs,pkba,pkr))
```

Chapter 6
Challenges and Solutions for DNS Security in IPv6

Hosnieh Rafiee
Hasso Plattner Institute, Germany

Martin von Löwis
Hasso Plattner Institute, Germany

Christoph Meinel
Hasso Plattner Institute, Germany

ABSTRACT

The Domain Name System (DNS) is a necessary component of the Internet that allows hosts on the Internet to communicate with other hosts without needing to know their cryptic IP addresses. When this protocol was first introduced it did not contain robust security features because scalability was an issue. One of the useful features added to DNS was the DNS update mechanism that allowed other hosts to dynamically change DNS entries. This feature, though, exposed new vulnerabilities to DNS servers which necessitated the implementation of new security protocols. Some of the security protocols introduced to address these issues were Transaction SIGnature (TSIG) and DNS Security Extension (DNSSEC). Although, in IPv4, these mechanisms did resolve most of the security issues dealing with authentication between a node and a DNS server, they are not viable in IPv6 networks. This is because the Neighbor Discovery Protocol (NDP) introduced to organize the large IPv6 address space automatically does not support DNS authentication or have an option for secure DNS updating. In this chapter, the authors first explain the common approaches used in IPv4 to address these security issues. Then they explain the differences between the use of these approaches in IPv4 and IPv6, where the focus is on new research with regard to authentication mechanisms between hosts and DNS servers.

DOI: 10.4018/978-1-4666-4514-1.ch006

INTRODUCTION

DNS (Mockapetris, 1987) establishes a naming system for computers, or any other service or device, connected to a network. Without the DNS protocol, Web addresses would become long, confusing, and difficult to remember. The importance of DNS lies in how it makes the Internet and other networks easier to use. It does this by translating domain names into IP addresses. For example, the domain name www.example.com might translate to the IP address 192.168.204.6. Therefore, changing an IP address of a server, such as Web or email, would have a profound effect on a large number of users and systems that make use of the services on those servers on the Internet.

Even though DNS is a very critical element of the Internet, it only supports basic security mechanisms. Also, new DNS functions, such as Dynamic DNS (DDNS), open up new security issues concerning DNS, such as to how to prevent attackers from changing DNS records–in other words, how to authenticate the host's desire to change Resource Records (RRs) on DNS servers. To address this problem, two different protocols were introduced: Transaction SIGnature (TSIG) (Vixie, Gudmundsson, Eastlake 3rd, & Wellington, 2000) and DNS Security Extension (DNSSEC) (Arends, Austein, Larson, Massey, & Rose, 2005). The extensions to these security protocols could thus resolve the authentication problems in Internet Protocol version 4 (IPv4). But the main problem that exists with the IPv4 network is a lack of IP addresses. According to the IANA exhaustion counter, the last blocks of IPv4 addresses have already been given to the local Internet registries. It is for this reason that the next generation of Internet Protocol, i.e. IPv6 (Deering, & Hinden, 1998) was proposed. The number of unique IPv6 addresses is 2^{128-32} times greater than those of IPv4. To organize this large address space, two different mechanisms have been proposed: Dynamic Host Configuration Protocol (DHCPv6) (Droms, Bound, Volz, Lemon, Perkins, & Carney, 2003) and Neighbor Discovery Protocol (NDP) (Narten, Nordmark, Simpson, & Soliman, 2007). These two mechanisms, together, are known as IPv6 Autoconfiguration. Unfortunately, security, in the DNS update process, is also the main issue with these two mechanisms. For example, when using DHCPv6, no options have been added to the DHCPv6 messages to handle host authentication of the DNS server. Another main problem, with these mechanisms, is the changeable nature of IPv6 addresses. Because of privacy reasons, and in order to prevent attackers from tracking a node in IPv6 networks, the IPv6 addresses are valid only for a short period of time, which is dependent on network policy. Moreover, in one of these addressing mechanisms, i.e., NDP, there is no control over the nodes that can join the IPv6 networks. These unmanageable and temporary addresses create several issues for the updating of DNS records. There is another issue which concerns resolver authentication. Usually, the DNS client (stub resolver) on the client's computer sends its queries to another recursive DNS server in order to recursively query other DNS servers and to translate a name to an IP address. It then sends back the result to this client. The DNS client often does not support any secure mechanisms, like DNSSEC, and thus only relies on the source IP address authentication process. An attacker is thus able to spoof this IP address and then send the wrong response to this client. The attacker will then direct the victim to a computer of his choice which, in fact, might be one of his own servers. On many occasions, like checking a bank account, it is important for users to ensure that the query response received from the DNS server was originated by the real recursive DNS server and has not been spoofed by an attacker.

The main focus of this chapter will be on the security mechanisms needed to ensure a securer DNS update and on the proper authentication process. Several books already discuss DNS implementation and configuration. We will therefore just briefly mention this background information. The remaining sections of this chapter are organized as follow:

First – DNS concepts and functions are briefly explained. Second – IPv6 autoconfiguration mechanisms, threats, and the differences between DNS in IPv4 and IPv6 are explained. Third – divides DNS functions into two categories, introduces DNS threats in each category, describes the current security mechanism in place for IPv6, introduces the most recent research on DNS security for IPv6, and explains future trends. The last section summarizes this chapter.

DOMAIN NAME SYSTEM (DNS)

DNS and its Functions

DNS is a hierarchical database that stores data in a particular format in what are called Resource Records (RRs). These RRs are distinguished by their types – MX, NS, AAAA, A, etc. Each RR specifies information about a particular object. The server uses these records to answer queries from hosts in its zone (Mockapetris, 1987).

To provide a host with DNS functionality, it is necessary to install software that implements the DNS protocol. One of these implementations is the Berkeley Internet Name Domain (BIND) that was first introduced in the early 1980s at the University of California at Berkeley. This implementation is also viewed as the reference implementation for the Internet's DNS. The latest versions (version 8+) of this implementation support Dynamic Update which will be explained in the next section.

A DNS-capable host is called a Name Server (NS). Name Servers can be divided into two categories: Authoritative and Recursive.

- **Authoritative:** An authoritative name server provides the answers to DNS queries. For example, it would respond to a query about a mail server IP address or Website IP address. It provides original, first-hand, definitive answers (authoritative answers) to DNS queries. It does not provide 'just cached' answers that were obtained from another name server. Therefore it only returns answers to queries about domain names that are installed in its system configuration.

  There are two types of Authoritative Name Servers:
  - **Master Server (Primary Name Server):** A master server stores the original master copies of all zone records. A host master is only allowed to change the master server's zone records. Each slave server gets updated via a special automatic updating mechanism within the DNS protocol. All slave servers maintain identical copies of the master records.
  - **Slave Server (Secondary Name Server):** A slave server is an exact replica of the master server. It is used to share the DNS server's load and to improve DNS zone availability in cases where the master server fails. It is recommended that there be at least 2 slave servers and one master server for each domain name.

- **Recursive (Something which Repeats or Refers Back to Itself):** A recursive name server responds to queries where the query does not contain an entry for the host in its database. It first checks its own records and cache for the answer to the query and then, if it cannot find an answer there, it may recursively query name servers higher up in the hierarchy and then pass the response back to the originator of the query. This is known as a *recursive query* or *recursive lookup*.

In principle, authoritative name servers suffice for the operation of the Internet. However, with only authoritative name-servers operating, every DNS query must start with recursive queries at the root zone of the Domain Name System and each user system must implement resolver software capable of a recursive operation. In fact, the majority of DNS query responses are generated from the cache of recursive servers, which are responsible for obtaining the IP address of the site or computer you are trying to reach. Many of the security compromises and breaches that occur today are the result of vulnerabilities in the recursive or caching DNS server code.

For example, when a user types something like "www.xxx.com" into his browser, in order to resolve this address, a request is sent to a Name Server. The IP address of this local DNS server is configured either via Dynamic Host Configuration Protocol (DHCP – a network protocol that is used to configure network devices so that they can communicate on an IP network) or by other mechanisms that were explained in the section entitled "DNS for IPv6". The Name Server resolves the address by the use of different types of queries which can be either recursive queries (the DNS server has to reply with the requested information or with an error message because the DNS server cannot provide a referral to a different DNS server [Microsoft Library, 2013]) or iterative queries (the DNS server provides the best answer which can be the resolved name or a referral to a different DNS server [Microsoft Library, 2013]). It will then return that Website's IP address. It is at this time that a connection will be established and the content on that Website will become visible.

Mechanisms to Update DNS

DNS update (Wellington, 2000) is a mechanism for adding, changing, or removing a RR record in a DNS zone file. There are two mechanisms used to update DNS RRs: manual updating and Dynamic DNS Update (DDNS) (Wellington, 2000). In manual updating, an administrator needs to edit the zone file in order to process the modifications. If the DNS service needs to restart in order to apply the modifications, then this would have an adverse effect on DNS performance. During the restart process of a DNS service, the DNS servers (name servers) will be unable to process DNS queries that are asked of it by other hosts on the Internet. To address this problem DDNS was introduced. By the use of this mechanism it is possible for the name server to change one or several records, in one particular zone, with just one DNS update request, while at the same time, being able to respond to user queries. The clients, or servers, can thus automatically send updates to the authoritative name servers in order to modify the records they want to modify. The authoritative name server then checks to make sure that certain prerequisites have been met. The prerequisites contain a set of RRs that must exist on the primary master server in the particular zone that needs to process this update packet. DDNS can also be used, in conjunction with DHCP, to update RR records when a computer's IP address is changed. To do this, clients send update messages, which should contain an additional DHCP option that provides their Fully Qualified Domain Name (FQDN) (Stapp & Volz, 2006), along with instructions to the DHCP server as to how to process the DNS dynamic updates. (For example, if the client name is "hostx" and the parent domain name is "mynetwork.com," then the FQDN is "hostx.mynetwork.com). An example of an application needing DDNS would be a small business, where a static IP address is not available for use by their servers, or the IP addresses are set dynamically by Neighbor Discovery Protocol (NDP) or DHCPv6.

DNS FOR IPV6

Internet Protocol Version 6 (IPv6)

Internet Protocol Version 6 (IPv6) (Deering, & Hinden, 1998) represents the next generation of Internet protocol. The main reason for its creation was due to the exhaustion of IP addresses that currently exists in the current version of the Internet

Protocol, Internet Protocol version 4 (IPv4). IPv4 allows for only about 4.2×10^9 unique addresses worldwide while IPv6 allows for about 3.40×10^{38} addresses – a number unlikely ever to run out. These IPv6 IP addresses are in a hexadecimal format – such as (fe08:1a63:2001:50e9::). It is because of this hexadecimal format that it is difficult to memorize IPv6 addresses. Administrators do not want to have to manually set these IP addresses for the hosts on their network and thus look for other mechanisms for their management. In order to organize such a large address space, two IPv6 autoconfiguration mechanisms were introduced: Dynamic Host Configuration Protocol v6 (DHCPv6) and Neighbor Discovery Protocol (NDP).

IPv6 Autoconfiguration

There are two different types of autoconfiguration mechanisms used in IPv6 – Stateful Autoconfiguration and Stateless Autoconfiguration. Stateful Autoconfiguration, DHCPv6, is the equivalent of IPv4's DHCP but for IPv6. It is used to pass out addresses and service information in the same manner that DHCP does it in IPv4. This is called "stateful" because both the DHCP server and the client must maintain state information in order to keep addresses from conflicting, to handle leases, and to renew addresses, over time. Stateless autoconfiguration allows a host to propose an address which will probably be unique and to offer it for use on the network. Because no server has to approve the use of the address, or pass it out, stateless autoconfiguration is simpler. This is the default mode of operation for most IPv6 systems, which includes servers.

Dynamic Host Configuration Protocol Version 6 (DHCPv6)

DHCPv6 (Droms et al., 2003) is a protocol that can be used to allow a DHCP server to automatically assign an IP address to a host from a defined range of IP addresses configured for that network. DHCPv6 operates in many modes compared to DHCPv4:

- **Stateless Mode:** In combination with stateless IP configuration, DHCPv6 delivers router advertisements to a host with DNS server information along with other information, like options for SIP phones and other services.
- **Stateful Mode:** A host can also configure it's IP address (as with DHCPv4) with DHCPv6
- **DHCPv6 Prefix Delegation (DHCPv6-PD) (Troan, & Droms, 2003):** This is an extension to DHCPv6 that enables an IPv6 host, running DHCPv6 protocol, to ask for a network prefix from that DHCPv6 server. This DHCPv6 server can be an Internet Service Provider ISP).

When a device connects to the IP network, it sends out a Router Solicitation (RS) message. The responding message, a Router Advertisement (RA) message, contains two flags. The O flag is set to indicate the existence of "other" information on the DHCPv6 servers. The M flag indicates the use of managed mode. Managed mode is the action where the client should ask DHCPv6 for an IP address and not configure one statelessly. The big difference between DHCPv4 and DHCPv6 is the way in which the device identifies itself if a host wants to assign the addresses itself, instead of selecting addresses dynamically from a pool.

Neighbor Discovery Protocol (NDP)

Neighbor Discovery (ND) (Narten et al., 2007) enables hosts to discover their neighboring routers and hosts and presents a technique which allows the host to obtain router information from routers. It also enables all nodes on the network to check for the reachability of other neighboring hosts and routers. ND and Stateless Address

AutoConfiguration (SLAAC) (Thomson, Narten, & Jinmei, 2007), together, comprise NDP. This protocol defines five different Internet Control Message Protocol version 6 (ICMPv6) message types, which perform functions for IPv6 similar to those of Address Resolution Protocol (ARP) and Internet Control Message Protocol (ICMP), Router Discovery, and Router Redirect protocols for IPv4.

A NDP-enabled node can configure its IP address automatically as soon as it is plugged into a new network. This newly joined node first generates its Interface Identifier (IID), which is represented by the 64 rightmost 128 bits of the IPv6 address. It concatenates the IID with the local link layer prefix that starts with fe08, and sets this on its network adapter. It then sends a RS message to all neighboring routers requesting router information. Routers respond to this message with a RA message that contains routing information and subnet prefixes (64 bits). The subnet prefix consists of the 64 leftmost 128 bits of the IPv6 addresses. The node then sets its global IP address (as a temporary address) with the subnet prefix obtained from the RA message, and sends a Neighbor Solicitation (NS) message to all nodes on that network in order to prevent the possibility of collisions with its IP address (process Duplicate Address Detection [DAD]). If it does not receive any Neighbor Advertisement (NA) messages after a certain time, (a standard of about 1 second) from any nodes claiming to own its IP address, then it changes the status of this IP address to permanent and starts using it. Otherwise, it will generate a new IID and repeat this process.

The Differences between DNS for IPv4 and IPv6

Even though DNS resides far above the Internet Protocol in the TCP/IP protocol architecture suite, it works intimately with IP addresses. For this reason, changes are necessary to afford it the ability to support the new IPv6. These changes include the definition of a new IPv6 address RR (AAAA) as a replacement for the A RR in IPv4. When a node wants to know the IP address of a sample domain, the response to this query will be obtained by retrieving that IP address from the AAAA RR record on the DNS server.

Another change occurs in Reverse mapping. Reverse mapping maps a particular IP address to a particular host and allows nodes, on the Internet, to look for a domain name associated with an IP address. An IPv4 reverse map uses IN-ADDR. ARPA Pointer Resource Records (PTR RRs) for reverse mapping. For example, if the IP address is 192.168.254.17, the reverse lookup domain name is 17.254.168.192.IN-ADDR.ARPA. On the other hand, IPv6 makes use of the IP6.ARPA domain PTR RRs for reverse mapping. Each hexadecimal digit of the 32-digit IPv6 address (zero compression and double-colon compression notation cannot be used) becomes a separate level, in inverse order, in the reverse domain hierarchy, when the namespace for reverse queries is created. For example, the IPv6 address is 2001:0db8:0000::/48 so the reverse lookup domain name is 0.0.0.0.8.b.d.0.1.0.0.2.IP6.ARPA.

Because IPv4 and IPv6 coexist, and because different formats are used for reverse mapping, the reverse zone files need to be defined separately.

DNS SECURITY

DNS is an essential protocol used on the Internet. When this protocol was first introduced it did not contain robust security features because of scalability issues (Scalability refers to the fact that the database, which must be kept in sync, is distributed over the entire Internet.). In today's environment, security has become a big issue for DNS. Safeguarding the DNS operation is a primary concern to everyone using the Internet today. DNS critical functions can be divided into two categories: reading data from a DNS server and writing data to a DNS server. There are some security issues associated with each of these functions. In the following sections these issues, and the current solution for them, will be described.

Reading Data from a DNS Server

Any host on the Internet can query DNS servers. No authentication is needed to do this. The host needs only to support a client DNS application called a resolver. When a host, such as a client or a mail server, wants to resolve the domain name or IP address of another host on the network, it sends its query to a resolver. The resolver can be a server, located in an Internet Service Provider's (ISP) network, which gives the host access to the Internet. The task of the resolver is to query, recursively, the root DNS server, and other DNS servers, to find the authoritative DNS server. The resolver then sends a query to that name server in order to read the content of RRs on that DNS server. The authoritative DNS server then responds to the query with the relevant content contained in the RRs. After receiving the response from the authoritative DNS server, the resolver forwards this response to the host that initiated the query. Figure 1 shows the process of querying name servers to find a sample domain (example.com). Some hosts do support the DNS resolving process themselves, while others rely on a resolver to resolve the query.

DNS Read Threats

DNS queries are exchanged in plain text. Attackers can easily sniff these messages, manipulate them for their own purposes and, then, forward them on to the resolvers. Resolvers have no way of verifying this data. They forward these DNS responses to the query initiator without authenticating them or ensuring their integrity.

Another problem exists for clients initiating these queries. The basic authentication mechanism uses the source IP address. If the source IP address of the query response is the same as that of the resolver, then the clients' computer will accept that response. The clients thus have no way of ensuring that the query responses were originated by the real resolver and not as the result of having been spoofed by an attacker. The DNS queries are thus vulnerable to several types of attack, which are explained below.

Man in the Middle (MITM) Attack

When a nameserver and a resolver initiate a DNS request and response, an attacker might intercept both, and then attempt to spoof the messages exchanged between the name server and resolver. The attacker reroutes communication between a nameserver and a resolver through the attacker's computer. The nameserver and resolver have no idea that the attack is being perpetrated. The attacker is thus able to monitor and read the traffic before sending it on to the intended recipient. This attack is possible because the DNS queries

Figure 1. Reading data from DNS server

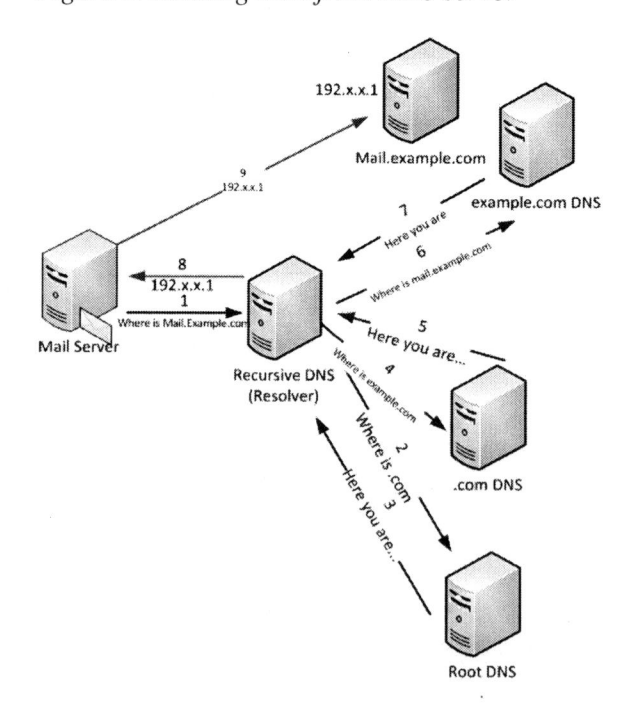

are only authenticated based on the source IP address. The attacker can thus spoof this IP address and initiate his attack. Other types of attack that are included in this category are packet sniffing and cache poisoning.

DNS Cache Poisoning Attacks

DNS cache poisoning is another form of MITM attack. Cache is a very important component of the DNS infrastructure. Many components within the DNS hierarchy maintain their own cache to avoid the necessity of accessing an external server's cache. A resolver nameserver receives a response and caches it for a certain period of time (dependent on network policy) so that further queries for the matching domain can be resolved using data from its cache. Not only does this reduce the amount of DNS traffic, but it makes the resolution process more efficient. An attacker might also respond to a requestor's DNS query with spoofed messages. Whenever a nameserver sends out a query to another nameserver, it verifies the response through the execution of the following steps:

- Ensure that the Query ID (16 bit identifier for the request) in the response matches the one contained in the request.
- Ensure that the response arrives on the same User Datagram Protocol (UDP) port that was used for sending the request.
- Ensure that the question section in the response matches that of the question contained in the query.
- Ensure that additional information contained in the response belongs to the same domain as that which was queried.

When the verification process is successful, the response is accepted and the cache is updated. An attacker can try to guess this data by sending a query for the domain name that it wants to hijack to the nameserver it wants to poison. Knowing that the nameserver will soon reach out to external nameservers for resolution, the attacker starts flooding the nameserver with forged responses. Nameservers are designed to accept the first valid response – the rest of the responses are ignored. The chance of the attacker's valid looking response reaching the nameserver is high if the attacker is able to generate responses that reach the resolver before a valid response does. This process redirects other user's queries, of that domain, to the attacker's computer.

Packet Sniffing

This attack occurs when DNS sends an entire query or response in a single, unsigned, unencrypted UDP packet. Messages sent this way make spoofing easy. An attacker can capture DNS query packets, generate wrong responses, and then send them quickly to the resolver, before the correct response is received from the name server. As no source authentication or data integrity checks are supported, this will not be detected by the resolver.

Transaction ID Guessing

A transaction ID is a 16-bit field which identifies a specific DNS transaction. The transaction ID is created by the DNS request initiator and is copied to the DNS response by a DNS query responder. Using the transaction ID, the DNS client can match responses to its requests. It is not hard to guess, from the DNS request, without having to intercept packets on the LAN, the transaction ID of a DNS response. In practice, the client UDP port and the Transaction ID can be predicted from previous DNS requests/responses (DNS queries). It is common for the client port to be a known fixed value, due to firewall restrictions, or the port number will increase incrementally due to resolver library behavior. The DNS transaction ID generated by a client usually increases incrementally. This reduces the search space for an attacker (Atkins & Austein, 2004).

Distributed Denial of Service (DDoS) Attack

A DDoS attack is an attempt to make a DNS server unavailable in the network. Over the past several months a series of Distributed Denial of Service (DDoS) attacks have victimized DNS root and Top Level Domain (TLD) name server operators. Suppose an attacker targets nameserver A on the Internet. The attacker initiates several DNS request messages, using nameserver A as the source IP address of these messages, for the purpose of initiating a DDoS attack on nameserver A. These messages are sent from different infected computers, called botnets, around the Internet. If the resolvers cannot find a response to that query in their cache, they issue a DNS request message of their own, to the compromised name servers, in order to retrieve the response. The compromised name servers return the DNS responses to the resolvers. The resolvers then send these DNS response messages to the spoofed IP address, i.e., nameserver A. Nameserver A is thus bombarded with many DNS response queries which prevents it from answering new DNS queries. The nameserver A's services would thus not be available to real users.

Secure DNS Read

There are some mechanisms that can be used to secure DNS queries. Two of these are the DNS Security Extension (DSNSEC) (Arends et al., 2005) and the Internet Protocol Security (IPsec) (Kent & Seo, 2005).

DNS Security Extension (DNSSEC)

DNSSEC (Arends et al., 2005) was introduced by the Internet Engineering Task Force (IETF) as an extension to the DNS used in validating DNS query operations. It verifies the authenticity and integrity of query results from a signed zone. In other words, if DNSSEC is available from the requestor client to the resolver/caching name server to the authoritative name servers, then the client has a level of assurance that the DNS query response is signed and trustworthy, starting from the root and chaining all the way down to the domain and sub domains. It uses asymmetrical cryptography. This means that separate keys are used to encrypt and decrypt data in order to provide security for certain name servers with their respective administrators. When DNSSEC is used, all answers include a digital signature. This will prevent DNS spoofing attacks because the attacker does not have the same private key as the server and thus will be unable to sign his own response and send it to the victim. But the problem with DNSSEC is that the signatures are not created on-the-fly because DNS itself does not have access to the keys needed to sign its own responses. Thus, the administrator of that zone should sign each domain and sub domain manually, ahead of time, and then store those signatures in the SIG RRs of the DNS server. Moreover, the zone private key should be stored offline. This is the reason that it cannot fully support the Dynamic Update process. It cannot generate the signature, on-the-fly, in order to respond to real-time queries. Also using DNSSEC cannot guarantee the data's confidentiality because it does not encrypt the data but just signs it.

Internet Protocol Security (IPsec)

The Internet Engineering Task Force (IETF) (Kent & Seo, 2005) proposed the use of IPsec in order to provide access control, data authentication, integrity, and confidentiality for the data that is sent between communication nodes across IP networks. IPsec insures data security at the IP packet level (IP datagram). A packet is a unit of data that is assembled and routed across the network, including a header and payload. Other protocols that assist IPsec in securing packets are:

Challenges and Solutions for DNS Security in IPv6

- **Encapsulating Security Payload (ESP):** A session protocol for data protection that provides confidentiality, authentication, and integrity.
- **Authentication Header (AH):** Provides authentication and integrity.
- **Internet Key Exchange (IKE):** Provides session key negotiation, key management, and Security Association (SA) management.

IPsec can be configured to operate in either of two modes: tunnel and transport mode. When the tunnel mode, the default IPsec mode, is used the entire original IP packet is protected by IPsec. This means that IPsec encapsulates the original packet, encrypts it, adds a new IP header to it and then sends it to the other side. In other words, the entire packet is the payload and this packet is then processed using IPsec. Tunnel mode is most commonly used to encrypt traffic between secure IPsec gateways – such as, between the Cisco router and PIX Firewall, or an end-station to a gateway, where the gateway acts as a proxy for the hosts behind it. Transport mode is used for end-to-end communications – such as, for a host to host IPsec SA. Only the original packet's payload is encrypted and protected using this mode. The IP header is not protected, so an attacker might eavesdrop to find the source and destination of this packet. A secure Telnet or secure Remote Desktop session, from a client to a server, are representative of the IPsec transport mode.

Even though IPsec is a good approach for securing data at the packet level, in practice, because of the complexities involved, it is not easy to configure or to implement. For example, public key authentication used in IKE requires the use, and hence understanding, of X.509 certificates (Cooper, Santesson, Farrell, Boeyen, Housley, & Polk, 2008). Moreover, the secret key distribution mechanism requires an infrastructure whereby the traditional methods for authentication are Pre-Shared Keys and Digital Signatures. The use of a Pre-Shared Key is only feasible when the number of communicating hosts is small. This is why, in practice, IPsec is not used to secure DNS messages. On the contrary, IPsec benefits from the use of DNSSEC records for authentication in IKE processing (Merino, Martínez, Organero, & Kloos, 2006), but this method is beyond the scope of this chapter.

Can Existing Secure DNS Read Mechanisms be used in IPv6?

Two DNS secure read mechanisms were introduced in the prior section. Unfortunately, the human intervention required to apply the configurations needed by these mechanisms makes them difficult to use in both IPv6 and IPv4 networks. For example, pre-configuring all DNSKEYs used in DNSSEC mechanisms, for every root island of security, is not practical because of scalability and key management, in each resolver, are major issues in today's fast-growing Internet. In other words, the current resolver (stub-resolvers) installed on most of the world's computers would need to be replaced with ones that could handle DNSSEC messages. The fact that replies to DNS requests exceeding 512 bytes (due to the use of older preconfigured equipment) are blocked, poses a second problem. Typically, DNSSEC replies are four times larger. The third reason is that zones whose parents do not deploy DNSSEC cannot use a DNSSEC approach. Thus, the communication between a non DNSSEC enabled zone with a DNSSEC enabled zone is not protected and is prone to read attacks as mentioned in the previous sections.

Writing Data to DNS Server

Writing data to a DNS server is the process of adding, changing, or removing a RR record in a zone's master file. This is called a DNS Update. This process can be for the transfer of the entire zone from a master to slave, or updating just a few RRs in the master name server. The old mechanism used to process updates consisted of a manual update process. But this manual process had a negative impact on the performance of DNS servers because of the need for human intervention. Human intervention also opened the door for an increase in DNS attacks that were the result of human error. For example, a long delay could result when an update is needed and the administrator is not available. Another problem, with some implementations of DNS, is that the DNS service will need to be restarted before the changes will take effect. During a restart, DNS servers are unable to process DNS queries. To address these issues the Dynamic DNS update (DDNS) (Wellington, 2000) was introduced. DDNS enables real-time, dynamic updates to entries in the DNS database. By using this mechanism, it is possible for the name server to change one or several records in one particular zone with the use of only one DNS update request, while at the same time, responding to user queries. The clients or servers can thus automatically send updates to the authoritative name servers in order to modify the records they want modified.

DNS Write Threats

DDNS uses a basic protection mechanism in order to prevent other nodes from making unauthorized updates. This is done by checking whether or not the source IP address is the same as that on the list of authorized updaters. But there is a flaw here because attackers can spoof this IP address and update DNS RRs and then redirect all traffic to their desired hosts rather than the intended hosts. The attackers can also execute other attacks – such as, phishing attacks, infection of other computers, Distributed Denial of Service (DDoS) attacks, etc. They can also redirect traffic to the victim's host which will inundate that server with messages and render its service unavailable (DoS). The list of DNS write threats include the vulnerabilities of the Operating System (unauthorized access to zone file), zone file configuration vulnerabilities (human mistakes), Source IP spoofing, DNS update spoofed messages, and Zone file corruption (accidentally).

Vulnerabilities of the Operating System

The bugs (bug – an error or mistake in software code that does not allow the software to perform its task correctly) in a server Operating System (OS) might give attackers access to computers on its network, especially when they are always connected to the Internet and the servers' service is accessible via the Internet. For example, unnecessary open ports in an OS could allow remote code execution.

When an attacker gains access to the OS, he might access critical data, such as a DNS zone file, and update RRs for his own advantage. Overflowing the code execution buffer is another type of attack against the OS. This attack calls a subroutine that returns to a point in the main program defined by the attacker. This is one of many, similar types of OS level attacks, which exploit OS vulnerabilities on which the DNS service is running (Rooney, 2011).

Zone File Configuration Vulnerabilities

When an administrator configures the DNS service, any misconfiguration might allow for the extraction of critical data from a zone file to the attacker's computer or might lead to an improperly configured server.

Source IP Spoofing

If a host wants to update a RR record residing in a zone file on the DNS server, the DNS server checks to see that the source IP address, of the DNS requestor, is the same as that stored in the DNS configuration file. If it is the same, the DNS server will process the update request. An attacker

Challenges and Solutions for DNS Security in IPv6

can listen to DNS traffic, intercept an IP address, and then, illegally update a RR in a DNS server. He can then redirect the traffic to the computer of his choice.

Spoofed Message Attack

This type of attack is usually classified as a source IP spoofing attack. In this attack, the attacker listens to the DNS traffic, and when a legitimate host wants to update a RR in a zone file on the DNS server, the attacker intercedes and changes the content of the DNS update and resends it to the DNS server. Since the source IP address is now actually the same as the legitimate host IP address, the update request will be processed by the DNS server.

Zone File Corruption

When the hard disk, where the zone file is stored, encounters a physical problem, which causes a part of data to be lost, a corrupted zone file is the result.

Secure DNS Write

Some security mechanisms and protocols were introduced to address the problems mentioned in earlier sections. TSIG (Vixie et al., 2000) is one such protocol that can be used to secure a Dynamic Update. The remainder of this section will explain the TSIG RR format and the messages exchanged between a client and a server when the DNS update is initialized.

Transaction SIGnature (TSIG)

TSIG is a protocol which provides endpoint authentication and data integrity by the use of one-way hashing and shared secret keys to establish a trust relationship between two hosts that can be either a client and a server or two servers. The TSIG keys are manually exchanged between these two hosts and must be kept in a secure place. This protocol can be used to secure a Dynamic Update or to give assurance to the slave name server that the zone transfer is from the original master name server and that it has not been spoofed by hackers. It does this by verifying the signature with a cryptographic key shared with that of the receiver.

The TSIG Resource Record (RR) has the same format as other records used in a DDNS update request. Some of the fields of this TSIG RR are: Name, Class, Type, Time To Live Resource Data (TTL RDATA), etc. For example, an RDATA field would specify the type of algorithm that would be used in a one-way hashing function. It could be a Hash-Based Message Authentication Code-Message-Digest algorithm (HMAC-MD5.SIG-ALG.REG.INT [HMAC-MD5]), a Generic Security Service Algorithm for Secret Key Transaction (GSS-TSIG), a Hash-Based Message Authentication Code-Secure Hash Algorithm (HMAC-SHA1), HMAC-SHA224, HMAC-SHA256, HMAC-SHA384 or HMAC-SHA512. These algorithms are defined by the Internet Assigned Numbers Authority (IANA). New algorithms should first be registered with IANA prior to their use. Some of the other fields residing in RDATA are; the time the data is signed, the Message Authentication Code (MAC) that contains a hash of the message being signed, and the Original ID which is the ID number of the original message.

Can Existing Secure DNS Write Mechanisms be used in IPv6?

As explained in prior sections, the new IPv6 addressing mechanism, NDP, creates a problem as to how to authenticate a DNS server during the DNS Update process without, or with minimal, human intervention, while staying within the goals of this protocol. The main reason NDP was proposed was to ease the management of the large address space in IPv6 networks and to reduce the need for human intervention in address configuration. This eliminates the need to memorize complex hexadecimal addresses. A node might join an IPv6 network and have its IP address automatically configured by the use of the NDP mechanism, which needs no further administrator intervention. Moreover, privacy is an important issue in IPv6 when nodes on the network need to frequently change their IP address in order to prevent being tracked by attackers. This makes it difficult to authenticate who the update requestor of the DNS RRs is, based solely on the source IP address. Other security mechanism, such as TSIG, need a manual key exchange or signature generation before starting the secure authentication process between the DNS server and a host. In IPv6 networks it becomes harder to apply this authentication mechanism. Although, in IPv6, the manual update process is a major concern, in IPv4 it is an acceptable procedure for the following reasons:

- Using Active Directory (AD) to simplify the authentication process
  - **Advantage:** Nodes are already authenticated so that they can update their DNS records
  - **Disadvantages:** The administrator manually adds the new node to this network.
- The addressing mechanism in IPv4 is not a completely automatic process – it is either totally manual or requires network administrator intervention for DHCPv4 server configuration. These administrators thus exchange the keys required for TSIG, or other current DNS update security mechanisms, between the DNS server and the DNS update requestor.

Two solutions for node authentication, when Secure Neighbor Discovery (SEND) is used with a DNS server, are Modified TSIG and Modified SEND. In Modified TSIG there are two different scenarios in play. One pertains to the authentication of a node, with a DNS server, in order to update the DNS records. The other pertains to the authentication of two DNS servers, such as a slave and a master. SEND can also be used to authenticate other DNS servers on the Internet. The solution offered in this chapter focuses primarily on the first scenario, but it can also be used to resolve the issues stated in the second scenario. To address the stated problem, the addition of an extension to the current TSIG protocol is proposed in order to automate the DNS Update authentication process when SEND is used.

In the second solution, modified SEND, there are again two different scenarios in play here – one where all the hosts are in the same local link with the DNS server and one where the DNS server is located outside the bounds of the local link.

In the following section we will explain the steps necessary to create and verify Update Messages.

Modified TSIG

The TSIG RR can be created by employing the same data used to generate a new IP address in a node – that is, from the key pairs (public/private keys), the output value of CGA generation function (Interface ID), and other required parameters. These values must be cached in the node's memory for later use.

The proposed solution to the Update Request vulnerability issue is presented by the following steps. As a node needs to change its IP address frequently in order to maintain privacy, key pairs and CGA parameters must be cached during the generation of the IP address when using SEND. The following steps show how to generate an IP address.

1. Use a RSA algorithm or other CGA supported algorithms in order to generate key pairs (public/private keys).
   The shared secrets generated in TSIG may be equivalent to key pair generation in the CGA process. When somebody wants to generate

Challenges and Solutions for DNS Security in IPv6

TSIG secrets, he uses the dnssec-keygen comment (in Linux) which then generates a set of .key and .private files in the current working directory. Then, from the content of the .private file, the base-64 string of data is obtained (starting from the word "key") and this is called the shared secret. However, this shared secret is only shared between two hosts, a client and a DNS server, and for each pair of hosts this process should be repeated. The DNS server must also be configured in order to know what key to use for which host. This means that every time a host changes its IP address this process must again be repeated. But when using the modified TSIG, the same key pairs used in the initial IP address generation are used in the modified TSIG process. These keys can be generated on the fly, for first time IP address generation, using the RSA algorithm or other types of algorithms, such as ECC (Brian, 2009). This way of using CGA is called the CGA-TSIG algorithm, which will be added as an algorithm type to TSIG RDARA. The algorithm which is used in the signed message, and key generation process, can be added to the algorithm type field, which is a part of the CGA-TSIG Data field in the other Data section of TSIG RDATA.

2. Call the CGA generation function in order to generate an IP address.

A newly joined node generates its IP address by calling the CGA generation function. The steps used for the generation of the CGA algorithm are, as depicted in Figure 2, as follows:

The node

a. Generates a random modifier
b. Concatenates a modifier consisting of a zero value for the prefix (64 bits), a zero value for the collision count (1 bit) and a RSA public key
c. Executes a Secure Hash Algorithm (SHA1) on the output of step 2 and takes the 112 bits of the resulting digest and names it Hash2
d. Compares the 16×Sec leftmost bits of Hash2 to zero. If the condition is not met, increments the modifier and repeats steps 2 thru 4. If the condition is met, then execute the next step.
e. Concatenates the modifier using the prefix, collision count, and public key. It then executes another SHA1 on that output and calls it Hash1. It takes the

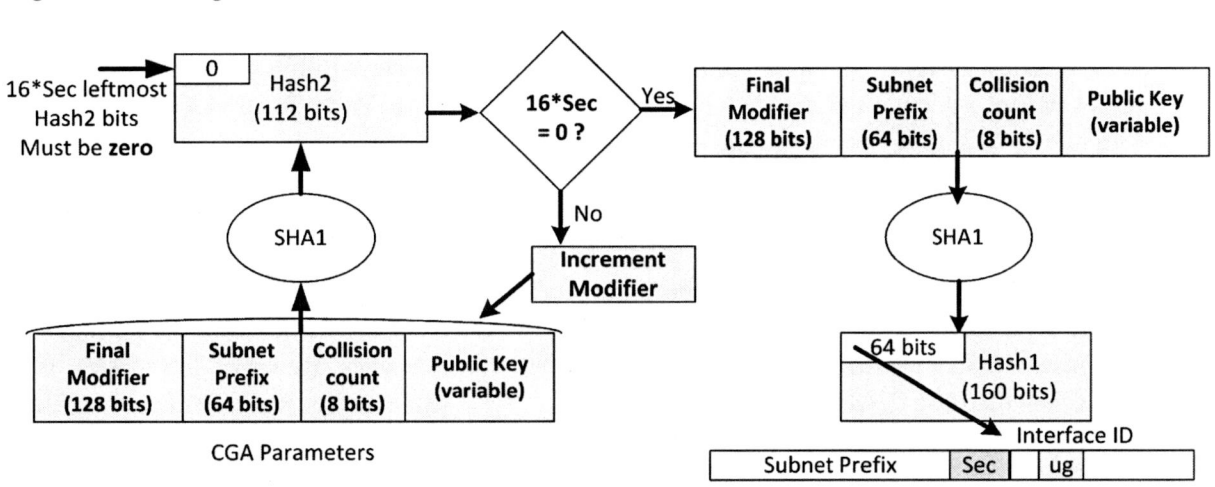

Figure 2. CGA algorithm

first 64 bits from the Hash1 output and calls this the Interface ID (IID). It then sets the first 3 left-most bits to the Sec value. It also sets bits 7 and 8 to one (called u and g).

f. Concatenates the subnet prefix with the IID and executes Duplicate Address Detection (DAD) in order to avoid address collision on the network. It sends all CGA parameters (modifier, subnet prefix, collision count, public key), along with the messages, so that other nodes will be able to verify its address ownership.

The steps necessary for the generation of the modified TSIG (CGA-TSIG) are as follows:

1. **Obtain Required Parameters from Cache:** The CGA-TSIG algorithm obtains the old IP address, modifier, subnet prefix, public key from the cache. It concatenates the old IP address with the CGA parameters, i.e., modifier, subnet prefix, public key and collision count (the order of the CGA parameters are shown in step 2 in the prior paragraph describing the IP address generation) and adds them to the initial part of the CGA-TSIG data.

In the case of multiple DNS servers (authentication of two DNS servers) there are three possible scenarios with regard to the authentication process, which differs from that of the authentication of a node (client) with one DNS server, because of the need for human intervention.

a. **Add the DNS Servers' IP Address to a Slave Configuration File:** A DNS server administrator will need to manually add the IP address of the master DNS server to the configuration file of the slave DNS server. When the DNS update message is processed, the slave DNS server can authenticate the master DNS server based on the source IP address, and prove the ownership of this address by the use of CGA. The disadvantage to the use of this approach occurs when the IP address of one of these DNS servers is changed. Then it becomes necessary to update the IP address in the DNS configuration file. Another possible solution for automating this process entails saving the public key, of the sender of the DNS Update message, on the other DNS server, after the source IP has been successfully verified for the first time. In this case, when the sender generates a new IP address by executing the CGA algorithm using the same public key, the other DNS server can still verify it and add its new IP address to the DNS configuration file automatically.

b. **Manually Exchange the Public/Private Keys:** A DNS server administrator will need to manually save the public/private keys, of a master DNS server, in the slave DNS server. This approach does not have the disadvantage of the first approach because any time any DNS server wants to change its IP address it will use the public/private keys which will be readily available for authentication purposes.

c. **Retrieve Public/Private Keys from a Third Party Trusted Authority (TA):** The message exchange option of SEND can be used for the retrieval of the certificate. This may be done automatically, from the TA, by using the Certificate Path Solicitation and the Certificate Path Advertisement messages. However, in practice, it is still not clear just how the hierarchical certificate will be processed. A second option has a DNS server administrator retrieving the certificate from a TA manually. Then, like in scenario 2, saving the certificate to the DNS server for use in the generation of its address, or in the DNS Update process. In this case, whenever any of these servers wants to generate a new IP address, the DNS update process can still be accomplished automatically, without the need for human intervention.

2. **Generate Signature:**

Before a node starts exchanging a shared secret, it first sends the DNS Transaction Key (TKEY) (Eastlake, 2000) query to the server in order to ask for the establishment of a shared secret session. In order to reduce the number of message exchanges needed between a DNS server and a host, a modified CGA signature is added to the first message sent by a host (a client). This will contain the required information needed for the DNS Update Request.

For the generation of this signature, all CGA parameters (modifier, public key, collision count and subnet prefix), that are concatenated with the IP tag, the DNS update message, and the Time Signed field, are then signed by using a RSA algorithm, or other algorithms that depend on what has been chosen for the CGA generation, and the private key, which was generated in the initial step of IP address generation and was cached for use in this step. This signature can be added as an extended option to the TSIG RDATA field. Figure 3 shows the format of the data in this signature. Time Signed is the same timestamp as that used in RDATA. This value is the UTC date and time value obtained from the signature generator. This approach will prevent replay attacks by changing the content of the signature each time a node wants to send a DNS Update Request. The Update Message contains the entire DNS update message, with the exclusion of the TSIG RR. A DNS update message consists of a header, a zone, a prerequisite, an update and additional data. The header contains the control information, the zone identifies the zones to which this update should be applied (Mockapetris, 1987b), the prerequisite prescribes the RRs that must be in the DNS database, the update contains the

Figure 3. Modified TSIG signature content

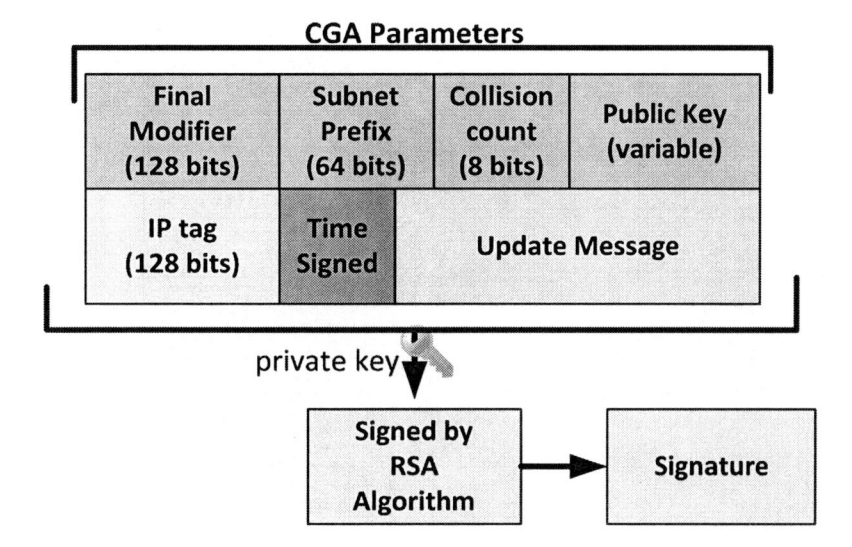

RR that needs to be modified or added, and the additional data is the data that is not a part of the DNS update, but is necessary in order to process this update.

3. **Generate Old Signature:**
   If the nodes generated new key pairs, then they need to add the old public key and message, signed by the old private key, to the CGA-TSIG Data. A node will retrieve the timestamp from Time Signed, will use the old private key to sign it, and then will add the content of this signature to the old signature field of the CGA-TSIG DATA. This step will be skipped when the node does not generate new key pairs. In this case, the length of the old signature field is set to zero.

As explained earlier, the TSIG RR contains fields such as Name, Class, etc. The TSIG RDATA field is extended to accommodate the addition of a CGA-TSIG Len and CGA-TSIG Data, as shown in Figure 4. The algorithm name is the same algorithm as that used for generating an IP address in IPv6 networks, i.e., the CGA algorithm which is referred to as CGA-TSIG. The Other Len field contains the overall length of the Other Data field, which will contain the CGA-TSIG Len, the CGA-TSIG Data and other options. CGA-TSIG Data contains the IP tag, the tag used to identify the node's old IP address, the Type used as the name of the algorithm used in SEND, i.e., CGA, the algorithm type used to generate key pairs and sign the message which, by default, would be the RSA, the signature (the format of this signature was explained in step 2 for the CGA-TSIG generation), the old public key, the old signature, and the length of each of them. The length of the CGA parameters will be variable and is dependent on the size of public key.

A client's public key can be associated with several IP addresses on a server. A DNS server keeps a client's public key and IP addresses in a data field formatted as shown in figure 4. This allows the client to update his own RRs using multiple IP addresses, while at the same time, allowing him to change IP addresses. If a client

Figure 4. Modified TSIG RR format

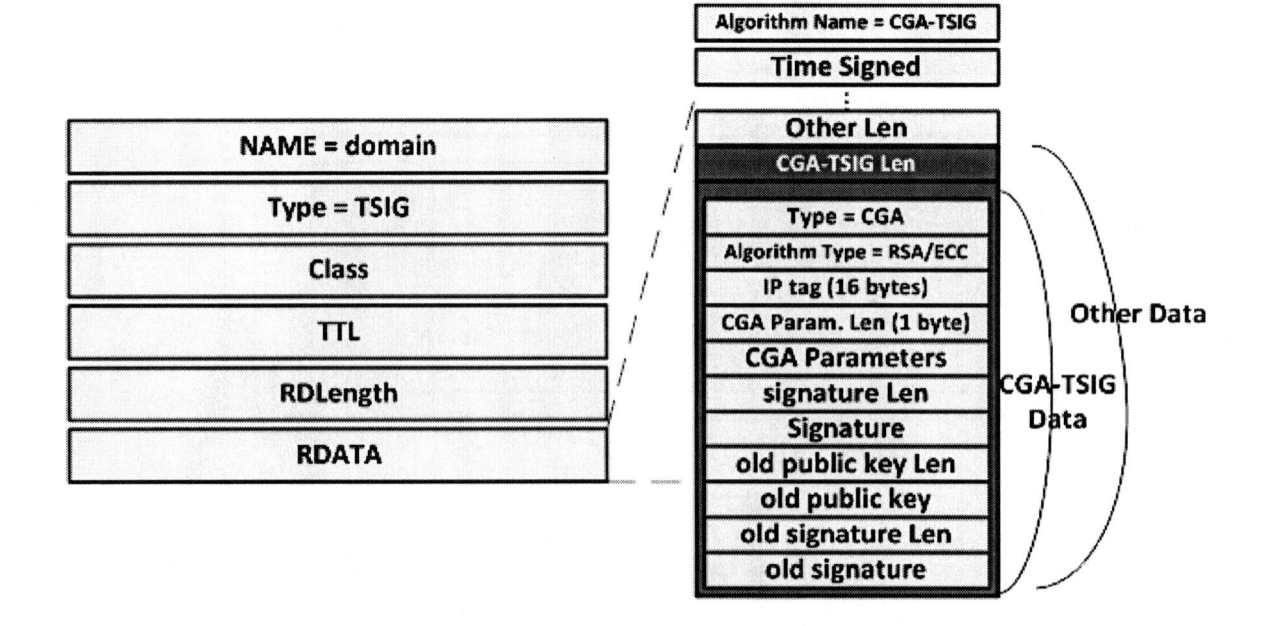

Challenges and Solutions for DNS Security in IPv6

wants to add RRs to the server by using a new IP address, then the IP tag field will be set to binary zeroes and the server will add the new IP address being passed to it to the CGATSIGIPs table in the database. If the client wants to replace an existing IP address in the CGATSIGIPs table (see Figure 5) on the server with a new one, then the IP tag field will be populated with the IP address which is to be replaced. The server will then look for the IP address referenced by the IP tag in the CGATSIGIPs Table (or file) and replace that IP address with the new one.

When a host sends a DNS Update message to a DNS server for the first time, the DNS server must save the public key for this client in CGATSIGkeys.

All DNS update requests/responses sent to the DNS server, or vice versa, should contain the modified TSIG RR in order to give other communicating nodes the ability to validate the sender. These update requests/responses will contain all the required information needed to process the DNS Update Request. Whenever a client, or a DNS server, generates a DNS update request, and uses either TCP or UDP as the transport layer to send this Update Request message to one DNS server, the DNS server should verify this message and, according to the verification result, discard it without further action or process the message. When the process is successful, the DNS server will send a DNS response message back to the sender informing the sender that the update process was completed successfully.

The query response sent back to the client from a resolver should also contain the modified TSIG RR. But the clients' query requests do not need to contain this option because a resolver responds to anonymous queries sent from any host. This enables a client to authenticate the resolver and to discard the responses that contain spoofed source IP addresses.

Modified TSIG Verification

To prevent attackers from making an unauthorized DNS update modification, authentication of the sender is very important. The verification process is as follows:

1. **Execute the CGA Verification:**
   In order to verify CGA a node needs to process the following steps:
   a. **Check the Subnet Prefix:**
      The 64 leftmost bits of IPv6 addresses constitute the subnet prefix. The receiver obtains the subnet prefix from the source IP address of the sender's message. Then the subnet prefix is obtained from the CGA parameters in the CGA-TSIG Data field of the received message. A comparison is then made between these two subnet prefixes. If the subnet prefixes match, then execute step 2. If there is not a match, then the node will be considered an attacker and the message will be discarded without further action.
   b. **Compare Hash1 to the Interface ID:**

Figure 5. CGA-TSIG tables on MySQL backend database

```
create table cgatsigkeys (
id        INT auto_increment,
pubkey VARCHAR(300),
primary key(id)
);

create table cgatsigips (
id        INT auto_increment,
idkey     INT,
IP        VARCHAR(20),
FOREIGN KEY (idkey) REFERENCES cgatsigkeys(id)
primary key(id)
);
```

The receiver will obtain all of the CGA parameters from the CGA-TSIG Data field. Then Hash1 will be calculated by executing SHA1 against these CGA parameters in order to obtain the 64 leftmost bits from the result. Hash1 is then compared to the 64 rightmost bits of the sender's IP address known as the Interface ID (IID). It will ignore any difference in the first three leftmost bits of the IID (Sec value) and the u and the g bits (see Figure 1). u and g are bits 7 and 8 of the first leftmost byte of the IID. If there is a match, execute step 3. If they do not match, then the source will be considered a spoofed source IP address and the message will be discarded without further action.

   c. **Evaluate Hash2 with CGA Parameters:**

The receiver obtains the CGA parameters. It sets the collision count and the subnet prefix to zero, and then execute SHA1, on the resulting data, in order to obtain a result. The 112 leftmost bits of the result is called Hash2. The 16×sec leftmost bits of Hash2 are compared to zero. If the condition is met, execute the next step in the CGA-TSIG verification process. If the condition is not met, then the CGA parameters will be consider as spoofed CGA parameters and the message will be discarded without further action.

2. **Check the Time Signed:**

The Time Signed value is obtained from the CGA-TSIG Data field and is called t1. The current system time is then obtained and converted to UTC time, and is called t2. If t1 is in the range of t2 and t2 minus x minutes (see formula 1: x minutes may vary according to the transmission lag time), execute step 3. If t1 is not in the range of t2, then the source will be considered a spoofed message, and the message will be discarded without further action. The range of x minutes is used because the update message may experience a delay during the transmission over TCP or UDP. Both times will use UTC time in order to avoid differences based on geographical location.

$$t2-x \leq t1 \leq t2 \quad (1)$$

3. **Verify the Signature:**

The signature, contained in the CGA-TSIG Data field of the DNS message, should be verified. This can be done by retrieving the public key from the CGA-TSIG Data field and using it to verify the signature. If the verification process is successful, and the node does not want to update another node's RR, then the Update Message will be processed. If the signature verification is successful and the node wants to update another node's RR(s), then the process will execute step 4. If the verification was not successful, the message will be discarded without further action.

4. **Verify the Source IP address:**

If a node wants to update a/many RR(s) on another DNS server, like a master DNS server wanting to update RRs on the slave DNS server, the requester's source IP address must be checked against the one in the DNS configuration file. If it is the same, the Update Message will be processed. If it is not the same, then step 5 will be executed.

5. **Verify the Public Key:**

The DNS server checks whether or not the public key retrieved from the CGA-TSIG Data field is the same as what was saved manually by the administrator or is in storage where the public keys and IP addresses are saved automatically after the first DNS update. If it is the same, then the Update Message will be processed. If it is not the same, then the message will be discarded without further action.

6. **Verify the Old Public Key:**
   If the old public key length is zero, then skip this step and discard the DNS update message without further action. If the old public key length is not zero, then the DNS server will retrieve the old public key from the CGA-TSIG DATA and will check whether or not it is the same as what was saved in the DNS server's storage where the public keys and IP addresses are saved. If it is the same, then step 7 will be executed. If they are not the same, then the message should be discarded without further action.
7. **Verify the Old Signature:**
   The old signature contained in the CGA-TSIG DATA should be verified. This can be done by retrieving the old public key and old signature from the CGA-TSIG DATA and using this old public key to verify the old signature. If the verification is successful, then the update message should be processed and the new public key should be replaced with the old public key in the DNS server. If the verification process fails, then the message should be discarded without further action.

The verification process for the resolver in a client also follows the same steps as above. With the use of the approach proposed in this chapter, the probability of the attacks, described earlier, being successful will be greatly diminished. This is because the DNS Update requestor's source IP address can be verified by the DNS server's use of the CGA algorithm. The CGA signature also prevents the spoofing of DNS update messages.

Modified TSIG Evaluation

We evaluated different algorithms as part of our proposed TSIG modification. For example, the average time to generate a key pair with a RSA key of 1024 bits using over 1000 samples on a computer with a 2.6 GHz CPU processor and 2 GB of RAM was less than 27.8 milliseconds. This value constitutes about 10% of the total CGA generation process time. The main problem with our proposed approach, thus, is the affect that the CGA algorithm computational process time will have on performance, i.e., the computational cost involved in creating the CGA. This will adversely impact both the address generator and the process used by the attacker. For the attacker, the cost of doing a brute force attack against a $(16 \times Sec + 59)$-bit hash value would have an algorithm processing time value estimated to be $O(2^{16 \times Sec + 59})$. But, in spite of the sequential nature of CGA, it is possible to improve the CGA generation performance with the application of parallelization techniques. To evaluate this approach, we did several experiments using two 64 bit VM operating systems. The first VM was a quad core CPU and the second was a single-core CPU. Both machines had 2 GB of RAM. All the measurements are done for a RSA key size equal to 1024 bits and Sec value of 1. The CGA creation process was called 1000 times to ensure sufficient sampling. The parallel approach sped up the CGA computation time by 70.1%, when using 4 cores. These results show that the CGA process does benefit by the use of a multicore processor utilizing parallelization techniques.

Moreover, when a node once generates a CGA, it does not need to re-generate it in order to send the DNS update message. As explained in prior sections, it can cache that value and fetch it from memory whenever it is needed. This means that, once it is generated, the CGA can then be available for different uses until it is time for the generation of another IP address. Another improvement results from the reduction in network traffic. Generally, to establish a secure DNS update, a minimum of four messages are exchanged between a DNS server and a client. With our approach, just two messages are needed. One is the DNS update request, the other is the DNS update response, both of which contain our proposed TSIG RR. This therefore lends itself to speeding up the DNS Update process.

Modified SEND

In this approach, the DNS update message is added to the SEND Neighbor Advertisement (NA) message (Rafiee et al., 2013) which means that the DNS server process, using this SEND implementation, will initiate the update process. The DNS service no longer needs to listen to extra ports because, with this implementation of SEND, after a successful verification, another intermediate service is called to add/modify/remove RRs on the DNS database. The NA message is the message that is sent by the node when the node generates its IP address and wants to advertise it. In this case, the node sets the S flag in the NA message to zero. This simplifies the DNS update mechanism for local networks and utilizes a secure authentication mechanism, i.e., the SEND verification process. The NA message format, with modified SEND options, is depicted in Figure 6. As the figure shows, the DNS update is a new message option. This is also included in the RSA signature so that the DNS server will be sure of the integrity of this data. It will also assure the DNS server that this node, with this IP address, actually owns this hostname. The checksum calculation for NA messages is also included in the DNS Update option.

When the DNS server is on another network, for transparency, a Controller Node (CN) is used. The task of the CN is to listen to NA messages sent by nodes and, after successful verification, generating DNS updates on behalf of these nodes. In this case the administrator of that network only needs to configure the CN node by using CGA-TSIG or the other currently available mechanisms instead of configuring all new nodes. In this approach, the CN node needs to maintain the public key, IP address, and domain names, of the nodes, in his database.

CONCLUSION

In this chapter DNS functions are classified into DNS read functions and DNS write functions. Attacks that might be initiated against each of these functions are then described. DNS Update is one of the essential functions used by DNS servers. It affords nodes the ability to update their DNS records dynamically. Unfortunately, it also creates new security issues for DNS servers as to how to authenticate the nodes who's RRs it wants to update. Another problem with this update process lies in maintaining data integrity and confidentiality during DNS queries. There have been three different protocols introduced for securing DNS

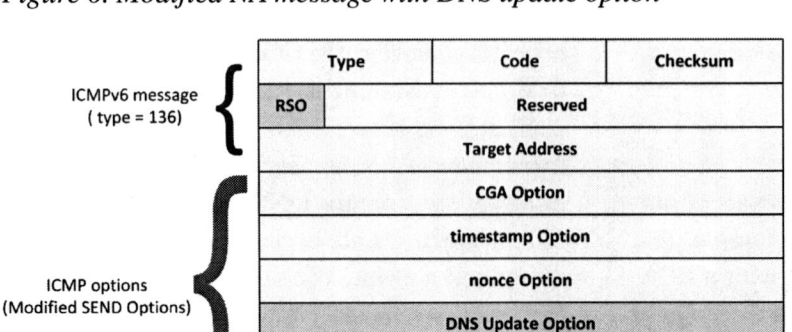

Figure 6. Modified NA message with DNS update option

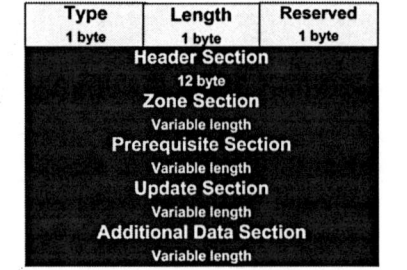

Updates and queries: TSIG, DNSSEC and IPSEC. But in IPv6, if StateLess Address AutoConfiguration (SLAAC) is used, these secure protocols will fail because, in SLAAC, there is no human intervention used to control what nodes join a network. Moreover, in TSIG or DNSSEC, not all processing is done automatically, and a few steps may need to be done offline. To address this problem two solutions were proposed. An extension to the TSIG protocol (CGA-TSIG) and an extension to SEND, which takes advantage of the use of CGA for the DNS authentication process of a node within a DNS server. Both approaches will also decrease the number of messages needed to be exchanged between the DNS server and the DNS client. This will result in enhanced performance for the DNS update process. These approaches might prevent several types of attack such as DNS Update spoofing, etc. These approaches also automate the authentication process between the communicating nodes (a client and a DNS server) since CGA does not need a Public Key Infrastructure (PKI) framework for the verification of the node's address ownership. CGA-TSIG can also be used for securing the DNS read process. The CGA-TSIG data structure can be added, as an extension, to DNS query responses sent by resolvers. This will thus prevent the types of attacks described in earlier sections.

REFERENCES

Arends, R., Austein, R., Larson, M., Massey, D., & Rose, S. (2005). DNS security introduction and requirements. *RFC*. Retrieved March 2005, from http://www.ietf.org/rfc/rfc4033.txt

Atkins, D., & Austein, R. (2004). Threat analysis of the domain name system (DNS). *RFC*. Retrieved August 2004, from http://www.ietf.org/rfc/rfc3833.txt

Brown, D. L. (n.d.). SEC 1: Elliptic curve cryptography. *Certicom Research*. Retrieved May 21, 2009, from www.secg.org/download/aid-780/sec1-v2.pdf

Cooper, D., Santesson, S., Farrell, S., Boeyen, S., Housley, R., & Polk, W. (2008). Internet X.509 public key infrastructure certificate and certificate revocation list (CRL) profile. *RFC*. Retrieved May 2008, from http://www.ietf.org/rfc/rfc5280.txt

Deering, S., & Hinden, R. (1998). Internet protocol, version 6 (IPv6) specification. *RFC*. Retrieved December 1998, from http://www.ietf.org/rfc/rfc2460.txt

Droms, R., Bound, J., Volz, B., Lemon, T., Perkins, C., & Carney, M. (2003). Dynamic host configuration protocol for IPv6 (DHCPv6). *RFC*. Retrieved July 2003, from http://www.ietf.org/rfc/rfc3315.txt

Eastlake, D. (2000). Secret key establishment for DNS (TKEY RR). *RFC*. Retrieved September 2000, from http://www.ietf.org/rfc/rfc2930.txt

Kent, S., & Seo, K. (2005). Security architecture for the internet protocol. *RFC*. Retrieved December 2005, from http://www.ietf.org/rfc/rfc4301.txt

Merino, P. J., Martínez, A. G., Organero, M. M., & Kloos, C. D. (2006). Enabling practical IPsec authentication for the internet. *Lecture Notes in Computer Science, 4277*, 392-403. Retrieved from http://rd.springer.com/chapter/10.1007/11915034_63

Microsoft Library. (n.d.). *Recursive and iterative queries*. Retrieved 2013, from http://technet.microsoft.com/en-us/library/cc961401.aspx

Mockapetris, P. (1987a). Domain names - Concepts and facilities. *RFC*. Retrieved November 1987, from http://www.ietf.org/rfc/rfc1034.txt

Mockapetris, P. (1987b). Domain names - Implementation and specification. *RFC*. Retrieved November 1987, from http://www.ietf.org/rfc/rfc1035.txt

Narten, T., Nordmark, E., Simpson, W., & Soliman, H. (2007). Neighbor discovery for IP version 6 (IPv6). *RFC*. Retrieved September 2007, from http://www.ietf.org/rfc/rfc4861.txt

Rafiee, H., Loewis, M. V., & Meinel, C. (2013). DNS update extension to IPv6 secure addressing. In *Proceeding of FINA Conference*. IEEE.

Rooney, T. (2011). Secure DNS (part I). In *IP address management: Principles and practice* (pp. 256–258). Hoboken, NJ: IEEE Press/Wiley.

Stapp, M., & Volz, B. (2006). Resolution of fully qualified domain name (FQDN) conflicts among dynamic host configuration protocol (DHCP) clients. *RFC*. Retrieved October 2006, from http://www.ietf.org/rfc/rfc4703.txt

Thomson, S., Narten, T., & Jinmei, T. (2007). IPv6 stateless address autoconfiguration. *RFC*. Retrieved September 2007, from http://www.ietf.org/rfc/rfc4862.txt

Troan, O., & Droms, R. (2003). IPv6 prefix options for dynamic host configuration protocol (DHCP) version 6. *RFC*. Retrieved December 2003, from http://www.ietf.org/rfc/rfc3633.txt

Vixie, P., Gudmundsson, O., Eastlake, D., III, & Wellington, B. (2000). Secret key transaction authentication for DNS (TSIG). *RFC*. Retrieved May 2000, from http://www.ietf.org/rfc/rfc2845.txt

Wellington, B. (2000). Secure domain name system (DNS) dynamic update. *RFC*. Retrieved November 2000, from http://www.ietf.org/rfc/rfc3007.txt

KEY TERMS AND DEFINITIONS

CGA-TSIG: A combination of CGA with TSIG. This modification of TSIG utilizes CGA as a means of authenticating a node with a DNS server.

DHCPv6: A protocol that can be used to allow a DHCP server to automatically assign an IP address to a host from a defined range of IP addresses configured for that network.

DNS Update: DNS update is a process of adding, removing, or modifying one or several Resource Records (RRs) on DNS servers.

DNSSEC: An extension to DNS which secures the DNS functions and verifies the authenticity and integrity of query results from a signed zone.

IPsec: Provides access control, data authentication, integrity, and confidentiality for the data that is sent between communication nodes across IP networks.

IPv6 Autoconfiguration: A node generates its IP address as soon as it connects to the network by using Stateless or Statefull mechanisms.

NDP: Neighbor Discovery (ND) and StateLess Address Autoconfiguration (SLAAC) mechanism, together, are called NDP. This mechanism allows hosts to discover their neighboring routers and hosts and obtain router information, and to generate and to set their IP address.

TSIG: TSIG is a protocol that provides endpoint authentication and data integrity by using one-way hashing and shared secret keys to establish a trust relationship between two hosts.

Section 3
Malware and Intrusion Detection Systems

Chapter 7
Host-Based Intrusion Detection Systems:
Architectures, Solutions, and Challenges

Vít Bukač
Masaryk University, Czech Republic

Vashek Matyáš
Masaryk University, Czech Republic

ABSTRACT

In this chapter, the reader explores both the founding ideas and the state-of-the-art research on host-based intrusion detection systems. HIDSs are categorized by their intrusion detection method. Each category is thoroughly investigated, and its limitations and benefits are discussed. Seminal research findings and ideas are presented and supplied with comments. Separate sections are devoted to the protection against tampering and to the HIDS evasion techniques that are employed by attackers. Existing research trends are highlighted, and possible future directions are suggested.

INTRODUCTION

Even if we employed the whole spectrum of available protective technologies, kept all our systems patched and regularly instructed all our users, security incidents would still happen. Therefore, we have been adding another piece into the puzzle of the layered computer security. A piece that is responsible for the detection of intrusions that penetrated our protective measures.

That piece is called an Intrusion Detection System (IDS). It is a device or a software application that monitors events occurring at a host and/or in a network, identifies malicious activities or policy violations and produces reports for further analyses. A Host-based IDS (HIDS) is "a program that monitors the characteristics of a single host and events occurring within that host to identify and stop suspicious activity" (Scarfone, 2012, p. 94). In practice, a HIDS usually monitors the

DOI: 10.4018/978-1-4666-4514-1.ch007

Host–Based Intrusion Detection Systems

behavior of running processes, enforces the integrity of critical system files and registry keys, performs complex log analyses, and monitors the host network traffic.

In the first section of this chapter, HIDSs are defined and their properties are outlined. Sections two to five focus on standalone HIDSs. Section two presents the traditional log analysis and SIEM systems. Section three focuses on the analysis of process behavior. Section four discusses the integrity checking and the transition from periodic to real-time checking. Section five is concerned with the analysis of host network traffic. Sections six to nine focus on collaborative HIDSs. Section six presents their overall properties. Section seven addresses the specifics of the trust-based collaborative HIDSs and section eight addresses the specifics of the collaborative HIDSs in mobile ad hoc networks. Section nine then deals with the cloud-based intrusion detection. Section ten addresses the problem of HIDS security with the latest evasion techniques being discussed in section eleven. The following sections summarize the work and the identified research trends and suggest new research directions.

This chapter is based on a survey conducted by Bukač, Tuček, and Deutsch (2012), and some work on this chapter was supported by the Czech research project VG20102014031.

BACKGROUND

Numerous intrusion detection systems taxonomies have been proposed in the past. Lazarevic et al. (2005) designates five criteria to be used to classify IDSs: information source, analysis strategy, time aspects, architecture and response. A more detailed taxonomy that also includes classification by alerts and adds further subcategories is outlined by Sabahi and Movaghar (2008).

We recognize two types of IDSs based on the analysis strategy: misuse-based IDSs (i.e., signature-based) and anomaly-based IDSs. Signature-based systems compare observed events with known patterns of malicious activities. Signature-based systems can effectively detect existing threats and, provided signatures were constructed efficiently, have a low false positives rate. Anomaly-based systems compare the actual behavior with pre-created profiles of normal behavior and observe any deviations. Anomaly-based systems can detect previously unknown attacks, but the identification of these attacks can be very vague. A training period without any ongoing intrusions is often required to construct normal profiles. Some anomaly-based systems are adaptive; therefore, they can update their normal profiles in a reaction to the changing properties of the observed system. Commercially available solutions can incorporate both detection approaches (e.g., common antivirus software is predominantly signature-based, but can also include the heuristic analysis that falls into the anomaly-based analysis strategy). Surveys of various intrusion detection analysis strategies as well as comparison of their strengths and weaknesses are provided by Murali and Rao (2005) and by Chandola, Banerjee, and Kumar (2009).

Scarfone and Mell (2012) distinguish four categories of IDSs based on information source (i.e., the type of events they monitor and the ways in which they are deployed): Network-based IDS (NIDS), Host-based IDS (HIDS), wireless IDS and a network behavior analysis system. Sometimes we can also encounter the term "hybrid IDS" that denotes a system that combines two or more IDS categories. In the following text we focus strictly on host-based IDSs.

Our taxonomy of standalone HIDSs is based on the work of de Boer and Pels (2005). They divide HIDSs into four groups: file system monitoring, log file analysis, connection analysis, and kernel-based IDSs. In our taxonomy, the file system monitoring is restricted only to the cryptographic integrity checking. Although we acknowledge the existence of other techniques (e.g., timestamp checking, file size checking) we do not believe that they are sufficient for today's needs and are no longer challenging research directions. In a similar fashion, we focus on the system calls analysis in the kernel-based IDSs group. We also extend the connection analysis group. Pels and de Boer perceive the connection analysis HIDSs as tools that can detect and monitor incoming network connections. We broaden this view and assume that the network-analysis HIDSs can inspect any traffic between the host and the network.

Architecture-wise, we divide host-based intrusion detection systems into standalone HIDSs and collaborative HIDSs. Standalone HIDSs have four subclasses that differentiate in their detection approach: log analysis, process monitoring, integrity checking, and network traffic monitoring. For collaborative HIDSs we designate three subclasses: trust-based collaborative HIDSs, collaborative HIDSs in mobile ad hoc networks (MANETs), and cloud IDSs. Trust-based collaborative HIDSs have been detached because of trust-related attacks that must be addressed. HIDSs for MANETs have been detached because of specific environment properties. Cloud IDS agents have been detached because in some cases their detection role can be minimized and they serve primarily as data collection units, but they still must fulfill other requirements on HIDSs (e.g., tamper resistance). Collaborative HIDSs may or may not comprise of nodes that are capable to operate standalone.

During the last several years a significantly greater research effort has been devoted to the development of network-based IDSs at the expense of host-based IDSs. Jiankun Hu (2010) gives two main reasons: real time and computing resource restraint, and networking factor. We add another three reasons: the ground truth problem, deployment and management issues, and single machine attack class limitation. The final list is then as follows:

- **Real-time and Computing Resource Restraint (Hu, 2010):** An intrusion should be detected during or immediately after it happened. However, traditional HIDS techniques (e.g., log analysis, offline integrity checking) bring undesirable delays and/or require a large amount of computing resources. NIDSs usually detect intrusions in real-time.
- **Networking Factor (Hu, 2010):** Nowadays, most applications are network-based. Over the years these applications became a primary attack vector against end hosts. Therefore, there is a strong tendency to protect the network applications in a well-arranged centralized manner.
- **Ground Truth Problem:** Information supplied to and from a HIDS could be forged or altered by an attacker who took control of an underlying operating system. Existing common privilege control mechanisms allow the administrator to modify every aspect of the system, including the kernel configuration and the code stored in programmable hardware. Also, an attacker with root privileges can alter logs to hide any traces of malicious actions.
- **Deployment and Management Issues:** Current networks are heterogeneous, comprising of hosts with different capabilities and different operating systems. Devising a tool which could be applied across the whole network is a difficult process. Managing dozens or hundreds of HIDSs is both organizationally and technically more challenging than managing several NIDSs.
- **Single Machine Attack Class Limitation:** Attacks that are manifested over multiple computers (e.g., horizontal port scans) might not be detected when our view of the events is limited to a single host. Network-based IDSs can correlate events from the entire network and detect such attacks accordingly. An alternative approach is to employ a collaborative HIDS that can benefit from exchanging messages and sharing views with other hosts in the network.

We believe that the importance of the real-time and computing resource restraint will decrease, because current fast hardware allows security researchers to develop new complex detection techniques with required properties. The ground truth problem is also well understood and steadily researched both by the academic community and the private sector. Deployment and management issues are sometimes reduced by the central management consoles. For example, some antivirus software vendors provide server applications with the aggregate view over all installed instances. Unfortunately, these administrative consoles are vendor-specific and are not compatible with other vendors' products. Single machine class limitation is an inherent problem. In global view, we believe HIDSs should always seek cooperation with already existing intrusion detection architecture, contribute to it and benefit from it.

HIDSs were traditionally used mostly on desktop client computers and laptops. However, modern smartphones and tablets have almost the same capabilities and, inevitably, the same weaknesses. These devices frequently traverse between networks with different levels of security, often hold sensitive company or personal data, and can be easily stolen or lost. Respected advisory company Gartner predicts over 320 million tablets sold just in 2015, with cumulatively over 900 million sold by the end of that year (Milanesi, 2011). We are convinced this boom presents a new ground for HIDSs.

HIDSs interact with ordinary users, not just network or security specialists. Therefore, it is necessary to take the user satisfaction into account when a HIDS is designed. Regardless of the employed detection method, we believe every HIDS should meet the following properties:

- **Low Resource Consumption:** Users perceiving slower responses of applications that they use after the HIDS was installed are likely to turn off the HIDS or at least limit its function. Therefore, overall CPU load and memory consumption should be kept low. An acceptable compromise is low overall resource consumption with occasional short peaks to verify or discard anomalies.
- **Low False Positives:** We argue that the false positives rate should be kept absolutely minimal, possibly zero, even at the expense of true positives rate, if necessary. In enterprise environments with dozens or hundreds of computers even just a single false positive from each HIDS every day can lead to security operators being overwhelmed. We support our view with the work of Axelsson (2000), who estimates the acceptable false positives rate of an IDS being surprisingly low, especially if there are many observed events. Moreover, repeating the warnings could ultimately lead to warnings being ignored by the users, as was suggested by Bravo-Lillo et al. (2011), rendering the HIDS wasteful.
- **Low Energy Consumption:** Low energy consumption is necessary for HIDSs to be useable on mobile devices. Bickford et al. (2011) refer to the tradeoff between security features and energy consumption of rootkit detectors that use integrity checking. They suggest creating profiles with different levels of protection and different levels of energy consumption. We support their conclusions and encourage HIDS researchers to include power consumption measurements in their experiments.
- **Interoperability:** Host-based IDSs should be designed to be able to supply their alerts or raw data to central monitoring entities and also be able to react on their feedback (e.g., show an alert message). Node trust and privacy issues must be addressed. Standard data exchange formats (e.g., IDMEF) and algorithms should be employed.

- **Look and Feel:** The HIDS must be easy to use for common users, but also should allow for an advanced management in enterprises (e.g., scripting via command line interface, unattended installations, remote control).

When these conditions are met, HIDSs will become an important complementary part of the overall intrusion detection architecture and will supply the following benefits:

- **Semantic Information:** HIDSs are close to the protected resources, in the best position to observe the behavior of the operating system or its applications. Alert reports can be very precise, including the name of a malicious process or an identity of a user under whose context the process was run.
- **Network Traffic Interpretation:** If we can solve the ground truth problem, the network traffic data is more precise than in case of NIDSs. Host-based IDSs interpret packets in the same way as applications. The majority of network traffic IDS evasion techniques (e.g., packet payload obfuscation, interpretation discrepancies) are not useable against HIDSs (Ptacek, 1998). HIDSs can inspect traffic which was end-to-end encrypted on network layer or transport layer (e.g., by TLS or IPsec), because it has access to the plaintext at the application layer.
- **Best Effort:** We often encounter situations in which other IDS categories are not useable (e.g., notebooks connecting through an untrusted Wi-Fi, 4G mobile devices). In some cases even if a malicious activity was detected, network administrators may not be willing to share that information with affected users. Then we must rely on HIDSs to provide at least a minimal level of protection.

Another HIDS survey was published by Vigna and Kruegel (2005). Our work partly explores one of the suggested research trends, namely the use of hardware-based mechanisms for trustworthy intrusion detection. We also discuss the integrity checking in the context of the real-time intrusion detection which was not considered a viable option previously. Zhou et al. (2010) presented an extensive survey of collaborative intrusion detection systems. In the part of our survey related to the collaborative IDS we take a rather different overall approach. We limit ourselves strictly to the cooperating HIDSs and we focus on exploring how the collaborative intrusion detection could be employed and what problems could be encountered in typical deployment scenarios (e.g., in mobile ad hoc networks).

Last but not least, our work explores the research effort of approximately the last five years, most notably the widespread of virtualization technologies, the emergence of cloud-based intrusion detection solutions and the whole direction of HIDSs research in situation when network-based IDSs are generally more preferred both by the academic community and by the users.

MAIN FOCUS OF THE CHAPTER

Log Analysis

Almost every application can produce one or more log files of its activity. A log consists of records that usually contain at least event identification, event originator, and time information. Log analysis has been traditionally used to identify security incidents, policy violations, and operational problems. Current research efforts aim towards intelligent log correlation, data mining, and SIEM systems (Security Information and Event Management).

Log correlation is primarily aimed to decrease the false positives rate and to identify stealthy attacks. Two different approaches can be followed (Abad, 2003). During bottom-up approach multiple logs are analyzed and anomalies are identified. Once an anomaly is discovered, its context is examined and it is decided whether the anomaly is a sign of an intrusion. Bottom-up approach can detect previously unknown attacks, but the analysis is complex and requires many log files to be parsed. With the top-down approach the attack has already been known and it is required to identify which logs could contain the related traces. The analysis is simpler and could reveal similarities between attacks of the same class.

"The SIEM system is a complex collection of technologies designed to provide vision and clarity on the corporate IT system as a whole, benefiting security analysts and IT administrators as well" (Miller, 2010, p. xxv). SIEM systems help both with security and operations management. From the security point of view, the primary purpose is to monitor, identify, document, and respond to security issues. SIEM systems comprise of five collections of services:

- **Log Management:** Log management components are responsible for collecting logs from various sources, their normalization, and storing in a centralized database. Subsequently, stored data is efficiently organized and retrieved on-demand.
- **IT Regulatory Compliance:** Building filters to enable automated audits and creation of reports.
- **Event Correlation:** Judging events in the context of other events. Each event is analyzed from multiple viewpoints determined by the collected log data. Events can therefore be interpreted with a deeper sense and possible causes can be identified.
- **Active Response:** Some SIEM systems enable automated reaction to observed events (e.g., modification of an access control list or firewall rules).
- **Endpoint Security:** Endpoint devices can be monitored to verify they remain in a secured state (e.g., local firewall is enabled, antivirus signature database has been updated).

Main problems encountered in log analysis systems nowadays are:

- **Inconsistent Log Formats** (Kent, 2006): There exist many different log formats (e.g., syslog format, comma-separated values, XML-based formats) with various orders of fields in records, different separators and different file formats. Audit records must be converted to a common format to enable the correlation of events. A special case is the timestamp information, which must be considered also with respect to time zones, standard/summer times and clock shifts between remote systems.
- **Audit Data Volume** (Kent, 2006): Correlation of events within each log file and also between different log files is often necessary for successful intrusion detection. However, the sheer volume of audit data from multiple sources makes the analysis difficult even for very powerful intrusion detection engines, because relevant security information is hidden under common operational status information.
- **Log Files Security:** Log files must be protected against threats that could compromise their integrity and availability. Without protection, attackers could remove traces of their activities or make logs unavailable altogether. If log files contain private data, providing confidentiality through encryption and/or access control is also recommended. Also, a near real-time log retransmission can be established to make unauthorized changes difficult and to sup-

port event analysis without unnecessary delays (e.g., Microsoft Windows Event log forwarding).

Asif-Iqbal et al. (2011) assume that normal events form big clusters (i.e., operational noise), whereas anomalous events form small clusters. They propose a framework capable to correlate heterogeneous logs from multiple sources. Log files are parsed individually, because their inner format may be different, and are converted into a standard Comma-Separated Value format. Log records are subsequently clustered using K-means partitional algorithm, while the number of clusters was decided by the Expectation Maximization algorithm. Next, during the filtering phase, big clusters are omitted and small clusters are forwarded to further processing. Clusters are clustered again, which leads to better true negative rates and true positives rates. The framework is fast and extensible, but as it is proposed it requires batch processing and therefore it is not very suitable for a real-time detection. A frequent incremental collecting of newly-added events could be employed to mitigate this issue.

Wang et al. (2009) address the problem of constructing important and suitable attributes from audit data to best characterize behavioral patterns of a subject so that abnormality can be clearly distinguished from normal activities. A new approach is proposed that constructs frequency attribute weights not only from the frequency information of events in each sequence of audit data, but also from the distribution of the event in the whole data. Principal component analysis, nearest neighbor method and chi-square test are employed for anomaly detection.

Park et al. (2010) argue that normal user behavior patterns cannot be summarized as a statistical profile with sufficient accuracy, because the profile models only static user behavior. A new anomaly detection method for an audit data stream is proposed. A grid-based clustering algorithm is employed to model user activity in real time. User behavior is represented as a data element in a transaction of the data stream. Any new user activity influences both intermediate clustering algorithm results and already established user profile. Unfortunately, adaptive profiling also allows a clever attacker to make the IDS include the malicious behavior in the statistical profile if the attacker can keep small incremental changes of this behavior.

A practical system for secured retention of anonymity service system logs is proposed by Köpsell and Švenda (2010). Protected records can be accessed only if a cryptographic smart card and its owner are present and the retained data is not outdated. An operator cannot be forced to reveal logged resources outside the data retention period, because the period is enforced directly on the smart card with the help of trusted time stamping servers.

Process Monitoring

Traditionally, process monitoring was mainly concerned whether a particular process is running, suspended or killed. Therefore, it could be noticed if important system processes, usually security-related (e.g., logging processes, antivirus software), were not tampered with. Subsequently, the interest in process monitoring shifted to discovering whether the process itself is exhibiting a malicious behavior. Observation techniques can range from rather simple (e.g., CPU and memory consumption measurements, file access monitoring) to quite complex (e.g., system calls monitoring). A careful balance between the method complexity and CPU and memory consumption is required. Often, a whitelisting principle for already examined applications is used to lower the resource demands. Process monitoring can be online or offline. Offline processing is usually performed in a sandbox environment, which allows running a potentially malicious application without risking harm to the computer. On the other hand, online monitoring can adapt to changes in the process behavior in real-time. Sandbox environments are frequently based on virtualization technologies.

Currently the most common method of process monitoring behavior is the analysis of invoked system calls as proposed by Hofmeyr et al. (1998). It is assumed that each program has a unique behavior specific to a particular architecture, software version and configuration, local administrative policies and usage patterns. A normal profile of the process behavior is built up during the training phase (i.e., all recorded system call sequences are stored in a database). During the detection phase, any deviations from the normal profile are considered anomalous. System calls can be analyzed with regards to their sequence order and/or accompanying parameters. The approach can be further enhanced with the analysis of instruction sequences between system calls and with interactions between multiple processes.

Baliga et al. (2008) proposed Paladin, a solution for a real-time automated detection and containment of rootkit attacks using the virtual machine technology. They developed a prototype using the VMware Workstation to illustrate the solution. Their analysis and experimental results indicate that this approach can successfully detect and contain effects of a large percentage of known Linux rootkits. They also demonstrate effectiveness of this approach, particularly against the malware that uses rootkits to hide.

An effective and efficient malware detector is presented by Kolbitsch et al. (2009). The detector is behavior-based. First, each program is executed in a controlled environment and its interactions with the operating system (i.e., system calls) are observed. The model is generated automatically. It is represented as a behavior graph with nodes being system calls that could be used for malicious activities. During subsequent executions, the model is compared with an actual program behavior in real-time. The described technique has an advantage that it detects whole malware families, not just a single instance of a malicious code. Also, it cannot be easily evaded by the obfuscation or polymorphic techniques.

A platform-independent HIDS based on an analysis of system calls is presented by Sujatha et al. (2008). The HIDS monitors system calls for both user and host activity. A set of relevant parameters, the behavior set, is established to distinguish between normal and anomaly events. These parameters are: CPU-usage, disk-usage, log-in-time, I/O activities, frequency of applications launched and network speed. Parameter values are processed with a neural network, specifically the self-organizing map. The self-organizing map is trained with the Simple Competitive Learning algorithm. The learning phase is unsupervised and spans over multiple training cycles. With more learning cycles the false positives rate and the true negatives rate are decreasing. Since the framework is platform-independent, the system is highly portable contrary to common system call analysis HIDSs. Unfortunately, malware that causes only minor changes to the system performance parameters cannot be detected with this technique. A hybrid HIDS that combines behavior set analysis with signature detection is advised.

Özyer et al. (2007) proposed a detection method based on an iterative rule learning using a fuzzy rule-based genetic classifier. Their approach consists of two main phases. During the first stage, many candidate rules are created for each class with a fuzzy association rules mining. Rules are pre-screened by a two-rule evaluation criterion in order to reduce the fuzzy rule search space. Candidate rules obtained after pre-screening are used in a genetic fuzzy classifier to generate rules for the classes specified in the IDS: normal, probe, denial of service, user to root and remote to local. During the second stage, a boosting genetic algorithm is employed for each class to find its fuzzy rules required to classify data each time a fuzzy rule is extracted and included in the system. A boosting mechanism evaluates the weight of each data item to help the rule extraction mechanism focus on data having relatively more weight.

PROBE by Kwon et al. (2008) is a HIDS based on an analysis of relationships between processes. The system consists of three components: tree builder, path checker and process controller. The tree builder constructs a tree with processes as nodes and child-parent relationships as edges. The path checker subsequently analyzes the tree to discover anomalous spawning of child processes. For each edge three weights identifying the child (application, shell, and clone) are calculated. If all three weights exceed predefined thresholds, the spawned process is considered abnormal. Analysis of relationships between child and parent processes limits types of malware that can be detected compared to a system call analysis. On the other hand, the graph analysis is lightweight, with memory and processing time requirements lower than common detection techniques based on system calls, while maintaining a reasonable precision.

Integrity Checking

Integrity checking is aimed to protect critical system files, configurations (e.g., user and group databases, registry) and runtime resources (i.e., kernel state, network stack state, system events) from unsolicited changes. Changes can be a result of hardware and software errors, intentional attacks or inadvertent harmful user actions. Control checksums are calculated with cryptographic hash functions both in keyed and unkeyed variants and stored in a secured database. During every subsequent check the stored value is compared with the newly calculated value. If the values differ, the file was tampered with (Sivathanu, 2005). Some integrity checkers also provide means to block file operations before they are finished or to restore files to their original states.

File changes can be detected periodically or in the real time. Real time integrity checkers require hooks in the kernel so that an HIDS could intercept system calls. Periodical integrity checkers are simple and can be implemented in the user space. However, they can provide only the attack detection, not the attack prevention. Periodic integrity checkers verify the integrity of protected resources once in a time period. With shorter time periods, attacks are detected sooner. However, overall system performance can be affected, because the stored value must be accessed from a slow persistent storage. The similar problem is encountered when we require integrity verification of many files. Therefore, it is recommended to identify the critical system files whose integrity would most likely be compromised during an intrusion and protect their integrity only. Another approach is to use caching. Hash values of files that are accessed repeatedly are kept in a fast dynamic memory and therefore can be recovered quickly.

Patil et al. (2004) proposed a real-time integrity checker called I3FS. The integrity of each file is verified before the file is made available to a requesting application. The proposed solution utilizes a layer of a virtual file system between user processes and an arbitrary real file system. I3FS is configurable by security policies which can be modified by host system administrators. It is implemented as a loadable kernel module for file systems. I3FS is comparable to the open-source integrity checker Tripwire. However, in contrast to Tripwire it is capable of real-time integrity checking, has low performance overhead and is more resistant to tampering due to its in-kernel approach.

The ICAR (Integrity Checking and Restoring) system was developed by Kaczmarek and Wróbel (2008). ICAR enables a real-time restoration of compromised system files from a read-only external memory. A kernel module monitors the application behavior. When a file is requested, an integrity check is performed. If the file was compromised and the backup is present on the external memory, the file is restored in real time and the event is logged. Access to the file is allowed only if the integrity checksum was correct or if the file was restored from the backup. Although ICAR idea is intriguing, its usability for most end systems is questionable, because operating system patches and application updates would require constant re-creating of the content of the read-only media.

Jin et al. (2010) propose a real time integrity checking method for virtual machines. The method does not require installation of kernel hooks or any other modifications of existing virtual machines, therefore it ensures a low dependency on a chosen operating system and a high attack resistance. A system call sensor module is inserted in the virtual machine manager. All file operations of protected virtual machines are intercepted by the module and rerouted to the integrity checker that runs in a secured privileged virtual machine. Files are monitored with regard to three policies. "Significant files" cannot be modified, modifications of "sensitive files" are always logged and "remaining files" are not monitored. Initially, the list of significant and sensitive files is provided by an administrator. Subsequently, a sensitivity weight is computed for each other file. If the weight of a file reaches a predefined threshold, the file is included in the significant set or the sensitive set. The weight is computed from the frequency of usage of the file and the significance of its parent directory.

A trusted persistent storage easily becomes a performance weak point. It usually has a limited capacity and read/write rates. Therefore, a careful design of integrity checking algorithms is required. Oprea and Reiter (2007) designed integrity constructions which require only a constant amount of trusted storage memory per file. The integrity checking is intended for use in cryptographic file systems and works on the memory block level. Performance requirements for the trusted storage are further decreased by exploiting the sequentiality of memory block writes.

Network Traffic Monitoring

A network traffic HIDS monitors incoming and outgoing packets for signs of unsolicited data flows. Data encryption on the network layer or the transport layer does not affect HIDS capability, because it can obtain the access to the decrypted payload at the application layer. The gathered traffic is interpreted by a HIDS similarly as by client applications, opposite to discrepancies that are typical for network intrusion detection systems.

When a host was incorporated in a botnet it could be misused for a variety of illegal activities (i.e., denial-of-service attacks, spamming, online fraud). Many of these activities cause changes in the host network behavior. Even when the bot does not exhibit any malicious activity, it still communicates with its command and control servers on the Internet. Upon discovering that the host participates in any of these specific data flows, we can assume the host was compromised and should be quarantined and examined.

HIDSs often perform the deep packet analysis of some data traffic. At a typical end host connection speed (i.e., 100 Mb/s Fast Ethernet, 1 Gb/s Gigabit Ethernet) it is often possible even without dedicated HW modules. A random packet sampling technique can be used to keep an acceptable CPU load even during traffic peaks.

A generic collaborative framework for bot detection is presented by Takemori et al. (2009). Victims of attacks report their IP addresses and timestamps of attacks to a central authority. Remaining nodes periodically download the list of victims and compare it with own outgoing packets. If there is a match, a compromised node knows it has been misused. Further inspection of compromised hosts allows discovering command and control servers even if the attack traffic itself has spoofed source IP addresses. Takemori's approach requires a massive collaboration to be truly functional. Storing the traffic history on the local host might raise privacy concerns when the host is shared among multiple users.

Bot infected hosts often request commands and updates from botnet command and control servers. Takemori et al. (2008) suggested comparing host outgoing traffic with whitelists in order to discover the computer-originated malicious data flows. Initially, whitelists are populated with IP addresses of well-known services (e.g., DNS servers, patch servers, antivirus servers) and of computers in a local network. After the first installation of the operating system a few days learning period takes place, during which users cannot work with the computer and intrusions must not take place. During this period the computer-originated outgoing packets are monitored and their destination domain names are added to the whitelists. After this quite lengthy learning period, packets that do not match any whitelist entry are dropped. To ensure that user-originated traffic is not affected, the traffic is allowed through during a short time after each interaction between the user and the computer (e.g., a keyboard operation). In large enterprise environments with multiple heterogeneous systems the whitelist maintenance can be problematic. A solution could be an automatic updating service that collaborates with well-known security vendors.

Kwon et al. (2011) assume the host compromise by a bot can be discovered from an outgoing traffic. They describe two properties that differentiate bot and human processes in a host machine. First condition is whether the behavior was initiated by a user. It can be decided from interaction with input devices and types of Windows GUI reports. Second condition is whether the behavior is malicious. Two types of malicious behavior are classified and used for detection: distributed denial-of-service attacks (DDoS attacks) and spamming. DDoS attacks are recognized by an incoming to outgoing packet count asymmetry and spamming hosts are identified by the quantity and the periodicity of the mail traffic. If both conditions hold for a packet, the responsible process is reliably identified as malicious by analyzing correlations between API calls and attack traffic, even if process' port-binding information is hidden from HIDS. We highlight this ability because it simplifies incident response and root cause analysis. As such, it makes the proposed system applicable in a high security enterprise environment.

Not-a-bot (NAB) system mitigates network attacks by an automatic validation of the user-originated traffic (Gummadi, 2009). For each request, the originator is automatically determined. If the originator is the user or an application running on user behalf, the request is allowed, otherwise the request is blocked. Decision on whether the request comes from the user is based on user's interactions with a computer. After each keystroke or mouse movement there is a short time window during which requests are allowed through. Allowed requests are attested with a digital signature. The attesting module cannot be altered because its integrity is protected by a Trusted Platform Module. The attestation is responder-specific, content-specific and challenger-specific. Attested requests are analyzed by verifiers in network who may take appropriate actions. NAB can be used with existing network protocols, however, client applications require modifications for NAB to be supported.

We acknowledge that large volume attacks (e.g., DDoS attacks, spamming campaigns, click fraud) can be successfully mitigated with the user-initiated traffic recognition. However, attacks with low traffic volume can be performed during the short period after each user operation, therefore being considered user-originated.

Modern malware often exploits HTTP traffic over TCP port 80 for its communication, because this port is usually open at firewalls on the path. Xiong et al. (2009) present a HIDS that parses the outgoing HTTP traffic for signs of intrusions and permits or denies the traffic according to a whitelist. Each HTTP request is processed independently of the requesting browser in case the browser was compromised. A source domain is identified for each HTTP object in the response. If the domain is already on the whitelist, the object is allowed. Otherwise the user is queried whether he explicitly requested the object and if so, the domain is added to the whitelist. An experiment has shown that users tend to visit a limited set of

IP addresses, but regularly. Authors claim that such result supports the usability of the presented HIDS. On the other hand, a common Webpage contains objects from several dozen domains (e.g., advertising sites, social networks, user satisfaction monitoring sites). HIDSs users, who are often inexperienced in terms of IT security, cannot be realistically asked to decide whether each of these domains should be allowed.

An active probing mechanism to detect the ARP spoofing, malformed ARP packets and the ARP denial-of-service attack in a local network without the need for a central entity is suggested by Barbhuiya et al. (2011). Received ARP requests and responses are verified by broadcasted confirmation requests. If IP and MAC addresses were already considered trustworthy, ARP packets are accepted. Otherwise a simple verification process is performed during which all hosts are queried. If the attacker is present in the network and attempts the ARP spoofing, query responses from hosts are not uniform and the spoofing is detected. Since ARP spoofing can be easily hindered by network switches, the proposed protocol is suitable especially for wireless ad hoc networks, for which it provides a good protection against ARP-related attacks with little communication overhead.

DDoSniffer from Laurens et al. (2009) is a tool for the detection of outgoing TCP SYN denial-of-service attacks. The tool parses outgoing TCP packets. If a packet begins a new TCP connection a new record is created in the Newconn table and in the Conn table. When a packet counter of a particular connection exceeds four (i.e., the TCP handshake was finished and the connection was fully established), the record is removed from the Newconn table. An alarm is reported when the number of records in the Newconn table exceeds predefined threshold or when any of the connections in the Conn table has incoming to outgoing packet ratio higher than four (i.e., the host sends outgoing packets at a high rate without receiving TCP acknowledgements). Alarms are also raised if the IP spoofing is taking place. DDoSniffer tool has a simple design, but it is able to detect only a minority of existing DDoS attacks. Also, fixed connection thresholds can be exploited by an attacker who can keep the attack traffic just below the threshold.

Collaborative IDS

Standalone HIDSs can provide a basic protection for individual computers. However, in an enterprise environment this approach might not be sufficient. Standalone HIDSs cannot provide data correlation, global overview of the infrastructure and usually cannot be centrally managed efficiently. Also, different types of IDSs are differently sensitive to various intrusions. HIDSs are not suitable for a detection of large-scale DDoS attacks, horizontal port scans or spamming campaigns. On the other hand, NIDSs have difficulties with identifying malware intrusions, privilege abuses or focused data thefts. A Collaborative Intrusion Detection System (CIDS) can be employed to address the shortcomings of standalone IDSs. Nodes in CIDS exchange relevant audit data (raw data, alerts, or both) and share information about intrusions and attackers. Data sharing and correlation are intended to improve the true positives rate and the false positives rate.

Recent research aims primarily to design generic frameworks that could incorporate both host-based IDSs and network-based IDSs. Integration could be either direct or indirect. Direct IDSs integration is tighter, usually centralized, and within products of one vendor. However, in case of failure the whole security system might be affected. Indirect integration is usually based on SIEM (Scarfone, 2012).

Collaborative IDSs are categorized according to their topology:

- **Centralized CIDS:** All audit data is aggregated at a single point. Centralized systems offer a global view of a security state of the infrastructure. Audit data analysis

is simplified, because the IDS detection engine has full knowledge of events in its security domain. However, centralized systems suffer from computational performance limitations and low scalability. Also, the central system presents a single point of failure and can itself become a target of knowledgeable attackers.
- **Distributed CIDS:** In distributed systems the audit data is shared equally among all nodes or among a set of neighbors of a local node. Single point of failure limitation and computational performance limitation are loosened, however detection rate improvement may be lower than in case of centralized IDS, because each node has access to a smaller amount of audit data.
- **Hierarchical CIDS:** Hierarchical intrusion detection systems combine properties of centralized and distributed IDSs. Among all nodes in a hierarchical IDS, a subset of privileged nodes with a higher trustworthiness exists. Privileged nodes usually collect audit data from their neighbors and then share it with other privileged nodes. More than one layer of privileged nodes may be present. We can perceive hierarchical IDS as a set of clusters where a privileged node is the cluster head and his neighbors are cluster members.
- **Cloud IDS:** Intrusion detection is offered as a service. IDS analysis engine is placed in the cloud, usually on a virtual server. Cloud clients provide system events and receive analysis results. IDS infrastructure is shared between cloud customers and cloud providers.

Development of collaborative IDSs presents many new problems and challenges:

- **Data Volume:** Amount of data intended for transmission, processing and storing is an important scalability factor. Collecting audit data from multiple independent IDS presents a significant increase of data traffic transmitted over network. This limitation is further emphasized if both alerts and raw data are transmitted. Processing of the data at the detection engine may pose a great burden on its computational resources. Maintaining audit data for a possible post-incident analysis is costly in terms of disk/tape storage capacity.
- **Trust and Privacy Issues:** Sharing sensitive data over networks requires a framework that supports confidentiality, integrity and authentication of entities. Moreover, each independent node may be compromised and directed to disrupt the whole CIDS. Trust management systems, often based on node reputation, must be established to compensate for malicious nodes. In some cases special privacy-preserving components must anonymize/pseudonymize the audit data before it is transmitted to the detection engine.
- **Scalability and Robustness:** Scalability and robustness challenges are closely related to the volume of processed data and trust issues. By their nature, hierarchical IDSs and distributed IDSs provide more scalability options than standalone IDSs or centralized IDSs. Spreading data analysis over multiple nodes lowers computational requirements on each single node. In case of a node failure another node can overtake its responsibilities. A careful design of decision schemes is necessary to support these properties.
- **Free-rider Problem:** A node can enjoy benefits of a collaborative IDS even without contributing.
- **Information Sharing:** Collaborative IDSs usually incorporate heterogeneous systems. Standardized models are necessary for smooth alert and audit data sharing. An example of such data model is the

Intrusion Detection Message Exchange Format (IDMEF), which defines data formats and exchange procedures for IDS information sharing.
- **Alerts and False Positives Notification:** An event in a domain of collaborative IDSs may be detected by multiple nodes. A reliable event correlation should be put in place that identifies similar intrusions and reports them in a unified fashion.
- **Denial of Service:** Given the distributed nature of collaborative IDSs and both technical and administrative difficulties in fully securing every node, the resistance of a collaborative IDS against denial of service attacks is required. Collaborative IDSs should be able to function even with a reasonable number of nodes being inaccessible or disabled.

Aussibal and Gallon (2008) proposed a distributed detection platform with an advanced alert processing system, capable of evaluating the severity of alerts. The system consists of probes and detection entities. Probes are common IDSs, both HIDSs and NIDSs. Detection entities serve as alert aggregators. Each anomaly detected by a probe is cross-referenced with the Common Vulnerability Scoring System (CVSS) and is assigned a score. If the probe is compatible with the Common Vulnerabilities and Exposures dictionary (CVE), the CVE information is added to the alert message. Alert messages are collected at detection entities. For each observed network flow the sum of alert scores is computed and if the sum exceeds a pre-set threshold, the flow is classified as "ALERT" and all other detection entities are notified. It is imperative to evaluate the reliability of each probe for each class of detectable attacks when using already existing IDSs. A rigorous comparative testing may be required so that IDSs could collaborate efficiently, benefiting from individual strengths of probes and eliminating their weaknesses.

A distributed IDS that utilizes mobile agents is proposed by Liu and Li (2008). The IDS incorporates both HIDSs and NIDSs. There are four types of agents – "host agents," "net agents," "manage agents," and "mobile agents." Static agents reside at the host, collect data and detect any possible host intrusions. Net agents detect intrusions within the network traffic. Reports from host agents and network agents are collected at manage agents. When a suspicious, but not necessarily intrusive, activity is detected, a manage agent spawns a new mobile agent. Mobile agent is a specialized piece of code that visits all hosts where the suspicious activity was reported, collects related contextual information, and possibly generates alerts. All information is summarized and transmitted to the manage agent that in turn may use it in the self-learning process. This detection method is inherently reactive, yet it can benefit from rich contextual data collected over multiple hosts.

Roschke et al. (2010) focus on improving performance of alert correlation through the use of fast databases and efficient algorithms. Basic clustering algorithms are evaluated and their performance is discussed. New memory-supported alert correlation and clustering algorithms using hash-based index tables are proposed. Authors conclude that for analytical operations like clustering or correlation, the column-oriented databases have a better performance than the row-oriented databases. However, the column-oriented databases have higher memory consumption and insert operation is slow. An Extensible Correlation Platform capable of real-time alert clustering and correlation is proposed on the basis of these findings.

Trust-Based Collaborative IDS

Utilization of node reputation is a common approach in collaborative IDSs. Alerts and raw data coming from nodes with a high reputation have more weight than those coming from nodes with a low reputation. Reputation thresholds can be established as a filtering mechanism for alerts from untrustworthy nodes.

A variety of attacks can disrupt the trust-based systems (Fung, 2009):

- **Sybil Attack:** During the Sybil attack the malicious node simulates a large number of identities with an intention to artificially improve its own reputation.
- **Newcomer Attack:** The malicious node presents itself under a new identity, therefore discarding previous (bad) reputation.
- **Betrayal Attack:** A previously trustworthy node become malicious and starts sending false alarms, stops sending legitimate alerts and begins to negatively influence its neighborhood.
- **Collusion Attack:** A group of malicious nodes cooperate by providing false alert rankings.
- **Inconsistency Attack:** A node alternates between the legitimate and malicious behavior.

Fung et al. (2009) propose a new trust-based framework for HIDSs collaboration, utilizing the concept of dynamically sent peer-to-peer test messages. Each HIDS sends requests for alert ranking or test messages to peer HIDSs. Test messages and real alert ranking requests are undistinguishable. The purpose of test messages is to evaluate the trustworthiness of a node, because the originating node already knows the true answer. Satisfaction score is calculated from the received answer, the expected answer and the difficulty of the test message. The framework is designed to cope with attacks against trust-based collaborative IDSs and is reasonably scalable, but it requires a lengthy training period.

RepCIDN, a Collaborative Intrusion Detection Network both for HIDSs and NIDSs with a partially-decentralized schema is proposed by Pérez et al. (2012). RepCIDN uses the signature detection model and supports a dissemination of signatures. The schema is enhanced with a reputation system that uses a Wise Committee (WC). WC members are several most trustworthy NIDSs. WC permission is required for any intra-domain information sharing. The trustworthiness of each node in the security domain is decided by WC members on the basis of interactions it had with the system in the past. Inter-domain communication is forwarded through wise committee leaders in a P2P fashion. We consider the Wise Committee idea promising. Highly secured NIDSs in the center of the infrastructure provide a solid source of trustworthy information, which can be supported with detailed contextual data from HIDSs.

Collaborative IDS in Mobile Ad Hoc Networks

Anantvalee and Wu (2006) define a mobile ad hoc network (MANET) as "a self-configuring network that is formed automatically by a collection of mobile nodes without the help of a fixed infrastructure or centralized management." Network nodes are communicating wirelessly on a multi-hop basis. Each node is able to forward other nodes' packets. The topology is dynamic with nodes frequently changing positions, leaving and re-entering the network and forming and dropping transient connections with nodes in range. The network structure may be flat or multi-layer, depending on the applications.

A number of both passive and active attacks for MANETs have been recognized. Passive attacks concern mainly eavesdropping and traffic analysis. Active attacks include routing attacks, changes of forwarded packets, masquerade attacks, denial of service attacks etc. Also, the nodes physical security is often poor. Therefore, attackers can capture one or more nodes and attempt internal attacks. IDSs in MANETs must be resistant to insider attacks from Byzantine nodes that may

Host–Based Intrusion Detection Systems

drop genuine alerts or oppositely make false alerts. Intrusion detection systems in MANETs are usually distributed cooperative, because each node can observe only its local neighborhood.

According to Zhou and Haas (1999), intrusion detection in MANETs is challenging due to communication over wireless media, placement of nodes in a potentially hostile environment, continual dynamic changes in topology, and a need for scalability over hundreds or thousands of nodes. Sahu and Shandilya (2010) also emphasize difficulties with centralized approach in an ad hoc network, node resource constraints, IDS accuracy issues, recommendation to use a trust model and necessity to protect the IDS itself. Another limitation is presented by Pérez et al. (2011). In collaborative intrusion detection networks HIDSs are allowed to travel between security domains. Data and alerts are exchanged within each security domain and also between security domains. It is difficult to assess the trustworthiness of alerts from a mobile HIDS that is arriving into a local security domain from another security domain. As a solution, authors suggest a reputation value formula, which takes into account the previous behavior of the HIDS in the local security domain and recommendations provided by other security domains weighted with subjective reliability of these security domains as perceived from the local security domain.

A number of surveys on intrusion detection in MANETs has been published in the past, for example by Brutch and Ko (2003), Mishra, Nadkarni, and Patcha (2004), Anantvalee and Wu (2006), and Sahu and Shandilya (2010).

A decentralized two-stage intrusion detection system HybrIDS for mobile ad hoc networks with minimal resource utilization was proposed by Lauf et al. (2010). Detection is based on an analysis of the application layer behavior. The system combines two detection strategies: Maxima Detection System (MDS) and Cross-Correlative Detection System (CCDS). MDS analyzes local maxima in probability distribution function of statistics generated from requests and compares them with a threshold value. MDS can function with zero knowledge of the protected system. However, it can detect only one deviant node. CCDS monitors the degree of correlation among node behaviors. It can reveal multiple malicious nodes, but a calibration period is required. MDS is therefore used to calibrate CCDS in early stages.

ExWatchdog from Nasser and Chen (2007) is an extension to a well-known Watchdog collaborative routing protocol-based intrusion detection system (Marti et al., 2000) for MANETs. ExWatchdog addresses Watchdog's inability to recognize malicious nodes that falsely report other nodes as misbehaving, while they themselves are actual culprits. Each node keeps a tab of paths between each two nodes and a sum of packets exchanged over each path. If any node is reported as misbehaving, the source node verifies the reputation report through confirmation packets over suboptimal routing paths that do not contain candidate malicious nodes. ExWatchdog solves Watchdog's issue with false reports and consequently decreases the overall system overhead, especially in situations with many misbehaving nodes.

Cloud-Based IDS

We differentiate between two primary classes of HIDSs in cloud environment, infrastructure HIDSs and cloud client HIDSs. Infrastructure HIDSs are placed at physical servers or inside cloud virtual machines and are intended to protect the server infrastructure of the cloud. Although infrastructure HIDSs are consistent from the technical point of view, their use is influenced by the specifics of cloud environment, specifically the separation of responsibilities. Cloud client HIDSs are subscribers of in-cloud intrusion detection services (intrusion detection as a service, IDSaaS). They serve primarily as simple data collection units that may optionally perform data preprocessing and filtering. Audit data is then transmitted to a central high availability detection engine placed in the cloud. The biggest limitation of IDSaaS is inability to detect intrusions in case of a failure of the link between the cloud service provider and the customer. Such failure may be inadvertent, but also the result of a deliberate (D)DoS attack.

Cloud Security Alliance white paper (2011) states that in addition to traditional functions, IDSs in cloud are required to provide virtualization layer workload monitoring, hypervisor and virtual machine manager integrity monitoring and virtual machine image repository monitoring. Cloud IDSs can be deployed at the system layer, the platform layer and the application layer. Correlation of audit data from each layer may improve the accuracy of detection. IDSs managed by cloud providers can detect attacks spanning over multiple customers or detect attacks on some customers using data received from other customers. Simultaneous usage of a single physical server by multiple customers is also common and could be considered a security threat by some organizations. Moreover, privacy-sensitive data aggregated at the IDS might subject to laws or internal organization policies. Enforcing these policies in cloud may be hard, especially in situations when the organization does not know the precise physical location where its data is stored (Mather, 2009).

Although cloud providers offer their own security services to customers, these services often lack necessary transparency and may not comply with organization's regional regulations or internal procedures. Consequently, cloud customers demand to be allowed to deploy their own security services in conjunction with provider's services. Subsequently, security management and responsibilities in cloud are divided between the cloud service provider and the customer. Customer's security specialists do not have full control over the underlying virtual machine or its physical infrastructure. Trust boundaries and areas of responsibility must therefore be established.

A comprehensive paper on cloud infrastructure security was published by Vaquero, Rodero-Merino and Morán (2011). Modi et al. presented a survey of intrusion detection techniques in cloud (2013).

Oberheide et al. (2008) propose CloudAV, an antivirus in the form of an in-cloud network service. Files from local computers are sent to the network service for analysis. A technique called "N-version protection" is employed. This technique checks each file by multiple signature detection engines and behavioral detection engines in parallel. Each engine runs in a separate virtualized Xen container. Results are aggregated and cached both at the server and at the client. The caching helps mitigate effects of a link failure between the host and CloudAV. The proposed approach has a high accuracy thanks to the parallel detection and enhanced forensics capabilities. Intrusion can be detected retrospectively by re-checking previously received files when the signature database has been updated.

Another system that uses N-version protection is uCLAWS by Martínez et al. (2010). uCLAWS employs a new malware and intrusion detection ontology implemented in OWL language. It is designed as a customer-oriented Web service accessible through XML messages using SOAP. Web services design allows an easy portability of client agents. uCLAWS's detection rate outperforms all other engines included in the results comparison.

It should be noted that a centralized antivirus service may be prone to the host-based IDS evasion techniques due to discrepancies between the host and the service system. Contextual metadata transferring (e.g., operating system identifier, list of installed patches) may be necessary for a correct file parsing. Moreover, the sent data should be considered private. The service provider could profile the user and monitor his activity, unless privacy-protecting measures are taken.

Houmansadr et al. (2011) propose a cloud-based system for a complex detection of malware in smartphones. A network proxy is established between Internet and the cell network. The smartphone environment is emulated in the cloud. All incoming traffic is duplicated by the proxy and sent simultaneously to the smartphone and to the emulation platform. High cloud performance allows complex IDS engines that are unsuitable for resource-constrained mobile devices to be used for a real-time in-depth analysis. Each smartphone has a lightweight agent installed that collects user and sensor input, sends it to the emulation engine, and optionally performs the intrusion response. Contrary to previous approaches the user input is replicated in real time, not in batches. Therefore, the cloud replica is always kept synchronized with little required bandwidth.

Paranoid Android (PA) by Portokalidis et al. (2010) is a scalable security model very similar to the work of Houmansadr. PA aims to minimize energy consumption and bandwidth requirements of the traces transmission from the smartphone to the cloud replica. PA's host tracer creates records of only those system calls that could introduce nondeterminism and compresses them in order to minimize the required bandwidth. PA also adopts a loose synchronization strategy. When smartphone network adapters are in a sleep mode, traces are not transmitted but rather stored in the local secure storage. Traces in the storage are protected by HMAC in order to make a removal or modification by an attacker detectable. Synchronization is continued once the connection is restored. Traces are verified by ClamAV signature detection and dynamic taint analysis at the cloud replica. Although only ClamAV antivirus has been used so far, the model is extensible to N-version protection. PA brings a low communication overhead, but in the current state it also significantly depletes the smartphone battery.

HIDS Security

The question of tamper-resistance should be raised during every HIDS-related discussion. Host-based intrusion detection systems reside directly at the protected hosts, therefore they are vulnerable when an attacker took control of the underlying operating system. A HIDS can be shut down, its analysis engine could be influenced, critical files changed or deleted, input data altered or output alerts dropped. Ensuring reliable input and output in a potentially hostile environment is a challenging task.

Molina and Cukier (2009) define the HIDS resiliency as "the probability that the HIDS will not be subverted in the event of an attack against the system under supervision." They argue that the resiliency is closely linked with the independency. HIDS should be most independent of the supervised system, because shared system elements can serve as attack vectors. The HIDS resiliency is defined as a quantitative, attack-dependent metric, whereas the HIDS independency is defined as a qualitative attack-independent metric. A sample independence analysis of Samhain integrity checker over Gentoo Linux is provided.

Laureano et al. (2007) suggested that HIDSs could be protected in a virtual environment. Processes and events are monitored inside a virtual machine, but the analysis is performed by a HIDS that is placed on an underlying physical machine. The HIDS is separated from the attacker but it still possesses all knowledge about the protected system.

XenFIT by Quynh and Takefuji (2007) is a new file integrity checker with a high tamper resistance. It is intended for virtual machines hosted on the Xen hypervisor. The HIDS is running in the user space in a separate highly secured privileged Virtual Machine (VM). From there it has access to file systems of protected virtual machines. Access to the protected virtual machine data is via breakpoints in chosen system calls in the kernel memory of the protected VM. Therefore, no program code is running inside the protected VM. An attacker who obtained root privileges to the protected VM can disable breakpoints, but cannot tamper with the HIDS itself. Also, minimal changes to the protected VM make XenFIT hardly detectable for the attacker.

VMwall, an application-level firewall for Xen virtual environments with a high tamper resistance is presented by Srivastava and Giffin (2008). VMwall's function is not affected even if the attacker takes control of the protected virtual machine. VMwall utilizes the virtual machine isolation and the virtual machine introspection for a secured monitoring of the network traffic of protected virtual machines. A kernel module intercepts packets destined to and coming from the protected VM and decides if they are forwarded. A user agent correlates packets with processes running inside the VM. Both the kernel module and the user agent are placed in a secured VM. Data structures which are necessary for VMwall function are secured with existing kernel integrity protection mechanisms.

Payne et al. (2008) present Lares, an architecture for a secured active monitoring in the virtualized environment. Lares allows for system hooks being placed in untrusted virtual machines, therefore enabling the active monitoring, opposite from the more common VM interspection technique. The protected VM contains system hooks and a "trampoline" code that mediates the communication with an analysis engine in a secured VM. The trampoline functionality is self-contained (i.e., does not depend on kernel functions), non-persistent (i.e., does not require data which was generated during previous hook activations) and atomical. Hooks are secured with a memory protection mechanism. When a guest VM requires a write change in a certain memory page, the hypervisor verifies whether the requested memory address is not designated as write-protected. If so, the change is not allowed and the required change from the guest VM is not propagated into the actual physical memory. A list of protected memory regions is stored and maintained by a Lares component.

Parno et al. (2009) argue that network devices devote a lot of their precious resources to reconstructing the state information that is already known to end hosts. Proliferation of TPM-equipped computers and secure smartphones encourages us to use these trusted elements of end hosts to support the host trustfulness. They designed an architecture where information from trusted clients is collected by trusted verifiers and verifiers make recommendations to network filters how to react on the traffic. Clients have a minimal-size hypervisor incorporated. The hypervisor ensures a secure boot of the client and that the agent application was not modified. Once clients authorize verifiers, clients can cryptographically attest their traffic by a hardware-based cryptographic attestation. Any change to the protective hypervisor layer makes the authentication token inaccessible, forbidding the client to further authenticate its traffic. Network filters allow, block, or inspect the network traffic based on the recommendations from verifiers.

Evasion Techniques

Evasion techniques are modifications to existing attacks, which allow these attacks to proceed undetected by intrusion detection systems. Usually, these modifications only marginally affect the core function of the attack, but simultaneously they significantly change its external properties. Evasion techniques were first described by Ptacek and Newsham (1998) as an approach to evade detection by a NIDS. Ptacek and Newsham distinguished "insertion," which involves injection of packets to the NIDS, "evasion," which involves rejection of packets by the NIDS and "denial-of-service," which represents an attempt to make the NIDS unable to function. Since then, the scope of evasion techniques widened to include also evasion of host-based IDSs. Modern IDSs can overcome some simple evasion techniques (e.g., path obfuscation, simple fragmentation), but the majority still remains problematic. Evasion techniques can be tailored to an IDS product, a signature database file or even to a specific IDS instance.

We identify five evasion approaches:

- **Code Morphing:** Malware signature is masked by compression, encryption, extraordinary encoding or polymorphic code.
- **Behavior Morphing:** The actual attack behavior is modified to distinguish from

expected malicious behavior (e.g., order of operations during the attack is shuffled; malicious operations are performed by separate processes seemingly without mutual relations).
- **Timing:** IDSs inherently observe intrusions in a distinguishable time window. By spreading the attack in sufficiently long time the boundaries of what is considered a "normal" behavior are not crossed. Also, anomaly IDSs which are constantly updating their normal profiles can be made to consider malicious activities harmless.
- **Denial of Service:** The ability of IDSs to detect or report intrusions is denied. HIDS or some of its components may be shut down, modified, or overwhelmed.
- **Duality of Interpretation:** The attacker exploits differences between how the input is interpreted by the IDS and by the application. IDS is persuaded that the input is either benign or it is corrupted and should be discarded.

A framework for an evaluation of evasion techniques for botnets is presented by Stinson and Mitchell (2008). The cost associated with evading IDSs consists of two components: implementation complexity and botnet utility. Implementation complexity represents the difficulty of making modifications to the botnet in order to evade detection, ranging from a simple command selection to extensive source code modifications. Botnet utility specifies the impact of modifications on the ability of the botnet to perform its activities. Modifications could influence diversity of attacks, time required to launch an attack, botnet size, attack rate and synchronization level. Authors suggest designing such detection methods where the evasion techniques against them negatively affect the botnet capabilities.

Shadow attacks, a new class of duality of interpretation evasion attacks against behavior-based malware detectors, are proposed by Ma et al. (2012). Behavior-based detectors usually analyze system calls to detect anomalies. Shadow attacks employ partitioning of sequences of malicious system calls into multiple processes. Therefore, unless the detector can correlate system calls from all shadow processes, the global system calls sequence remains undetected. To conceal their relationship, shadow processes can communicate through ordinary channels (e.g., sockets, shared memory, shared file, remote network coordination) or through special covert channels. A compiler-level tool AutoShadow for an automatic transformation of an arbitrary malware source code to a shadow malware executable is created.

Another two new classes of duality of interpretation attacks against signature-based malware detectors are presented by Jana and Shmatikov (2012). Chameleon attacks exploit differences between the heuristics used by detectors to determine the type of file and those used by end hosts. The type of the file presented to the detector is incorrectly recognized and therefore an inappropriate signature matching is performed, without regard to specific requirements of the file type (e.g., an archive is considered to be a monolithic file). Werewolf attacks exploit differences between how executables and application-specific formats are parsed between detectors and actual applications or operating systems. Even though the file is recognized, the detector's parsing ability is usually limited in comparison to the application's parser. Both classes of attacks require only the file metadata to be modified, allowing a simple masquerading of an arbitrary malware file. Authors conclude that host-based IDSs could be more resistant to some types of chameleon and werewolf attacks, especially when on-access file scanning is employed and when HIDSs are closely integrated with the application (e.g., application itself provides access to an already parsed file).

We believe that at least some classes of attack tools that employ shadow, werewolf, or chameleon evasion techniques could be detected by HIDSs capable of analyzing the host's network traffic. Adapting the network behavior of tools responsible for example for (D)DoS attacks, port scans or malware spreading is rather difficult task. Modification could also lead to a lower effectiveness of the attack tools, in compliance with recommendations from Stinson and Mitchell (2008). Although this approach is predominantly followed by NIDSs, we encourage adopting this technique also for HIDSs, bearing in mind both HIDS advantages and disadvantages.

FUTURE RESEARCH DIRECTIONS

In our view, the future of HIDSs lies mainly in smartphones, tablets and other general-purpose mobile devices. These devices regularly connect to untrusted networks, communicate with possibly infected peers in their range and often contain both valuable personal and enterprise data.

We are convinced that host-based intrusion detection systems should always be considered an important part of an overall intrusion detection architecture. On the other hand, HIDSs may also work separately, without the support, and still provide a decent level of protection. HIDSs should not aim to replace network-based IDSs, but rather serve as a complementary tool. In this architecture, their tasks will be to confirm and stop the intrusion, identify attack vectors and help to restore the secured state. The ability to identify attack vectors may be even enhanced to the point where HIDS output can be used as a guideline where to find a forensics evidence of the malicious activity.

We have identified two main research trends across all HIDSs: the utilization of virtualization technologies and the shift towards a real-time detection. Achieving the real-time detection is a necessary step towards functional host-based intrusion prevention systems. It is also a logical progression towards an efficient collaboration with NIDSs. Virtualization can affect virtually every aspect of HIDSs, with attack detection, management simplification and tamper resistance being the most notable. However, in most cases changes must be made to the virtualization layer or a custom-based hypervisor must be created. This may limit the usability and flexibility of virtualization-based solutions. Virtualization-based approaches are indeed functional; however, usually they can be used only for VMs hosted in datacenters. Another important problem to address is how to masquerade the virtual environment as a real environment. Otherwise, the malware that determines it is running in the virtual machine could alter its behavior and evade detection.

Another fruitful area of research that we have identified concerns the ways how trusted platform modules or cryptographic smartcards could be used in connection with a HIDS to (at least partially) solve the ground truth problem. We are in favor of hardware attestations and tamper-resistant integrity verification. For a standalone HIDS the ability to reason about the validity of provided information would be invaluable. Collaborative HIDSs can also solve the ground truth problem with reputation systems, but they are often slow to discover misbehaving hosts.

Considering specific subclasses of HIDSs, the log analysis systems are now mature and ready for massive deployments in real environments as can be proved by a number of existing commercial applications. Basic problems with inconsistent log formats and alert correlation were mostly solved. Scalability remains an issue, but hierarchical log analysis models and faster hardware make the costs acceptable. Future research will enhance the event correlation capabilities up to the point of semantic correlation.

The focus of integrity checkers has shifted from a periodic checking to an online checking during the past several years. Online checkers do not have a window of vulnerability between two subsequent checks, during which an attacker could modify critical system files, perform any malicious activity and then restore the files to the former state without being detected. On the other hand, online checking brings an increased complexity and often requires modification of existing systems. A problematic part of integrity checking is to determine which files/resources should be protected. An incomplete set could lead to intrusions going undetected, whereas a large set could produce many false positives. Currently, file lists are supplied by integrity checker vendors. An interesting idea for further research could be to apply anomaly techniques in order to determine the list of critical but not frequently modified files.

Process monitoring is currently almost solely directed towards the system call analysis. Differences between works of research teams are mainly in their approaches how anomalies are analyzed. We are convinced that process monitoring area is promising. Ever-increasing number of malware presses to employ automated malware detectors even for end devices. Behavior detection is especially beneficial in the context of polymorphic malware.

Network traffic analysis HIDSs deal with the same problems as NIDSs. We are convinced that aggregating host contextual information with a view of host network traffic provides a new promising research challenge. The challenge is emphasized with collaborative systems. Designing protocols and schemes for intrusion data exchange with regards to privacy requirements, limited node trust and frequent node movements will be particularly demanding. Existing systems that incorporate both HIDSs and NIDSs usually put more trust on NIDSs and HIDSs serve as an additional source of information. It is a logical solution and we expect to see more similar models. We do not expect a wide deployment of purely collaborative network analysis HIDSs. They are suitable only for corporate networks, which is a traditional domain of NIDSs and they do not bring enough benefits to overcome this fact.

Cloud-based intrusion detection is a fostering concept. Low client resources requirements combined with minimal user knowledge requirements predetermine the cloud-based IDS to become very popular, particularly among home users and small companies that cannot afford own IT security specialists. As with collaborative systems, privacy and trust issues must be addressed. Using cloud-based IDS could be somewhat problematic on mobile devices with pay-per-use Internet connection, because the IDS can generate potentially huge network traffic. We believe the number of cloud-based IDS services will grow and so will their diversity.

Interesting findings are linked with user-friendliness. Since HIDSs directly impact common users, user-friendliness is a determining factor in HIDSs popularity. Our survey has shown that keeping reasonable memory requirements is an important goal of almost every HIDS, and CPU and memory consumption is usually indeed low. On the other hand, many solutions have a very high false positives rate (i.e., several percent). We are convinced that a system that disturbs users from their ordinary work is unacceptable and cannot be deployed in real environment. Especially, large organizations with hundreds of client computers do not want their security specialists to waste time with repeating false alarms. The same situation is with HIDSs that require some form of human input (i.e., solve a puzzle, confirm change) unless they are carefully balanced.

During security experiments, the emphasis is put on the false positives rate and the false negatives rate. Our informal observations confirm the findings of Killrouhy and Maxion (2011), who claim that only around 50% of security research papers use comparative experiments. We hypothesize that the reason is the unavailability of shared test data, but also the unavailability of actual HIDS implementations.

We are currently investigating an option for the design of an anomaly-based HIDS capable of detecting outgoing denial-of-service attacks, types of these attacks, intended targets and originator processes. Therefore, when an ongoing attack is detected, we can inform the administrator of the computer that the computer was either infected with malware or the operator is deliberately misusing computer resources. The detection will be based on an analysis of host data traffic, combined with the knowledge of basic system properties (e.g., host IP address, logged user name). We believe that such a self-contained detection module can function independently, providing a best effort service, but can also be incorporated in a large intrusion detection architecture, where it can serve as a complementary source of information.

CONCLUSION

In this chapter, we explored the current state of host-based intrusion detection. The reasons behind low HIDS popularity were argued. Requirements for an optimal HIDS were formulated. A HIDS taxonomy of both standalone and collaborative HIDSs was presented. Standalone HIDSs include log analysis systems, integrity checkers, process monitoring systems and host network traffic analyzers. Collaborative HIDSs contain but are not limited to trust-based systems, specific collaborative HIDSs for mobile ad hoc networks and cloud-based IDSs. Overall characteristics of each class were presented and related issues were examined in detail. Research advances in each class were thoroughly analyzed. Both contemporary trends and future challenges were formulated. The HIDS ground truth problem was presented and techniques that can be used to increase HIDS resistance against tampering were discussed.

REFERENCES

Abad, C., Taylor, J., Sengul, C., Yurcik, W., Zhou, Y., & Rowe, K. (2003). Log correlation for intrusion detection: A proof of concept. In *Proceedings of the 19th Annual Computer Security Applications Conference* (pp. 255-264). Washington, DC: IEEE Computer Society.

Anantvalee, T., & Wu, J. (2006). A survey on intrusion detection in mobile ad hoc networks. In Xiao, Y., Shen, X., & Du, D.-Z. (Eds.), *Wireless/Mobile Network Security* (pp. 170–196). Berlin: Springer.

Asif-Iqbal, H., Udzir, N. I., Mahmod, R., & Ghani, A. A. A. (2011). Filtering events using clustering in heterogeneous security logs. *Information Technology Journal*, *10*(4), 798–806. doi:10.3923/itj.2011.798.806.

Aussibal, J., & Gallon, L. (2008). A new distributed IDS based on CVSS framework. In *Proceedings of the 2008 IEEE International Conference on Signal Image Technology and Internet Based Systems* (pp. 701-707). Washington, DC: IEEE Computer Society.

Axelsson, S. (2000). The base-rate fallacy and the difficulty of intrusion detection. *ACM Transactions on Information and System Security*, *3*(3), 186–205. doi:10.1145/357830.357849.

Baliga, A., Iftode, L., & Chen, X. (2008). Automated containment of rootkits attacks. *Computers & Security*, *27*(7-8), 323–334. doi:10.1016/j.cose.2008.06.003.

Barbhuiya, F. A., Roopa, S., Ratti, R., Hubballi, N., Biswas, S., Sur, A., & Ramachandran, V. (2011). An active host-based detection mechanism for ARP-related attacks. In Meghanathan, N, Kaushik, B.K, & Nagamalai, D (Eds.), *Communications in Computer and Information Science: Advances in Networks and Communications* (pp. 432-443). Berlin: Springer. doi:10.1007/978-3-642-17878-8_44.

Bickford, J., Lagar-Cavilla, H. A., Varshavsky, A., Ganapathy, V., & Iftode, L. (2011). Security versus energy tradeoffs in host-based mobile malware detection. In *Proceedings of the 9th International Conference on Mobile Systems, Applications, and Services* (pp. 225-238). New York, NY: ACM.

Bravo-Lillo, C., Cranor, L. F., Downs, J., Komanduri, S., & Sleeper, M. (2011). Improving computer security dialogs. *Lecture Notes in Computer Science, 6949*, 18–35. doi:10.1007/978-3-642-23768-3_2.

Brutch, P., & Ko, C. (2003). Challenges in intrusion detection for wireless ad-hoc networks. In *Proceedings of the 2003 Symposium on Applications and Internet Workshops* (pp. 368-373). Washington, DC: IEEE Computer Society.

Bukač, V., Tuček, P., & Deutsch, M. (2012). Advances and challenges in standalone host-based intrusion detection systems. *Lecture Notes in Computer Science, 7449*, 105–117. doi:10.1007/978-3-642-32287-7_9.

Chandola, V., Banerjee, A., & Kumar, V. (2009). Anomaly detection: A survey. *ACM Computing Surveys, 41*(3). doi:10.1145/1541880.1541882.

Cloud Security Alliance. (2011). *Security guidance for critical areas of focus in cloud computing v3.0 (Technical report)*. Cloud Security Alliance.

De Boer, P., & Pels, M. (2005). *Host-based intrusion detection systems (Technical report, Revision 1.10)*. Amsterdam: Informatics Institute, University of Amsterdam.

Fung, C. J., Zhang, J., Aib, I., & Boutaba, R. (2009). Robust and scalable trust management for collaborative intrusion detection. [Piscataway, NJ: IEEE Press.]. *Proceedings of Integrated Network Management, IM, 2009*, 33–40.

Gummadi, R., Balakrishnan, H., Maniatis, P., & Ratnasamy, S. (2009). Not-a-bot: Improving service availability in the face of botnet attacks. In *Proceedings of the 6th USENIX Symposium on Networked Systems Design and Implementation* (pp. 307-320). Berkeley, CA: USENIX Association.

Hofmeyr, S. A., Forrest, S., & Somayaji, A. (1998). Intrusion detection using sequences of system calls. *Journal of Computer Security, 6*(3), 151–180.

Houmansadr, A., Zonouz, S. A., & Berthier, R. (2011). A cloud-based intrusion detection and response system for mobile phones. In *Proceedings of the 2011 IEEE/IFIP 41st International Conference on Dependable Systems and Networks Workshops* (pp. 31-32). Washington, DC: IEEE Computer Society.

Hu, J. (2010). Host-based anomaly intrusion detection. In Stavroulakis, P. P., & Stamp, M. (Eds.), *Handbook of Information and Communication Security* (pp. 235–255). Berlin: Springer-Verlag. doi:10.1007/978-3-642-04117-4_13.

Jana, S., & Shmatikov, V. (2012). Abusing file processing in malware detectors for fun and profit. In *Proceedings of the 33rd IEEE Symposium on Security & Privacy* (pp. 80-94). IEEE.

Jin, H., Xiang, G., Zou, D., Zhao, F., Li, M., & Yu, C. (2010). A guest-transparent file integrity monitoring method in virtualization environment. *Computers & Mathematics with Applications (Oxford, England), 60*(2), 256–266. doi:10.1016/j.camwa.2010.01.007.

Kaczmarek, J., & Wróbel, M. (2008). Modern approaches to file system integrity checking. [*st International Conference on Information Technology*. IEEE.]. *Proceedings of the, 2008*, 1.

Kent, K., & Souppaya, M. (2006). *Guide to computer security log management (NIST Special Publication 800-92)*. Gaithersburg, MD: National Institute of Standards and Technology.

Killrouhy, K. S., & Maxion, R. A. (2011). Should security researchers experiment more and draw more inferences? In *Proceedings of the 4th Conference on Cyber Security Experimentation and Test*. Berkeley, CA: USENIX Association.

Kolbitsch, C., Comparetti, P. M., Kruegel, C., Kirda, E., Zhou, X., & Wang, X. (2009). Effective and efficient malware detection at the end host. In *Proceedings of the 18th USENIX Security Symposium* (pp. 351-366). Berkeley, CA: USENIX Association.

Köpsell, S., & Švenda, P. (2010). Secure logging of retained data for an anonymity service. In Bezzi, M., Duquenoy, P., Fischer-Hübner, S., Hansen, M., & Zhang, G. (Eds.), *IFIP Advances in Information and Communication Technology: Privacy and Identity Management for Life* (pp. 284–298). Berlin: Springer. doi:10.1007/978-3-642-14282-6_24.

Kwon, J., Lee, J., & Lee, H. (2011). Hidden bot detection by tracing non-human generated traffic at the zombie host. In *Proceedings of the 7th International Conference on Information Security Practice and Experience* (pp. 343-361). Berlin: Springer.

Kwon, M., Jeong, K., & Lee, H. (2008). PROBE: A process behavior-based host intrusion prevention system. In *Proceedings of the 4th International Conference on Information Security Practice and Experience* (pp. 203-217). Berlin: Springer.

Lauf, A. P., Peters, R. A., & Robinson, W. H. (2010). A distributed intrusion detection system for resource-constrained devices in ad-hoc networks. *Ad Hoc Networks*, 8(3), 253–266. doi:10.1016/j.adhoc.2009.08.002.

Laureano, M., Maziero, C., & Jamhour, E. (2007). Protecting host-based intrusion detectors through virtual machines. *Computer Networks: The International Journal of Computer and Telecommunications Networking*, 51(5), 1275–1283.

Laurens, V., Miége, A., El Saddik, A., & Dhar, P. (2009). DDoSniffer: Detecting DDOS attack at the source agents. *International Journal of Advanced Media and Communication*, 3(3), 290–311. doi:10.1504/IJAMC.2009.027014.

Lazarevic, A., Kumar, V., & Srivastava, J. (2005). Intrusion detection: A survey. In Kumar, V, Srivastava, J, & Lazarevic, A (Eds.), *Managing Cyber Threats: Issues, Approaches, and Challenges* (pp. 19-81). New York, NY: Springer Science+Business Media, Inc. doi:10.1007/0-387-24230-9_2.

Liu, J., & Li, L. (2008). A distributed intrusion detection system based on agents. *Computational Intelligence and Industrial Application*, 1, 553–557.

Ma, W., Duan, P., Liu, S., Gu, G., & Liu, J.-C. (2012). Shadow attacks: Automatically evading system-call-behavior based malware detection. *Journal in Computer Virology*, 8(1-2), 1–13. doi:10.1007/s11416-011-0157-5.

Marti, S., Giuli, T. J., Lai, K., & Baker, M. (2000). Mitigating routing misbehavior in mobile ad hoc networks. In *Proceedings of the 6th Annual International Conference on Mobile Computing and Networking* (pp. 255-265). New York, NY: ACM.

Martinez, C. A., Echeverri, G. I., & Sanz, A. G. C. (2010). Malware detection based on cloud computing integrating intrusion ontology representation. In C. E. Velasquez & Y. A. Rodriguez (Eds.), *2010 IEEE Latin-American Conference on Communications* (pp. 1-6). IEEE Communications Society.

Mather, T., Kumaraswamy, S., & Latif, S. (2009). *Cloud security and privacy*. Sebastopol, CA: O'Reilly Media, Inc..

Milanesi, C. (2011). iPad and beyond: The future of the tablet market (Technical report). Washington, DC: Gartner, Inc.

Miller, D. R., Harris, S., Harper, A. A., Vandyke, S., & Blask, C. (2010). *Security information and event management (SIEM) implementation*. New York: The McGraw-Hill Companies.

Mishra, A., Nadkarni, K., & Patcha, A. (2004). Intrusion detection in wireless ad hoc networks. *IEEE Wireless Communications, 11*(1), 48–60. doi:10.1109/MWC.2004.1269717.

Modi, C., Patel, D., Borisaniya, B., Patel, H., Patel, A., & Rajarajan, M. (2013). A survey of intrusion detection techniques in cloud. *Journal of Network and Computer Applications, 36*(1), 42–57. doi:10.1016/j.jnca.2012.05.003.

Molina, J., & Cukier, M. (2009). Evaluating attack resiliency for host intrusion detection systems. *Journal of Information Assurance and Security, 4*(1), 1–9.

Murali, A., & Rao, M. (2005). A survey on intrusion detection approaches. In *Proceedings of the 1st International Conference on Information and Communication Technologies* (pp. 233-240). Washington, DC: IEEE Computer Society.

Nasser, N., & Chen, Y. (2007). Enhanced intrusion detection system for discovering malicious nodes in mobile ad hoc networks. In *Proceedings of 2007 IEEE International Conference on Communications* (pp. 1154-1159). IEEE.

Oberheide, J., Cooke, E., & Jahanian, F. (2008). CloudAV: N-version antivirus in the network cloud. In *Proceedings of the 17th USENIX Security Symposium* (pp. 91-106). Berkeley, CA: USENIX Association.

Oprea, A., & Reiter, M. K. (2007). Integrity checking in cryptographic file systems with constant trusted storage. In *Proceedings of 16th USENIX Security Symposium*. Berkeley, CA: USENIX Association.

Özyer, T., Alhajj, R., & Barker, K. (2007). Intrusion detection by integrating boosting genetic fuzzy classifier and data mining criteria for rule pre-screening. *Journal of Network and Computer Applications, 30*(1), 99–113. doi:10.1016/j.jnca.2005.06.002.

Park, N. H., Oh, S. H., & Lee, W. S. (2010). Anomaly intrusion detection by clustering transactional audit streams in a host computer. *Information Sciences, 180*(12), 2375–2389. doi:10.1016/j.ins.2010.03.001.

Parno, B., Zhou, Z., & Perrig, A. (2009). *Help me help you: Using trustworthy host-based information in the network (Technical report)*. Pittsburgh, PA: CyLab, Carnegie Mellon University.

Patil, S., Kashyap, A., Sivathanu, G., & Zadok, E. (2004). I3FS: An in-kernel integrity checker and intrusion detection file system. In *Proceedings of the 18th USENIX Conference on System Administration* (pp. 67-78). Berkeley, CA: USENIX Association.

Payne, B. D., Carbone, M., Sharif, M., & Lee, W. (2008). Lares: An architecture for secure active monitoring using virtualization. In *Proceedings of the 2008 IEEE Symposium on Security and Privacy* (pp. 233-247). Washington, DC: IEEE Computer Society.

Pérez, M. G., Mármol, F. G., Pérez, G. M., & Gómez, A. F. S. (2012). RepCIDN: A reputation-based collaborative intrusion detection network to lessen the impact of malicious alarms. *Journal of Network and Systems Management*, 1–40.

Pérez, M. G., Mármol, F. G., Pérez, G. M., & Skarmeta, G. A. (2011). Mobility in collaborative alert systems: Building trust through reputation. In Casares-Giner, V., Manzoni, P., & Pont, A. (Eds.), *NETWORKING 2011 Workshops* (pp. 251–262). Berlin: Springer. doi:10.1007/978-3-642-23041-7_24.

Portokalidis, G., Homburg, P., Anagnostakis, K., & Bos, H. (2010). Paranoid android: Versatile protection for smartphones. In *Proceedings of the 26th Annual Computer Security Applications Conference* (pp. 347-356). New York, NY: ACM.

Ptacek, T. H., & Newsham, T. N. (1998). *Insertion, evasion and denial of service: Eluding network intrusion detection (Technical report)*. Secure Networks, Inc..

Quynh, N. A., & Takefuji, Y. (2007). A novel approach for a file-system integrity monitor tool of Xen virtual machine. In *Proceedings of the 2nd ACM Symposium on Information, Computer and Communications Security* (pp. 194-202). New York, NY: ACM.

Roschke, S., Cheng, F., & Meinel, C. (2010). A flexible and efficient alert correlation platform for distributed IDS. In *Proceedings of the 4th International Conference on Network and System Security (NSS)* (pp. 24-31). NSS.

Sabahi, F., & Movaghar, A. (2008). Intrusion detection: A survey. In *Proceedings of the 3rd International Conference on Systems and Networks Communications* (pp. 23-26). Washington, DC: IEEE Computer Society.

Sahu, S., & Shandilya, S. K. (2010). A comprehensive survey on anomaly-based intrusion detection in MANET. *International Journal of Information Technology and Knowledge Management, 2*(2), 305–310.

Scarfone, K., & Mell, P. (2012). *Guide to intrusion detection and prevention systems (IDPS) (NIST Special Publication 800-94 Revision 1)*. Gaithersburg, MD: National Institute of Standards and Technology.

Sivathanu, G., Wright, C. P., & Zadok, E. (2005). Ensuring data integrity in storage: techniques and applications. In *Proceedings of the 2005 ACM Workshop on Storage Security and Survivability* (pp. 26-36). New York, NY: ACM.

Srivastava, A., & Giffin, J. (2008). Tamper-resistant, application-aware blocking of malicious network connections. In *Proceedings of the 11th International Symposium on Recent Advances in Intrusion Detection* (pp. 39-58). Berlin: Springer-Verlag.

Stinson, E., & Mitchell, J. C. (2008). Towards systematic evaluation of the evadability of bot/botnet detection methods. In D. Boneh, T. Garfinkel, & D. Song (Eds.), *Proceedings of the 2nd Conference on USENIX Workshop on Offensive Technologies*. Berkeley, CA: USENIX Association.

Sujatha, P. K., Kannan, A., Ragunath, S., Bargavi, K. S., & Githanjali, S. (2008). A behavior based approach to host-level intrusion detection using self-organizing maps. In *Proceedings of the First International Conference on Emerging Trends in Engineering and Technology* (pp. 1267-1271). Washington, DC: IEEE Computer Society.

Takemori, K., Fujinaga, M., Sayama, T., & Nishigaki, M. (2009). Host-based traceback, tracking bot and C&C server. In *Proceedings of the 3rd International Conference on Ubiquitous Information Management and Communication* (pp. 400-405). New York, NY: ACM.

Takemori, K., Nishigaki, M., Tomohiro, T., & Yutaka, M. (2008). Detection of bot infected PCs using destination-based IP and domain whitelists during a non-operating term. In *Proceedings of the 2008 Global Communications Conference* (pp. 2072-2077). Washington, DC: IEEE Computer Society.

Vaquero, L. M., Rodero-Merino, L., & Morán, D. (2011). Locking the sky: A survey on IaaS cloud security. *Journal of Computing – Cloud Computing, 91*(1), 93-118.

Vigna, G., & Kruegel, C. (2005). Host-based intrusion detection. In *Handbook of Information Security (Vol. III)*. New York: John Wiley & Sons.

Wang, W., Zhang, X., & Gombault, S. (2009). Constructing attribute weights from computer audit data for effective intrusion detection. *Journal of Systems and Software*, *82*(12), 1974–1981. doi:10.1016/j.jss.2009.06.040.

Xiong, H., Malhotra, P., Stefan, D., Wu, C., & Yao, D. (2009). User-assisted host-based detection of outbound malware traffic. In *Proceedings of the 11th International Conference on Information and Communications Security* (pp. 293-307). Berlin: Springer-Verlag.

Zhou, L., & Haas, Z. J. (1999). Securing ad hoc networks. *IEEE Network*, *13*(6), 24–30. doi:10.1109/65.806983.

Zhou, V. C., Leckie, C., & Karunasekera, S. (2010). A survey of coordinated attacks and collaborative intrusion detection. *Computers & Security*, *29*(1), 124–140. doi:10.1016/j.cose.2009.06.008.

ADDITIONAL READING

Alpcan, T., & Basar, T. (2004). A game theoretic analysis of intrusion detection in access control systems. In *Proceedings of the 43rd IEEE Conference on Decision and Control* (pp. 1568-1573). IEEE.

Basin, D., Schaller, P., & Schläpfer, M. (2011). Logging and log analysis. In *Proceedings of Applied Information Security* (pp. 69–80). Berlin: Springer. doi:10.1007/978-3-642-24474-2_5.

Chen, P. M., & Noble, B. D. (2001). When virtual is better than real. In *Proceedings of the Eighth Workshop on Hot Topics in Operating Systems* (pp. 133-138). Washington, DC: IEEE Computer Society.

Christodorescu, M., & Jha, S. (2004). Testing malware detectors. In *Proceedings of the 2004 ACM SIGSOFT International Symposium on Software Testing and Analysis* (pp. 34-44). New York, NY: ACM.

Denning, D. E. (1987). An intrusion-detection model. *IEEE Transactions on Software Engineering*, *13*(2), 222–232. doi:10.1109/TSE.1987.232894.

Garfinkel, T., & Rosenblum, M. (2003). A virtual machine introspection based architecture for intrusion detection. In *Proceedings of 10th Network and Distributed Systems Security Symposium* (pp. 191-206). IEEE.

Giuseppini, G., & Burnett, M. (2004). *Microsoft log parser toolkit*. Rockland, MA: Syngress Publishing, Inc..

Grimaila, M. R., Myers, J., Mills, R. F., & Peterson, G. (2012). Design and analysis of a dynamically configured log-based distributed security event detection methodology. *The Journal of Defense Modeling and Simulation: Applications, Methodology. Technology (Elmsford, N.Y.)*, *9*(3), 219–241.

Hay, A., Cid, D., & Bray, R. (2008). *OSSEC host-based intrusion detection guide*. Burlington, MA: Syngress Publishing, Inc..

Hsu, F.-H., Wu, M.-H., Tso, C.-K., Hsu, C.-H., & Chen, C.-W. (2012). Antivirus software shield against antivirus terminators. *IEEE Transactions on Information Forensics and Security*, *7*(5), 1439–1447. doi:10.1109/TIFS.2012.2206028.

Kim, G. H., & Spafford, E. H. (1994). The design and implementation of tripwire: A file system integrity checker. In *Proceedings of the 2nd ACM Conference on Computer and Communications Security* (pp. 18-29). New York, NY: ACM.

Kolias, C., Kambourakis, G., & Maragoudakis, M. (2011). Swarm intelligence in intrusion detection: A survey. *Computers & Security, 30*(8), 625–642. doi:10.1016/j.cose.2011.08.009.

Kotsiantis, S. B., Zaharakis, I. D., & Pintelas, P. E. (2007). Supervised machine learning: A review of classification techniques. *Frontiers in Artificial Intelligence and Applications, 160*, 3–24.

Law, F. Y. W., Chow, K., Lai, P. K. Y., & Tse, H. (2009). A host-based approach to botnet investigation? In S. Goel (Ed.), *Lecture Notes of the Institute for Computer Sciences, Social Informatics and Telecommunications Engineering: Digital Forensics and Cyber Crime – First International ICST Conference* (pp. 161-170). Springer.

Malan, D. J., & Smith, M. D. (2005). Host-based detection of worms through peer-to-peer cooperation. In *Proceedings of the 2005 ACM Workshop on Rapid Malcode* (pp. 72-80). New York, NY: ACM.

Marty, R. (2011). Cloud application logging for forensics. In *Proceedings of the 2011 ACM Symposium on Applied Computing* (pp. 178-184). New York, NY: ACM.

Mutz, D., Valeur, F., Vigna, G., & Kruegel, C. (2006). Anomalous system call detection. *ACM Transactions on Information and System Security, 9*(1), 61–93. doi:10.1145/1127345.1127348.

Patwardhan, A., Parker, J., Joshi, A., Iorga, M., & Karygiannis, T. (2005). Secure routing and intrusion detection in ad hoc networks. In *Proceedings of the Third IEEE International Conference on Pervasive Computing and Communications (PerCom 2005)* (pp. 191-199). IEEE.

Roschke, S., Cheng, F., & Meinel, C. (2009). Intrusion detection in the cloud. In *Proceedings of the Eighth IEEE International Conference on Dependable, Autonomic and Secure Computing* (pp. 729-734). IEEE.

Schneier, B., & Kelsey, J. (1999). Secure audit logs to support computer forensics. *ACM Transactions on Information and System Security, 2*(2), 159–176. doi:10.1145/317087.317089.

Wagner, D., & Soto, P. (2002). Mimicry attacks on host-based intrusion detection systems. In *Proceedings of the 9th ACM Conference on Computer and Communications Security* (pp. 255-264). New York, NY: ACM.

Werlinger, R., Hawkey, K., Muldner, K., Jaferian, P., & Beznosov, K. (2008). The challenges of using an intrusion detection system: Is it worth the effort? In *Proceedings of the 4th Symposium on Usable Privacy and Security* (pp. 107-118). New York, NY: ACM.

Wu, S. X., & Banzhaf, W. (2010). The use of computational intelligence in intrusion detection systems: A review. *Applied Soft Computing, 10*(1), 1–35. doi:10.1016/j.asoc.2009.06.019.

KEY TERMS AND DEFINITIONS

Cloud-Based IDS: An IDS where the analysis engine is offered as a cloud service and raw data is collected from agents that are placed on client machines.

Collaborative HIDS: A HIDS that exchanges information with other HIDSs in the network and uses these data to improve its detection capability.

Evasion Technique: A modification to an existing attack, which allow this attack to proceed undetected by intrusion detection systems.

Host-Based IDS (HIDS): "An IDS that monitors the characteristics of a single host and events occurring within that host for suspicious activities" (Scarfone, 2012, p. 94).

Intrusion Detection System (IDS): A device or a software application that monitors events occurring at a host or in a network, identifies malicious activities or policy violations and produces reports for further analyses.

Reputation System: A system that accepts information about the behavior of nodes (e.g., client computers) as its input and gives out the confidence in their behavior in the future, usually in the form of a reputation score.

Security Information and Event Management (SIEM) System: "A complex collection of technologies designed to provide vision and clarity on the corporate IT system as a whole, benefiting security analysts and IT administrators as well" (Miller, 2010, p. xxv).

Standalone HIDS: A HIDS that does not receive any input from other HIDS instances in the network.

Chapter 8
Enhancing Intrusion Detection Systems Using Intelligent False Alarm Filter:
Selecting the Best Machine Learning Algorithm

Yuxin Meng
City University of Hong Kong, China

Lam-For Kwok
City University of Hong Kong, China

ABSTRACT

Intrusion Detection Systems (IDSs) have been widely implemented in various network environments as an essential component for current Information and Communications Technologies (ICT). However, false alarms are a big problem for these systems, in which a large number of IDS alarms, especially false positives, could be generated during their detection. This issue greatly decreases the effectiveness and the efficiency of an IDS and heavily increases the burden on analyzing real alarms. To mitigate this problem, in this chapter, the authors identify and analyze the reasons for causing this problem, present a survey through reviewing some related work in the aspect of false alarm reduction, and introduce a promising solution of constructing an intelligent false alarm filter to refine false alarms for an IDS.

DOI: 10.4018/978-1-4666-4514-1.ch008

1. INTRODUCTION

Intrusion detection is a process of monitoring the events occurring in a computer system or network, analyzing them for signs of security problems (Bace, 2000) and this concept is evolved from audit. To conduct the process of intrusion detection, *Intrusion Detection Systems* (IDSs) have been developed with the purpose of automatically detecting intrusions (e.g., Malware, Virus, Trojan) by monitoring local systems or network events.

Traditionally, there are two major types of intrusion detection systems: *Host-based IDS* (HIDS) and *Network-based IDS* (NIDS). A host-based IDS mainly monitors the events which occurred in a local computer system, and then reports its findings. On the other hand, a network-based IDS aims to monitor network traffic and detect network attacks through analyzing incoming network packets. HIDS and NIDS can be regarded as two aspects of an intrusion detection process. In real deployment, a security administrator usually implements both of them with the purpose of providing a more comprehensive protection in a network environment or in a computer system.

Nowadays, IDSs are being widely deployed in various business environments (e.g., bank, insurance company) to protect network security. In general, the specific detection approaches can be classified into three folders: *signature-based IDS*, *anomaly-based IDS* and *hybrid IDS*. A signature-based IDS (or called *misuse-based IDS*) (Roesch, 1999) detects an attack by comparing its signatures with current network events (e.g., network packets). A signature (or called *rule*) is a kind of descriptions to describe a known attack or exploit. An anomaly-based IDS (Paxson, 1999) identifies anomalies by means of pre-established *normal profile*. Note that anomalies are patterns in data that do not conform to a well defined notion of normal behavior and a normal profile is used to describe a normal event (e.g., a normal network connection). A hybrid IDS (Ali, Halim, & G¨okhan, 2009) is capable of conducting both signature-based detection and anomaly-based detection. Through combining these two detection approaches, a hybrid IDS is expected to provide much more information about network traffic and identify network attacks more powerfully.

However, a false alarm is a very challenging problem in information and communications technologies (ICT) (i.e., designing any secure and practical protocols, deploying and setting a network, evaluating any network architectures or systems), and especially a key limiting factor for an intrusion detection system (Axelsson, 2000). In real-world applications, a large number of false alarms could be generated by these IDSs during the detection (McHugh, 2000), which can greatly reduce the effectiveness of an IDS and heavily increase the burden of identifying true alarms and analyzing helpful information. In particular, we identify that this problem stems primarily from three reasons as below:

- **Protocol Issues:** In a network, some protocols and packets (e.g., UDP) can be easily spoofed and modified, which provide a chance for attackers to bypass the examination of an IDS, or mislead the analysis work.
- **Network Architecture Issues:** There is a lack of contextual information about their protected network environment for current IDSs.
- **Inherent Challenging Issues in an IDS:** Both a signature-based IDS and an anomaly-based IDS are suffering from inherent limitations (i.e., it is hard to accurately identify an attack).

To mitigate the problem of false alarms, in this chapter, we introduce a promising method of using intelligent false alarm filter, by adaptively selecting an appropriate machine learning algorithm, to filter out IDS false alarms and to improve the performance of these detection systems. In theory, a false alarm can be referred to either a *false positive* or a *false negative*. But for constructing a false alarm filter, a false alarm mainly refers to a false positive. The generation of false negatives is mainly due to the detection capability of an IDS, thus, the reduction of false negatives is out of scope in this chapter. On the whole, our contributions in this chapter can be summarized as below:

- We investigate the recent development of false alarm reduction and identify three major factors in the field of intrusion detection, such as *protocol issues*, *network architecture issues* and *inherent issues in an IDS*.
- We present a survey regarding the reduction of false alarms in the three aspects: *signature and profile improvement*, *alert verification and correlation techniques*, and *machine learning-based alarm filter construction*.
- To improve the performance of an IDS, we propose a promising and flexible solution of constructing a *machine learning-based intelligent false alarm filter* to help refine alarms. The proposed approach is easy for implementation by deploying behind an IDS as an additional component and can be adaptive to traffic changes by intelligently selecting the most appropriate machine learning algorithm.
- In the evaluation, we gave a case study of our proposed false alarm filter and the experimental results indicate that our proposed alarm filter could maintain filtration rate and filtration accuracy at a stable and high level.

The remaining parts of this chapter are organized as follows. In the second section, we give a survey by reviewing some related work about mitigating the false alarm problem (e.g., new algorithm design, IDS signature improvement). In the third section, we analyze the major reasons in causing the false alarm problem. We describe our approach of constructing an intelligent false alarm filter by means of machine learning algorithms and present a case study in the fourth section. Finally, we conclude our work with future directions in the last section.

BACKGROUND AND RELATED WORK

In the field of intrusion detection, as shown in Table 1, there are four situations about inputs (e.g., whether there is an intrusion) and outputs (e.g., whether there is an alert) for an IDS.

Based on this table, we describe the four types of alarms as below:

- **True Positive (TP):** Making an alarm when there is an intrusion;
- **False Negative (FN):** Making no alarm when there is an intrusion;
- **False Positive (FP):** Making an alarm when there is no intrusion;
- **True Negative (TN):** Making no alarm when there is no intrusion.

As discussed above, a false alarm is either a false positive or a false negative. In this chapter, we focus on *false positive*, which indicates the possibility of making an alarm when there is no intrusion. In real-world applications, false posi-

Table 1. Four types of alarms for an intrusion detection system

Intrusion Detection System (IDS)	Alert	No Alert
Intrusion	True Positive	False Negative
No Intrusion	False Positive	True Negative

tives are a big problem for an IDS, and it is a key limiting factor to encumber the further development of an IDS (Axelsson, 2000).

A lot of efforts and approaches have been made and proposed in order to resolve this problem. Generally, we can classify these efforts into three folders: 1) *signature and profile improvement*, 2) *alert verification and correlation techniques*, and 3) *machine learning-based alarm filter construction*. In the remaining parts, we present a short survey about each category.

Signature and Profile Improvement

The idea of *signature and profile improvement* aims to reduce false positives by enhancing the accuracy of IDS's signatures and the modeling of normal profiles. For a signature-based IDS, the two most important signature improvements are: *contextual signatures* and *vulnerability signatures*.

Sommer and Paxson (2003) first developed a type of *contextual signatures* by adding additional contextual information (i.e., knowledge of the environment, defining dependencies between signatures to model step-wise attacks, and recognizing exploit scans) in the matching process. They designed an efficient *Bro* signature engine incorporative: low-level context by using regular expressions for matching; and high-level context by taking advantage of the semantic information. Through interpreting a signature-match only as an event, rather than as an alert, their work showed that the designed *Bro* engine was able to leverage Bro's context and state-management mechanisms to improve the quality of alerts.

Later, Brumley et al. (2006) further proposed a concept of *vulnerability signatures* that is a representation (e.g., a regular expression) of a vulnerability language. More specifically, a vulnerability signature matches a set of inputs (or strings) which satisfy a vulnerability condition in the program. A vulnerability condition is a specification of a particular type of program bug (e.g., buffer overflow). Formally, let P denotes a program, c denotes a vulnerability condition, $T(P,x)$ denotes the execution trace and D denotes the domain of inputs. Thus, vulnerability signatures (denote as $L(P,c)$) can be represented as:

$$L(P,c) = \{x \in D \mid T(P,x) \rightarrow c\}$$

To generate a vulnerability signature, the steps are described as below:

1. **To Pre-process the Program Before any Exploit is Received:**
   a) Disassembling the program P and
   b) Converting the assembly into an intermediate representation.
2. **To Compute a Chop with Respect to the Trace T:** The chop includes all paths to the vulnerability point including that taken by the sample exploit.
3. **To Compute the Signature L:**
   a) Compute the Turing machine signature,
   b) Compute the symbolic constraint signature and
   c) Compute the regular expression signature.

In the evaluation, these two new types of signatures presented positive results regarding improving the quality of alerts and reducing false positives. The regular expression (Friedl, 2002; Gruber & Holzer, 2008) is a formal language that is widely used in the field of intrusion detection.

For the application of contextual signatures, (Zaidi, Bayse, & Cavalli, 2009) presented a new methodology for interoperability testing based on contextual signatures and passive testing with invariants. The use of contextual signatures eases the expression of interoperability testing properties. There are two types of interoperability properties: vertical and horizontal that can be described by contextual signatures. In the case study, they showed that contextual signatures were very useful to check interoperation between layers of the same protocol stack and check that distant entities of the same layer.

Other related work about the applications of contextual signatures can be referred to (Meng & Kwok, 2011b; Meng & Li, 2012).

For the applications of vulnerability signatures, (Brumley et al., 2007) presented an efficient and practical way of creating vulnerability signatures based on binary program analysis. They pointed out that previous approach (Brumley et al., 2006) of vulnerability signature generation were sound, but exponential in size to the number of program paths in the unrolled program. Particularly, loops and other cyclic structures in the previous work are explored (unrolled) a fixed number of times, so that previously generated vulnerability signatures are not scalable when there are many paths that an exploit may take. To mitigate the issue, they proposed an automatic technique to generate vulnerability signatures with the same properties as the previous research, but to reduce the overall signature size and generation time from exponential to quadratic in the size of the unrolled program. At a high level, their approach summarized multiple program paths, while previous approaches only enumerated them. By more efficiently representing a program path, the proposed approach was more scalable as the generated signatures could encompass more program paths with fewer false negatives.

To speed up the process of vulnerability signature matching, (Schear, Albrecht, & Borisov, 2008) developed a matching architecture based on three points: 1) the use of high-speed pattern matchers, together with control logic, instead of recursive parsing, 2) the limited nature and careful management of implicit state, and 3) the ability to avoid parsing large fragments of the message not relevant to a vulnerability. They further built a prototype called VESPA, which was capable of detecting vulnerabilities in both text and binary protocols. Compared to full protocol parsing, VESPA could achieve 3x or better speedup, and thus detect vulnerabilities in most protocols at a speed of 1 Gbps or more. In addition, the proposed architecture was also well adapted to being integrated with network processors or other special-purpose hardware.

Then, Caballero et al. (2009) proposed *protocol-level constraint-guided exploration*, a new approach towards generating high coverage vulnerability-based signatures. They indicated that the key technical challenge to effective signature-based defense was to automatically and quickly generate signatures that have both low false positives and low false negatives. Their approach has three main characteristics: 1) it is constraint-guided, 2) the constraint-guided exploration works at the protocol-level and generates protocol-level signatures at the end, and 3) it effectively merges explored execution paths to remove redundant exploration. They further designed and developed a tool called *Elcano* to realize the above idea. In their experiments, *Elcano* achieved optimal or close-to-optimal results in terms of coverage. In addition, the generated signatures are compact.

Later, Li et al. (2010) presented the design of *NetShield* which is a vulnerability signature based NIDS/NIPS with the purpose of providing an efficient way to match a large vulnerability ruleset. This system could obtain multigigabit throughput while offering much better accuracy. Their experimental results showed that the designed engine in *NetShield* achieved at least 1.9+Gbps signature matching throughput on a 3.8GHz single-core PC, and could scale-up to at least 11+Gbps under a 8-core machine for 794 HTTP vulnerability signatures. Several other related work can be referred to (Xu et al., 2005; Cadar et al., 2006; Yang et al., 2006; Yu, Alkhalaf, & Bultan, 2009).

On the other hand, for an anomaly-based IDS, improving the accuracy of establishing a normal profile is the major way to reduce its false positives. Usually, normal profiles can be built by means of various machine learning schemes. The main modes are *supervised anomaly detection*, *semi-supervised anomaly detection* and *unsupervised anomaly detection* (Chandola, Banerjee, & Kumar, 2009).

- The *supervised anomaly detection* (Joshi, Agarwal, & Kumar, 2001; Joshi, Agarwal, & Kumar, 2002; Phua, Alahakoon, & Lee, 2004) is to build a predictive model for normal events and anomaly events. Any unseen data-instance is compared against this model to determine which class (normal or abnormal) it belongs to. However, there are two big issues related to this method. (1) The anomalous instances should be far less compared to the normal instances in the training data; (2) obtaining accurate and representative labels, especially for the anomaly class is usually challenging.
- The mode of *semi-supervised anomaly detection* (Dasgupta & Majumdar, 2002) is to assume that the training data has labeled instances for only the normal class. The key point is to build a model for the class corresponding to normal behavior, and use the model to identify anomalies in the test data.
- The mode of *unsupervised anomaly detection* is applicable in the situation that normal instances are far more frequent than anomalies in the test data. Several related articles or surveys about the anomaly detection can be referred to other work (Markou & Singh, 2003; Bakar et al., 2006; Patcha & Park, 2007).

Alert Verification and Correlation Techniques

The notion of *alert verification* was first proposed by Kruegel and Robertson (2004) which is a process of verifying the success of attacks. That is, given an attack (and a corresponding alert raised by an intrusion detection system), it is the task of the alert verification to determine whether this attack is succeeded or not. They further defined two modes of the alert verification: *active verification* and *passive verification*.

In particular, *active verification* is defined as gathering configuration data or forensic traces after an alert occurs, whereas *passive verification* is defined as gathering configuration data once (or at regular, scheduled intervals) and have data available before the attack occurs. Both active and passive mechanisms can be used to check attack requirements against victim configurations. However, only active verification can be employed when check for traces that might be left after an attack. The reason is that passive verification performs its task before an alert is received while active verification is performed as a reaction to a received alert.

Kruegel and Robertson (2004) additionally indicated two requirements for this process. The most important requirement for the alert verification process is accuracy. An accurate verification process will keep the number of false negatives (i.e., an alert is marked as non-relevant, when in fact it is) and false positives (i.e., an alert is marked as relevant, although it is not) low. Another requirement is a low cost of the verification process.

Following the concept of alert verification, Zhou et al. (2005) proposed a method to verify the result of attacks using lightweight protocol analysis based on the observation: network protocols often have short meaningful status codes saved at the beginning of server responses upon client requests. That is, a successful intrusion that alters the behavior of a network application server often results in an unexpected server response, which does not contain a valid protocol status code. In the off-line experiment, they modified Snort signatures and used a real-world dataset for evaluation. The results showed that their approach could effectively verify the results of intrusion attempts against network application servers, thus improving the quality of alerts reported by an IDS.

Then, Bolzoni et al. (2007) presented an architecture designed for alert verification (i.e., to reduce false positives) in network intrusion detection systems, which is based on a systematic anomaly based analysis of the system outputs. Their main idea is that: a successful attack often causes an anomaly in the output of the service, therefore modifying the normal output outcome. To detect this anomaly can help reduce false alerts. They gave an example that a successful SQL injection attack against a Web application often causes the output of SQL table content (e.g., user/admin credentials).

Alert correlation is another way to improve the quality of IDS alarms by correlating several alarms to provide a high-level view of malicious activities on a network. In this case, an alert correlation system often focuses on alert clusters and discards all alerts that have not been correlated. Ning and Xu (2003) identified that false alerts generated by IDSs have a negative impact on alert correlation, so that alert verification can be regarded as an important prerequisite to help an alert correlation system achieve good correlation results.

For the application of alert correlation, Ning et al. (2001) presented an approach to help understand generated IDS alarms which is based on the obersevations that most intrusions are not isolated but related as different stages of attack sequences, with the early stages preparing for the later ones. In this case, they proposed an approach of correlating alerts using prerequisites of intrusions by identifying necessary conditions leading the intrusion to be successful. For example, the existence of a vulnerable service is the prerequisite of a remote buffer overflow attack against the service. In total, their approach can: 1) provide a high-level representation of the correlated alerts, and thus reveals the structure of series of attacks; 2) reduce the impact of false alerts by only keeping correlated alerts; and 3) allow the intrusion response systems to take appropriate actions to stop the ongoing attacks.

In addition, Valdes and Skinner (2001) presented a probabilistic approach to alert correlation, extending the ideas from multi-sensor data fusion. This probabilistic approach provided a unified mathematical framework for correlating alerts that match closely but not perfectly, in which the minimum degree of match required to fuse alerts is controlled by a single configurable parameter. For each feature, they defined a similarity function and overall similarity is weighted by a specifiable expectation of similarity. Features in this set must match at least as well as the minimum similarity specification in order to combine alerts, regardless of the goodness of match on the feature set as a whole.

Later, Cuppens and Miège (2002) developed a cooperation module, called CRIM, between several IDSs to analyze alerts and generate more global and synthetic alerts, which can reduce the total number of alerts and increase the detection rate of attacks. Specifically, there are three functions in the module: alert clustering function, alert merging function, and alert correlation function. The clustering function can have an access to the alert database and generate clusters of alerts. The merging function is to create a new alert that is representative of the information contained in the various alerts belonging to this cluster. At last, the correlation function is to correlate alerts in order to provide a security administrator with more synthetic information. The result of the correlation function is a set of candidate plans that correspond to the intrusion under execution by the intruder.

Later, Valeur et al. (2004) presented a general correlation model that included a comprehensive set of components and a framework based on this model. They further built a framework that implemented the correlation process and used a tool based on the framework to analyze a number of data sets. Instead of just focusing on the overall effectiveness of correlation, they paid more attention to each aspect of the process separately, and to provide insights into how each component of the correlation process contributes to alert reduction. Their experimental results showed that different parts of the process contribute to correlation in different ways, depending on the nature of the data being analyzed.

Xu and Ning (2006) presented three privacy-preserving schemes of alert correlation (called *alert anonymization techniques*). To evaluate privacy protection and guide alert anonymization, they defined local privacy and global privacy, and used entropy to compute the values of attributes. Later, Hofmann et al. (2007) proposed a completely distributed intrusion detection system by means of distributed hash tables to efficiently exchange and aggregate alerts. Using this distributed system, it is possible to distribute the alert processing and correlation load among all participating ID agents, thus increasing scalability and effectiveness of the overall system. Tedesco and Aickelin (2008) developed an automated alert correlation algorithm using attack type graphs which is suitable for deployment in a real-time setting.

Specifically, they presented a novel type-graph algorithm which unified correlation and hypothesizing into a single operation. The algorithm was implemented and validated through a series of experiments, which showed that a good implementation was suitable for real-time correlation even in cases where the IDS alert rate is alarmingly high.

Ren, Stakhanova, and Ghorbani (2010) then proposed an online approach for alert correlation. In particular, their approach for online correlation of intrusion alerts has two stages. In the first online stage, they employed a Bayesian network to automatically extract information about the constraints and causal relationships among alerts. Based on the extracted information, they then reconstructed attack scenarios on-the-fly providing network administrator with the current network view and predicting the next potential steps of the attacker. The major advantage of the proposed approach is that it can dynamically adjust to the current alert behavior and reflect it in the correlation process.

Roschke, Cheng, and Meinel (2011a) designed an alert correlation algorithm based on attack graphs that was capable of detecting multiple attack scenarios for forensic analysis. In particular, the designed algorithm worked with implicit alert correlations, considering only the last alert of a certain type per node in the attack graph. The algorithm consisted of a mapping of alerts to nodes in the attack graph, an alert aggregation, a building of an alert dependency graph, and a function for finding suspicious alert subsets.

Alserhani et al. (2011) presented a "require/provide" model that established a cooperation between statistical and knowledge-based model in order to achieve higher detection rate with the minimal false positives. They advocated that a knowledge-based model with vulnerability and extensional conditions could provide manageable and meaningful attack graphs. Their proposed model has been implemented in real-time mode and has successfully generated security events on establishing a correlation between attack signatures. Moreover, their system could be used to detect one of the most serious multi-stage attacks in cyber crime, namely SQLIA (SQL Injection Attack). Several other related work about the applications of alert correlation can be referred to Debar and Wespi (2001), Morin et al. (2002), and Roschke, Cheng, & Meinel (2011b).

Machine Learning-Based Alarm Filter Construction

Constructing an alarm filter is also a popular method in reducing false alarms, which can achieve a good filtration rate and provide excellent flexibility by deploying behind an IDS. A lot of machine learning algorithms have been applied to constructing such a filter.

Lee and Stolfo (2000) first proposed a data-mining based framework to extract features, improve attack detection and maintain a low false positive rate. Then, Pietraszek (2004) presented a machine learning-based system of ALAC (Adaptive Learner for Alert Classification) to reduce false positives by classifying alerts into true positives and false positives. During the training phase, the ALAC classifies alerts into two labels: true or false positive. Then, this system computes a parameter of *classification confidence* and presents this classification to a human analyst. The analyst's feedback is used to generate training examples and to build and update the classifiers. After the training phase, the classifiers are expected to classify new incoming alerts.

Later, Law and Kwok (2004) proposed a promising method to reduce the number of false alarms by using KNN (K-Nearest-Neighbor) classifier. They model the normal alarm patterns to describe the sequence of incoming alarms, and then identified deviations from that model to identify the anomalies. The KNN classifier is used to classify new data points into normal or abnormal based on the Euclidean distances. Alharby and Imai (2005) mined historical alarms for characterizing the "normal" stream of alarms and proposed a method of reducing false alarms by using continuous and discontinuous sequential patterns. They believed that every single element in the sequence had a value and contained important information, so that they considered all possible subsequences to make sure that each single alarm within the sequence was included in the normal model. The normal model can be used to classify the next incoming sequence with a satisfactory threshold.

Following the idea of applying machine learning to false alarm reduction, many supervised learning algorithms such as Support Vector Machine (Davenport, Baraniuk, & Scott, 2006), Neural Networks (Wang, Wang, & Dai, 2004), Fuzzy Set (Dickerson & Dickerson, 2000; El-Semary et al., 2005) have been studied. However, these supervised learning algorithms demand a number of labeled instances during the training process. To mitigate this issue, *semi-supervised learning*, which can automatically label instances without human intervention, has been applied in this field.

For example, Chiu et al. (2010) introduced a semi-supervised learning based mechanism to build an alert filter. The semi-supervised learning only needs a very small amount of label information and can make the alert filter be more practical for the real systems. In particular, they used a Network Connection Feature instance (NCF instance) to represent the corresponding cluster of alerts. These NCF instances will be used to train the machine learning-based analysis engine for classifying alerts into suspicious alerts or false alarms. Then, Meng and Kwok (2012) implemented a disagreement-based semi-supervised learning algorithm to improve both detection accuracy and false alarm reduction. The disagreement-based semi-supervised learning is a promising method in which multiple learners are trained for the task and the disagreements among the learners are exploited during the semi-supervised learning process. This algorithm has many advantages like avoiding the model assumption violation, the non-convexity of the loss function, and the poor scalability of the learning algorithms.

In the community of machine learning, active learning is a form of supervised machine learning in which a learning algorithm has the capability of interactively querying a user for some useful information to obtain the desired outputs. It usually consists of two components: a classifier and a query function. By combining active learning and semi-supervised learning, unlabeled data can be more effectively used in intrusion detection. (Meng & Kwok, 2012) further implemented a false alarm filter by combining semi-supervised learning with active learning. The experimental results indicated that semi-supervised learning could become more effective co-working with active learning.

Li and Guo (2007) also identified that it was a difficult task to obtain adequate attack data for supervised classifiers to model the attack patterns, and the data acquisition task is always time-consuming and greatly relies on the domain experts.

They then proposed a novel supervised network intrusion detection method based on TCM-KNN (Transductive Confidence Machines for K-Nearest Neighbors) machine learning algorithm and active learning based training data selection method. In the experiment, they compared the performance of SVM, Neural Network, KNN, and TCM-KNN. The experimental results indicated that TCM-KNN could effectively detect anomalies with high detection rate, low false positives under the circumstance of using much fewer selected data as well as selected features for training.

OUR PROPOSED METHOD

In this section, we begin by analyzing the reasons for causing false alarms, and we then introduce a promising solution of constructing an intelligent false alarm filter in mitigating this problem.

False Alarm Problem

As mentioned above, we identify three main reasons for false alarm generation such as *Protocol issues*, *Network architecture issues* and *Inherent challenging issues in an IDS*. We describe each reason as below:

1. Protocol Issues: This issue mainly refers to network protocols in that a network-based IDS utilizes protocol analysis to detect network attacks or exploits. In other words, these detection systems should analyze network protocols to obtain meaningful information for signature matching or profile matching. However, it is very difficult to build a full signature database and establish an accurate normal profile (Axelsson, 2000).

For a signature-based IDS, its detection capability is equal to its stored signatures. A signature is a kind of descriptions for a known attack and is usually constructed by expert knowledge (i.e., knowledge from security experts) so that it is very hard to cover all potential protocol vulnerabilities by means of human efforts (i.e., the number of signatures is always limited as compared to various protocols in real-world applications). For example, by simply modifying a packet's format such as modifying the destination IP address of an ICMP, a signature-based NIDS may generate a lot of false alarms (e.g., the type with "ICMP Destination Unreachable Communication with Destination Host is Administratively Prohibited").

The situation is similar to an anomaly-based IDS, these systems usually attempt to build a normal profile for current network events, however, a normal profile cannot cover all network accidents (e.g., traffic mutation) so that some unknown protocol events may easily trigger these systems to generate a number of false alarms. For instance, some traffic mutations may easily cause an anomaly-based NIDS to produce many false alarms. In addition, Sommer and Paxson (2010) identify that for an anomaly-based IDS, the number of false positives generated is far higher than that of a signature-based IDS.

On the whole, this issue has a great relationship with the *Inherent challenging issues in an IDS*. Due to the limitations of IDSs, an attacker can utilize these protocol issues to lower the efficiency of an IDS.

2. Network Architecture Issues: Several researches (Ptacek & Newsham, 1998; Kruegel & Robertson, 2004) have identified the problem that intrusion detection systems are often run without any (or very limited) information of the network resources that they protect. A classic example is that: a Code Red attack that targets a Linux Web server is of no use as it can only exploit vulnerabilities in Microsoft's IIS Web Server.

To mitigate this issue, a promising way is to design a system that establishes an overview of the protected hosts and services. For example, the system contains some contextual information to distinguish between Linux and Windows servers, thus enabling a "network-aware" IDS to discard a Code Red attack against a Linux machine.

The example of Code Red attack shows that an event may be harmless in a certain environment whereas may be harmful in other environments, according to some certain conditions. To mitigate this issue, adding some contextual information to current IDSs is a promising method. Some related work about contextual signatures can be referred to the above survey.

3. Inherent Challenging Issues in an IDS: As discussed above, this reason has a close relationship with *protocol issues*. The difference is that *Inherent challenging issues in an IDS* can be regarded as a subjective reason (i.e., the detection approach used in an IDS) while the *protocol issues* (i.e., the implementation environment for an IDS) can be treated as an objective reason.

For a signature-based IDS, signatures may either be "tight" or "loose" in real settings (Sommer & Paxson, 2003). If using tight signatures, the IDS may have no capability to detect attacks other than those for which it has explicit signatures. An example is that, for the Snort signature #1042 which aims to detect an exploit of CVE-2000-0778 by searching for "Translate: F" in Web requests, it turns out that this header is regularly used by certain applications. If using loose signatures, the alerts generated in fact may not reflect an actual attack so that a lot of false positives can be produced.

For an anomaly-based IDS, it is very hard to establish an accurate normal profile, since the network traffic is volatile and is hard to predict. In addition, this kind of detection systems usually uses machine learning algorithms to construct normal profiles in which a large number of labeled instances should be given in advance. But in real settings, it is impossible to provide such a number of instances, so that an unseen event may cause a lot of false positives.

Intelligent False Alarm Filter

As illustrated above, we summarize three major techniques in reducing false alarms: *signature and profile improvement*, *alert verification and cor-* *relation techniques*, and *machine learning-based alarm filter construction*. We briefly analyze these approaches as follows:

- **Signature and Profile Improvement:** This approach is very effective to improve the detection accuracy of an IDS and thus reduce false alarms, but this approach is rather complex and needs major modifications on an IDS. But in real settings, it is extremely hard to modify some IDSs (e.g., commercial IDSs) without the source files.
- **Alert Verification and Correlation Techniques:** This approach uses additional contextual information of protected environment to refine false alarms. Although several works have shown that this approach was feasible and effective, the major problem is how to determine and collect appropriate and widely available contextual information.
- **Machine Learning-Based Alarm Filter:** To construct an alarm filter by means of machine learning algorithms is a simple and effective method in reducing false alarms, and is also flexible for implementation behind an IDS. The problem is how to measure different machine learning algorithms and select an appropriate algorithm. New measures should be defined for this approach.

In this chapter, we advocate the approach of constructing an alarm filter, and we further propose a promising solution of constructing an intelligent false alarm filter that can adaptively select the most appropriate machine learning algorithm from a pool of algorithms in reducing false alarms. The merits of this intelligent approach are described as below:

- **Flexibility:** The alarm filter is often deployed behind an IDS to launch alarm reduction without affecting the structure of an intrusion detection system. According to different security requirements, this alarm filter can be easily designed and changed. For example, the alarm filter can be easily deployed behind a Snort or a Bro and can also be selected to work online or off-line in terms of actual requirements. Particularly, the alarm filter is very promising for a commercial IDS, since it is usually hard to obtain its source codes in which direct modifications are impossible.

- **Automation and Adaptation:** The proposed false alarm filter can intelligently select the most appropriate machine learning algorithms in false alarm reduction, which can keep filtration accuracy and filtration rate at a high and stable level. This approach solves the problem of unstable performance caused by applying only one specific machine learning scheme to constructing an alarm filter and filtering out false alarms.
- **Scalability:** The contextual information can be used in an alarm filter to further filter out false alarms or non-critical alarms (Meng & Li, 2012). A non-critical alarm is neither related to a malicious activity nor related to a successful attack. In other words, a non-critical alarm is either a false positive or a non-relevant positive. Therefore, constructing an alarm filter can provide an interface to involve other techniques.

A high-level architecture of constructing an intelligent false alarm filter is described in Figure 1. There are mainly four components: *Data Standardization, Data Storage, Machine Learning Algorithm Selection* and *False Alarm Filtration*. The component of *Data Standardization* is responsible for extracting features and converting incoming IDS alarms into *formal* alarm formats (i.e., representing by a pre-defined feature-set) that machine learning algorithms can handle. The component of *Data Storage* is responsible for providing a database to store converted alarms. The component of *Machine Learning Algorithm Selection* is responsible for selecting the most appropriate machine learning schemes to reduce alarms. Finally, the component of *False Alarm Filtration* is responsible for reducing false alarms based on selected algorithms. The outputs of the alarm filter are true alarms. By intelligently selecting the most appropriate (best) machine learning algorithms, the filter is capable of maintaining the filtration rate and the filtration accuracy at a high level. Details of each component are describes as follows:

Data Standardization: In real-world applications, an IDS alarm may have different formats (e.g., Snort, Bro). Therefore, the first task is to standardize the alarm format through feature selection and feature extraction. In the step of feature selection, we should select some common and important features from IDS alarms. In addition, we should consider their meanings to a machine learning classifier. Then, in the step of feature extraction, we should extract these selected features for each incoming alarm.

Figure 1. The high-level architecture of an intelligent false alarm filter

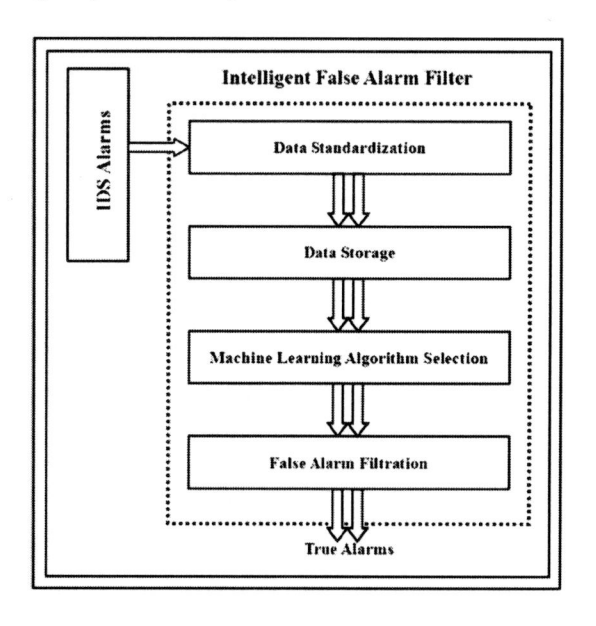

Data Storage: After standardization, all converted alarms should be stored in a database waiting for filtration. In addition, if we use an active learning algorithm, the database can be utilized as a pool to store and provide unlabeled alarm data. After filtration, some labeled alarms can be stored to another database as historical data.

Machine Learning Algorithm Selection: In this component, all algorithm candidates will be trained using available labeled data and then the component selects the most appropriate algorithm with the best performance periodically. To measure the performance of an algorithm, some metrics can be used such as classification accuracy, false alarm detection accuracy etc. Take classification accuracy as an example, the algorithm with the best classification accuracy can be selected and output as the most appropriate algorithm. In a new round, the classification accuracy can be re-calculated for all algorithms. To improve the accuracy of detection, in the new round of algorithm selection, we can add some new labeled data (i.e., extracting from previous filtration) in the process of training.

False Alarm Filtration: In this component, all alarms will be filtered out by means of selected machine learning algorithm. Note that in each round, the component should select an appropriate algorithm again which can maintain the filtration accuracy of the whole system.

As shown in Figure 2, we describe the deployment of the intelligent false alarm filter. Generally, the alarm filter is deployed behind an IDS to perform alarm filtration. In this scenario, network traffic first arrives at the IDS. The IDS then inspects packet payloads and produces alarms to alert potential attacks. To conduct alarm filtration, all produced alarms will be forwarded to the alarm filter first.

In particular, the false alarm filter can conduct alarm filtration in two ways: off-line and online. The off-line implementation is usually easier than the online implementation.

- **Off-line Filtration:** To implement the alarm filter off-line, we only need to consider the accuracy of identifying false alarms. Therefore, more complex algorithms can be used to achieve higher classification accuracy without considering the limit of runtime.
- **Online Filtration:** To implement the alarm filter online, we should balance more factors such as runtime, memory circles, detection accuracy etc. In different scenarios, we should employ distinct strategies to ensure the balance between accuracy and resources.

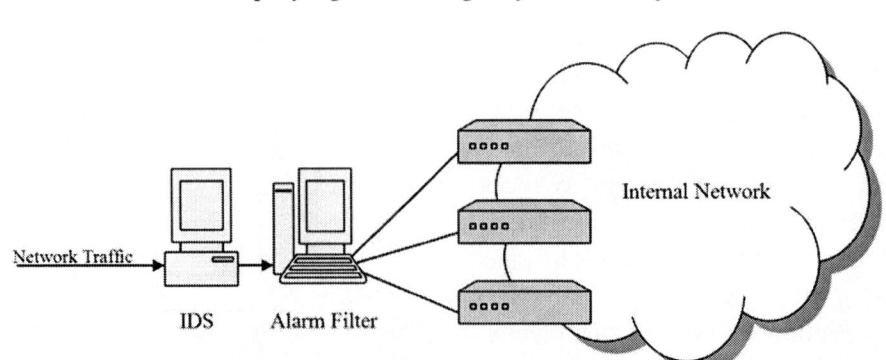

Figure 2. The network structure: deploying the intelligent false alarm filter

Case Study

To better illustrate the intelligent false alarm filter, we give a specific example using Snort alarms as described in our previous work (Meng & Kwok, 2011a), in which we designed an adaptive (intelligent) false alarm filter to filter out false alarms with the best machine learning algorithm.

The specific false alarm filter is presented in Figure 3. There are four major components in the alarm filter: *feature selection, format conversion, machine learning comparison* and *machine learning selection*. The function of each component is similar to the architecture as shown in Figure 1. When alarms come from an IDS, the false alarm filter will extract features at first and convert selected features into the common format. These two components are derived from the process of *Data Standardization*.

Then, these standardized alarms (called *standard alarms*) will be stored in a database and can be used as training data to re-train the filter with the purpose of intelligently selecting the best machine learning algorithm. In the component of *performance comparisons*, the alarm filter compares the performance of different algorithms using the same datasets and determines the best algorithm.

Finally, the selected algorithm will be applied to the filter to help filter out false alarms. In addition, the algorithm selection is actively and repeatedly choosing the best machine learning algorithm in terms of the input alarms within a fixed time slot. The outputs of the adaptive false alarm filter are true alarms, while the false alarms can be saved into another database for back-up and future analysis.

Feature Extraction: Snort (Roesch, 1999) is a lightweight open-source signature-based network intrusion detection system which is very popular and widely used in the intrusion detection community. When Snort detects an attack, it thus generates an alarm or several alarms to alert this situation. We give several examples of Snort alarms in Figure 4.

In Figure 4(a), this alarm is to alert *ICMP PING* which is classified into the type of *Miscellaneous activity*. The target packets of this alarm are ICMP packets and the priority of this alarm is set to 3. In general, low priority numbers show high priority alarms. The statement of "194.7.248.153 -> 172.16.113.204" shows the source IP address and the destination IP address,

Figure 3. Intelligent machine-learning based false alarm filter

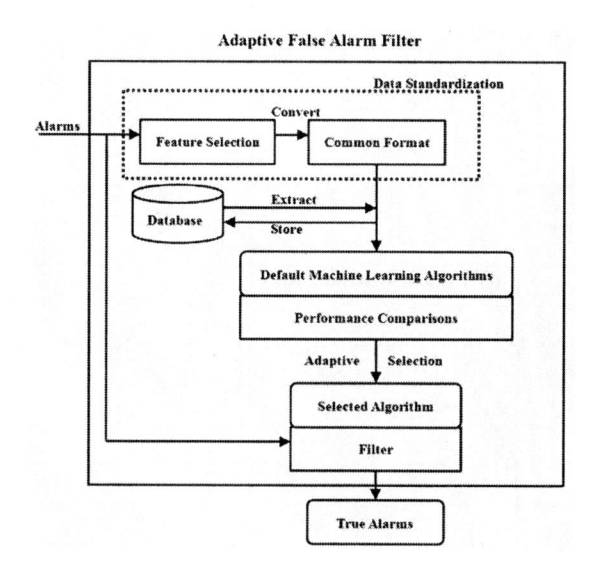

Figure 4. Examples of snort alarms (Meng & Kwok, 2011a)

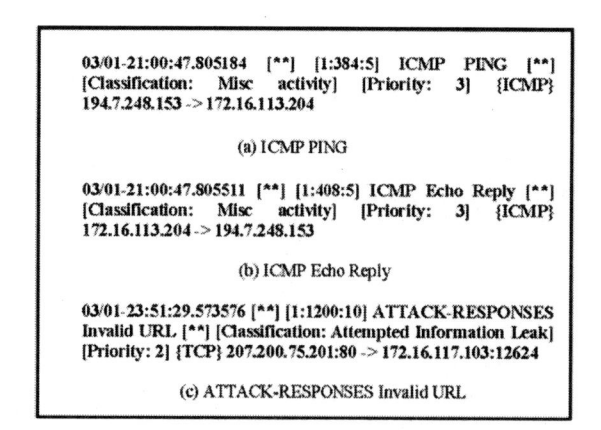

```
03/01-21:00:47.805184 [**] [1:384:5] ICMP PING [**]
[Classification: Misc activity] [Priority: 3] {ICMP}
194.7.248.153 -> 172.16.113.204
```
(a) ICMP PING

```
03/01-21:00:47.805511 [**] [1:408:5] ICMP Echo Reply [**]
[Classification: Misc activity] [Priority: 3] {ICMP}
172.16.113.204 -> 194.7.248.153
```
(b) ICMP Echo Reply

```
03/01-23:51:29.573576 [**] [1:1200:10] ATTACK-RESPONSES
Invalid URL [**] [Classification: Attempted Information Leak]
[Priority: 2] {TCP} 207.200.75.201:80 -> 172.16.117.103:12624
```
(c) ATTACK-RESPONSES Invalid URL

and points out the direction of network flow. The occurred time of this alarm is "03/01-21:00:47.805184".

The alarm in Figure 4(b) is similar to the first one which is to alert the *Miscellaneous activity of ICMP Echo Reply*. In Figure 4(c), this alarm alerts the TCP packets for *ATTACK-RESPONSES Invalid URL* belonging to the classification of *Attempted Information Leak*. The difference is that this alarm does not only give the source IP address and the destination IP address, but also points out the source port number 80 and the destination port number 12624. The priority number 2 means that the priority of this alarm is higher than the above two alarms.

Before the alarm filtration, we should first standardize the Snort alarms into a common format that can be processed by different machine learning schemes. With the understanding of the Snort alarms, we select and construct 8 features to represent the Snort alarms: *description, classification, priority, packet type, source IP address, source port number, destination IP address* and *destination port number*. The initial results of converting Snort alarms into standard alarms are presented in Table 2.

This table shows that the features of *source port number* and *destination port number* will be set to "0" if no specific port numbers are specified in the Snort alarms. To train different machine learning algorithms, these features should be further processed to their *appearance possibility* in the whole training dataset, making sure that these features are meaningful to the machine learning schemes.

Measurement: To determine the best performance among different machine learning algorithms, a *decision value* is defined as below. (*DV* represents the decision value, *CA* represents the classification accuracy and *PFA* represents the precision of false alarm)

$$DV = 0.4 \times CA + 0.6 \times PFA$$

The Classification Accuracy (*CA*) is the correct classification rate of both false alarms and true alarms while the Precision of False Alarm (*PFA*) is defined as follows:

$$PFA = \frac{\text{the number of false alarms classified as false alarm}}{\text{the number of alarms classified as false alarm}}$$

A desirable algorithm is expected to have a PFA of 1. We prefer a higher precision of false alarm than classification accuracy because a higher accuracy of identifying false alarms is very critical and effective to be used to construct a false alarm filter. That is, the decrease of PFA (i.e., a true alarm is classified and filtered out as a false alarm) is more harmful. For instance, in our previous work (Meng & Kwok, 2011a), we

Table 2. Feature selection of snort alarms

Features	Figure 4(a)	Figure 4(b)	Figure 4(c)
Description	ICMP PING	ICMP Echo Reply	ATTACK-RESPONSES Invalid URL
Classification	Misc activity	Misc activity	Attempted Information Leak
Priority	3	3	2
Packet type	ICMP	ICMP	TCP
Source IP	194.7.248.153	172.16.113.204	207.200.75.201
Source port	0	0	80
Destination IP	172.16.113.204	194.7.248.153	172.16.117.103
Destination port	0	0	12624

set weight values of (0.4, 0.6) for *CA* and *PFA* respectively. Accordingly, we denote the most appropriate machine learning algorithm as the one with the highest Decision Value (*DV*).

By means of the decision value, in each round of algorithm selection, the best algorithm can be used in alarm filtration. Thus, the alarm filtration can perform false alarm filtration at a stable and high level. More specific results can be referred to Meng and Kwok (2011a).

In addition, the equation of computing the decision value can be further presented as:

$$DV = W1 \times CA + W2 \times PFA$$

In the above equation, *W1* and *W2* are weight values. In real deployment, these weight values can be determined by conducting some simulations in advance with the purpose of identifying the most appropriate values in various environments. Meng and Kwok (2011a) showed that the weight values of (0.4, 0.6) were effective in the evaluation, but in other environments (i.e., different network deployment), it is better to select and evaluate the values again.

Scalability: As shown in Figure 3, it is not very difficult to implement different machine learning algorithms into the proposed intelligent false alarm filter by modifying the component of *machine learning algorithm selection*. For instance, in Meng and Kwok (2012), we give a case study of implementing an if-then rules based fuzzy algorithm into the intelligent false alarm filter. By conducting a set of simulations, we find that this specific fuzzy algorithm can be deployed in the alarm filter through setting the number of fuzzy subsets to 3 or 4.

Note that, before implementing other algorithms, we should check whether current alarm features are suitable to the new algorithm. We should also check whether it is necessary to add or modify current components. For example, if we need to implement a pool-based active learning algorithm, we may need to develop a component to store unlabeled data (as a *pool*).

CONCLUSION AND FUTURE WORK

False alarms are a big challenging issue in different kinds of systems in ICT, which are relevant to both network protocols and network architectures. In intrusion detection, false alarms are also a key limiting factor in encumbering the development of an IDS. In this chapter, we present a short survey on reviewing some recent work in mitigating the false alarm problem (e.g., signature and profile improvement, alert verification and correlation techniques, and machine learning-based alarm filter construction), analyze the major reasons in causing the false alarm problem, and introduce a promising solution of constructing an intelligent false alarm filter to filter out false alarms by selecting the most appropriate machine learning algorithm and introduce a case study of how to deploy such an alarm filter.

Particularly, we advocate that the construction of an intelligent false alarm filter is a promising method in reducing false alarms (i.e., easy to deploy and design). In the case study, we specifically give an example of building an adaptive machine learning-based false alarm filter to filter out false alarms in an adaptive way. The major issue for constructing such an alarm filter is how to objectively measure the performance of different machine learning algorithms, since the weight values of (0.4, 0.6) used in our case study are subjective based on expert experiences. In different network environments, the effective weight values may be varied and should be decided accordingly.

Future work could include determining how to set an appropriate weight value, or measuring the performance of machine learning algorithms with new designed parameters (i.e., using information theory). Future work could also include extending the false alarm filter to incorporate ensemble approach, which can generally achieve a better result than a single machine learning algorithm. In addition, constructing an alarm filter with contextual information is also an interesting topic in this area (i.e., establishing a two-tier filtration process).

REFERENCES

Alharby, A., & Imai, H. (2005). IDS false alarm reduction using continuous and discontinuous patterns. In *Proceedings of the 3rd International Conference on Applied Cryptography and Network Security* (pp. 192-205). Springer-Verlag.

Ali, A. M., Halim, Z. A., & G¨okhan, C. K. (2009). A hybrid intrusion detection system design for computer network security. *Computers & Electrical Engineering*, *35*(3), 517–526. doi:10.1016/j.compeleceng.2008.12.005.

Alserhani, F., Akhlaq, M., Awan, I. U., & Cullen, A. J. (2011). Event-based alert correlation system to detect SQLI activities. In *Proceedings of the 2011 International Conference on Advanced Information Networking and Applications* (pp. 175-182). IEEE Press.

Axelsson, S. (2000). The base-rate fallacy and the difficulty of intrusion detection. *ACM Transactions on Information and System Security*, *3*(3), 186–205. doi:10.1145/357830.357849.

Bace, R. G. (2000). *Intrusion detection*. Indianapolis, IN: Sams.

Bakar, Z., Mohemad, R., Ahmad, A., & Deris, M. (2006). A comparative study for outlier detection techniques in data mining. In *Proceedings of the 2006 IEEE Conference on Cybernetics and Intelligent Systems* (pp. 1-6). IEEE Press.

Bolzoni, D., Crispo, B., & Etalle, S. (2007). ATLANTIDES: An architecture for alert verification in network intrusion detection systems. In *Proceedings of the 2007 Large Installation System Administration Conference* (pp. 141-152). Usenix Press.

Brumley, D., Newsome, J., Song, D., Wang, H., & Jha, S. (2006). Towards automatic generation of vulnerability based signatures. In *Proceedings of the 2006 IEEE Symposium on Security and Privacy* (pp. 2-16). IEEE Press.

Brumley, D., Wang, H., Jha, S., & Song, D. (2007). Creating vulnerability signatures using weakest preconditions. In *Proceedings of the 20th IEEE Computer Security Foundations Symposium* (pp. 311-325). IEEE Press.

Caballero, J., Liang, Z., Poosankam, P., & Song, D. (2009). Towards generating high coverage vulnerability-based signatures with protocol-level constraint-guided exploration. In *Proceedings of the 12th Symposium on Recent Advances in Intrusion Detection* (pp. 161-181). Springer-Verlag.

Cadar, C., Ganesh, V., Pawlowski, P., Dill, D., & Engler, D. (2006). EXE: Automatically generating inputs of death. In *Proceedings of 13th ACM Conference on Computer and Communications Security* (pp. 322-335). ACM Press.

Chandola, V., Banerjee, A., & Kumar, V. (2009). Anomaly detection: A survey. *ACM Computing Surveys*, *41*(3), 1–58. doi:10.1145/1541880.1541882.

Chiu, C.-Y., Lee, Y.-J., Chang, C.-C., Luo, W.-Y., & Huang, H.-C. (2010). Semi-supervised learning for false alarm reduction. In *Proceedings of the 10th Industrial Conference on Advances in Data Mining: Applications and Theoretical Aspects* (pp. 595-605). Springer-Verlag.

Cuppens, F., & Miege, A. (2002). Alert correlation in a cooperative intrusion detection framework. In *Proceedings of the 2002 IEEE Symposium on Security and Privacy* (pp. 202-215). IEEE Press.

Dasgupta, D., & Majumdar, N. (2002). Anomaly detection in multidimensional data using negative selection algorithm. In *Proceedings of the IEEE Conference on Evolutionary Computation* (pp. 1039-1044). IEEE Press.

Davenport, M. A., Baraniuk, R. G., & Scott, C. D. (2006). Controlling false alarms with support vector machines. In *Proceedings of the 2006 International Conference on Acoustics, Speech and Signal* (pp. 589-592). IEEE Press.

Debar, H., & Wespi, A. (2001). Aggregation and correlation of intrusion-detection alerts. In *Proceedings of the 2001 International Conference on Recent Advances in Intrusion Detection* (pp. 85-103). Springer-Verlag.

Dickerson, J. E., & Dickerson, J. A. (2000). Fuzzy network profiling for intrusion detection. In *Proceedings of the 2000 International Conference of the North American Fuzzy Information Society* (pp. 301-306). IEEE Press.

El-Semary, A., Edmonds, J., Gonzalez, J., & Papa, M. (2005). A framework for hybrid fuzzy logic intrusion detection systems. In *Proceedings of the 2005 International Conference on Fuzzy Systems* (pp. 325-330). IEEE Press.

Friedl, J. (2002). *Mastering regular expressions*. Sebastopol, CA: O'Reilly.

Gruber, H., & Holzer, M. (2008). Finite automata, digraph connectivity, and regular expression size. In *Proceedings of the 35th International Colloquium on Automata, Languages and Programming* (pp. 39-50). Springer-Verlag.

Hofmann, A., Dedinski, I., Sick, B., & de Meer, H. (2007). A novelty-driven approach to intrusion alert correlation based on distributed hash tables. In *Proceedings of the 12th IEEE Symposium on Computers and Communications* (pp. 71-78). IEEE Press.

Joshi, M. V., Agarwal, R. C., & Kumar, V. (2001). Mining needle in a haystack: Classifying rare classes via two-phase rule induction. In *Proceedings of the 2001 ACM SIGMOD International Conference on Management of Data* (pp. 91-102). ACM Press.

Joshi, M. V., Agarwal, R. C., & Kumar, V. (2002). Predicting rare classes: can boosting make any weak learner strong? In *Proceedings of the 8th ACM SIGKDD International Conference on Knowledge Discovery and Data Mining* (pp. 297-306). ACM Press.

Kruegel, C., & Robertson, W. (2004). Alert verification: Determining the success of intrusion attempts. In *Proceedings of the 1st Workshop on Detection of Intrusions and Malware and Vulnerability Assessment* (pp. 25-38). Springer-Verlag.

Law, K.-H., & Kwok, L.-F. (2004). IDS false alarm filtering using KNN classifier. In *Proceedings of the 5th International Workshop on Information Security Applications* (pp. 114-121). Springer-Verlag.

Lee, W., & Stolfo, S. J. (2000). A framework for constructing features and models for intrusion detection systems. *ACM Transactions on Information and System Security*, *3*(4), 227–261. doi:10.1145/382912.382914.

Li, Y., & Guo, L. (2007). An active learning based TCM-KNN algorithm for supervised network intrusion detection. *Computers & Security*, *26*(7-8), 459–467. doi:10.1016/j.cose.2007.10.002.

Li, Z., Xia, G., Gao, H., Tang, Y., Chen, Y., & Liu, B. (2010). NetShield: Matching with a large vulnerability signature ruleset for high performance network defense. In *Proceedings of ACM Conference on Applications, Technologies, Architectures, and Protocols for Computer Communications* (pp. 279-290). ACM Press.

Markou, M., & Singh, S. (2003). Novelty detection: A review-part 1: Statistical approaches. *Signal Processing, 83*(12), 2481–2497. doi:10.1016/j.sigpro.2003.07.018.

McHugh, J. (2000). Testing intrusion detection systems: A critique of the 1998 and 1999 DARPA off-line intrusion detection system evaluation as performed by Lincoln laboratory. *ACM Transactions on Information and System Security, 3*(4), 262–294. doi:10.1145/382912.382923.

Meng, Y., & Kwok, L.-F. (2011a). Adaptive false alarm filter using machine learning in intrusion detection. In *Proceedings of the 6th International Conference on Intelligent Systems and Knowledge Engineering* (pp. 573-584). Springer-Verlag.

Meng, Y., & Kwok, L.-F. (2011b). A generic scheme for the construction of contextual signatures with hash function in intrusion detection. In *Proceedings of the 2012 International Conference on Computational Intelligence and Security* (pp. 978-982). IEEE Press.

Meng, Y., & Kwok, L.-F. (2012). A case study: Intelligent false alarm reduction using fuzzy if-then rules in network intrusion detection. In *Proceedings of the 9th International Conference on Fuzzy Systems and Knowledge Discovery* (pp. 505-509). IEEE Press.

Meng, Y., & Li, W. (2012). Constructing context-based non-critical alarm filter in intrusion detection. In *Proceedings of the 7th International Conference on Internet Monitoring and Protection* (pp. 75-81). IARIA Press.

Morin, B., Mé, L., Debar, H., & Ducassé, M. (2002). M2D2: A formal data model for IDS alert correlation. In *Proceedings of the 5th International Conference on Recent Advances in Intrusion Detection* (pp. 115-137). Springer-Verlag.

Ning, P., Reeves, D., & Cui, Y. (2001). *Correlating alerts using prerequisites of intrusions* (Technical Report TR-2001-13). Raleigh, NC: North Carolina State University.

Ning, P., & Xu, D. (2003). Learning attack strategies from intrusion alert. In *Proceedings of the 2003 ACM Conference on Computer and Communications Security* (pp. 200-209). ACM Press.

Patcha, A., & Park, J.-M. (2007). An overview of anomaly detection techniques: Existing solutions and latest technological trends. *Computer Networks, 51*(12), 3448–3470. doi:10.1016/j.comnet.2007.02.001.

Paxson, V. (1999). Bro: A system for detecting network intruders in real-time. *Computer Networks, 31*(23-24), 2435–2463. doi:10.1016/S1389-1286(99)00112-7.

Phua, C., Alahakoon, D., & Lee, V. (2004). Minority report in fraud detection: Classification of skewed data. *SIGKDD Explorer Newsletter, 6*(1), 50–59. doi:10.1145/1007730.1007738.

Pietraszek, T. (2004). Using adaptive alert classification to reduce false positives in intrusion detection. In *Proceedings of the 7th Symposium on Recent Advances in Intrusion Detection* (pp. 102-124). Springer-Verlag.

Ptacek, T. H., & Newsham, T. N. (1998). *Insertion, evation, and denial of service: Eluding network intrusion detection (Technical Report)*. Secure Networks.

Ren, H., Stakhanova, N., & Ghorbani, A. A. (2010). An online adaptive approach to alert correlation. In *Proceedings of the 7th International Conference on Detection of Intrusions and Malware, and Vulnerability Assessment* (pp. 153-172). Springer-Verlag.

Roesch, M. (1999). Snort-lightweight intrusion detection for networks. In *Proceedings of the 1999 Large Installation System Administration Conference* (pp. 229-238). USENIX Association.

Roschke, S., Cheng, F., & Meinel, C. (2011a). A new alert correlation algorithm based on attack graph. In *Proceedings of the 4th International Conference on Computational Intelligence in Security for Information Systems* (pp. 58-67). Springer-Verlag.

Roschke, S., Cheng, F., & Meinel, C. (2011b). An alert correlation platform for memory-supported techniques. *Concurrency and Computation, 24*(10), 1123–1136. doi:10.1002/cpe.1750.

Schear, N., Albrecht, D. R., & Borisov, N. (2008). High-speed matching of vulnerability signatures. In *Proceedings of the 11th Symposium on Recent Advances in Intrusion Detection* (pp. 155-174). Springer-Verlag.

Sommer, R., & Paxson, V. (2003). Enhancing byte-level network intrusion detection signatures with context. In *Proceedings of the 10th ACM Conference on Computer and Communications Security* (pp. 262-271). ACM Press.

Sommer, R., & Paxson, V. (2010). Outside the closed world: On using machine learning for network intrusion detection. In *Proceedings of the 2010 IEEE Symposium on Security and Privacy* (pp. 305-316). IEEE Press.

Tedesco, G., & Aickelin, U. (2008). Real-time alert correlation with type graphs. In *Proceedings of the 4th International Conference on Information Systems Security* (pp. 173-187). Springer-Verlag.

Valdes, A., & Skinner, K. (2001). Probabilistic alert correlation. In *Proceedings of the 4th International Symposium on Recent Advances in Intrusion Detection* (pp. 54-68). Springer-Verlag.

Valeur, F., Vigna, G., Kruegel, C., & Kemmerer, R. A. (2004). Comprehensive approach to intrusion detection alert correlation. *IEEE Transactions on Dependable and Secure Computing, 1*(3), 146–169. doi:10.1109/TDSC.2004.21.

Wang, J., Wang, Z., & Dai, K. (2004). A network intrusion detection system based on the artificial neural networks. In *Proceedings of the 3rd International Conference on Information Security* (pp. 166-170). ACM Press.

Xu, D., & Ning, P. (2006). A flexible approach to intrusion alert anonymization and correlation. In *Proceedings of the 2nd International Conference on Security and Privacy in Communication Networks and the Workshops* (pp. 1-10). IEEE Press.

Xu, J., Ning, P., Kil, C., Zhai, Y., & Bookholt, C. (2005). Automatic diagnosis and response to memory corruption vulnerabilities. In *Proceedings of the 12th ACM Conference on Computer and Communication Security* (pp. 223-234). ACM Press.

Yang, J., Sar, C., Twohey, P., Cadar, C., & Engler, D. (2006). Automatically generating malicious disks using symbolic execution. In *Proceedings of the 2006 IEEE Symposium on Security and Privacy* (pp. 243-257). ACM Press.

Yu, F., Alkhalaf, M., & Bultan, T. (2009). *Generating vulnerability signatures for string manipulating programs using automata-based forward and backward symbolic analyses* (Technical Report 2009-11). UCSB CS.

Zaidi, F., Bayse, E., & Cavalli, A. (2009). Network protocol interoperability testing based on contextual signatures and passive testing. In *Proceedings of the 2009 ACM Symposium on Applied Computing* (pp. 2-7). ACM Press.

Zhou, J., Carlson, A., & Bishop, M. (2005). Verify results of network intrusion alerts using lightweight protocol analysis. In *Proceedings of the 21st Annual Computer Security Applications Conference* (pp. 117-126). ACM Press.

ADDITIONAL READING

Amoroso, E. (1999). Intrusion detection: An introduction to internet surveillance, correlation, trace back, traps, and response. Sparta, NJ: Intrusion.Net Books.

Anderson, R. (2001). *Security engineering: A guide to building dependable distributed systems*. New York: John Wiley & Sons.

Axelsson, S. (2000). The base-rate fallacy and the difficulty of intrusion detection. *ACM Transactions on Information and System Security*, *3*(3), 186–205. doi:10.1145/357830.357849.

Bace, R. G. (2000). *Intrusion detection*. Indianapolis, IN: Sams.

Bakar, Z., Mohemad, R., Ahmad, A., & Deris, M. (2006). A comparative study for outlier detection techniques in data mining. In *Proceedings of the 2006 IEEE Conference on Cybernetics and Intelligent Systems* (pp. 1-6). IEEE Press.

Boggs, N., Hiremagalore, S., Stavrou, A., & Stolfo, S. (2011). Cross-domain collaborative anomaly detection: So far yet so close. In *Proceedings of the 2011 Recent Advances in Intrusion Detection* (pp. 142-160). Springer-Verlag.

Cheng, B.-C., & Tseng, R.-Y. (2011). A context adaptive intrusion detection system for MANET. *Computer Communications*, *34*(3), 310–318. doi:10.1016/j.comcom.2010.06.015.

Denning, D. (1987). An intrusion-detection model. *IEEE Transactions on Software Engineering*, *13*(2), 222–232. doi:10.1109/TSE.1987.232894.

Elshoush, H. T., & Osman, I. M. (2011). Alert correlation in collaborative intelligent intrusion detection systems - A survey. *Applied Soft Computing Journal*, *11*(7), 4349–4365. doi:10.1016/j.asoc.2010.12.004.

Estevez-Tapiador, J. M., Garcia-Teodoro, P., & Diaz-Verdejo, J. E. (2004). Anomaly detection methods in wired networks: A survey and taxonomy. *Computer Communications*, *27*(16), 1569–1584. doi:10.1016/j.comcom.2004.07.002.

Frias-Martinez, V., Stolfo, S. J., & Keromytis, A. D. (2010). Behavior-profile clustering for false alert reduction in anomaly detection sensors. In *Proceedings of the 2010 Annual Computer Security Applications Conference* (pp. 367-376). IEEE Press.

Helman, P., & Liepins, G. (1993). Statistical foundations of audit trail analysis for the detection of computer misuse. *IEEE Transactions on Software Engineering*, *19*(9), 886–901. doi:10.1109/32.241771.

Ilgun, K., Kemmerer, R. A., & Porras, P. A. (1995). State transition analysis: A rule-based intrusion detection approach. *IEEE Transactions on Software Engineering*, *21*(3), 181–199. doi:10.1109/32.372146.

Ko, C., Ruschitzka, M., & Levitt, K. (1997). Execution monitoring of security-critical programs in distributed systems: A specification-based approach. In *Proceedings of the 1997 IEEE Symposium on Security and Privacy* (pp. 175-187). IEEE Press.

Kolias, C., Kambourakis, G., & Maragoudakis, M. (2011). Swarm intelligence in intrusion detection: A survey. *Computers & Security*, *30*(8), 625–642. doi:10.1016/j.cose.2011.08.009.

Kumar, S., & Spafford, E. H. (1994). *An application of pattern matching in intrusion detection* (Technical Report CSD-TR-94-013). West Lafayette, IN: Purdue University.

Lane, T., & Brodley, C. E. (1999). Temporal sequence learning and data reduction for anomaly detection. *ACM Transactions on Information and System Security, 2*(3), 295–331. doi:10.1145/322510.322526.

Lee, W., Fan, W., Miller, M., Stolfo, S., & Zadok, E. (2002). Toward cost-sensitive modeling for intrusion detection and response. *Journal of Computer Security, 10*(1-2), 5–22.

Lee, W., & Stolfo, S. J. (2000). A framework for constructing features and models for intrusion detection systems. *ACM Transactions on Information and System Security, 3*(4), 227–261. doi:10.1145/382912.382914.

Li, Z., Xia, G., Gao, H., Tang, Y., Chen, Y., & Liu, B. (2010). NetShield: Matching with a large vulnerability signature ruleset for high performance network defense. In *Proceedings of ACM Conference on Applications, Technologies, Architectures, and Protocols for Computer Communications* (pp. 279-290). ACM Press.

Manganaris, S., Christensen, M., Zerkle, D., & Hermiz, K. (2000). A data mining analysis of RTID alarms. *Computer Networks, 34*(4), 571–577. doi:10.1016/S1389-1286(00)00138-9.

Massicotte, F., Labiche, Y., & Briand, L. C. (2008). Toward automatic generation of intrusion detection verification rules. In *Proceedings of 2008 Annual Computer Security Applications Conference* (pp. 279-288). IEEE Press.

McHugh, J. (2000). Testing intrusion detection systems: A critique of the 1998 and 1999 DARPA off-line intrusion detection system evaluation as performed by Lincoln laboratory. *ACM Transactions on Information and System Security, 3*(4), 262–294. doi:10.1145/382912.382923.

Meng, Y. (2012). Measuring intelligent false alarm reduction using an ROC curve-based approach in network intrusion detection. In *Proceedings of the 5th IEEE International Conference on Computational Intelligence for Measurement Systems and Applications* (pp. 108-113). IEEE Press.

Meng, Y., & Kwok, L.-F. (2012). A case study: Intelligent false alarm reduction using fuzzy if-then rules in network intrusion detection. In *Proceedings of the 9th International Conference on Fuzzy Systems and Knowledge Discovery* (pp. 505-509). IEEE Press.

Ning, P., Reeves, D., & Cui, Y. (2001). *Correlating alerts using prerequisites of intrusions* (Technical Report TR-2001-13). Raleigh, NC: North Carolina State University.

Ning, P., & Xu, D. (2003). Learning attack strategies from intrusion alert. In *Proceedings of the 2003 ACM Conference on Computer and Communications Security* (pp. 200-209). ACM Press.

Patcha, A., & Park, J.-M. (2007). An overview of anomaly detection techniques: Existing solutions and latest technological trends. *Computer Networks, 51*(12), 3448–3470. doi:10.1016/j.comnet.2007.02.001.

Puketza, N. J., Zhang, K., Chung, M., Mukherjee, B., & Olsson, R. A. (1996). A methodology for testing intrusion detection systems. *IEEE Transactions on Software Engineering, 22*(10), 719–729. doi:10.1109/32.544350.

Qin, X., & Lee, W. (2004). Attack plan recognition and prediction using causal networks. In *Proceedings of the 20th Annual Computer Security Applications Conference* (pp. 370-379). IEEE Press.

Rajasegarar, S., Leckie, C., & Palaniswami, M. (2008). Anomaly detection in wireless sensor networks. *IEEE Wireless Communications, 15*(4), 34–40. doi:10.1109/MWC.2008.4599219.

Scarfone, K., & Mell, P. (2007). *Guide to intrusion detection and prevention systems (IDPS)*. NIST Special Publication.

Sperotto, A., Schaffrath, G., Sadre, R., Morariu, C., Pras, A., & Stiller, B. (2010). An overview of IP flow-based intrusion detection. *IEEE Communications Surveys and Tutorials, 12*(3), 343–356. doi:10.1109/SURV.2010.032210.00054.

Sun, B., Osborne, L., Xiao, Y., & Guizani, S. (2007). Intrusion detection techniques in mobile ad hoc and wireless sensor networks. *IEEE Wireless Communications, 14*(5), 56–63. doi:10.1109/MWC.2007.4396943.

Wagner, D., & Dean, D. (2001). Intrusion detection via static analysis. In *Proceedings of the 2001 IEEE Symposium on Security and Privacy* (pp. 156-168). IEEE Press.

Wang, K., Cretu, G., & Stolfo, S. J. (2005). Anomalous payload-based worm detection and signature generation. In *Proceedings of the 8th International Conference on Recent Advances in Intrusion Detection* (pp. 227-246). Springer-Verlag.

Warrender, C., Forrest, S., & Perlmutter, B. (1999). Detecting intrusion using system calls: Alternative data models. In *Proceedings of the 1999 IEEE Symposium on Security and Privacy* (pp. 133-145). IEEE Press.

Wu, S. X., & Banzhaf, W. (2010). The use of computational intelligence in intrusion detection systems: A review. *Applied Soft Computing Journal, 10*(1), 1–35. doi:10.1016/j.asoc.2009.06.019.

Zhou, C. V., Leckie, C., & Karunasekera, S. (2010). A survey of coordinated attacks and collaborative intrusion detection. *Computers & Security, 29*(1), 124–140. doi:10.1016/j.cose.2009.06.008.

Zhou, J., Carlson, A., & Bishop, M. (2005). Verify results of network intrusion alerts using lightweight protocol analysis. In *Proceedings of the 21st Annual Computer Security Applications Conference* (pp. 117-126). ACM Press.

KEY TERMS AND DEFINITIONS

Alert Correlation: Correlate several alarms to a more comprehensive alarm.

Alert Verification: Verify whether an alert is successful.

False Alarm Reduction: Reducing false alarms.

Intelligent Technique: An automatic way of completing a task.

Intrusion Detection System: A system to automatically detect intrusions.

Intrusion Detection: A process of identifying intrusions.

Machine Learning: A branch of artificial intelligence.

Chapter 9
Towards Building Efficient Malware Detection Engines Using Hybrid CPU/GPU-Accelerated Approaches

Ciprian Pungila
West University of Timişoara, Romania

Viorel Negru
West University of Timişoara, Romania

ABSTRACT

This chapter presents an outline of the challenges involved in constructing efficient malware detection engines using hybrid CPU/GPU-accelerated architectures and discusses how one can overcome such challenges. Starting with a general problem description for malware detection and moving on to the algorithmic background involved for solving it, the authors present a review of the existing approaches for detecting malware and discuss how such approaches may be improved through GPU-accelerated processing. They describe and discuss several hybrid hardware architectures built for detecting malicious software and outline the particular characteristics of each, separately, followed by a debate on their performance and most suitable application in real-world environments. Finally, the authors tackle the problem of performing real-time malware detection and present the most important aspects that need to be taken into account in intrusion detection systems.

DOI: 10.4018/978-1-4666-4514-1.ch009

INTRODUCTION

Malware detection is a highly common and computationally intensive problem in intrusion detection systems nowadays. The term *malware* comes from the combination of two separate terms, *malicious* and *software*. Suggestively enough, the malware detection problem aims to identify malicious software and is an intensely active field of research in computer security (Idika et al., 2007; Vinod et al., 2009; Egele et al., 2012). With the ever-growing number of threats nowadays given the market boost of mobile devices and the increasing variety of operating systems, it is becoming more and more challenging to track down and identify threats on all mobile, desktop, and server-oriented platforms. Nonetheless, malware has continued to evolve and spread to the desktop and server segment as well, as a result being more than 17.7 million known malware threats today according to Bott (2012).

Efficient malware detection engines have been subject to intensive research in the past few years, and as the graphics processing units (also commonly called GPUs) have been improved significantly and could theoretically surpass, in terms of bandwidth performance, contemporary CPUs (where CPU is the acronym for Central Processing Unit, the kernel of basic operations in computers nowadays), hybrid architectures have evolved which aim to detect malware faster and better. Given the highly parallel nature of GPUs today, taking advantage of such high-degree of parallelism seemed to be the best course of action for solving computational intensive tasks. Considering the complexity required to achieve accurate malware detection, GPU-based implementations have started to emerge even beginning with the launch of the first GPU-oriented programming framework by NVIDIA in 2007, called CUDA (Compute Unified Device Architecture), and later variants have also been ported to compatible graphics cards from ATI.

The objectives of this chapter are the following: we will formulate the problem of malware detection, outlining the general architecture used for performing malware detection in common intrusion detection systems today; we move on to presenting the algorithmic background for performing malware detection and discuss its applicability in real-world scenarios, exemplifying with an overview of the functionality implemented in the ClamAV open-source antivirus; we then present a general overview of the GPU computing capabilities, moving on to a discussion of the CUDA framework and how it may be used to solve computationally-challenging problems; we present and discuss the particular features of several different hybrid architectures which are GPU-based and which aim to solve the same problem of malware detection, outlining the applicability, benefits and drawbacks of each; finally, we present a conclusion of the subjects covered and suggest future research opportunities and on-going work in the field.

BACKGROUND

This section introduces the concept of malware, presenting the different forms under which the concept is found today, and presents a few common approaches for achieving malware detection. We also present the algorithmic background required for achieving malware detection, beginning with the most commonly used multiple pattern-matching algorithm and discussing a few common architectures: in particular, we present the RMAS (Run-time Malware Analysis System) and ClamAV approaches, also outlining known solutions to employing different heuristics for detecting malicious program behavior at run-time. The last part of this section covers NVIDIA's CUDA framework and architecture.

A Short Definition of Malware

According to Wikipedia (2012), *malware* refers to "software used or created to disrupt computer operation, gather sensitive information, or gain access to private computer systems." Basically, a malware program is intended to do damage, and the form under which such a program does its work can vary from one implementation to another – which is also the primary reason of the existence of the different types of malware nowadays, including its most wide-spread form as *viruses*, a type of software commonly distributed through the Internet and e-mails, known as *worms*, disguised functionality also referred to as *Trojan horse*, intrusive software also called *adware*, a form of software designed for spying activities commonly known as *spyware* (including *rootkits, keyloggers,* and others), and the list can continue.

Malware has received constant attention throughout the past 10 years as operating systems started to evolve and become increasingly complex and bigger (as a rule of thumb, the higher the complexity of a software, the more prone that software is to attacks and faults), but mostly in the past few years with the highly spread nature of mobile operating systems and the variety of hardware platforms hosting them. While the initial startup of malware was in the early form of *viruses*, with the explosion of the Internet *worms, spyware* and *Trojan horses* began to emerge and soon were wildly spread through email and social networks. On the other hand, *adware* was a common form of aggressive marketing until not long ago (and still is sometimes nowadays, although its tolerance policy has been reduced drastically), which led for example to many programs being bundled with intrusive programs that were trying to convince the user to purchase one or more services.

One of the most resilient forms of malware that has been spotted recently in the wild comes in the form of *metamorphic viruses*, such as Stuxnet (McMillan, 2012) and Flame (CrySyS Lab, 2012), the latter being recently considered to be "the most complex malware ever found" up to this day (Crysis Lab, 2012).

Towards Detecting Malware

Detecting malware is performed nowadays through several techniques, but the general approach as also pointed out by Kaspersky (2012) is making heavy use of two primary techniques: *static* and *dynamic analysis*. The *static analysis* engine in a malware detection intrusion detection system (also commonly abbreviated IDS in literature) handles the accurate (exact) matching of malware functionality inside a program's executable code. The *dynamic analysis* counterpart performs *heuristic analysis* of the program's executable code and attempts to classify it as anomalous or safe-to-execute based on a threat level, which is computed during the analysis.

The current trend in modern antivirus programs is to combine the two approaches mentioned above into a *hybrid analysis* methodology, which makes use of several hardware-supported features, such as *emulation* or *virtualization*. Emulating a program ensures that its functionality is reproduced to a certain degree of accuracy on the running hardware (which is simulated through software), while the emulator can track down any anomalous activity during the execution stages. Virtualizing a program refers to analyzing the program's execution while partially (but not completely, like emulation does) obstructing access to the underlying hardware. As a special technique of virtualization, *sandboxing* is a common approach for tracing the execution of a program in a simulated environment, which is partially connected to the underlying hardware, with no real impact or damage to the real operating system or its software components. Basically, using a simulated, sandboxed environment, a program may be executed and its threat level assessed with no security risks or implications for the end-user.

Algorithmic Background

While not entirely defined as a widely accepted standard in literature, performing *static analysis* in malware detection usually refers to accurately matching malicious signs of activity in a program's executable code. Given that in real-world scenarios the analysis is performed without direct access to the program's source code, when we are discussing about *viruses, Trojans,* or other forms of malware, most antivirus programs use one or more forms of signature-based matching which aim to identify malicious portions of code inside a program. This is in fact directly related to the problem of *pattern matching*, or the problem of locating one or more patterns (also called the *initial dictionary*) into an input data string: in our case, the *dictionary* is comprised from the malware signatures and the input data string is the program's executable code.

The *dynamic analysis* performed on an executable refers to employing different heuristics, as mentioned above, and virtualization techniques (such as *sandboxing* discussed earlier), for computing the threat level of a program by emulating it in a confined environment. There are however several techniques which do not require the program to be ran, usually relying on graphs and employing different analysis methods (e.g. through the construction of program dependence graphs, or by performing system call analysis, etc.) for attempting to determine the runtime behavior of the code. The threat level computed highly relies on the accuracy of the analysis methods proposed, but also on the known malicious behaviors (defined *a-priori*, as in most machine-based learning approaches) used throughout the process. As with all approaches related to artificial intelligence, there is room for further debate and improvement in this area, making it one of the most challenging aspects in malware detection.

There are numerous algorithms dedicated to solving the *pattern-matching* problem mentioned above, however given the high number of signatures used in the detection process, such algorithms require intensive computational resources to process all the information. For instance, the ClamAV open-source antivirus (ClamAV, 2012) uses signatures in different forms and has a total of over 2,5 million signatures in its four signature databases (ClamAV Database, 2012). From these signatures, a little over 60,000 (Cha et al., 2010; Pungila, 2012a) are used to perform virus signature matching (while the others are MD5 hashes - used for accurate matching of malware files, or regular expressions for tracking down malicious scripts inside HTML or other types of documents). As pointed out by Pungila et al. (Pungila, 2012a), only a small fraction (about 11%) of these are regular expressions, which are more complex to detect, while the others are simple patterns.

Solving the problem of *multiple pattern matching* can be done by employing *simple pattern matching* techniques, with many dedicated algorithms existing here, such as the naive, Karp-Rabin, Knuth-Morris-Pratt or Boyer-Moore approaches (Karp et al., 1987; Knuth et al., 1977; Boyer et al., 1977). Nevertheless, a simple analysis shows that even though the simple pattern matching problem may be solved efficiently using for instance a sublinear (in the average case) implementation of the Boyer-Moore algorithm (which has a running time performance of $O\left(\frac{N}{M}\right)$ in the best case, where N is the input string length and M is the pattern length), extending the approach to multiple pattern matching requires would basically mean applying the same algorithm multiple times for all K patterns, resulting in a best-case performance of $O\left(\frac{N \times K}{M_{avg}}\right)$, where M_{avg} is the average length of all patterns in the dictionary. Given that in real-world scenarios K is very high (60,000 in the case of ClamAV signatures and possibly higher in other antivirus implementations), such a solution is not feasible for efficient implementations and real-time scanning engines.

Figure 1. a) A representation of the Aho-Corasick automaton for the input dictionary {0xAA 0xBB 0xAA, 0xAA 0xCC 0xBB, 0xBB 0xAA 0xBB, 0xBB 0xBB 0xAA 0xAA }, where dashed lines are showing a few example failure functions. b) The same representation of the Commentz-Walter tree for the same dictionary (notice the reversed trie tree) with the shift distances computed are stored as [shift1, shift2].

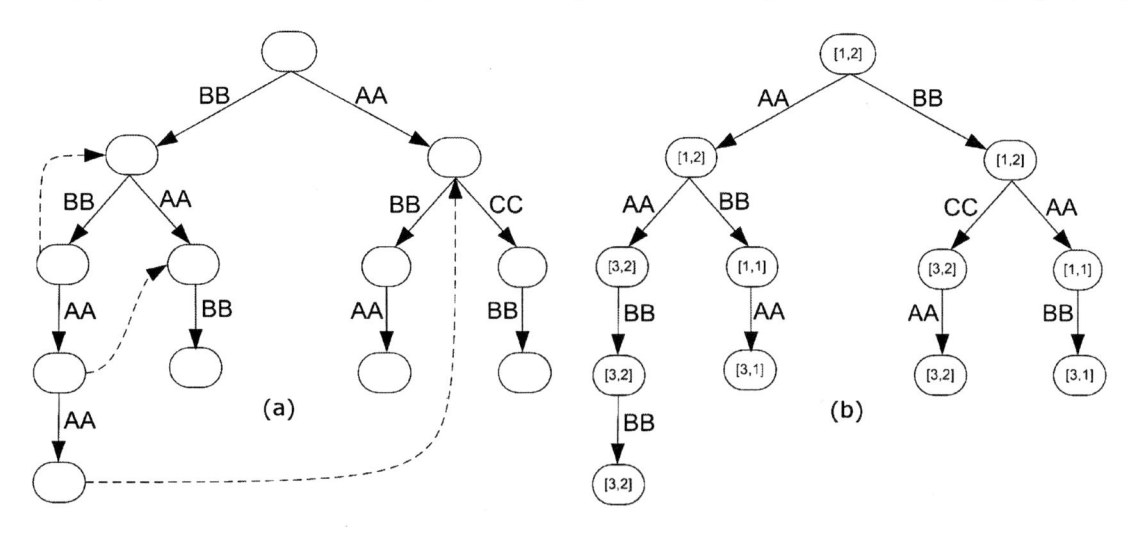

Fortunately, several algorithms have been designed and existed for a long time now, with the most popular approaches being: the Aho-Corasick algorithm, the Commentz-Walter approach and the Wu-Manber variant (Aho et al, 1975; Commentz-Walter, 1979; Wu et al., 1994). These algorithms overcome the limitation of single pattern matching and attempt, by precomputing a model for processing the data, to scan the entire input using the precomputed model and therefore achieve much better running times.

The Aho-Corasick Algorithm

The Aho-Corasick algorithm (Aho et al, 1975) builds an automaton (a finite state machine) from a trie tree constructed from the input dictionary (see Figure 1a). The first stage in building the automaton is represented by the construction of the trie tree from the set of input patterns, which is also commonly used in dictionary-matching applications. The next step is represented by the precomputation of a *failure function*, for each node in the automaton, as follows: for word *w* at the current node *z* in the automaton, determine the longest suffix s_w of *w* for which the following is verified: there exists a node *n* in the automaton for which the word at *n* is equal to s_w. If such a suffix is found and not empty, the failure function for node *z* points to node *n*. If there was no suffix found, the failure function always points back to the root of the automaton (state 0).

During runtime, the algorithm takes each input character (matching is performed left-to-right), from the input data set and matches it against the current node – if there is a transition for it, the new state of the automaton becomes the state indicated by the transition, otherwise the same character is applied to the state indicated to by the failure function of the node. This is a recursive process that terminates in the root of the automaton. In essence, the automaton parses each of the input characters in the input data and jumps from one location to another in the automaton, with the highest *local hit average* being observed in the root (initial) state, in case of mismatches (the most common situations).

One particularly interesting observation here is that the algorithm's performance is optimal in the worst-case: $O\left(N + \sum_{i=0}^{K-1} M_i + Z\right)$, where N is the input data length, M_i is the length of pattern i, and Z is the number of occurrences in the input data. This shows that in the worst situation, the algorithm performs in linear time, which makes it very fast for real-world applications, one of the reasons why it is so popular in several fields relying on pattern-matching applications, such as bioinformatics (Rahman et al., 2007; Nordin et al., 2009; Horak, 2010) or natural language processing (Zaslawskiy et al., 2010; Zha et al., 2011; Kumar et al., 2011).

The Commentz-Walter Algorithm

Starting from the idea of the single pattern matching Boyer-Moore algorithm, which offers sublinear performance in the average case and the best performance known up-to-date for a pattern matching algorithm in the best-case scenario, the Commentz-Walter algorithm (Commentz-Walter, 1979) is based on the same trie tree concept as its Aho-Corasick counterpart, however the tree is now built from the reversed set of patterns instead of the usual ones (see Figure 1b). The algorithm begins the matching process by performing right-to-left matching, just as the Boyer-Moore algorithm does, and aims to identify portions of text, which may be skipped when performing the matching, in order to avoid unnecessary comparisons. Therefore, the algorithm precomputes a model based on two *shifting* distances, intuitively called *shift1* and *shift2*. These distances are being used to perform longer jumps in the input text in case of mismatches (the Aho-Corasick algorithm only does a jump of one single position for every character).

The shifting distances are computed as follows: *shift1* is representing the minimal distance between the depth of the current node z of the automaton (which has the word w assigned to it), and the depth of a node y (with the word v) of a higher depth, so that w is a suffix of v. The distance may not exceed however w_{min}, the length of the shortest keyword in the input dictionary. The *shift2* distance is computed in a similar manner, except that in the definition above node y must be a leaf in the tree and the *shift2* distance must be lower or equal to the *shift2* distance of the parent node. When performing the matching process, the algorithm begins the scanning starting at position w_{min} -1 in the input string *text*, from right to left, and in case of mismatches at node v in the tree it jumps in the input string by $min\{shift2(v), max\{shift1(v), char(text[pos-j])-j-1\}\}$, where $char(c)$ is computed as the minimum of $w_{min}+1$ and the depth of all nodes having c as a label.

The algorithm outperforms the Aho-Corasick approach in real-world situations (Watson, 1994, 1995; Pungila, 2012b), yet it highly relies on longer patterns for achieving better skip rates in the input string. When used with short patterns, the algorithm can perform worse than the previous.

The Wu-Manber Algorithm

The Wu-Manber algorithm combines the hashing ideas used in the Karp-Rabin approach (Karp et al., 1987) with the jump idea used in the Boyer-Moore algorithm (Boyer et al., 1977) into an algorithm that performs jumps by comparing hashes of blocks of text in the input string and determining jumping positions according to these. The overall idea is to no longer perform comparisons using single characters in the input string, but instead use blocks of text to compute hashes, which get retrieved from a previously computed hashtable and contain jumping distances in the input string in case of mismatches.

The authors recommend different variants for performing efficient computation of the hash, specifically they recommend using a block of two characters for a low number of patterns in the dictionary, and three characters for a high number of patterns. Nonetheless, the storage requirements for this algorithm are $O(c^B)$, where c is the alphabet size (for virus signatures, the alphabet is the entire ASCII charset, so the alphabet size is 256) and B is the block size (which is 3 as recommended for the authors, given we are using a large set of patterns). In total, a number of 2^{24} elements are being stored as key-pair values, which results in a memory usage (considering that pointers occupy 32 bits in hardware memory) of 128 MB of memory for storing the entire hashtable before it is being precomputed. If the pointer size is 64 bits, the memory requirements would double, using 256 MB of memory in total. An improved version of the algorithm aimed at virus scanning was recently proposed by Lin et al. (2011) using a backward hashing approach.

The algorithm outperforms in real-world scenarios both the Aho-Corasick and Commentz-Walter counterparts (Aho & Corasick, 1975; Commentz-Walter, 1979), but given the high memory requirements its implementation becomes challenging on low-memory devices, including GPUs. The average amount of memory a GPU has nowadays is around 1 GB, with some parts of the memory being used to hold the screen pixel data and color formats. On an average GeForce GTX 560Ti graphics card (running on the GF114 Streaming Multiprocessor) having 1 GB of DDR5 RAM, about 360 MB of RAM are reserved to be used by the operating system, with the rest being available to the user. For large data processing, the remaining memory may become insufficient in very short time and, unlike a normal computer where virtual memory mechanism are employed when the physical memory runs out, GPUs cannot go beyond their actual memory capacity. Similarly, other devices (such as mobile devices) have low performance in situations where virtual memory mechanisms are employed, therefore it is ideal in both these scenarios to restrain the memory usage as much as possible and limit the amounts to the actual usable amount. It is therefore feasible to implement memory efficient algorithms in order to ensure the best use of the memory capacity and avoid situations where the program cannot be run at all because of such resource constraints.

The differences and particular capabilities of each algorithm are presented in Table 1.

RMAS: A Run-Time Malware Analysis System Framework

Sponchioni (2011) presented the RMAS, or Run-Time Malware Analysis System, a framework designed to analyze and detect malware. The purpose of the framework is to help analysts with viral analysis by detecting new, customized malware. Given the constant struggle among virus writers to improve the efficiency of their malware and keep it hidden from detection by antivirus software, the framework focuses on the dynamic analysis of executable programs in order to be able to assess their threat level in the Windows operating system. Their modular system performs

Table 1. Classification of common multiple pattern matching algorithms

Pattern Matching Algorithm	Construction Stage	Pre-computation	Run-time Performance	Memory Usage	Matching Regular Expressions
Aho-Corasick	Trie tree	Failure functions	Linear in input data size	Varies with number of nodes in trie	Yes
Commentz-Walter	Reversed trie tree	Shifting distances	Varies with input, usually sub-linear	Varies with number of nodes in reversed trie	Yes
Wu-Manber	Hash-table of prefixes	Hash table computation	Varies with input, sub-linear, usually the fastest	High, constant, depends on machine's pointer size (32/64-bit)	No

both static and dynamic analysis, but the focus is primarily on the latter. It has a component, which performs behavior analysis and computes the dangerousness level of the program.

The main components are comprised of a static module (written in PHP/Python), a dynamic analysis engine written in C and a detection engine built in Python. Their approach is based on file-hashing, integration with virus-checking Websites such as VirusTotal.com, PE (Portable Executable, the format of the executable files built for Windows NT-based platforms such as Windows XP and onwards) information extraction (through import table analysis for example), automatic detection of the packer used when producing the executable, detecting the entropy of a file and so on. Their approach is only applicable to the Windows operating system, since it employs three components for performing dynamic analysis which rely on user-level system-wide hooking (a feature in the Windows operating system which allows hooks to be installed whenever a system-call is being made in a program) for tracing down registry, file, network and process-related activity, and a kernel-level hook system for performing the same operations, on a more privileged level of access to the operating system.

ClamAV: An Open-Source Antivirus

A wide-spread open-source antivirus program today is the ClamAV software (ClamAV, 2012). ClamAV has a daily updated database totaling over 2,5 million signatures on the 26th of September, 2012. From these signatures, a little over 62,000 are used for viruses, Trojans and worms (Cha, 2010; Pungila, 2012a, 2012b), while the others are designed for detecting malicious scripts or for comparing file hashes. Even further, from that amount only about 11% are coming in the form of regular expressions, while the remaining are comprised of simple characters.

Virus Signature Matching

Matching virus signatures begins with the construction of a signature for that particular virus, which ideally uniquely identifies the virus once matched inside the corpus of an executable piece of code. The signatures are actually comprised of the hexadecimal encoding of the mnemonics used in the disassembly process by virus analysts and usually refer to unique instructions which may be traced only inside infected files. Most type of viruses may be detected through this approach, but more complicated viruses, such as *polymorphic* or *metamorphic* threats require additional detection stages. Polymorphic viruses are viruses which can shift or encrypt their code partially from one infection to another. The weak spot of such an approach however is the decryption part of the virus code, which is always the same for each infection - which is why virus analysts usually build signatures for these infections based on the decryption module of the code. However, for metamorphic threats, or viruses which can encrypt their code entirely from one infection to another, heuristic methods are required in order to achieve partial or complete detection.

The simplest signature format is the following:

AABBCCDDEEFF00112233

and is comprised of a sequence of characters from the input alphabet in hexadecimal format (in this case, the characters are AA, BB, CC and so on). The typical regular expression signature format is found in Box 1 and it contains several sub-signatures which are linked together through different types of constraints. For example, the AABBCCDD sub-signature is linked to EEFF00 through a constraint of type *, meaning that any number of characters may exist between two matching positions of these two sub-signatures. The {4-} constraint specifies that at least 4 characters must be present between two matching positions of EEFF00 and 112233, while {-24} specifies at most 24 characters, and {6-12} specifies between 6 and 12 characters. ClamAV also supports other tags in regular expressions, such as ?? (meaning a full character match), or ? (meaning a half-byte, or partial matching of the first or last 4 bits only). Nevertheless, as observed in several research studies (Vasiliadis et al., 2010; Cha et al., 2010; Pungila et al., 2012b), most of the signatures in the ClamAV database are comprised of these three types of constraints: at least n bytes between sub-signatures, at most m bytes between them, or anything from n to m bytes between these.

Detection Process

The ClamAV detection process as pointed out by Miretskyi et al. (2004) is comprised of a combination of the Aho-Corasick automaton presented earlier and the Wu-Manber matching technique discussed. In essence, ClamAV uses a depth-limited trie tree, where the limit is a depth of 2 (the reason being that the smallest sub-signature of a virus in the ClamAV database has only two bytes). From this depth onwards, ClamAV keeps linked list of all the patterns and attempts to match them using the Wu-Manber algorithm. Nevertheless, regular expressions are being scanned using still the slower Aho-Corasick approach (Cha, 2010).

Detecting regular expressions through the Aho-Corasick automaton has been widely studied in the past years and several approaches exist. However, for limited constraints, such as the ones imposed by the ClamAV database, simpler variants have emerged (Pungila, 2009; Vasiliadis et al, 2010; Lin et al., 2011; Pungila, 2012b). With an on-going interest in digital forensics and data recovery and tracking, similar approaches have emerged for this particular field of research also (Zha et al., 2011; Pungila, 2012c).

Employing Heuristics for Classifying Run-Time Behavior

Employing heuristics on top of the pattern matching approaches known today is a subject commonly debated in several areas of research, including signal processing and digital forensics (Pungila, 2009, 2010; Zha, 2010). In malware detection engines, heuristics are employed mostly in the dynamic analysis process.

Several heuristics are used nowadays to classify run-time behavior, some of them involving running the program upfront (through emulation or virtualization), while others do not require the program to be ran and attempt to determine its output through a static analysis process, after which heuristics are employed for matching malicious behavior.

One common approach to classifying malicious behavior is through the analysis of system calls (Pungila, 2009; Maggi et al., 2010). This approach has the advantage of being able to be applied both in online and offline processing, meaning it can be executed while the program is running or before its actual execution. When employed during program runtime, efficiency drops and is highly depending on the *look-ahead* abilities of the heuristic to determine "what comes next" in terms of system calls. In other words, by looking ahead in the program and extracting the upcoming system calls, one can classify anomalous behavior based on a predefined set of known samples. When

Box 1.

```
AABBCCDD*EEFF00{4-}112233{6-12}445566{-24}FFEEDDCC
```

employed in offline processing, static analysis methods such as those based on control flow and program dependence graphs (CFG and PDG) are employed, after which relevant system calls are extracted as sequences and then compared to the known malicious samples for assessing the threat level.

Zanero (2004) proposed a Bayesian approach for classifying program behavior based on quantitative methods. A fuzzy approach based on the N-grams technique was also suggested by Cha (2005). Mutz et al. (2006) have also applied multiple detection models to the system call analysis technique and propose a Bayesian network approach to classify behavior. Maggi et al. (2010) propose an architecture for detecting malicious behavior by analyzing sequences of system calls that a program makes, along with their arguments, using several stochastic models and analyzing the best performance of each. A distributed model for system call analysis based on the MapReduce model was proposed by Liu et al. (2011), where the clients are offloaded with the task of performing the complex analysis by outsourcing it to a dedicated processing server.

Since dynamic analysis is the primary focus of all metamorphic virus analysts, as these heuristic-based techniques have proven to be the only ones capable of successfully identifying metamorphic and some polymorphic behavior, this field of research is still widely open for future contributions, especially in hybrid implementations.

NVIDIA's CUDA Architecture

The CUDA framework architecture for GPU programming was first presented by NVIDIA in 2007 and soon became of great interest due to its simplicity and ease of use. CUDA's framework makes use of an extension of the C99 programming language and allows developers to build programs, which run directly on the GPU (see Figure 2).

There are a few notions commonly used in CUDA terminology. First, there is the notion of a *thread*, or a sequential piece of code which gets executed by the GPU. A GPU has multiple threads running in parallel at the same time, executing the same piece of code called a *kernel*. Threads are organized into *warps*, which are groups of threads. Warps are being scheduled periodically by an internal scheduler. GPUs nowadays have one or more Streaming Multiprocessors (SMs). Threads are organized into blocks and cooperate, in the same block, through a limited amount of

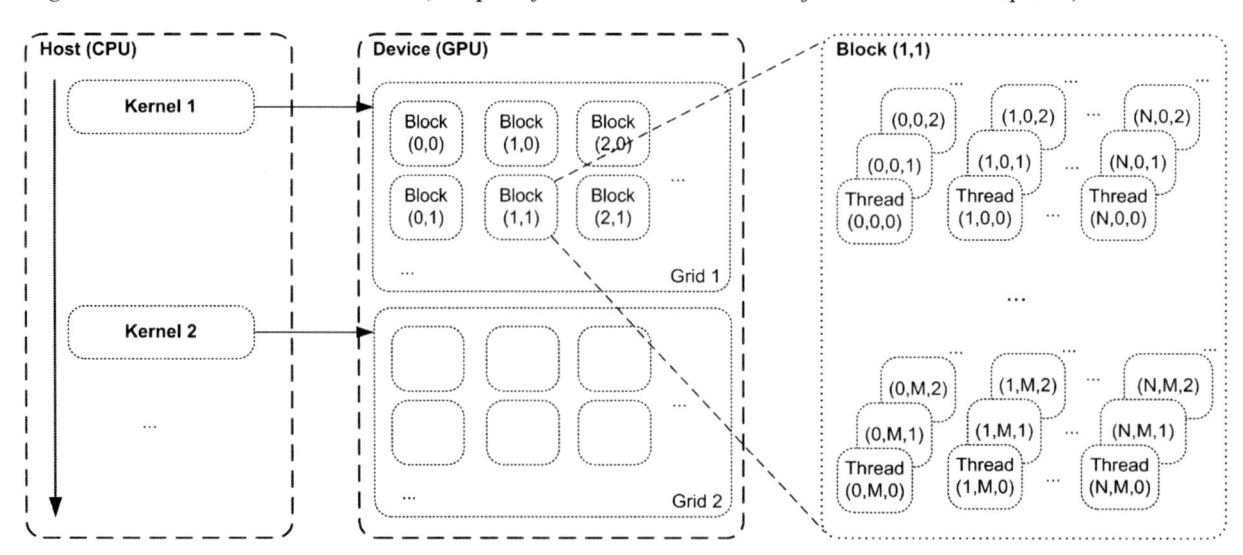

Figure 2. The CUDA architecture (adapted from NVIDIA's CUDA framework description)

shared memory. Threads can also synchronize within a block, however threads in different blocks cannot cooperate. Blocks are organized into grids, but only one kernel can execute on a device at a time, which is an important limitation (latest versions of CUDA allow execution of a limited number of multiple kernels concurrently).

For example, the GeForce GTX 560Ti uses the GF114 streaming multiprocessors (having a total of 8 SMs) with 48 warps per SM and 32 threads per warp. In theory, the GPU can actively schedule up to 8 x 48 x 32 = 12,288 threads at a time (Pungila, 2012b).

In literature, CPU-related hardware is usually called the *host side*, while that which is GPU-related is referred to as *device side*. Both the host and the device have their own separate memory spaces, and while the CPU can perform different memory operations on the system RAM (including implementing virtual memory mechanism), the GPU's internal memory is much more limited, is generally much faster and is usually used for storing textures and other types of data related to graphics rendering. As a result, all data which is required for algorithmic implementations on the GPU must first be copied from the host RAM memory to the device's video RAM. The copy process is performed through blocking calls, meaning while the copying is taking place, the CPU waits and performs no other tasks.

TOWARDS EFFICIENT HYBRID CPU/GPU ARCHITECTURES FOR MALWARE DETECTION

This section covers, in the beginning, the most important challenges that need to be overcome for achieving efficient malware detection using hybrid implementations, moving on to a discussion about a few known architectures, such as GrAVity, MiDEA, and PFAC. We then present a few efficient storage methodologies for hybrid CPU/GPU implementations of very large automata (particularly emphasizing the multiple pattern matching automata used in the malware detection process) and, at the end of the section, we discuss the most important aspects required in order to construct a real-time hybrid malware detection architecture and propose a general layout of such an architecture.

Challenges

Implementing hybrid hardware architectures has always been a challenge due to the different nature of designs and goals of the different devices involved in the computational process. For CPU/GPU hybrid solutions, this is no different: GPUs were initially built to perform intensive graphics (both 2D and 3D) computations and have only recently received attention for usage in general-purpose programming (GPGPU, or General Purpose computation on Graphics Processing Units). At the moment, GPUs and their corresponding frameworks (both in NVIDIA and ATI architectures) have important limitations, which may impose significant bottlenecks in algorithmic implementations and real-world scenarios. We will attempt to present some of these limitations with respect to the CUDA architecture, which is the most popular given its simplicity and direct hardware mapping.

Usability Limitations on GPGPU Devices

Once a kernel is being executed inside the GPU through the CUDA framework, all processing done on the host-side is still on-going, however the screen does not refresh and no activity is shown there until the GPU finishes its task. This can cause several problems, especially when dealing with debugging the code (infinite loops may actually cause the system to become unresponsive, unless the TDR feature discuss below is active and resets the driver) on the device. Furthermore, since *kernel* function calls (acting as constructors of the threads in the GPU, with each thread executing the kernel) are non-blocking, unlike the memory transfer calls, the CPU may have to wait and synchronize with the GPU in certain situations, in which case an infinite loop would mean a full system stall. The primary disadvantage to the end-user is that during longer processing performed in the GPU, the system appears to be unresponsive and uncontrollable, which sometimes may generate the false impression of stalling and may cause the user to perform a cold reboot when, in fact, there are still computations taking place in the background (see Figure 3.)

A partial solution to this problem would be implementing a host-side watchdog mechanism that could restore control to the operating system for ensuring screen refreshes, by forcefully terminating GPU operations and saving upfront the state in the computations performed, then resuming them after the UI refreshing has completed.

This is far from an elegant solution, as unobtrusive screen refreshes will require a frequency of at least 24 checks per second in the watchdog mechanism to ensure that no visible stalling is experienced by the end-user. The ideal solution here would be to implement hardware support for multiple kernel concurrency, as discussed below.

Timeout Detection and Recovery

The Windows Driver Model (WDM) in the Windows operating system requests all drivers to implement a feature called *Timeout Detection and Recovery* (TDR), which acts like a watchdog of the overall driver functionality. In particular, for GPU processing, if the GPU is non-responsive for more than 3 seconds in the TDR-based driver model, the driver is being reset so control can be restored to the operating system. This is usually followed by a notification in the operating system itself saying

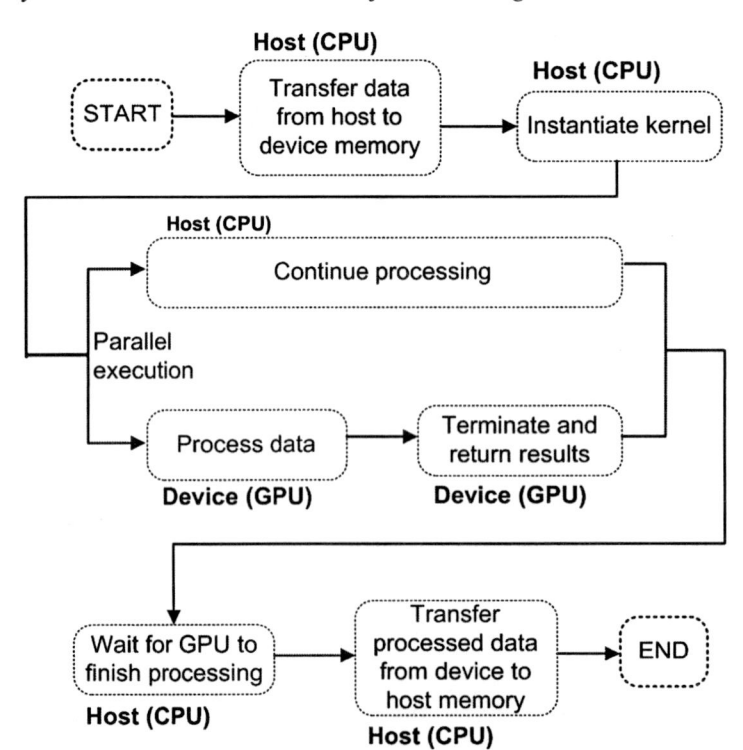

Figure 3. A generic hybrid CPU/GPU architecture for executing code on both the host and device

that the "Display driver stopped responding and has recovered" in Windows Vista or Windows 7 and is meant to increase the stability and reliability of the system in case of bugs, crashes or hardware incompatibilities. Nevertheless, when performing GPU programming, results can sometimes take much more than 3 seconds to be obtained, which renders this particular feature to become useless. Windows offers a registry-based hack for turning off the TDR feature by resetting the counter to 0 (or by increasing it to a higher TDR value), however a reboot is necessary in order to achieve this. As a result, the system is more prone to errors and instability caused by faulty drivers or hardware, even if not related to the graphics driver itself. Ideally, a hybrid architecture should not operate any changes on the default TDR settings in the operating system.

Limited Memory and Thread-Interaction

One important hardware limitation in GPUs nowadays is that the memory available to the processing stage is severely limited compared to equivalent RAM memories in the host. Although much faster usually than host memory, the memory used in the GPUs has only grown in the recent years to an average of 1-1.5 GB of RAM per GPU. When performing CUDA programming on a GeForce GTX 560 Ti using the GF114 SM, from the total of 1 GB of device RAM on the card and with no other programs using the GPU, only about 368 MB were used for reserved purposes and only about 632 MB were available to the end-user for programming purposes and storing data. With such important limitations, and taking into account the fact that most algorithms processing massive amounts of data, such as those involving a large number of signatures in automaton-based pattern matching applications (including, but not limited to intrusion detection systems), the need for designing memory-efficient algorithms becomes more stringent than ever.

Another important limitation is that there is limited threat interaction in CUDA. In fact, the safest way to communicate between threads in a CUDA program is when threads are part of the same block. In Figure 4, the CUDA memory model shows that the fastest way to achieve thread-communication is through the shared memory available to a block. As multiple blocks may be running at the same time on the same SM, the amount of shared memory available per block is drastically reduced (the shared memory per SM is usually around 16KB, and it becomes even smaller when dealing with a large number of blocks running in parallel). As a result, there is very little thread interaction because of the low shared-memory available to a block. Another possible mean of interaction is through global memory – although slower, this is accessible by all threads and diverse synchronization mechanisms may be used (which were available only in the latest versions of CUDA though) to perform Inter-Thread Communication (ITC). Using this approach does cause the program to be more error-prone and sometimes difficult to debug, given the highly asynchronous nature of kernel code execution on the GPU.

Figure 4. The CUDA memory model (adapted from Andrews, 2012)

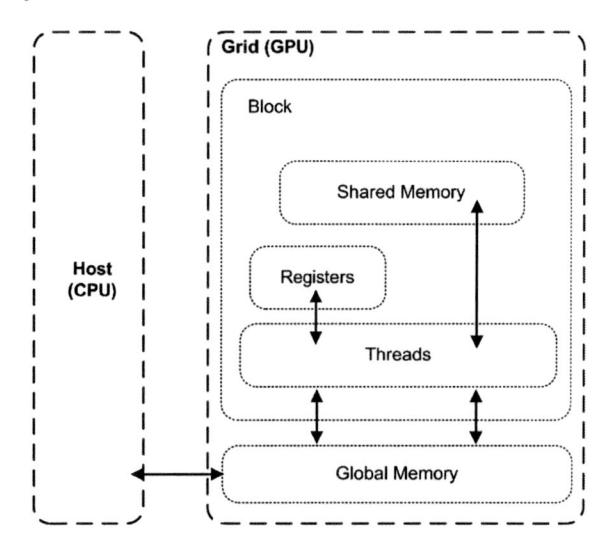

Limited Kernel Concurrency

CUDA devices which have compute capabilities of version 2.0 or later (e.g. based on the Kepler and Fermi architectures) may execute multiple kernels simultaneously, however at the moment the maximum number of kernel launches executing on a device is limited to 16 (on CUDA compatibility version 2.1), and a kernel from one CUDA context cannot execute in parallel with a kernel from another CUDA context. Additionally, kernels using larger amounts of memory are less likely to execute concurrently with other kernels, and the fact that there is no dependence between the kernels executing must be specified manually by the programmer. As a consequence, there is little room to execute task-parallel algorithms and even so, the number of tasks is limited by hardware design. Nonetheless, future versions will undoubtedly address this issue as well so that the execution paradigm resembles the one currently used in modern CPUs. To partially solve this problem, the Kepler architecture (the latest released at the moment) and the upcoming CUDA 5 framework allow the use of *dynamic parallelism*, or the ability to launch kernels from inside a thread.

High-Degree of Parallelism

The CUDA architecture is a highly parallel hardware device which can execute thousands (or tens of thousands) of threads concurrently. As a result, a high-degree of parallelism is necessary for the algorithms that are ported to CUDA, otherwise the processing bandwidth of the GPU may not be fully saturated and the outcome may offer worse performance than single CPU implementations. As an immediate consequence, algorithms that run on CUDA must be parallelized upfront and only then ran on the device. This can of course bring the main focus to the degree of parallelism that an algorithm may offer - not all algorithms are efficiently parallelizable and in fact, in parallel complexity theory the class *NC* (which is a set of languages decidable in parallel time) includes such examples, for instance the *parallel binary search* (Tvrdik, 2012). Therefore, only highly-parallelizable algorithms are suitable for hardware architectures such as CUDA and produce better performance and speedups compared to sequential implementations.

Optimizing Throughput

The host-device memory transfers are blocking calls and that basically imposes restrictions on the amount of memory transfers performed. Currently, such transfers have high throughput thanks to the PCI Express architecture improvements, but mostly when transferring large amounts of data between the host and the device. In our custom-built tests for instance, when transferring a large number of data structures (occupying in average 40 bytes per structure) corresponding to the nodes in a large automaton (of about 350,000 nodes) on a high-end desktop machine, about 3 hours were required in total, which makes such transfers completely inefficient and avoidable at all costs. Therefore, the need to maximize the throughput is imperative and shows that it is not always sufficient to build efficient algorithms in terms of performance, but also in terms of storage and throughput transfers. We also need to point (Pungila, 2012a, 2012b) here the problem of sparse pointer locations throughout memory.

Whenever allocating memory, both on the host and the device, pointers are used to indicate memory locations and, for a large number of allocations, are highly spread throughout memory. This may not seem like a problem at first, but at a closer look after careful analysis of the spreading degree, a trie-based structure that should occupy about 100 MB of RAM took almost 250 MB of RAM in host memory. Through a somewhat similar approach, a higher amount of about 160 MB was occupied in the device memory when attempting to perform the same allocation. It is worth observing that these amounts are not fixed: they vary according to the operating system available memory (for the host) and according to the device's internal memory management routines (for the device), so the numbers may be higher or lower (however, as an empirical observation we have made during the tests performed in previous research on the host, they are usually occupying about 40% at least of the total memory requirements, resulting in at least 140% higher memory requirements than initially estimated; more plausible scenarios for higher number of structures tend to double the amount of memory, leading to up to 200% higher memory than the estimated). These gaps which appear between consecutive memory allocations (shown in Figure 5a as unused spaces) are reserved for future memory allocations or re-allocations of existing structures, so their purpose is well-intended, however given that memory-prone algorithms on the device tend to avoid memory reallocations and prefer to instead fully use the PCI Express throughput by allocating all the memory in the beginning and later on just accessing it, such behavior is no longer needed. As a result, all approaches based on sequential memory allocations are slowing down the processing considerably and are to be avoided in real-time implementations or critical performance environments.

Considering the malware detection stages and the fact that pattern matching automata are being used to perform virus signature matching for example, and that such automata have a very high number of nodes - about 7 million nodes (Pungila, 2012a), it is desirable to avoid performing 7 million allocation routines and instead find efficient approaches to transferring the automata in one burst, if at all possible. Work performed earlier by Mark Norton of the Snort intrusion detection system team (Norton, 2004) has outlined several efficient ways to store very large automata in memory with minimal extra-storage, which was later on successfully applied in several architectures (Lee, 2008; Vasiliadis, 2011; Lin, 2012) while recent work outlined models designed specifically for maximizing throughput (Pungila, 2012b) in hybrid CPU/GPU architectures. In the following sections we will present recent architectures designed for GPU-acceleration and discuss their storage model, as well as an analysis of the efficiency and applicability to malware detection.

Figure 5. a) Sparse memory locations resulted after allocating memory through classic allocation routines; b) ideal memory layout for maximizing throughput in host-to-device and vice-versa transfers (adapted from Pungila, 2012a, 2012b)

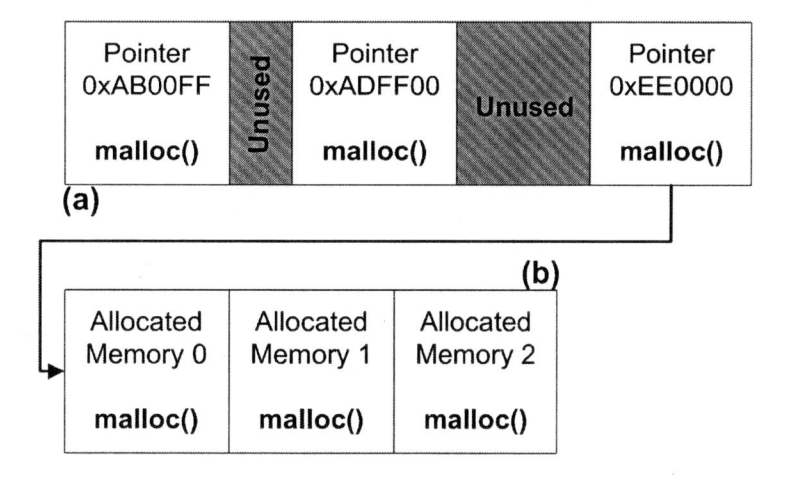

Detecting Malware through Efficient Hybrid Implementations

There have been many architectures proposed which benefit from GPU acceleration in the malware detection stages of intrusion detection systems, and in this section we will present and discuss recent work performed in this direction. The final goal is to familiarize the reader with the different layouts and scenarios for which these architectures were built, outlining both their benefits and weaknesses at the same time.

GrAVity: A Massively Parallel Antivirus Engine

Vasiliadis et al. (Vasiliadis, 2010) have proposed an architecture for implementing an antivirus engine using the massively parallel GPU processing capabilities. Their approach modifies the ClamAV engine so that the input files are being scanned initially on the GPU by using a depth-limited implementation of the Aho-Corasick automaton. By using a depth-limited search approach, only a prefix of each virus signature is being scanned, and in case of a match a dedicated verification module is being executed for further accurate matching. In their approach, the GPU acts like a high-pass filter.

Their approach is somewhat similar to the depth-limited scanning performed by the ClamAV engine (Miretskiy et al., 2004); however, they use a depth of 8 for implementing the automaton. As a consequence, they have observed that the false positive rate when using depth-limited scanning is lower than 0,0001% in real-world scenarios, which makes the approach more feasible for implementation in real-time engines because the processing is performed faster with a depth-limited tree and the memory usage is lower.

The primary disadvantage of their implementation however lies in the inefficient node structure of the automaton. Each node occupies 256 pointers, leading to a total of more than 4 x 256 = 1,024 bytes for each node to be stored, assuming a 32-bit pointer (for 64-bit pointers, the memory requirements double). For 350,000 nodes, that would lead to a memory usage of about 350 MB, which is very high given that there are still plenty of 128 and 256 MB graphics cards on the wild which will not be able to store that data. The authors did not focus however on the memory efficiency of the implementation, but rather on the actual performance improvements that emerged. The final performance of the GrAVity architecture obtained a speed-up of 100x the performance of the original ClamAV implementation on a CPU.

One of the first solutions for reducing storage requirements was proposed by Tuck et al. (2004). Their approach involves a path-compression technique which compressed consecutive single-childed nodes in the tree into a unique compressed node. The compressed transitions in the automaton are stored as a sequence in the compressed node. The approach poses additional challenges, especially when dealing with the Aho-Corasick automaton (where failure functions may point inside a compressed node, in which case an additional failure offset must be specified to point to the exact character in the compressed sequence to which the failure function indicates) or the Commentz-Walter algorithm (where shifting distances become much more difficult to compute and an overall re-arrangement of the tree is necessary).

The path-compression approach has been tested on the Snort IDS (Tuck, 2004; Zha, 2011) making use of bitmapped nodes (nodes which store a bitmap for the entire alphabet and compute child node locations in an array of children by computing the population counts, or *popcounts* as they are called in literature, which is the number of bits of 1 in a given binary word) while more recent work (Pungila, 2012a) has implemented the approach in a hybrid-compression version of the Aho-Corasick automaton for the ClamAV signature database. The latter implementation makes use of bitmapped nodes, path-compression and a new technique called "pattern-compression" or "pattern-fragmentation", where patterns are decomposed according to their longest common subsequences in order to reduce storage in total by up to almost 75% compared to other non-optimized implementations (using as little as 37.5 MB of memory for over 62,000 signatures from the ClamAV database). The implementation makes use of the memory model layout presented earlier (Pungila, 2012b), making the implementation feasible for GPUs as well. However, as the authors have observed, GPU implementations are more challenging because of slower performance in memory-prone operations.

MiDEA: A Multi-Parallel Intrusion Detection Architecture

Vasiliadis et al. (Vasiliadis, 2011) have proposed through MiDEA a multi-parallel architecture which can benefit of network, CPU and GPU parallelization. While not directly aimed at malware detection but rather designed for network intrusion detection systems (and based on the Snort signature dataset), their approach is of particular interest because of the storage methodology used in the implementation.

MiDEA uses the banded-row format (first proposed by Norton, 2004) for storing the Aho-Corasick automaton in a modified version of the algorithm that the authors call *AC-Compact*. This version only stores, for each row in the state table of the Aho-Corasick automaton, the information from the lower to the upper characters for a given state, which forms the *bandwidth* of the row in the state table. In essence, for each state in the automaton, the algorithm only stores the elements beginning with the first character in the alphabet that produces a valid transition, and up to the last character in the alphabet that also produces a valid transition. This approach has the advantage of reducing the memory usage by an important factor for certain alphabets, however it induces some additional processing required in order to determine whether a match is found for a transition at a given state, at run-time. Additionally, the approach does not scale well to widely sparse state tables, since the bandwidth would be getting closer to the length of the alphabet while in fact only a few characters are used throughout it. Further work in this field has been done (Lee & Huang, 2008) and showed that the state table can be further compressed through some reduction stages, making the storage space requirements significantly lower, at the expense of the additional pre-processing stage and having the disadvantage of not being able to easily perform regular expression matching. The storage benchmarks in MiDEA have shown a reduction of storage space by almost 37x compared to the non-optimized Aho-Corasick implementation.

The PFAC Pattern Matching Library

The PFAC pattern-matching library is a GPU-based framework for performing efficient pattern matching and was proposed by Lin et al. (2012). Their methodology is based on the *Parallel Failureless Aho-Corasick* algorithm (PFAC), which is aimed specifically at GPU implementations and only scales well on highly parallel platforms, because it eliminates the failure function in the automaton and performs, in each thread launched in the GPU grid, a search in the resulting structure at each byte in the input data, and stops fully when a match or mismatch is found. Since most characters produce mismatches, the algorithm scales well and works fine, but does not scale well to heterogeneous implementations and uses a large amount of memory, comparable to the non-optimized version of the automaton.

An improvement in the algorithm is suggested through a hashing function (*perfect hashing*), where only valid transitions in the state machine are stored in the hash table. Their approach scales well to hardware, using bitwise and shift operations, however collisions may still appear due to the subjective nature of the hashing function used.

For solving this, the authors propose a double-hashing technique (*two-level perfect hashing*) and prove an inequality showing the maximum amount of storage required for the automaton using this implementation. An immediate disadvantage here is the dependability of the implementation on the hashing function used, the variable storage space which is also tied to the actual hashing function and the computational overhead introduced by the hashing computation.

To summarize the differences between the different architectures we discussed, Table 2 presents an outline of the basic characteristics of each as per the challenges discussed earlier.

Efficiently Storing Large Automata in Hybrid CPU/GPU Architectures

Recent work (Pungila, 2012b) has outlined that achieving storage efficiency in hybrid CPU/GPU-based solutions is possible through the use of a simple model that allows maximum-throughout transfers between the host and the device, based on the construction of the trie tree. The steps involved in the construction of the model are shown in Figure 6.

According to Figure 6, the construction stages are implying the following steps: a) construction of the trie tree corresponding to the automaton (working for both the Aho-Corasick version or the Commentz-Walter algorithm), which is performed on the host-side because of the higher performance of memory allocation

Figure 6. The steps required for a model (Pungila, 2012b) designed for maximum throughput of large automata in hybrid CPU/GPU architectures

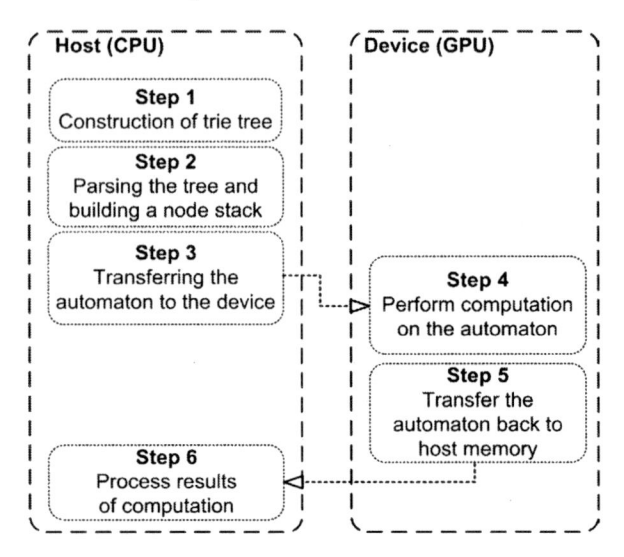

routines required to build the nodes of the tree; b) parsing of the tree (for instance using in-order, pre-order or post-order) and construction of a compact stack of nodes, where each element in the stack is a node structure; in this model, all children of a node are stored in consecutive locations and an offset is kept from the parent to the starting offset of the first child; c) the automaton obtained now only requires one single external pointer, all internal pointers are stored as offsets; the original tree can be discarded from host memory; as a consequence, it is ready to be transferred for further processing on the device through a single memory transfer; d) the transfer is full-

Table 2. Characteristics of each architecture as related to the challenges discussed earlier

Architecture Name	Usability Limitations on GPGPU Devices	Time-out Detection and Recovery	Memory Efficiency	Degree of Algorithmic Parallelism	Throughout Optimized
GrAVity	No support	No support	No	High	No
MiDEA	No support	No support	Yes, fixed space (AC-Full vs. AC-Compact)	High	Partially (for AC-Compact)
PFAC	No support	No support	Yes, variable space (parallel failureless Aho-Corasick)	Very high	Yes (by design)

duplex, meaning both the host can send the automaton to the device, and the device can send back the automaton to the host; this ensures a dual-processing capability which fully benefits from the available bandwidth.

The tests performed on the Aho-Corasick, Commentz-Walter and Wu-Manber pattern matching algorithms have taken into account the following ideas already discussed in literature: a) a depth-limited tree implementation covering depths of 8, 12 and 16, similar to the GrAVity approach (Vasiliadis, 2010); b) a hybrid-parallel scanning engine where the task-parallel scanning is ensured through two different pattern matching sub-engines (the first is scanning for regular-expressions using the Aho-Corasick automaton, while the second scans for the remaining patterns which are simple signatures), each implementing a data-parallel scan of the input data.

The advantages of this storage format are numerous: the approach only uses a single external pointer to memory (all internal pointers are replaced by offsets, making machine-dependant implementations possible and using less storage on hardware that uses pointers which occupy 64 or more bits), maximum throughput is ensured for host-to-device and device-to-host transfers of the entire automaton with no performance impact and constant storage space is required for the automaton (depending on the total number of states in the automaton and the size of the alphabet). The benchmarks performed showed that the hybrid-parallel scanning architecture proposed behaves very well and uses very little memory compared to other approaches (19x less memory than the GrAVity approach and 1.6x less storage than the PFAC implementation). The lowest memory obtained for the same set of 62,000 signatures in the ClamAV database (as of March, 2012) was of about 14.75 MB for the task-parallel implementation of Aho-Corasick (for scanning regular expressions) and Commentz-Walter (for scanning regular patterns) algorithms, with depth-limited automata (to a depth of 8) and no performance penalties compared to other existing approaches.

Towards Building Real-Time Malware Scanners in Hybrid CPU/GPU Systems

Performing real-time malware scanning is a challenging task given the complexity of the operations involved. Modern operating systems nowadays include support for installing hooks (or traps) that can execute before a system call is taking place, with the pioneering design (in terms of support, efficiency and high-degrees of applicability) in this area being the Windows operating system (other systems, such as Linux-based ones or MacOS offer limited, early-stage support for achieving the same). The immediate advantage of such an approach is that a real-time malware scanner may be employed even before a program gets executed, network data may be analyzed before it is being processed and so on, elements which are vital in order to implement proactive protection against threats in nowadays computing. In fact, most antivirus programs use the system-wide hooking concept provided in Windows for setting up real-time malware scanners that assess threat levels before programs are executed and allow the termination (or disinfection) of such programs in case they are found to be of malicious nature. The immediate disadvantage of course is that the same approach may in itself be used for malicious purposes, e.g. it may allow a perpetrator to hide itself from detection if the system gets infected before the installation of an antivirus program. An overall approach for achieving malware scanning is shown in Figure 7. A more specific approach for detecting malware behavior has been proposed by Chuan et al. (2012).

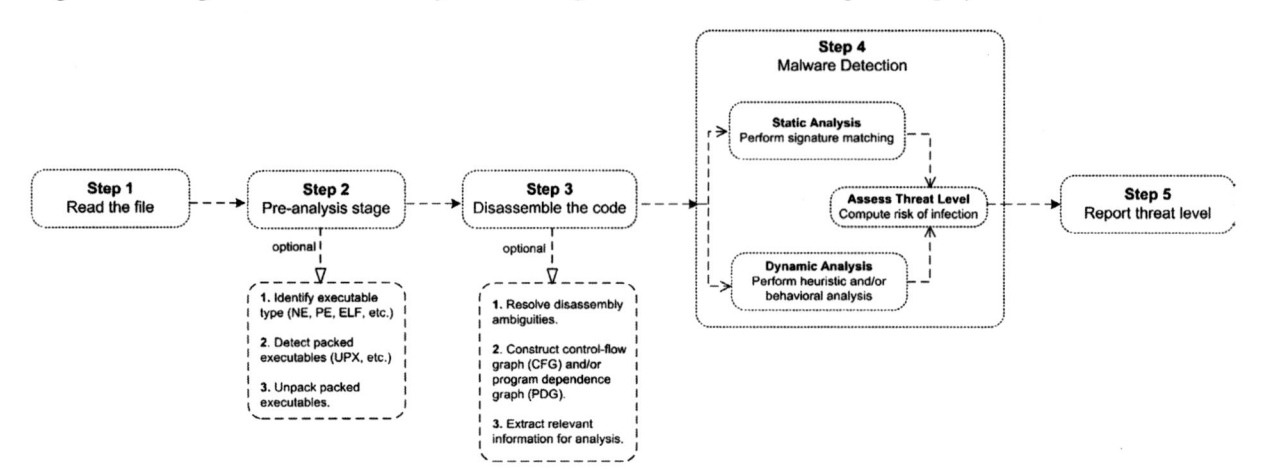

Figure 7. The generic architecture for detecting malware in modern operating systems

In order to take advantage of GPU acceleration in the implementation, we consider an efficient malware scanner needs to tackle with the challenges involved in developing hybrid implementations, as pointed out earlier, and believe that it should comply with the following minimal guidelines for overcoming them:

- **Minimally Intrusive:** A real-time scanner must be as less intrusive as possible. Malware detection can be, as we have seen, a very complex task and may sometime take a significant amount of time, especially if in-depth dynamic analysis is involved, which results in slower response times of the operating system to the end-user, specifically when hooking system calls. Ideally, a real-time scanner should minimize the impact on the usability aspects while maximizing the scanning performance. We believe the future will also bring better hardware support for improving this area, for instance allowing the GPU to perform general-purpose computations in parallel with the video processing, so that the user does not experience any discomfort during the processing by having their screen frozen.

- **Resource Efficiency:** Since malware engines have two different components in general for performing the analysis, and both can become highly demanding in terms of resources (e.g. the static and dynamic analysis engines may use very large automata in the detection stages), it is desirable for a real-time malware scanner to be as resource-efficient as possible, both in terms of computational and storage resources. Ideally, the scanner should minimize the impact on resources with little to no compromise at all on the malware detection rate.

- **Heterogeneous Processing:** Heterogeneous processing capabilities should apply, for best performance, to both the scanner architecture and also to each individual hardware component in the system. An efficient scanner should be able to schedule work using proper load-balancing algorithms which choose the best distribution of work on the hardware available to the user. Furthermore, data heterogeneity must also apply to each computational unit in the architecture, so that for instance both the CPU and the GPU can process different tasks in parallel. The first steps have already been taken by NVIDIA (and also ATI, with its upcoming HSA) so that in the near future the upcoming GPU architectures will allow better interaction between threads, a larger amount of shared memory and better kernel concurrency.

Based on the above observations, we can conclude that a generic architecture for achieving real-time malware scanning in hybrid, GPU-accelerated platforms may be built using a similar approach as in Figure 8.

The proposed architecture separates the operating system processing layer from the logic of the engine itself in a modular layout. The interrupt routines are called whenever system calls with potential risk are being used in a user-process, while risk-free system calls are directly communicating with the kernel in order to execute and speed-up performance. For risk assessment, the hybrid architecture employs a load-balancing and scheduling module which makes decisions referring to the work distribution on the computational units available to the user (CPUs or GPUs) and assigns static/dynamic analysis work tasks to each, while keeping the work-load balanced with special emphasis on obtaining high-performance and aiming to keep the memory usage as low as possible. Memory transfers between the host and the device are handled through the PCI Express architecture, outlined separately because of its significant importance in achieving high throughput between the two, as we have also pointed out previously.

TOWARDS MOBILE IMPLEMENTATIONS

One of the primary benefits of low-memory, high-throughput architectures are most resource-constrained mobile devices. While the malware threat on such devices is currently much lower than on desktop systems, it is an emerging field of research and efficient mobile implementations are of high interest currently.

Probably the most important aspect of a mobile implementation of a generic malware detection architecture is resource-balancing: on a device with a low amount of memory, the highest pos-

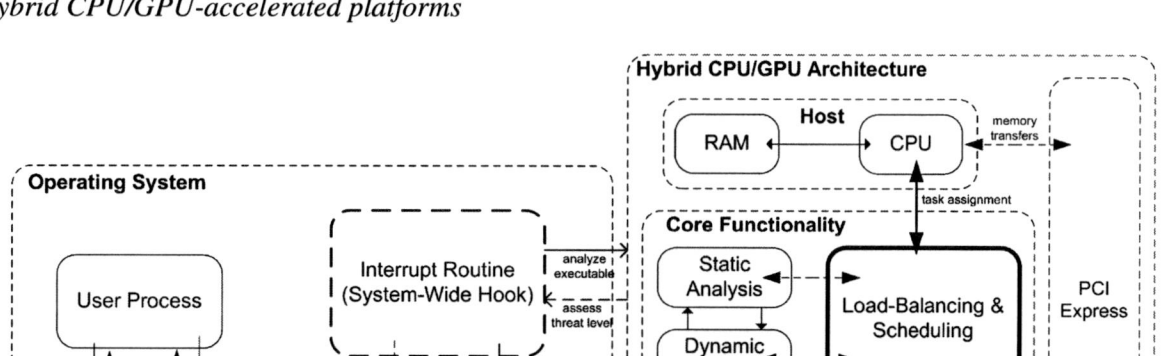

Figure 8. The generic architecture for achieving real-time malware scanning of executable programs in hybrid CPU/GPU-accelerated platforms

sible throughput is desired, while keeping the ratio throughput/memory usage higher than a minimally acceptable threshold. It is also known that GPUs inside mobile hardware platforms are also generally capable of outrunning in terms of bandwidth the performance of their attached CPUs, which is why a greater shift towards hybrid architectures will come as no surprise in the near future.

Although the discussion employed in this chapter has been focused on the CUDA framework (since it is also the most widespread in terms of GPGPU implementations nowadays), discussing its particular characteristics and outlining the primary challenges involved in developing malware detection architectures, the concepts remain primarily the same for mobile platforms. In particular, the high degree of parallelism and throughput optimization are to be desired for all implementations, and the efficient storage models presented earlier may still be used in mobile solutions. However, it is still worth mentioning that mobile implementations may pose additional challenges, the primary being the load-balancing mechanism (whose primary aim could be the efficient consumption of power at run-time to ensure a smaller battery-drain), along with highly-improved response times to minimize the lag in the user-frontend experience, all which may be subject to further debate until such platforms may offer a more popular, standardized framework for hybrid development.

FUTURE RESEARCH DIRECTIONS

Building hybrid architectures that fully benefit from GPU acceleration and bypass the limitations of the classic hardware designs today is a very challenging topic and could definitely be improved in the near future. NVIDIA has already made the first small, but important steps in their upcoming CUDA 5 framework through the implementation of *dynamic parallelism*, while ATI has also announced an upcoming hybrid hardware architecture (called HSA, or Heterogeneous Systems Architecture) for their APU-based platform in 2014, according to Shimpi (2012).

Future research directions in the field could be focusing on building a seamless integration of both the CPU and the GPU into a hybrid approach that can successfully overcome the existing synchronization boundaries today, which are also a partial bottleneck of the system, so that the CPU can be programmed to focus on other tasks while the GPU delivers the results of the computation. Additionally, real-time architectures will greatly benefit from improved throughout-oriented models which allow real-time transfers of tree-based data structures to be performed more efficiently and faster. Even further, employing the use of cached texture memory in the GPU would improve overall performance of the system. Additional work could also focus on efficient ways of solving the problem of coalesced reads and writes through better thread-level cache management, by building an approach that implements better branch prediction in the hardware device itself, or by adding a custom-built software prediction model on top of the pattern-matching layer. Another possible direction of research could refer to the construction of better, hardware-aware architectures that reduce computational delays through different hardware-dependant mechanisms.

CONCLUSION

As we strive to reach the physical limitations of contemporary hardware, it is becoming even clearer that the future is dedicated to hybrid hardware solutions, where different computational devices interact and schedule tasks according to fine-tuned load-balancing algorithms that can enhance power consumption with minimal compromise on performance. This chapter's aim was to propose an insight on efficient ways to build malware detection engines using hybrid CPU/GPU-accelerated architectures and discusses several recent models for achieving that goal. We also outlined several characteristics of hybrid architectures and how these influence the design and development of malware detection engines.

This chapter tackled with the problem of efficient malware detection in hybrid hardware implementations, where computationally intensive tasks may fully benefit from the massively parallel architectures of GPUs and use that to build better, more efficient intrusion detection systems. We presented a short definition and introduction to malware at the start of the chapter, moving on to presenting the most commonly used pattern matching algorithms for detecting it, and finally outlined recent existing hybrid approaches to building malware detection engines in intrusion detection systems. We discuss the challenges and implications of constructing hybrid architectures and debate the advantages and disadvantages of each of the solutions proposed. Finally, we propose a few future research topics which may be addressed in the future and show how these could contribute to the overall design and efficiency of GPU-accelerated architectures.

It is our belief that there is still much room for improvement in the field of hybrid architectures, both in terms of hardware and software designs. As of now, given the enormous computational resources that GPUs offer, and the highly-demanding implementations of malware detection engines, upcoming designs of intrusion detection systems will most certainly take into account hybrid implementations that can significantly accelerate and improve the overall performance, leading to better runtimes and less memory usage.

REFERENCES

Aho, A., & Corasick, M. (1975). Efficient string matching: An aid to bibliographic search. *Communications of the ACM, 18*(6), 333–340. doi:10.1145/360825.360855.

Bott, E. (2012). The malware numbers game: how many viruses are out there? *ZDNet.com*. Retrieved 25th of September, 2012 from http://www.zdnet.com/blog/bott/the-malware-numbers-game-how-many-viruses-are-out-there/4783

Boyer, R. S., & Moore, J. S. (1977). A fast string searching algorithm. *Communications of the ACM, 20*, 726–777. doi:10.1145/359842.359859.

Cha, B. (2005). Host anomaly detection performance analysis based on system call of neuro-fuzzy using Soundex algorithm and N-gram technique. In *Proceedings of Systems Communications* (pp. 116–121). Systems Communications.

Cha, S. K., Moraru, I., Jang, J., Truelove, J., Brumley, D., & Andersen, D. G. (2010). Split-screen: Enabling efficient, distributed malware detection. In *Proceedings of the 7th USENIX Conference on Networked Systems Design and Implementation (NSDI)* (p. 25). USENIX.

Chuan, L. L., Ismail, M., Yee, C. L., & Jumari, K. (2012). A new generic taxonomy of malware behavioral detection and removal techniques. *Journal of Theoretical and Applied Information Technology, 42*(2), 260–270.

Clam, A. V. (2012a). The ClamAV open-source antivirus. *ClamAV.com*. Retrieved 25th of September, 2012 from http://www.clamav.org

Clam, A. V. Database. (2012b). The ClamAV virus database. *ClamAV.com*. Retrieved 25th of September, 2012 from http://www.clamav.net/lang/en/ and http://database.clamav.net/

Commentz-Walter, B. (1979). A string-matching algorithm fast on the average. In *Proceedings of the 6th International Collection on Automata, Languages and Programming* (pp. 118-132). Springer-Verlag.

CrySyS Lab. (2012). *sKyWIper (a.k.a. Flame a.k.a. Flamer): A complex malware for targeted attacks* (Technical Report). Retrieved 25th of September, 2012 from http://www.crysys.hu/skywiper/skywiper.pdf

Egele, M., Scholte, T., Kirda, E., & Kruegel, C. (2012). A survey on automated dynamic malware-analysis techniques and tools. *ACM Journal of Computing Surveys, 44*(2).

Horak, Z. (2010). Fuzzified Aho-Corasick search automata. In *Proceedings of the Sixth International Conference on Information Assurance and Security (IAS)* (pp. 338-342). IAS.

Idika, N., & Mathur, A. P. (2007). *A survey of malware detection techniques*. Retrieved 16th of January, 2013 from http://www.serc.net/system/files/SERC-TR-286.pdf

Karp, R. M., & Rabin, M. O. (1987). *Efficient randomized pattern-matching algorithms*. Retrieved 14th of October, 2008 from http://www.research.ibm.com/journal/rd/312/ibmrd3102P.pdf

Kaspersky. (2012). Heuristic analysis in Kaspersky anti-virus 2012. *Kaspersky.com*. Retrieved 25th of September, 2012 from http://support.kaspersky.com/kav2012/tech?qid=208284682

Knuth, D., Morris, J. H., & Pratt, V. (1977). Fast pattern matching in strings. *SIAM Journal on Computing, 6*(2), 323–350. doi:10.1137/0206024.

Kumar, P. J. S., Knananna, M. R., Shine, H., & Arun, S. (2011). Implementing high performance lexical analyzer using CELL broadband engine processor. *International Journal of Engineering Science and Technology, 3*(9), 6907–6913.

Lee, T. H., & Huang, N. L. (2008). An efficient and scalable pattern matching scheme for network security applications. In *Proceedings of 17th International Conference on Computer Communications and Networks (ICCN)* (pp. 1-7). ICCN.

Lin, C. H., Chien, L. S., Liu, C. H., Chang, S. C., & Hon, W. K. (2012). *PFAC library: GPU-based string matching algorithm*. Paper presented at the GPU Technology Conference 2012. New York, NY.

Lin, P. C., Lin, Y. D., & Lai, Y. C. (2011). A hybrid algorithm of backward hashing and automaton tracking for virus scanning. *IEEE Transactions on Computers, 60*(4), 594–601. doi:10.1109/TC.2010.95.

Liu, S. T., Huang, H. C., & Chen, Y. M. (2011). A system call analysis method with MapReduce for malware detection. In *Proceedings of the IEEE 17th International Conference on Parallel and Distributed Systems (ICPADS)* (pp. 631-637). IEEE.

Maggi, F., Matteucci, M., & Zanero, S. (2010). Detecting intrusions through system call sequence and argument analysis. *IEEE Transactions on Dependable and Secure Computing, 7*(4), 381–395. doi:10.1109/TDSC.2008.69.

McMillan, R. (2012). Siemens: Stuxnet worm hit industrial systems. *ComputerWorld.com*. Retrieved 25th of September, 2012 from http://www.computerworld.com/s/article/print/9185419/Siemens_Stuxnet_worm_hit_industrial_systems?taxonomyName=Network+Security&taxonomyId=142

Miretskiy, Y., Das, A., Wright, C. P., & Zadok, E. (2004). AVFS: An on-access anti-virus file system. In *Proceedings of the 13th Conference on USENIX Security Symposium* (p. 6). Berkeley, CA: USENIX Association.

Mutz, D., Valeur, F., Vigna, G., & Kruegel, C. (2006). Anomalous system call detection. *Journal ACM Transactions on Information and System Security, 9*(1), 61–93. doi:10.1145/1127345.1127348.

Nordin, M., Rahman, A., Yazid, M., & Saman, M., Ahmad, Osman, A., & Tap, M. (2009). A filtering algorithm for efficient retrieving of DNA sequence. *International Journal of Computer Theory and Engineering, 1*(2), 102–109.

Norton, M. (2004). *Optimizing pattern matching for intrusion detection*. SourceFire Inc..

Pungila, C. (2009). A Bray-Curtis weighted automaton for detecting malicious code through system-call analysis. In *Proceedings of the 11th International Symposium on Symbolic and Numeric Algorithms for Scientific Computing (SYNASC)* (pp. 392-400). IEEE Xplore Digital Library.

Pungila, C. (2010). A model for energy-efficient household maintenance through behavioral analysis of electrical appliances. In *Proceedings of the 7th International Conference on e-Business Engineering (ICEBE)* (pp. 409-414). ICEBE.

Pungila, C. (2012a). Hybrid compression of the Aho-Corasick automaton for static analysis in intrusion detection systems. In *Proceedings of the International Joint Conference CISIS'12-ICEUTE'12-SOCO'12 Special Sessions* in *Advances in Intelligent Systems and Computing* (pp. 77-86). Springer-Verlag.

Pungila, C. (2012c). Improved file-carving through data-parallel pattern matching for data forensics. In *Proceedings of the 7th IEEE International Symposium on Applied Computational Intelligence and Informatics (SACI)* (pp. 197-202). IEEE.

Pungila, C., & Negru, V. (2012b). A highly-efficient memory-compression approach for GPU-accelerated virus signature matching. In *Proceedings of the 15th International Conference, ISC 2012* (LNCS), (pp. 354-369). Berlin: Springer-Verlag.

Rahman, M., Costas, S., & Laurent, M. (2007). Pattern matching in degenerate DNA/RNA sequences. In *Proceedings of the Workshop on Algorithms and Computation (WALCOM)* (pp. 109-120). WALCOM.

Shimpi, A. L. (2012). AMD outlines HSA roadmap: Unified memory for CPU/GPU in 2013, HSA GPUs in 2014. *AnandTech.com*. Retrieved 25th of September, 2012 from http://www.anandtech.com/show/5493/amd-outlines-hsa-roadmap-unified-memory-for-cpugpu-in-2013-hsa-gpus-in-2014

Sponchioni, R. (2011). *RMAS (run-time malware analysis system)*. Paper presented at the IT Security for the Next Generation International Students Conference, Kaspersky International Cup 2011. New York, NY.

Tuck, N., Sherwood, T., Calder, B., & Varghese, G. (2004). Deterministic memory-efficient string matching algorithms for intrusion detection. In *Proceedings of INFOCOM* (pp. 2628-2639). IEEE.

Tvrdik, P. (2012). *Parallel complexity theory: CS838: Topics in parallel computing, CS1221*. Retrieved 26th of September, 2012 from http://pages.cs.wisc.edu/~tvrdik/3/html/Section3.html

Vasiliadis, G., & Ioannidis, S. (2010). GrAVity: A massively parallel antivirus engine. In *Proceedings of the 13th International Conference on Recent Advances in Intrusion Detection (RAID)* (pp. 79-96). Berlin: Springer-Verlag.

Vasiliadis, G., Polychronakis, M., & Ioannidis, S. (2011). MIDeA: A multi-parallel intrusion detection architecture. In *Proceedings of the 18th ACM Conference on Computer and Communications Security (CCS)* (pp. 297-308). ACM.

Vinod, P., Laxmi, V., & Gaur, M. S. (2009). Survey on malware detection methods. In *Proceedings of the IIT Kanpur Hackers' Workshop 2009 (IITKHACK09)*. Retrieved 16th of January, 2013 from http://www.security.iitk.ac.in/contents/events/workshops/iitkhack09/papers/vinod.pdf

Watson, W. B. (1994). *The performance of single-keyword and multiple-keyword pattern matching algorithms*. Retrieved 27th of September, 2012 from http://alexandria.tue.nl/extra1/wskrap/publichtml/9411074.pdf

Watson, W. B. (1995). *Taxonomies and toolkits of regular language algorithms*. Eindhoven, The Netherlands: Eindhoven University of Technology, Department of Mathematics and Computer Science.

Wu, S., & Manber, U. (1994). *A fast algorithm for multi-pattern searching* (Technical Report TR-94-17). Phoenix, AZ: University of Arizona.

Zanero, S. (2004). Behavioral intrusion detection. In *Proceedings of the 19th International Symposium of Computer and Information Sciences (ISCIS)* (pp. 657-666). ISCIS.

Zaslawskiy, I., Abtisyan, A., & Gevorgyan, V. (2010). Implementation of dictionary lookup automata for UNL analysis. *International Journal Information Theories and Applications*, *17*(2), 141–150.

Zha, X. (2011). Multipattern string matching on a GPU. In *Proceedings of the IEEE Symposium on Computers and Communications (ISCC)* (pp. 277-282). IEEE.

Zha, X., & Sahni, S. (2010). Fast in-place file carving for digital forensics. In *Proceedings of the e-Forensics'10* (pp. 141-158). E-Forensics.

Zha, X., & Sahni, S. (2011). Fast in-place file carving for digital forensics. In *Proceedings of Forensics in Telecommunications, Information, and Multimedia* (pp. 141–158). Berlin: Springer-Verlag. doi:10.1007/978-3-642-23602-0_13.

ADDITIONAL READING

Alshawabkeh, M., Jang, B., & Kaeli, D. (2010). Accelerating the local outlier factor algorithm on a GPU for intrusion detection systems. In *Proceedings of the 3rd Workshop on General-Purpose Computation on Graphics Processing Units* (pp. 104-110). ACM.

Beaucamps, P., & Filiol, E. (2007). On the possibility of practically obfuscating programs towards a unified perspective of code protection. *Journal in Computer Virology*, *3*(1), 3–21. doi:10.1007/s11416-006-0029-6.

Bonfante, G., Kaczmarek, M., & Marion, J. Y. (2007). Control flow graphs as malware signatures. In *Proceedings of the International Workshop on the Theory of Computer Viruses*. Retrieved 27th of September, 2012 from http://hal.inria.fr/docs/00/17/62/35/PDF/tcv07b.pdf

Bonfante, G., Kaczmarek, M., & Marion, J. Y. (2009). Architecture of a morphological malware detector. *Journal in Computer Virology*, *5*(3), 263–270. doi:10.1007/s11416-008-0102-4.

Cheng, Y. W. (2010). Fast virus signature matching based on the high performance computing of GPU. In *Proceedings of the Second International Conference on Communication Software and Networks (ICCSN)* (p. 513). ICCSN.

Farmer, D., & Venema, W. (2005). *Forensic discovery: Malware analysis basics*. Retrieved 26th of September, 2012 from http://www.porcupine.org/forensics/forensic-discovery/chapter6.html

Huang, N. F., Wung, H. W., Lai, S. H., Chu, Y. M., & Tsai, W. Y. (2008). A GPU-based multiple-pattern matching algorithm for network intrusion detection systems. In *Proceedings of the 22nd International Conference on Advanced Information Networking and Applications - Workshops (AINAW)* (pp. 62-67). AINAW.

Jacob, N. (2006). Offloading IDS computation to the GPU. In *Proceedings of the 22nd Annual Computer Security Applications Conference (ACSAC'06)* (pp. 371-380). ACSAC.

Jamsed, M., Lee, J., Moon, S., Yun, I., & Kim, D. (2012). Kargus: A highly-scalable software-based intrusion detection system. In *Proceedings of the 19th ACM Conference on Computer and Communications Security (CCS '12)*. CCS.

Jana, S., & Shmatikov, V. (2012). Abusing file processing in malware detectors for fun and profit. In *Proceedings of the IEEE Symposium on Security and Privacy* (pp. 80-94). IEEE.

Konstantinou, E. (2008). *Metamorphic virus: Analysis and detection* (Technical Report RHUL-MA-2008-02). London, UK: University of London.

Lin, C. H., Tsai, S. Y., Liu, C. H., Chang, S. H., & Shyu, J. M. (2010). Accelerating string matching using multi-threaded algorithm on GPU. In *Proceedings of Global Telecommunications Conference (GLOBECOM 2010)* (pp. 1-5). ACM.

Lindorfer, M., Kolbitsch, C., & Comparetti, P. M. (2011). Detecting environment-sensitive malware. In *Proceedings of the 14th International Conference on Recent Advances in Intrusion Detection* (pp. 338-357). Berlin: Springer-Verlag.

Qian, Q., Che, H., Zhang, R., & Xin, M. (2010). The comparison of the relative entropy for intrusion detection on CPU and GPU. In *Proceedings of the 2010 IEEE/ACIS 9th International Conference on Computer and Information Science* (pp. 141-146). IEEE Computer Society.

Roundy, K. A., & Miller, B. P. (2010). Hybrid analysis and control of malware. In *Proceedings of the 13th International Conference on Recent Advances in Intrusion Detection* (pp. 317-338). Berlin: Springer-Verlag.

Schultz, M. G., Eskin, E., Zadok, E., & Stolfo, S. J. (2001). Data mining methods for detection of new malicious executables. In *Proceedings of the IEEE Symposium on Security and Privacy* (pp. 38). IEEE.

Srivastava, A., & Giffin, J. (2010). Automatic discovery of parasitic malware. In *Proceedings of the 13th International Conference on Recent Advances in Intrusion Detection* (pp. 97-117). Berlin: Springer-Verlag.

Szor, P. (2005). *The art of computer virus research and defense*. Reading, MA: Addison-Wesley Professional.

Tumeo, A., Villa, O., & Sciuto, D. (2010). Efficient pattern matching on GPUs for intrusion detection systems. In *Proceedings of the 7th ACM International Conference on Computing Frontiers* (p. 87). ACM.

Valgenti, V. C., Chhugani, J., Sun, Y., Satish, N., Kim, M. S., Kim, C., & Dubey, P. (2012). GPP-grep: High-speed regular expression processing engine on general purpose processors. In *Proceedings of the Research in Attacks, Intrusions and Defenses 15th International Symposium, RAID 2012*. RAID.

Vasiliadis, G., Antonatos, S., Polychronakis, M., Evangelos, P., & Ioannidis, S. (2008). Gnort: High performance network intrusion detection using graphics processors. In *Proceedings of the 11th International Symposium on Recent Advances in Intrusion Detection* (pp. 116-134). IEEE.

Vasiliadis, G., Antonatos, S., Polychronakis, M., Evangelos, P., & Ioannidis, S. (2009). Regular expression matching on graphics hardware for intrusion detection. In *Proceedings of Recent Advances in Intrusion Detection (LNCS)* (pp. 265–283). Berlin: Springer. doi:10.1007/978-3-642-04342-0_14.

Wu, C., Yin, J., Cai, Z., Zhu, E., & Cheng, J. (2009). An efficient pre-filtering mechanism for parallel intrusion detection based on many-core GPU. *Security Technology - Communications in Computer and Information Science, 58*, 298-305.

Zha, X., & Sahni, J. (2012). GPU-to-GPU and host-to-host multipattern string matching on a GPU. *IEEE Transactions on Computers*.

Zhang, X., Zhao, C., Wu, J., & Song, C. (2011). A GPU-RSVM based intrusion detection classifier. In *Proceedings of the Second International Conference, ICTMF* (pp. 92-100). ICTMF.

KEY TERMS AND DEFINITIONS

APU: Acronym for *Accelerated Processing Units*, referring to processing systems capable of performing additional computations by offloading the CPU and assigning through load-balancing the computations to other resources, such as a GPU.

CPU: Acronym for *Central Processing Unit*, representing the core of computers nowadays as a silicon-based microchip which can perform different logical, arithmetical and input/output operations through custom programming.

GPGPU: Abbreviation for *General Purpose computation on Graphics Processing Units*, refers to graphics cards which may be used to perform additional custom computations on top of the graphics processing abilities for which they were designed.

GPU: Acronym for *Graphics Processing Units*, a term referring to graphics cards inside a user's computer.

Malware: Also known as *malicious software*, a type of software designed with malicious intent.

Pattern: A sequence of characters forming a text of fixed length. The term is commonly used in *pattern matching* applications.

Virus: A self-replicating type of software that infects executable files, usually by modifying the entry point of the code and making its code execute first, only afterwards allowing the execution of the original program. To the end-user, an infection is almost never observable since the program runs in the same way, except that the virus had already executed its code even before the real program ran.

Section 4
Secure Platforms and Frameworks

Chapter 10
A Mobile-Based Attribute Aggregation Architecture for User-Centric Identity Management

Alexandre B. Augusto
University of Porto, Portugal

Manuel E. Correia
University of Porto, Portugal

ABSTRACT

The massive growth of the Internet and its services is currently being sustained by the mercantilization of users' identities and private data. Traditional services on the Web require the user to disclose many unnecessary sensitive identity attributes like bankcards, geographic position, or even personal health records in order to provide a service. In essence, the services are presented as free and constitute a means by which the user is mercantilized, often without realizing the real value of its data to the market. In this chapter the auhors describe OFELIA (Open Federated Environment for Leveraging of Identity and Authorization), a digital identity architecture designed from the ground up to be user centric. OFELIA is an identity/authorization versatile infrastructure that does not depend upon the massive aggregation of users' identity attributes to offer a highly versatile set of identity services but relies instead on having those attributes distributed among and protected by several otherwise unrelated Attribute Authorities. Only the end user, with his smartphone, knows how to aggregate these scattered Attribute Authorities' identity attributes back into some useful identifiable and authenticated entity identity that can then be used by Internet services in a secure and interoperable way.

DOI: 10.4018/978-1-4666-4514-1.ch010

1. INTRODUCTION

The explosive growth of the Internet is accelerating the migration of essential real world and monetary infrastructures to the virtual world, with digital identity playing a central catalyzing role for this societal transformative process. Arguably, the digital world is radically different from the real world, but there are some essential concepts that are readily transposed. Very much like in the physical world, in the Internet we have people interacting with other people and non-human computerised entities, under highly diverse situations. In the real world, people behave rather differently when they are at work, in the grocery store or at the gym, where they assume different roles in the face of different contextual situations. This essential social ability to contextually change the way we relate with others is what must be transposed from the physical world to the Internet every time we try to dematerialise societal real world processes to the virtual world.

A digital Identity can thus be readily defined has the "set of characteristics that uniquely describes a digital subject or entity and its relations with other entities or digital subjects in a virtual world." A digital subject, or entity, is therefore something, not necessarily human, that makes a request in order to access a particular resource (a Web page, an item from a database...) and is composed by a set of personal data attributes that in some sense characterizes that person or entity, usually referred to as a "user." The subset of personal data attributes needed for a specific role (or "user") depends on the situation and context at hand and is usually referred to as an identity persona (Baden, Bender, Spring, Bhattacharjee, & Starin, 2009). The association between an identity persona and a user is done by the means of an authentication process that can also be conducted by an Identity Management System (IdMS) (Hai-Binh & Bouzefrane, 2008).

Digital identity management systems, like their real world analogues, are essential in ensuring that a network infrastructure is capable to scale and meet the basic interoperable expectations and functionalities concerning security, privacy and reliability that emerge every time there is a need to plan and deploy a well engineered Internet service.

1.1. Digital Identity Management

Digital identity is maintained by identity Management Systems (IdMS). These are composed by governing organization policies, economic model, business processes and technologies that implement and manage the personal identity users attributes that are needed to establish and manage access rights to organizational digital assets (Chadwick, 2009). Moreover Identity management systems are also responsible for the digital identity lifecycle management within organizations, as they provide the flexible and scalable means by which it is possible to validate and exchange the digital personal data attributes that one needs in order to establish and promote interoperability among different systems, in accordance with some set of pre-established organizational security and legal policies. According to Kim Cameron, every useful IdMS should follow the seven "Laws of Identity" (Cameron, 2005) that can be observed on Table 1.

Identity management systems are employed by Identity Providers (IdP) (Clauß & Köhntopp, 2001) to manage digital identity within an organization, group of organizations or even the whole Internet. Depending on the scale, their interim structure and the social and/or financial benefits accrued by their deployment; IdPs can be further classified as:

- **Traditional (digital silo):** Where each service domain deploys its own IdP, thus forcing the user to create multiple independent accounts in order to access different services.
- **Centralized:** Bringing the concept of single sign-on (David, 2006), later extended with the usage of information cards (Cameron & Jones, 2007) in order to es-

Table 1. The seven "laws of identity"

"Law" Number:	Description:	Comments:
One	User consent	An identity is identified and used only when the user agrees to it.
Two	Limited disclosure	The system provides the minimum identifying information required for the transaction.
Three	Fewest parties	Only rely parties that need to know receive identifying information.
Four	Directional identity	Omni-directional versus unidirectional
Five	IdMS should work with a variety of identity technologies, run by multiple providers.	Designers cannot assume the feasibility of a universal identity or the availability of a single expression of an identity.
Six	Human integration	High levels of reliability between the human user and the system
Seven	Consistent experience across platforms	Similar to the way the Web appears to users.

tablish a way to dismiss the typical login/password scenario. In this model only one centralized IdP is needed to provides the necessary user credentials to grant authentication for different domains (OpenID (Sakimura, Bradley, Jones, Medeiros, & Jay, 2012)).

- **Federated:** Where there exists a pre-negotiated circle of trust between the participating administrative domains whose IdPs can then grant access to any one of the service domain that falls within the federation authority as a whole. Authentication within the federation is achieved by presenting a valid identifier emitted and authenticated by any IdP that falls in the circle of trust, creating an asymmetric trust relationships among the members of the federation (Orawiwattanakul, Yamaji, Nakamura, Kataoka, & Sonehara, 2010).
- **User-centric:** Its main objective is empowering users by returning the identity data control back to the user, the legitimate owner (Hai-Binh & Bouzefrane, 2008; Bhargav-Spantzel, Camenisch, Gross, & Sommer, 2007).

1.2. Identity Providers Evolution

The old traditional IdP silo model is still the most commonly deployed type of IdP currently in use on the Internet. It requires the user to manage a set of different credentials for different services, which leads to well known security issues (Hovav & Berger, 2009) and intractable interoperability problems. There is however one positive property that emerges from the widespread usage of silo based IdPs, which is the real and effective fragmentation of the user digital identity attributes among different unrelated Identity providers. This is positive from the users' privacy point of view, since under the silo model no single system can own a complete full set of the user's identity attributes. In other words, the users' personal data is naturally decentralized and this helps to protect and improve upon the users' privacy. However, the silo model in its current form does not scale in the Internet. Not only it makes it very difficult to build effective interoperability among otherwise unrelated systems but it also constitute an obstacle to the implementation of secure single-sign-on (David, 2006) mechanisms in a standardized way.

More recently the interest on housing more comprehensive sets of users identity attributes under the same roof, has been increasing dramatically due to the discovery of their highly strategic and commercial value for the Internet market (Schwartz, 2004). Massive centralized identity providers have started to flourish on the Internet. Companies like Google, Facebook and even Microsoft, are currently under a fierce competition over the hearts and minds of users for their personal data. One of their main strategic purposes is to create enormous monopolized centralized databases of their users identity attributes, as they allow them to produce highly accurate user profiles that they can then monetize very efficiently for marketing and further lock-in purposes (Schwartz, 2004). These global companies harvest and aggregate personal data in such a massive scale that, lest it is put under some kind of restrain, it will very soon represent a major global threat to personal security and privacy the like of which the world has never seen.

This competition over digital identity led to the emergence of new standardized identity management protocols like OpenID (Sakimura et al., 2012), for interoperable users authentication and identity management and OAuth (Hammer-Lahav., 2012), for authorization management. These protocols opened the way for new network infrastructures that help cater the need Web applications have for data interoperability. These protocols provide the necessary means for centralized identity providers to operate in standardised and interoperable ways and are employed as standard mechanisms upon which it becomes feasible to build interoperable single sign-on systems and attribute sharing based on the concept of valet keys in an effective way. More recently a new open standard, OpenID Connect (Sakimura et al., 2012), has emerged as a single solution for combining both authentication and authorization within a single standardised infrastructure protocol.

In the middle of this dispute lies the user, most of the time unaware that it is his valuable identity and privacy that is paying for the set of otherwise "free" essential Internet services (Facebook, Google, etc.) that he is using on a daily basis, most of the time without his explicit consent or control (Mont, Pearson, & Bramhall, 2003). The user is rarely provided with the opportunity and means to negotiate the real value of something as intrinsically vital as his identity. However, this privacy abuse is not the only problem that results from unrestrained data aggregation. If a massive centralized identity provider suffers an attack, millions of highly detailed personal attributes can be immediately compromised with highly severe consequences for the users. All these issues constitute the main motivation behind our proposal for a real time fully distributed mobile based user-centric aggregation IdMS for authentication and authorization.

1.3. User Centric as a Solution for User Privacy

More recently, the general tendency has been to concentrate development efforts on identity management models. These are being structured around user-centric concepts, totally in concert with a more interventive and democratic digital society ever more focused on empowering individuals with tools for a more reliable, responsible and secure user-centric management of private digital data. Recent incidents related with the unauthorized disclosure of sensitive information also show how important it is for users to be able to exercise some control on how much about them is publicly known and disseminated on the Internet. It is therefore crucial to promote the development of standardised interoperable systems that enable the user-centric management of private information and help secure the users basic right for privacy.

There are also some types of sensitive personal data that by their very nature can be subjected to change and thus become stale, sometimes very quickly. With a centralized and "distant" identity provider, it can therefore become quite difficult to manage the degree of staleness for highly dynamic personal data like GPS, heart beating, etc. For these reasons, we believe that all users' private information should be kept as much as close as possible to their owners' primary source, under the user´s direct control. For example if the data is the user´s current GPS position, this data should not be shared with a third party node like the *Fire Eagle* (Inc, 2007) in order to deploy the information to a relying party (a service that consumes the users' identity in order to obtain a set of users' identity attributes). In order words, the relying party should be able to directly request the GPS coordinate from the users original data source (in this case his GPS device) and not the last time that this individual or application remembered to update its value from an otherwise stale source of information (in this case, a positioning identity attribute stored in a traditional IdPs). Highly dynamic personal data should therefore be securely disclosed on demand by the owner's original data source directly to the requester relying party at the users discretion.

Access to the owners data primary source is managed by the user by engaging the help of a personal Authoritative Authority (AA) (Paci, Shang, Fernando, & Bertino, 2009). These AAs are entities in the network that disclose personal data to other relying applications at the users discretion after their explicit consent, which must be informed in the sense that it must be based on a reliable trusted identity for the original requester at the relying party. These authorization consents should also be limited in time and be easily revoked. These constitute basic essential assumptions for a well-designed user-centric attribute aggregating identity management system.

1.4. Attribute Aggregation Model to Decentralize Data

As previously discussed, silo identity management models suffer from serious security issues common to all centralized systems. If the identity attribute storage model is fully centralized it could potentially become a victim of targeted attacks that could compromise the entire user's digital identity. It is therefore an intrinsic design directive for our aggregation model to have the user's digital identity split and distributed between different data primary sources. There are many user centric attribute aggregation models to choose from. The most relevant in the literature are:

- **Identity Relay (Inman & Chadwick, 2010):** The Relying Party (RP) trusts a single master federated IdP, that is responsible to request and relay all attributes to the RP, who is then responsible for their aggregation.
- **RP Mediated Attribute Aggregation (Sakimura et al., 2012):** The RP redirects the user-agent to each IdP thus obliging the users to a high level of interaction and making the user-agent responsible for attribute aggregation.
- **Client Mediated Assertion (Inman & Chadwick, 2010):** Based on an intelligent user agent that guide the user to the different IdPs, obliging the users a high level of interaction, the user agent is responsible for the attribute aggregation and the delivery to the Relying Party.
- **Identity Federation Model (David, 2006):** After user authentication, a secret is generated and shared between all federated IdPs by the user-agent thus allowing the RP to request the needed attributes from all the federated IdPs.
- **Identity Proxying/Chaining (Gemmill, Robinson, Scavo, & Bangalore, 2009):** The RP fully trusts in a single master federated IdP that is responsible to request and aggregate all requested attributes.
- **Linking Service (Chadwick & Inman, 2009):** In this model only the user knows about all his IdPs, a service called linking service is responsible to hold minimal information that allows RPs to obtain their

queries from the other IdPs via the linking service. After user authentication, the IdP offers the possibility of attribute aggregation and if the user accepts it, the information to access the linking service is shared with the RP. The aggregation of attributes can be done by the linking service itself or at the RP.

Our proposal, OFELIA, is based on a user identity attribute aggregation infrastructure that falls within the "Linking service" category (Augusto & Correia, 2012). In OFELIA attribute aggregation is realised by the means of a secure mobile authentication and authorization broker, running on smartphones, where users exercise discretionary asynchronous control over access requests to their personal identity attributes. These are distributed and located among several different attribute storage network nodes that have been previously established as Authorization Authorities (AA). The smartphone thus provides the user with the means to also exercise aggregated management control of his AAs, by conditionally making them accessible to Web applications (Relying parties) on behalf of its authorised trusted users and during a predetermined, but revocable, well-defined period of time.

The adoption of smartphones as a user-centric management platform is highly appropriate because these devices are nowadays ubiquitous, have more than adequate processing power, provide Internet connectivity and follows his owner everywhere, thus providing a practical solution for the users Internet reachability challenge (Barkhuus & Polichar, 2011). The use of smartphones for identity management is currently also recognized as essential for enhancing security and privacy (Adi, Al-Qayedi, Zarooni, & Mabrouk, 2004; Paci et al., 2009; Zhikui, 2007) and has been proved to play a crucial role on the more flexible user-centric models (Augusto & Correia, 2013).

1.5. The OFELIA Proposal

Our overall goal is to define and specify a fully decentralized privacy and user-centric infrastructure for identity management based on the distributed aggregation of users private data and protected by a set of personal AAs. In OFELIA, the user personal smartphone acts as the Linking Service where the user directly manages attribute aggregation and access authorization.

We also intend to deploy the user smartphone as a secure authorization broker where attribute aggregation is achieved by securely enrolling the users AAs and their respective managed identity attributes into the users smartphone. To implement and deploy OFELIA we relied on already proven and standardised protocols/infrastructures like:

- **Extensible Messaging and Presence Protocol (XMPP) and Restful Web services:** To authenticate, validate and establish the communication between the intervening network nodes.
- **OpenID:** Employed as an authenticator and provider of the necessary bootstrapping information about the user.
- **Quick Response Code:** To quickly exchange digital information with the smartphones in order to simplify user experience.
- **Valet Key Based Protocols:** To create the necessary means for managing and conveying conditional, but revocable access authorizations to Relying Parties.
- **Public Key Infrastructure:** To manage trust among the different participating network nodes.
- **MicroSD Mobile Security Cards:** A smartphone mobile smartcard to better secure the linking service privately held keys and provide second level token based authentication capabilities to the Identity Attribute Aggregation service.

We are currently actively engaged in developing and deploying the following four different components: (1) one application programming interface (API), to allow for a faster and simpler deployment of third party Relying Parties and Service providers into OFELIA; (2) other API for the enrollment of third party Attribute Authorities, thus helping to diversify the universe of available identity attributes; (3) an implementation for an Identity Broker (Augusto & Correia, 2012), another component of our linking service aggregation model; (4) and an android application, implementing the secure mobile authorization broker to enroll and aggregate AAs and authorize, manage and revoke access to users identity attributes that are being managed and secured by the enrolled AAs.

The rest of this chapter is organised as follows. In section 2, we review the proposed architecture, describing each technology and their functionality in the architecture components that are described as well. In section 3 we describe in detail our protocol responsible to establish the connection between the architecture components and describe a usage case scenario, which can be quite useful to help to better understand the different components interaction. In section 4 we described what has already been accomplished and present some preliminary conclusions for the work we have already developed thus far within our project OFELIA (Open Federated Environments Leveraging Identity and Authorization). We finalize with a brief outline of our future development and discuss some implementation notes about libraries and software that we have used during the course of the implementation of OFELIA.

2. ARCHITECTURE

In this section, we describe in detail the main technological components we have employed in OFELIA. We also discuss the main aspects behind some of the alternatives and compromises we had to make to integrate our vision with already existing real world services and devices (ex: Google XMPP infrastructure, Android devices, etc.). We also take some time to describe the conceptual data model for attribute aggregation and its most relevant aspects like the protocols and services we have employed to integrate the different components that compose the proposed architecture. Figure 1 shows the main relationships between the principal components and the type of communications and the data exchanges that can occur between them in a simplified way. In what follows we provide a more detailed description of the functional role played by each one of these parts.

2.1. The Relying Party/Service Provider (RP/SP)

The RP/SP is a Web application that requires user's identity attributes that are being held by the user AAs aggregation. We plan to develop and implement RP/SP software library components to allow for a much more simple integration of current existing Web application into our proposed infrastructure.

The software library components must provide functionalities for X509/PGP certificate management, support OpenID Connect authentication and be capable of asynchronously, discover, request, access and store users identity attributes and securely manage authorization tokens. These are issued by the user's smartphone, at the user's discretion, whenever a RP/SP asks authorization to access a set of users identity attributes. They contain, among other elements, validity semantic assertions determined by the user that must hold true when the requesting RP/SP presents it to an AA as proof of access entitlement. These tokens are digitally signed by the user at the smartphone to guarantee their integrity and authenticity. An RP/SP must also be capable of secure crypto session

Figure 1. OFELIA architecture

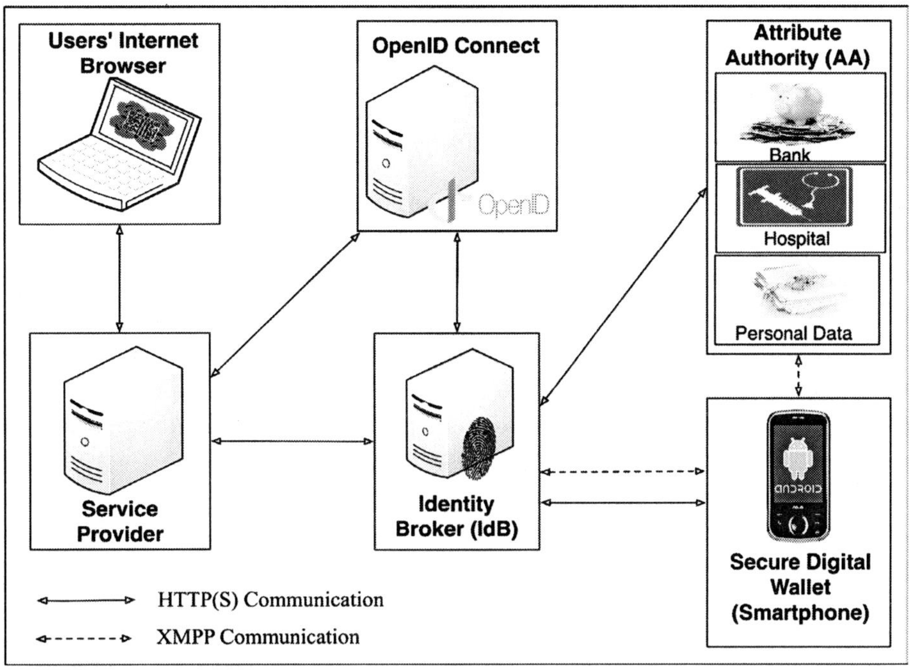

keys negotiation with the users AAs by using the IdB as a relay. It must also provide encryption/decryption functionalities for sensitive identity attributes and be capable of parsing and analysing AAs identity assertions according to digital identity XML semantic specifications. The RP/SP should also provide safe caching of authorization tokens while their validity assertions holds true.

2.2. Attribute Authorities

The Attribute Authorities (AAs) are independent network entities responsible for the security and management of personal data. The user smartphone needs to be enrolled into each one of the AAs in order to establish the data aggregation. In order to determine which personal attributes are being held at the AA, the user smartphone is provided with a XML semantic description of the identity attributes that are being held at each enrolled AA. The smartphone then merges the description of the AA identity resources into the user's personal data aggregation and announces to the IdB that it is the custodian aggregator for that data and is now ready to act as a personal authorization broker and issue authorization tokens at the users discretion.

The participating AAs must also be provided with appropriate security mechanisms for authentication and authorization to ensure the appropriate level of access control necessary to protect these assets from unauthorized access and provide the RP/SP with the means to search for identity attributes and negotiate with the IdBs and user smartphone the authorization tokens needed to be able to access the resources being held by the users aggregation.

This type of framework allows for a simple and scalable integration of an already existing infrastructure of personal data repositories as AAs. For authentication reasons, each participating AA must be provided with a public key pair whose authenticity must be attested by a valid PKI X509 or PGP certificate containing the AA's identity.

Each AA must also store a list of the emitted authorization tokens whose validity assertions still hold true but have been for some reason revoked by the user.

2.3. The Identity Broker

The Identity Broker (IdB) exists to cater for privacy-enhanced contexts where the RP/SP cannot be fully trusted and to prevent the more popular AAs to directly track users while they navigate through Web applications that use as part of their digital identity and personal data infrastructure. Moreover, for privacy and security reasons the IdB must also not know the content of the personal data it is relaying. This is accomplished by having the RP/SP and AA to negotiate session keys and then encrypt all personal data that is being relayed by the IdB.

The proposed architecture aims for a trust balance where the RP/SP does not have to know about the aggregation of AAs and the IdB does not need to know about the nature and value of the personal attributes being requested by the RP/SP. For authentication purposes and to prevent men in the middle attacks it is mandatory for the IdB to be in the possession of a public key pair whose legitimacy can be attested by a valid PKI X509/PGP certificate with the IdB identity.

2.4. The Smart-Phone as an Authorization Broker

In OFELIA, we are employing android smart phones as highly decentralized personal access authorization management devices for identity management, empowering the user by allowing the creation of customized access control policies that the user finds most adequate for his personal data. This means that the user is no longer obliged to comply with the abusive identity management policies, normally in place at major sites where the user have to share or give full control of his data to network entities he does not fully know or does not fully trust, as happens with the majority of current Internet applications. OFELIA also brings some advantages in security due to the full "hidden" decentralization it imposes on the storage of identity attributes.

This application is the critical component of the user digital identity access and should thus be always reachable over the Internet. Unfortunately, this is not always possible. Network aware smartphone applications are highly demanding in terms of phone battery and network signal usage and therefore cannot be always left running. In order to circumvent this problem the identity broker can be configured by the user to send a SMS message requesting the smartphone to reconnect. This is archived by the SMS handler service installed on the smartphone in the same time the application is installed. When the SMS handler receives a reconnect SMS message, it launches our application thus reconnecting the smartphone. After a certain period of inactivity our application terminates itself to save on phone battery.

All mechanisms related to authorization token creation, token revocation, attribute access authorization, and the enrollment into attribute authorities and the identity broker are conducted by the user interacting with smartphone application. More details about tokens authorization and attribute authorities and identity broker enrollment process are discussed in section 3.

2.5. XML Schema

In order to create the right semantics for interoperability, between different nodes with different implementations, it is essential to have an efficient and highly expressive semantic model for digital identity. This process is highly complex and still requires more comprehensive research from the community as a whole to reach a state where it becomes more practical to automatically reason with identity attributes (Cao & Yang, 2011).

Despite the importance in establishing efficient semantic models for digital identity, this chapter focus is on identity attribute aggregation, so the more complex process involved with digital identity semantics will be addressed as future work. Meanwhile we have designed a more simplified digital identity data representation, based on a XML Schema, which we employ throughout our implementation to keep and promote interoperability for data exchange within OFELIA. The Figure 2 shows the designed XML Schema skeletal structure that consists in a root element named *OfeliaDataExchange* and it is composed by three main elements: *Header*, *User* and *Data*.

The *Header* element has two attributes: the *State* used to describe the current operation and the *Type* to define the actual stage of the operation. The *State* operations are classified as: (1) *DATALIST* used to exchange the list of existing attributes between the smartphone and the identity broker; (2) *TOKENS* to handle the process of authorization token request; and (3) *DATA* used to process the data request when data access was previously conceived. The *Type* is defined in 3 stages: REQ, ASW and ERR that represent respectively request, answer and error.

The *User* element is composed by three attributes and one element. The attributes are: the *JabberID* to hold the requester XMPP contact; the *OpenID* to hold the requester OpenID address and the *PubKey* to hold requester public key. The element is named *Tokens* and is composed by three attributes: the *AuthToken* that is responsible to hold the authorization token; the *Secret* that acts as a *nonce* (Badra, Guillet, & Serrhrouchni, 2009); and the *ExpireDate* as its own name suggests holds the token expire date.

The *Data* element is composed by optional elements. Currently we have a *gps* element defined with the following attributes: *Latitude*, *Longitude,* and *timestamp*. We are currently defining several other elements to describe other dynamic attributes like heart beat, blood pressure and among others that could prove to be useful for remote monitoring Web applications. The *Data* element can thus contain highly diverse types of

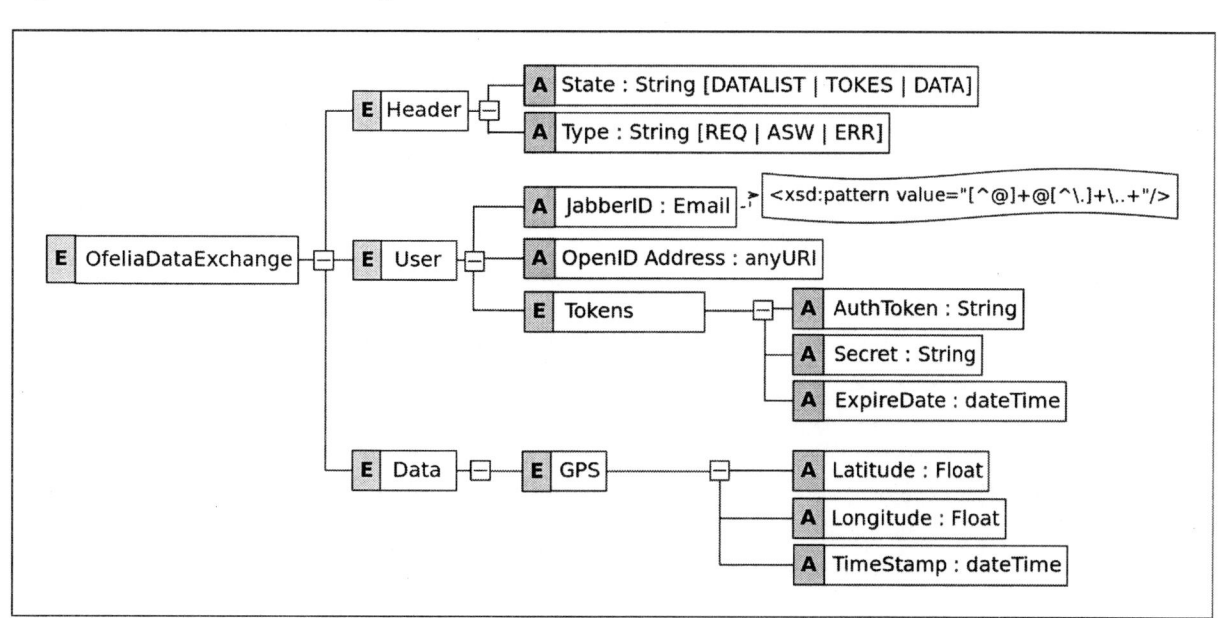

Figure 2. OFELIA data exchange schema

formalised dynamic data types, to cover a highly diverse range of application areas. In other words, we can provide for all kind of personal dynamic attributes so long as its data type is formalised in the *OfeliaDataExchange* XML Schema. It is also mandatory that all *Data* elements have a valid timestamp attribute, not only to be able to maintain an historic value for its values but also to prevent the resending of the same value during different data exchanges.

2.6. XMPP: Extensible Messaging and Presence Protocol

XMPP is an open technology for real-time communication that uses the eXtensible Markup Language (XML) as a base format for exchanging information formatted as XML documents. These documents are sent from one entity to another (Saint-Andre, Smith, & Tronon, 2009) by using an appropriate application level transport protocol according to network availability. XMPP servers provide a very flexible set of standard services that can be used by many different types of applications like network games, chat system, etc.

Arguably, in the mobile world, there is some difficulty in directly addressing and communicating with Internet enabled mobile devices. In the mobile world an implicit direct communication with the device is almost impossible due to the shortage of public IPs addresses faced by Internet service providers and mobile operators. In the future, IPv6 is supposed to solve this problem however it is our strong belief that the mobile Telecommunications operators will still not allow this kind of direct communication to mobile phones due to their very inflexible business plans, where the mobile phone is nowadays mostly regarded simply as a consumer device and never as a provider of services. In fact Telecommunications operators restrict even the ports available to initiate communications and the most restrictive only allow direct communication with the Internet over port 80 (HTTP port).

A neutral rendezvous point on the Internet where our architecture nodes can meet to exchange messages is thus obviously necessary. Towards this end, a XMPP messaging infrastructure proves to be an almost ideal communication asset for our needs because of its core services, namely:

1. Almost real time messaging. Essential to maintain accurate and updated the dynamic data types that are being maintained and exchange between the Identity Broker, the Authorization Authorities and the Authorization Broker (smartphone).
2. Authentication by digital certificates. Guarantees a high level of trust and non-repudiation between architecture nodes and users.
3. Ability to efficiently operate over HTTP by the means of the BOSH (Bidirectional-streams Over Synchronous HTTP) protocol (Paterson & Saint-Andre, 2007), where two non directly addressable devices located on private closed intranets, with minimal Internet access, can locate each other over the Internet and then directly exchange messages in a reliable and safe way.
4. Its capacity to store and forward messages in case any of the nodes becomes offline. This proved to be a very strong and convenient asset to have for asynchronous communications with mobile devices. It is important to have in mind that cellular phones are often located in areas with bad data coverage, which results in severe communication problems that have to be dealt in an asynchronous manner.
5. Its scalability, to avoid bottleneck problems and the fact that it is a mature, fully supported and approved Internet standard that is widely deployed and is currently a very important part of the communication operations and infrastructure of large distinct companies like: Google, Facebook, Blizzard, Steam, among others.

2.7. OpenID

The OpenID provides a decentralized protocol for user authentication. It is deployed as part of Identity Managers that allows a user to sign into distinct domains with a single OpenID account (single sign on) and at the same time let the user control what of his identity attributes will be disclosed in order to identify and authenticate himself into the domain that is acting as an OpenID consumer.

In order for a user to authenticate into a domain with OpenID, he needs to be redirected to his OpenID provider where he is asked to authenticate (usually via a login/password method) and then authorise the identity attribute exchange requested by the domain. If this proves to be successful, the user is then redirected to the originating requesting domain and granted access. In order to standardise and define appropriate semantics for a minimum useful set of user attributes that could be universally recognised by all RPs, the full set of standardised and widely recognised identity attributes for OpenID is unfortunately substantially small. This decreases the usefulness of the protocol and has so far limited its deployment almost exclusively to the authentication domain.

Recently the OpenID foundation started to work in a new protocol named OpenID Connect that aims to unify authentication and authorization in a single service protocol. This unification will create the right means for data access authorization and it will prove to be a firm step towards solving the issues resulting from a too limited set of widely recognized identity attributes.

In OFELIA we employ OpenID as an authenticator and as the provider of the bootstrapping information required by the Relying Party to enroll into the Identity Broker. The users essential information that is needed for bootstrapping consists in two key identity attributes, the Identity Broker Internet domain address and the user's public key.

2.8. Quick Response Code

A Quick Response code (QR code) is a two-dimensional square shape that encodes a reasonable amount of digital information into a small amount of 2D space. The encoding is achieved with the careful positioning of varying size black and white smaller squares within the 2D space defined by the QR square. These 2D codes are normally displayed within Web pages or printed in paper posters and are employed to quickly exchange digital information with mobile devices that would otherwise had to be entered by hand. This is accomplished by having the mobile device to digitally scan and decode the displayed QR code with its built-in optical camera (Hsiang-Cheh, Feng-Cheng, & Wai-Chi, 2011).

In our architecture, QR codes are displayed at computers displays to expedite in a secure way the enrollment process of smartphones into the Identity Broker and Attribute Authorities. QR codes are a very convenient way of conveying a reasonably amount of secret shared information to a smartphone that would otherwise be extremely cumbersome to input by hand by the user.

The usage of QR codes to share secret information can, in a way, be seen as the establishment of a rather new secure communication channel that takes advantage of the analog security properties of the optical channel that is employed during the scanning of the QR codes by the smartphone. In practice QR codes are used to simplify and make practical the enrollment process between our authorization broker (smartphone) and the other nodes of the OFELIA infrastructure.

2.9. Valet Key-Based Protocol

Nowadays many common authorization protocols like *Kerberos* and *OAuth* are based on a valet key concept. They all employ a token as a secure digital object that a pre-authorized entity needs to present in order to have direct access to some restricted resource. In other words, these tokens look like a valet key for data access in the sense that any entity that possesses the key has temporary and restricted access to the protected resource. One of the most common scenarios is a token based authorization scheme involving three distinct actors: The data owner (User), a third party application (Relying Party) and the user data storage (Attribute Authority). In this scenario a user wants to provide a relying party with an authorisation to access his data that resides on a certain attribute authority. To achieve this, the relying party redirects the user to the attribute authority with a formalised request where the user is asked to authorise it, this request includes the data that the relying party desires to obtain and for how long time he wants to access it. After authorisation, the attribute authority returns to the relying party a signed authorisation token that allow the relying party to access the requested data by presenting the signed authorisation token while it remains valid. These tokens can be revoked at anytime by the user that owns or manages the data.

For security reasons, the authorisation token must be very hard to falsify. In OFELIA it takes the form of a base64 encoded XML excerpt, containing elements for a large pseudo-random number (Eastlake & Schiller, 2005) and a simple semantic statement element, describing the authorization validity restrictions that apply to this particular authorization. This statement can express for example temporal restrictions. In order to ensure a right level of authentication and non-repudiation, this XML excerpt is always digitally signed by the user's smartphone private key. The resulting XML document is then encoded into a base64 string, which then constitutes a well formed OFELIA token.

These valet key tokens provide a very flexible security mechanism for the Attribute Authority to more easily manage access control to restricted resources. At the same time these tokens provide the Relying Parties with the means to access otherwise restricted resources without the need to obtain, share and manage other types of credentials like login/passwords. In OFELIA these authorisation tokens are issued by the authority broker (user's smartphone) and are only shared with the Identity Broker and the Attribute Authority, in order to provide for data access. It is also important to clarify that in our model the user maintains the revocation rights by being able to unconditionally revoke these tokens, at any given moment, by the means of his personal smartphone that acts as an Authority Broker.

2.10. Public Key Infrastructure

One of the key critical components of our proposed architecture is the management of trust among the participating components. To establish the necessary level of trust we rely on a Public Key Infrastructure (PKI) that is responsible for the management of the certificates that are at the core of the privacy, trust, non-repudiation and authentication infrastructure mechanisms that we need to put in place to secure our architecture.

To establish a stronger and therefore more trustworthy identity/authentication between the different actors, namely: the relying party (data requester), the attribute authority (data storage), the identity broker (identity manager), and the authorization broker (user's smartphone), we rely on the deployment of a well managed standard compliant PKI that can also sign PGP (Pretty Good Privacy) and X509 certificates. These certificates are then used as securely vouched identity credentials that are employed to establish highly secure communication channels, with a reasonable degree of non-repudiation properties and trust between the different actors involved in the communication.

2.11. MicroSD Mobile Security Card

Due to its potential economical factor (Barkhuus & Polichar, 2011), the hunger for mobile devices that can act as an authentication/authorization node are daily increasing. Mobile operators like

Orange started to explore the usage of smartphone as authorization brokers. Despite the fact that mobile operator have the best profile to provide a service like that since they already have a whole system prepared for this means, this service will require an extra fee for their customers. In order to not rely on single mobile operators and flee from the extras fees an alternative path is the usage of smartcards on the smartphones.

A smartcard is a pocket-sized device with an embedded microprocessor that can provide secure: identification, authentication, data storage and application processing. The chip of the microprocessor guarantees tamper-resistance (Maia & Correia, 2012) and its protocol interface assure the security over its data access by being logically impossible to extract information without the appropriate keys. The protocol interface set a strict control over what can be directly accessed from the smartcard (even with the appropriate pin) making almost impossible to clone it.

Nowadays almost all smartphones accept the microSD card in order to expand its storage capacity. This card provides an interesting technical standard known as SmartSD, which provides the necessary crypto components and device physical non-tampering for our architecture. This process is archived by adding a smartcard component besides the flash component inside the SD card.

The mobile security card is a microSD card that explores the SmartSD standard by embedding a smartcard chip with JavaCard OS. This card has a special place in our architecture since its responsible for guaranteeing a strong user authentication and trustworthy protection of data. Otherwise, we would to rely on a regular file based keystore, turning the smartphone in a desirable target of attacks where the keystore file would be easily compromised. So it is reasonable to put the file based keystore level of security in tandem with the security provided by a much simpler login/password based scheme. In fact an attack on a password protected keystore involves a password guessing attack completely analogous in terms of complexity to what happens with an attack directed towards a login/password scheme, the only thing really different in this case being the need to possess a copy of the keystore file in order to proceed with the attack.

3. ENROLLMENT PROCESSES AND USAGE CASE SCENARIO

In OFELIA the smartphone plays a key role by acting as the user personal authorization broker. The user starts by enrolling his smartphone into each one of the aggregations participating Attribute Authorities that manage the user's personal data. This process allows the mobile device to create an aggregated list of all possible identity data attributes available for that particular user. This list remains solely within the local province of each user personal mobile device and is not disclosed to the network. This helps prevents the massive aggregation of personal data by the Internet operators and gives back to the user some degree of control over his identity attributes.

The smartphone must also be enrolled into an Identity Broker so that the user can then announce and manage the list of attributes names and respective types that can then be made available to the requesting Relying Parties (RP). The authorization tokens needed to access the attributes that are being maintained within the AAs are issued by the user's smartphone at the user's discretion, after an access request is made by some RP. The creation of the available attributes list is dynamic and must thus be updated each time the smartphone is enrolled or unrolled from an AA, thus increasing or decreasing the number of attributes announced by the identity broker for relying parties, all this under the strict control of the user. In this section, we provide a detailed explanation of the different kind of enrollments in a step-by-step fashion, in order to allow for a better and more comprehensive understanding of the main features provided by the OFELIA architecture.

3.1. Attribute Authority Enrollment

In order to start managing access to his identity attributes, the user first needs to enroll his smartphone with each one of the participating AAs. This process can be done at any time, and should be as effortless and automatic as possible, giving more freedom to the user to painless add or remove AAs as he so wishes. All participating AAs must therefore be OFELIA ready, in other words they must use the AA OFELIA framework and API (mentioned in subsection 2) to properly engage with the other infrastructure participants.

OFELIA provides AAs with an easy and secure method to help the user link his smartphone to the AAs accounts that make up the user's attribute aggregation. This is achieved with the help of a specially built AA enrolling Web page, where the set of parameters that must be provided to the smartphone to instantiate the linkage with the AA is codified into a specially built QR-code that is displayed on the computer screen as part of the user's AA Web session. This QR-code is then conveyed to the smartphone by the means of its digital camera. It provides all the necessary URL locations, the AA X509 certificate and the access token the smartphone needs to instantiate the linkage with the AA in a secure way. To enroll the smartphone with a particular AA the user only has to start an authenticated Web session with the particular AA and then use his smartphone to scan the Web session QR-code that is displayed for the enrollment process with the OFELIA application that has already been previously installed in the users personal device. Figure 3 exemplifies the AA enrolment process providing a more technically detailed description of the whole process.

1. User requests authorization by sending the necessary credential using a Web browser.
2. The Attribute Authority grants access if the user credentials are valid.
3. The user request a full access token in order to establish a data access link for the smartphone.
4. The Attribute Authority answers with a data access token and the AA access Web services addresses encrypted with the user's public key, all compiled and encoded as a QR code.
5. The user uses the OFELIA application in his smartphone to scan the QR-code from the computer screen. The OFELIA App will then automatically proceed and finalize the enrolment process without the need of any further help from the user.

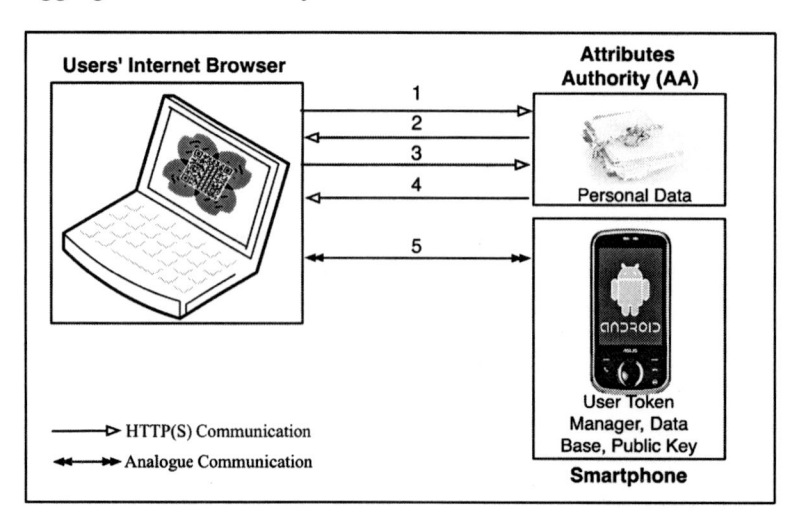

Figure 3. Attribute aggregation enrollment flow

3.2. Identity Broker Enrollment

In order to establish a communication channel between the relying parties and the user attributes stored in the AAs, the user must also have his smartphone enrolled with an OFELIA identity broker.

This enrollment process between the user's smartphone and the identity broker is very similar to the enrollment process described for the AAs. But first the user must use an Internet browser to logins/authenticate into the IdB with OpenID Connect account, which provides the IdB with the XMPP identity (jabber address) and the public key of the user's smartphone. The user is then presented with a QR-code at the computer screen that can then be scanned by its smartphone using the OFELIA App. This QR-code contains all the information the smartphone needs to automatically enroll into the IdB. The IdB also provides the user with a Web interface where he can list the history of all the RP/SP attribute requests interactions that have been performed by other third parties. This enrollment process is demonstrated on Figure 4.

After completing the IdB enrollment process, the user is then free to interact with the mobile OFELIA application to decide upon and determine the restrictions that should be associated with each access requests being made by third party RP/SP Web applications. The user can also use the OFELIA App to revoke previously issued and still valid authorizations tokens.

1. The user authenticates at IdB via Openid Connect account and allows the IdB to request the user XMPP address and its public key.
2. The Openid Connect answers to the IdB with the requested data.
3. The IdB sends back to the user computer screen an image of a QR-code of a temporary random link to the IdB session enrollment required data: X509 Certificate, users identification and IdB addresses (XMPP and Web addresses) For security reasons this link can only be used once and his discarded by the IdB immediately after use.

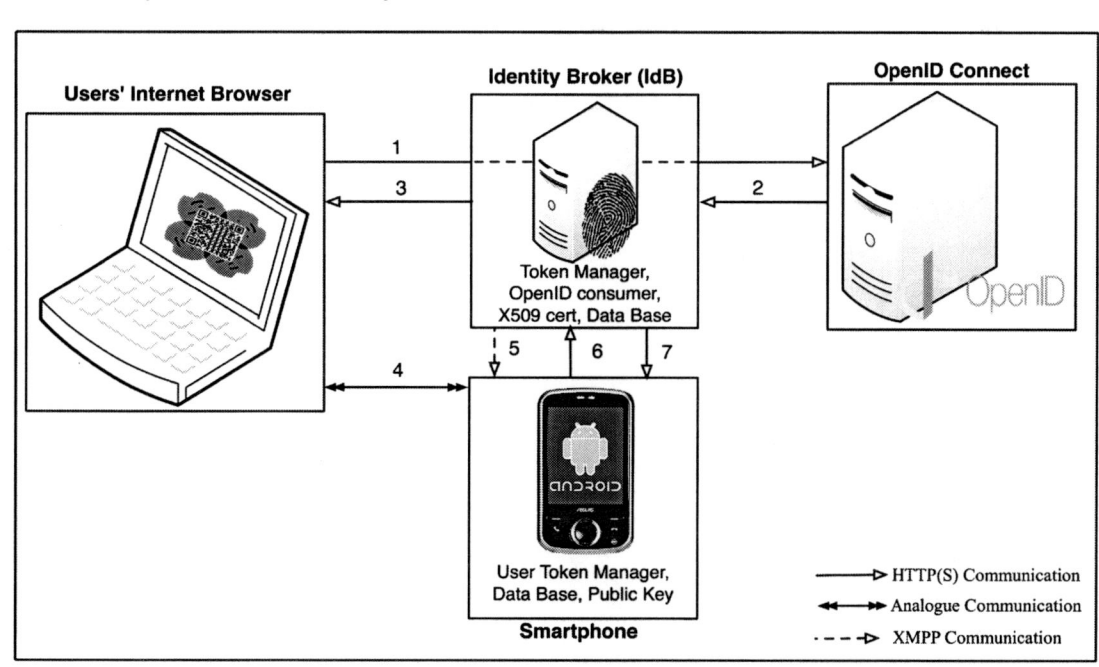

Figure 4. Identity broker enrollment flow

4. The OFELIA App scans the QR-code, obtains the link, and uses it to retrieve the enrollment data directly from the Internet.
5. The IdB sends to the smartphone an XMPP signed challenge, encrypted with the smartphone public key that has been previously obtained by OpenID Connect.
6. The OFELIA App on the smartphone answers the IdB challenge by sending an XMPP reply containing the list of all the attribute names and respective types that are being aggregated by the users smartphone.
7. The IdB confirms the registration to the user's smartphone and this concludes the mobile phone IdB enrollment process.

3.3. Relying Service Enrollment

Every time the user decides to register a new RP, another enrollment process is triggered in order to allow for the OFELIA requests and data exchange to take place. This process is a bit longer than the other enrollments since we have the participation all OFELIA components.

The user employs an Internet browser to logins/authenticates into the RP with its OpenID Connect account, which provides the IdB address as part of one of the user's identity attributes and allows the RP to enroll with IdB as a user's authorized RP application that can ask for the values of a subset of identity attributes approved for that particular RP. After enrollment the RP can then request to the IdB a list of personal attributes. This is done via a XMPP message from the RP to the IdB requesting the list of the available user's data for that RP. This triggers an authorization request from the IdB to the user's' smartphone that must be acted upon by the user and leads to the issuing of authorization tokens by the smart phone.

On the user's approval, the OFELIA application creates signed access tokens for each one of the involved data storages (AAs) and also sends an encrypted copy of these access tokens to the RP via the IdB. In this case the encryption is done with the RP public key. This prevents a malicious IdB from issuing data requests on its own. This scenario is exemplified in Figure 5. Now the RP can request attributes from IdB while the authorization given by the user remains valid.

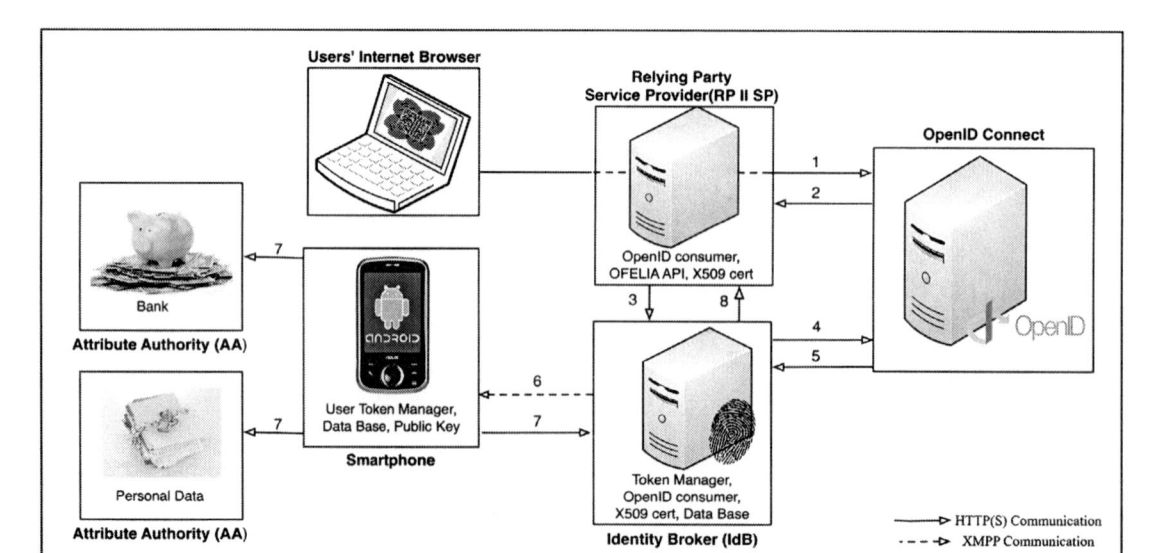

Figure 5. Relying party enrollment flow

1. The user authenticates to the RP via its Openid Connect account allowing the RP to request his public key and the IdB URL HTTP location.
2. Openid Connect answers to the RP with the requested data.
3. The RP makes a TLS REST registration request to the IdB, providing its certificate as the client cert for the TLS connection that is established from the RP to the IdB. The registration request contains the OpenID request link some descriptive information details (to be displayed at the user's mobile phone) about the RP service and a list of the requested data enciphered with the user's public key.
4. The IdB tests the OpenID request link in order to verify if the request is valid.
5. Openid Connect answers the IdB, If the answer from the OpenID server comes as a replay-attack (Badra et al., 2009) attempt, it in fact confirms to the IdB that the user has been previously authenticate with OpenID at the requesting RP and therefore this RP enrollment attempt is legitimate. This is a widespread OpenID hack that allows a service to verify if the user has already been previously OpenID authenticated at some other site. The IdB can then pre-register the RP by generating an RP identifier token.
6. The IdB sends a XMPP message to the smartphone containing a signed request message with the encrypted RP data request plus other requesting RP details (identifier token, certificate, details of service and RP URL HTTP location).
7. At the user's discretion, an access authorization token is generated by the smartphone and sent back to the IdB encrypted with the RP public key and encrypted with each AA public key to each one of the involved AA with the RP details.
8. The IdB validates the RP registration by sending to the RP the encrypted access token that has been issued by the smartphone.

3.4. Usage Case Scenario

For a credible illustrative OFELIA aggregation scenario, imagine an online bookstore as a Relying Party and for example a credit card company and university acting as Attribute Authorities. Now let's assume the user is online shopping at the online bookstore and upon completion of his purchase, if he can prove that he has a specific bank card and is a student of certain university, the online bookstore gives him an immediate special discount on books of his study domain.

At the moment of purchase and after the user had already been authenticated via OpenID Connect, the online bookstore, acting as a RP, will request the IdB of that user for proof of bank card and university membership for that particular user. This triggers an authorization request made by the IdB that is displayed at the user smartphone, to authorize the necessary AAs to disclose this information. The user can then use the OFELIA App application installed at his smartphone to authorize both AAs (university and bank card) to disclose the user's membership status (signed by the AAs X509 certificates) to the bookstore. These authorizations take the form of digitally signed authorization tokens that are registered on the respective AAs and delivered to the IdB encrypted with the RP public keys. The IdB then acts as a relay and sends the signed encrypted authorization tokens back to the Relying online bookstore (RP).

The RP, now in possession of these digitally signed authorization tokens, can then sent them to the IdB, encrypted with the respective AA public key each time the online bookstore wants to get evidence the user is still a valid customer of the bank and member of an university. These access tokens together with the identity consultation requests are then digitally signed and relayed by the IdB into the appropriate AAs, which upon analyzing the validity of the accompanying authorization tokens can deliver the requested information back to the IdB, digitally signed by the AAs and encrypted for the RP. This encryption step is important in order to establish a high level of privacy and security. The IdB should not know the value of the identity attributes, otherwise the entity responsible for the IdB would be in a position of doing massive data aggregation with their users' data, and that aggregation by itself would become a much more prized target for attacks. This constitutes two of the main reasons for OFELIA to have been developed in the first place, i.e. to provide an identity/authorization versatile infrastructure that does not depend upon the massive aggregation of users identity attributes.

Finally the IdB relays the requested encrypted information to the RP that can verify its integrity and validity by decrypting the attributes values and verifying the validity of its digital signatures and thus letting the online bookstore (RP) apply the special discount on books of the buyer subject studies domains.

4. CONCLUSION

With the proposed infrastructure, it is possible to securely dynamically manage the aggregation of identity attributes from different Authorization Authorities into a single user centric digital identity whose authorizations can be managed in a novel versatile way involving temporal constraints by the arbitrage of the user's smartphone.

OFELIA also possesses innovative mechanisms to protect users' privacy by preventing the massive aggregation of users identity attributes into a single place. We have taken special care to prevent the disclosure of identity attributes values at the IdB precisely to prevent the massive disclosure of user data lest the IdB be compromised.

In OFELIA if an attacker compromises the IdB he will not have disclosed the user's identity attributes values that should therefore continue to remain safe in a privacy aware way. Furthermore, since the identity attributes are always held by their original source (the attribute authority) the identity attributes maintains a kind of freshness state. This opens a whole new range of opportunities and possibilities due the ability to allow data be processed as requested. In other words every time a relying party requests an identity attribute, this data value is processed in real time, becoming an essential feature for dynamic attributes that for its own nature is volatile.

4.1. Future Work

We are currently extending OFELIA with smartphone to smartphone communication mechanisms parameterized by QR codes to cater for side channel authorization requests in the case where some OFELIA user, enrolled in a relying party and acting as some predefined role wants to directly ask to some other user, permission to access some of his OFELIA managed identity attributes.

Interoperability between different identity management systems is the key for usability. Therefore we intend to research and develop a novel XML based digital Identity model to improve upon the main ideas present on other semantic models for user-centric identity and base it on SAML (Saklikar & Saha, 2007), metadata identity semantics and other alternative distributed digital identity semantic models (Cao & Yang, 2011).

4.2. Development Notes

As already mentioned, to implement OFELIA architecture we relied in some libraries and software. In this subsection we exposed the libraries, their versions and if possible their respective download links:

OpenID Consumer Library:

- Openid4java
- Version: 0.9.5.593
- Download link: http://openid4java.google-code.com/files/openid4java
- -full-0.9.5.593.tar.gz

XMPP BOSH Client Connector:

- Ignite realtime SMACK API
- Revision: 12894
- Svn link: http://svn.igniterealtime.org/svn/repos/smack/branches/bosh/

XMPP Test Server:

- Ignite realtime Openfire
- Version: 3.6.4
- Linux download link: http://www.igniterealtime.org/downloads/download-landing.jsp?
- file=openfire/openfire_3_6_4.tar.gz

Android API 10 for android 2.3.3:

- Android SDK
- Version: 20.0.3
- Linux download link: http://dl.google.com/android/android-sdk_r20.0.3-linux.tgz

ACKNOWLEDGMENT

This work is funded by the ERDF through the Programme COMPETE and by the Portuguese Government through FCT – Foundation for Science and Technology, project OFELIA ref. PTDC/EIA-EIA/104328/2008 and is being conducted with the institutional support provided by DCC/FCUP and the facilities and research environment gracefully provided by the CRACS (Center for Research in Advanced Computing Systems) research unit, an INESC TEC associate of the Faculty of Science, University of Porto.

REFERENCES

Adi, W., Al-Qayedi, A., Zarooni, A. A., & Mabrouk, A. (2004). *Secured multi-identity mobile infrastructure and offline mobile-assisted micro-payment application.* Paper presented at the Wireless Communications and Networking Conference. New York, NY.

Augusto, A. B., & Correia, M. E. (2012). OFELIA – A secure mobile attribute aggregation infrastructure for user-centric identity management. In Gritzalis, D., Furnell, S., & Theoharidou, M. (Eds.), *Information Security and Privacy Research* (Vol. 376, pp. 61–74). Berlin: Springer. doi:10.1007/978-3-642-30436-1_6.

Augusto, A. B., & Correia, M. E. (2013). A secure and dynamic mobile identity wallet authorization architecture based on a XMPP. In *Messaging Infrastructure Innovations in XML Applications and Metadata Management: Advancing Technologies* (pp. 21–37). Hershey, PA: IGI Global.

Baden, R., Bender, A., Spring, N., Bhattacharjee, B., & Starin, D. (2009). Persona: An online social network with user-defined privacy. *SIGCOMM Computing and Communications Review, 39*(4), 135–146. doi:10.1145/1594977.1592585.

Badra, M., Guillet, T., & Serhrouchni, A. (2009). *Random values, nonce and challenges: Semantic meaning versus opaque and strings of data.* Paper presented at the Vehicular Technology Conference Fall (VTC 2009-Fall). New York, NY.

Barkhuus, L., & Polichar, V. (2011). Empowerment through seamfulness: Smart phones in everyday life. *Personal and Ubiquitous Computing, 15*(6), 629–639. doi:10.1007/s00779-010-0342-4.

Bhargav-Spantzel, A., Camenisch, J., Gross, T., & Sommer, D. (2007). User centricity: A taxonomy and open issues. *Journal of Computer Security, 15*(5), 493–527.

Cameron, K. (2005). *The laws of identity (Whitepaper).* Albuquerque, NM: Microsoft.

Cameron, K., & Jones, M. (2007). Design rationale behind the identity metasystem architecture. In *Proceedings of ISSE/SECURE 2007 Securing Electronic Business Processes* (pp. 117-129). Vieweg.

Cao, Y., & Yang, L. (2011). *GISL: A generalized identity specification language based on XML schema*. Paper presented at the 7th ACM Workshop on Digital Identity Management. Chicago, IL.

Chadwick, D. W. (2009). Federated identity management. In Alessandro, A., Gilles, B., & Roberto, G. (Eds.), *Foundations of Security Analysis and Design V* (pp. 96–120). Springer-Verlag. doi:10.1007/978-3-642-03829-7_3.

Chadwick, D. W., & Inman, G. (2009). Attribute aggregation in federated identity management. *Computer*, *42*(5), 33–40. doi:10.1109/MC.2009.143.

Clauß, S., & Köhntopp, M. (2001). Identity management and its support of multilateral security. *Computer Networking*, *37*(2), 205–219. doi:10.1016/S1389-1286(01)00217-1.

David, W. C. (2006). *Authorisation using attributes from multiple authorities*. Paper presented at the Enabling Technologies: Infrastructure for Collaborative Enterprises. New York, NY.

Eastlake, D. E., & Schiller, J. I. (2005). *Randomness requirements for security*. Retrieved from https://ietf.org/rfc/rfc4086.txt

Gemmill, J., Robinson, J.-P., Scavo, T., & Bangalore, P. (2009). Cross-domain authorization for federated virtual organizations using the myVocs collaboration environment. *Concurrent Computing: Practical Experience*, *21*(4), 509–532. doi:10.1002/cpe.1350.

Hai-Binh, L., & Bouzefrane, S. (2008). *Identity management systems and interoperability in a heterogeneous environment*. Paper presented at the Advanced Technologies for Communications. New York, NY.

Hammer-Lahav. E. (2012). *The oauth 2.0 authorization protocol*. Retrieved from https://tools.ietf.org/html/rfc6749

Hovav, A., & Berger, R. (2009). *Tutorial: Identity management systems and secured access control*. Academic Press.

Hsiang-Cheh, H., Feng-Cheng, C., & Wai-Chi, F. (2011). Reversible data hiding with histogram-based difference expansion for QR code applications. *IEEE Transactions on Consumer Electronics*, *57*(2), 779–787. doi:10.1109/TCE.2011.5955222.

Inc, Y. (2007). *Fire eagle*. Retrieved from http://fireeagle.yahoo.net/

Inman, G., & Chadwick, D. (2010). A privacy preserving attribute aggregation model for federated identity managements systems. *Upgrade. Privacy and Identity Management*, *11*(1), 6.

Maia, L. A., & Correia, M. E. (2012). *Java JCA/JCE programming in Android with SD smart cards*. Paper presented at the Information Systems and Technologies (CISTI), 2012. New York, NY.

Mont, M., Pearson, S., & Bramhall, P. (2003). Towards accountable management of privacy and identity information. In Snekkenes, E., & Gollmann, D. (Eds.), *Computer Security – ESORICS 2003* (Vol. 2808, pp. 146–161). Berlin: Springer. doi:10.1007/978-3-540-39650-5_9.

Orawiwattanakul, T., Yamaji, K., Nakamura, M., Kataoka, T., & Sonehara, N. (2010). *User-controlled privacy protection with attribute-filter mechanism for a federated SSO environment using shibboleth*. Paper presented at the 2010 International Conference on P2P, Parallel, Grid, Cloud and Internet Computing. New York, NY.

Paci, F., & Shang, N., Jr. K. S., Fernando, R., & Bertino, E. (2009). *VeryIDX - A privacy preserving digital identity management system for mobile devices*. Paper presented at the 2009 Tenth International Conference on Mobile Data Management: Systems, Services and Middleware. New York, NY.

Paterson, I., & Saint-Andre, P. (2007). *XEP-0206: XMPP: Over BOSH*. Retrieved Jun 2012, from http://xmpp.org/extensions/xep-0206.html

Saint-Andre, P., Smith, K., & Tronon, R. (2009). *XMPP: The definitive guide building real-time applications with jabber technologies*. Sebastopol, CA: O'Reilly Media, Inc..

Sakimura, N., Bradley, J., Jones, M., Medeiros, B., & Jay, E. (2012). *Openid connect standard 1.0*.

Saklikar, S., & Saha, S. (2007). *Next steps for security assertion markup language (SAML)*. Paper presented at the 2007 ACM Workshop on Secure Web Services. Fairfax, VA.

Schwartz, P. M. (2004). *Property, privacy, and personal data*. Academic Press.

Zhikui, C. (2007). *A privacy enabled service authorization based on a user-centric virtual identity management system*. Paper presented at the Communications and Networking in China, 2007. Beijing, China.

Chapter 11
The Austrian Identity Ecosystem:
An E-Government Experience

Klaus Stranacher
Graz University of Technology, Austria

Thomas Zefferer
Graz University of Technology, Austria

Arne Tauber
Graz University of Technology, Austria

Bernd Zwattendorfer
Graz University of Technology, Austria

ABSTRACT

Architectures and protocols for secure information technology are crucial to satisfy security requirements of current e-government solutions. Identity plays a central role in most e-government solutions, as users typically need to be reliably identified and authenticated. User identification and authentication approaches usually rely on complex cryptographic methods and sophisticated technical solutions. Additionally, these solutions need to be backed by appropriate organizational and legal frameworks that assure the legal validity of provided identification and authentication approaches. In this chapter, the authors introduce the Austrian identity ecosystem that represents one of the main pillars of the Austrian e-government infrastructure. They discuss underlying concepts and main building blocks of this comprehensive ecosystem and show how architectures and protocols for secure information technology are employed to assure the security of user identification and authentication processes. By discussing concrete use cases, the authors illustrate the applicability of the Austrian identity ecosystem for both Austrian and foreign citizens.

DOI: 10.4018/978-1-4666-4514-1.ch011

INTRODUCTION

Identity is an important concept of various scientific disciplines and has also become common in popular discourse (Fearon, 1999). Due to its frequent use, the term 'identity' is often used without any further explanations and definitions, ignoring its multiple meanings. Given the complexity of the term and concept of identity, it is unsurprising that various different definitions can be found in literature. Hogg et al. (1988) define identity as *'people's concepts of who they are, of what sort of people they are, and how they relate to others'*. According to Katzenstein (1996), *'the term [identity] (by convention) references mutually constructed and evolving images of self and other'*. White (1992) states that *'identity is any source of action not explicable from biophysical regularities, and to which observers can attribute meaning'*. The different definitions of the term 'identity' emphasize the multiple meanings and interpretations of this term and its relevance for many scientific disciplines.

Identity plays also a central role for governments and public administrations. Usually, such institutions have a rather pragmatic view on the abstract term identity. For these institutions, identity is basically a necessary concept that facilitates the implementation of governmental and administrative procedures. Each person that participates in such a procedure is assigned a unique identifier (e.g. a number) that unambiguously distinguishes this person from others. This concept is applied to both natural and legal persons in the same way. The use of abstract numbers is necessary as in large administrative districts (such as states or nations) the name and date of birth of citizens are usually not sufficient to allow for an unambiguous distinction of users.

Identity has played an important role in the accomplishment of governmental and administrative procedures for a long time. Citizens have become used to identify themselves by showing an ID or passport when participating in official procedures or applying for official services. During the past years, Information and Communication Technologies (ICT) have significantly changed the way administrative procedures are conducted by both public administrations and citizens. Attempts to leverage ICT in order to improve the efficiency of governmental procedures are subsumed under the term e-Government. E-Government allows citizens to carry out administrative procedures over the Internet without the need to personally show up at administrative offices. One of the biggest challenges in e-Government is the development and deployment of appropriate means to reliably identify persons that actively participate in Internet-based e-Government procedures. This typically involves the deployment of an electronic ID (eID) that is linked to the person's identity and is used to unambiguously identify this person in electronic governmental procedures.

Many European countries have rolled-out electronic IDs to their citizens on national level since years. In the special case of Austria, the so called Citizen Card represents the national eID that allows citizens to securely identify and authenticate at online procedures. The Austrian Citizen Card concept has already been introduced in 2002 and has been designed to be applicable in both the public and the private sector. Public administrations use the Citizen Card concept to reliably identify and authenticate citizens in e-Government procedures. At the same time, the Citizen Card concept is also used by the private sector to protect access to security sensitive applications such as e-Banking. This way, the Citizen Card has emerged being a key concept and core component of various security sensitive online services in Austria.

During the past ten years, a complex and powerful ecosystem of Citizen Card related concepts and components has evolved to address emerging challenges such as integration of legal identities, electronic mandates, or interoperability with foreign eID solutions. In this article we introduce the Austrian identity ecosystem in detail. Starting from the Citizen Card concept, which represents the key element of the entire ecosystem, related concepts and components of the Austrian identity ecosystem are introduced and discussed. We show how the set of well-established concepts and components is used to securely authenticate national and foreign citizens and how advanced concepts such as legal identities and electronic mandates are considered. We will especially elaborate on security and privacy requirements of electronic identities and discuss how these issues are addressed by the Austrian identity ecosystem.

E-GOVERNMENT IN AUSTRIA

Austria has been working on appropriate e-Government solutions for a couple of years and has invested significant effort in their development. The main aim of these efforts is to support Austrian citizens and businesses in online procedures and thereby facilitating access to public authorities or public administrations with the help of ICT. Austria follows a well-defined and sustainable e-Government strategy, which is aligned along several initiatives and regulations of the European Union. The main strategy dates back to the year 2000 and is based on agreements achieved in the EU summit in Feira (European Parliament, 2000a) and Lisbon (European Parliament, 2000b). In this summit, common objectives such as online availability of main governmental services by the year 2005 had been agreed. These agreements have been anchored in the Austrian government program to join forces and to spur e-Government in Austria. Several EU initiatives dealing with e-Government agreements to strengthen the European internal market have followed. Examples of such European initiatives are the European Union action plan "eEurope" (European Commission, 2002) or the "i2010" initiative of the European Commission (European Commission, 2006), representing a successor initiative of this action plan. Currently, the European Commission has published new guidelines in its "Digital Agenda for Europe 2020" (European Commission, 2010). These guidelines especially focus on strengthening the digital European internal market by providing faster Internet connections and interoperable online services.

All these directives and regulations have yielded according amendments of the Austrian e-Government strategy and implementations based on well-established information and communication technologies. However, the main vision for successful and sustainable e-Government in Austria, which has been elaborated in the year 2000, is still valid. This vision envisages that all Austrian citizens and businesses must be able to conduct all governmental processes and transactions electronically, fast and in a simply manner, and without any special or detailed knowledge on technology (Federal Chancellery of Austria, 2010a). This vision foresees a simple, secure, and transparent implementation of e-Government services by means of modern information and communication technologies.

Basic Objectives

From this overall vision and from the general Austrian e-Government strategy, the following basic objectives of e-Government solutions in Austria can be derived:

- Assure trust in provided services by appropriately informing citizen on the security-, privacy-, and transparency-preserving features of provided solutions.
- Include all relevant authorities to avoid silo solutions, i.e. separated solutions of different authorities, which hinder interoperability between them.
- Iteratively transform services to achieve complete transactional services without media-breaks.

One major aim of the Austrian e-Government strategy is to inform citizens about the availability and the maturity of electronic governmental services. This way, citizens should be able to recognize the added value such as higher comfort and flexibility, and should also gain an appropriate level of trust in these services. Therefore, it is important that e-Government applications are easily accessible and follow common and approved approaches to assure an adequate degree of usability. Moreover, e-Government applications should be easily locatable by citizens and any existing barriers that threaten to aggravate access to services should be removed. The use of existing and well-established standards helps to decrease such barriers. Another important criterion with respect to citizen information is security. Security and privacy are essential to assure trust in governmental online services that usually transfer or process sensitive data. Citizens must believe and give credit to the same level of trust for online services as they do for traditional paper-based procedures. Citizens must be appropriately informed about the strengths and security features of used technologies.

Another main pillar of the Austrian e-Government strategy constitutes the inclusion of all relevant authorities. This requirement involves the implementation of e-Government on different public administrative levels. This means that e-Government should be implemented on national, regional, and local level involving federal states, municipalities, and cities. All levels must cooperate with each other to guarantee consistency and to avoid silo solutions. Existing infrastructures should be conjointly re-used to benefit as much as possible from the advantages offered by e-Government.

Existing e-Government infrastructures and solutions should not be abandoned, but moreover integrated into new and emerging services. The aim is to develop fully-fledged transactional solutions and services without media breaks. This means that citizens should be able to electronically apply for governmental procedures and at the same time receive the results without the need for paper-based post mail. To achieve this goal, governmental services should be transformed iteratively to electronic pendants. This means to set up simple and pure informational services at the beginning and to steadily increase the complexity and sophistication of these services. The final goal is to roll out complete transactional services in the end. The step-wise transformation necessitates continuous amendments that are facilitated by fast technological improvements. The fulfillment of this requirement can be facilitated by a modular design of services and by the definition of appropriate interfaces.

Besides the definition of technological concepts and solutions, the realization of a comprehensive e-Government strategy requires the implementation of long-term and fundamental structures in several areas. By the help of an e-Government strategy, concepts and guidelines are worked out, which need to be further implemented step-wise. To implement those concepts, a general framework, not only on technical but also on organizational and legal level, has to be implemented. This guarantees the necessary basis for a successful and sustainable e-Government infrastructure.

The following sub-sections briefly describe the organizational, legal, and technical frameworks that have been defined to guarantee successful e-Government solutions in Austria.

Organizational Framework

To achieve the ambitioned objectives defined by the Austrian e-Government strategy, efficient and collaborative organizational structures are required. Therefore, Austria relies on a dynamic and flexible organizational model. The most important entities of this organizational model are the:

- E-Government Platform
- E-Cooperation Board

- Platform Digital Austria
- E-Government Innovation Centre

The *E-Government Platform* consists of the Austrian vice chancellor, several ministries, the president of the Austrian Federal Economic Chamber, the presidents of social insurance carriers, and governing actors of e-Government working groups, which have strong relations to the federal states in Austria. The major objective of this platform is the organization of e-Government initiatives and activities in Austria on political level.

The *E-Cooperation Board* is combined of ministries, federal states, associations of Austrian cities and towns, and advocacy groups. The E-Cooperation Board coordinates ongoing work in the field of e-Government and determines the responsibility for carrying out e-Government implementation plans.

The *Platform Digital Austria* constitutes the coordination and strategy council of the federal government for e-Government in Austria. All e-Government projects converge in this council. Hence, this council represents one of the central entities of the Austrian e-Government strategy.

The *E-Government Innovation Centre* has been founded in parallel to the Platform Digital Austria. It is responsible for technology observation and technical innovations with respect to e-Government. Furthermore, federal states, cities, or municipalities are supported in their e-Government activities. In addition, the E-Government Innovation Centre has been a partner in several European-wide e-Government projects, such as STORK[1] (Secure Secure idenTity acrOss boRders linKed) or SPOCS[2] (Simple Procedures Online for Cross- Border Services).

Legal Framework

Besides a mature organizational structure, a consistent legal framework represents a relevant factor for successful and sustainable e-Government in Austria. The main pillar of the Austrian legal framework for e-Government constitutes the Austrian E-Government Act (Federal Chancellery of Austria, 2004), which has been especially stipulated according to the Austrian e-Government strategy. However, the legal framework is not based on the Austrian E-Government Act only, but includes several additional relevant laws and regulations. Basically, the main legal framework components of the Austrian e-Government are the:

- E-Government Act
- Signature Act
- General Administrative Procedures Act
- Service of Documents Act

Within the European Union, Austria is one of the first Member States that has adopted a comprehensive e-Government law. The Austrian E-Government Act has come into force on March 1, 2004 and has been amended on January 1, 2008. The three main principles of the Austrian E-Government Act are freedom of choice regarding citizens' interaction with the government and public authorities, guaranteeing security and data protection, and assurance of barrier-free access to e-Government services for all citizens.

The Austrian Signature Act (Federal Chancellery of Austria, 1999) constitutes the implementation of the EU Signature Directive (European Union, 1999), which was published by the European Commission in 1999. This directive specifies a common legal framework for electronic signatures in the European Union. In general, the Austrian Signature Act distinguishes between simple, advanced, and qualified electronic signatures. Qualified electronic signatures are legally equivalent to hand-written signatures according to the EU Signature Directive. Qualified electronic signatures play a major role in the Austrian eID concept, as they are also used for secure electronic authentication of citizens in online procedures.

The General Administrative Procedures Act (Federal Chancellery of Austria, 1991) regulates procedures of nearly all public administrations and authorities in Austria. For instance, this act regulates how citizens can contact public authorities. In electronic processes, this can be done e.g. via e-mail or Web forms.

The Service of Documents Act (Federal Chancellery of Austria, 1982) defines the postal and electronic delivery of authoritative documents to citizens. Similar to the paper-based world, in electronic delivery a differentiation between verifiable and non-verifiable delivery exists. In a verifiable delivery scenario the recipient confirms the receipt of a document by his or her signature. In Austria, verifiable deliveries can be also carried out using electronic means.

Technical Framework

The technical framework to be applied for e-Government in Austria is based on modern and approved information and communication technologies. By the help of these technologies, data and message exchange between citizens, businesses, and public authorities can be organized in a secure and transparent way. The technical core component within the Austrian e-Government strategy constitutes the Austrian Citizen Card concept. The Austrian Citizen Card is an electronic ID (eID), which allows for secure and reliable authentication of citizens in online procedures and enables citizens to create qualified electronic signatures.

Smart cards are currently a popular technology that can be used to practically implement the Austrian Citizen Card concept. National health insurance cards, which are applicable as Citizen Card, have been rolled-out nation-wide. However, the Austrian Citizen Card concept is technology agnostic, hence alternative implementations are also possible. An increasing number of citizens use the Austrian Mobile Phone Signature (Orthacker et al., 2010). In this solution, Citizen Card functionality is not implemented by a smart card but by a central server with attached hardware security module (HSM). Citizens authorize access to personal data stored and processed in the central HSM by means of a two-factor authentication with the help of their mobile phones.

In general, Austria tries to guarantee technology neutrality in its e-Government solutions. This neutrality is guaranteed by open interfaces and easy exchangeability of single modules. One major aspect thereby is the use of international standards (e.g. well-known standards SOAP/WSDL Web services, SSL, SAML[3] or electronic signature standards such as XMLDSIG[4] or XAdES[5]). On the one hand, such standards ensure interoperability between cross-domain applications of public authorities. On the other hand, well-established and proven standards ascertain a high level of security and privacy for citizens.

THE AUSTRIAN E-ID CONCEPT

The Austrian eID concept aims to achieve the basic goals of the Austrian e-Government strategy that have been discussed in the previous section. To achieve these goals, the Austrian eID concept has been based on the organizational, legal, and technical frameworks provided by the Austrian e-Government strategy. In this section we discuss the Austrian eID concept in detail. We do so by discussing the Austrian Citizen Card concept, which represents the backbone of the Austrian eID concept, first. We then introduce different concepts and components that are based on the Austrian Citizen Card concepts and that build the Austrian identity ecosystem.

The Austrian Citizen Card Concept

The Austrian eID concept (Federal Chancellery of Austria, 2008) constitutes one of the key concepts of the Austrian e-Government strategy. The Austrian Citizen Card, in turn, defines the key concept of the Austrian eID concept. Representing the official eID in Austria, the Citizen

Card is basically an abstract definition of a secure eID token that is in possession of the citizen. Its main capabilities are secure identification and authentication of citizens as well as the creation of qualified electronic signatures according to the EU Signature Directive (European Union, 1999).

As mentioned above, the Citizen Card concept is a technology-neutral concept that allows for several different implementations. Currently, smart cards and mobile phones can be used as Citizen Card. However, the technology neutral approach guarantees that also alternative approaches and implementations can be developed and deployed in the future.

Citizen Card Functions

Irrespective of the actual implementation of the Citizen Card concept, the Austrian Citizen Card provides a well-defined set of functionality. We elaborate on the supported features in the following.

Identification and Authentication of Citizens

Unique identification and secure authentication are essential components of governmental processes. In e-Government processes, the Citizen Card provides technical means for carrying out identification and authentication electronically. By using the Citizen Card in online applications, user identification is based on the so-called *Identity Link*. The Identity Link is a special data structure including the citizen's first name, last name, date of birth, and a unique identifier. Although the included identifier is unique, it must not be used directly for identification at online applications due to legal privacy restrictions. Therefore, the unique identifier is derived for a specific sector the application belongs to. On the one hand, this derivation still guarantees uniqueness; on the other hand, applications are not able to track citizens.

This way, the concept of sector-specific identifiers assures privacy preservation. The sector specific identification approach followed in Austria is discussed in more detail later in this article.

The unique identifier stored on the Citizen Card allows for a unique identification of users in online procedures. However, security sensitive applications usually require user not only to identify but to also authenticate. Identification and authentication are actually related processes. The claim to be a person is typically referred to as identification, while the proof of this claim is referred to as authentication. In Austria, the Citizen Card is not only used for identification but also for electronic authentication. In online processes, authentication is carried out by creating an electronic signature by applying Citizen Card functionality. The functionality to create electronic signatures using the Austrian Citizen Card is described in the following.

Secure and Qualified Electronic Signatures

Besides proofing his or her identity, citizens often need to express a written declaration of intent in governmental processes or transactions. This requirement can occur, for instance, when applying for a governmental process or at the end of such a process, when confirming the receipt of results. In traditional paper-based processes, a written expression of declaration of intent is carried out through hand-written signatures. In electronic processes, the hand-written signature needs some equivalent.

According to the Austrian Signature Act, which constitutes the Austrian implementation of the EU Signature Directive, the electronic pendants to hand-written signatures are qualified electronic signatures. Qualified electronic signatures are fully equivalent to hand-written signatures by law. In general, electronic signatures are cryptographic mechanisms to express a declaration of intent electronically. According to the EU Signature Directive, qualified electronic signatures are created by using a qualified digital certificate and by invoking a Secure Signature Creation Device (SSCD). A qualified digital certificate needs to include some specific information according to the EU Signature Directive. All requirements for qualified digital certificates are defined in this directive. An SSCD is usually a cryptographic hardware token that needs to fulfil several requirements also defined in the EU Signature Directive.

Data Storage

The third functionality of the Austrian Citizen Card constitutes simple data storage. The Citizen Card provides a readable and writeable data storage. The data storage is divided into logical entities, which are irrespective of the physical storage location. Possible physical storage locations are the Citizen Card itself, the citizen's hard drive, or data storage accessible over the Internet, e.g. cloud storage solutions. Data to be stored can be of arbitrary format, such as other digital certificates, XML data, or similar data formats.

Citizen Card Model

Figure 1 illustrates the general Citizen Card model (Federal Chancellery of Austria, 2008) and shows all participating parties and components in Citizen Card-based transactions. The central component of the Citizen Card model is the so-called *Citizen Card Software (CCS)*, which constitutes a middleware residing between the citizen and the online application. All involved entities are briefly described below.

- **Citizen:** A citizen is a natural person who wants to access a governmental application by using Citizen Card functionality. The Citizen Card functionality is invoked through the Citizen Card software.
- **Online Application:** This as a governmental or business application offering specific services to citizens, which may require Citizen Card functionality. For instance, restricted access to services is protected through Citizen Card authentication.
- **Citizen Card Software:** The Citizen Card Software constitutes a software, which is either locally installed on the citizen's computer or provided remotely on server-side. This software provides Citizen Card functionality to the citizen. Amongst others, Citizen Card functionality includes identification, authentication, or the creation of electronic signatures. The Citizen Card Software is the core component of this model, facilitating access to Citizen Card functions and operations.
- **User Interface:** The user interface is the interface between the user and the Citizen Card Software. Required credentials to au-

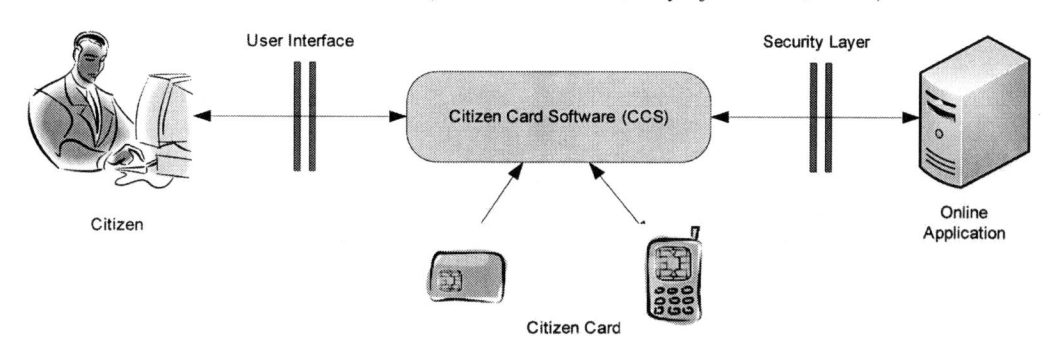

Figure 1. The Austrian citizen card model (Federal Chancellery of Austria, 2008)

thorize access to Citizen Card functionality are collected from the user through this interface.
- **Security Layer:** The *Security Layer* is a well-defined interface between the online application and the Citizen Card Software. Via this interface, applications are able to access Citizen Card functionality. This interface can be used without paying attention to the underlying Citizen Card implementation. Implementation specifics are encapsulated by the Citizen Card Software.

The Identity Ecosystem in Austria

Based on the Austrian Citizen Card concept, that has been discussed above in more detail, a complex ecosystem of related concepts and solutions has evolved during the past years. We give an overview of this ecosystem in the following.

As elaborated above, secure identification and authentication are key features of the Austrian Citizen Card. The Citizen Card representing the Austrian national eID relies on existing unique identifiers that are further used to derive sector-specific identifiers. Unique identifiers are essential as identification based on first name, last name, and date of birth may be ambitious, especially when the number of users increases. Therefore, in Austria all citizens are registered in the *Central Register of Residence (CRR)* and have a unique number assigned (*CRR Number*). The CCR Number acts as unique identifier.

Due to data protection restrictions, the CRR Number must not be directly used in e-Government processes. Therefore, the CRR Number is encrypted to derive a new unique identifier. This new identifier is created by the *SourcePIN Register Authority*, a subdivision of the *Austrian Data Protection Commission*. The derived identifier is named *sourcePIN* and is also unique for all citizens. In addition, the sourcePIN is stored on the Citizen Card together with other identity related data such as first name, last name, and date of birth. Those identification data and the corresponding citizen's qualified certificate are wrapped within a special XML-based data structure. This data structure, which has already been briefly mentioned above, is called *Identity Link* and is electronically signed by the SourcePIN Register Authority. This signature establishes and certifies a link between the identity data and the qualified certificate stored on the Citizen Card. The Identity Link can be further used for unique identification at online applications.

According to the Austrian E-Government Act, the unique identifying sourcePIN requires special protection to preserve citizen's privacy. A permanent storage of this identifier is only allowed within the Identity Link stored on the Citizen Card. Hence, for identification at online applications it is forbidden to use the sourcePIN directly. Because of this restriction - due to data protection reasons - the Austrian e-Government strategy foresees a sector-specific model for identification at online applications. Instead of using the sourcePIN directly, a sector-specific identifier is derived from the sourcePIN. This so-called *sector-specific PIN (ssPIN)* is derived from the combination of the sourcePIN and a governmental sector identifier (e.g. finance, tax, etc.) by using cryptographic one-way hash functions. The use of cryptographic hash functions allows for special privacy protection, as the sourcePIN cannot be calculated from a given ssPIN. In addition, an authority from a specific governmental sector is not able to calculate the ssPIN of another sector, e.g. the ssPIN of the finance sector differs from the ssPIN of the tax sector.

Hence, within the Austrian eID concept the ssPIN constitutes the identifier to be finally used for identification at online applications.

The entire Austrian eID concept for natural persons relies on the unique identifier stored in Austria's Central Register of Residence. Austrian citizens living in Austria, and hence being

The Austrian Identity Ecosystem

registered in the CRR, are usually the typical use case and basic assumption when developing e-Government strategies and concepts in Austria. However, the Austrian eID concept also foresees e-Government applications for persons not listed in the CRR (e.g. foreign citizens or Austrian citizens currently residing in a foreign country). Such persons are not registered in the CRR but can be registered in the so-called *Supplementary Register for Natural Persons (SR)*. The Supplementary Register for Natural Persons constitutes an additional register for foreign citizens or Austrian citizens living abroad. Through the Supplementary Register for Natural Persons, these persons become part of the Austrian eID infrastructure and thus get the possibility to use e-Government applications in Austria. In more detail, by registering in the Supplementary Register for Natural Persons, they also get a unique sourcePIN assigned. This way, foreign citizens can be treated equivalently to domestic Austrian citizens in online e-Government applications. In fact, foreign citizens get the same rights in online applications and e-Government processes as Austrian citizens. The legal basis for that is the so-called *E-Government Equivalence Decree* (Federal Chancellery of Austria, 2010b), which was published and became law in 2010. This decree specifies which foreign electronic IDs can be treated equally to the Austrian eID, i.e. the Austrian Citizen Card.

Another main pillar of the Austrian eID ecosystem is the usage of electronic mandates. Electronic mandates can be used as electronic representations for natural and legal persons, or for professional representatives. In case of representation of natural persons, the sourcePIN of both the representative and the represented person are taken for modelling the mandate process electronically. However, also legal persons such as companies get a unique number for governmental processes in Austria. This unique number of a legal person and the sourcePIN of the representative (natural person) are used for mandate generation. We will discuss the use case on electronic mandates in more detail below.

The Austrian identity ecosystem allows unique identification and secure authentication for both natural and legal persons. To ease an integration of the rather complex Austrian eID ecosystem into security sensitive applications, a set of software modules has been developed, which cover most functionality and hide complex details. Figure 2 illustrates main components and entities of the Austrian identity ecosystem. We skip a full description of the individual components in this section. However, we are going to describe the individual organizations interacting with each other as well as basic technical building blocks in more detail in the following section.

USE CASES FOR IDENTIFICATION AND AUTHENTICATION

To better illustrate the practical application of the various components of the Austrian identity ecosystem, several concrete use cases, in which different users are securely identified and authenticated, are discussed in this section.

Figure 2 provides a general overview of the Austrian identity ecosystem by showing relevant involved components and their relations to each other. Irrespective of that actual use case, a citizen wants to log in to an online application, which runs in the domain of a service provider. The central element to grant access to the online application is the component *MOA-ID* (Federal Chancellery of Austria, 2003). MOA-ID provides secure identification and authentication of citizens based on the Austrian eID concept. In addition to MOA-ID, several other components exist, which are needed to cover all uses cases within the Austrian identity ecosystem. In general, the Austrian identity ecosystem distinguishes three use cases:

- Identification and Authentication of Austrian citizens
- Identification and Authentication of foreign citizens

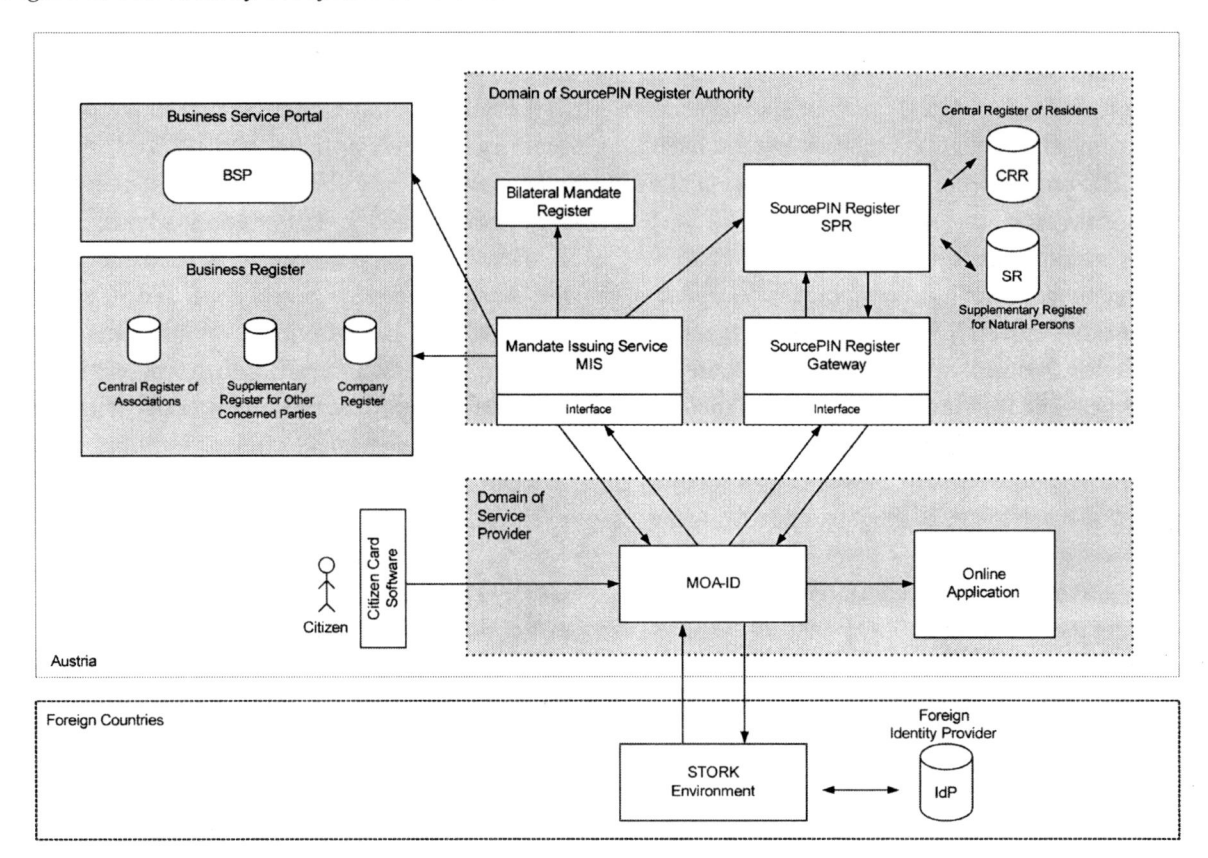

Figure 2. The identity ecosystem in Austria

- Identification and Authentication of legal identities and electronic mandates

In the following subsections, these use cases are explained in detail, involved components are introduced, and interaction between these components is discussed.

Identification and Authentication of Austrian Citizens

The Austrian e-Government concept foresees user identification based on sector-specific identifiers. This concept guarantees uniqueness while preserving privacy. Authentication of citizens is based on the creation of qualified electronic signatures to state the willingness to access protected services provided by online applications.

As shown in Figure 2, the central component MOA-ID plays a major role for identifying and authenticating citizens, who want to access protected services of an online application. In general, the entire process is divided into two steps, identification, and authentication of the citizen. For identification, the Identity Link of the citizen is used. For authentication, the citizen needs to apply an electronic signature.

Figure 3 shows the sequence diagram for this use case in detail. Secure authentication of a citizen consists of the following steps:

1. The citizen wants to access an application, which is run by a service provider. The application performs an access check and – if has not been successfully authenticated yet

The Austrian Identity Ecosystem

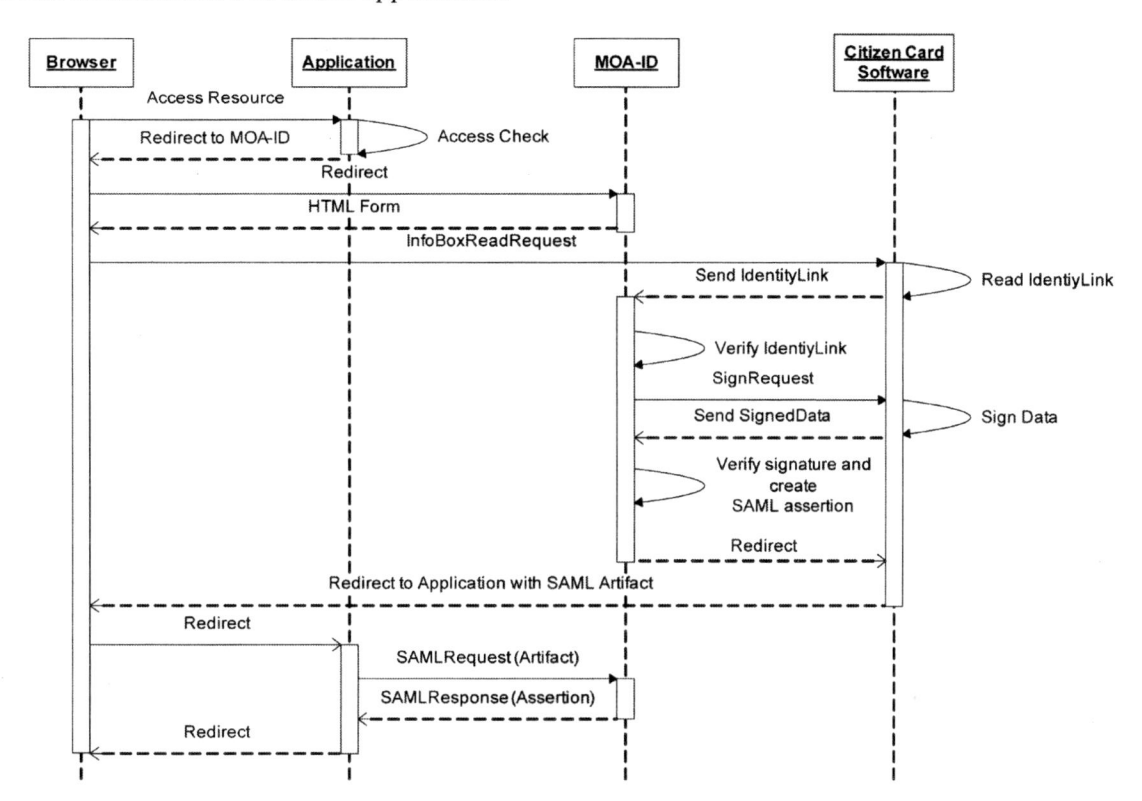

Figure 3. Sequence diagram showing relevant steps to be carried out by Austrian citizens for identification and authentication at online applications

- redirects the citizen to MOA-ID for identification and authentication.
2. MOA-ID returns an HTML form, which includes an XML request to read the Identity Link from the citizen's Citizen Card (InfoBoxReadRequest). This request is sent to the Citizen Card Software.
3. The Citizen Card Software reads the Identity Link and returns it to MOA-ID.
4. MOA-ID verifies the Identity Link as the Identity Link is signed by the SourcePIN Register Authority. At this stage the citizen is successfully identified.
5. Based on the information gathered from the Identity Link, MOA-ID sends an XML request to create an electronic signature to the Citizen Card Software.
6. The citizen is requested to sign the data included in the XML request. The data basically textually describes the willing to intend to authenticate at the applications. After this step, the Citizen Card Software returns the signed data to MOA-ID.
7. MOA-ID verifies the signed data, creates a SAML assertion, and redirects the citizen to the online application (via the Citizen Card Software and the citizen's Web browser). This redirect also includes a SAML artifact, a pointer to the SAML assertion temporally stored at MOA-ID.
8. The online application uses the SAML artifact as a reference to gather the SAML assertion from MOA-ID.
9. Based on the information in the SAML assertion, the online application decides whether the citizen is granted access or not. Finally, the citizen is redirected to the requested protected resource.

Identification and Authentication of Foreign Citizens

In 2008, the Austrian E-Government Act (Federal Chancellery of Austria, 2004) was amended. This revision allows foreign citizens to be treated equally to Austrian citizens in Austrian e-Government processes by amending the following statement:

[...] Data subjects who are not registered in the Central Register of Residents nor in the Supplementary Register may be entered in the Supplementary Register in the course of an application for the issue of a Citizen Card without proof of the data in accordance with paragraph 4 if the application is provided with a qualified electronic signature which is linked to an equivalent electronic verification of that person's unique identity in his or her country of origin. The Federal Chancellor shall lay down by Order further conditions for equivalence. The SourcePIN Authority shall, upon application of the data subject, provide the SourcePIN of the data subject directly to the Citizen Card enabled application where the official procedure is carried out. The SourcePIN may be used by the SourcePIN Register Authority only to calculate ssPINs [...]

Based on this statement, foreign electronic identities are fully integrated in the Austrian identity ecosystem. As a requirement, foreign citizens must be registered in the Supplementary Register for Natural Persons (SR) in case they are not already registered in the Central Register of Residents (CRR). Based on that registration, the SourcePIN Register Authority is able to derive a sourcePIN from the information extractable of the foreign eID. Additionally, a temporary[6] Identity Link can be created and further used for identification of foreign citizen at Austrian online applications.

For the integration of foreign citizens into the Austrian identity ecosystem, the respective foreign eID needs to provide an appropriate level of equivalence to the Austrian eID. This equivalence is stated in the *E-Government Equivalence Decree* (Federal Chancellery of Austria, 2010b), which has come into force in June 2010. All countries listed in this decree have in common that they rely on a unique identifier for identifying persons and store this identifier in the citizen's digital certificate. This identifier can be, depending on the country, the tax number, the social insurance number, the health care user number, or an arbitrary personal identification number. Table 1 lists all foreign electronic identities that are equivalent to the Austrian eID according to the E-Government Equivalence Decree.

The identification and authentication process for foreign citizens is based on the identification and authentication use case for Austrian citizens. Therefore, the foreign citizen to be authenticated must be identified via the Central Register of Residents or the Supplementary Register for Natural Persons. Each foreign citizen, who wants to become part of the Austrian eID ecosystem, needs to undergo a registration process. During this registration process, identification attributes are read from the foreign eID card. The foreign citizen is automatically registered in the Supplementary Register during the first login. The registration is based on the citizen's qualified certificate and the data included in this certificate. The registration process is conduced completely online. Hence, personal presence of foreign users in public administrations is not required.

Regarding the identification and authentication of foreign users, two scenarios are distinguished (Login via SourcePIN Register Gateway and Login via STORK). Both scenarios base on the same legal framework, but differ (partly) in the technical implementation. The two scenarios are discussed in more detail in the following subsections.

The Austrian Identity Ecosystem

Table 1. Equivalent foreign electronic identities (Federal Chancellery of Austria, 2010b)

Country	Unique Identifier	Name of eID Token
Belgium	RRN number (Rijksregister-Registre National)	Belgian Personal Identity Card (Elektronische identiteitskaart BELPIC)
Estonia	PIC number (Personal Identification Code)	Estonian ID Card (Isikutunnistus ID-kaart ESTEID)
Finland	FINUID number (Finnish Unique Identifier)	Finnish Electronic Identity Card (FINEID)
Iceland	SSN number (Social Security Number)	Icelandic bank card
Italy	Tax identification number	Electronic Identity Card (Carta d'identità elettronica)
		National Service Card (Carta nazionale dei servizi)
Liechtenstein	Serial number of the certificate in conjunction with PEID number (Personal Identification Number)	Lisign
Lithuania	Personal ID code	Lithuanian Personal Identity Card (Asmens Tapatybės Kortelė)
Portugal	Personal identification number	Personal Identity Card (Cartão do Cidadão)
	Social insurance number	
	Tax number	
	Healthcare user number	
Sweden	Personal ID number	Nationellt id-kort
Slovenia	Serial number of the certificate in conjunction with PRN number (Personal Registration Number) or tax identification number	SIGOV Card
	Tax identification number	Halcom ONE FOR ALL!
		Postarca smart card
Spain	Personal ID number	DNI electronic (DNI electrónico)

Login via SourcePIN Register Gateway

Basically, the login for foreign citizens is based on the login for Austrian. For the registration of a foreign citizen in the Supplementary Register for Natural Persons, a so called SourcePIN Register Authority Gateway is used. This gateway is contacted by MOA-ID during the authentication process and provides simple access to the SourcePIN Register Authority, which is responsible for the registration of foreign citizens and the creation of the temporary Identity Link. As a basic requirement, foreign eID token specifics must be integrated in the Citizen Card Software. Amongst others, the open source Citizen Card Software MOCCA[7], which represents another key component of the Austrian identity ecosystem, supports eID tokens from the following countries: Belgium, Estonia, Finland, Italy, Liechtenstein, Lithuania, Portugal, and Sweden.

Figure 4 illustrates the sequence diagram for this login scenario. The following process steps need to be carried out to successfully identify and authenticate a foreign citizen according at an Austrian online application:

1. The start of the authentication process is equal to the steps 1-2 from the authentication process for Austrian citizens (see section *Identification and Authentication of Austrian Citizens*). There, an XML request for retriev-

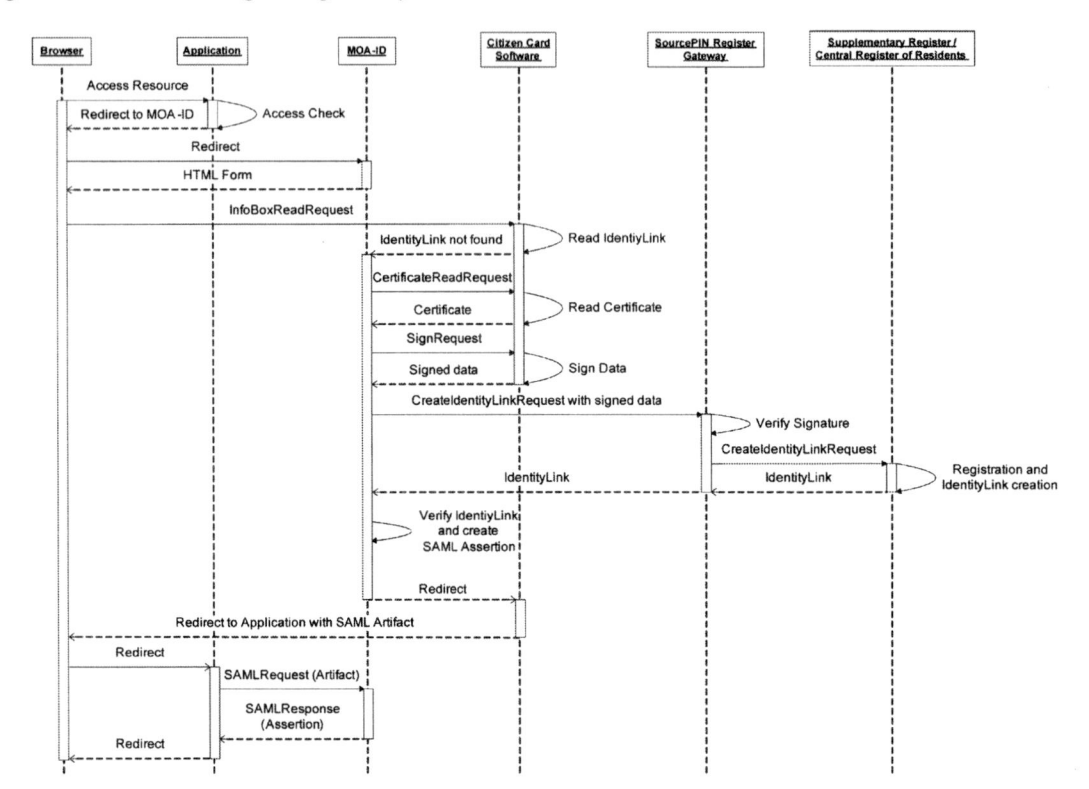

Figure 4. Sequence diagram showing relevant steps to be carried out for foreign citizen authentication through the SourcePIN register gateway

ing the Identity Link is sent via HTTP Post to the Citizen Card Software.
2. The Citizen Card Software tries to read the Identity Link. As a foreign eID token is used instead of an Austrian Citizen Card, this read process fails. A well-defined error message is sent back to MOA-ID.
3. Instead reading the Identity Link, MOA-ID creates an XML request to get the qualified certificate from the foreign citizen's eID token. This request is sent to the Citizen Card Software, which reads the certificate form the citizen's eID token and returns the certificate to MOA-ID.
4. Based on the information within the signer certificate, MOA-ID sends an XML request (to create an electronic signature) to the Citizen Card Software.
5. The foreign citizen is requested to sign the data, which textually states the willingness for authentication at the online application. The Citizen Card Software returns the signed data to MOA-ID.
6. MOA-ID creates an XML request including the signed data and sends this request to the SourcePIN Register Gateway.
7. The gateway verifies the signature and forwards the request to the SourcePIN Register.
8. The SourcePIN Register searches the Central Register of Residents and the Supplementary Register for Natural Persons in order to find the entry of the foreign citizen. At this point, two scenarios need to be distinguished:
   a. The foreign citizen is already registered in one of the two registers. Therefore, an Identity Link can be generated and returned to the gateway.

The Austrian Identity Ecosystem

b. The foreign citizen is not registered in one of the registers. In this case, the citizen is automatically registered in the Supplementary Register for Natural Persons. After completion of the registration process, an Identity Link can be generated and returned to the gateway.
9. The gateway receives the Identity Link from the SourcePIN Register and sends it to MOA-ID.
10. MOA-ID verifies the electronic signature of the Identity Link, creates a SAML assertion including citizen's identity and authentication information, and redirects the citizen to the online application. This redirect also includes a SAML artifact, being a point to the SAML assertion temporally stored at MOA-ID.
11. These process steps are equal to the steps 8-9 from the authentication process for Austrian citizens (see section *Identification and Authentication of Austrian Citizens*).

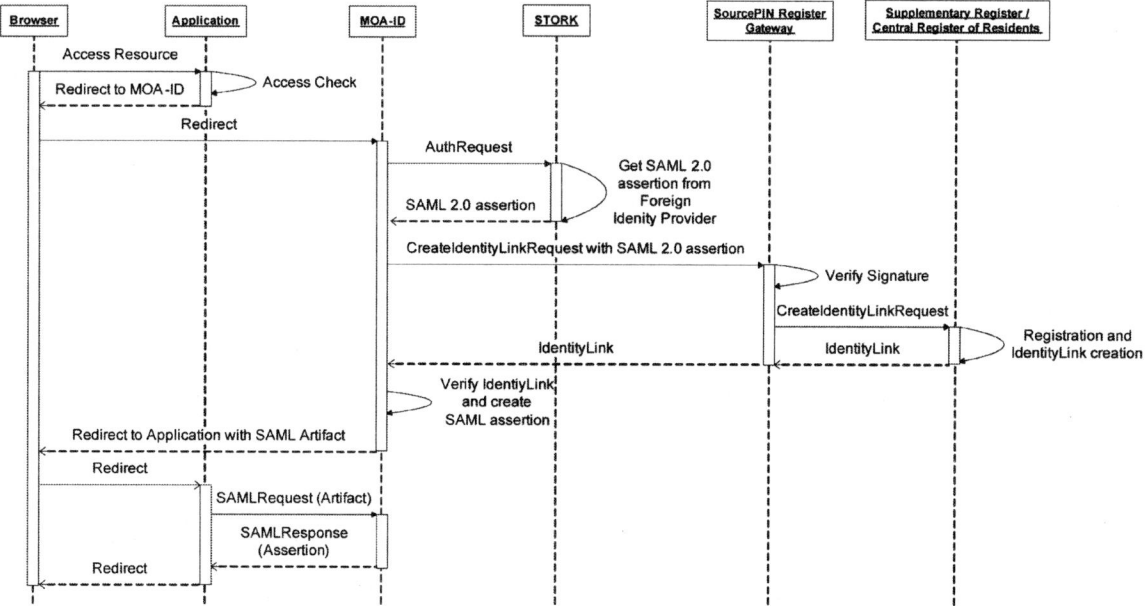

Login via STORK

STORK was an EU large scale pilot project aiming on the interoperability of national eID solutions in cross-border scenarios. During the STORK project, a framework has been developed, which enables citizens to log in at foreign applications using their national eID and domestic infrastructure.

In contrast to the scenario shown above, the Citizen Card Software is not involved in the authentication process. Therefore, this scenario does not require foreign eID tokens to be integrated in Citizen Card Software solutions. Figure 5 shows the sequence diagram for this scenario. The following process steps need to be carried out to successfully identify and authenticate a foreign citizen according to this scenario:

1. See process step 1 from the authentication process for Austrian citizens (see section *Identification and Authentication of Austrian Citizens*).

Figure 5. Sequence diagram showing relevant steps to be carried out for foreign citizen authentication through the STORK framework

2. In this step, the citizen selects his or her home country. MOA-ID sends a well-defined authentication request to the STORK environment of the selected home country.
3. The STORK environment contacts the national identity provider to get a SAML 2.0 assertion. The citizen identifies at the identity provider using his or her national eID infrastructure. The SAML 2.0 assertion includes several requested citizen identity information. In particular, the assertion contains a citizen's signature representing the willingness to login at the Austrian online application.
4. The identity provider returns the SAML 2.0 assertion to the national STORK environment and sends it back to MOA-ID.
5. MOA-ID creates an XML request based on extracted data out of the SAML 2.0 assertion (including the citizen's signature) and sends this request to der SourcePIN Register Gateway.
6. The gateway verifies the signature of the citizen, which is part of the SAML 2.0 assertion, and forwards the request to the SourcePIN Register.
7. See process step 9-11 of the scenario for foreign citizens discussed above (see section *Login via SourcePIN Register Gateway*).

Legal Identities and Electronic Mandates

Representation and mandates are important vehicles in public procedures and business processes. We usually use mandates to empower other persons to act on behalf of ourselves. Typical examples are health care proxies or mandates to carry out bank transactions on behalf of another person. Particularly in e-Government processes many contacts are initiated by companies or other organisations whereby a natural person, e.g. a company manager, is representing the legal person. Another use case is professional representation. Lawyers, notaries, clerks, or tax consultants are representing their clients in various matters.

The Austrian e-Government initiative considered representation from the very beginning. Art. 5 of the Austrian e-Government Act (Federal Chancellery of Austria, 2004) states that

[...] where the Citizen Card is to be used for submissions by a representative, a reference to the permissibility of the representation must be entered in the Citizen Card of the representative. This occurs where the sourcePIN Register Authority having been presented with proof of an existing authority to represent or in cases of statutory representation, enters in the Citizen Card of the representative, upon application by the representative, the sourcePIN of the principal and a reference to the existence of an authority to represent, including any relevant material or temporal limitations [...]

and

[...] in cases of professional representation in which no particular proof of authority to represent is required, enters in the Citizen Card of the representative, in a form which can be verified electronically, a reference to the fact that he has been authorised to act as professional representative [...]

Since professional representatives may represent hundreds or thousands of clients, it is inconvenient to enter the power of representation for each client in the Citizen Card environment. Further, it does not match practice in traditional proceedings or business processes where - due to their professional license - professional representatives may just claim to represent a particular client. Therefore, in Austrian e-Government professional representatives are identified with a special object identifier (OID), which is included in the qualified certificate of their Citizen Card. Each occupational group has a different value, so different types of professional representatives can be distinguished according to the OID in their certificate.

For all other types of representations the Austrian e-Government initiative has published a specification for electronic mandates. This specification is based on XML and aims for creating an electronic image of traditional mandates. One might think that representation and electronic mandates might not be a complex task. Popular existing approaches for representation are the permission-based delegation model (PBDM) in role-based access control (RBAC) (Khambhammettu et al., 2006) or delegation in RBAC (Zhang et al., 2003). These models are intra-organisational and do not meet the requirements for an identity management system on a national scale. Attribute certificates used in Public Key Infrastructures (PKI) are also often used for representation. However, representation is usually not limited to a single role, but might be more complex as discussed by Rössler (2009). Representation can be categorised into

- **Bilateral Representations:** Where a mandator empowers the proxy to act in her name.
- **Substitution:** Where an intermediary is indirectly empowered by the mandator to delegate the power of representation to a proxy.
- **Delegation:** Which is similar to substitution, but in this case the proxy does not act in the intermediary's name, but the mandator's name.

The Austrian specification for electronic mandates is able to model all mentioned representation scenarios. The XML structure of an electronic mandate is illustrated in Figure 6. An electronic mandate holds the following core information:

- The proxy's (representative) identification data. This includes the sourcePIN, name, and date of birth.
- The mandator's identification data. In case of natural persons these are the sourcePIN, name, and date of birth. In case of legal persons the full name (e.g. company name) and the register number (e.g. company number) are included.
- In case an intermediary (delegate or substitute) is involved, the according identification data are included.
- Date and time of issuance of the mandate.
- Mandate content as a textual description defining the scope of application, e.g. that the mandate can only be used for certain bank transactions.
- Financial or timely constraints, e.g. that a mandate is only valid up to a certain date or that a transaction can only be carried out up to a certain amount.

This XML structure must be electronically signed by the SourcePIN Register Authority. For authenticity, only mandates signed by this authority are valid mandates in the context of Austrian e-Government.

The Austrian mandate management system is illustrated in Figure 2. The system can be characterized as a central system with just-in-time generation of electronic mandates on the basis of live information retrieved from constitutive registers. The core of the system is the so-called Mandate Issuing Service (MIS). It handles most process steps in the mandate management workflow. The main duties are:

- To accept incoming requests by identity providers, e.g. MOA-ID. Requests have to contain the proxy's identity link and a set of mandate identifiers. In case of professional representative the proxy's certificate has also to be provided. Mandate identifiers are a kind of search filter. For example, an identity provider may only want to accept mandates for bank transactions or tax affairs.

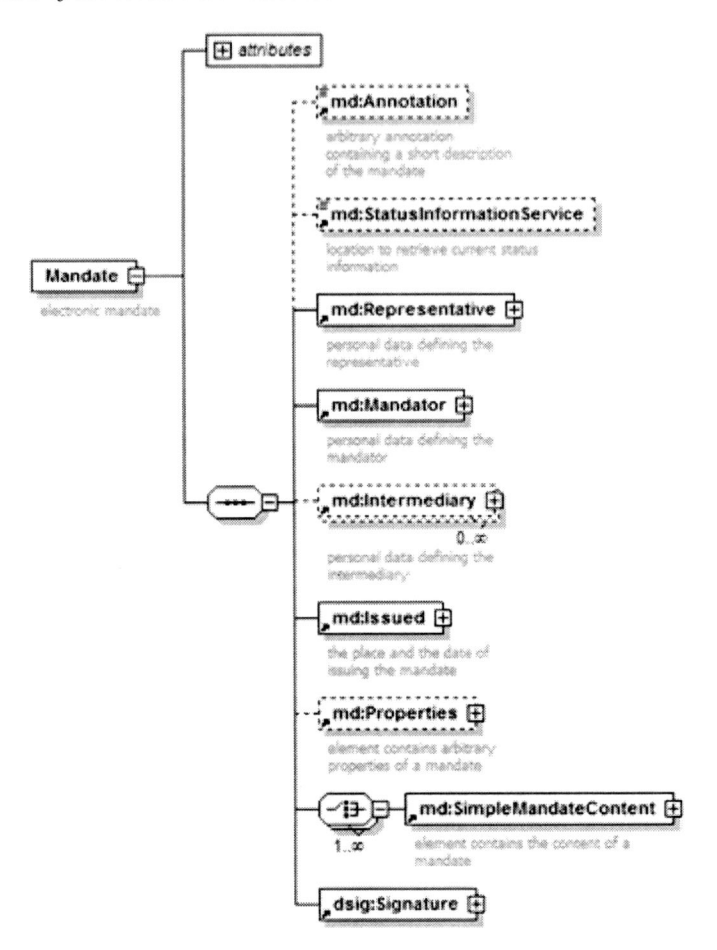

Figure 6. XML structure of an electronic mandate

- To search for a proxy's mandates. The MIS distinguishes between bilateral mandates, i.e. mandates between natural persons, and mandates for legal persons. The SourcePIN Register Authority provides a central service for bilateral mandates. Mandators can access this service with their Citizen Card and register a new mandate, i.e. empower another person. In case of legal persons several (constitutive) registers are accessed. For example, the service searches the company register, the central register for associations, or the supplementary register for legal persons whether the proxy is authorized to solely represent a legal person or not. By using the business service portal, authorized persons of a company can designate certain persons to carry out specific transaction on behalf of the company, e.g. to accept certified electronic mail items. This mandate source is also queried by the MIS.
- Retrieve the mandator's sourcePIN. In case of a bilateral mandate, the mandator's identification data has to be provided in the mandate. This also includes the sourcePIN. Since the register only stores the ssPIN to identify a mandator's mandate, the MIS has to retrieve the mandator's sourcePIN from the SourcePIN register.

How does the authentication process in case of a proxy work? We assume that access to a particular e-Government resource is restricted to certain persons and protected by MOA-ID. When a proxy is trying to access the resource on behalf of another person, the following steps are carried out by MOA-ID and the mandate management system:

- MOA-ID reads the Identity Link from the proxy's Citizen Card.
- The proxy creates a qualified electronic signature and signs a statement (including a unique reference value) that she wants to act on behalf of another person.
- MOA-ID submits the Identity Link, the signature certificate, and a list of mandate identifiers as search filters to the MIS.
- The MIS searches all sources for mandates belonging to the proxy by considering the search filters.
- The MIS returns a URL to MOA-ID, which redirects the proxy to this URL.
- The proxy selects a mandate from the list of available mandates from the sources.
- The MIS electronically signs the selected mandate and redirects the proxy back to MOA-ID.
- MOA-ID fetches the selected mandate from the MIS and finishes the proxy's authentication.

In comparison to the standard MOA-ID authentication without representation (see section *Identification and Authentication of Austrian Citizens*), the proxy is faced with only one more single step.

In case of professional representatives, the MIS presents the proxy a further option when selecting a mandate. The professional representative can choose to represent either a natural or legal person. In case of a natural person, the representative has to enter the client's name and date of birth. The MIS fetches the sourcePIN from the SourcePIN Register and creates the electronic mandate. In case of legal persons, the professional representative can search the constitutive register for company information. For example, by entering the company's name or the company number, the MIS searches the company register for this specific company and creates a dedicated mandate for this company.

CONCLUSION

The Austrian identity ecosystem and its core concepts and building blocks support a broad spectrum of different use cases regarding the secure and reliable identification and authentication of users. Austrian citizens are authenticated by means of their personal Citizen Card, which can be implemented by means of smart cards or mobile phones. Additionally, foreign citizens can make use of the Austrian identity ecosystem to securely authenticate at Austrian e-Government services. Finally, the Austrian identity ecosystem also provides appropriate concepts for the integration of legal identities and electronic mandates.

The comprehensive Austrian identity ecosystem allows for a secure and reliable identification and authentication of national and foreign citizens. Identification and authentication of users are key requirements of most transactional e-Government services. By providing well-designed solutions for various use cases, the Austrian identity ecosystem facilitates the fulfillment of these requirements.

The Austrian identity ecosystem and its core concepts and building blocks is a prime example of a successful application of secure information technology to establish appropriate solutions for security sensitive applications. By relying on approved protocols and architectures, the Austrian identity ecosystem contributes to the overall security of the Austrian e-Government strategy and assures the future success of e-Government in Austria.

REFERENCES

ETSI TS 101 903. (2010). *Electronic signatures and infrastructures (ESI), XML advanced electronic signatures (XAdES) V1.4.2.*

European Commission. (2002). *eEurope 2005: An information society for all*. Geneva, Switzerland: European Commission.

European Commission. (2006). *i2010 eGovernment action plan: Accelerating eGovernment in Europe for the benefit of all*. Geneva, Switzerland: European Commission.

European Commission. (2010). *A digital agenda for Europe*. Geneva, Switzerland: European Commission.

European Parliament. (2000a). *Santa maria de feira European Council. Conclusions of the Presidency*. Geneva, Switzerland: Author.

European Parliament. (2000b). *Lisbon European council. Presidency Conclusions*. Geneva, Switzerland: Author.

European Union. (1999). *Directive 1999/93/EC of the European parliament and of the council of 13: December 1999 on a community framework for electronic signatures*. Brussels, Belgium: European Union.

Fearon, J. D. (1999). *What is identity (as we now use the word)?* Palo Alto, CA: Stanford University.

Federal Chancellery of Austria. (1982). *Service of documents act*. Federal Law Gazette No. 200/1982 as amended by: Federal Law Gazette I No. 5/2008.

Federal Chancellery of Austria. (1991). *General administrative procedure act 1991–AVG*. Federal Law Gazette No. 51/1991 as amended by: Federal Law Gazette I No. 135/2009.

Federal Chancellery of Austria. (1999). *The Austrian signature act*. Federal Law Gazette I No. 190/1999.

Federal Chancellery of Austria. (2003). *Module for online applications (MOA) - Identification (ID)*. Retrieved from https://joinup.ec.europa.eu/software/moa-idspss/description

Federal Chancellery of Austria. (2004). The Austrian egovernment act: Federal act on provisions facilitating electronic communications with public bodies, entered into force on 1 March 2004, last amended part I, Nr. 111/2010. *Austrian Federal Law Gazette (BGBl) part I Nr. 10/2004.*

Federal Chancellery of Austria. (2008). *The Austrian citizen card*. Retrieved from http://www.buergerkarte.at/konzept/securitylayer/spezifikation/aktuell/

Federal Chancellery of Austria. (2010a). *Implementation of the i2010 initiative in Austria*. Retrieved from http://www.bka.gv.at/DocView.axd?CobId=16635

Federal Chancellery of Austria. (2010b). E-government equivalence decree, decree of the federal chancellor laying down conditions for equivalence under section 6(5) of the e-government act, 2010. *Austrian Federal Law Gazette (BGBl) Nr. 170/2010.*

Hogg, M., & Abrams, D. (1988). *Social indentifications: A social psychology of intergroup relations and group processes*. London: Routledge.

Katzenstein, P. (1996). *The culture of national security: Norms and identity in world politics*. New York: Columbia University Press.

Khambhammettu, H., & Crampton, J. (2006). Delegation in role-based access control. [ESORICS.]. *Proceedings of ESORICS*, *2006*, 174–191.

OASIS. (2012). *Security assertion markup language (SAML), OASIS security services (SAML) TC*. Retrieved from http://www.oasis-open.org/committees/tc_home.php?wg_abbrev= security

Orthacker, C., Centner, M., & Kittl, C. (2010). Qualified mobile server signature. In Meyer, H. M., & Turner, J. A. (Eds.), *IFIP Advances in Information and Communication Technology Series*. Springer.

Rössler, T. (2009). Empowerment through electronic mandate – Best practice Austria. In *Proceedings of 9th IFIP WG 6.1 Conference on e-Business, e-Services and e-Society, I3E 2009*, (vol. 305, pp. 148-160). Berlin: Springer.

White, H. C. (1992). *Identity and control: A structural theory of social action*. Princeton, NJ: Princeton University Press.

World Wide Web Consortium. (2008). *XML signature syntax and processing* (2nd ed). Retrieved from http://www.w3.org/TR/xmldsig-core/

Zhang, X., Oh, S., & Sandhu, R. (2003). PBDM: A flexible delegation model in RBAC. In *Proceedings of the Eighth ACM Symposium on Access Control Models and Technologies SACMAT 2003*, (pp. 149-157). ACM.

ENDNOTES

1. http://www.eid-stork.eu/
2. http://www.eu-spocs.eu/
3. SAML (OASIS, 2012) is a widely used XML standard and framework for the secure exchange of identity and authentication information.
4. XMLDSIG (World Wide Web Consortium, 2008) is a recommendation of the World Wide Web Consortium for XML digital signature processing rules and syntax.
5. XAdES (ETSI TS 101 903, 2010) is an open standard for XLM based advanced electronic signatures.
6. The identity link is repeatedly generated and not permanently stored on a foreign eID card.
7. https://joinup.ec.europa.eu/software/mocca/description

Chapter 12
Developing Secure, Unified, Multi-Device, and Multi-Domain Platforms:
A Case Study from the Webinos Project

Andrea Atzeni
Politecnico di Torino, Italy

John Lyle
University of Oxford, UK

Shamal Faily
University of Oxford, UK

ABSTRACT

The need for integrated cross-platform systems is growing. Such systems can enrich the user experience, but also lead to greater security and privacy concerns than the sum of their existing components. To provide practical insights and suggest viable solutions for the development, implementation, and deployment of complex cross-domain systems, in this chapter, the authors analyse and critically discuss the security-relevant decisions made developing the Webinos security framework. Webinos is an EU-funded FP7 project, which aims to become a universal Web application platform for enabling development and usage of cross domain applications. Presently, Webinos runs on a number of different devices (e.g. mobile, tables, PC, in-car systems, etc.) and different Operating Systems (e.g. various Linux distributions, different Windows and MacOSx versions, Android 4.x, iOS). Thus, Webinos is a representative example of cross-platform framework, and even if yet at beta level, is presently one of the most mature, as a prototype has been publicly available since February 2012. Distilling the lessons learned in the development of the Webinos public specification and prototype, the authors describe how potential threats and risks are identified and mitigated, and how techniques from user-centred design are used to inform the usability of security decisions made while developing the alpha and beta versions of the platform.

DOI: 10.4018/978-1-4666-4514-1.ch012

INTRODUCTION

People use multiple devices with different form factors every day. These devices provide access to similar services but in different ways - native apps, Websites, mobile-specific Websites, etc. As such, these devices are interacting with each other more often, either to synchronize data or to provide cross-device user experiences, e.g., using a smart phone as a remote control for a smart TV, or having a companion application to a live TV programme. These new activities, scenarios and cross-domain user experiences require greater communication and increase the potential for misuse.

For example, *Gloria likes to personalize her online experience by setting application preferences, but also for privacy reasons she retains separate online identities. Gloria may be used to adopting a mobile device for one identity and a laptop for another, each of which covers two separate contexts. With smart systems and identity providers both available, Gloria's device may switch from one identity to another, but Gloria may be unaware of this switch if she set up her device to move between services without any intervention. In fact, she may not be aware which identity is exposed unless her activities are such that she would be conscious of an identity switch.*

Every different device may make a different trade-off considering authentication, authorization, and usability. For example, some devices may only infrequently ask the user to authenticate in order to minimize the use of a small keyboard or screen. However, when devices are used together, their different settings may conflict and either harm the user experience or reduce the system's security.

Security control can introduce usability problems (Schneier, 2009) as configuring and then using complex security features, like access control systems, can be difficult, time-consuming and fundamentally at odds with the primary goals of the end user. As each new platform may have a different system and interface for doing this, the access control problems in cross-device systems are magnified.

How security problems can be addressed in such a complex scenario without losing focus on the usability of the system is the topic of this chapter. The chapter describes a case study in multi and cross-device access control based on the *Webinos* project. The *Webinos* project has designed and implemented a cross-platform application environment which allows developers to create applications which can communicate seamlessly between each platform. This includes the development of a personal device network (Niemegeers and Heemstra de Groot, 2002) which attempts to solve many of the related problems. User-centred design techniques are one of the most important points in our approach. Users are personified as specific entities (like Gloria), with skills, attitudes and motivations, to avoid talking about generic users" who might become contradictory when based on solely on the imagination of developers.

This chapter is structured as follows: section 2 introduces the *Webinos* project and gives a high-level technical overview, as well as listing desired goals, implementation details and the most important concepts related to the *Webinos* architecture. Section 2 also introduces related work on similar architectures to inform our security framework. Section 3 explains in detail how we approached the key usability problems. Section 4 states the main threats we identified in the cross-domain *Webinos* platform. Section 5 introduces the security of the *Webinos* execution environment. Section 6 describes the different types of authentication mechanisms introduced in *Webinos*. Section 7 highlights how to secure a communication session to avoid confidentiality and integrity losses. Section 8 addresses the core of the access control system: the policy framework. Section 9 approaches another task performed as part of *Webinos*: the security analysis of the APIs introduced in *Webinos* so far. Section 10 briefly describes the need for a secure storage to keep confidential information in our cross-device system. Section 11 finally discuss our findings in a multi-platform system and draws conclusions.

BACKGROUND

Webinos

Webinos is a cross-device application platform for mobile Web applications and widgets. It provides applications with a set of APIs for accessing local resources, such as sensors and address books, as well as APIs for communication with other devices and services. The platform aims to create a seamless multi-device user experience through data synchronization and a consistent access control system. *Webinos* is supported on four main device domains: PCs, smartphones, in-car systems and set-top boxes. The *Webinos* project (The *Webinos* Consortium, 2012c) consists of a consortium of over twenty partners, including mobile network operators, device manufacturers, industry research institutions, universities and software companies.

Webinos is suitable for augmenting common scenarios like the following: *Helen and her family see an advert on television for a skiing holiday and decide to book it using their TV. Automatically, their calendars are updated, the car navigation system adds the destination, and a post is added to Helen's social network. On the long car journey, Helen plays a game with her children using their in-car entertainment system and her smartphone. A few minutes later, Helen's parents call, and she invites them to take over playing the game with the children remotely, giving her a much-needed break* (a set of scenarios and use cases are available in the Webinos deliverables [The Webinos consortium, 2012d]).

The platform was designed with the following high-level goals in mind:

- Interoperability of applications across the four device domains. Each application can communicate with others on the same device, with another device belonging to the same user, or with an unknown device elsewhere.
- Compatibility achieved through standard JavaScript APIs. This allows applications to run on multiple devices with minimal modification.
- Security and privacy for users and application developers.
- Adaptability allowing applications and devices to take advantage of information about the current environment.
- Usability through the creation of a *seamless experience* for users of applications across multiple devices.

The *Webinos* runtime has been officially implemented so far for three target platforms: Android for smartphones and tablets, Windows for PC, and Linux variants for in-car systems and set-top boxes (other unofficial versions exist, e.g., for MacOSX and iOS).

Webinos is based around the concept of *personal zones*, as shown in Figure 1, and consists broadly of three components, as listed in Table 1.

A user's personal zone is the set of all their devices. Each personal zone has a *personal zone hub* (PZH), which coordinates communication, synchronizes data and provides access to devices from the Internet. All other devices have a *Web Runtime* (WRT) (much like a browser) which displays Web applications and process widgets. The Web runtime has been extended with a *Webinos* plug-in to connect it to a local *Personal Zone Proxy* (PZP), which implements APIs, provides local access control and communicates with the personal zone hub.

The hub is responsible for discovering Internet services and appropriately routing requests from and to each device in the zone. The hub must be constantly online and addressable, so that any device on the Internet can potentially communicate with devices within the zone. This allows for remote data sharing and resource usage both within and between personal zones. The proxy will cache all routing information, so that when a hub is not accessible (e.g. when a device loses network

Developing Secure, Unified, Multi-Device, and Multi-Domain Platforms

Figure 1. Overview of Webinos

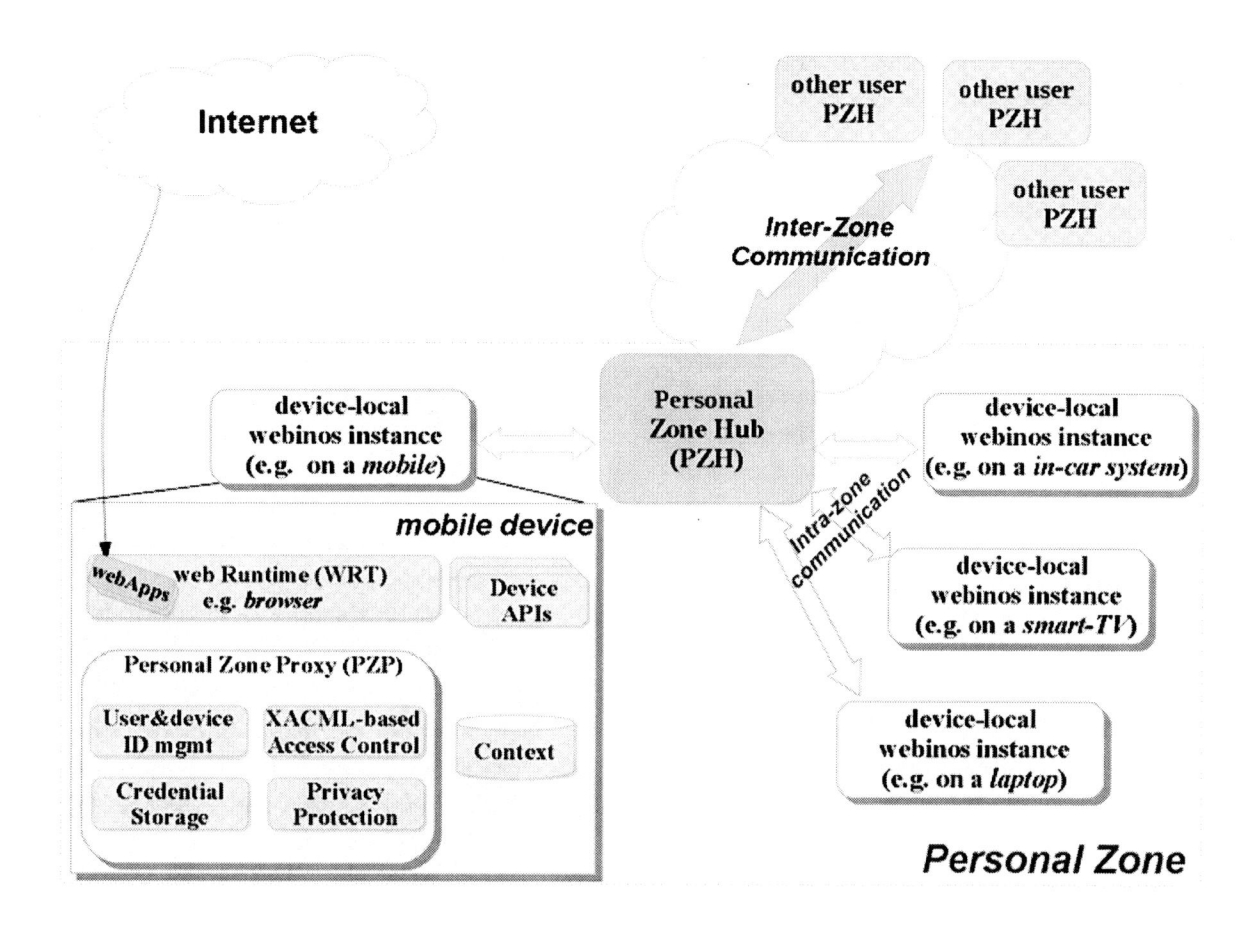

access) the proxy can perform many of the same tasks and support peer-to-peer communication. The *Webinos* architecture is therefore federated: each user has their own personal zone hub and each device has its own proxy. The hub is a key component in the architecture because it provides a central location for storing and synchronizing data, but also because it has many useful security features. The hub can act as a trusted party. In one example application it is used to host personal data rather than trusting it to the application provider.

The hub can be installed on any device, but we have implemented it to be either a cloud-based virtual platform or installed on a home router. The personal zone hub is an essential component within *Webinos* and potentially useful for any Web application middleware.

Table 1. Personal zone components

Component	Key Features and Capabilities
Personal Zone Hub (PZH)	Constantly available and addressable, routes messages, acts as a certificate authority. The hub provides a Web-based user interface to control the personal zone and audit activity.
Personal Zone Proxy (PZP)	Implements most of the Webinos JavaScript APIs, and provides policy-driven access control. As the name suggests, it proxies requests between the PZH and the Web runtime
Web Runtime (WRT)	The user interface to Web applications and widgets.

Component Technologies

The Webinos project makes use of several existing technologies and frameworks.

For initial user registration and subsequent management of the personal zone through a Web interface on the personal zone hub, Webinos uses *OpenID*. OpenID is a decentralised identity and authentication system for Web-based systems. It allows users to register with an *identity provider (IdP)* and then re-use this provider when authenticating to other Websites. For example, when registering with an online Web forum, the end user can specify their identity provider and then will be redirected to this provider to authenticate. The identity provider will send the forum an *identity assertion* proving that the user has ownership of the claimed identity. This allows users to have fewer identities and authentication credentials, and means that they do not have to give passwords to potentially untrustworthy third party services.

The Webinos implementation uses NodeJS, an open source JavaScript runtime for distributed network applications (Joyent, Inc., 2012). NodeJS had to be ported to Android, but was then available on all target platforms. The rest of the platform was written in device-agnostic JavaScript as well as some native C++.

RELATED WORK

The emerging field of cross-platform security is only partially covered by well-established security research on home and personal area networks, which focus on logically or physically co-located collection of devices, like in a home wireless network. Security is only partially covered since, for example, a home network tends to use only one medium, such as WiFi, and therefore cannot encompass mobile devices and connection via mobile device networks.

Since the *Webinos* project is an attempt to make the creation of secure cross-device platform, it addresses the security and privacy issues of the new scenarios' increased connectivity, applying some concepts and adapting and evolving previous security solutions when needed.

In particular,

- Kinkelin et al. (2011) adopted a method to create device-user link and trust relationship among different (home) networks. We extend the solution to the mobile world and add certificates exchange.
- UPnP Device Protection Service (UPnP Forum, 2011) is interesting for combination of certificates and device pairings, which is also our approach, but we adopted a simpler schema of level of privileges and hierarchies.
- SHAMAN (Mitchell and Schaffelhofer, 2004; SHAMAN Project, 2002) investigated the personal CA concept that we borrowed, but we make different assumptions about the place of the personal CA, which is cloud based and in principle always available.
- UIA (Ford et al., 2006) proposed a similar but more general solution. We argue that, in practice, a *Webinos*-like structure would be the most common way in which this solution would be realised, considering the necessity of dealing with Network Address Translation and mobile networks. Differently from UIA, we introduce a further step of usability leveraging on existing user identities when available (e.g. in social networks).

Where previous proposal failed to convincingly cover a particular usage scenario, we tried to fill the gap. The main gaps we identified are mostly related with user acceptability of the security mechanisms.

- Web PKI are not suitable for users of Web servers and their devices, as the scarce use

of client certificates on the public Web demonstrates. This means that two users of the Web cannot identify each other with secure and robust mechanisms.
- A home network tends to use only one medium, such as WiFi, thus Home PKI cannot interoperate with mobile networks, and therefore cannot encompass mobile devices which often connect from remote locations via mobile data
- User PKIs have usability problem, and are not integrated with social networks

Our focus on user experience in Webinos is motivated by some milestone articles on usable security: Whitten and Tygar (1999) suggests that security needs a usability standard that is different from those applied to 'general consumer software', while Sasse et al. (2001) advocates properly applying standard usability design techniques for addressing security problems, interest in HCI-security is also witnessed by specific sessions at major conferences (e.g. Faily et al., 2013).

The decision to use domain certificates to bootstrap a PKI is based on what we believe users will accept. By incorporating the complex PKI mechanisms into the underlying Webinos middleware, specifically in the PZH (in principle always available in the "cloud"), we have made the PKI metaphor usable for end users who might otherwise be unwilling to invest in PKI management.

Mobile Application Projects

Android is an open source platform derived from Linux 2.6, shaped for mobile devices. Android security (And, 2012) is based on two different mechanisms: *sandboxing* and access control based on read-write-execute permission tuple.

Each Android application is hosted in a Dalvik VM, which is an optimized interpreter for resource (power, memory) scarce devices. Each application runs sandboxed (isolated) from each other in its own instance of the Dalvik virtual machine. The kernel is responsible for sandboxing management. Each instance of the Dalvik virtual machine represents a Linux kernel process. Applications must declare needed permissions for capabilities not provided by the sandbox, so the system prompts the user for consent (at install time). Permission may be enforced at the time of a call into the system, starting an activity (i.e. an application component), sending and receiving broadcasts, accessing and operating on a content provider, and binding to or starting a service.

The second security mechanism is essentially the same of Linux OS. Files and data held by an application are isolated from other applications enforced by the Android Linux kernel and traditional Unix file permissions. To access data from another application, it must first be exposed via a content provider accessed by the message bus.

To ensure application integrity and authenticity, applications must be signed with a certificate whose private key is held by their developer. The certificate identifies the author of the application and does not need to be signed by a certificate authority.

iOS previously known as iPhone OS (iOS, 2010), is a Unix-like operating system developed by Apple for its smartphones and tablets. In iOS, every application is sandboxed during installation. The application, its preferences, and its data are restricted to a unique location in the file system and no application can access another application's preferences or data. In addition, an application running in iOS can see only its own keychain items. The keychain is used to store passwords, keys, certificates, and other secrets.

Its implementation, therefore, requires both cryptographic functions to encrypt and decrypt secrets, and data storage functions to store the secrets and related data in files. To achieve these aims, Keychain Services calls the Common Crypto dynamic library. Digital signatures are required on all applications for iOS. In addition, Apple adds its own signature before distributing an iOS application. Apple does not sign applications that have not been signed by the developer, and applications not signed by Apple simply will not run (Mac, 2010a, 2010b).

Webinos has incorporated several useful ideas from mobile operating systems' security:

- *Code signing*, to prevent installation/instantiation of non-trusted applications (i.e. not authenticated and/or not modified by non-authorized parties and/or provided by untrusted parties).
- *Sandboxing*, to prevent unwanted influences of one application to another one and or to the runtime.
- A *security policy framework*, that is as simple as possible to avoid usability problems and lead to misconfiguration, but expressive enough to allow detailed access control to any key features and functions.

BONDI (bon, 2009) is a composite specification allowing Web applications (widget and Web pages) to interoperate over BONDI defined execution environments. The security framework introduced in BONDI allows different forms of security policy to be expressed based on widget resource signatures (compliant with W3C Widgets 1.0 digital signature specification [W3C Widgets, 2011]). Signatures associated to each widget are also used to assure provenance and integrity. It allows blacklisting and/or whitelisting of widgets, authors, and Websites. The model identifies identity types, resources, attributes and conditions that can be expressed in an XML-based interchange format.

While *Webinos* took inspiration from this work, he management of a security policies can be a source of usability problems, particularly given BONDI's focus on mobile devices rather than device owners. In the following section we will describe how we improved access control system to cope with these multiple domains, and studies were carried out to improve usability.

Usability

In addition to enabling the convergence of different device platforms, we also designed *Webinos* to meet the expectations of a broad user base. This meant that not only would *Webinos* need to be secure in light of a broad range of risks, these risks would need to be addressed without compromising the user experience of *Webinos*-enabled applications. The consequences of failing to do this are well reported in the HCI Security literature. For example, Whitten & Tyger's seminal work on the usability of PGP (Whitten and Tygar, 1999) illustrates how, despite developing an aesthetically pleasing graphical user interface, users were unable to correctly configure and use PGP to encrypt email; this was because the mental models used by the developers of PGP were at odds with those associated with its end users. Surprisingly, insights into how to incorporate human factors into the design of secure systems have been limited, despite the growing interest in HCI-Security at both Information Security and HCI conferences. This is slowly beginning to change, as evidenced by dedicated sessions at major conferences (e.g. Faily et al., 2013); however, the state-of-the-art for designing usable security remains the application of classic user-centred design techniques to voice the security expectations of a system's stakeholders.

To account for these user expectations, we created and extensively used behavioural specification of archetypical users called *personas*. Personas (Cooper, 1999) are artefacts designed to deal with programmer biases arising from the word *user*. These biases can lead to programmers bending and stretching assumptions about users to meet their own expectation. To address these biases, designers explicitly develop for specific user profiles; these represent the target segment of the system or product being designed. This approach brings two benefits. First, designers only have to focus on those requirements necessary to keep the target persona happy. Second, the idiosyncratic detail associated with personas makes them communicative to a variety of stakeholders. Since their initial proposal over a decade ago, Personas have become a mainstay in User-Centred Design, with articles, book-chapters, and even a book (Pruitt and Adlin, 2006) devoted to the subject of developing and applying them to support usability design. Personas have also been found to be useful as a tool for eliciting requirements for secure systems (Faily and Fléchais, 2010).

When designing *Webinos*, personas were used to surface assumptions that different project team members held about prospective users.

Despite their popularity, the process for developing personas is often methodologically weak, with little concrete guidance available about how to begin personas development effort, and how to structure their analysis. To address these weaknesses, we devised methodologically grounded process to develop them. This led to several "end-user" and "developer" personas (The *Webinos* Consortium, 2011).

Personas were also used to inform threat modelling by the creation of *attacker personas*. The adversarial element is an intrinsic part of the design of secure systems, but usually assumptions about attackers and threat is often limited or stereotypical. One component of a threat is a threat agent, the person or organisation who is motivated to fulfil the threat by attacking the system. We used attacker personas to model these agents, using an approach for developing them which is both grounded and validated by structured data about attackers (Atzeni et al., 2011).

These personas were created in the same way as other *Webinos* personas, but their characteristics were based on data sources about known attackers. The attacker personas were chosen to be representative of OWASP (OWASP Foundation, 2011) human threat agents. To mitigate the risk of developing irrational attacker models, we chose not to model rare but possibly very dangerous attackers, such as government or organised-crime sponsored professional hackers; accurate information about such attackers is not generally available.

The grounding of attacker personas is based on three important characteristics: they are representative of known attacker classes; they are representative of criminals convicted for common online crimes; and they are situated within the context of *Webinos* by design and workshop discussions. As a result, supplemental threat modelling artefacts appeared more realistic, because they were grounded in what a concrete attacker can and is willing to do.

THREAT MODEL

As detailed in section 2, the *Webinos* platform can be split into two key components:

- An application runtime environment (the WRT, essentially an environment providing Web browser's functionalities) for executing applications securely and providing APIs for accessing local resources.
- An overlay network connecting devices belonging to different people and on different networks to support multi-device use cases.

As such, threats tend to exist either at the application execution or network layer. In addition, we must consider the impact of physical threats such as device loss, theft or interference during maintenance. We also consider threats to data storage.

Threats were identified by approaching the problem through a structured risk-analysis approach, which also addressed human factors. We developed a model of *Webinos* based on the IRIS (Integrated Requirement and Information Security) meta-model (Faily and Fléchais, 2010), fed by the *Webinos* user and attacker personas. The attacker personas were grounded in data sources accredited by the security community, such as the Common Attack Pattern Enumeration (CAPEC) (The MITRE Corporation, 2012) and The Open Web Application Security Project (OWASP) 'Top Ten Project' (OWASP foundation, 2011). In addition, as part of the development of *Webinos*, we identified misuse and misusability cases (Faily and Fléchais, 2011) and threats early on in the design phase and applied security *pre-mortems* (Faily et al., 2012) to elicit sources of threats.

Application Environment Threats

Threats to the application environment are broadly the same as threats to any Web browser, but with the added impact of new device APIs and services being misused. We identified *Webinos*-specific threats and attacks including:

1. **Unauthorised use of APIs and remote resources through content injection (XSS/CSRF):** A vulnerable application could be trusted by the end user but load malicious JavaScript from a third party. This JavaScript could take advantage of the application's privileged status and misuse the APIs that it has access to. For example, misusing the messaging API to send unauthorised text messages to premium numbers.
2. **Vulnerability exploitation in the underlying device platform through Webinos APIs:** If a *Webinos* API to access a local resource, such as a sensor, was implemented in native code and contain a buffer overrun or similar attack, a Web application could exploit this to gain access to the system. This would allow the machine to be added to a botnet, or for user data to be stolen.
3. **Eavesdropping on communication between applications and Webinos:** Applications served over HTTP are vulnerable to requests and responses (which may contain valuable data or credentials) being intercepted and modified.
4. Application Denial of Service by competing application developers. If Web applications are competing for users, then one might attempt to exploit a vulnerability to render the other unusable and drive people to alternatives. For example, a content injection attack could deface the Web application or crash on start-up.
5. Applications capturing hidden analytics about end users. In particular, *Webinos* allows for recording of user context evolution, and provides an API (the context API [The *Webinos* Consortium, 2012b]) to allow application to access these data. This might be misused to track the user's activities and behaviour in unwanted and privacy-invasive ways.
6. **Device availability loss through battery exhaustion:** Malicious or poorly developed Web applications might run resource-intensive code and exhaust the battery of a mobile device, rendering it temporarily unusable.
7. **Cross-site scripting (XSS):** If an insecure application loads JavaScript injected by a malicious third party, it could result in loss of data or cause the Web application to misbehave.
8. **Theft of identity credentials:** If an attacker gains access to the user's OpenID credentials used to log into the PZH, this could result in loss of confidentiality and integrity of stored data, loss of access to administration console, impersonation, loss of other credentials.
9. **Man in the Browser' attacks:** Malicious plugins might be installed which are able to steal Web application data.
10. **Evasion of access control policies through use of non-Webinos APIs:** If the underlying device platform offers alternative ways of accessing device resources, a *Webinos*

Developing Secure, Unified, Multi-Device, and Multi-Domain Platforms

application might use them to circumvent the access control system.

11. **Spoofing of PZH administration page to steal user credentials:** The user might be tricked into entering credentials into an unauthorised page through spoofing.
12. **Use of accidentally-enabled test code and experimental APIs in Webinos deployments:** If the *Webinos* platform was developed with test code that remained enabled after deployment, attackers could misuse this capability to bypass policy controls or exploit the platform.
13. **User linkability through fingerprinting browser APIs:** The addition of new browser APIs would make it easier for advertisers to track the same user between sites; they would have a similar set of APIs available.
14. **Two-factor authentication defeat through misuse of Webinos messaging APIs:** The *Webinos* messaging APIs might allow a Web application to view SMS messages used as a second factor of authentication.
15. **Misconfigured access controls exploitation:** if users set overly permissive access control policies, applications may be able to gain unexpected access to resources.
16. **Identification of weak policies through context framework:** Since the context framework log also policy usage, poorly restricted access to context data can allow policy related information leakage.
17. **Insecure storage of Webinos data:** Offline Web application data might become available to local malware, or to a thief who has gained physical access to a device.
18. **Failure to check permissions on access requests:** A weakness in the *Webinos* implementation could be exploited to gain unauthorised access to APIs.

While several more threats and attacks still remain, this list does provide useful coverage of threats to the *Webinos* application environment and test cases for the specification and requirements.

Network Threats

Threats to a *Webinos* personal zone may impact the security of every device within it. The following threats and attacks have been identified and must be mitigated in the architecture.

1. **Insecure key storage and use:** The *Webinos* platform uses PKI to identify devices. If a device key was stolen or copied by an attacker, they would be able to join another device to the personal zone and either impersonate the user or gain access to other services.
2. **Unauthorised joining of a personal zone:** A user's PZH might allow an unauthorised user to add a new device to the personal zone. This attack might be hard to detect and would allow a range of misuses of personal devices.
3. **Impersonating a friend when requesting access the user's personal zone:** If Mallory is able to impersonate Bob, he could do this to create a connection to Alice's personal zone and access her resources. This may be possible if Alice is not sure of how Bob can be identified, or if Bob's user credentials are easy to guess or steal.
4. **Unauthorised enrolment of a user device to a malicious personal zone hub:** Before a personal zone proxy is configured to point to the user's personal zone hub, an attacker might force it to join another, malicious hub without the user realising. This would then give the attacker access to Alice's device and allow the attacker to impersonate Alice.
5. **Unauthorised transfer of data from secure to insecure devices:** If one *Webinos* device is well-secured and difficult to access, an attacker might use a less secure device to access it via *Webinos*.

Physical and Environmental Threats

1. **Misuse of physical access to access data stored on remote devices:** Similarly to the previous attack, this involves a malicious engineer or technician misusing their access to a device during maintenance (such as a car during its annual service) to access data stored on the rest of the personal zone.
2. **Exploiting NFC capabilities to impersonate users via a relay attack:** Alice's NFC reader might be made available over *Webinos* and then relay attacks could allow Eve to impersonate her NFC device for mobile payment or identity theft.
3. **Exploiting Bluetooth capabilities:** Since Bluetooth is developed for easy connectivity, often it is used in "mode 1" (no encryption and authentication), and thus bluetooth connections allow for impersonation, eavesdropping and connection hijacking.

Data at Rest

The following components in *Webinos* will be storing data.

1. Applications may store data locally on each device, as well as using data (such as media files) exposed by each device. To support this, an application specific, isolated storage area is made available to each *Webinos* application. In addition, *Webinos* can also expose arbitrary data storage. Access to arbitrary data storage will be mediated by policies and require a different permission. Isolated storage from one application is never exposed to another.
2. Devices. Each device with a PZP will store some or more of the following:
   a. Application data
   b. Data in policies, certificates, and preferences. This may include the names of applications the user has installed, the devices they use and their friends' identities. It is therefore considered private.
   c. Browser histories and system logs
   d. Context data (a temporary log file), if enabled.
   e. Downloaded widget data containing potentially valuable intellectual property
3. Cloud-based components (PZH, online services) may store:
   a. Context data
   b. Data in policies, certificates, and preferences. This may include the names of applications the user has installed, the devices they use and their friends' identities. It is therefore considered private.
   c. Application data (outside of *Webinos* control)

We therefore identify the following threats in Table 2.

In the sections that follow, we will describe how these threats have been addressed.

Trusted Execution Environment

Threats like unauthorized use of APIs and resources, application denial of service, cross site scripting, man in the browser demand a trusted environment of execution to be mitigated.

The security of the *Webinos* execution environment is specified to achieve security properties, starting from some assumptions. The *Webinos* core components, i.e. the PZH, the PZP and the *Webinos* runtime system are assumed as trusted, so, threats involving the corruption of code while on the device or modification of the runtime itself are not considered.

However, these components are considered at different level of security. While the PZH is the core of the security framework, it is usually placed in particularly secure place (e.g. in the cloud

Developing Secure, Unified, Multi-Device, and Multi-Domain Platforms

Table 2. Reference threats for data at rest

Threat	Description	Attacker	Motivation
Native malware	Malware is installed on *Webinos*-enabled device and is used to access and transmit application data to a third party. This may be targeted to particular apps or users	Irwin	Corporate espionage or discrediting an existing application. Monetary gain.
Device theft	A *Webinos*-enabled device is stolen and data is down loaded by the thief.	David	Most likely selling the device, but this could be a targeted attack on an individual or corporation
Webinos malware	A malicious *Webinos* application accesses user data	Frankie	Stealing personal data for personal or monetary gain, may be looking for credentials or credit card details.
Online data leak	A PZH provider exposes their entire file system by mistake. This compromises the certificates, keys and settings of each user	Gary	May be discrediting former employee, or may be looking for recognition from the user community
App content theft	A *Webinos* widget data is stolen by another developer	Jimmy	Monetary gain – copying valuable IPR
Data blackmail	User data is encrypted and the key held by an attacker. The user is extorted to get back their personal data	Ethan	Monetary gain

under control of personal zone provider) and little can be done in case of its violation, information available to the PZP and the WRT are minimized to mitigate information leakage if compromised.

Webinos components of the runtime system allows execution on the base of the application trust, which can be given through certificates signed by a recognised authorities and/or through user authorisation (secured by a previous authentication) at application install or runtime. The only authorised applications shall be from signed, trusted sources, which may be defined by the manufacturer, network provider, or end user.

The *Webinos* runtime must be able to control all application (origin) authenticity and integrity, and this for the firun time before being installed or updated, and *Webinos* must protect the integrity of application instances as they are transferred between devices. Application integrity and authenticity is enforced by the *Webinos* system, in particular the personal zone proxy which acts also as policy enforcement point.

At the same time the system must restrict the application from loading untrustworthy external code, when embedded in a downloaded page (e.g. in a <*script*> tag) The external source must either be an HTTPS location, trusted by the *Webinos* system, or the script must has a signature file linked in the HTML.

Ambiguities in security information must be avoided, i.e. *Webinos* personas shall be able to easily recognize *Webinos* applications running and the authority that certified them and *Webinos* personas should be able to the *Webinos* policy editing tool shall allow policy specification based on assets recognizable by the user and based on comprehensible actions and effects.

The *Webinos* runtime shall protect policies from tampering or modification by unauthorised applications, by exploiting mechanisms to isolate them in memory and in the file system.

Default behaviour should be set to a conservative posture, to avoid common problem of weak configuration left untouched. The installation (or filef use) of an application is the time when a trust decision must be made. By default, unless there are good reasons (based on a conscious decision of the end user), applications should not be installed. If there is doubt about the provenance of the application—whether it is from the right source and has the right name—it should also not be installed

IDENTITY AND AUTHENTICATION

The problem of user authentication and identity management was identified as one of the most sensitive within the *Webinos* security group. Threats like unauthorised joining of a personal zone, spoofing of PZH page, friend impersonation, and unauthorised enrolment can be mitigated by proper authentication mechanisms.

Since *Webinos* provides for local and remote access, in different domains, and from different platform, the provided identity management mechanisms should be usable by a large variety of users and for a large variety of purposes (i.e. it should be suitable in principle for all end user personas, difficult to trespass for attacker personas, and possible to exploit for developer personas).

Webinos should allow for identification of the user to any *Webinos* device and application while paying attention to privacy issues. (e.g. a blind answer to any identity request would allow for information leakage, thus there is the choice to not respond to any request by any device, at least not before some trust relationship has been established).

The unusual *Webinos* approach requires identification for devices with multiple users on one device (e.g. TV system), thus a one-to-one device-user relationship cannot be always assumed

Many reference personas developed in *Webinos* (e.g. Peter), would distressingly manage multiple authentications and multiple authentication systems. Thus, *Webinos* should expose a single sign-on experience when possible. This problem is even more difficult, as *Webinos* must interact with services on the Web which adopt different authentication schemes (e.g. OAuth), as much seamlessly as possible, while preserving the security of the authentication.

To allow for transparency, the user should know the less of different identities (to not mention of different identity providers) while the appropriate identity required to access services should be always accessible.

To allow for simplicity, existing identities (e.g. Google) should be re-used when possible, but only if appropriate. For example, authentication to a specific device often depends on an identity agreed between the user and the device OS (e.g. finger print, user name/password, etc.), and the device does not need to rely on a third party identity provider to perform authentication. In this case, adopting a third party identities could enable denial of service attacks due to unavailability of the third party identity provider, while not reducing the identities already adopted by the person.

Identity management through certificates and public key infrastructure is also a valuable point, since it allows for a solid framework and for securing communications, with the strong contraindication that almost all *Webinos* reference personas cannot understand the PKI metaphor, due to their technical background.

Final aspect to consider is that authentication is a requirement to solve security problems, but has its own security requirements that must be addressed, in particular is desirable to carry it on a secure channel, to achieve integrity and confidentiality of the exchanged authentication credentials. To challenge these requirements, in *Webinos* we developed five independent authentication mechanisms to handle the combination of users, devices and applications, while hiding complexities and re-using identities. In the next sections we detail these five mechanisms, two related to the users, two to the devices and one to applications.

Users

Users in *Webinos* are primarily identified via an OpenID (OpenID, 2013) account URI. This may be a URL or email address. This identity is used to authenticate the user to the personal zone hub's Web interface and administer the personal zone. How the authentication occurs is up to the OpenID provider. However, on some devices users may forego the OpenID authentication in favour of they device-held private key and certificate. For devices with constrained user interfaces, this prevents users from repeatedly having to enter passwords. Furthermore, allow for re-use of existing identities if so desired by the user.

Users may also authenticate to the underlying platform via a device specific mechanism, wrapped using the *Webinos authentication API*. This allows them to take advantage of any fingerprint readers, screen-locks or other systems. This authentication is only used by the authentication API and to authenticate the user if they want to make changes to the local platform. E.g., enabling or disabling a local service. Also in this case, the choice is to not introduce new identities but instead re-use what already available and known by the user.

Devices

Devices are identified by their public key certificate, issued by the personal zone hub. The private key is stored using a platform-provided key store facility, such as Gnome Keyring on Linux or Keychain Services on OS X. Certificates and keys are used as part of the mutually-authenticated TLS connections established between devices in the personal zone.

Certificates are granted to devices when they are enrolled into the personal zone. Enrolment happens through the user visiting their personal zone hub and obtaining a temporary short authentication token. This token is then used when the device connects over TLS to the hub, who exchanges it for a certificate. The authentication metaphor is here more complex, but it is acceptable since it is performed transparently by the end user that likely could misunderstand and misuse certificates and public key mechanisms.

Applications

Applications are identified by the name they are given in the widget manifest, as well as a set of signatures from various authorities. When running in a widget runtime, they have a *recognised origin* referring to the author's own domain, if it exists. The signature scheme is based on the W3C Widget Signatures standard w3c-widget and recognised origins are described in WAC core specifications (The Wholesale Application Community, 2012).

SESSION MANAGEMENT

A functioning *Webinos* network consists of multiple devices, multiple servers, and multiple applications. It requires the interaction of PZPs and PZHs belonging to different users, over multiple different networks.

In *Webinos* there are many notions of session at different levels, due to the different types of possible communications. In particular,

- *Intra Personal Zone Sessions* that are established among PZPs and PZH for any type of communication, particularly for authentication and exchange of data information. The PZH is permanently addressable on the Internet, and requires that the information exchanged in the session are secure.
- *Synchronization* is special case of intra zone sessions, which is required to seamlessly migrate information among different devices in the personal zone, like user data and identity information, certificates, context events and stream, application data and so on. Since synchronisation touches a number of sensitive objects, it can create major issues if leaked.

- *Inter Personal Zone Sessions* which can be created when accessing services on devices/servers outside the user personal zone (e.g. a service on a friend's device). These sessions (for example, between two applications in two different zones) are mediated by a suitable enforcement point entity in each of the two zones personal zone (for anyone of the two zones, a PZP on the device where the service is provided or is requested, and/or the PZH of the other zone). As special case, it is sometimes necessary to route messages between two PZH's to allow monitored communications between applications and services on different zones

Different sessions for different usage enables threats like eavesdropping on communication between applications, Spoofing of PZH administration pages as well as unauthorized joining of a personal zone and friend impersonation.

Another aspect is that the developer personas we elicited (namely, Jessica and Jimmy) are not incline to pay attention to the security and privacy of the users, unless legally obliged to. Thus, *Webinos* should provide a mechanism both easy to use, and to implement. While lack of care in protecting user security and privacy may have many roots (from time pressure to inexperience), and while a systematic re-education of Web developers would greatly improve user security, still sessions require protection now, since session data may contain private information, and may be even possible to use a hijacked session to impersonate a user on an application. From the other hand, the hijacking or unauthorised disclosure of Web session is feasible even inexperienced attackers, as widely available tools like Firesheep and FaceNiff can show.

In *Webinos* we mitigate this by imposing privacy and authentication protocols to implement the following properties.

- Traffic between zones and services is encrypted to make snooping traffic more difficult.
- Client-server sessions are mutually authenticated. This mutual authentication includes, user and device.
- Traffic can be monitored at the PZH for anomalies. For example sudden changes in IP address, can be challenged be asking the device to re-authenticate. This helps mitigate against real time token stealing attacks.

To achieve this goal we impose a mandatory use of Transport Layer Security (TLS) (Dierks and Rescorla, 2008) and relevant extensions, and to allow this PZPs need to be installed securely on devices PZP installation bootstrap. Once this "Intra Personal Zone Pairing" is done, the established long term trust relationship between that PZP and the PZH can be exploited to build up secure sessions.

DISTRIBUTED ACCESS CONTROL POLICIES

A key security feature provided by *Webinos* is a policy-based access control system. This mediates every attempt by an application, device and user to use a *Webinos* API. This is designed to limit the privileges of applications which may be trusted to access certain features but not others. For example, a 'news' application might request access to geolocation data in order to find the most relevant stories, but does not require the ability to send SMS or use the camera. Following the principle of least privilege has been proven effective in other application frameworks (Felt et al., 2011) and *Webinos* attempts to do the same. We believe a properly developed access control system would limit a number of identified threats, like unauthorised use of APIs and remote resources, improper use of non-*Webinos* APIs, exploitation of poor access control configuration.

However, the distributed and heterogeneous nature of *Webinos*, along with the ability to form ad-hoc peer-to-peer collaborations creates challenges, as described in previous work (Lyle et al., 2012).

Firstly, the devices in a user's personal zone must have a synchronised and consistent set of policies. Because different devices come online and offline at different times (a car, for example, might not be used for a week or two) it is necessary to aggressively check that the most recent policies are in place before making access control decisions. Although a *default-deny* policy would prevent out-of-date devices from doing too much harm, revocation of application permissions becomes a slower process. Synchronisation is therefore a core requirement of the *Webinos* policy framework.

Another challenge is integrating privacy controls. Rather than simple access control for confidentiality, users of applications may want assurance that their personal data is not misused or disclosed to third parties. While these requirements are ultimately impractical to enforce—Web applications given access to personal data will always be capable of sharing them with remote servers—it would be helpful for users to be informed of how applications *intend* to use their data.

For example, the news application might state that it only uses *geolocation* to filter results, and that this is not shared with any third party. Such statements can then be matched against the user's preferences and a more informed decision can be made about whether to grant the application access to this resource. The challenge that *Webinos* is facing is to integrate security and privacy controls without introducing excessive complexity.

While *Webinos* tries to build on existing work in policy enforcement, another challenge is adapting more limited access control systems to a more complicated environment. The initial plan for *Webinos* was to use the BONDI-defined (bon, 2009) XACML-based (Godik and Moses, 2005) policy enforcement language and framework, but this turned out to need modification. BONDI policies do not support cross-device interaction or multiple users. Policies must also be able to refer to a dynamically changing set of features, as new APIs may be added by new applications.

Finally, the policy framework had to take into account the different level of confidence in user identity that each application has. For example, a mobile device may be assumed to always belong and be used by one person. However, a shared television might regularly be used by several people, including guests. This means that policies need to refer to the authentication level of the user, and may need to request re-authentication before permission can be granted.

The *Webinos* policy framework is based on XACML, but with the reduced vocabulary defined by the BONDI policy engine (bon, 2009). The BONDI approach has also been adapted to allow the *subject* of policies to refer to the device and user. Abstractly, *Webinos* policies are usually composed in the following way, where device T is the *target device* and device R is the *requesting device*:

User U can access Feature F of Device T through application A on Device R.

An example using XACML syntax is shown in Table 3, for user *jessica@example.com*'s mobile device, denying access to the contacts API. Taken from the *Webinos* Consortium (2012a).

Note that policies refer to *features* of APIs rather than APIs themselves. This is because APIs may include both low- and high-risk functions, such as reading SMS versus sending SMS. Policies are defined in the *policy.xml* file on each platform. New policies are created through user actions: when an application is installed, it prompts the user to allow or deny the application installation and to grant access to requested APIs. This approval is translated into XACML and added to the policy file. The policy implementation architecture also follows from XACML, with policy enforcement (PEP), decision (PDP), information (PIP), and access (PAP) points. On *Webinos*,

Table 3. Example of denying access policy

```
<policy-set combine="deny-overrides">
    <policy combine="first-applicable">
        <target>
            <subject>
                <subject-match attr="id" match="appID"/>
                <subject-match attr="version" match="1.0"/>
                <subject-match attr="user-id"
                    match="pzh.isp.com/jessica@example.com/Jessica's+Mobile/App"/>
            </subject>
        </target>
        <rule effect="deny">
            <condition combine="or">
                <resource-match attr="api-feature"
                    match="http://www.w3.org/ns/api-perms/contacts.read"/>
            </condition>
        </rule>
        <rule effect="permit"> ...</rule>
        <rule effect="deny" />
    </policy>
</policy-set>
```

policy caching is required for requests to remote devices in order to improve efficiency, making the PDP cache (PDPc) a core component.

Synchronisation of policies is implemented through the PZH, which each proxy queries when it starts to receive changes. Each proxy may also make changes to policies (for example, installing a new application) but these require authorisation at the PZH. PZPs also contain an *exceptions.xml* file in the same format.

This file is not synchronised between devices, and is designed to set broad policies that do not need to be changed remotely. This limits the impact of one malicious device attempting to change policies for the whole personal zone.

To describe data handling policies, the XACML-based architecture has been adapted using extensions from the PrimeLife project (Ardagna et al., 2009). This allows *Webinos* to make access control decisions based on both the request context and user preferences. *Webinos* applications contain a *manifest* which let developers give reasons for requesting access to APIs as well as stating obligations with regards to how they will store data. An example excerpt from a manifest is given in Table 4.

THREAT-AWARE API DEVELOPMENT

The *Webinos* platform offers a set of APIs to expose the device and the personal zone's capabilities to applications. These include an *authentication*

Table 4. Privacy-related excerpt of the manifest file

```
<ProvisionalAction>
    <AttributeValue>http://Webinos.org/geolocation</AttributeValue>
    <AttributeValue>#pseudo-analysisDHP</AttributeValue>
    <DeveloperProvidedDescription language="EN">
        The geolocation feature is required by this application in
        order to customise search results.
    </DeveloperProvidedDescription>
</ProvisionalAction>
```

API, which provides to authorized applications the current authentication status of users, and may ask the runtime to (re)authenticate the user; *discovery* which allow applications to discover services without any previous knowledge of the service, and many others (the complete list and description is available in the official deliverable (The *Webinos* Consortium, 2012b).

Each API may have unique security and privacy concerns. Each must be considered in turn and any API-specific threats need to be mitigated. This process also helps to mitigate one of the bigger threats identified in section 4: the exploitation of the underlying platform through misuse of *Webinos* APIs. To approach this problem, we performed a risk analysis process shared among several partners of the project. Selected parties reviewed each API, either due to their security expertise or their involvement with the development of the API and therefore insights into potential threats. Most analysis data was reviewed by another partner before it was considered finished. Creativity was encouraged as part of this exercise, as well as other suitable data sources, like The Mozilla WebAPI security analysis (Mozilla, 2012) and, since many APIs derive from previous efforts by the W3C and WAC, their original considerations on security and privacy.

The findings of this process were conveyed as a series of recommendations and reported to the API developers to inform and modify the API (which within the project is an iterative process). Since API developers were often aware of performance issues, but more rarely of the security implications, this analysis allows for a threat-aware development.

Analysts structured their feedback in a manner that was quick to read, following a specifically developed template. The template suggested that analysts consider various personas, data sources and attack vectors. More specifically, the template allowed obvious threats that misuse of this API could cause to users to be highlighted, taking into account the assets the API gives access to, as well as what happens if the API is excessively used. This considered several *Webinos* personas and took advantage of any persona-specific security and privacy consideration (developed in *Webinos* in parallel to the specification development).

The template has a specific section for threats based on remote invocation of the API (i.e., when called from another device and/or by another user, what are the additional security concerns?). It also allowed analysts with implementation experience to describe their concerns. Developer-specific threats were considered through use of the two developer personas. For instance, analysts were asked how a developer or their application might be caused harm if they used or relied on a certain AP. Finally, threats to device manufacturers, operators, and other stakeholders were also considered: e.g. excessive bandwidth consumption for telecommunications operators.

As a result of the threat analysis several mitigations were recommended. These primarily involved setting default permissions or identifying excessive use of an API, but others were also suggested.

Example Analysis

As an example, we consider the Context API (other API's threat analyses are described in the *Webinos* official deliverable). This API allows access to a user's context data through either explicit queries or a subscription model. Context events include all API calls. Specific threats identified include privacy, confidentiality and non-repudiation topics:

- Any application can monitor what the user is doing and has done, and can react to particular events. This might be used for targeted adverts, physical or cyber stalking, targeted theft or burglary and identity theft.
- Any application can potentially see which files have been opened, where the user has been, contact information, and so on. Depending on implementation, this could

include the content of files and more. An application might use this to gain access to APIs and resources it does not have permission for.
- Users may want to go unmonitored and need to turn off context collection at times. If this is hard to do or unclear, it might result in embarrassment or a loss of reputation.

No specific threats have been identified for remote invocation of this API, because this API primarily uses a central database.

From implementation experience, two availability risks were raised: subscribing to common context events might slow down the platform considerably, making it unusable, and too many queries to the context API might over-use bandwidth and cause either a loss of battery power of expensive mobile phone bills.

Developers using this API should be aware that context data could be inconsistent or misused, thus provide a false impression for developers. For example, if a user turns on and off their context data, it may make them appear to have different behaviour to reality.

Finally, from other stakeholders' point of view, too many queries to the context API might over-use bandwidth and reduce battery life.

Mitigations suggested varied from conservative prevention, turning off context collection by default and providing controls for turning on/off collection and clearing the database, to allowing for fine grained controls and deletion of data (suitable for users aware of what context aspect make available). To enable awareness of the API usage, the system should provide feedback for when applications query context data. Another suggestion was the creation of a figr-grained taxonomy of context data, to allow strict integration with the access control system, and allowing for a bare minimum collection of information about API calls.

Finally, as default policy, access to this API should be denied by default to trusted sources (this allow user to be aware when the requests are done) and always denied to untrusted (unknown) sources.

Analysis Results

The API threat analysis highlighted the fact that APIs should be more privacy aware, e.g. the Discovery API is privacy-invasive due to its use of persistent identifiers for *Webinos* services; this facilitates user fingerprinting, and is unnecessary for "impersonal" services, while the Calendar API and the Messaging API expose a great deal of information to requesting applications, even if not always required. e.g. for Calendar, an application which requires only the free/busy status of a user will still be given details of every calendar entry. Privacy friendliness could be achieved by a finer grained detail of the API interface (so application can obtain only the interface which exposes the minimum required user information) and the use of an Intent-style approach where the application is unaware of the service fulfilling a request.

It is also useful to make a clear distinction between types of application: 'system level' and 'Web level'. These have different potential security levels, and address the two types of use case considered within *Webinos*. On the one hand, applications requiring only slightly more functionality than that provided by the Web browser. On the other, system-level applications which are more trusted and need to have greater access to device features. Web applications could be executed in a normal Web browser and should be given access to a limited set of APIs in a more privacy-friendly way (e.g. discovery). This is because Web applications are vulnerable to a wide range of attacks which are difficult to mediate at the API level. By contrast, system level applications will run in a secure execution environment (a widget runtime) which protects them from attacks by plugins, or through cross-site scripting. They have the potential to access more APIs and may have fewer privacy constraints. These apps should only be installed from app stores and must be pre-vetted, but when they are installed they are able to do much more.

SECURE STORAGE

The *Webinos* platform uses and stores data which may have security and privacy requirements. For example, many of the personas may use applications to monitor health data, to read personal emails, or to store valuable work fipla. As such, it is important to address threats and mitigations to vulnerabilities affecting data at rest.

Because most platforms already provide some mitigation to attacks on stored data, *Webinos* does not attempt to solve every problem. Table 5 shows how the threats from section 4 may be mitigated. In the case of Application content theft, we do not attempt to provide a DRM solution but expect that one could be implemented over the top of *Webinos*.

DISCUSSION

We sum up now a set of principles the lessons learned from two years of work in developing the security framework.

Tablets, smartphones, laptops, and cars are all designed to be mobile. This significantly increases the risk of a device being lost or stolen. Sensitive data should either not be stored in mobile devices or protected by secure storage available on the devices. More sensibly, revocation must be primarily concerned with removing a lost and potentially rogue device from the personal network, recalling the security inclination of the potential users (for many *Webinos* personas revocation must be a one-click process, and must also not rely on the user having another enrolled device to hand).

The interoperability of Web applications—which provide a common, accessible Web server for communication—should be re-used to make personal networks available to any device capable of making outgoing connections to Web servers. Mechanisms which requires an always-on connection (e.g. for authentication, synchronization, PKI management) would greatly benefit of this availability, while the management cost would be outsourced to the Internet infrastructure and to the provider. We believe this is an enabler for a efficient scaling of complex security solutions (like PKI) on mobile networks with frequently changing IP addresses.

It is better to delegate the tasks to the underlying OS when a security mechanisms is platform specific and low-level. It is time consuming to design an application middleware, which is capable of interacting with all low-level security

Table 5. Examples of suggested mitigation for data-at-rest's reference threats

Threat	Mitigation
Native malware	Provide anti-malware tools and allocate each native application in its own private storage area
Device theft	Provide full disk encryption
Webinos malware	*Webinos* will provide isolated storage for each application, require additional permissions to access shared areas
Online data leak	The PZH can be designed to minimize risk by storing as little data as possible. PZH providers should provide disk encryption and should follow best practice guidelines to avoid vulnerabilities. Keys should be stored privately using either a trusted hardware device or a separate fipr system.
App content theft	No mitigation
Data blackmail	Offer backup and recovery tools.

mechanisms on all platforms. Each platform has different application security infrastructures, so protection from malware is hard to achieve in a truly cross-platform manner.

Furthermore, the underlying OS can use a device-specific solution, with the advantage that this should be well tested by frequent use. For example, the best way to protect private keys is likely to be device-specific. Some devices support secure hardware which may provide a high level of protection. Furthermore, devices in different contexts will have different authentication requirements: e.g., a shared PC might only unlock private keys after authenticating the end user, whereas a mobile device may be assumed to belong to one person only.

The use of secure hardware capabilities should be the object of further investigation inside *Webinos*. It would be useful because hosted applications may be running on insecure remote platforms and this could be assessed through use of attestation on the host and verification on the user's device (Lyle, 2010). If the host is found to be running an untrustworthy configuration then the application may not be installed, or if the host changes configuration it could result in a new assessment.

The emerging cross-platform scenarios are young and admit misinterpretation as the security implications of these scenarios are unclear. For example, device keys are not always a factor of user authentication, this is because personal devices are designed to be mobile, thus is more secure to use a device key to identify the device only, and only as a second factor when the device is appropriate: e.g., a laptop or mobile phone with a single user and a login prompt. This contrasts with some literature (e.g. Balfanz et al., 2005), which identifies that certificates could be treated like capabilities, but is corroborated by some threat scenarios we investigated, e.g. when a device is stolen and then access to core security zone management is admitted only on the basis of the private key.

CONCLUSION AND FUTURE WORK

In this paper we presented the design of *Webinos*, providing insights into the motivation behind security choices and the overall architecture, as well as the literature which inspired our work

We used *personas* in order to support usable security design. Most of the *Webinos* personas we expect to already have identities on the Web (e.g. from social networks, email accounts, and homepages). Some were tech-savvy, and thus not comfortable with having multiple online accounts in different contexts. A mapping from Web-based identity to a public key or certificate is therefore a good way to allow users to find each other through acceptable Web identities (obtained by a combination of user and device as suggested by (Ford et al., 2006)), while benefitting from the stronger security guarantees inherent in a public key infrastructure. This leverages existing relationships and avoids the discovery and bootstrapping problems often associated with PKI (Balfanz et al., 2005). It also minimizes the need for passwords. Since PKI terminology must not be exposed to end users, all keys and certificates should be generated automatically, and there should never be a prompt or question asked to users referring to these things. However, even if we conceal details of the authentication and identity management *Webinos* system, we believe that further research is needed in this field, especially to develop empirical evidence of the usefulness of our proposed approach.

We also plan further studies on authentication and identity classification, as well as investigations into stronger integration with social networks. For example, adopting a social network reputation and review system could be a way to reduce reliance on the public key infrastructure for *application* security. Application certificates are one source of information on trustworthiness, but social networks may provide more useful information, e.g. if 90% of the user's friends rate an application highly, this information may help the user decide whether to trust the application or not. On a similar theme, recommendations from particular users might trigger policy settings which allow the application to be installed with minimal authorisation. In this way, *Webinos* could present to the end user a comfortable security model, since similar to today's social network model, and thus could enhance acceptability, avoid misinterpretation and enable user's security-wise behaviour.

ACKNOWLEDGMENT

The research described in this chapter was funded by EU FP7 *Webinos* Project (FP7-ICT-2009-5 Objective 1.2). We thank all our project partners as this chapter draws upon their work.

REFERENCES

Android. (2012). *Developer guide: Security and permissions, October 2012*. Retrieved from http://developer.android.com/guide/topics/security/security.html

Ardagna, C. A., di Vimercati, S. D. C., Paraboschi, S., Pedrini, E., & Samarati, P. (2009). An XACML-based privacy-centered access control system. In *Proceedings of the First ACM Workshop on Information Security Governance, WISG '09*, (pp. 49–58). ACM.

Atzeni, A., Cameroni, C., Faily, S., Lyle, J., & Fléchais, I. (2011). Here's Johnny: A methodology for developing attacker personas. In *Proceedings of the 6th International Conference on Availability, Reliability and Security*, (pp. 722–727). IEEE.

Balfanz, D., Durfee, G., & Smetters, D. (2005). Making the impossible easy: Usable PKI. In *Security and Usability: Designing Secure Systems that People Can Use* (pp. 319–334). Sebastopol, CA: O'Reilly.

BONDI. (n.d.). *Architecture and security requirements appendices*. Retrieved from http://bondi.omtp.org/1.01/security/BONDI_Architecture_and_Security_Appendices_v1_01.pdf

Cooper, A. (1999). *The inmates are running the asylum: Why high tech products drive us crazy and how to restore the sanity* (2nd ed.). Upper Saddle River, NJ: Pearson Higher Education.

Dierks, T., & Rescorla, E. (2008). *The transport layer security (TLS) protocol version 1.2*. RFC 5246 (Proposed Standard). Retrieved from http://www.ietf.org/rfc/rfc5246.txt

Faily, S., Coles-Kemp, L., Dunphy, P., Just, M., Akama, Y., & De Luca, A. (2013). Designing interactive secure systems: CHI 2013 special interest group. In *CHI '13 Extended Abstracts on Human Factors in Computing Systems*. ACM. doi:10.1145/2468356.2468807.

Faily, S., & Fléchais, I. (2010a). A meta-model for usable secure requirements engineering. In *Proceedings of the 2010 ICSE Workshop on Software Engineering for Secure Systems*, (pp. 29–35). ACM.

Faily, S., & Fléchais, I. (2010b). Barry is not the weakest link: Eliciting secure system requirements with personas. In *Proceedings of the 24th BCS Interaction Specialist Group Conference, BCS '10*, (pp. 124-132). London: British Computer Society.

Faily, S., & Fléchais, I. (2011). Eliciting usable security requirements with misusability cases. In *Proceedings of the 19th IEEE International Requirements Engineering Conference*, (pp. 339–340). IEEE Computer Society.

Faily, S., Lyle, J., & Parkin, S. (2012). Secure system? Challenge accepted: Finding and resolving security failures using security premortems. In *Proceedings of Designing Interactive Secure Systems: Workshop at British HCI 2012*. London: HCI.

Felt, A. P., Greenwood, K., & Wagner, D. (2011). The effectiveness of application permissions. In *Proceedings of the 2nd USENIX Conference on Web Application Development, WebApps'11*. Berkeley, CA: USENIX Association. Retrieved from http://dl.acm.org/citation.cfm?id=2002168.2002175

Ford, B., Strauss, J., Lesniewski-Laas, C., Rhea, S., Kaashoek, F., & Morris, R. (2006). Persistent personal names for globally connected mobile devices. In *Proceedings of the 7th Symposium on Operating Systems Design and Implementation, OSDI '06*, (pp. 233–248). Berkeley, CA: USENIX Association. Retrieved from http://dl.acm.org/citation.cfm

Godik, S., & Moses, T. (2005). *Extensible access control markup language (XACML) version 1.1, May 2005*. Retrieved from http://www.oasis-open.org

iOS. (n.d.). *Developer library: iOS technology overview introduction*. Retrieved from http://developer.apple.com/library/ios/documentation/Miscellaneous/Conceptual/iPhoneOSTechOverview/Introduction/Introduction.html

Joyent, Inc. (2012). *Nodejs website*. Retrieved from http://nodejs.org/

Kinkelin, H., Holz, R., Niedermayer, H., Mittelberger, S., & Carle, G. (2011). On using TPM for secure identities in future home networks. *Future Internet, 3*(1), 1–13. Retrieved from http://www.mdpi.com/1999-5903/3/1/1/

Lyle, J. (2010). *Trustable services through attestation*. (PhD thesis). University of Oxford, Oxford, UK. Retrieved from http://www.cs.ox.ac.uk/people/John.Lyle/thesis-final-25-06-11.pdf

Lyle, J., Monteleone, S., Faily, S., Patti, D., & Ricciato, F. (2012). Cross-platform access control for mobile web applications. In *Proceedings of the IEEE International Symposium on Policies for Distributed Systems & Networks*. IEEE.

Mac. (n.d.a). *OS X developer library: Security architecture*. Retrieved from http://developer.apple.com/library/mac/documentation/Security/Conceptual/Security_Overview/Introduction/Introduction.html

Mac. (n.d.b). *OS X developer library: Security services*. Retrieved from http://developer.apple.com/library/mac/documentation/Security/Conceptual/Security_Overview/Security_Services/Security_Services.html

Mitchell, C.J., & Schaffelhofer, R. (2004). *Security for mobility: The personal PKI*. Institution of Engineering and Technology.

MITRE Corporation. (n.d.). *Common attack pattern enumeration and classification (CAPEC)*. Retrieved from http://capec.mitre.org/

Mozilla. (n.d.). *Boot to gecko project website*. Retrieved from http://www.mozilla.org/en-US/b2g/

Niemegeers, I.G., & de Groot, S.M.H. (2002). From personal area networks to personal networks: A user oriented approach. *Wireless Personal Communications, 22*, 175–186. Retrieved from http://dx.doi.org/10.1023/A:1019912421877

Open, I. D. (n.d.). *What is OpenId?* Retrieved from http://openid.net/get-an-openid/what-is-openid/

OWASP Foundation. (n.d.). *The open web application security project*. Retrieved from http://www.owasp.org/index.php/

Pruitt, J., & Adlin, T. (2006). *The persona lifecycle: Keeping people in mind throughout product design*. Amsterdam: Elsevier.

Sasse, M. A., Brostoff, S., & Weirich, D. (2001). Transforming the 'weakest link': A human-computer interaction approach to usable and effective security. *BT Technology Journal, 19*, 122–131. doi:10.1023/A:1011902718709.

Schneier, B. (2009). *Security versus usability*. Retrieved from http://www.schneier.com/blog/archives/2009/08/security_vs_usa.html

SHAMAN Project. (2002). *Deliverable 13, work package 3, November 2002*. Retrieved from http://www.isrc.rhul.ac.uk/shaman/docs/d13a3v1.pdf

UPnP Forum. (2011). *UPnP device protection service* (Technical report). Retrieved from http://upnp.org/specs/gw/deviceprotection1.w3c-widget

Webinos Consortium. (2011). *User expectations on security and privacy phase 1, February 2011*. Retrieved from http://Webinos.org/content/Webinos-User_Expectations_on_Security_and_Privacy_v1.pdf

Webinos Consortium. (2012a). *Phase 2 platform Specifications: Policy*. Retrieved from http://webinos.org

Webinos Consortium. (2012b). *Phase 2 API specification*. Retrieved from http://Webinos.org/blog/2012/09/24/Webinos-report-phase-ii-api-specifications

Webinos Consortium. (2012c). *The webinos project website*. Retrieved from http://Webinos.org/

Webinos Consortium. (2012d). *Updates on scenarios and use-cases*. Retrieved from http://www.webinos.org/wp-content/uploads/2012/06/D2.4-Updates-on-Scenarios-and-Use-Cases.public.pdf

Whitten, A., & Tygar, J. D. (1999). Why Johnny can't encrypt: A usability evaluation of PGP 5.0. In *Proceedings of the 8th Conference on USENIX Security Symposium*, (pp. 169–184). Berkeley, CA: USENIX Association.

Wholesale Application Community. (2012). *WAC core specifications 2.1: Security and privacy*. Retrieved from http://specs.wacapps.net/core/

World Wide Web Consortium. (W3C). (2011, August 11). *XML digital signatures for widgets, W3C proposed recommendation*. Retrieved from http://www.w3.org/TR/2011/PR-widgets-digsig-20110811/

Chapter 13
Securing XML with Role-Based Access Control:
Case Study in Health Care

Alberto De la Rosa Algarín
University of Connecticut, USA

Timoteus B. Ziminski
University of Connecticut, USA

Steven A. Demurjian
University of Connecticut, USA

Yaira K. Rivera Sánchez
University of Connecticut, USA

Robert Kuykendall
Texas State University, USA

ABSTRACT

Today's applications are often constructed by bringing together functionality from multiple systems that utilize varied technologies (e.g. application programming interfaces, Web services, cloud computing, data mining) and alternative standards (e.g. XML, RDF, OWL, JSON, etc.) for communication. Most such applications achieve interoperability via the eXtensible Markup Language (XML), the de facto document standard for information exchange in domains such as library repositories, collaborative software development, health informatics, etc. The use of a common data format facilitates exchange and interoperability across heterogeneous systems, but challenges in the aspect of security arise (e.g. sharing policies, ownership, permissions, etc.). In such situations, one key security challenge is to integrate the local security (existing systems) into a global solution for the application being constructed and deployed. In this chapter, the authors present a Role-Based Access Control (RBAC) security framework for XML, which utilizes extensions to the Unified Modeling Language (UML) to generate eXtensible Access Control Markup Language (XACML) policies that target XML schemas and instances for any application, and provides both the separation and reconciliation of local and global security policies across systems. To demonstrate the framework, they provide a case study in health care, using the XML standards Health Level Seven's (HL7) Clinical Document Architecture (CDA) and the Continuity of Care Record (CCR). These standards are utilized for the transportation of private and identifiable information between stakeholders (e.g. a hospital with an electronic health record, a clinic's electronic health record, a pharmacy system, etc.), requiring not only a high level of security but also compliance to legal

DOI: 10.4018/978-1-4666-4514-1.ch013

entities. For this reason, it is not only necessary to secure private information, but for its application to be flexible enough so that updating security policies that affect millions of documents does not incur a large monetary or computational cost; such privacy could similarly involve large banks and credit card companies that have similar information to protect to deter identity theft. The authors demonstrate the security framework with two in-house developed applications: a mobile medication management application and a medication reconciliation application. They also detail future trends that present even more challenges in providing security at global and local levels for platforms such as Microsoft HealthVault, Harvard SMART, Open mHealth, and open electronic health record systems. These platforms utilize XML, equivalent information exchange document standards (e.g., JSON), or semantically augmented structures (e.g., RDF and OWL). Even though the primary use of these platforms is in healthcare, they present a clear picture of how diverse the information exchange process can be. As a result, they represent challenges that are domain independent, thus becoming concrete examples of future trends and issues that require a robust approach towards security.

1. INTRODUCTION

Today's world is dominated by systems with a wide range of technological approaches (e.g. application programming interfaces, Web services, cloud computing, data mining, etc.), where one major objective is to support information sharing and exchange as applications are constructed as meta-systems (systems of systems), with new applications interfacing with multiple technologies, comprised of many interacting components. In such an environment, the one major challenge is to ensure that local security policies (of constituent systems) are satisfied not only when the application accesses a single system, but also when considered from a higher-level perspective. That is, an application's security is the combination of the security that must be attained within each constituent system that is accessed. What happens when security privileges of individual systems are in conflict with one another? How do we reconcile these local security policies? Is it possible to define a global encompassing security process or framework that provides a level of guarantee to the local security policies from an enforcement perspective? As today's applications continue to become more and more complex, interacting with many other systems (or applications) using varied technological paradigms, there will be a need to provide some degree of assurance that security for the application (global) satisfies the sum of the parts (local security of constituent systems). Information exchange has increased exponentially, due to the development of generic data standards (e.g., XML, JSON, RDF, OWL, etc.) and the ease of interconnection across systems, in domains such as biomedical, health informatics, library repositories, collaborative software development, etc. All of these domains present security challenges that, though not unique, have yet to be sufficiently addressed; often neither in the specific format or system (local security), and definitely not across multiple formats and meta-systems (global security).

In this effort to facilitate the intercommunication between heterogeneous systems, the *eXtensible Markup Language (XML)*[1] has become the de facto document standard for information exchange. In health care, which will serve as the case study for this chapter, XML is used for standards such as: the Health Level Seven's (HL7) Clinical Document Architecture (CDA) (Dolin, 2006) that underlies many Health Information Exchange (HIE) approaches; and, the Continuity of Care

Record[2] (CCR), used for storage of administrative, patient demographics, and clinical data. In Health Information Technology (HIT), the clinical document architecture and the continuity of care record come together in systems such as Electronic Health Records (EHR) and Personal Health Records (PHR) (e.g., Microsoft HealthVault[3]). The clinical document architecture is used to support health information exchange among hospitals, clinics, physician practices, laboratories, etc., with the continuity of care record providing the means to model the data that needs to be exchanged. As documents derived from standards such as these are circulated among various systems and made available to particular users with specific needs, we must expand security from each individual system to a focus that is more expansive in controlling the document and its content, particularly for health information exchange. Current approaches to security only do so from the system's perspective, in which the security policies that govern it are the final authority, and no consideration is given to the policies that govern the data repositories or constituent systems. This level of security is inadequate to scenarios such as information exchange in which the data utilized could not be owned by any particular user, but by an external party. Added to this is the rapidly emerging mobile applications domain where, in the case of health care, patients manage personal health information for chronic diseases, and a need to securely access information and authorize its exchange with medical providers via mobile applications, electronic health records, secure emails, or other means is a key concern. A solution that achieves this will require document-level access control of XML schemas to allow XML instances to appear differently to authorized users at specific times based on criteria that include, but are not limited to, a user's role, time and value constraints on data usage, collaboration for sharing data, delegation of authority as privileges are passed among authorized users, etc.

The challenge of attaining customized XML security enforcement necessitates the addressing of legal and adaptability requirements. In health care, the Health Insurance Portability and Accountability Act[4] (HIPAA) provides a set of security guidelines in the usage, transmission, and sharing of Protected Health Information (PHI); in e-commerce, there would be a need to protect Personally Identifiable Information (PII) including names, addresses, accounts, credit card numbers, etc. Protected health information and personally identifiable information must be strictly adhered to in many applications and settings. From an adaptability perspective, XML security policies must be defined at the XML schema level to support the definitions of users grouped in different roles, each with possible different sets of permissions that act on the specific parts of the information (an XML instance), across millions of records (XML instances). For the purposes of this chapter, we focus on the attainment of the National Institute for Standards and Technology's[5] (NIST) standard Role-Based Access Control (RBAC) (Ferraiolo, 1995, 2001) for XML, which would support the definition of security policies at the XML schema level (for example, the continuity of care record document (patient data) at the schema) that can then be used to specify (allow or deny) different permissions on certain portions of an XML instance (for example, a continuity of care record's instance), allowing the same instance to appear differently to specific users (patients and medical providers) acting in a chosen role at different times. To accomplish this, we leverage a secure software engineering process that promotes the consideration of security at an early stage and throughout the process. The usage of an XML schema via a new Unified Modeling Language (UML) schema diagrams requires a security framework for XML that allows the design, implementation, and deployment of enforceable security policies to allow access to XML instances to be precisely controlled by role. The definition of security at the

XML schema level via an external security policy separates the security from the XML instances, which avoids the overhead required when updating security policies that are otherwise embedded in instances and target a large amount of these.

In this chapter, we present our security framework for XML (De la Rosa Algarín, 2012) defined at the schema level and realized at the instance level through the creation and generation of eXtensible Access Control Markup Language (XACML)[6] policies, and demonstrate the work (design, mapping of policy and enforcement) via a case study of an in-house health care scenario composed of a set of health information technology applications. As shown in Figure 1, this generalized framework achieves granular security by taking the XML schemas and instances for any application (right hand side of Figure 1) and using them to define UML[7] diagrams for the respective XML schemas and the associated roles in order to create an enforcement XACML security policy that will be able to generate role-restricted (RR) instances that limit the information in the original instances based on the defined security (left hand side of Figure 1). Our approach provides separation of security concerns to tackle the challenge of changing security policies that can apply to millions of XML instances. In support of this framework, we leverage our prior work on secure software engineering using UML (Pavlich-Mariscal, 2008) and have created new UML diagrams: an XML Schema Class Diagram that captures the structure of the applications XML schemas; and an XML Role Slice Diagram that allows privileges on an XML schema's entities and attributes to be allowed/denied to different users by role at different times, thereby creating a role-restricted instance that is customized for that user. We note that Figure 1 is referring to any XML schemas, instances, and security definitions regardless of domain. In this chapter, after briefly reviewing our security framework for XML schemas and documents, we apply it to a case study of health care, consisting of the continuity of care record standard, utilized as the information exchange document, coupled with two in-house developed applications: the Personal Health Assistant (PHA), which consists of two mobile applications that support the exchange of information stored in a personal health record (Microsoft HealthVault) between patients and providers; and, SMARTSync (Ziminski, 2012), a medication reconciliation application, built as a meta-system utilizing Microsoft HealthVault and the Harvard SMART Platform[8], that generates a list of potential overmedication, adverse interactions, and adverse reactions for the patient and provider. All of these applications require that the XML that is delivered be restricted by role (a filtering of the content of the instance) in order to insure that only the authorized information is provided to the user. Our in-house mobile and Web apps both share the same server, with the Web app accessing another server, using well accepted Web standards (XML, RDF, JSON) for information modeling and exchange; thus our work is applicable to any such architecture. The use of these in-house applications supports our ability to apply and experiment with our XML security solutions with actual working systems that, while health care based, are just mobile/Web apps and servers.

The remainder of this chapter has five sections. In Section 2, background is provided on the NIST RBAC standard, XML, and the continuity of care record for the reader's benefit and understanding of the examples used throughout the chapter. In Section 3, we briefly describe our existing security framework for XML (De la Rosa Algarín, 2012) with a review of the new UML diagrams (XML Schema Class Diagram and XML Role Slice Diagram in Figure 1) for XML schemas and security definition, the generation of enforcement XACML policy schemas from these new diagrams, and relevant related work. Section 4 presents our case study in health care using two in-house developed applications, Personal Health Assistant (PHA) and SMARTSync, by detailing: the overall architecture and associated technologies (An-

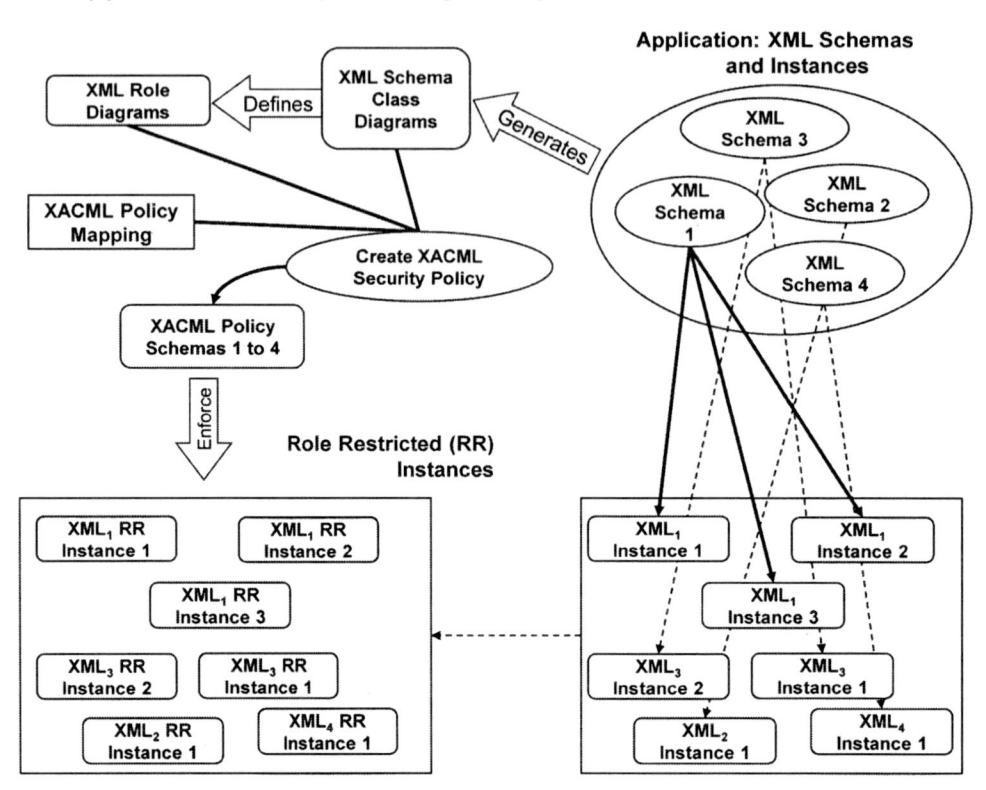

Figure 1. Security framework and enforcement process for XML

droid[9], JSON[10], Microsoft HealthVault, and Harvard's SMART Platform), the Personal Health Assistant and SMARTSync applications, and the attainment of security for these applications using our security framework from Section 3. Note that while we utilize the health care domain as the case study for our demonstration, this security framework can be applied in any domain where the document structure to be secured is XML and an XML schema that validates the instances is available. Following our case study of the health care domain, Section 5 presents future trends by detailing a large scale view of health information technology systems and applications, with an emphasis on the interplay of health information exchange among the various systems; and the role of security at global and local levels across such a complex architecture. As part of this discussion, accessible health information technology platforms are explored, including: Microsoft Health-Vault personal health record; Open *m*Health[11], which promotes mobile health via an open architecture; and, the Harvard SMART platform for substitutable medical applications that promote reuse, are explored. The wide range of open electronic health records, the myriad of XML standards, and the way that applications like Personal Health Assistant and SMARTSync interact to gather data effectively are also explored. These platforms, their role in the health information exchange process, and the large amount of data formats, standards and usage of data present concrete examples of research problems not unique to the health care domain, but present in domains that utilize information exchange, meta-systems or traditional system interoperability, as part of their daily workflow, requiring the intercommunication of information stored in different repositories with different formats and security policies. The end result is the recognition of a greater need for a comprehensive approach to security operating under information exchange. Towards this end, in Section 5, we also include a number of recommendations for the health care discipline and health information technology for improvements towards a more cohesive and shared future that promotes patient's health via electronic means. These recommendations, though directed to the health care domain as part of the case study, are presented in a general way so that the underlying, common application construction and interoperations issues are evident, and the proposed recommendation can be likewise achieved in this setting. We finish the chapter by offering concluding remarks in Section 6.

2. BACKGROUND

In support of this chapter, we provide background in three key areas: the National Institute for Standards and Technology (NIST) Role-Based Access Control (RBAC) model (Ferraiolo, 1995, 2001) which is intended to allow a user to be assigned permissions (read, write, etc.) to access objects (or portions of objects) based on his/her responsibilities as defined by a role; the eXtensible Markup Language (XML) a well-established standard for data representation that facilitates ease of exchange among users and systems; and, the health standard Continuity of Care Record (CCR) the represents data on patients (demographic, medications, allergies, medical history, etc.) using XML. Collectively, all three of these background areas establish the concepts and terms that are utilized throughout the paper. Health care is also an easy-to-understand domain, since most readers have experience with the stakeholders (medical providers) and their venues (offices, clinics, hospital, labs, etc.).

Role-based access control has long been utilized in the industry to represent permissions to an application based on a user's responsibilities. A role (e.g., Physician or Nurse) represents a category of permissions against objects (e.g., the way the role can access the data in a patient medical record), and by assigning permissions to roles, we can authorize users to roles against specific objects (e.g., Dr. Smith with Physician role can access objects of Patient Jones). When a role needs to change, we can change its permissions without impacting its authorization. The NIST RBAC (Ferraiolo, 1995, 2001) model organizes roles into different levels. First, $RBAC_0$ defines permissions on a role and authorizes a role to a user. Second, $RBAC_1$ allows for role hierarchies where permissions defined at the parent role can pass down to the child roles, e.g., the Nurse is a parent role with Staff_RN a role for taking care of patients, Discharge_RN a role for handling patient's upon leaving a hospital, Education_RN would teach patients about managing their chronic disease, etc. Third, $RBAC_2$ supports constraints, such as separation of duty and mutual exclusion, e.g., the roles Staff_RN and Physician are not allowed to assigned to the same individual (user); this prevents a user assigned a Staff_RN being assigned a Physician role in the future. Finally, from an authorization perspective, a user can be assigned multiple roles, but is only allowed to play a single role at any given time, which corresponds to the concept of sessions in $RBAC_3$, which provide the enforcement of permissions on specific objects authorized to a user playing a role at runtime. For example, Dr. Smith may have a Primary_MD role when treating patients in his practice while have an Attending_MD role when treating patients at a hospital.

XML is intended as a unifying means for data in terms of its representation to allow for it to be collected, transmitted, displayed, and exchanged among users and systems with ease. XML is a modeling language with the ability to define an *XML Schema* for the structure of the data being modeled (akin to a class in a UML diagram) which can then be instantiated to create *XML Instances* that are also referred to as XML documents. Collectively, a given application (like an electronic medical record) can have a set of XML schemas that describe the application and all of its instances. In this context, each XML schema serves as both the blueprint and validation agent for instances seeking to comply and be used for information representation and exchange. XML schemas support the definition of information to be hierarchically structured and tagged, and the tags themselves can be exploited to capture and represent the semantics of the information. The main modeling capability of XML schemas is the XML Schema Definition and associated XML Schema language. As an example, an XML schema can be composed of multiple xs:simpleType, xs:sequence, xs:element, etc, and these can be combined and nested in any way to form a more encompassing xs:complexType, a characteristic shared with classes in UML.

A continuity of care record document includes both protected health information and personally identifiable information such as demographics, social security number, insurance policy details, and health related information (such as medications, procedures, psychological notes, etc.). The continuity of care record schema defines all of the structure and interdependencies of information, but in practice, not all of the information at the schema level is available to all users based neither on role, nor at the instance level available to be written by some users based on role. For example, a Secretary role at a private practice performing financial operations might only need to see the patient's demographics and insurance policy details (personally identifiable information), whereas the Primary_MD role may to access the entire patient's information, but not the social security number. Select protected health information, such as psychiatric notes may not be available to the Primary_MD role, but be more constrained. Thus, when given information modeled using XML schemas (like the continuity of care record) and the associated instances (data for actual patients), the intent of the work presented in this chapter is to allow for the continuity of care record instances to be authorized to a user by role which will allow the instances appear differently at particular times and will also limit if the user (by the permissions of the role) will be able to read and/or write the authorized portions of an instance.

3. SECURITY FRAMEWORK FOR XML

Our security framework for XML schemas and instances (see Figure 1 again) separates the security policies from the schema by utilizing extended UML diagrams and a mapping algorithm that places the XACML policies at the same layer of the UML diagrams. These two diagrams, the XML Schema Class Diagram (XSCD) and the XML Role Slice Diagram (XRSD), are XML representative artifacts in the UML model, as we detail in Section 3.1, to address XML security from a software engineering perspective. Tackling the problem this way allows for the change of policies affecting large numbers of XML instances without the inherent cost of updating each instance. With our framework, designers can follow both a secure software engineering approach (Pavlich-Mariscal, 2008), and a secure information engineering approach for a more complete and secure solution. As a result, from the XSCD and XRSD artifacts, we generate a XACML policy that can enforce the defined security at the schema level, as we present in Section 3.2. To complete the discussion, Section 3.3 reviews related research. Note that we again stress that the security approach that is being demonstrated focuses on XML schemas and instances, and the generation of XACML policies; health care is simply an explanation vehicle.

3.1. XML Schema Class and Role Slice Diagrams in UML

UML provides multiple diagrams to visually model applications, but there is a lack of integrating security. Our prior work has defined new UML security diagrams for supporting RBAC (Pavlich-Mariscal, 2008) via the UML meta-model. Using this as a basis, we have extended this work to define two new UML artifacts (De la Rosa Algarín, 2012): the XML Schema Class Diagram (XSCD) in Figure 2a that contains architecture, structure characteristics, and constraints of an XML schema; and, the XML Role Slice Diagram (XRSD) in Figure 2b which has the ability to add permissions to the various elements of the XSCD, i.e. read/write, read/nowrite, noread/write, noread/nowrite. The set of all XML schemas for a given application are converted into a corresponding set of XSCDs. As a result, we provide secure software engineering to the XML design process where the creation of an XML schema is placed into the UML context alongside other diagrams. XSCD, in Figure 2a, presents the way that the XSCD for the continuity of care record's schema xs:complexType 'StructuredProductType' would be represented in an UML-like XSCD diagram. The XSCD allows for customized access control policies to be generated for the respective concepts of the XML schema. The XRSD in Figure 2b is capable of applying access control policies or permissions on the attributes of the XSCD based on role, thereby achieving fine-grained control. Permissions on XML documents are read, no read, write, and no write permissions with respective stereotypes, <<read/write>>, <<read/nowrite>>, <<noread/write>>, and <<noread/nowrite>>. Figure 2b defines Physician and Nurse XRSDs with permissions against the XSCD in Figure 2a. Note that in Figure 2b, the continuity of care record's complexType 'StructuredProductType' element Product allows a Physician role all of the

Figure 2. XSCD of a continuity of care record schema segment (a) and XRSD of the XSCD in a health care scenario (b)

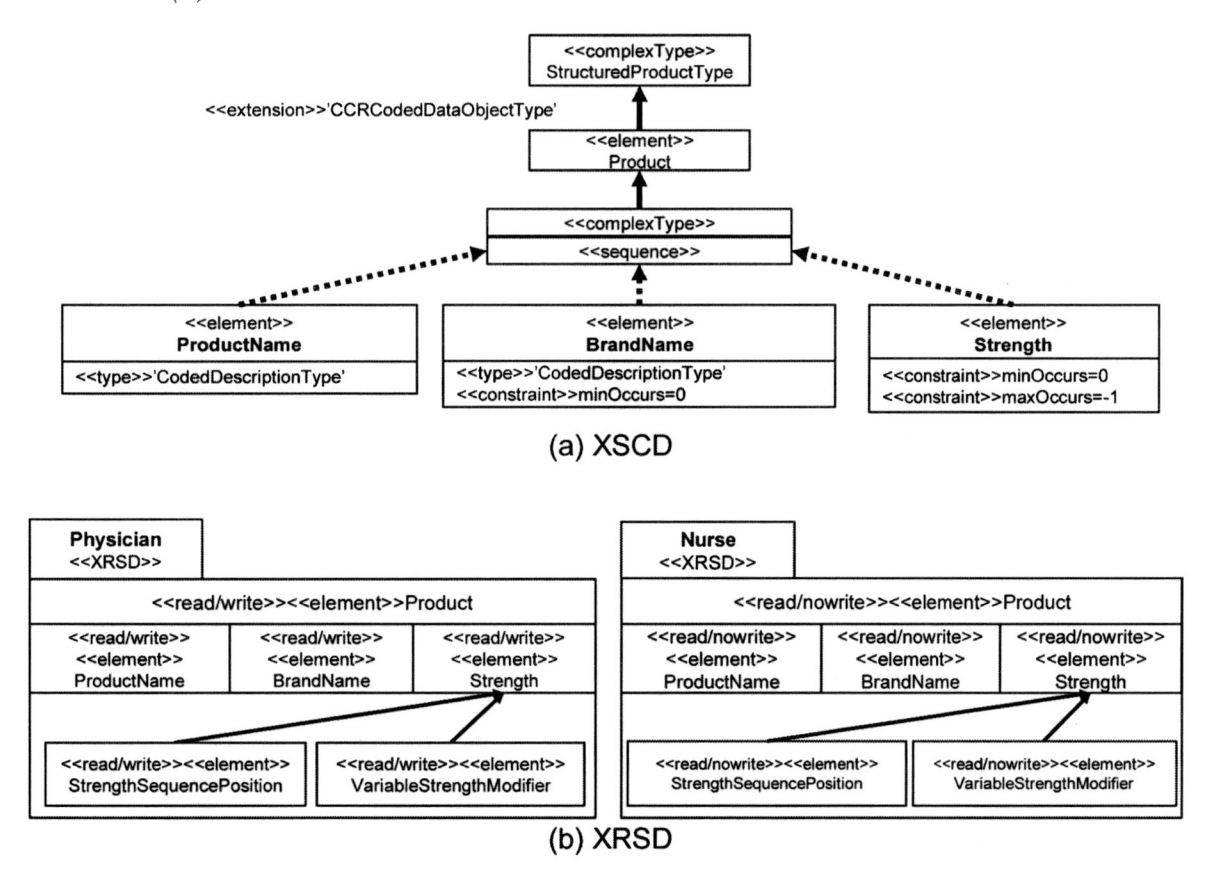

information on a drug and be able to create new instances following the continuity of care record schema, with the Nurse role limited to read the drug details and cannot create new records. Note that the XSCD (Figure 2a) and the XRSD (Figure 2b) do not cover the whole continuity of care record schema representation due to space limitations.

3.2. Generating XACML Policies from XSCD and XRSD

As given in Figure 2b, XRSDs act as the blueprint of the access-control policy for reading and writing permissions for a specific element or component of an XML schema for any given role, and are used to represent the portions of the application's XSCD (Figure 2a) that are to be allowed (or denied) access at an instance level to create role restricted instances (Figure 1), which can then be used to generate an XACML policy using the XACML Policy Mapping process in Figure 3. The architecture has a number of components: Policy Enforcement Point (PEP) allows a request to be made on a resource (a user playing a Physician role to access an continuity of care record instance); Policy Decision Point (PDP), which evaluates the request and provides a response according to the policies in place (evaluate if a Physician role can access (read and/or write) a portion of a continuity of care record schema); the Policy Administration Point (PAP) is utilized to write and manage policies (a realization of the XRSD against the continuity of care record schema and its associated instances); and, the Policy Information Point (PIP) to arbitrate very fine grained security issues (control access to psychiatric data). To map the XRSD in Figure 2b into an XACML policy, we utilize an XACML PolicySet to make the authorization decision via a set of rules in order to allow for access control decisions that may contain multiple Policies, and each Policy contains the access control rules. Note that multiple XACML Polices may be generated, resulting in a PolicySet for a specific set of XML schemas that comprise a given application. Our prior work (De la Rosa Algarín, 2012) has all of the details for this mapping process to generate XACML policies; and while we omit this discussion due to length considerations, in Figure 4 we present the generated XACML policy for the Physician XRCD in Figure 2b.

Briefly, we explain the generated XACML. First, the Policy's PolicyId attribute value is the Physician XRSD is concatenated to 'AccessControlPolicy'; the Rule's RuleId attribute value is the Physician XRSD value concatenated to the XRSD's higher order element (in Figure 4 it would be Product as defined in the XSCD in Figure 2b) and concatenated to 'ProductRule'; the Rule's Description value is the Physician XRSD is concatenated to 'Access Control Policy Rule'; and, the XACML Policy and Rules target and match the role (*Subject*, e.g., *Physician* in Figure 2b and 4), the schema elements (*Resources*, e.g., ProductName, BrandName and Strength in Figure 2a, 2b and 4), and the permissions (*Actions*, e.g., read and write in Figure 2b and 4). Second the

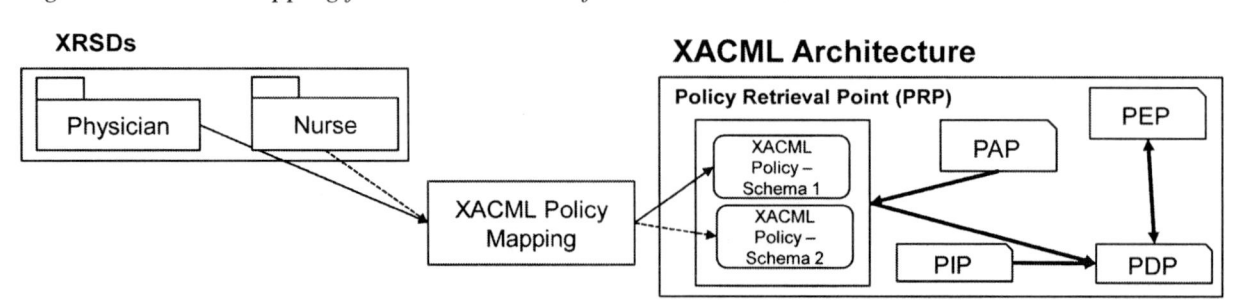

Figure 3. XACML mapping from XRSD's and enforcement architecture

Figure 4. Mapped XACML policy from physician XRSD

```xml
<?xml version="1.0" encoding="UTF-8"?>
  <Policy xmlns="urn:oasis:names:tc:xacml:2.0:policy:schema:os"
    xmlns:xsi="http://www.w3.org/2001/XMLSchema-instance"
    xsi:schemaLocation="urn:oasis:names:tc:xacml:2.0:policy:schema:os
    http://docs.oasis-open.org/xacml/access_control-xacml-2.0-policy-schema-os.xsd"
    xmlns:md="http:www.med.example.com/schemas/record.xsd"
    PolicyId="urn:oasis:names:tc:xacml:2.0:example:policyid:PhysicianAccessControlPolicy"
    RuleCombiningAlgId="urn:oasis:names:tc:xacml:1.0:rule-combining-algorithm:deny-overrides">
    <Target/>
      <Rule RuleId="urn:oasis:names:tc:xacml:2.0:example:ruleid:PhysicianProductRule" Effect="Permit">
      <Description>Physician Access Control Policy Rule</Description>
      <Target>
        <Subjects>
          <Subject>
            <SubjectMatch MatchId="urn:oasis:names:tc:xacml:1.0:function:string-equal">
              <AttributeValue DataType="http://www.w3.org/2001/XMLSchema#string">
                Physician
              </AttributeValue>
              <SubjectAttributeDesignator AttributeId="urn:oasis:names:tc:xacml:2.0:example:attribute:role"
                DataType="http://www.w3.org/2001/XMLSchema#string"/>
            </SubjectMatch>
          </Subject>
        </Subjects>
        <Resources>
          <Resource>
            <ResourceMatch MatchId="urn:oasis:names:tc:xacml:1.0:function:string-equal">
              <AttributeValue DataType="http://www.w3.org/2001/XMLSchema#string">
                ccr:schema:product:productname
              </AttributeValue>
              <ResourceAttributeDesignator
                AttributeId="urn:oasis:names:tc:xacml:1.0:resource:target-namespace"
                DataType="http://www.w3.org/2001/XMLSchema#string"/>
            </ResourceMatch>
          </Resource>
          <Resource>
            <ResourceMatch MatchId="urn:oasis:names:tc:xacml:1.0:function:string-equal">
              <AttributeValue DataType="http://www.w3.org/2001/XMLSchema#string">
                ccr:schema:product:brandname
              </AttributeValue>
              <ResourceAttributeDesignator
                AttributeId="urn:oasis:names:tc:xacml:1.0:resource:target-namespace"
                DataType="http://www.w3.org/2001/XMLSchema#string"/>
            </ResourceMatch>
          </Resource>
          <Resource>
            <ResourceMatch MatchId="urn:oasis:names:tc:xacml:1.0:function:string-equal">
              <AttributeValue DataType="http://www.w3.org/2001/XMLSchema#string">
                ccr:schema:product:strength
              </AttributeValue>
              <ResourceAttributeDesignator
                AttributeId="urn:oasis:names:tc:xacml:1.0:resource:target-namespace"
                DataType="http://www.w3.org/2001/XMLSchema#string"/>
            </ResourceMatch>
          </Resource>
        </Resources>
        <Actions>
          <Action>
            <ActionMatch MatchId="urn:oasis:names:tc:xacml:1.0:function:string-equal">
              <AttributeValue DataType="http://www.w3.org/2001/XMLSchema#string">
                read
              </AttributeValue>
              <ActionAttributeDesignator
                  AttributeId="urn:oasis:names:tc:xacml:1.0:action:action-read"
                DataType="http://www.w3.org/2001/XMLSchema#string"/>
            </ActionMatch>
          </Action>
          <Action>
            <ActionMatch MatchId="urn:oasis:names:tc:xacml:1.0:function:string-equal">
              <AttributeValue DataType="http://www.w3.org/2001/XMLSchema#string">
                write
              </AttributeValue>
              <ActionAttributeDesignator AttributeId="urn:oasis:names:tc:xacml:1.0:action:action-write"
                DataType="http://www.w3.org/2001/XMLSchema#string"/>
            </ActionMatch>
          </Action>
        </Actions>
      </Target>
    </Rule>
  </Policy>
```

XACML *Subject* Physician is identified as an attribute. Third, the resources are identified; namely, the *AttributeValue's* value is the Physician XRSD's element names from the XSCD (e.g., ProductName, BrandName and Strength in Figure 2a, 2b and 4). Finally, the XACML *Actions* as operations and values (read and write in Figure 2b and 4) are defined. The end result in Figure 4 is an XACML policy that when applied to a continuity of care record instance for the Physician role will generated a role restricted XML instance that limits the visibility and usage of the continuity of care record instance for a particular patient.

3.3. Related Work

In this section, we present related work in a number of areas. First in, XML security frameworks, one effort on enterprise resource planning consists of an integrated packaged software that serves as a single solution for database and communication utilizing XML (Chandrakumar, 2012) by focusing on the XML Signature specification (Ardagna, 2007), and another effort (Ammari, 2010) presents an architecture capable of handling the receiving of XML messages from heterogeneous systems. Second, in embedded XML security, the work of (Damiani, 2000) presents an access control system that embeds the definition and enforcement of the security policies in the structure of the XML documents in order to provide customizable security using document type definitions (outmoded XML) that incurs high overhead since security changes impact all instances, while the work of (Damiani, 2008.) details a model that combines the embedding of policies and rewriting of access queries to provide security to XML datasets.

Third, in XML and access control, one effort (Bertino, 2002; Bertino, 2004) presents Author-X, a Java-based system for discretionary access control in XML documents (using document type definitions) that provides customizable protection to the documents with positive and negative authorizations. A second effort (Leonardi, 2010) considers the scenario of a federated access control model, in which the data provider and policy enforcement are handled by different organizations, while a third effort (Kuper, 2005) presents a model consisting of access control policies over a document type definition with XPath expressions in order to achieve XML security. Last, the work of (Müldner, 2009) uses an approach of supporting RBAC to handle the special case of role proliferation, which is an administrative issue that happens in RBAC when roles are changed, added, and evolve over time, making security of an organization difficult to manage. Finally, in encryption-based XML security, the XML Security Working Group[12] (SWG) works on three different security aspects: XML signatures, XML encryption, and XML Security Maintenance, a second effort (Bertino, 2002) encrypts different sections of an XML document with different encryption keys which are distributed to the specific users based on the access control policies in place, and a third effort (Rahaman, 2008) presents a distributed access control model for collaborative environments where XML documents are used.

4. CASE STUDY OF HEALTHCARE APPLICATIONS

In this section, we present a case study of attaining security in XML for two in-house developed health applications, demonstrating the generation and enforcement of XACML policies on XML instances based on an a subset of the continuity of care record schema. The first, a mobile health application, the Personal Health Assistant (PHA), consists of two perspectives for medication management. One perspective allows a patient to keep track of their medications, nutritional supplements, allergies, etc., and also authorize that protected health information (continuity of care record information), which is stored in Microsoft HealthVault, to his/her specific medical providers at different times. The second perspective allows a provider to select and view the authorized protected health information on a patient-by-patient basis as determined by his/her assigned role. The second application, SMARTSync for medication reconciliation (Ziminski, 2012), takes patient medications from HealthVault and the Harvard SMART Platform Reference Electronic Health Record and from this information is able to generate a summary list of medications/supplements added by patients (in HealthVault) with those prescribed by a patient's medical provider. The intent is to generate a color-coded list of potential overmedication, adverse interactions, and adverse reactions for the patient and provider. Both applications have been coded by undergraduate, masters, and doctoral students as part of research related to biomedical and health informatics and its security and interoperability issues. The remainder of this section begins the case study by presenting the overall architecture of Personal Health Assistant and SMARTSync in Section 4.1. Then, Personal Health Assistant and SMARTSync are described in Sections 4.2 and 4.3, respectively, with a focus on their functional capabilities and user interfaces. Finally, in Section 4.4, we explore the way that XACML based security is achieved in the Personal Health Assistant application (where the documents to secure are XML instances) and in SMARTSync (where information is represented in RDF/XML and JSON-DL that must then be converted to XML in order to allow the information to be appropriately secured). Note, from a generalized perspective, we have a mobile app (PHA) and Web-based app that both interact with a server (MSHV) using JSON with XML conversion occurring to retrieve data entered by the end-user (patient), with the Web app (SMARTSync) also interacting with another external system (SMART EHR) which is effectively a database controlled by a third party (physician's office with patient data). If you reread the prior sentence without the parenthetical remarks, you have a mobile app and Web app interacting with one server, and the Web app interacting with another, all with information flowing with standard formats (XML, JSON, RDF); clearly the architecture is generalizable in this way to many other business and industrial domains.

4.1. Overall Architecture

The overall architecture of the two healthcare applications is given in Figure 5, where the bottom of the figure indicates Personal Health Assistant and SMARTSync. Microsoft HealthVault acts as the data source (server) for both applications, and stores information in a proprietary format which to be exported via a .NET API which can then be used to generate a continuity of care record compliant document in XML. The HealthVault Middle-Layer Server (center of Figure 5) acts as the contained solution of policy access, information, decision, and enforcement points (see right hand side of Figure 3). The XACML policies created and stored in the account of each respective user limits access to HealthVault through the HealthVault Middle-Layer Server, which handles the requests (where data is sent as JSON) of both applications. To store the relations between the authorized list of providers and their respective patients, the Middle-Layer Server uses MySQL[13]. JSON is utilized for the communication of the two applications and the Middle-Layer Server, allowing us to insure a uniform communication with any application (not only with Personal Health Assistant) that can be created for users. The communication between the Personal Health Assistant (patient version) and the Middle-Layer Server is done with unmodified JSON objects, while the communication between the Personal Health Assistant - (provider) version and SMARTSync and the Middle-Layer Server is a combination of unmodified (for the initial request of patients) and filtered (for the resulting data allowed by the policies enforced) JSON. From HealthVault, XML role restricted instances are generated. Requests done by the provider application determine the format of the data. If a provider is requesting

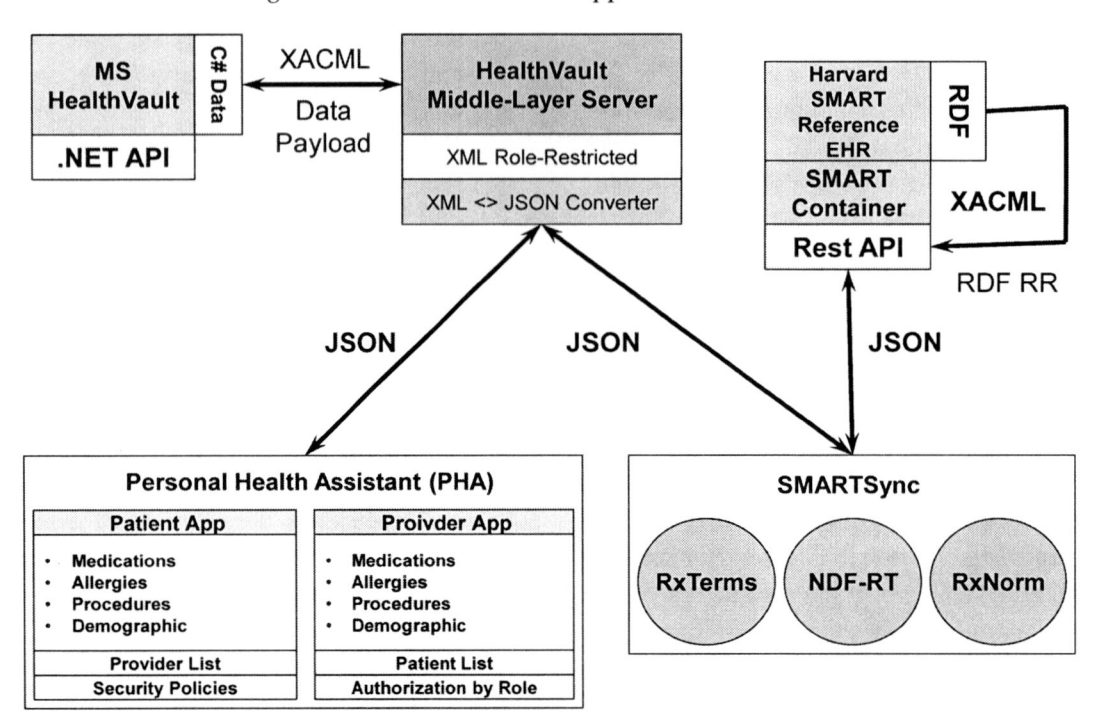

Figure 5. Medication management and reconciliation applications

information in the patient's continuity of care record document, then data from HealthVault is exported as a continuity of care record schema compliant XML document with policy enforcement performed, whereas any input from the provider to HealthVault is first received as a JSON payload, converted to an XML document based on the continuity of care record schema, enforced with policies (Section 4.3), and once authorized, translated to HealthVault objects for write back. A similar process occurs on the SMARTSync side to merge and save the data from HealthVault and SMART Reference Electronic Health Record (another server) back into HealthVault.

4.2. Personal Health Assistant (PHA)

Personal Health Assistant (PHA) is an in-house developed mobile (not publicly available), test-bed Android application for medication management that allows: patients to view and update their personal health record stored in their HealthVault account and authorize medical providers to access certain portion of protected health information; and, for providers to obtain the permitted information from their respective patients that they have been authorized to view. The patient version of Personal Health Assistant allows users to perform a set of actions regarding their health information. Users can view and edit their medication list, allergies, observations of daily living, and set security policies for read/write permissions on their medical providers by role per the discussion in Section 3. Security settings can be set at a fine granular level, and each provider gets view/update authorizations to the different information components available in Personal Health Assistant. The provider version of Personal Health Assistant allows the users (health professionals or medical providers) to view and edit the medical information of their patients as long as they are permitted to do so as dictated by the security set by the user (patient).

4.3. SMARTSync Application

SMARTSync is an in-house developed (not publicly available), Web-based test-bed medication reconciliation application used to create and preserve a patient's medication list through transfers among locations of care, preventing immediate interactions, and avoiding dosage errors in situations where brand and generic drugs are received or multi-component drugs are used (Barnsteiner, 2005; Poon, 2006). Significant risks include (Huang, 2004): *overmedication* when a provider prescribes a new medication (or one from the same class) or when an interacting medication is prescribed; *adverse interactions*, the result of conflicts between medications, which can change effect strength or serum concentration; and *adverse reactions*, allergic/other effects, experienced by patients which can result in a patient being wrongly labeled as allergic to a medication, unnecessarily excluding it as a treatment option in the future. To accomplish this, we gather data form HealthVault and SMART Reference Electronic Health Record as shown in Figure 5. Any medical data source (e.g., an electronic medical record, a personal health record, etc.) can be turned into a SMART container by exposing the SMART REST API, the SMART Connect API, and the related RDF/XML based data model[14].

In the SMART framework, applications are grouped on the SMART dashboard, which offers authentication and a set of basic services based on RDF/SPARQL for accessing the underlying medical data source in the SMART container. SMARTSync is also operated through this user interface component. In addition, SMARTSync communicates with HealthVault and takes advantage of the RxNorm, RxTerms, and the National Drug File – Reference Terminology[15] nomenclature/terminologies for semantic navigation of clinical drugs. The graphical user interface for SMARTSync is designed provide the alert information to the user in a quick and easily recognizable fashion, geared towards simplicity in order to serve a wide range of patients and to be easily portable to mobile devices. The main application screen is currently divided in two tabs, visualizing the personal health record (HealthVault) and the SMART Reference Electronic Health Record. Patients can switch between the tabs to see the list of medications stored in each record. The *Reconcile Medications* and the *Find Medication Interactions* buttons perform on-demand reconciliation and interaction searches. In the HealthVault tab, the user is presented with the reconciled list of medications. If any of the entries interact, the severity of interaction is indicated by a yellow (significant interaction) or red (critical interaction) background. Entries for which no interactions are found are displayed with a neutral background color. There are up to three buttons located next to each of the medications, over the counters, and natural supplements on either tab: *View Interactions*, *Details*, and *Remove*. Since a patient cannot modify the information located in the provider's EMR, the only button visible in this tab is *Details*. *View Interactions* presents the user with a listing of cross-interactions between the specified medication (over the counter/natural supplement) and any other reconciled entry. *Details* presents information of the medication ingredients, generic names, and the dates when the user started and stopped taking the medication. *Remove*, only available in the personal health record tab, allows the user to permanently delete the medication from their personal health record.

4.4. Achieving Security in Personal Health Assistant and SMARTSync

Securing the protected health information in Personal Health Assistant and SMARTSync is accomplished by utilizing the new UML-like XSCD and XRSD diagrams that define the security (see Section 3.1) in order to generate the XACML security policies (see Section 3.2). While

Personal Health Assistant strictly uses HealthVault to store and retrieve information, SMARTSync (by the nature and objective of the SMART Platform) is capable of obtaining information from heterogeneous data sources that do not share the same XML standard. These two cases present the diversity of formats and standards (sometimes equivalent, often non-equivalent) on which not only the health care domain operates, and must be considered in order to effectively secure information that is being exchanged in different formats among a range of health information technology systems. This approach of using XML to exchange and share information is occurring using a mobile app, a Web app, and multiple servers; this is a very typical model for any application domain. In the remainder of this section, we describe the way that the XACML policy is enforced when handling reading and writing requests on XML instances whose schema has been secured in Personal Health Assistant, as well as the realization of the security framework in SMARTSync which requires additional steps to deal with additional data formats.

Providing security on the continuity of care record utilized by Personal Health Assistant is achieved by the enforcement in the HealthVault Middle-Layer server (see Figure 5). The read and write operations to be enforced are initialized by the provider perspective of Personal Health Assistant, handled by the HealthVault Middle-Layer server, and realized in the generated XACML (see Figure 4 in Section 3.2). When a request is initiated from a provider to read the protected health information of a patient, the Middle-Layer Server retrieves the patient's information exported as a continuity of care record along with the targeting XACML policy. After this step, enforcement is performed and those elements with read permissions denied for the provider are filtered out and deleted from the continuity of care record using the XACML policy (Figure 4). Once this has occurred, the filtered instance of the patient's continuity of care record is then converted into an equivalent JSON object for Personal Health Assistant utilization; JSON is utilized to provide a common abstraction layer in data model for any other developed application that wishes to utilize HealthVault data. Consider an example scenario where a user with a role of Nurse is requesting information on a patient's personal health record. The permission of read for the Nurse role has been allowed for medications and allergies, and denied for medical procedures. The permission of write has been disallowed for all data elements. When a nurse utilizes the provider's Personal Health Assistant, s/he selects the patient named Jane Doe. As explained, the Middle-Layer Server retrieves the Jane Doe continuity of care record along with the XACML policy, and enforces security by filtering the continuity of care record as directed by the XACML policy. The filtered continuity of care record is then converted into a JSON object so that the Personal Health Assistant application can present the information to the user.

The steps to enforce security on writing operations done by a provider are similar. Starting with a write-back request with the JSON payload of new information, the Middle-Layer Server utilizes the XACML (see Figure 4) to evaluate which elements the provider is allowed to update. Only these elements are then updated in the continuity of care record, which goes through a validation process with the continuity of care record schema (for consistency in structure and integrity), and then written back to HealthVault in their respective objects. If the user requesting a write operation has a role with a permission that allows it to occur, the continuity of care record instance is updated with the sent data, and validated with the continuity of care record schema before the write-back to HealthVault. If validation against the schema is successful, then the write-back occurs, and the update performed by the provider is saved in the patient's HealthVault record. If the requester has a role that is not allowed to perform writing operations on the desired element, the Middle-Layer Server drops the request. Our approach provides a means for updating XML documents (in this case continuity of care record instances) that is controlled via an XACML security policy with the assistance of the Middle-Layer Server.

While HealthVault provides the information in continuity of care record, the SMART Platform's data model is capable of providing information in RDF/XML[16], N-TRIPLES[17], TURTLE[18] and JSON-LD[19]. RDF[20], which is a semantically augmented extension to XML, shares similar design, structure and hierarchical characteristics. The RDF/XML format provides XML syntax for RDF. This syntax is defined with respect to the XML namespaces, information set, and base. By using N-TRIPLES, the formal grammar for RDF/XML is annotated from the RDF graph. N-TRIPLES is an RDF graph-serializing format that enables the precise recording of the RDF graph mapping to machine-readable form. TURTLE allows the writing of RDF graphs in textual form, consisting of directives and triple-generating statements. Finally, JSON-LD is a linked data format utilized to provide context to data. Based on JSON, JSON-LD is capable of augmenting RESTful[21] services into providing data to the semantic-Web (Lanthaler, 2012). To secure the information obtained from the SMART Platform that is utilized by SMARTSync, we make use of the JSON-LD format. While an RDF/XML instance is at its core an XML instance annotated with RDF, it lacks a unique serialization from which an XML schema can be abstracted. That is, multiple XML schemas exist that validate against the different RDF/XML serializations. This presents a scalability problem in our approach, as we only consider a unique and valid XML schema to secure. The use of JSON-LD provides a unique JSON representation from which an equivalent XML instance can be generated using a variety of tools that are available for this purpose. To properly apply our security framework to JSON-LD, we first apply an XML transformation to the JSON-LD instance.

Since JSON-LD is extended JSON, any JSON to XML transformation tool will do the conversion and create an equivalent XML document, from which an XML schema can then be generated. To demonstrate, the Figure 6a has JSON-LD for the medication AMITRIPTYLINE (for depression), while the right hand side has the resulting XML instance. Since the generated XML instance only has one serialization, the one obtained from the transformation operation, abstracting a unique XML schema that can validate is possible using an XML schema generator or tool, e.g., Microsoft's Visual Studio[22], Stylus Studio[23], Eclipse's Oxygen XML Plugin[24], Trang[25], etc. This XML Schema abstracted from AMITRIPTYLINE instance is shown in Figure 7a.

To complete the process, we again leverage the XSCD and XRSD's from Section 3.1 to generate XACML Policies (using the process in Section 3.2). In Figure 7, the XML Schema for the medication (Figure 7a) is then enforced using an XACML policy (Figure 7b). The XACML Policy only changes, with respect to the continuity of care record targeting policy, in the resources and their references. Note that we utilize the same color-coding scheme from Section 3.2 to illustrate the different aspects of the XACML with respect to the shading for policy, and blue and red lettering for read and write, respectively. While the SMART Platform does not currently support writing data back to the data sources, we still provide the mechanism to enforce security on write operations. That is, the Action elements in the XACML policy are still defined for read and write operations (and evaluated to Deny or Permit based on the credentials deduced from the XRSD). The SMARTSync example clearly illustrates that it is possible for our XACML security framework to work in many different settings, as long as there are tools available to allow the data translation to occur and the appropriate XML schema to be generated.

Figure 6. SMART JSON-LD for medication (a) and transformed XML instance (b)

```
{
  "@context": ".../contexts/smart_context.jsonld",
  "@graph": [
    {
      "@type": "Medication",
      "belongsTo": {
        "@id": "http://sandbox-api.smartplatforms.org/records/2169591"
      },
      "drugName": {
        "@type": "CodedValue",
        "code": {
          "@id": "http://purl.bioontology.org/ontology/RXNORM/856845"
        },
        "dcterms__title": "AMITRIPTYLINE HCL 50 MG TAB"
      },
      "endDate": "2007-08-14",
      "frequency": {
        "@type": "ValueAndUnit",
        "unit": "/d",
        "value": "2"
      },
      "instructions": "Take two tablets twice daily as needed for pain",
      "quantity": {
        "@type": "ValueAndUnit",
        "unit": "{tablet}",
        "value": "2"
      },
      "startDate": "2007-03-14"
    },
    {
      "@id": "http://purl.bioontology.org/ontology/RXNORM/856845",
      "@type": [
        "spcode__RxNorm_Semantic",
        "Code"
      ],
      "dcterms__identifier": "856845",
      "dcterms__title": "AMITRIPTYLINE HCL 50 MG TAB",
      "system": "http://purl.bioontology.org/ontology/RXNORM/"
    }
  ]
}
```

(a) JSON-LD

```xml
<?xml version="1.0" encoding="UTF-8" ?>
<@context>
    .../contexts/smart_context.jsonld
</@context>
<@graph>
    <@type>Medication</@type>
    <belongsTo>
        <@id>http://sandbox-api.smartplatforms.org/records/2169591</@id>
    </belongsTo>
    <drugName>
        <@type>CodedValue</@type>
        <code>
            <@id>http://purl.bioontology.org/ontology/RXNORM/856845</@id>
        </code>
        <dcterms__title>AMITRIPTYLINE HCL 50 MG TAB</dcterms__title>
    </drugName>
    <endDate>2007-08-14</endDate>
    <frequency>
        <@type>ValueAndUnit</@type>
        <unit>/d</unit>
        <value>2</value>
    </frequency>
    <instructions>Take two tablets twice daily as needed for pain</instructions>
    <quantity>
        <@type>ValueAndUnit</@type>
        <unit>{tablet}</unit>
        <value>2</value>
    </quantity>
    <startDate>2007-03-14</startDate>
</@graph>
<@graph>
    <@id>http://purl.bioontology.org/ontology/RXNORM/856845</@id>
    <@type>spcode__RxNorm_Semantic</@type>
    <@type>Code</@type>
    <dcterms__identifier>856845</dcterms__identifier>
    <dcterms__title>AMITRIPTYLINE HCL 50 MG TAB</dcterms__title>
    <system>http://purl.bioontology.org/ontology/RXNORM/</system>
</@graph>
```

(b) Transformed XML

Figure 7. Segment of XML schema (a) and a segment of the targeting XACML policy (b)

```xml
<?xml version="1.0" encoding="UTF-8"?>
<xs:schema xmlns:xs="http://www.w3.org/2001/XMLSchema"
 elementFormDefault="qualified">
  <xs:element name="graph">
    <xs:complexType>
      <xs:sequence>
        <xs:element ref="type"/>
        <xs:element ref="belongsTo"/>
        <xs:element ref="drugName"/>
        <xs:element ref="endDate"/>
        <xs:element ref="frequency"/>
        <xs:element ref="instructions"/>
        <xs:element ref="quantity"/>
        <xs:element ref="startDate"/>
      </xs:sequence>
    </xs:complexType>
  </xs:element>
  <xs:element name="belongsTo" type="id"/>
  <xs:element name="drugName">
    <xs:complexType>
      <xs:sequence>
        <xs:element ref="type"/>
        <xs:element ref="code"/>
        <xs:element ref="dctermstitle"/>
      </xs:sequence>
    </xs:complexType>
  </xs:element>
  <xs:element name="code" type="id"/>
  <xs:element name="dctermstitle" type="xs:string"/>
  <xs:element name="endDate" type="xs:NMTOKEN"/>
  <xs:element name="frequency">
    <xs:complexType>
      <xs:sequence>
        <xs:element ref="type"/>
        <xs:element ref="unit"/>
        <xs:element ref="value"/>
      </xs:sequence>
    </xs:complexType>
  </xs:element>
  <xs:element name="instructions" type="xs:string"/>
  <xs:element name="quantity">
    <xs:complexType>
      <xs:sequence>
        <xs:element ref="type"/>
        <xs:element ref="unit"/>
        <xs:element ref="value"/>
      </xs:sequence>
    </xs:complexType>
  </xs:element>
  <xs:element name="startDate" type="xs:NMTOKEN"/>
  <xs:element name="type" type="xs:NCName"/>
  <xs:complexType name="id">
```

```xml
<?xml version="1.0" encoding="UTF-8"?>
<Policy xmlns="urn:oasis:names:tc:xacml:2.0:policy:schema:os"
 xmlns:xsi="http://www.w3.org/2001/XMLSchema-instance"
 xsi:schemaLocation="urn:oasis:names:tc:xacml:2.0:policy:schema:os
 http://docs.oasis-open.org/xacml/access_control-xacml-2.0-policy-schema-os.xsd"
 xmlns:md="http:www.med.example.com/schemas/record.xsd"
 PolicyId="urn:oasis:names:tc:xacml:2.0:example:policyid:PhysicianAccessControlPolicy"
 RuleCombiningAlgId="urn:oasis:names:tc:xacml:1.0:rule-combining-algorithm:deny-overrides">
  <Target/>
  <Rule RuleId="urn:oasis:names:tc:xacml:2.0:example:ruleid:PhysicianProductRule"
        Effect="Permit">
    <Description>Physician Access Control Policy Rule</Description>
    <Target>
      <Subjects>
        <Subject>
          <SubjectMatch MatchId="urn:oasis:names:tc:xacml:1.0:function:string-equal">
            <AttributeValue DataType="http://www.w3.org/2001/XMLSchema#string">
              Physician
            </AttributeValue>
            <SubjectAttributeDesignator
              AttributeId="urn:oasis:names:tc:xacml:2.0:example:attribute:role"
              DataType="http://www.w3.org/2001/XMLSchema#string"/>
          </SubjectMatch>
        </Subject>
      </Subjects>
      <Resources>
        <Resource>
          <ResourceMatch MatchId="urn:oasis:names:tc:xacml:1.0:function:string-equal">
            <AttributeValue DataType="http://www.w3.org/2001/XMLSchema#string">
              generated:schema:graph:type
            </AttributeValue>
            <ResourceAttributeDesignator
              AttributeId="urn:oasis:names:tc:xacml:1.0:resource:target-namespace"
              DataType="http://www.w3.org/2001/XMLSchema#string"/>
          </ResourceMatch>
        </Resource>
        <Resource>
          <ResourceMatch MatchId="urn:oasis:names:tc:xacml:1.0:function:string-equal">
            <AttributeValue DataType="http://www.w3.org/2001/XMLSchema#string">
              generated:schema:graph:belongsTo
            </AttributeValue>
            <ResourceAttributeDesignator
              AttributeId="urn:oasis:names:tc:xacml:1.0:resource:target-namespace"
              DataType="http://www.w3.org/2001/XMLSchema#string"/>
          </ResourceMatch>
        </Resource>
        <Resource>
          <ResourceMatch MatchId="urn:oasis:names:tc:xacml:1.0:function:string-equal">
            <AttributeValue DataType="http://www.w3.org/2001/XMLSchema#string">
              generated:schema:graph:drugName
            </AttributeValue>
            <ResourceAttributeDesignator
```

5. FUTURE TRENDS AND RESEARCH DIRECTIONS

Future trends and research directions in security are related to taking a high-level view of the information data exchange process, in general, and its application to the healthcare domain, in particular. Our focus in this section, with respect to health care as shown in Figure 8, considers all of the different health information technology systems and relevant standards that are utilized in the care and treatment of patients, with an emphasis on the interplay of health information exchange among various health information technology systems with security at global and local levels across such a complex architecture. Content wise, the lower left of Figure 8 contains open electronic health record systems (openEHR[26], PatientOS[27], VistA[28]) that all share an ability to export patient data in XML formats (XML, continuity of care record, and clinical document architecture); this is in contrast to commercial electronic health records (GE Centricity) which often have proprietary formats that hinder health information exchange. The upper left of Figure 8 contains various emerging platforms: Open *m*Health to promote mobile health via an open architecture, the Harvard SMART platform for substitutable medical applications that promote reuse), and Microsoft HealthVault, a personal health record. Open mHealth and SMART have JSON and JSON-LD, respectively, to model patient data, which must be converted (XML-C diamond) before it can be secured. HealthVault has .NET classes that can export to XML instances. The bottom right contains the medical applications that must be securely managed, Personal Health Assistant and SMARTSync, as reviewed in Section 4. The upper right contains the various standards and services involving medications (RxTerms[29] and RxNorm[30]), medical codes (SNOMED[31]), medical nomenclature (UMLS[32] and MeSH[33]), and laboratory codes (LOINC[34]) that are used by all of the systems and applications. Again, we note that the architecture shown in Figure 8 has many servers (left side), access to standards (upper right), and end user applications (lower right); this can logically be mapped to another domain that has a similar architecture.

The two complementary aspects to allow all of the interactions to occur across the diagram is overlaid in Figure 8 via: health information exchange (pentagon) that uses dotted lines to indicate the need to share information among health information technology systems and applications; and, the Global Security Policy and Control (octagon) that provides a centralized location from which secure interactions can locally occur within the framework. The end result and major challenge, represented in Figure 8 for the health

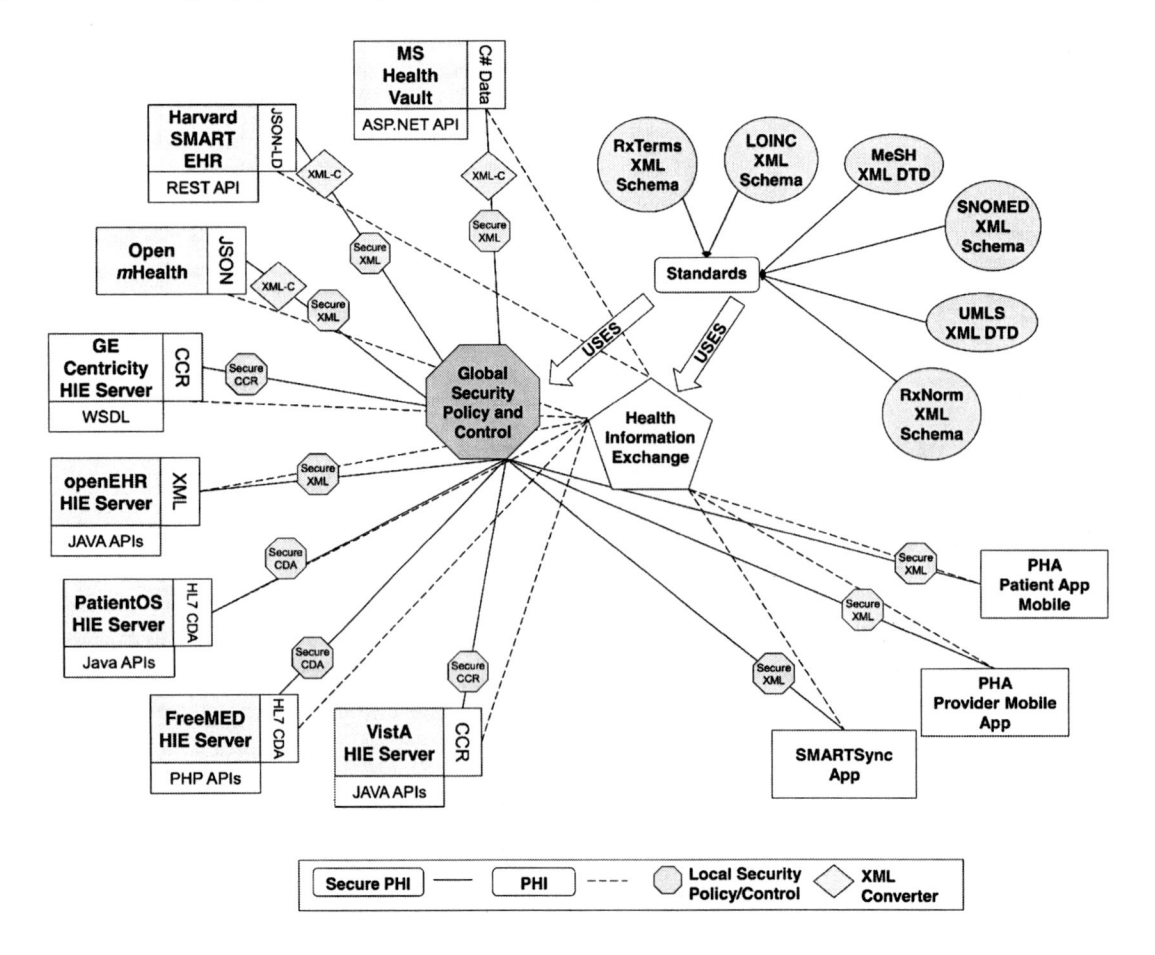

Figure 8. The interplay of health information exchange and security

care domain, is the recognition of a greater need for a comprehensive approach to security at global and local levels operating within an environment that is driven to share data through health information exchange. This need for a global approach towards security, addressed at the document-level, is not unique to healthcare, as other domains (such as e-commerce, etc.) also make use of data found in distributed repositories, each with their own local and global security policies to enforce. Note that Figure 8 does not contain all of the possible scenarios and possibilities that can arise from the interplay of information exchange in healthcare or another domain with a similar architecture. First, other security threats (intrusion detection, name server attacks, etc.) can take place. These vulnerabilities and the effects they have in the information exchange process must be protected proactively. We have realized that, in current security approaches, these types of attacks are found retroactively (e.g., when audits of systems are performed). The impact of these attacks can create a disparity between system trust and sharing policies (local and global security). For example, as shown in the lower left of Figure 8, electronic health record systems that share information typically do so via the use of a Health Information Exchange (HIE) server that contains data from the production counterpart offloaded at regular intervals. In the event of a security compromise, only the information deemed sharable would be breached. This layer of defense allows the systems to only share the data they seem comfortable with in case of a security threat such as intrusion or server attacks.

Second, another major component in health information exchange is the data analytics and mining across the entire interoperating systems to allow clinicians and clinical researchers to query the data in support of analyzing health data towards improving medical care. Institutions and individuals who are placed under this component typically use data dispersed throughout repositories under a set of terms of conditions and agreement of fair usage. The case of such data analytics and mining presents a challenge in terms of security since the users of the data are not usually the owners, and therefore must abide by the security policies set in each individual system. In the case of health care, privacy of protected health information and personal identifiable information is controlled by an array of policy enforcement or computational methods, some which prove sufficient for a set of cases, but not all. For example, there exist generic data publishing methods (e.g., k-anonymity and (α, k)-anonymity) that are not useful for cases with demographic data and the specific needs of electronic health records. An example of this is that, if age is not to be disclosed, removing the age from the shared dataset might not be enough since health codes (e.g., International Classification of Diseases – 9[35] codes) can reveal a person's age. Towards the goal of providing proper security while maintaining data usefulness, several machine learning techniques have been developed not only as mechanisms of verification for privacy enforcement, but also as mechanisms for feedback on the quality and completeness of the desired security policies.

Third, a scenario, which is not typically discussed, is what happens in the event where information providers decide to enter and/or leave the information exchange architecture. In these situations, global and local security is impacted in not only the constituent systems of the information exchange process, but also in those meta-systems already deployed that make use of resources found on information providers that left; in this case, both outdated resources and information from new systems can skew data analysis. Such events require the constant need of updating the security policies on those systems that share and utilize share data. Currently, when such an event happens, each information provider still part of the architecture must scramble to update their sharing and security policies to the new architecture's components.

In Section 4, we reviewed security for XML as attained with Personal Health Assistant and SMARTSync. Our intent in this section is to provide a look at future trends in regards to the attainment of security for XML data exchange in health care from two perspectives. First, in Section 5.1, we explore the accessible technology platforms in the health care domain, more specifically we focus on Open mHealth, Harvard SMART, and Microsoft HealthVault, that are all intended for widespread use by different users and in different contexts, to provide a means for various stakeholders (patients, clinicians, medical researchers, medical vendors, health information technology companies, etc.) to more easily interact with one another in different ways. These are concrete examples of the variety of platforms that can be found in an information exchange process, and while we focus on the healthcare counterpart as part of our case study, the content can be generalized to other domains with respect to the different platforms available to them. Next, in Section 5.2, we examine the open and free data repositories in the form of open electronic health records, namely, openEHR, PatientOS, and VistA. These repositories are intended to promote an environment of open access and sharing via a community approach, as viable alternatives to commercial products that are difficult to install and maintain, particularly for medical providers that lack information technology staff. In the same manner as Section 5.1, these electronic health records serve as concrete examples of the diversity and distributed nature of repositories in the information exchange process found across domains. Collectively, both perspectives demonstrate the significant level of complexity needed in regards to information exchange, and the diverse scenarios under which a security policy and control approach with both global and local components must effectively operate. Finally, Section 5.3 takes a concerted look at the information exchange and security issues from the health care perspective, their underlying computational issues, and makes recommendations that stakeholders in any domain would need to pursue in order to utilize information exchange process to insure that information can be successfully shared, exchanged, and secured. Again, many applications will have accessible platforms (open), proprietary systems (commercial), require the use of standards (in XML, RDF, OWL), and interact with Web-based and mobile apps via different protocols (JSON, SOAP, Web services, etc.); our work is generalizable.

5.1. Accessible Technology Platforms

In terms of accessible health information technology platforms, we focus on Microsoft HealthVault, Open mHealth, and Havard SMART, all of which offer different capabilities to specific stakeholders for particular purposes. HealthVault, launched in 2007, is a personal health record intended to allow patients to manage their own medical information including demographic data, personal data (height, weight), medications, allergies, etc. The larger scale intent is to provide a means for this to be stored securely (protected health information and HIPAA compliant) while simultaneously facilitating interactions with health care providers, medical device companies, health information technology applications, etc. For example, there are a wide range of applications and devices[36] for managing medical conditions such as diabetes meters, blood pressure monitors, etc. that can connect to HealthVault. Also, major pharmacies (CVS and Walgreens) allow patients to be able to link their prescription records into HealthVault. Such a capability would greatly improve our Personal Health Assistant Patient and Provider applications, and the accuracy of medication reconciliation in SMARTSync. Other HealthVault partners include the American Cancer Society, American Diabetes Association, and the American Heart Association. The reach of HealthVault from a patient centered personal health record to one that can reach out into application, devices, and the medical provider community at large is an important future trend.

Harvard University's SMART (Sustainable Medical Applications, Reusable Technologies) is one of the projects funded by The Office of the National Coordinator for Health Information Technology through the Strategic Health IT Advanced Research Projects[37] (SHARP) program. The goal of the SMART project is to provide a uniform, well-defined, reusable infrastructure for applications to interact with medical-record data. The creators of SMART motivate their work with the argument that environments which are constantly changing and evolving such as the health care system have the inherit need for information technology infrastructures that are of general purpose nature rather than monolithic and pre-designed (Mandl, 2009). SMART has a diverse range of partners, including Microsoft, CVS/Caremark, Athena Health, the Massachusetts Department of Public Health, etc.; all share the objective of improving the delivery of health care to patients via technology. However, SMART's focus differs from HealthVault since it is emphasizing the promotion of the platform for research endeavors with the recent launch of a SMART app at Boston Children's hospital. The future trend to promote the exchange and sharing of information to positively impact patient care is a laudable objective.

Lastly, the Open *m*Health organization has defined an open source architecture with mix and match components for mobile health applications to be constructed from reusable units; the intent is to use the architecture to make data an information more meaningful to patients and clinicians via personal evidence that is provided by patients and analyzing by clinicians. To support this, Open *m*Health provides *Data Processing Units (DPU)* and *Data Visualization Units (DVU)* (Estrin, 2012). A data processing unit is a Web service that defines a set of data inputs and outputs (via an application programming interface) and provides an underlying algorithmic capability to extract, infer, and analyze a data set from one or more sources. For example, a data processing unit may take as input a set of glucose readings and insulin dosages with date time stamps, along with patient time (weight, age, etc.) and be able to output an analysis to determine the trends in terms of diabetes care (e.g., low glucose levels too often, etc.). A data visualization unit provides the means via a returned browser component to display information from a data processing unit in a form that is conducive to the recipient (patient, provider, researcher, etc.). Open *m*Health, via its data processing and visualization units, will provide access to a myriad of information including sensors from mobile devices, sensor data collected from the cloud (via glucose meters that update values to cloud repository), data from public sources (Food and Drug Administration DailyMed[38], nutrition), data from electronic health records, etc. One of their major initiatives is the Post Traumatic Stress Disorder collaboration with the Department of Veteran Affairs, having a mobile post-traumatic stress disorder Coach to help veterans cope with post-traumatic stress disorder. This future trend has the features of HealthVault (putting care under a patient's control) with a simultaneous eye to providers and researchers interested in treating patients or analyzing data sets.

These three platforms present the diversity of purpose and orientation (user-oriented for HealthVault, developer oriented for Open *m*Health, developer and user-oriented for SMART) in platforms that are constituents of the information exchange process, yet must act in harmony in order to provide the best and/or intended functionality and results for their end users. They also demonstrate the differences in the use of technologies and standards that can be found across platforms, from completely proprietary products (HealthVault) to community driven efforts (SMART) to semi-private/collaborative approaches (Open *m*Health). These differences result in different policies for usage and data sharing, and in turn result in conflicts of which policy should be enforced completely, partially, or not at all.

5.2. Open and Free Data Repositories

The adoption of electronic health records has increased in the previous years because of the benefits they provide and enacted laws, such as the Affordable Care Act of 2010[39]. The shift from paperwork to electronic data has pushed vendors to seize the opportunity and create their own respective versions of electronic health records for consumer adoption. We focus on those alternatives that are open source and free to implement: openEHR, PatientOS and VistA. openEHR[40] serves as a framework and standard to describe the administration and storage of patient data for electronic clinic history. This electronic clinic history acts as the repository of patient information, and is independent of the technology utilized for its access. The openEHR specifications are maintained by the openEHR foundation. These specifications, which arise from research done throughout a decade, include information and data models for the electronic clinic history, demographic information, clinical procedures, etc., and are implemented to provide a base for health information exchange. With the ongoing binding of Systematized Nomenclature of Medicine – Clinical Terms to openEHR, as well as the addition of a virtual electronic health record for the user interface, openEHR serves as an open source, complete solution framework for users and institutions to implement their own EHRs capable of complying with information exchange standards and data storage. This important future trend sets the standard for all electronic health records to target.

The objective of PatientOS[41] is to make the user's (medical provider) workflow a rapid one. To achieve this, PatientOS provides detailed observations on which values should be default in which forms, an almost never-changing user interface (as the tool is updated), automated functions and using the least amounts of clicks necessary to complete a task. PatientOS permits the user workflow to be customized based on the user, his/her role, and the institution in which the user works. While other software solutions are plagued by a scarce maintenance and update schedule, PatientOS has been designed to be scalable and easily maintained. These two factors reduce the bar on updating the electronic health record to a newer version by assuring users that the backend does not change. For developers, PatientOS offers a Java application programming interface that permits the development of plugins, customized forms, and user interface themes. By partnering with businesses such as MResult Healthcare, new alternatives to reducing the cost of implementation of electronic health records are possible. As a future trend, PatientOS targets the ease of both deploying and integrating health information technology into medical practices for usage by providers, a vital problem that hinders adoption of electronic health records.

Lastly, VistA[42] (Veterans Health Information Systems and Technology Architecture) is an open source information system built around an electronic health record. Developed by the United States Department of Veterans Affairs (VA), VistA consists of hundreds of clinical, financial, infrastructure and patient-Web functions. Clinical functions range from Admission Discharge Transfer, clinical procedures, pharmaceutical, laboratories, and mental health. Financial and administrative functions include an automated information collection system, incident reporting, fugitive felon program, and others. The infrastructure functions cover the maintenance of the backend, as well as communication standards, e.g., capacity management tools, Health Level 7 (messaging), broker, an SQL interface, and a network health exchange. The last sets of functions, the patient-Web functions, provide clinical information decision support, health record keeping, and a personal finance system. With the Veterans Health Administration utilizing VistA, the electronic health record is considered the largest medical system in the United States, spanning the largest health information exchange system and covering over 8 million patients. This widespread use also translates to physician usage: 60% of United States trained physicians rotate through the Veterans Health Administration, making VistA the most familiar and widely used electronic health record in the country. The widespread use of VistA has spanned different iterations, including Austronaut VistA[43], WorldVistA[44], OpenVistA[45], and vxVistA[46]. As a future trend, VistA is often cited as the "trend setting" and model for electronic health records and their adoption across the world.

VistA, openEHR and PatientOS demonstrate the way that data formats utilized for export and import functionalities, as well as internal operations, can differ between solutions intended for the same domain. These differences in data structures and formats utilized by repositories is not unique to the health care domain, and demonstrate a need to present an encompassing approach that handles all of the possibilities in term of document standards and secure information exchange. Added to this are the proprietary solutions that are widespread (for example, in the health care domain GE Centricity[47]) that could only support one of the many available standards due to development and economic reasons.

5.3. Recommendations for Success

The computing profession operates in the world where standards are the norm rather than the exception. After a tumultuous period in the late 1980s/early 1990s, where there were many different incompatible versions of C++, the profession has striven to an emphasis and strong reliance on the standards definition and approval process. In the early years of UML, every vendor's tool was incompatible; today, the UML via OMG has a standard of not just the language but the structure of the diagrams, allowing XMI to be exported for importing into any other UML tool. The same is true for database systems, which easily allow the porting of relational schemas and databases of all sizes via XML and XMI, allowing data to easily move from MySQL to Oracle or to SQL Server. In the process, the standards community in computing has provided the tools, and all of the vendors have accepted the responsibility to allow for designs, information, and data of all formats to be easily and effectively exchanged.

One troubling trend in widespread information exchange, especially in health care, is the lack of such a commitment by vendors and a promotion of data exchange. Clearly, as shown in Figure 8 for health care, there are many standards that have been adopted and are in use, ranging from JSON to RDF to XML to the continuity of care record and clinical document architecture standards; but those standards and the modeling of data have not been unified. Further, when one attempts to share information across commercial vendors (for example, between the electronic health records such as GE Centricity, AllScripts[48], etc.), it ends up requiring n^2 custom mappings of data between n different systems, as vendors are more concerned with proprietary protection of information as opposed to facilitating sharing; one major issue is competition as hospitals in a region see sharing information leading to the potential of losing patients. In health care this is clearly evident, as vendors do not want to provide the ability to export to a common XML format for medical data, since then it would allow the medical provider to potentially change vendors (akin to changing from Oracle to SQL Server in order to save licensing costs).

Another troubling trend is the inability to access information in repositories (for example, electronic health records) in a manner that would be able to present information that cuts across multiple instances of common information (patient's record); patient's visit multiple providers, labs, health facilities, etc., and if each has their own repository, the ability to get a complete collection of all of the information has not been achievable to date. Following the theme of health care, consider than an electronic health record is set up to manage individual patients and their medical records electronically including medications, allergies, immunizations, etc. However, suppose a medication is recalled, as Vioxx[49] was back in 2004, then every medical provider would need to contact his/her patients to switch their medication. But, electronic health records don't provide the ability to easily do this. In fact, for it to occur, one would need to have enough technical expertise to understand and access the underlying relational schema and database to write an ad-hoc query. There is a further hindrance in regards to supporting analysis of a medical provider's practice from a data and treatment perspective. For example, if you are a medical provider who wants to check on all of the diabetes patients in your practice taking a specific medication and determine commonalities related to other diseases (say congestive heart failure) or conditions (obesity), there is no way for you to make such an investigation without sophisticated ad-hoc queries.

Another issue to consider is the legal implications involved in data sharing and exchange, especially data that is confidential or otherwise protected by legal statues. For example, the Ethical, legal and social implications (ELSI) of human genomics are tied to the Genetic Information Nondiscrimination Act (GINA) of 2008[50] and the Health Insurance Portability and Accountability Act of 1996 (HIPAA). GINA protects a patient's genetic information against discrimination in health insurance and employment; this includes: genetic test of patient, his/her family members, fetus of individual or family member, family medical history, and request/receipt of genetic services that may including clinical research trials. HIPAA's Privacy Rule insures that protected health information is securely maintained by entries with patients retaining rights to access that information while still allowing entities to disclose the information under certain situations. HIPAA's Security Rule defines the "series of administrative, physical, and technical safeguards for covered entities to use to assure the confidentiality, integrity, and availability of electronic protected health information". For ELSI, protection of information must be reconciled across HIPAA and GINA to securely deliver the appropriate combination of clinical, genomic, and phenotypic information to all of the involved stakeholders (medical, researchers, clinical providers, support personnel, insurers, and patients).

Based on these issues and their underlying computational, political and acceptance limitations, we propose three major recommendations to facilitate information exchange in domains clouded by different standards, platforms, purposes and orientations. *First*, we note that there is a need for a *formal and unifying standards process* for data to allow the easy exporting and importing of data across information technology systems. This does not only mean to achieve a common format, but also one that uses the most up-to-date technologies. For example, in the health care scenario (see Figure 8), there are not just XML schemas used in current standards, but outdated and outmoded standards such as the document type definitions (XML DTD). One unifying standard or a set of standards with the most up-to-date features is a must to successfully achieve information exchange. We know this works well, since the UML community with its standard allows the easy exchange of UML designs between different tools and the database community provides export in XML to allow ease of porting a database across vendor products.

Second, open source and commercial data repositories need to be more conducive towards *cross platform access*, providing the potential for more effective tools and applications that improve the functionality, analysis or usage of information to improve end-user experience. In the case of health care, this involves open and commercial electronic health record vendors to provide *cross patient access* in order to provide better tools for medical providers so patient care and treatment improves. The computing community has been a leader in this regard, and these successful approaches need to be applied.

Third, involving the combination of legal statutes on domains that utilize and exchange data that is protected (for example, in health care with GINA and HIPAA for ELSI), will require careful consideration of the *policy, cost, usage, and exchange of information in a secure manner* across a wider range of data (for example, clinical, genomic, and phenotypic) than has normally been required. HIPAA gets involved in many non-medical settings, as does the need to manage personal identifiable information for many domains.

6. CONCLUSION

This chapter has presented a security framework for XML (see Section 1 and Figure 1) that is intended to allow security to be defined at the XML schema level to be enforced on XML instances using NIST Role-Based Access Control (RBAC) in Section 2. In the process, the XML instances delivered to users (by role) are customized to insure that a user is only able to see and/or modify what has been authorized, effectively yielding role restricted XML instances. To achieve the security, we leverage XACML to define policies against XML schemas that can then be enforced on all XML instances; our approach separates the security privileges from both the XML schema and their instances, allowing changes as security policies evolve to have no impact on schemas and existing instances. Our approach has been demonstrated on a healthcare domain case study with an emphasis on medical or clinical patient data as represented by the continuity of care record standard (see Section 2 and Figure 2), and we have briefly reviewed our earlier work (De la Rosa Algarín, 2012) that has created UML diagrams: an XML Schema Class Diagram (XSCD) to graphically represent an XML schema, and XML role slice diagram (XRSD) to define roles and their privileges (read, write, etc.) against XML schema elements (see Section 3.1). Using this as a basis, we described the generation of an XACML security policy for enforcement purposes, as detailed in Section 3.2, and illustrated in Figure 6. Collectively, the work in Section 3 was applied to in Section 4 to two applications: the Personal Health Assistant (PHA) in Section 4.2 hooked to Microsoft HealthVault for a patient to track of medications, nutritional supplements, allergies, etc., and also authorize that protected health information to his/her specific medical providers who can use their own app to select and view the authorized protected health information on a patient-by-patient basis as determined by his/he assigned role; and SMARTSync, an application for medication reconciliation in Section 4.3 hooked to Microsoft HealthVault and Harvard SMART's Reference Electronic Health Record to gather information from multiple sources. For each application, we demonstrated the generation of XACML policies in different ways from an eventual XML representation (Section 4.4). While we demonstrated the work in a health care domain, our architecture is simply servers, mobile, and Web apps, interacting with one another using many different mans (XML, JSON, SOAP, Web services, etc.). The XML security approach that we have presented is intended to target the wide array of apps on the World Wide Web.

Our future trends in Section 5 has taken a larger scale view of the security process for XML in regards to secure data sharing and exchange; while the work in this chapter (Section 3) is applicable to any domain, Section 5 focuses on the health care domain and the unique challenges of security at global and local levels that must interact with health information exchange across a myriad of health information technology systems and applications that have differing data formats that must be reconciled. The emerging trends in Sections 5.1 and 5.2 include accessible information technology platforms: the HealthVault system that allow patients to manage their health information with increasing linkages to applications, medical devices, pharmaceutical records, etc.; the Harvard SMART platform promoting a reusable infrastructure for health care data sharing and exchange, with diverse partners and roll out of research tools at a major medical center; the Open *m*Health platform trending to both satisfy patient, provider, and research requirements through an innovative and open means to collect and visualize information; and, a set of open and free data repositories, more specifically the electronic health records openEHR, PatientOS, and VistA, all striving to promote open access and sharing via a community approach, as viable alternatives to commercial products that are difficult to install and maintain. These platforms and systems served as concrete examples to pinpoint the major issues currently present to attain information exchange, and in Section 5.3 we presented a number of recommendations, some controversial, chastising the adoption of standards and free exchange of information by commercial information technology vendors, and hindering the attempt to utilize and exchange information in information technology systems for more effective usability, such as patient care in health care. Many of these recommendations are accepted practice in computing and information technology, and there needs to be a migration of these successes by applying those approaches to health care and other domains.

REFERENCES

Ammari, F., & Lu, J. (2010). Advanced XML security: Framework for building secure XML management system (SXMS). In *Proceedings of the 2010 Seventh International Conference on Information Technology: New Generations (ITNG)* (pp. 120-125). ITNG.

Ardagna, C., Damiani, E., Capitani di Vimercati, S., & Samarati, P. (2007). XML security. In *Proceedings of Security, Privacy, and Trust in Modern Data Management* (pp. 71-86). Springer. doi:10.1007/978-3-540-69861-6_6.

Barnsteiner, J. (2005). Medication reconciliation: Transfer of medication information across settings-keeping it free from error. *The American Journal of Nursing*, *105*(3), 31. doi:10.1097/00000446-200503001-00007 PMID:15802996.

Bertino, E., Carminati, B., & Ferrari, E. (2004). Access control for XML documents and data. *Information Security Technical Report*, (9): 19–34. doi:10.1016/S1363-4127(04)00029-9.

Bertino, E., Castano, S., Ferrari, E., & Mesiti, M. (2002). Protection and administration of XML data sources. *Data & Knowledge Engineering*, (43): 237–260. doi:10.1016/S0169-023X(02)00127-1.

Bertino, E., & Ferrari, E. (2002). Secure and selective dissemination of XML documents. *ACM Transactions on Information and System Security*, (5): 290–331. doi:10.1145/545186.545190.

Chandrakumar, T., & Parthasarathy, S. (2012). Enhancing data security in ERP projects using XML. *International Journal of Enterprise Information Systems*, (8): 51–65. doi:10.4018/jeis.2012010104.

Damiani, E., De Capitani di Vimercati, S., Paraboschi, S., & Samarati, P. (2000). Design and implementation of an access control processor for XML documents. *Computer Networks*, *33*(1), 59–75. doi:10.1016/S1389-1286(00)00053-0.

Damiani, E., Fansi, M., Gabillon, A., & Marrara, S. (2008). A general approach to securely querying XML. *Computer Standards & Interfaces*, *30*(6), 379–389. doi:10.1016/j.csi.2008.03.006.

De la Rosa Algarín, A., Demurjian, S. A., Berhe, S., & Pavlich-Mariscal, J. (2012). A security framework for XML schemas and documents for healthcare. In *Proceedings of 2012 International Workshop on Biomedical and Health Informatics (BHI 2012)*, (pp. 782-789). BHI.

Dolin, R. H., Alschuler, L., Boyer, S., Beebe, C., Behlen, F. M., Biron, P. V., & Shvo, A. S. (2006). HL7 clinical document architecture, release 2. *Journal of the American Medical Informatics Association*, *13*(1), 30–39. doi:10.1197/jamia.M1888 PMID:16221939.

Estrin, D., & Sim, I. (2010). Open mHealth architecture: An engine for health care innovation. *Science*, *330*(6005), 759–760. doi:10.1126/science.1196187 PMID:21051617.

Ferraiolo, D., Cugini, J., & Kuhn, D. R. (1995). Role-based access control (RBAC): Features and motivations. In *Proceedings of 11th Annual Computer Security Application Conference* (pp. 241-248). CSAC.

Ferraiolo, D. F., Sandhu, R., Gavrila, S., Kuhn, D. R., & Chandramouli, R. (2001). Proposed NIST standard for role-based access control. *ACM Transactions on Information and System Security*, *4*(3), 224–274. doi:10.1145/501978.501980.

Huang, S., & Lesko, L. (2004). Drug-drug, drug-dietary supplement, and drug-citrus fruit and other food interactions: What have we learned? *Journal of Clinical Pharmacology*, *44*(6), 559. doi:10.1177/0091270004265367 PMID:15145962.

Kuper, G., Massacci, F., & Rassadko, N. (2005). Generalized XML security views. In *Proceedings of the 10th ACM Symposium on Access Control Models and Technologies* (pp. 77-84). ACM.

Lanthaler, M., & Gütl, C. (2012). On using JSON-LD to create evolvable RESTful services. In *Proceedings of the 3rd International Workshop on RESTful Design (WS-REST 2012) at WWW2012* (pp. 25-32). Lyon, France: ACM Press.

Leonardi, E., Bhowmick, S., & Iwaihara, M. (2010). Efficient database-driven evaluation of security clearance for federated access control of dynamic XML documents. In *Database Systems for Advanced Applications* (pp. 299–306). Academic Press. doi:10.1007/978-3-642-12026-8_24.

Mandl, K., & Kohane, I. (2009). No small change for the health information economy. *The New England Journal of Medicine*, *360*(13), 1278–1281. doi:10.1056/NEJMp0900411 PMID:19321867.

Müldner, T., Leighton, G., & Miziołek, J. (2009). Parameterized role-based access control policies for XML documents. Information Security Journal: A Global Perspective, Taylor & Francis, (18), 282-296.

Pavlich-Mariscal, J., Demurjian, S., & Michel, L. (2008). A framework of composable access control definition, enforcement and assurance. In *Proceedings of the SCCC'08. International Conference of the IEEE* (pp. 13–22). IEEE.

Poon, E., Blumenfeld, B., & Hamann, C. et al. (2006). Design and implementation of an application and associated services to support interdisciplinary medication reconciliation efforts at an integrated healthcare delivery network. *Journal of the American Medical Informatics Association*, *13*(6), 581–592. doi:10.1197/jamia.M2142 PMID:17114640.

Rahaman, M., Roudier, Y., & Schaad, A. (2008). Distributed access control for XML document centric collaborations. In *Proceedings of the EDOC'08. 12th International IEEE* (pp. 267-276). IEEE.

Ziminski, T. B., De la Rosa Algarín, A., Saripalle, R., Demurjian, S. A., & Jackson, E. (2012). SMARTSync: Towards patient-driven medication reconciliation using the SMART framework. In *Proceedings of 2012 International Workshop on Biomedical and Health Informatics (BHI 2012)*, (pp. 806-813). BHI.

ADDITIONAL READING

Baumer, D., Earp, J., & Payton, F. (2000). Privacy of medical records: IT implications of HIPAA. *ACM SIGCAS Computers and Society*, *30*(4), 40–47. doi:10.1145/572260.572261.

Berhe, S., Demurjian, S., & Agresta, T. (2009). Emerging trends in health care delivery: Towards collaborative security for NIST RBAC. In *Proceedings of Research Directions in Data and Applications Security LNCS* (Vol. 5645, pp. 283–290). Berlin: Springer. doi:10.1007/978-3-642-03007-9_19.

Berhe, S., Demurjian, S., Gokhale, S., Pavlich-Mariscal, J., & Saripalle, R. (2011). Leveraging UML for security engineering and enforcement in a collaboration on duty and adaptive workflow model that extends NIST RBAC. [LNCS]. *Proceedings of Research Directions in Data and Applications Security, 6818*, 293–300.

Berhe, S., Demurjian, S., Saripalle, R., Agresta, T., Liu, J., & Cusano, A. ... Gedarovich, J. (2010). Secure, obligated and coordinated collaboration in health care for the patient-centered medical home. In *Proceedings of the AMIA Annual Symposium* (p. 36). AMIA.

Bernauer, M., Kappel, G., & Kramler, G. (2003). *Representing XML schema in UML - An UML profile for XML schema (Tech. Rep.)*. Citeseer.

Bernauer, M., Kappel, G., & Kramler, G. (2004). Representing XML schema in UML – A comparison of approaches. In *Proceedings of Web Engineering* (pp. 767–769). Web Engineering. doi:10.1007/978-3-540-27834-4_54.

Blechner, M., Sariapalle, R., & Demurjian, S. (2012). A proposed star schema and extraction process to enhance the collection of contextual and semantic information for clinical research data warehouses. In *Proceedings of 2012 International Workshop on Biomedical and Health Informatics (BHI 2012)*. BHI.

Demurjian, S., Ren, H., Berhe, S., Devineni, M., Vegad, S., & Polineni, K. (2010). Improving the information security of collaborative web portals via fine-grained role-based access control. In Murugesan, S. (Ed.), *Handbook of Research on Web 2.0, 3.0 and X.0: Technologies, Business and Social Applications* (pp. 430–448). Hershey, PA: IGI Global.

Demurjian, S., Saripalle, R., & Berhe, S. (2009). An integrated ontology framework for health information exchange. In *Proceedings of 21st International Conference on Software Engineering and Knowledge Engineering (SEKE09)* (pp. 575–580). SEKE.

Doan, T., Demurjian, S., Ting, T. C., & Phillips, C. (2004). RBAC/MAC security for UML. *Research Directions in Data and Applications Security, 144*, 189–204. doi:10.1007/1-4020-8128-6_13.

Klyne, G., Carroll, J. J., & McBride, B. (2004). *Resource description framework (RDF), concepts and abstract syntax*. W3C Recommendation, 10.

Mandl, K., Mandel, J., & Murphy, S. et al. (2012). The SMART platform: Early experience enabling substitutable applications for electronic health records. *Journal of the American Medical Informatics Association, 19*(4), 597. doi:10.1136/amiajnl-2011-000622 PMID:22427539.

Montelius, E., Astrand, B., Hovstadius, B., & Petersson, G. (2008). Individuals appreciate having their medication record on the web: A survey of attitudes to a national pharmacy register. *Journal of Medical Internet Research, 10*(4). doi:10.2196/jmir.1022 PMID:19000978.

Pavlich-Mariscal, J., Demurjian, S., & Michel, L. (2010). A framework for security assurance of access control enforcement code. *Computer & Security Journal, 29*(7), 770–784. doi:10.1016/j.cose.2010.03.004.

Pavlich-Mariscal, J., Demurjian, S., & Michel, L. (n.d.). A framework of composable security features: Preserving separation of security concerns from models to code. *Computer & Security Journal, 29*(3), 350-379.

Pavlich-Mariscal, J., Doan, T., Michel, L., Demurjian, S., & Ting, T. C. (2005). *Role slices: A notation for RBAC permission assignment and enforcement. Research Directions in Data and Applications Security (LNCS)* (Vol. 3654, pp. 40–53). Berlin: Springer.

Phillips, C., Demurjian, S., & Bessette, K. (2005). A service-based approach for RBAC and MAC security. In Stojanovic, Z., & Dahanayake, A. (Eds.), *Service-Oriented Software System Engineering: Challenges and Practices* (pp. 317–339). Hershey, PA: IGI Global.

Routledge, N., Bird, L., & Goodchild, A. (2002). UML and XML schema. *Australian Computer Science Communications, 24*(2), 157–166.

Saripalle, R. Knath, Demrjian, S., & Berhe, S. (2011). Towards a software design process for ontologies. In *Proceedings of 2011 International Conference on Software and Intelligent Information (ICSII 2011)*. ICSII.

Skogan, D. (1999). UML as a schema language for XML based data interchange. In *Proceedings of the 2nd International Conference on the Unified Modeling Language (UML'99)*. UML.

KEY TERMS AND DEFINITIONS

Continuity of Care Record (CCR): A document standard for health information typically used for Personal Health Records (PHR) with the intended purpose of information exchange. It provides a universal structure to the patient's information that can be utilized by different personal health records, applications and systems.

Electronic Health Record (EHR): An electronic version of the patient's medical record. An electronic health record contains all related health information, from medications to procedures, and is managed by the institution in which it is stored (e.g. hospital, private practice, clinic, etc).

eXtensible Access Control Markup Language (XACML): A security policy language designed from XML. Its specifications allow for a uniform policy language that can be enforced in heterogeneous systems. XACML policies can be enforced at a systems level, software level, or information level, depending on the policies' targets and rules.

eXtensible Markup Language (XML): A structured language utilized for information exchange, standards and information validation via the use of schemas. Its extensibility allows developers and experts to design and implement common standards for the use across systems and domains.

Health Information Exchange (HIE): The ability to share information among health information technology systems by linking information for the same patient across multiple repositories to provide a complete health care view.

Health Information Technology (HIT): Information technologies (e.g. mobile applications, computer programs, decision support systems, etc.) whose use is intended for the healthcare domain.

Meta-System: A system or platform built from many constituent systems that makes use of functionality or data distributed among its components or external data repositories.

Personal Health Record (PHR): An electronic version of a medical record that is managed by the patient. PHRs typically provide the means to manage medication lists, allergies, procedures, emergency contacts, and other clinical data.

Personal Identifiable Information (PII): Information that contains attributes and values that can help determine a person's identity.

Protected Health Information (PHI): Clinical and other health related information regarding a patient that is protected under laws, or must be protected as dictated by laws.

Role-Based Access Control (RBAC): An access control model where permissions are assigned directly to roles, which are assigned to users.

Role-Restricted (RR): A filtered version of a document. Its filtering depends on the role of the user requesting the information, and the security policies in place.

Substitutable Medical Apps, Reusable Technologies (SMART): A platform that permits the development and reusability of applications by targeting a common abstraction layer, removing the need to target specific data repositories.

XML Role-Slice Diagram (XRSD): The XRSD is a diagram containing the role's credentials and the elements of the XML schema on which these credentials act.

XML Schema Class Diagram (XSCD): The XSCD is an UML artifact that serves as an equivalent representation of an XML schema in a UML diagram.

ENDNOTES

1. eXtensible Markup Language, http://www.w3.org.com/XML/
2. Continuity of Care Record (CCR), http://www.astm.org/Standards/E2369.htm
3. Microsoft HealthVault, http://www.microsoft.com/en-us/healthvault/
4. Health Insurance Portability and Accountability Act of 1996 (HIPAA), http://www.hhs.gov/ocr/privacy/
5. National Institute of Standards and Technology, http://www.nist.gov/index.html
6. OASIS XACML, https://www.oasis-open.org/committees/xacml/
7. Unified Modeling Language, http://www.uml.org/
8. SMART Platforms, http://www.smartplatforms.org/
9. Android, http://www.android.com/
10. JavaScript Object Notation, http://www.json.org/
11. Open *m*Health, http://openmhealth.org/
12. XML Security Working Group (SWG), http://www.w3.org/2008/xmlsec/
13. MySQL, http://www.mysql.com/
14. SMART RDF/XML Data Model, http://dev.smartplatforms.org/reference/data_model/
15. NDF-RT, http://www.pbm.va.gov/NationalFormulary.aspx
16. RDF/XML, http://www.w3.org/TR/REC-rdf-syntax/
17. N-TRIPLES, http://www.w3.org/2001/sw/RDFCore/ntriples/
18. Terse RDF Triple Language (TURTLE), http://www.w3.org/TeamSubmission/turtle/
19. JSON for Linking Data (JSON-LD), http://json-ld.org/
20. Resource Description Framework (RDF), http://www.w3.org/RDF/
21. RESTful Services, http://www.ibm.com/developerworks/Webservices/library/ws-restful/
22. MS VisualStudio XML Schema Definition Tool, http://msdn.microsoft.com/en-us/library/x6c1kb0s(v=vs.80).aspx
23. StylusStudio, http://www.stylusstudio.com/
24. Eclipse's Oxygen XML Plugin, http://oxygenxml.com/eclipse_plugin.html
25. Trang, http://www.thaiopensource.com/relaxng/trang.html
26. openEHR, http://www.openehr.org/home.html
27. PatientOS, http://www.patientos.org/
28. VistA, http://worldvista.org/AboutVistA
29. RxTerms, http://wwwcf.nlm.nih.gov/umlslicense/rxtermApp/rxTerm.cfm
30. RxNorm, http://www.nlm.nih.gov/research/umls/rxnorm/
31. SNOMED, http://www.ihtsdo.org/snomed-ct/

32. UMLS, http://www.nlm.nih.gov/research/umls/
33. MeSH, http://www.ncbi.nlm.nih.gov/mesh
34. LOINC, http://loinc.org/
35. ICD-9 codes, http://www.icd9data.com/
36. HealthVault App Directory, https://account.healthvault.com/Directory
37. Strategic Health IT Advanced Research Projects, http://goo.gl/62K5d
38. FDA DailyMed, http://dailymed.nlm.nih.gov/dailymed/about.cfm
39. Affordable Care Act of 2010, http://www.healthcare.gov/law/full/
40. openEHR, http://www.openehr.org/home.html
41. PatientOS, http://www.patientos.org/index.html
42. VistA, http://worldvista.org/AboutVistA
43. Austronaut VistA, http://astronautvista.com/
44. WorldVistA, http://www.worldvista.org/
45. OpenVistA, http://www.medsphere.com/solutions/openvista-for-the-enterprise
46. vxVista, https://www.vxvista.org/display/vx4h/Welcome
47. GE Centricity, http://goo.gl/LCvU7
48. AllScripts, http://www.allscripts.com/
49. Vioxx, http://www.merck.com/newsroom/vioxx/
50. Genetic Information Nondiscrimination Act of 2008, http://www.genome.gov/24519851/

Compilation of References

Abad, C., Taylor, J., Sengul, C., Yurcik, W., Zhou, Y., & Rowe, K. (2003). Log correlation for intrusion detection: A proof of concept. In *Proceedings of the 19th Annual Computer Security Applications Conference* (pp. 255-264). Washington, DC: IEEE Computer Society.

Abadi, M., & Fournet, C. (2001). Mobile values, new names, and secure communication. In *Proceedings of the 28th ACM SIGPLAN-SIGACT Symposium on Principles of Programming Languages (POPL'01)*, (pp. 104-115). ACM Press.

Abadi, M., Glew, N., Horne, B., & Pinkas, B. (2002). Certified email with a light on-line trusted third party: Design and implementation. In *Proceedings of the 11th international World Wide Web conference* (pp. 387-395). ACM Press.

Abd El-Wahed, M., Mesbah, S., & Shoukry, A. (2008). Efficiency and security of some image encryption algorithms. In *Proceedings of the World Congress on Engineering* (Vol. 1, pp. 561-564). IEEE.

Aboba, B., Simon, D., & Eronen, P. (2008). *Extensible authentication protocol (EAP) key management framework*. Internet Engineering Task Force (IETF), Request for Comments: 5247. Retrieved from http://tools.ietf.org/html/rfc5247

Adi, W., Al-Qayedi, A., Zarooni, A. A., & Mabrouk, A. (2004). *Secured multi-identity mobile infrastructure and offline mobile-assisted micro-payment application*. Paper presented at the Wireless Communications and Networking Conference. New York, NY.

Adida, B. (2008). Helios: Web-based open-audit voting. In *Proceedings of the Seventeenth Usenix Security Symposium*, (pp. 335-348). USENIX Association.

Aho, A., & Corasick, M. (1975). Efficient string matching: An aid to bibliographic search. *Communications of the ACM, 18*(6), 333–340. doi:10.1145/360825.360855.

Alharby, A., & Imai, H. (2005). IDS false alarm reduction using continuous and discontinuous patterns. In *Proceedings of the 3rd International Conference on Applied Cryptography and Network Security* (pp. 192-205). Springer-Verlag.

Ali, A. M., Halim, Z. A., & G̈okhan, C. K. (2009). A hybrid intrusion detection system design for computer network security. *Computers & Electrical Engineering, 35*(3), 517–526. doi:10.1016/j.compeleceng.2008.12.005.

Alliance for Telecommunications Industry Solutions. (n.d.). *Homepage*. Retrieved from http://www.atis.org

Alserhani, F., Akhlaq, M., Awan, I. U., & Cullen, A. J. (2011). Event-based alert correlation system to detect SQLI activities. In *Proceedings of the 2011 International Conference on Advanced Information Networking and Applications* (pp. 175-182). IEEE Press.

Alvarez, G., Montoya, F., Romera, M., & Pastor, G. (1999). Chaotic cryptosystems. In L. D. Sanson (Ed.), *Proceedings of the 33rd Annual International Carnahan Conference on Security Technology*, (pp. 332–338). IEEE.

Alvarez, G., & Li, S. (2006). Some basic cryptographic requirements for chaos-based cryptosystems. *International Journal of Bifurcation and Chaos in Applied Sciences and Engineering, 16*(8), 2129–2151. doi:10.1142/S0218127406015970.

Amazon S3 Availability Event. (2008). Retrieved from http://status.aws.amazon.com/s3-20080720.html

Compilation of References

Ammari, F., & Lu, J. (2010). Advanced XML security: Framework for building secure XML management system (SXMS). In *Proceedings of the 2010 Seventh International Conference on Information Technology: New Generations (ITNG)* (pp. 120-125). ITNG.

Anantvalee, T., & Wu, J. (2006). A survey on intrusion detection in mobile ad hoc networks. In Xiao, Y., Shen, X., & Du, D.-Z. (Eds.), *Wireless/Mobile Network Security* (pp. 170–196). Berlin: Springer.

Anastasi, G., Conti, M., Francesco, M. D., & Passarella, A. (2009). Energy conservation in wireless sensor networks: A survey. *Ad Hoc Networks*, 7(3), 537–568. doi:10.1016/j.adhoc.2008.06.003.

Android. (2012). *Developer guide: Security and permissions, October 2012*. Retrieved from http://developer.android.com/guide/topics/security/security.html

AOL Apologizes for Release of User Search Data. (2006). Retrieved from news.cnet.com/2010-1030_3-6102793.html

Ardagna, C. A., di Vimercati, S. D. C., Paraboschi, S., Pedrini, E., & Samarati, P. (2009). An XACML-based privacy-centered access control system. In *Proceedings of the First ACM Workshop on Information Security Governance, WISG '09*, (pp. 49–58). ACM.

Ardagna, C., Damiani, E., Capitani di Vimercati, S., & Samarati, P. (2007). XML security. In *Proceedings of Security, Privacy, and Trust in Modern Data Management* (pp. 71-86). Springer. doi:10.1007/978-3-540-69861-6_6.

Arends, R., Austein, R., Larson, M., Massey, D., & Rose, S. (2005). DNS security introduction and requirements. *RFC*. Retrieved March 2005, from http://www.ietf.org/rfc/rfc4033.txt

Arkko, J., Devarapalli, V., & Dupont, F. (2004). *Using IPsec to protect mobile IPv6 signaling between mobile nodes and home agents*. Internet Engineering Task Force (IETF), Request for Comments: 3776. Retrieved from http://tools.ietf.org/html/rfc3776

Arkko, J., Kempf, J., Zill, B., & Nikander, P. (2005). *Secure neighbor discovery (SEND)*. Internet Engineering Task Force (IETF), Request for Comments: 3971. Retrieved from http://tools.ietf.org/html/rfc3971

Armbrust, M., Fox, A., Griffith, R., Joseph, A. D., Katz, R. H., & Konwinsky, A. ... Zaharia, M. (2009). *Above the clouds: A Berkeley view of cloud computing* (Technical Report No. UCB/EECS-2009-28). Berkeley, CA: University of California at Berkeley. Retrieved from http://www.eecs.berkeley.edu/Pubs/TechRpts/2009/EECS-2009-28.pdf

Asif-Iqbal, H., Udzir, N. I., Mahmod, R., & Ghani, A. A. A. (2011). Filtering events using clustering in heterogeneous security logs. *Information Technology Journal*, 10(4), 798–806. doi:10.3923/itj.2011.798.806.

Asokan, N., Shoup, V., & Waidner, M. (1998). Asynchronous protocols for optimistic fair exchange. In *Proceedings of the IEEE Symposium on Security and Privacy*, (pp. 86-99). Washington, DC: IEEE Computer Society.

Asokan, N., Shoup, V., & Waidner, M. (1998). Optimistic fair exchange of digital signatures. In *Proceedings of Advances in Cryptology - Eurocrypt'98* (Vol. 1403, pp. 591–606). Berlin: Springer. doi:10.1007/BFb0054156.

Association for Retail Technology Standards (ARTS). (n.d.). *Homepage*. Retrieved from http://www.nrf-arts.org

Ateniese, G. (1999). Efficient verifiable encryption (and fair exchange) of digital signatures. In *Proceedings of the 6th ACM Conference on Computer and Communications Security* (pp. 138-146). New York: ACM Press.

Ateniese, G., & Nita-Rotaru, C. (2002). Stateless-recipient certified e-mail system based on verifiable encryption. In *Proceedings of the Cryptographer's Track at the RSA Conference on Topics in Cryptology* (pp. 182-199). London, UK: Springer-Verlag.

Ateniese, G., de Medeiros, B., & Goodrich, M. T. (2001). TRICERT: A distributed certified e-mail scheme. In *Proceedings of ISOC 2001 Network and Distributed System Security Symposium (NDSS'01)*. NDSS.

Atkins, D., & Austein, R. (2004). Threat analysis of the domain name system (DNS). *RFC*. Retrieved August 2004, from http://www.ietf.org/rfc/rfc3833.txt

Atkinson, R. (1995). *Security architecture for the internet protocol*. Internet Engineering Task Force (IETF), Request for Comments: 1825. Retrieved from http://tools.ietf.org/html/rfc1825

Atzeni, A., Cameroni, C., Faily, S., Lyle, J., & Fléchais, I. (2011). Here's Johnny: A methodology for developing attacker personas. In *Proceedings of the 6th International Conference on Availability, Reliability and Security*, (pp. 722–727). IEEE.

Augusto, A. B., & Correia, M. E. (2012). OFELIA – A secure mobile attribute aggregation infrastructure for user-centric identity management. In Gritzalis, D., Furnell, S., & Theoharidou, M. (Eds.), *Information Security and Privacy Research* (Vol. 376, pp. 61–74). Berlin: Springer. doi:10.1007/978-3-642-30436-1_6.

Augusto, A. B., & Correia, M. E. (2013). A secure and dynamic mobile identity wallet authorization architecture based on a XMPP. In *Messaging Infrastructure Innovations in XML Applications and Metadata Management: Advancing Technologies* (pp. 21–37). Hershey, PA: IGI Global.

Aura, T. (2005). *Cryptographically generated addresses (CGA)*. Internet Engineering Task Force (IETF), Request for Comments: 3972. Retrieved from http://tools.ietf.org/html/rfc3972

Aura, T., & Roe, M. (2006). Designing the mobile IPv6 security protocol. *Annales des Télécommunications*, 61(3-4), 332–356. doi:10.1007/BF03219911.

Aussibal, J., & Gallon, L. (2008). A new distributed IDS based on CVSS framework. In *Proceedings of the 2008 IEEE International Conference on Signal Image Technology and Internet Based Systems* (pp. 701-707). Washington, DC: IEEE Computer Society.

Awad, A., El Assad, S., & Carragata, D. (2008). *A robust cryptosystem based chaos for secure data*. Paper presented at IEEE, ISIVC Conference on Image/Video Communications over Fixed and Mobile Networks. Bilbao, Spain.

Axelsson, S. (2000). The base-rate fallacy and the difficulty of intrusion detection. *ACM Transactions on Information and System Security*, 3(3), 186–205. doi:10.1145/357830.357849.

Bace, R. G. (2000). *Intrusion detection*. Indianapolis, IN: Sams.

Backes, M., Hritcu, C., & Maffei, M. (2008). Automated verification of remote electronic voting protocols in the applied pi-calculus. In *Proceedings of the 21st IEEE Computer Security Foundations Symposium*, (pp. 195-209). Washington, DC: IEEE.

Baden, R., Bender, A., Spring, N., Bhattacharjee, B., & Starin, D. (2009). Persona: An online social network with user-defined privacy. *SIGCOMM Computing and Communications Review*, 39(4), 135–146. doi:10.1145/1594977.1592585.

Badger, L., Grance, T., Patt-Corner, R., & Voas, J. (2011). *Draft cloud computing synopsis and recommendations* (Special Publication 800-146). National Institute of Standards and Technology (NIST). US Department of Commerce. Retrieved from http://csrc.nist.gov/publications/drafts/800-146/Draft-NIST-SP800-146.pdf

Badra, M., Guillet, T., & Serhrouchni, A. (2009). *Random values, nonce and challenges: Semantic meaning versus opaque and strings of data*. Paper presented at the Vehicular Technology Conference Fall (VTC 2009-Fall). New York, NY.

Bahreman, A., & Tygar, J. (1994). Certified electronic mail. In *Proceedings of Network and Distributed System Security Conference* (pp. 3-19). Pittsburgh, PA: Carnegie Mellon University.

Bakar, Z., Mohemad, R., Ahmad, A., & Deris, M. (2006). A comparative study for outlier detection techniques in data mining. In *Proceedings of the 2006 IEEE Conference on Cybernetics and Intelligent Systems* (pp. 1-6). IEEE Press.

Balfanz, D., Durfee, G., & Smetters, D. (2005). Making the impossible easy: Usable PKI. In *Security and Usability: Designing Secure Systems that People Can Use* (pp. 319–334). Sebastopol, CA: O'Reilly.

Baliga, A., Iftode, L., & Chen, X. (2008). Automated containment of rootkits attacks. *Computers & Security*, 27(7-8), 323–334. doi:10.1016/j.cose.2008.06.003.

Barbhuiya, F. A., Roopa, S., Ratti, R., Hubballi, N., Biswas, S., Sur, A., & Ramachandran, V. (2011). An active host-based detection mechanism for ARP-related attacks. In Meghanathan, N, Kaushik, B.K, & Nagamalai, D (Eds.), *Communications in Computer and Information Science: Advances in Networks and Communications* (pp. 432-443). Berlin: Springer. doi:10.1007/978-3-642-17878-8_44.

Barkhuus, L., & Polichar, V. (2011). Empowerment through seamfulness: Smart phones in everyday life. *Personal and Ubiquitous Computing*, 15(6), 629–639. doi:10.1007/s00779-010-0342-4.

Compilation of References

Barnsteiner, J. (2005). Medication reconciliation: Transfer of medication information across settings-keeping it free from error. *The American Journal of Nursing, 105*(3), 31. doi:10.1097/00000446-200503001-00007 PMID:15802996.

Based, M. A., & Mjølsnes, S. F. (2009). A non-interactive zero knowledge proof protocol in an internet voting scheme. In *Proceedings of the 2nd Norwegian Information Security Conference (NISK 2009)*, (pp. 148-160). Tapir Akademisk Forlag.

Based, M. A., & Mjølsnes, S. F. (2010). Universally composable NIZK protocol in an internet voting scheme. In Cuellar, J. et al. (Eds.), *STM 2010 (LNCS)* (Vol. 6710, pp. 147–162). Berlin: Springer-Verlag.

Based, M. A., & Mjølsnes, S. F. (2011). A secure internet voting scheme. In Xiang, Y. et al. (Eds.), *ICA3PP (LNCS)* (Vol. 7017, pp. 141–152). Berlin: Springer.

Based, M. A., Tsay, J. K., & Mjølsnes, S. F. (2012). PEVS: A secure electronic voting scheme using polling booths. In Xiang, Y. et al. (Eds.), *ICDKE 2012 (Co-located with NSS 2012) (LNCS)* (Vol. 7696, pp. 189–205). Berlin: Springer-Verlag. doi:10.1007/978-3-642-34679-8_18.

Benaloh, J. (2006). Simple verifiable elections. In *Proceedings of the USENIX/ACCURATE Electronic Voting Technology Workshop*. USENIX/ACCURATE.

Benaloh, J., & Tuinstra, D. (1994). Receipt-free secret-ballot elections (extended abstract). In *Proceedings of the 26th Annual Symposium on Theory of Computing (STOC'94)*, (pp. 544-553). ACM Press.

Ben-Or, M., Goldreich, O., Micali, S., & Rivest, R. (1990). A fair protocol for signing contracts. *IEEE Transactions on Information Theory, 36*(1), 40–46. doi:10.1109/18.50372.

Bertino, E., Carminati, B., & Ferrari, E. (2004). Access control for XML documents and data. *Information Security Technical Report*, (9): 19–34. doi:10.1016/S1363-4127(04)00029-9.

Bertino, E., Castano, S., Ferrari, E., & Mesiti, M. (2002). Protection and administration of XML data sources. *Data & Knowledge Engineering*, (43): 237–260. doi:10.1016/S0169-023X(02)00127-1.

Bertino, E., & Ferrari, E. (2002). Secure and selective dissemination of XML documents. *ACM Transactions on Information and System Security*, (5): 290–331. doi:10.1145/545186.545190.

Bertion, E., Paci, F., & Ferrini, R. (2009, March). Privacy-preserving digital identity management for cloud computing. *IEEE Computer Society Data Engineering Bulletin*, 1-4.

Bhargav-Spantzel, A., Camenisch, J., Gross, T., & Sommer, D. (2007). User centricity: A taxonomy and open issues. *Journal of Computer Security, 15*(5), 493–527.

Bickford, J., Lagar-Cavilla, H. A., Varshavsky, A., Ganapathy, V., & Iftode, L. (2011). Security versus energy tradeoffs in host-based mobile malware detection. In *Proceedings of the 9th International Conference on Mobile Systems, Applications, and Services* (pp. 225-238). New York, NY: ACM.

Biggs & Vidalis. (2009). Cloud computing: The impact on digital forensic investigations. In *Proceedings of the 7th International Conference for Internet Technology and Secured Transactions (ICITST'09)*. London, UK: ICITST.

Blanchet, B. (2001). An efficient cryptographic protocol verifier based on prolog rules. In *Proceedings of the 14th IEEE Computer Security Foundations Workshop (CSFW)*, (pp. 82-96). IEEE Computer Society Press.

Blanchet, B., Cheval, V., Allamigeon, X., & Smyth, B. (2012). *ProVerif: Cryptographic protocol verifier in the formal model*. Retrieved from http://www.proverif.ens.fr/

Blaze, M., Kannan, S., Lee, I., Sokolsky, O., Smith, J. M., Keromytis, A. D., & Lee, W. (2009). Dynamic trust management. *IEEE Computer, 42*(2), 44–52. doi:10.1109/MC.2009.51.

Bohli, J. M., Mueller-Quade, J., & Roehrich, S. (2007). *Bingo voting: Secure and coercion-free voting using a trusted random number generator*. Retrieved from http://eprint.iacr.org/2007/162

Bolzoni, D., Crispo, B., & Etalle, S. (2007). ATLANTIDES: An architecture for alert verification in network intrusion detection systems. In *Proceedings of the 2007 Large Installation System Administration Conference* (pp. 141-152). Usenix Press.

BONDI. (n.d.). *Architecture and security requirements appendices*. Retrieved from http://bondi.omtp.org/1.01/security/BONDI_Architecture_and_Security_Appendices_v1_01.pdf

Boneh, D., Gentry, C., Lynn, B., & Shacham, H. (2003). Aggregate and verifiably encrypted signatures from bilinear maps. In *Proceedings of the 22nd International Conference on Theory and Applications of Cryptographic Techniques* (pp. 416-432). Berlin: Springer-Verlag.

Bose, R., & Pathak, S. (2006). A novel compression and encryption scheme using variable model arithmetic coding and coupled chaotic system. Transactions on Circuits and Systems, 53(4).

Bott, E. (2012). The malware numbers game: how many viruses are out there? *ZDNet.com*. Retrieved 25th of September, 2012 from http://www.zdnet.com/blog/bott/the-malware-numbers-game-how-many-viruses-are-out-there/4783

Boyer, R. S., & Moore, J. S. (1977). A fast string searching algorithm. *Communications of the ACM, 20*, 726–777. doi:10.1145/359842.359859.

Bravo-Lillo, C., Cranor, L. F., Downs, J., Komanduri, S., & Sleeper, M. (2011). Improving computer security dialogs. *Lecture Notes in Computer Science, 6949*, 18–35. doi:10.1007/978-3-642-23768-3_2.

Brown, D. L. (n.d.). SEC 1: Elliptic curve cryptography. *Certicom Research*. Retrieved May 21, 2009, from www.secg.org/download/aid-780/sec1-v2.pdf

Brown, M. J. (1999). *Users guide developed for the JBREWS project* (Technical Report LA-UR- 99-4676). Los Alamos, CA: Los Alamos National Laboratory of California University.

Bruening, P. J., & Treacy, B. C. (2009). *Cloud computing: Privacy, security challenges*. Washington, DC: Bureau of National Affairs.

Brumley, D., Newsome, J., Song, D., Wang, H., & Jha, S. (2006). Towards automatic generation of vulnerability based signatures. In *Proceedings of the 2006 IEEE Symposium on Security and Privacy* (pp. 2-16). IEEE Press.

Brumley, D., Wang, H., Jha, S., & Song, D. (2007). Creating vulnerability signatures using weakest preconditions. In *Proceedings of the 20th IEEE Computer Security Foundations Symposium* (pp. 311-325). IEEE Press.

Brutch, P., & Ko, C. (2003). Challenges in intrusion detection for wireless ad-hoc networks. In *Proceedings of the 2003 Symposium on Applications and Internet Workshops* (pp. 368-373). Washington, DC: IEEE Computer Society.

Bukač, V., Tuček, P., & Deutsch, M. (2012). Advances and challenges in standalone host-based intrusion detection systems. *Lecture Notes in Computer Science, 7449*, 105–117. doi:10.1007/978-3-642-32287-7_9.

Caballero, J., Liang, Z., Poosankam, P., & Song, D. (2009). Towards generating high coverage vulnerability-based signatures with protocol-level constraint-guided exploration. In *Proceedings of the 12th Symposium on Recent Advances in Intrusion Detection* (pp. 161-181). Springer-Verlag.

Cadar, C., Ganesh, V., Pawlowski, P., Dill, D., & Engler, D. (2006). EXE: Automatically generating inputs of death. In *Proceedings of 13th ACM Conference on Computer and Communications Security* (pp. 322-335). ACM Press.

Cameron, K., & Jones, M. (2007). Design rationale behind the identity metasystem architecture. In *Proceedings of ISSE/SECURE 2007 Securing Electronic Business Processes* (pp. 117-129). Vieweg.

Cameron, K. (2005). *The laws of identity (Whitepaper)*. Albuquerque, NM: Microsoft.

Cao, Y., & Yang, L. (2011). *GISL: A generalized identity specification language based on XML schema*. Paper presented at the 7th ACM Workshop on Digital Identity Management. Chicago, IL.

Cederquist, J., Dashti, M. T., & Mauw, S. (2007). A certified email protocol using key chains. In *Proceedings of the 21st International Conference on Advanced Information Networking and Applications Workshops*, (vol. 1, pp. 525-530). Washington, DC: IEEE Computer Society.

Center for the Protection of Natural Infrastructure (CPNI). (2010). *Information security briefing on cloud computing, 01/2010*. Retrieved from http://www.cpni.gov.uk/Documents/Publications/2010/2010007-ISB_cloud_computing.pdf

Compilation of References

Cha, S. K., Moraru, I., Jang, J., Truelove, J., Brumley, D., & Andersen, D. G. (2010). Split-screen: Enabling efficient, distributed malware detection. In *Proceedings of the 7th USENIX Conference on Networked Systems Design and Implementation (NSDI)* (p. 25). USENIX.

Cha, B. (2005). Host anomaly detection performance analysis based on system call of neuro-fuzzy using Soundex algorithm and N-gram technique. In *Proceedings of Systems Communications* (pp. 116–121). Systems Communications.

Chaballier, C. (2008). *SensLab D1.1a: SensLAB node hardware*. Retrieved from www.senslab.info

Chadwick, D. W. (2009). Federated identity management. In Alessandro, A., Gilles, B., & Roberto, G. (Eds.), *Foundations of Security Analysis and Design V* (pp. 96–120). Springer-Verlag. doi:10.1007/978-3-642-03829-7_3.

Chadwick, D. W., & Inman, G. (2009). Attribute aggregation in federated identity management. *Computer*, *42*(5), 33–40. doi:10.1109/MC.2009.143.

Chandola, V., Banerjee, A., & Kumar, V. (2009). Anomaly detection: A survey. *ACM Computing Surveys*, *41*(3), 1–58. doi:10.1145/1541880.1541882.

Chandrakumar, T., & Parthasarathy, S. (2012). Enhancing data security in ERP projects using XML. *International Journal of Enterprise Information Systems*, (8): 51–65. doi:10.4018/jeis.2012010104.

Chen, Y., Paxson, V., & Katz, R. H. (2010). *What's new about cloud computing security?* (Technical Report UCB/EECS-2010-5). Berkeley, CA: EECS Department, University of California, Berkeley. Retrieved from http://www.eecs.berkeley.edu/Pubs/TechRpts/2010/EECS-2010-5.html

Chen, S., Zhong, X. X., & Wu, Z. Z. (2008). Block chaos cipher for wireless sensor network. *Science in China Series F – Information Science*, *51*, 1055–1063. doi:10.1007/s11432-008-0102-5.

Chiu, C.-Y., Lee, Y.-J., Chang, C.-C., Luo, W.-Y., & Huang, H.-C. (2010). Semi-supervised learning for false alarm reduction. In *Proceedings of the 10th Industrial Conference on Advances in Data Mining: Applications and Theoretical Aspects* (pp. 595-605). Springer-Verlag.

Choi, H.-Y., Kim, K.-R., Lee, H.-B., Min, S.-G., & Han, Y.-H. (2011). Smart buffering for seamless handover in proxy mobile IPv6. *Wireless Communication and Mobile Computing*, *11*(4), 491–499. doi:10.1002/wcm.843.

Chor, B., Kushilevitz, E., Goldreich, O., & Sudan, M. (1998). Private information retrieval. *Journal of the ACM*, *45*(9), 965–981. doi:10.1145/293347.293350.

Chow, R., Golle, P., Jakobsson, M., Shi, E., Staddon, J., Masuoka, R., & Molina, J. (2009). Controlling data in the cloud: Outsourcing computation without outsourcing control. In *Proceedings of the ACM Workshop on Cloud Computing Security (CCSW'09)*, (pp. 85-90). Chicago, IL: ACM Press.

Chuan, L. L., Ismail, M., Yee, C. L., & Jumari, K. (2012). A new generic taxonomy of malware behavioral detection and removal techniques. *Journal of Theoretical and Applied Information Technology*, *42*(2), 260–270.

Clam, A. V. (2012). The ClamAV open-source antivirus. *ClamAV.com*. Retrieved 25th of September, 2012 from http://www.clamav.org

Clam, A. V. Database. (2012). The ClamAV virus database. *ClamAV.com*. Retrieved 25th of September, 2012 from http://www.clamav.net/lang/en/ and http://database.clamav.net/

Clarkson, M. R., Chong, S., & Myers, A. C. (2008). Civitas: Toward a secure voting system. In *Proceedings of the 2008 IEEE Symposium on Security and Privacy*, (pp. 354-368). Washington, DC: IEEE Computer Society.

Clauß, S., & Köhntopp, M. (2001). Identity management and its support of multilateral security. *Computer Networking*, *37*(2), 205–219. doi:10.1016/S1389-1286(01)00217-1.

Cloud Security Alliance (CSA). (2009). Security guidance for critical areas of focus in cloud computing. *CSA*. Retrieved from https://cloudsecurityalliance.org/csaguide.pdf

Cloud Security Alliance. (2011). *Security guidance for critical areas of focus in cloud computing v3.0 (Technical report)*. Cloud Security Alliance.

Cloud Security Alliance. (n.d.). *Homepage*. Retrieved from https://cloudsecurityalliance.org

CNet. (2009). *FTC questions cloud computing security*. Retrieved from http://news.cnet.com/8301-13578_3-10198577-38.html?part=rss&subj=news&tag=2547-1_3-0-20

Commentz-Walter, B. (1979). A string-matching algorithm fast on the average. In *Proceedings of the 6th International Collection on Automata, Languages and Programming* (pp. 118-132). Springer-Verlag.

Conta, A., Deering, S., & Gupta, M. (2006). *Internet control message protocol (ICMPv6) for the internet protocol version 6 (IPv6) specification*. Internet Engineering Task Force (IETF), Request for Comments: 4443. Retrieved from http://tools.ietf.org/html/rfc4443

Cooper, D., Santesson, S., Farrell, S., Boeyen, S., Housley, R., & Polk, W. (2008). Internet X.509 public key infrastructure certificate and certificate revocation list (CRL) profile. *RFC*. Retrieved May 2008, from http://www.ietf.org/rfc/rfc5280.txt

Cooper, A. (1999). *The inmates are running the asylum: Why high tech products drive us crazy and how to restore the sanity* (2nd ed.). Upper Saddle River, NJ: Pearson Higher Education.

Cortier, V., & Wiedling, C. (2012). *A formal analysis of the Norwegian e-voting protocol*. Paper presented at ETAPS 2012. Tallinn, Estonia.

Cryptographic Key Management Project. (n.d.). *Website*. Retrieved from http://csrc.nist.gov/groups/ST/key_mgmt/

CrySyS Lab. (2012). *sKyWIper (a.k.a. Flame a.k.a. Flamer): A complex malware for targeted attacks* (Technical Report). Retrieved 25th of September, 2012 from http://www.crysys.hu/skywiper/skywiper.pdf

Cuppens, F., & Miege, A. (2002). Alert correlation in a cooperative intrusion detection framework. In *Proceedings of the 2002 IEEE Symposium on Security and Privacy* (pp. 202-215). IEEE Press.

Damiani, E., De Capitani di Vimercati, S., Paraboschi, S., & Samarati, P. (2000). Design and implementation of an access control processor for XML documents. *Computer Networks*, *33*(1), 59–75. doi:10.1016/S1389-1286(00)00053-0

Damiani, E., Fansi, M., Gabillon, A., & Marrara, S. (2008). A general approach to securely querying XML. *Computer Standards & Interfaces*, *30*(6), 379–389. doi:10.1016/j.csi.2008.03.006

Dasgupta, D., & Majumdar, N. (2002). Anomaly detection in multidimensional data using negative selection algorithm. In *Proceedings of the IEEE Conference on Evolutionary Computation* (pp. 1039-1044). IEEE Press.

Davenport, M. A., Baraniuk, R. G., & Scott, C. D. (2006). Controlling false alarms with support vector machines. In *Proceedings of the 2006 International Conference on Acoustics, Speech and Signal* (pp. 589-592). IEEE Press.

David, W. C. (2006). *Authorisation using attributes from multiple authorities*. Paper presented at the Enabling Technologies: Infrastructure for Collaborative Enterprises. New York, NY.

Davies, E., & Mohacsi, J. (2007). *Recommendations for filtering ICMPv6 messages in firewalls*. Internet Engineering Task Force (IETF), Request for Comments: 4890. Retrieved from http://tools.ietf.org/html/rfc4890

De Boer, P., & Pels, M. (2005). *Host-based intrusion detection systems (Technical report, Revision 1.10)*. Amsterdam: Informatics Institute, University of Amsterdam.

De la Rosa Algarín, A., Demurjian, S. A., Berhe, S., & Pavlich-Mariscal, J. (2012). A security framework for XML schemas and documents for healthcare. In *Proceedings of 2012 International Workshop on Biomedical and Health Informatics (BHI 2012)*, (pp. 782-789). BHI.

Debar, H., & Wespi, A. (2001). Aggregation and correlation of intrusion-detection alerts. In *Proceedings of the 2001 International Conference on Recent Advances in Intrusion Detection* (pp. 85-103). Springer-Verlag.

Deering, S., & Hinden, R. (1998). Internet protocol, version 6 (IPv6) specification. *RFC*. Retrieved December 1998, from http://www.ietf.org/rfc/rfc2460.txt

Delaune, S., Kremer, S., & Ryan, M. D. (2008). *Verifying privacy-type properties of electronic voting protocols* (Research Report LSV-08-01). Paris: Laboratorie Specification et Verification, ENS Cachan.

Deng, R. H., Zhou, J., & Bao, F. (2002). Defending against redirect attacks in mobile IP. In *Proceedings of the 9th ACM Conference on Computer and Communications Security*, (pp. 59–67). New York, NY: ACM.

Deng, R., Gong, L., Lazar, A., & Wang, W. (1996). Practical protocols for certified electronic mail. *Journal of Network and Systems Management, 4*(3), 279–297. doi:10.1007/BF02139147.

Devarapalli, V., & Dupont, F. (2007). *Mobile IPv6 operation with IKEv2 and the revised IPsec architecture*. Internet Engineering Task Force (IETF), Request for Comments: 4877. Retrieved from http://tools.ietf.org/html/rfc4877

Devarapalli, V., Wakikawa, R., Petrescu, A., & Thubert, P. (2005). *Network mobility (NEMO) basic support protocol*. Internet Engineering Task Force (IETF), Request for Comments: 3963. Retrieved from http://tools.ietf.org/html/rfc3963

Dickerson, J. E., & Dickerson, J. A. (2000). Fuzzy network profiling for intrusion detection. In *Proceedings of the 2000 International Conference of the North American Fuzzy Information Society* (pp. 301-306). IEEE Press.

Dierks, T., & Rescorla, E. (2008). *The transport layer security (TLS) protocol version 1.2*. RFC 5246 (Proposed Standard). Retrieved from http://www.ietf.org/rfc/rfc5246.txt

Distributed Management Task Force. (n.d.). *Homepage*. Retrieved from http://www.dmtf.org

Dolin, R. H., Alschuler, L., Boyer, S., Beebe, C., Behlen, F. M., Biron, P. V., & Shvo, A. S. (2006). HL7 clinical document architecture, release 2. *Journal of the American Medical Informatics Association, 13*(1), 30–39. doi:10.1197/jamia.M1888 PMID:16221939.

Don't Cloud Your Vision. (n.d.). Retrieved from http://www.ft.com/cms/s/0/303680a6-bf51-11dd-ae63-0000779fd18c.html?nclick_check=1

Dossogne, J., & Lafitte, F. (2012). Mental voting booths. In Laud, P. (Ed.), *NordSec 2011 (LNCS)* (Vol. 7161, pp. 82–97). Berlin: Springer-Verlag.

Droms, R., Bound, E. J., Volz, B., Lemon, T., Perkins, C., & Carney, M. (2003). *Dynamic host configuration protocol for IPv6 (DHCPv6)*. Internet Engineering Task Force (IETF), Request for Comments: 3315. Retrieved from http://tools.ietf.org/html/rfc3315

Eastlake, D. (2000). Secret key establishment for DNS (TKEY RR). *RFC*. Retrieved September 2000, from http://www.ietf.org/rfc/rfc2930.txt

Eastlake, D. E., & Schiller, J. I. (2005). *Randomness requirements for security*. Retrieved from https://ietf.org/rfc/rfc4086.txt

Ebrahimi, T., Leprévost, F., & Warusfel, B. (2006). *Cryptographie et sécurité des systèmes et réseaux: Sous la direction de Touradj Ebrahimi, Franck Leprévost, Bertrand Warusfel*. Paris: Hermès Science.

Egele, M., Scholte, T., Kirda, E., & Kruegel, C. (2012). A survey on automated dynamic malware-analysis techniques and tools. *ACM Journal of Computing Surveys, 44*(2).

El-Semary, A., Edmonds, J., Gonzalez, J., & Papa, M. (2005). A framework for hybrid fuzzy logic intrusion detection systems. In *Proceedings of the 2005 International Conference on Fuzzy Systems* (pp. 325-330). IEEE Press.

Ernst, T. (2007). *Network mobility support goals and requirements*. Internet Engineering Task Force (IETF), Request for Comments: 4886. Retrieved from http://tools.ietf.org/html/rfc4886

Eronen, P., Tschofenig, H., & Sheffer, Y. (2010). *An extension for EAP-only authentication in IKEv2*. Internet Engineering Task Force (IETF), Request for Comments: 5998. Retrieved from http://tools.ietf.org/html/rfc5998

Estrin, D., & Sim, I. (2010). Open mHealth architecture: An engine for health care innovation. *Science, 330*(6005), 759–760. doi:10.1126/science.1196187 PMID:21051617.

ETSI TS 101 903. (2010). *Electronic signatures and infrastructures (ESI), XML advanced electronic signatures (XAdES) V1.4.2*.

ETSI TS 102 640-1. (n.d.). *Electronic signatures and infrastructures (ESI), registered electronic mail (REM), part 1: Architecture* (Tech. Rep.). Paris: Sophia Antipolis Cedex.

ETSI TS 102 640-2. (n.d.). *Electronic signatures and infrastructures (ESI), registered electronic mail (REM), part 2: Data requirements, formats and signatures for REM* (Tech. Rep.). Paris: Sophia Antipolis Cedex.

ETSI TS 102 640-3. (n.d.). *Electronic signatures and infrastructures (ESI), registered electronic mail (REM), part 3: Information security policy requirements for REM management domains* (Tech. Rep.). Paris: Sophia Antipolis Cedex.

ETSI TS 102 640-4. (n.d.). *Electronic signatures and infrastructures (ESI), registered electronic mail (REM), part 4: REM-md conformance profiles* (Tech. Rep.). Paris: Sophia Antipolis Cedex.

ETSI TS 102 640-5. (n.d.). *Electronic signatures and infrastructures (ESI), registered electronic mail (REM), part 5: REM-md interoperability profiles* (Tech. Rep.). Paris: Sophia Antipolis Cedex.

European Commission. (2002). *eEurope 2005: An information society for all*.Geneva, Switzerland: European Commission.

European Commission. (2006). *i2010 eGovernment action plan: Accelerating eGovernment in Europe for the benefit of all*.Geneva, Switzerland: European Commission.

European Commission. (2010). *A digital agenda for Europe*. Geneva, Switzerland: European Commission.

European Network and Information Security Agency (ENISA). (2009). *Cloud computing: Benefits, risks and recommendations for information security*. Geneva, Switzerland: ENISA.

European Parliament. (2000). *Santa maria de feira European Council. Conclusions of the Presidency*. Geneva, Switzerland: Author.

European Parliament. (2000). *Lisbon European council. Presidency Conclusions*. Geneva, Switzerland: Author.

European Telecommunication Standards Institute. (n.d.). *Homepage*. Retrieved from http://www.etsi.org

European Union. (1999). *Directive 1999/93/EC of the European parliament and of the council of 13: December 1999 on a community framework for electronic signatures*. Brussels, Belgium: European Union.

European University Institute. (2007). *Internet voting in the March 2007 parliamentary elections in Estonia*. Robert Schuman Center for Advanced Studies, Report for the Council of Europe.

Even, S., Goldreich, O., & Lempel, A. (1985). A randomized protocol for signing contracts. *Communications of the ACM*, 28, 637–647. doi:10.1145/3812.3818.

Faily, S., & Fléchais, I. (2010). A meta-model for usable secure requirements engineering. In *Proceedings of the 2010 ICSE Workshop on Software Engineering for Secure Systems*, (pp. 29–35). ACM.

Faily, S., & Fléchais, I. (2010). Barry is not the weakest link: Eliciting secure system requirements with personas. In *Proceedings of the 24th BCS Interaction Specialist Group Conference, BCS '10*, (pp. 124-132). London: British Computer Society.

Faily, S., & Fléchais, I. (2011). Eliciting usable security requirements with misusability cases. In *Proceedings of the 19th IEEE International Requirements Engineering Conference*, (pp. 339–340). IEEE Computer Society.

Faily, S., Coles-Kemp, L., Dunphy, P., Just, M., Akama, Y., & De Luca, A. (2013). Designing interactive secure systems: CHI 2013 special interest group. In *CHI '13 Extended Abstracts on Human Factors in Computing Systems*. ACM. doi:10.1145/2468356.2468807.

Faily, S., Lyle, J., & Parkin, S. (2012). Secure system? Challenge accepted: Finding and resolving security failures using security premortems. In *Proceedings of Designing Interactive Secure Systems: Workshop at British HCI 2012*. London: HCI.

Fang, Q., Liu, Y., & Zhao, X. (2008). A chaos-based secure cluster protocol for wireless sensor networks. *International Journal of the Institute of Information Theory and Automation Kybernetika*, 44(4), 522–533.

Fearon, J. D. (1999). *What is identity (as we now use the word)?* Palo Alto, CA: Stanford University.

Federal Chancellery of Austria. (1982). *Service of documents act*. Federal Law Gazette No. 200/1982 as amended by: Federal Law Gazette I No. 5/2008.

Federal Chancellery of Austria. (1991). *General administrative procedure act 1991 – AVG*. Federal Law Gazette No. 51/1991 as amended by: Federal Law Gazette I No. 135/2009.

Federal Chancellery of Austria. (1999). *The Austrian signature act*. Federal Law Gazette I No. 190/1999.

Federal Chancellery of Austria. (2003). *Module for online applications (MOA) - Identification (ID)*. Retrieved from https://joinup.ec.europa.eu/software/moa-idspss/description

Federal Chancellery of Austria. (2004). The Austrian egovernment act: Federal act on provisions facilitating electronic communications with public bodies, entered into force on 1 March 2004, last amended part I, Nr. 111/2010. *Austrian Federal Law Gazette (BGBl) part I Nr. 10/2004*.

Federal Chancellery of Austria. (2008). *The Austrian citizen card*. Retrieved from http://www.buergerkarte.at/konzept/securitylayer/spezifikation/aktuell/

Federal Chancellery of Austria. (2010). *Implementation of the i2010 initiative in Austria*. Retrieved from http://www.bka.gv.at/DocView.axd?CobId=16635

Federal Chancellery of Austria. (2010). E-government equivalence decree, decree of the federal chancellor laying down conditions for equivalence under section 6(5) of the e-government act, 2010. *Austrian Federal Law Gazette (BGBl) Nr. 170/2010*.

Felt, A. P., Greenwood, K., & Wagner, D. (2011). The effectiveness of application permissions. In *Proceedings of the 2nd USENIX Conference on Web Application Development, WebApps'11*. Berkeley, CA: USENIX Association. Retrieved from http://dl.acm.org/citation.cfm?id=2002168.2002175

Ferraiolo, D., Cugini, J., & Kuhn, D. R. (1995). Role-based access control (RBAC): Features and motivations. In *Proceedings of 11th Annual Computer Security Application Conference* (pp. 241-248). CSAC.

Ferraiolo, D. F., Sandhu, R., Gavrila, S., Kuhn, D. R., & Chandramouli, R. (2001). Proposed NIST standard for role-based access control. *ACM Transactions on Information and System Security*, 4(3), 224–274. doi:10.1145/501978.501980.

Ferrer-Gomila, J. L., Payeras-Capella, M., & Huguet i Rotger, L. (2000). An efficient protocol for certified electronic mail. In *Proceedings of the Third International Workshop on Information Security* (pp. 237-248). London, UK: Springer-Verlag.

Ferrer-Gomila, J. L., Payeras-Capella, M., & Huguet i Rotger, L. (2002). A realistic protocol for multi-party certified electronic mail. In *Proceedings of the 5th International Conference on Information Security* (pp. 210-219). London, UK: Springer-Verlag.

Ferrer-Gomilla, J. L., Onieva, J. A., Payeras, M., & Lopez, J. (2010). Certified electronic mail: Properties revisited. *Computers & Security*, 29, 167–179. doi:10.1016/j.cose.2009.06.009.

Flexiscale Suffers 18-Hour Outage. (2008). Retrieved from http://www.thewhir.com/web-hosting-news/flexiscale-suffers-18-hour-outage

Ford, B., Strauss, J., Lesniewski-Laas, C., Rhea, S., Kaashoek, F., & Morris, R. (2006). Persistent personal names for globally connected mobile devices. In *Proceedings of the 7th Symposium on Operating Systems Design and Implementation, OSDI '06*, (pp. 233–248). Berkeley, CA: USENIX Association. Retrieved from http://dl.acm.org/citation.cfm

Forum, T. M. (n.d.). *Homepage*. Retrieved from http://www.tmforum.org

Fournel, N., Fraboulet, A., & Feautrier, P. (2007). eSimu: A fast and accurate energy consumption simulator for real embedded system. In *Proceedings of WOWMOM: IEEE International Symposium on a World of Wireless Mobile and Multimedia Networks*. IEEE.

Frankel, S., & Herbert, H. (2003). *The AES-XCBC-MAC-96 algorithm and its use with IPsec*. Internet Engineering Task Force (IETF), Request for Comments: 3566. Retrieved from http://tools.ietf.org/html/rfc3566

Frankel, S., Glenn, R., & Kelly, S. (2003). *The AES-CBC cipher algorithm and its use with IPsec*. Internet Engineering Task Force (IETF), Request for Comments: 3602. Retrieved from http://tools.ietf.org/html/rfc3602

Franklin, M. K., & Reiter, M. K. (1997). Fair exchange with a semi-trusted third party (extended abstract). In *Proceedings of the 4th ACM Conference on Computer and Communications Security* (pp. 1-5). New York, NY: ACM.

Friedl, J. (2002). *Mastering regular expressions*. Sebastopol, CA: O'Reilly.

Fujioka, A., Okamoto, T., & Ohta, K. (1992). A practical secret voting scheme for large scale elections. In Seberry, J., & Zheng, Y. (Eds.), *Advances in Cryptology - AUSCRYPT '92 (LNCS)* (Vol. 718, pp. 244–251). Berlin: Springer. doi:10.1007/3-540-57220-1_66.

Fung, C. J., Zhang, J., Aib, I., & Boutaba, R. (2009). Robust and scalable trust management for collaborative intrusion detection.[Piscataway, NJ: IEEE Press.]. *Proceedings of Integrated Network Management, IM, 2009*, 33–40.

Furht, B., Socek, D., & Eskicioglu, A. M. (2004). Fundamentals of multimedia encryption techniques. In Furht, B., & Kirovski, D. (Eds.), *Multimedia Security Handbook*. Boca Raton, FL: CRC Press. doi:10.1201/9781420038262.

Gajek, S., Jensen, M., Liao, L., & Schwenk, J. (2009). Analysis of signature wrapping attacks and countermeasures. In *Proceedings of the IEEE International Conference on Web Services*, (pp. 575-582). Los Angeles, CA: IEEE.

Gao, Y.-X., Peng, D.-Y., & Yan, L.-L. (2010). Design and formal analysis of a new fair multi-party certified mail protocol. In *Proceedings of the 2010 International Conference on Machine Learning and Cybernetics (ICMLC)*, (pp. 3101-3106). IEEE Computer Society.

Garfinkel, S., & Shelat, A. (2003). Remembrance of data passed: A study of disk sanitization practices. *IEEE Security and Privacy*, *1*(1), 17–27. doi:10.1109/MSECP.2003.1176992.

Gartner Hype-Cycle. (2012). *Cloud computing and big data*. Retrieved from http://www.gartner.com/technology/research/hype-cycles/

Gemmill, J., Robinson, J.-P., Scavo, T., & Bangalore, P. (2009). Cross-domain authorization for federated virtual organizations using the myVocs collaboration environment. *Concurrent Computing: Practical Experience*, *21*(4), 509–532. doi:10.1002/cpe.1350.

Gentry, C. (2009). Fully homomorphic encryption using ideal lattices. In *Proceedings of the 41st Annual ACM Symposium on Theory of Computing (STOC'09)*, (pp. 169-178). Bethesda, MD: ACM.

Gjøsteen, K. (2010). *Analysis of an internet voting protocol*. Cryptology ePrint Archive, Report 2010/380.

Glenn, R., & Kent, S. (1998). *The NULL encryption algorithm and its use with IPsec*. Internet Engineering Task Force (IETF), Request for Comments: 2410. Retrieved from http://tools.ietf.org/html/rfc2410

Godik, S., & Moses, T. (2005). *Extensible access control markup language (XACML) version 1.1, May 2005*. Retrieved from http://www.oasis-open.org

Gosnell, T. B., Hall, J. M., Ham, C. L., Knapp, D. A., Koenig, Z. M., & Luke, S. J. ... Wolford, J.K. (1997). *Gamma-ray identification of nuclear weapon materials* (Technical Report DE97053424). Livermore, CA: Lawrence Livermore National Lab.

Gruber, H., & Holzer, M. (2008). Finite automata, digraph connectivity, and regular expression size. In *Proceedings of the 35th International Colloquium on Automata, Languages and Programming* (pp. 39-50). Springer-Verlag.

Gruschka, N., & Iacono, L. L. (2009). Vulnerable cloud: SOAP message security validation revisited. In *Proceedings of IEEE International Conference on Web Services (ICWS'09)*, (pp. 625-631). Los Angeles, CA: IEEE.

Gummadi, R., Balakrishnan, H., Maniatis, P., & Ratnasamy, S. (2009). Not-a-bot: Improving service availability in the face of botnet attacks. In *Proceedings of the 6th USENIX Symposium on Networked Systems Design and Implementation* (pp. 307-320). Berkeley, CA: USENIX Association.

Gundavelli, S., Leung, K., Devarapalli, V., Chowdhury, K., & Patil, B. (2008). *Proxy mobile IPv6*. Internet Engineering Task Force (IETF), Request for Comments: 5213. Retrieved from http://tools.ietf.org/html/rfc5213

Haddad, W., Madour, L., Arkko, J., & Dupont, J. (2004). *Applying cryptographically generated addresses to optimize MIPv6 (CGA-OMIPv6)*. Expired Internet Engineering Task Force (IETF) Internet draft. Retrieved from http://tools.ietf.org/html/draft-haddad-mip6-cga-omipv6-04

Hai-Binh, L., & Bouzefrane, S. (2008). *Identity management systems and interoperability in a heterogeneous environment*. Paper presented at the Advanced Technologies for Communications. New York, NY.

Hammer-Lahav. E. (2012). *The oauth 2.0 authorization protocol*. Retrieved from https://tools.ietf.org/html/rfc6749

Heys, H., & Adams, C. (Eds.). (1999). *Proceedings of Selected Areas in Cryptography: 6th Annual International Workshop*. Berlin: Springer.

Hofmann, A., Dedinski, I., Sick, B., & de Meer, H. (2007). A novelty-driven approach to intrusion alert correlation based on distributed hash tables. In *Proceedings of the 12th IEEE Symposium on Computers and Communications* (pp. 71-78). IEEE Press.

Hofmeyr, S. A., Forrest, S., & Somayaji, A. (1998). Intrusion detection using sequences of system calls. *Journal of Computer Security*, *6*(3), 151–180.

Hogg, M., & Abrams, D. (1988). *Social indentifications: A social psychology of intergroup relations and group processes*. London: Routledge.

Horak, Z. (2010). Fuzzified Aho-Corasick search automata. In *Proceedings of the Sixth International Conference on Information Assurance and Security (IAS)* (pp. 338-342). IAS.

Houmansadr, A., Zonouz, S. A., & Berthier, R. (2011). A cloud-based intrusion detection and response system for mobile phones. In *Proceedings of the 2011 IEEE/IFIP 41st International Conference on Dependable Systems and Networks Workshops* (pp. 31-32). Washington, DC: IEEE Computer Society.

Housley, R. (2005). *Using advanced encryption standard (AES) CCM mode with IPsec encapsulating security payload (ESP)*. Internet Engineering Task Force (IETF), Request for Comments: 4309. Retrieved from http://tools.ietf.org/html/rfc4309

Hovav, A., & Berger, R. (2009). *Tutorial: Identity management systems and secured access control*. Academic Press.

Hsiang-Cheh, H., Feng-Cheng, C., & Wai-Chi, F. (2011). Reversible data hiding with histogram-based difference expansion for QR code applications. *IEEE Transactions on Consumer Electronics*, *57*(2), 779–787. doi:10.1109/TCE.2011.5955222.

Huang, S., & Lesko, L. (2004). Drug-drug, drug-dietary supplement, and drug-citrus fruit and other food interactions: What have we learned? *Journal of Clinical Pharmacology*, *44*(6), 559. doi:10.1177/0091270004265367 PMID:15145962.

Hu, J. (2010). Host-based anomaly intrusion detection. In Stavroulakis, P. P., & Stamp, M. (Eds.), *Handbook of Information and Communication Security* (pp. 235–255). Berlin: Springer-Verlag. doi:10.1007/978-3-642-04117-4_13.

Hwang, R.-J., & Lai, C.-H. (2008). Efficient and secure protocol in fair certified e-mail delivery. *WSEAS Transactions on Information Science and Applications*, *5*(9), 1385–1394.

IBM Blue Cloud Initiative Advances Enterprise Cloud Computing. (n.d.). Retrieved from http://www-03.ibm.com/press/us/en/pressrelease/26642.wss

Idika, N., & Mathur, A. P. (2007). *A survey of malware detection techniques*. Retrieved 16th of January, 2013 from http://www.serc.net/system/files/SERC-TR-286.pdf

Imamoto, K., & Sakurai, K. (2002). A certified e-mail system with receiver's selective usage of delivery authority. In *Proceedings of the Third International Conference on Cryptology: Progress in Cryptology* (pp. 326-338). London, UK: Springer-Verlag.

Inc, Y. (2007). *Fire eagle*. Retrieved from http://fireeagle.yahoo.net/

Inman, G., & Chadwick, D. (2010). A privacy preserving attribute aggregation model for federated identity managements systems. *Upgrade. Privacy and Identity Management*, *11*(1), 6.

Institute of Electrical and Electronics Engineers (IEEE). (n.d.). *Homepage*. Retrieved from http://www.ieee.org

International Telecommunication Union – Telecommunication Standardization Sector (ITU-T). (n.d.). *Homepage*. Retrieved form http://www.itu.int/ITU-T

Internet Engineering Task Force. (n.d.). *Homepage*. Retrieved from http://www.ietf.org

iOS. (n.d.). *Developer library: iOS technology overview introduction*. Retrieved from http://developer.apple.com/library/ios/documentation/Miscellaneous/Conceptual/iPhoneOSTechOverview/Introduction/Introduction.html

Iyengar, S. S. (2011). *Fundamentals of sensor network programming: Applications and technology.* Oxford, UK: Wiley-Blackwell.

Jakimoski, G., & Kocarev, L. (2001). Chaos and cryptography: Block encryption ciphers based on chaotic maps. *IEEE Transactions on Circuits and Systems: Fundamental Theory and Applications, 48*(2), 163–169. doi:10.1109/81.904880.

Jana, S., & Shmatikov, V. (2012). Abusing file processing in malware detectors for fun and profit. In *Proceedings of the 33rd IEEE Symposium on Security & Privacy* (pp. 80-94). IEEE.

Jin, H., Xiang, G., Zou, D., Zhao, F., Li, M., & Yu, C. (2010). A guest-transparent file integrity monitoring method in virtualization environment. *Computers & Mathematics with Applications (Oxford, England), 60*(2), 256–266. doi:10.1016/j.camwa.2010.01.007.

Joshi, M. V., Agarwal, R. C., & Kumar, V. (2001). Mining needle in a haystack: Classifying rare classes via two-phase rule induction. In *Proceedings of the 2001 ACM SIGMOD International Conference on Management of Data* (pp. 91-102). ACM Press.

Joshi, M. V., Agarwal, R. C., & Kumar, V. (2002). Predicting rare classes: can boosting make any weak learner strong? In *Proceedings of the 8th ACM SIGKDD International Conference on Knowledge Discovery and Data Mining* (pp. 297-306). ACM Press.

Joshi, J. B. D., Bhatti, R., Bertino, E., & Ghafoor, A. (2004). Access control language for multi-domain environments. *IEEE Internet Computing, 8*(6), 40–50. doi:10.1109/MIC.2004.53.

Joyent, Inc. (2012). *Nodejs website.* Retrieved from http://nodejs.org/

Juels, A., Catalano, D., & Jakobsson, M. (2005). Coercion-resistant electronic elections. In *Proceedings of the 2005 ACM Workshop on Privacy in the Electronic Society,* (pp. 61-70). New York, NY: ACM.

Juels, A., Catalano, D., & Jakobsson, M. (2002). *Coercion-resistant electronic elections.* Cryptology ePrint Archive. Report, 2002(165), 2002.

Jung, H., Soliman, H., Koh, S., & Lee, J. Y. (2005). *Fast handover for hierarchical MIPv6 (F-HMIPv6).* Expired Internet Engineering Task Force (IETF) Internet draft. Retrieved from http://tools.ietf.org/html/draft-jung-mobopts-fhmipv6-00

Kaczmarek, J., & Wróbel, M. (2008). Modern approaches to file system integrity checking.[*st International Conference on Information Technology.* IEEE.]. *Proceedings of the, 2008,* 1.

Kaps, J. P., & Sunar, B. (2006). Energy comparison of AES and SHA-1 for ubiquitous computing. *Lecture Notes in Computer Science, 4097,* 372–380. doi:10.1007/11807964_38.

Karp, R. M., & Rabin, M. O. (1987). *Efficient randomized pattern-matching algorithms.* Retrieved 14th of October, 2008 from http://www.research.ibm.com/journal/rd/312/ibmrd3102P.pdf

Kaspersky. (2012). Heuristic analysis in Kaspersky antivirus 2012. *Kaspersky.com.* Retrieved 25th of September, 2012 from http://support.kaspersky.com/kav2012/tech?qid=208284682

Katzenstein, P. (1996). *The culture of national security: Norms and identity in world politics.* New York: Columbia University Press.

Kaufman, C., Hoffman, P., Nir, Y., & Eronen, P. (2010). *Internet key exchange protocol version 2 (IKEv2).* Internet Engineering Task Force (IETF), Request for Comments: 5996. Retrieved from http://tools.ietf.org/html/rfc5996

Kavitha, T., & Sridharan, D. (2010). Security vulnerabilities in wireless sensor networks: A survey. Journal of Information Assurance and Security, (5), 31-44.

Kent, S. (2005). *IP authentication header.* Internet Engineering Task Force (IETF), Request for Comments: 4302. Retrieved from http://tools.ietf.org/html/rfc4302

Kent, S. (2005). *IP encapsulating security payload (ESP).* Internet Engineering Task Force (IETF), Request for Comments: 4303. Retrieved from http://tools.ietf.org/html/rfc4303

Compilation of References

Kent, S., & Atkinson, R. (1998). *Security architecture for the internet protocol*. Internet Engineering Task Force (IETF), Request for Comments: 2401. Retrieved from http://tools.ietf.org/html/rfc2401

Kent, S., & Seo, K. (2005). *Security architecture for the internet protocol*. Internet Engineering Task Force (IETF), Request for Comments: 4301. Retrieved from http://tools.ietf.org/html/rfc4301

Kent, S., Kong, D., Seo, K., & Watro, R. (2012). *Certificate policy (CP) for the resource public key infrastructure (RPKI)*. Internet Engineering Task Force (IETF), Request for Comments: 6484. Retrieved from http://tools.ietf.org/html/rfc6484

Kent, K., & Souppaya, M. (2006). *Guide to computer security log management (NIST Special Publication 800-92)*. Gaithersburg, MD: National Institute of Standards and Technology.

Khambhammettu, H., & Crampton, J. (2006). Delegation in role-based access control.[ESORICS.]. *Proceedings of ESORICS, 2006*, 174–191.

Killrouhy, K. S., & Maxion, R. A. (2011). Should security researchers experiment more and draw more inferences? In *Proceedings of the 4th Conference on Cyber Security Experimentation and Test*. Berkeley, CA: USENIX Association.

Kinkelin, H., Holz, R., Niedermayer, H., Mittelberger, S., & Carle, G. (2011). On using TPM for secure identities in future home networks. *Future Internet, 3*(1), 1–13. Retrieved from http://www.mdpi.com/1999-5903/3/1/1/

Knuth, D., Morris, J. H., & Pratt, V. (1977). Fast pattern matching in strings. *SIAM Journal on Computing, 6*(2), 323–350. doi:10.1137/0206024.

Ko, M., Ahn, G.-J., & Shehab, M. (2009). Privacy-enhanced user-centric identity management. In *Proceedings of IEEE International Conference on Communications*, (pp. 998-1002). Dresden, Germany: IEEE.

Kolbitsch, C., Comparetti, P. M., Kruegel, C., Kirda, E., Zhou, X., & Wang, X. (2009). Effective and efficient malware detection at the end host. In *Proceedings of the 18th USENIX Security Symposium* (pp. 351-366). Berkeley, CA: USENIX Association.

Koodli, R. (2009). *Mobile IPv6 fast handovers*. Internet Engineering Task Force (IETF), Request for Comments: 5568. Retrieved from http://tools.ietf.org/html/rfc5568

Köpsell, S., & Švenda, P. (2010). Secure logging of retained data for an anonymity service. In Bezzi, M., Duquenoy, P., Fischer-Hübner, S., Hansen, M., & Zhang, G. (Eds.), *IFIP Advances in Information and Communication Technology: Privacy and Identity Management for Life* (pp. 284–298). Berlin: Springer. doi:10.1007/978-3-642-14282-6_24.

Kremer, S., & Markowitch, O. (2001). Selective receipt in certified e-mail. In *Proceedings of Progress in Cryptology Indocrypt 2001* (Vol. 2247, pp. 136–148). Berlin: Springer. doi:10.1007/3-540-45311-3_14.

Kremer, S., Markowitch, O., & Zhou, J. (2002). An intensive survey of fair non-repudiation protocols. *Computer Communications, 25*, 1606–1621. doi:10.1016/S0140-3664(02)00049-X.

Kremer, S., & Ryan, M. (2005). Analysis of an electronic voting protocol in the applied pi calculus. In *Programming Languages and Systems (LNCS)*. Berlin: Springer. doi:10.1007/978-3-540-31987-0_14.

Kruegel, C., & Robertson, W. (2004). Alert verification: Determining the success of intrusion attempts. In *Proceedings of the 1st Workshop on Detection of Intrusions and Malware and Vulnerability Assessment* (pp. 25-38). Springer-Verlag.

Kumar, P. J. S., Knananna, M. R., Shine, H., & Arun, S. (2011). Implementing high performance lexical analyzer using CELL broadband engine processor. *International Journal of Engineering Science and Technology, 3*(9), 6907–6913.

Kuper, G., Massacci, F., & Rassadko, N. (2005). Generalized XML security views. In *Proceedings of the 10th ACM Symposium on Access Control Models and Technologies* (pp. 77-84). ACM.

Kwon, J., Lee, J., & Lee, H. (2011). Hidden bot detection by tracing non-human generated traffic at the zombie host. In *Proceedings of the 7th International Conference on Information Security Practice and Experience* (pp. 343-361). Berlin: Springer.

Kwon, M., Jeong, K., & Lee, H. (2008). PROBE: A process behavior-based host intrusion prevention system. In *Proceedings of the 4th International Conference on Information Security Practice and Experience* (pp. 203-217). Berlin: Springer.

Lamport, L. (1981). Password authentication with insecure communication. *Communications of the ACM, 24*(11), 770–772. doi:10.1145/358790.358797.

Lanthaler, M., & Gütl, C. (2012). On using JSON-LD to create evolvable RESTful services. In *Proceedings of the 3rd International Workshop on RESTful Design (WS-REST 2012) at WWW2012* (pp. 25-32). Lyon, France: ACM Press.

Latest Cloud Storage Hiccups Prompts Data Security Questions. (n.d.). Retrieved from http://www.computerworld.com/action/article.do?command=viewArticleBasic&articleId=9130682&source=NLT_PM

Lauf, A. P., Peters, R. A., & Robinson, W. H. (2010). A distributed intrusion detection system for resource-constrained devices in ad-hoc networks. *Ad Hoc Networks, 8*(3), 253–266. doi:10.1016/j.adhoc.2009.08.002.

Laureano, M., Maziero, C., & Jamhour, E. (2007). Protecting host-based intrusion detectors through virtual machines. *Computer Networks: The International Journal of Computer and Telecommunications Networking, 51*(5), 1275–1283.

Laurens, V., Miége, A., El Saddik, A., & Dhar, P. (2009). DDoSniffer: Detecting DDOS attack at the source agents. *International Journal of Advanced Media and Communication, 3*(3), 290–311. doi:10.1504/IJAMC.2009.027014.

Law, K.-H., & Kwok, L.-F. (2004). IDS false alarm filtering using KNN classifier. In *Proceedings of the 5th International Workshop on Information Security Applications* (pp. 114-121). Springer-Verlag.

Lazarevic, A., Kumar, V., & Srivastava, J. (2005). Intrusion detection: A survey. InKumar, V, Srivastava, J, & Lazarevic, A (Eds.), *Managing Cyber Threats: Issues, Approaches, and Challenges* (pp. 19-81). New York, NY: Springer Science+Business Media, Inc. doi:10.1007/0-387-24230-9_2.

Leavitt, N. (2009). Is cloud computing really ready for prime time? *IEEE Computer, 42*(1), 15–20. doi:10.1109/MC.2009.20.

Lee, B., Boyd, C., Dawson, E., Kim, K., Yang, J., & Yoo, S. (2004). Providing receipt-freeness in mixnet-based voting protocols. In *Proceedings of Information Security and Cryptology (ICISC'03)* (LNCS), (vol. 2971, pp. 245-258). Berlin: Springer.

Lee, T. H., & Huang, N. L. (2008). An efficient and scalable pattern matching scheme for network security applications. In *Proceedings of 17th International Conference on Computer Communications and Networks (ICCN)* (pp. 1-7). ICCN.

Lee, W., & Stolfo, S. J. (2000). A framework for constructing features and models for intrusion detection systems. *ACM Transactions on Information and System Security, 3*(4), 227–261. doi:10.1145/382912.382914.

Leighon, T. (2009). Akamai and cloud computing: A perspective from the edge of the cloud (White Paper). *Akamai Technologies*. Retrieved from http://www.essextec.com/assets/cloud/akamai/cloud-computing-perspective-wp.pdf

Leonardi, E., Bhowmick, S., & Iwaihara, M. (2010). Efficient database-driven evaluation of security clearance for federated access control of dynamic XML documents. In *Database Systems for Advanced Applications* (pp. 299–306). Academic Press. doi:10.1007/978-3-642-12026-8_24.

Li, S. (2003). *Analyses and new designs of digital chaotic ciphers*. (Ph. D. Dissertation). Xi'an Jiaotong University, Shaanxi, China.

Li, Z., Xia, G., Gao, H., Tang, Y., Chen, Y., & Liu, B. ... Lv, Y. (2010). NetShield: Matching with a large vulnerability signature ruleset for high performance network defense. In *Proceedings of ACM Conference on Applications, Technologies, Architectures, and Protocols for Computer Communications* (pp. 279-290). ACM Press.

Liang, X., Cao, Z., Lu, R., & Qin, L. (2008). Efficient and secure protocol in fair document exchange. *Computer Standards & Interfaces, 30*(3), 167–176. doi:10.1016/j.csi.2007.08.003.

Compilation of References

Lian, S. (2009). A block cipher based on chaotic neural networks. *Neurocomputing*, *72*, 1296–1301. doi:10.1016/j.neucom.2008.11.005.

Li, G., Ling, H., Znati, T., & Wu, W. (2006). A robust on-demand path-key establishment framework via random key predistribution for wireless sensor network. *EURASIP Journal on Wireless Communications and Networking*, *2*, 1–10. doi:10.1155/WCN/2006/91304.

Lin, C. H., Chien, L. S., Liu, C. H., Chang, S. C., & Hon, W. K. (2012). *PFAC library: GPU-based string matching algorithm*. Paper presented at the GPU Technology Conference 2012. New York, NY.

Lin, P. C., Lin, Y. D., & Lai, Y. C. (2011). A hybrid algorithm of backward hashing and automaton tracking for virus scanning. *IEEE Transactions on Computers*, *60*(4), 594–601. doi:10.1109/TC.2010.95.

Liu, D., Qing, S., Li, P., & Yuan, C. (2008). A practical certified e-mail system with temporal authentication based on transparent TSS. In *Proceedings of the 2008 Ninth ACIS International Conference on Software Engineering, Artificial Intelligence, Networking, and Parallel/Distributed Computing* (pp. 285-290). Washington, DC: IEEE Computer Society.

Liu, S. T., Huang, H. C., & Chen, Y. M. (2011). A system call analysis method with MapReduce for malware detection. In *Proceedings of the IEEE 17th International Conference on Parallel and Distributed Systems (ICPADS)* (pp. 631-637). IEEE.

Liu, Z., Pang, J., & Zhang, C. (2010). Extending a keychain based certified email protocol with transparent TTP. In *Proceedings of the 2010 IEEE/IFIP International Conference on Embedded and Ubiquitous Computing* (pp. 630-636). Washington, DC: IEEE Computer Society.

Liu, J., & Li, L. (2008). A distributed intrusion detection system based on agents. *Computational Intelligence and Industrial Application*, *1*, 553–557.

Li, Y., & Guo, L. (2007). An active learning based TCM-KNN algorithm for supervised network intrusion detection. *Computers & Security*, *26*(7-8), 459–467. doi:10.1016/j.cose.2007.10.002.

Lopez, J., Onieva, J. A., & Zhou, J. (2004). Enhancing certified email service for timeliness and multicast. In *Proceedings of 2004 International Network Conference* (pp. 327-335). Plymouth, UK: University of Plymouth.

Lowensohn, J., & McCarthy, C. (2009). *Lessons from Twitter's security breach*. Retrieved from http://news.cnet.com/8301-17939_109-10287558-2.html

Lyle, J. (2010). *Trustable services through attestation*. (PhD thesis). University of Oxford, Oxford, UK. Retrieved from http://www.cs.ox.ac.uk/people/John.Lyle/thesis-final-25-06-11.pdf

Lyle, J., Monteleone, S., Faily, S., Patti, D., & Ricciato, F. (2012). Cross-platform access control for mobile web applications. In *Proceedings of the IEEE International Symposium on Policies for Distributed Systems & Networks*. IEEE.

Mac. (n.d.). *OS X developer library: Security architecture*. Retrieved from http://developer.apple.com/library/mac/documentation/Security/Conceptual/Security_Overview/Introduction/Introduction.html

Mac. (n.d.). *OS X developer library: Security services*. Retrieved from http://developer.apple.com/library/mac/documentation/Security/Conceptual/Security_Overview/Security_Services/Security_Services.html

Ma, C., Li, S., Chen, K., & Liu, S. (2006). Analysis and improvement of fair certified e-mail delivery protocol. *Computer Standards & Interfaces*, *28*(4), 467–474. doi:10.1016/j.csi.2005.03.002.

Madson, C., & Glenn, R. (1998). *The use of HMAC-MD5-96 within ESP and AH*. Internet Engineering Task Force (IETF) Request for Comments: 2403. Retrieved from http://tools.ietf.org/html/rfc2403

Madson, C., & Glenn, R. (1998). *The use of HMAC-SHA-1-96 within ESP and AH*. Internet Engineering Task Force (IETF) Request for Comments: 2404. Retrieved from http://tools.ietf.org/html/rfc2404

Maggi, F., Matteucci, M., & Zanero, S. (2010). Detecting intrusions through system call sequence and argument analysis. *IEEE Transactions on Dependable and Secure Computing*, *7*(4), 381–395. doi:10.1109/TDSC.2008.69.

Maia, L. A., & Correia, M. E. (2012). *Java JCA/JCE programming in Android with SD smart cards*. Paper presented at the Information Systems and Technologies (CISTI), 2012. New York, NY.

Mandl, K., & Kohane, I. (2009). No small change for the health information economy. *The New England Journal of Medicine, 360*(13), 1278–1281. doi:10.1056/NEJMp0900411 PMID:19321867.

Manral, V. (2007). *Cryptographic algorithm implementation requirements for encapsulating security payload (ESP) and authentication header (AH)*. Internet Engineering Task Force (IETF) Request for Comments: 4835. Retrieved from http://tools.ietf.org/html/rfc4835

Mansour, I., Chalhoub, G., & Bakhache, B. (2012). *Evaluation of a fast symmetric cryptographic algorithm based on the chaos theory for wireless sensor networks*. Paper presented at MWNS International Symposium on Mobile Wireless Network Security. New York, NY.

Markou, M., & Singh, S. (2003). Novelty detection: A review-part 1: Statistical approaches. *Signal Processing, 83*(12), 2481–2497. doi:10.1016/j.sigpro.2003.07.018.

Markowitch, O., & Roggeman, Y. (1999). Probabilistic non-repudiation without trusted third party. In *Proceedings of the 2nd Conference on Security in Communication Networks*. IEEE.

Marti, S., Giuli, T. J., Lai, K., & Baker, M. (2000). Mitigating routing misbehavior in mobile ad hoc networks. In *Proceedings of the 6th Annual International Conference on Mobile Computing and Networking* (pp. 255-265). New York, NY: ACM.

Martinez, C. A., Echeverri, G. I., & Sanz, A. G. C. (2010). Malware detection based on cloud computing integrating intrusion ontology representation. In C. E. Velasquez & Y. A. Rodriguez (Eds.), *2010 IEEE Latin-American Conference on Communications* (pp. 1-6). IEEE Communications Society.

Masuda, N., & Aihara, K. (2002). Cryptosystems with discretized chaotic maps. *IEEE Transactions on Circuits and Systems, 49*, 28–40. doi:10.1109/81.974872.

Mather, T., Kumaraswamy, S., & Latif, S. (2009). *Cloud security and privacy*. Sebastopol, CA: O'Reilly Media, Inc..

Ma, W., Duan, P., Liu, S., Gu, G., & Liu, J.-C. (2012). Shadow attacks: Automatically evading system-call-behavior based malware detection. *Journal in Computer Virology, 8*(1-2), 1–13. doi:10.1007/s11416-011-0157-5.

McHugh, J. (2000). Testing intrusion detection systems: A critique of the 1998 and 1999 DARPA off-line intrusion detection system evaluation as performed by Lincoln laboratory. *ACM Transactions on Information and System Security, 3*(4), 262–294. doi:10.1145/382912.382923.

McMillan, R. (2012). Siemens: Stuxnet worm hit industrial systems. *ComputerWorld.com*. Retrieved 25th of September, 2012 from http://www.computerworld.com/s/article/print/9185419/Siemens_Stuxnet_worm_hit_industrial_systems?taxonomyName=Network+Security&taxonomyId=142

Meng, Y., & Kwok, L.-F. (2011). Adaptive false alarm filter using machine learning in intrusion detection. In *Proceedings of the 6th International Conference on Intelligent Systems and Knowledge Engineering* (pp. 573-584). Springer-Verlag.

Meng, Y., & Kwok, L.-F. (2011). A generic scheme for the construction of contextual signatures with hash function in intrusion detection. In *Proceedings of the 2012 International Conference on Computational Intelligence and Security* (pp. 978-982). IEEE Press.

Meng, Y., & Kwok, L.-F. (2012). A case study: Intelligent false alarm reduction using fuzzy if-then rules in network intrusion detection. In *Proceedings of the 9th International Conference on Fuzzy Systems and Knowledge Discovery* (pp. 505-509). IEEE Press.

Meng, Y., & Li, W. (2012). Constructing context-based non-critical alarm filter in intrusion detection. In *Proceedings of the 7th International Conference on Internet Monitoring and Protection* (pp. 75-81). IARIA Press.

Merino, P. J., Martínez, A. G., Organero, M. M., & Kloos, C. D. (2006). Enabling practical IPsec authentication for the internet. *Lecture Notes in Computer Science, 4277*, 392-403. Retrieved from http://rd.springer.com/chapter/10.1007/11915034_63

Micali, S. (2003). Simple and fast optimistic protocols for fair electronic exchange. In *Proceedings of the Twenty Second Annual Symposium on Principles of Distributed Computing* (pp. 12–19). New York, NY: ACM.

Compilation of References

Microsoft Library. (n.d.). *Recursive and iterative queries.* Retrieved 2013, from http://technet.microsoft.com/en-us/library/cc961401.aspx

Milanesi, C. (2011). iPad and beyond: The future of the tablet market (Technical report). Washington, DC: Gartner, Inc.

Miller, D. R., Harris, S., Harper, A. A., Vandyke, S., & Blask, C. (2010). *Security information and event management (SIEM) implementation.* New York: The McGraw-Hill Companies.

Miretskiy, Y., Das, A., Wright, C. P., & Zadok, E. (2004). AVFS: An on-access anti-virus file system. In *Proceedings of the 13th Conference on USENIX Security Symposium* (p. 6). Berkeley, CA: USENIX Association.

Mishra, A., Nadkarni, K., & Patcha, A. (2004). Intrusion detection in wireless ad hoc networks. *IEEE Wireless Communications*, *11*(1), 48–60. doi:10.1109/MWC.2004.1269717.

Mitchell, C.J., & Schaffelhofer, R. (2004). *Security for mobility: The personal PKI.* Institution of Engineering and Technology.

MITRE Corporation. (n.d.). *Common attack pattern enumeration and classification (CAPEC).* Retrieved from http://capec.mitre.org/

Mockapetris, P. (1987). Domain names - Concepts and facilities. *RFC*. Retrieved November 1987, from http://www.ietf.org/rfc/rfc1034.txt

Mockapetris, P. (1987). Domain names - Implementation and specification. *RFC*. Retrieved November 1987, from http://www.ietf.org/rfc/rfc1035.txt

Modi, C., Patel, D., Borisaniya, B., Patel, H., Patel, A., & Rajarajan, M. (2013). A survey of intrusion detection techniques in cloud. *Journal of Network and Computer Applications*, *36*(1), 42–57. doi:10.1016/j.jnca.2012.05.003.

Molina, J., & Cukier, M. (2009). Evaluating attack resiliency for host intrusion detection systems. *Journal of Information Assurance and Security*, *4*(1), 1–9.

Molnar, D., & Schechter, S. (2010). Self hosting vs. cloud hosting: Accounting for the security impact of hosting in the cloud. In *Proceedings of the Workshop on the Economics of Information Security*. Retrieved from http://weis2010.econinfosec.org/papers/session5/weis2010_schechter.pdf

Monteiro, J. R. M., & Dahab, R. (2002). An attack on a protocol for certified delivery. In *Proceedings of the 5th International Conference on Information Security* (pp. 428-436). London, UK: Springer-Verlag.

Mont, M., Pearson, S., & Bramhall, P. (2003). Towards accountable management of privacy and identity information. In Snekkenes, E., & Gollmann, D. (Eds.), *Computer Security – ESORICS 2003* (Vol. 2808, pp. 146–161). Berlin: Springer. doi:10.1007/978-3-540-39650-5_9.

Morin, B., Mé, L., Debar, H., & Ducassé, M. (2002). M2D2: A formal data model for IDS alert correlation. In *Proceedings of the 5th International Conference on Recent Advances in Intrusion Detection* (pp. 115-137). Springer-Verlag.

Mozilla. (n.d.). *Boot to gecko project website.* Retrieved from http://www.mozilla.org/en-US/b2g/

Müldner, T., Leighton, G., & Miziołek, J. (2009). Parameterized role-based access control policies for XML documents. Information Security Journal: A Global Perspective, Taylor & Francis, (18), 282-296.

Murali, A., & Rao, M. (2005). A survey on intrusion detection approaches. In *Proceedings of the 1st International Conference on Information and Communication Technologies* (pp. 233-240). Washington, DC: IEEE Computer Society.

Mut Puigserver, M., Ferrer Gomila, J., & Huguet i Rotger, L. (2000). Certified electronic mail protocol resistant to a minority of malicious third parties. In *Proceedings of the Nineteenth Annual Joint Conference of the IEEE Computer and Communications Societies* (pp. 1401-1405). IEEE.

Mutz, D., Valeur, F., Vigna, G., & Kruegel, C. (2006). Anomalous system call detection. *Journal ACM Transactions on Information and System Security*, *9*(1), 61–93. doi:10.1145/1127345.1127348.

Na, J., Ryu, S., Lee, K., & Mun, Y. (2010). Enhanced PMIPv6 route optimization handover using PFMIPv6. *IEICE Transactions on Communications. E (Norwalk, Conn.)*, *93-B*(11), 3144–3147.

Narten, T., Draves, R., & Krishnan, S. (2007). *Privacy extensions for stateless address autoconfiguration in IPv6, RFC 4941*. Internet Engineering Task Force (IETF). Retrieved from http://tools.ietf.org/html/rfc4941

Narten, T., Nordmark, E., Simpson, W., & Soliman, H. (2007). *Neighbor discovery for IP version 6 (IPv6)*. IETF Request for Comments: 4861. Retrieved from http://tools.ietf.org/html/rfc4861

Nasser, N., & Chen, Y. (2007). Enhanced intrusion detection system for discovering malicious nodes in mobile ad hoc networks. In *Proceedings of 2007 IEEE International Conference on Communications* (pp. 1154-1159). IEEE.

Nenadic, A., Zhang, N., & Barton, S. (2004). Fair certified e-mail delivery. In *Proceedings of the 2004 ACM Symposium on Applied Computing* (pp. 391-396). New York, NY: ACM.

Netflix Prize. (n.d.). Retrieved from http://www.netflixprize.com/

Network World. (2008). *Loss of customer data spurs closure of online storage service the linkup*. Retrieved from http://www.networkworld.com/news/2008/081108-linkup-failure.html?page=1

News, B. B. C. (2009). *Facebook users suffer viral surge*. Retrieved from http://news.bbc.co.uk/2/hi/technology/7918839.stm

Nielsen, C. R., Andersen, E. H., & Nielson, H. R. (1996). Static analysis of a voting protocol. In *Proceedings of the IFIP World Conference in IT Tools*, (pp. 21-30). IFIP.

Niemegeers, I.G., & de Groot, S.M.H. (2002). From personal area networks to personal networks: A user oriented approach. *Wireless Personal Communications*, *22*, 175–186. Retrieved from http://dx.doi.org/10.1023/A:1019912421877

Nikander, P., Arkko, J., Aura, T., Montenegro, G., & Nordmark, E. (2005). *Mobile IP version 6 route optimization security design background*. Internet Engineering Task Force (IETF), Request for Comments: 4225, Dec. 2005. Retrieved from http://tools.ietf.org/html/rfc4225

Nikander, P., Kempf, J., & Nordmark, E. (2004). *IPv6 neighbor discovery (ND) trust models and threats*. Internet Engineering Task Force (IETF) Request for Comments: 3756. Retrieved from http://tools.ietf.org/html/rfc3756

Ning, P., & Xu, D. (2003). Learning attack strategies from intrusion alert. In *Proceedings of the 2003 ACM Conference on Computer and Communications Security* (pp. 200-209). ACM Press.

Ning, P., Reeves, D., & Cui, Y. (2001). *Correlating alerts using prerequisites of intrusions* (Technical Report TR-2001-13). Raleigh, NC: North Carolina State University.

Nordin, M., Rahman, A., Yazid, M., & Saman, M., Ahmad, Osman, A., & Tap, M. (2009). A filtering algorithm for efficient retrieving of DNA sequence. *International Journal of Computer Theory and Engineering*, *1*(2), 102–109.

Norton, M. (2004). *Optimizing pattern matching for intrusion detection*. SourceFire Inc..

Noura, H., El Assad, S., Vladeanu, C., & Caragata, D. (2011). *An efficient and secure SPN cryptosystem based on chaotic control parameters*. Paper presented at the 6th International Conference on Internet Technology and Secured Transactions. Abu Dhabi, UAE.

O'Shea, G., & Roe, M. (2001). Child-proof authentication for MIPv6 (CAM). *SIGCOMM Computer Communications Review*, *31*(2), 4–8. doi:10.1145/505666.505668

OASIS. (2012). *Security assertion markup language (SAML), OASIS security services (SAML) TC*. Retrieved from http://www.oasis-open.org/committees/tc_home.php?wg_abbrev= security

Oberheide, J., Cooke, E., & Jahanian, F. (2008). CloudAV: N-version antivirus in the network cloud. In *Proceedings of the 17th USENIX Security Symposium* (pp. 91-106). Berkeley, CA: USENIX Association.

Object Management Group. (n.d.). *Homepage*. Retrieved from http://www.omg.org

Okamoto, T. (1996). An electronic voting scheme. In N. Terashima, et al. (Ed.), *IFIP World Congress*, (pp. 21-30). London: Chapman & Hall Publications.

Okamoto, T., & Ohta, K. (1994). How to simultaneously exchange secrets by general assumptions. In *Proceedings of the 2nd ACM Conference on Computer and Communications Security* (pp. 184 - 192). New York, NY: ACM.

Onieva, J. A., Zhou, J., & Lopez, J. (2009). Multiparty nonrepudiation: A survey. *ACM Computing Surveys, 41*(1), 5:1-5:43.

Onieva, J. A., Lopez, J., & Zhou, J. (2009). *Secure multiparty non-repudiation protocols and applications (Vol. 43)*. London: Springer Publishing Company, Incorporated. doi:10.1007/978-0-387-75630-1.

Open Cloud Computing Interface. (n.d.). *Homepage*. Retrieved from http://occi-wg.org

Open Cloud Consortium. (n.d.). *Homepage*. Retrieved from http://opencloudconsortium.org

Open, I. D. (n.d.). *What is OpenId?* Retrieved from http://openid.net/get-an-openid/what-is-openid/

Oppliger, R., & Stadlin, P. (2004). A certified mail system (CMS) for the internet. *Computer Communications, 27*(13), 1229–1235. doi:10.1016/j.comcom.2004.04.006.

Oprea, A., & Reiter, M. K. (2007). Integrity checking in cryptographic file systems with constant trusted storage. In *Proceedings of 16th USENIX Security Symposium*. Berkeley, CA: USENIX Association.

Orawiwattanakul, T., Yamaji, K., Nakamura, M., Kataoka, T., & Sonehara, N. (2010). *User-controlled privacy protection with attribute-filter mechanism for a federated SSO environment using shibboleth*. Paper presented at the 2010 International Conference on P2P, Parallel, Grid, Cloud and Internet Computing. New York, NY.

Organization for the Advancement of Structured Information Standards. (n.d.). *Homepage*. Retrieved from http://www.oasis-open.org

Orthacker, C., Centner, M., & Kittl, C. (2010). Qualified mobile server signature. In Meyer, H. M., & Turner, J. A. (Eds.), *IFIP Advances in Information and Communication Technology Series*. Springer.

OWASP Foundation. (n.d.). *The open web application security project*. Retrieved from http://www.owasp.org/index.php/

Özyer, T., Alhajj, R., & Barker, K. (2007). Intrusion detection by integrating boosting genetic fuzzy classifier and data mining criteria for rule pre-screening. *Journal of Network and Computer Applications, 30*(1), 99–113. doi:10.1016/j.jnca.2005.06.002.

Paci, F., & Shang, N., Jr. K. S., Fernando, R., & Bertino, E. (2009). *VeryIDX - A privacy preserving digital identity management system for mobile devices*. Paper presented at the 2009 Tenth International Conference on Mobile Data Management: Systems, Services and Middleware. New York, NY.

Pareek, N. K., Patidar, V., & Sud, K. K. (2003). Discrete chaotic cryptography using external key. *Physics Letters. [Part A], 309*, 75–82. doi:10.1016/S0375-9601(03)00122-1.

Park, N. H., Oh, S. H., & Lee, W. S. (2010). Anomaly intrusion detection by clustering transactional audit streams in a host computer. *Information Sciences, 180*(12), 2375–2389. doi:10.1016/j.ins.2010.03.001.

Park, Y., & Cho, Y. (2004). Fair certified e-mail protocols with delivery deadline agreement. In *Proceedings of Computational Science and its Applications - ICCSA 2004 (Vol. 3043*, pp. 978–987). Berlin: Springer. doi:10.1007/978-3-540-24707-4_110.

Parno, B., Zhou, Z., & Perrig, A. (2009). *Help me help you: Using trustworthy host-based information in the network (Technical report)*. Pittsburgh, PA: CyLab, Carnegie Mellon University.

Patcha, A., & Park, J.-M. (2007). An overview of anomaly detection techniques: Existing solutions and latest technological trends. *Computer Networks, 51*(12), 3448–3470. doi:10.1016/j.comnet.2007.02.001.

Paterson, I., & Saint-Andre, P. (2007). *XEP-0206: XMPP: Over BOSH*. Retrieved Jun 2012, from http://xmpp.org/extensions/xep-0206.html

Patidar, V., Pareek, N. K., Purohit, G., & Sud, K. K. (2011). A robust and secure chaotic standard map based pseudorandom permutation-substitution scheme for image encryption. *Optics Communications, 284*, 4331–4339. doi:10.1016/j.optcom.2011.05.028.

Patil, S., Kashyap, A., Sivathanu, G., & Zadok, E. (2004). I3FS: An in-kernel integrity checker and intrusion detection file system. In *Proceedings of the 18th USENIX Conference on System Administration* (pp. 67-78). Berkeley, CA: USENIX Association.

Pavlich-Mariscal, J., Demurjian, S., & Michel, L. (2008). A framework of composable access control definition, enforcement and assurance. In *Proceedings of the SCCC'08. International Conference of the IEEE* (pp. 13–22). IEEE.

Paxson, V. (1999). Bro: A system for detecting network intruders in real-time. *Computer Networks*, *31*(23-24), 2435–2463. doi:10.1016/S1389-1286(99)00112-7.

Payne, B. D., Carbone, M., Sharif, M., & Lee, W. (2008). Lares: An architecture for secure active monitoring using virtualization. In *Proceedings of the 2008 IEEE Symposium on Security and Privacy* (pp. 233-247). Washington, DC: IEEE Computer Society.

Pecorra, L., & Carrol, T. (1990). Synchronization in chaotic systems. *Physical Review Letters*, *64*(8), 821–824. doi:10.1103/PhysRevLett.64.821 PMID:10042089.

Pereira, R., & Adams, R. (1998). *The ESP CBC-mode cipher algorithms*. Internet Engineering Task Force (IETF) Request for Comments: 2451. Retrieved from http://tools.ietf.org/html/rfc2451

Pérez, M. G., Mármol, F. G., Pérez, G. M., & Gómez, A. F. S. (2012). RepCIDN: A reputation-based collaborative intrusion detection network to lessen the impact of malicious alarms. *Journal of Network and Systems Management*, 1–40.

Pérez, M. G., Mármol, F. G., Pérez, G. M., & Skarmeta, G. A. (2011). Mobility in collaborative alert systems: Building trust through reputation. In Casares-Giner, V., Manzoni, P., & Pont, A. (Eds.), *NETWORKING 2011 Workshops* (pp. 251–262). Berlin: Springer. doi:10.1007/978-3-642-23041-7_24.

Perkins, C., Johnson, D., & Arkko, J. (2011). *Mobility support in IPv6*. Internet Engineering Task Force (IETF), Request for Comments: 6275. Retrieved from http://tools.ietf.org/html/rfc6275

Permpoontanalarp, Y., & Kanokkanjanapong, J. (2008). Dynamic undeniable fair certified email with DDOS protection. In *Proceedings of the 22nd International Conference on Advanced Information Networking and Applications* (pp. 763-770). Washington, DC: IEEE Computer Society.

Philip, M., & Das, A. (2011). Survey: Image encryption using chaotic cryptography schemes. *International Journal of Computers and Applications*, (1): 1–4.

Phua, C., Alahakoon, D., & Lee, V. (2004). Minority report in fraud detection: Classification of skewed data. *SIGKDD Explorer Newsletter*, *6*(1), 50–59. doi:10.1145/1007730.1007738.

Pietraszek, T. (2004). Using adaptive alert classification to reduce false positives in intrusion detection. In *Proceedings of the 7th Symposium on Recent Advances in Intrusion Detection* (pp. 102-124). Springer-Verlag.

Poon, E., Blumenfeld, B., & Hamann, C. et al. (2006). Design and implementation of an application and associated services to support interdisciplinary medication reconciliation efforts at an integrated healthcare delivery network. *Journal of the American Medical Informatics Association*, *13*(6), 581–592. doi:10.1197/jamia.M2142 PMID:17114640.

Portokalidis, G., Homburg, P., Anagnostakis, K., & Bos, H. (2010). Paranoid android: Versatile protection for smartphones. In *Proceedings of the 26th Annual Computer Security Applications Conference* (pp. 347-356). New York, NY: ACM.

Post, W. (2008). *Lithuania weathers cyber attack, braces for round 2*. Retrieved from http://blog.washingtonpost.com/securityfix/2008/07/lithuania_weathers_cyber_attac_1.html

Pruitt, J., & Adlin, T. (2006). *The persona lifecycle: Keeping people in mind throughout product design*. Amsterdam: Elsevier.

Ptacek, T. H., & Newsham, T. N. (1998). *Insertion, evasion and denial of service: Eluding network intrusion detection (Technical report)*. Secure Networks, Inc..

Pungila, C. (2009). A Bray-Curtis weighted automaton for detecting malicious code through system-call analysis. In *Proceedings of the 11th International Symposium on Symbolic and Numeric Algorithms for Scientific Computing (SYNASC)* (pp. 392-400). IEEE Xplore Digital Library.

Pungila, C. (2010). A model for energy-efficient household maintenance through behavioral analysis of electrical appliances. In *Proceedings of the 7th International Conference on e-Business Engineering (ICEBE)* (pp. 409-414). ICEBE.

Pungila, C. (2012). Hybrid compression of the Aho-Corasick automaton for static analysis in intrusion detection systems. In *Proceedings of the International Joint Conference CISIS'12-ICEUTE'12-SOCO'12 Special Sessions* in *Advances in Intelligent Systems and Computing* (pp. 77-86). Springer-Verlag.

Pungila, C. (2012). Improved file-carving through data-parallel pattern matching for data forensics. In *Proceedings of the 7th IEEE International Symposium on Applied Computational Intelligence and Informatics (SACI)* (pp. 197-202). IEEE.

Pungila, C., & Negru, V. (2012). A highly-efficient memory-compression approach for GPU-accelerated virus signature matching. In *Proceedings of the 15th International Conference, ISC 2012* (LNCS), (pp. 354-369). Berlin: Springer-Verlag.

Quynh, N. A., & Takefuji, Y. (2007). A novel approach for a file-system integrity monitor tool of Xen virtual machine. In *Proceedings of the 2nd ACM Symposium on Information, Computer and Communications Security* (pp. 194-202). New York, NY: ACM.

Rafiee, H., Loewis, M. V., & Meinel, C. (2013). DNS update extension to IPv6 secure addressing. In *Proceeding of FINA Conference.* IEEE.

Rahaman, M., Roudier, Y., & Schaad, A. (2008). Distributed access control for XML document centric collaborations. In *Proceedings of the EDOC'08. 12th International IEEE* (pp. 267-276). IEEE.

Rahman, M., Costas, S., & Laurent, M. (2007). Pattern matching in degenerate DNA/RNA sequences. In *Proceedings of the Workshop on Algorithms and Computation (WALCOM)* (pp. 109-120). WALCOM.

Ren, H., Stakhanova, N., & Ghorbani, A. A. (2010). An online adaptive approach to alert correlation. In *Proceedings of the 7th International Conference on Detection of Intrusions and Malware, and Vulnerability Assessment* (pp. 153-172). Springer-Verlag.

Ren, K., Lou, W., Zeng, K., Bao, F., Zhou, J., & Deng, R. H. (2006). Routing optimization security in mobile IPv6. *Computer Networks*, *50*(13), 2401–2419. doi:10.1016/j.comnet.2005.09.019.

Ristenpart, T., Tromer, E., Shacham, H., & Savage, S. (2009). Hey, you, get off of my cloud: Exploring information leakage in third-party compute clouds. In *Proceedings of the 16th ACM Conference on Computer and Communications Security (CCS'09)*, (pp. 199-212). Chicago: ACM Press.

Rivest, R. L. (2006). *The threeballot voting system*. Retrieved from http://people.csail.mit.edu/rivest/Rivest-TheThreeBallotVotingSystem.pdf

Rivest, R., Robshaw, M., & Yiqun Lisa Yin, R. S. (1998). *The RC6 block cipher, v1.1*. Retrieved from http://theory.lcs.mit.edu/~rivest/

Rivest, R. L. (1995). The RC5 encryption algorithm. In *Proceedings of Fast Software Encryption (LNCS)* (pp. 86–96). Berlin: Springer. doi:10.1007/3-540-60590-8_7.

Roesch, M. (1999). Snort-lightweight intrusion detection for networks. In *Proceedings of the 1999 Large Installation System Administration Conference* (pp. 229-238). USENIX Association.

Rooney, T. (2011). Secure DNS (part I). In *IP address management: Principles and practice* (pp. 256–258). Hoboken, NJ: IEEE Press/Wiley.

Roschke, S., Cheng, F., & Meinel, C. (2010). A flexible and efficient alert correlation platform for distributed IDS. In *Proceedings of the 4th International Conference on Network and System Security (NSS)* (pp. 24-31). NSS.

Roschke, S., Cheng, F., & Meinel, C. (2011). A new alert correlation algorithm based on attack graph. In *Proceedings of the 4th International Conference on Computational Intelligence in Security for Information Systems* (pp. 58-67). Springer-Verlag.

Roschke, S., Cheng, F., & Meinel, C. (2011). An alert correlation platform for memory-supported techniques. *Concurrency and Computation*, *24*(10), 1123–1136. doi:10.1002/cpe.1750.

Rössler, T. (2009). Empowerment through electronic mandate – Best practice Austria. In *Proceedings of 9th IFIP WG 6.1 Conference on e-Business, e-Services and e-Society, I3E 2009*, (vol. 305, pp. 148-160). Berlin: Springer.

Ryan, P. Y. A., & Teague, V. (2009). Pretty good democracy. In *Proceedings of the 17th International Workshop on Security Protocols* (LNCS). Cambridge, UK: Springer.

Ryu, S., & Mun, Y. (2005). The tentative and early binding update for mobile IPv6 fast handover. In *Proceedings of the First International Conference on Mobile Ad-Hoc and Sensor Networks*, (pp. 825–835). Berlin: Springer-Verlag.

Ryu, S., & Mun, Y. (2007). A scheme to enhance TEBU scheme of fast handovers for mobile IPv6. In *Proceedings of the 3rd International Conference on Embedded Software and Systems*, (pp. 773–782). Berlin: Springer-Verlag.

Sabahi, F., & Movaghar, A. (2008). Intrusion detection: A survey. In *Proceedings of the 3rd International Conference on Systems and Networks Communications* (pp. 23-26). Washington, DC: IEEE Computer Society.

Sahu, S., & Shandilya, S. K. (2010). A comprehensive survey on anomaly-based intrusion detection in MANET. *International Journal of Information Technology and Knowledge Management*, *2*(2), 305–310.

Saint-Andre, P., Smith, K., & Tronon, R. (2009). *XMPP: The definitive guide building real-time applications with jabber technologies*. Sebastopol, CA: O'Reilly Media, Inc..

Sakimura, N., Bradley, J., Jones, M., Medeiros, B., & Jay, E. (2012). *Openid connect standard 1.0*.

Saklikar, S., & Saha, S. (2007). *Next steps for security assertion markup language (SAML)*. Paper presented at the 2007 ACM Workshop on Secure Web Services. Fairfax, VA.

Sandler, D., Derr, K., & Wallach, D. S. (2008). Votebox: A tamper-evident, verifiable electronic voting system. In *Proceedings of the 17th Conference on Security Symposium (SS'08)*, (pp. 349-364). Berkeley, CA: USENIX Association.

Sasse, M. A., Brostoff, S., & Weirich, D. (2001). Transforming the 'weakest link': A human-computer interaction approach to usable and effective security. *BT Technology Journal*, *19*, 122–131. doi:10.1023/A:1011902718709.

Scarfone, K., & Mell, P. (2012). *Guide to intrusion detection and prevention systems (IDPS) (NIST Special Publication 800-94 Revision 1)*. Gaithersburg, MD: National Institute of Standards and Technology.

Schear, N., Albrecht, D. R., & Borisov, N. (2008). High-speed matching of vulnerability signatures. In *Proceedings of the 11th Symposium on Recent Advances in Intrusion Detection* (pp. 155-174). Springer-Verlag.

Schiller, J. (2005). *Cryptographic algorithms for use in the internet key exchange version 2 (IKEv2)*. IETF Request for Comments: 4307. Retrieved from http://tools.ietf.org/html/rfc4307

Schneier, B. (2009). *Security versus usability*. Retrieved from http://www.schneier.com/blog/archives/2009/08/security_vs_usa.html

Schneier, B., & Riordan, J. (1998). A certified e-mail protocol. In *Proceedings of the 14th Annual Computer Security Applications Conference* (pp. 347-352). Washington, DC: IEEE Computer Society.

Schneier, B. (1996). *Applied cryptography: Protocols, algorithms, and source code in C (cloth)* (2nd ed.). New York: John Wiley & Sons, Inc..

Schoenmakers, B. (1999). A simple publicly verifiable secret sharing scheme and its application to electronic voting. In *Advances in Cryptology-CRYPTO'99 (LNCS)* (Vol. 1966, pp. 148–164). Berlin: Springer-Verlag. doi:10.1007/3-540-48405-1_10.

Schwartz, P. M. (2004). *Property, privacy, and personal data*. Academic Press.

Security Bulletin, M. MS07-049. (2007). *Vulnerability in virtual PC and virtual server could allow elevation of privilege (937986)*. Retrieved from http://www.microsoft.com/technet/security/bulletin/ms07-049.mspx

Security Evaluation of Grid Environments. (n.d.). Retrieved from http://www.slideworld.com/slideshows.aspx/Security-Evaluation-of-Grid-Environments-ppt-217556

Sen, J. (2010). An intrusion detection architecture for clustered wireless ad hoc networks. In *Proceedings of the 2nd IEEE International Conference on Intelligence in Communication Systems and Networks (CICSyN'10)*, (pp. 202-207). Liverpool, UK: CICsyN.

Sen, J. (2010). A robust and fault-tolerant distributed intrusion detection system. In *Proceedings of the 1st International Conference on Parallel, Distributed and Grid Computing (PDGC'10)*, (pp. 123-128). Waknaghat, India: PDGC.

Sen, J. (2010). A distributed trust management framework for detecting malicious packet dropping nodes in a mobile ad hoc network. *International Journal of Network Security and its Applications, 2*(4), 92-104.

Sen, J. (2010). A distributed trust and reputation framework for mobile ad hoc networks. In *Proceedings of the 1st International Workshop on Trust Management in Peer-to-Peer Systems (IWTMP2PS)*, (pp. 538-547). Chennai, India: Springer.

Sen, J. (2010). A trust-based robust and efficient searching scheme for peer-to-peer networks. In *Proceedings of the 12th International Conference on Information and Communication Security (ICICS)* (LNCS), (vol. 6476, pp. 77-91). Barcelona, Spain: Springer.

Sen, J. (2011). A robust mechanism for defending distributed denial of service attacks on web servers. *International Journal of Network Security and its Applications, 3*(2), 162-179.

Sen, J. (2011). A novel mechanism for detection of distributed denial of service attacks. In *Proceedings of the 1st International Conference on Computer Science and Information Technology (CCSIT'11)*, (pp. 247-257). Springer.

Sen, J. (2011). A secure and efficient searching for trusted nodes in peer-to-peer network. In *Proceedings of the 4th International Conference on Computational Intelligence in Security for Information Systems (CISIS'11)* (LNCS), (vol. 6694, pp. 101-109). Berlin: Springer.

Sen, J., & Sengupta, I. (2005). Autonomous agent-based distributed fault-tolerant intrusion detection system. In *Proceedings of the 2nd International Conference on Distributed Computing and Internet Technology (ICDCIT'05)* (LNCS), (vol. 3186, pp. 125-131). Bhubaneswar, India: Springer.

Sen, J., Chowdhury, P. R., & Sengupta, I. (2006). A distributed trust mechanism for mobile ad hoc networks. In *Proceedings of the International Symposium on Ad Hoc and Ubiquitous Computing (ISAHUC'06)*, (pp. 62-67). Surathkal, India: ISAHUC.

Sen, J., Chowdhury, P. R., & Sengupta, I. (2007). A distributed trust establishment scheme for mobile ad hoc networks. In *Proceedings of the International Conference on Computation: Theory and Applications (ICCTA'07)*, (pp. 51-57). Kolkata, India: ICCTA.

Sen, J., Sengupta, I., & Chowdhury, P. R. (2006). A mechanism for detection and prevention of distributed denial of service attacks. In *Proceedings of the 8th International Conference on Distributed Computing and Networking (ICDCN'06)* (LNCS), (vol. 4308, pp. 139-144). Berlin: Springer.

Sen, J., Sengupta, I., & Chowdhury, P. R. (2006). An architecture of a distributed intrusion detection system using cooperating agents. In *Proceedings of the International Conference on Computing and Informatics (ICOCI'06)*, (pp. 1-6). Kuala Lumpur, Malaysia: ICOCI.

Sen, J., Ukil, A., Bera, D., & Pal, A. (2008). A distributed intrusion detection system for wireless ad hoc networks. In *Proceedings of the 16th IEEE International Conference on Networking (ICON'08)*, (pp. 1-5). New Delhi, India: IEEE.

Sen, J. (2010). An agent-based intrusion detection system for local area networks. *International Journal of Communication Networks and Information Security, 2*(2), 128–140.

Sen, J. (2010g). Reputation- and trust-based systems for wireless self-organizing networks. In *Security of Self-Organizing Networks: MANET, WSN, WMN, VANET* (pp. 91–122). Boca Raton, FL: CRC Press. doi:10.1201/EBK1439819197-7.

Shacham, H., & Waters, B. (2008). Compact proofs of retrievability. In *Proceedings of the 14th International Conference on the Theory and Application of Cryptology and Information Security: (ASIACRYPT'08)* (LNCS), (vol. 5350, pp. 90-107). Melbourne, Australia: Springer.

SHAMAN Project. (2002). *Deliverable 13, work package 3, November 2002*. Retrieved from http://www.isrc.rhul.ac.uk/shaman/docs/d13a3v1.pdf

Shannon, C. E. (1949). Communication theory of secrecy system. *The Bell System Technical Journal, 28*, 656–715.

Shih, C.-H., Kuo, J.-L., Huang, C.-H., & Chen, Y.-C. (2011). A proxy-based fast handover scheme for hierarchical mobile IPv6. In *Proceedings of the 5th International Conference on Ubiquitous Information Management and Communication*, (pp. 21:1–21:10). New York, NY: ACM.

Shimpi, A. L. (2012). AMD outlines HSA roadmap: Unified memory for CPU/GPU in 2013, HSA GPUs in 2014. *AnandTech.com*. Retrieved 25th of September, 2012 from http://www.anandtech.com/show/5493/amd-outlines-hsa-roadmap-unified-memory-for-cpugpu-in-2013-hsa-gpus-in-2014

Shin, D., & Ahn, G.-J. (2005). Role-based privilege and trust management. *Computer Systems Science and Engineering Journal, 20*(6), 401–410.

Silva, R. M., Crespo, R. G., & Nunes, M. S. (2010). Enhanced chaotic stream cipher for WSNs. In *Proceedings of the IEEE International Conference on Availability, Reliability and Security*, (pp. 210-215). IEEE.

Silva, R. M., Crespo, R. G., & Nunes, M. S. (2009). LoBa128, a lorenz based PRNG for wireless sensor networks. *International Journal of Communication Networks and Distributed Systems, 3*(4), 301–318. doi:10.1504/IJCNDS.2009.027596.

Sinclair, S., & Smith, S. W. (2008). Preventive directions for insider threat mitigation using access control. In Stolfo, S., Bellovin, S. M., Hershkop, S., Keromytis, A. D., Sinclair, S., & Smith, W. (Eds.), *Insider Attack and Cyber Security: Beyond the Hacker*. London: Springer. doi:10.1007/978-0-387-77322-3_10.

Sivathanu, G., Wright, C. P., & Zadok, E. (2005). Ensuring data integrity in storage: techniques and applications. In *Proceedings of the 2005 ACM Workshop on Storage Security and Survivability* (pp. 26-36). New York, NY: ACM.

Socek, D., Li, S., Magliveras, S. S., & Furht, B. (2005). Enhanced 1-D chaotic key based algorithm for image encryption. In *Proceedings of the IEEE Security and Privacy for Emerging Areas in Communications Networks* (pp. 406-407). IEEE.

Soliman, H., Castelluccia, C., ElMalki, K., & Bellier, L. (2008). *Hierarchical mobile IPv6 (HMIPv6) mobility management*. Internet Engineering Task Force (IETF), Request for Comments: 5380. Retrieved from http://tools.ietf.org/html/rfc5380

Sommer, R., & Paxson, V. (2003). Enhancing byte-level network intrusion detection signatures with context. In *Proceedings of the 10th ACM Conference on Computer and Communications Security* (pp. 262-271). ACM Press.

Sommer, R., & Paxson, V. (2010). Outside the closed world: On using machine learning for network intrusion detection. In *Proceedings of the 2010 IEEE Symposium on Security and Privacy* (pp. 305-316). IEEE Press.

Song, D., Wagner, D., & Perrig, A. (2000). Practical techniques for searches on encrypted data. In *Proceedings of the IEEE Symposium on Research in Security and Privacy*, (pp. 44-55). Oakland, CA: IEEE.

Sponchioni, R. (2011). *RMAS (run-time malware analysis system)*. Paper presented at the IT Security for the Next Generation International Students Conference, Kaspersky International Cup 2011. New York, NY.

Srivastava, A., & Giffin, J. (2008). Tamper-resistant, application-aware blocking of malicious network connections. In *Proceedings of the 11th International Symposium on Recent Advances in Intrusion Detection* (pp. 39-58). Berlin: Springer-Verlag.

Stapp, M., & Volz, B. (2006). Resolution of fully qualified domain name (FQDN) conflicts among dynamic host configuration protocol (DHCP) clients. *RFC*. Retrieved October 2006, from http://www.ietf.org/rfc/rfc4703.txt

Stavroulakis, P. (2006). *Chaos applications in telecommunications*. Boca Raton, FL: CRC.

Stinson, E., & Mitchell, J. C. (2008). Towards systematic evaluation of the evadability of bot/botnet detection methods. In D. Boneh, T. Garfinkel, & D. Song (Eds.), *Proceedings of the 2nd Conference on USENIX Workshop on Offensive Technologies*. Berkeley, CA: USENIX Association.

Storage Networking Industry Association. (n.d.). *Homepage*. Retrieved from http://www.snia.org

Sujatha, P. K., Kannan, A., Ragunath, S., Bargavi, K. S., & Githanjali, S. (2008). A behavior based approach to host-level intrusion detection using self-organizing maps. In *Proceedings of the First International Conference on Emerging Trends in Engineering and Technology* (pp. 1267-1271). Washington, DC: IEEE Computer Society.

Takabi, H., Joshi, J. B. D., & Ahn, G.-J. (2010). Security and privacy challenges in cloud computing environments. *IEEE Security and Privacy, 8*(6), 24–31. doi:10.1109/MSP.2010.186.

Takemori, K., Fujinaga, M., Sayama, T., & Nishigaki, M. (2009). Host-based traceback, tracking bot and C&C server. In *Proceedings of the 3rd International Conference on Ubiquitous Information Management and Communication* (pp. 400-405). New York, NY: ACM.

Takemori, K., Nishigaki, M., Tomohiro, T., & Yutaka, M. (2008). Detection of bot infected PCs using destination-based IP and domain whitelists during a non-operating term. In *Proceedings of the 2008 Global Communications Conference* (pp. 2072-2077). Washington, DC: IEEE Computer Society.

Tao, S., Ruili, W., & Yixun, Y. (1998). Perturbance-based algorithm to expand cycle length of chaotic key stream. *Electronics Letters, 34*(9), 873–874. doi:10.1049/el:19980680.

Tauber, A. (2012). *Cross-border certified electronic mailing*. (Thesis). Graz University of Technology, Graz, Austria.

Tauber, A. (2011). A survey of certified mail systems provided on the Internet. *Computers & Security, 30*(6-7), 464–485. doi:10.1016/j.cose.2011.05.001.

Tedesco, G., & Aickelin, U. (2008). Real-time alert correlation with type graphs. In *Proceedings of the 4th International Conference on Information Systems Security* (pp. 173-187). Springer-Verlag.

The Internet Rights Forum. (2003). Retrieved from http://www.forumInternet.org/telechargement/documents/reco-evote-en-20030926.pdf

Thomson, S., Narten, T., & Jinmei, T. (2007). *IPv6 stateless address autoconfiguration*. RFC 4862. Internet Engineering Task Force (IETF). Retrieved from http://tools.ietf.org/html/rfc4862

Tracker, S. (n.d.). *VMWare shared folder bug lets local users on the guest OS gain elevated privileges on the host OS*. Security Tracker ID: 1019493. Retrieved from http://securitytracker.com/id/1019493

Troan, O., & Droms, R. (2003). IPv6 prefix options for dynamic host configuration protocol (DHCP) version 6. *RFC*. Retrieved December 2003, from http://www.ietf.org/rfc/rfc3633.txt

Trusted Computing Group (TCG). (2010). *Cloud computing and security- A natural match*. Retrieved from http://www.trustedcomputinggroup.org

Tuck, N., Sherwood, T., Calder, B., & Varghese, G. (2004). Deterministic memory-efficient string matching algorithms for intrusion detection. In *Proceedings of INFOCOM* (pp. 2628-2639). IEEE.

Tvrdik, P. (2012). *Parallel complexity theory: CS838: Topics in parallel computing, CS1221*. Retrieved 26th of September, 2012 from http://pages.cs.wisc.edu/~tvrdik/3/html/Section3.html

UPnP Forum. (2011). *UPnP device protection service* (Technical report). Retrieved from http://upnp.org/specs/gw/deviceprotection1.w3c-widget

Valdes, A., & Skinner, K. (2001). Probabilistic alert correlation. In *Proceedings of the 4th International Symposium on Recent Advances in Intrusion Detection* (pp. 54-68). Springer-Verlag.

Valeur, F., Vigna, G., Kruegel, C., & Kemmerer, R. A. (2004). Comprehensive approach to intrusion detection alert correlation. *IEEE Transactions on Dependable and Secure Computing, 1*(3), 146–169. doi:10.1109/TDSC.2004.21.

Vaquero, L. M., Rodero-Merino, L., & Morán, D. (2011). Locking the sky: A survey on IaaS cloud security. *Journal of Computing – Cloud Computing, 91*(1), 93-118.

Vasiliadis, G., & Ioannidis, S. (2010). GrAVity: A massively parallel antivirus engine. In *Proceedings of the 13th International Conference on Recent Advances in Intrusion Detection (RAID)* (pp. 79-96). Berlin: Springer-Verlag.

Vasiliadis, G., Polychronakis, M., & Ioannidis, S. (2011). MIDeA: A multi-parallel intrusion detection architecture. In *Proceedings of the 18th ACM Conference on Computer and Communications Security (CCS)* (pp. 297-308). ACM.

Viega, J., & McGrew, D. (2005). *The use of galois/counter mode (GCM) in IPsec encapsulating security payload (ESP)*. IETF Request for Comments: 4106. Retrieved from http://tools.ietf.org/html/rfc4106

Vigna, G., & Kruegel, C. (2005). Host-based intrusion detection. In *Handbook of Information Security (Vol. III)*. New York: John Wiley & Sons.

Vinod, P., Laxmi, V., & Gaur, M. S. (2009). Survey on malware detection methods. In *Proceedings of the IIT Kanpur Hackers' Workshop 2009 (IITKHACK09)*. Retrieved 16th of January, 2013 from http://www.security.iitk.ac.in/contents/events/workshops/iitkhack09/papers/vinod.pdf

Vixie, P., Gudmundsson, O., Eastlake, D., III, & Wellington, B. (2000). Secret key transaction authentication for DNS (TSIG). *RFC*. Retrieved May 2000, from http://www.ietf.org/rfc/rfc2845.txt

Vogt, C., Bless, R., Doll, M., & Kuefner, T. (2004). *Early binding updates for mobile IPv6*. Expired Internet Engineering Task Force (IETF) Internet draft. Retrieved from http://tools.ietf.org/html/draft-vogt-mip6-early-binding-updates-00

Wang, C., Lan, C., Niu, S., & Cao, X. (2011). An id-based certified e-mail protocol suitable for wireless mobile environments. In *Proceedings of the 2011 Fourth International Symposium on Parallel Architectures, Algorithms and Programming* (pp. 146-150). Washington, DC: IEEE Computer Society.

Wang, C., Yang, X., Lan, C., & Cao, X. (2009). An efficient identity-based certified e-mail protocol. In *Proceedings of the 2009 Fifth International Conference on Intelligent Information Hiding and Multimedia Signal Processing* (pp. 1197-1200). Washington, DC: IEEE Computer Society.

Wang, H., Ou, Y., Ling, J., Xu, X., & Guo, H. (2007). A new certified email protocol. In *Proceedings of the 18th International Conference on Database and Expert Systems Applications* (pp. 683-687). Washington, DC: IEEE Computer Society.

Wang, J., Wang, Z., & Dai, K. (2004). A network intrusion detection system based on the artificial neural networks. In *Proceedings of the 3rd International Conference on Information Security* (pp. 166-170). ACM Press.

Wang, G., Bao, F., & Zhou, J. (2005). On the security of a certified e-mail scheme. In *Proceedings of Progress in Cryptology - Indocrypt 2004* (Vol. 3348, pp. 48–60). Berlin: Springer. doi:10.1007/978-3-540-30556-9_5.

Wang, W., Zhang, X., & Gombault, S. (2009). Constructing attribute weights from computer audit data for effective intrusion detection. *Journal of Systems and Software*, 82(12), 1974–1981. doi:10.1016/j.jss.2009.06.040.

Watson, W. B. (1994). *The performance of single-keyword and multiple-keyword pattern matching algorithms*. Retrieved 27th of September, 2012 from http://alexandria.tue.nl/extra1/wskrap/publichtml/9411074.pdf

Watson, W. B. (1995). *Taxonomies and toolkits of regular language algorithms*. Eindhoven, The Netherlands: Eindhoven University of Technology, Department of Mathematics and Computer Science.

Webinos Consortium. (2011). *User expectations on security and privacy phase 1, February 2011*. Retrieved from http://Webinos.org/content/Webinos-User_Expectations_on_Security_and_Privacy_v1.pdf

Webinos Consortium. (2012). *Phase 2 platform Specifications: Policy*. Retrieved from http://webinos.org

Webinos Consortium. (2012). *Phase 2 API specification*. Retrieved from http://Webinos.org/blog/2012/09/24/Webinos-report-phase-ii-api-specifications

Webinos Consortium. (2012). *The webinos project website*. Retrieved from http://Webinos.org/

Webinos Consortium. (2012). *Updates on scenarios and use-cases*. Retrieved from http://www.webinos.org/wp-content/uploads/2012/06/D2.4-Updates-on-Scenarios-and-Use-Cases.public.pdf

Wellington, B. (2000). Secure domain name system (DNS) dynamic update. *RFC*. Retrieved November 2000, from http://www.ietf.org/rfc/rfc3007.txt

White, H. C. (1992). *Identity and control: A structural theory of social action*. Princeton, NJ: Princeton University Press.

Compilation of References

Whitten, A., & Tygar, J. D. (1999). Why Johnny can't encrypt: A usability evaluation of PGP 5.0. In *Proceedings of the 8th Conference on USENIX Security Symposium*, (pp. 169–184). Berkeley, CA: USENIX Association.

Wholesale Application Community. (2012). *WAC core specifications 2.1: Security and privacy*. Retrieved from http://specs.wacapps.net/core/

Woo, T. Y. C., & Lam, S. S. (1993). A semantic model for authentication protocols. In *Proceedings IEEE Symposium on Research in Security and Privacy*, (pp. 178-194). Oakland, CA: IEEE.

World Wide Web Consortium. (2008). *XML signature syntax and processing* (2nd ed). Retrieved from http://www.w3.org/TR/xmldsig-core/

World Wide Web Consortium. (W3C). (2011, August 11). *XML digital signatures for widgets, W3C proposed recommendation*. Retrieved from http://www.w3.org/TR/2011/PR-widgets-digsig-20110811/

World, C. (2008). *Extended gmail outage hits apps admins*. Retrieved from http://www.computerworld.com/s/article/9117322/Extended_Gmail_outage_hits_Apps_admins

World, P. C. (2007). *Salesforce.com warns customers of phishing scam*. Retrieved from http://www.pcworld.com/businesscenter/article/139353/article.html

Wu, S., & Manber, U. (1994). *A fast algorithm for multi-pattern searching* (Technical Report TR-94-17). Phoenix, AZ: University of Arizona.

Xen Vulnerability. (n.d.). Retrieved from http://secunia.com/advisories/26986/

Xiang, T. (2007). A novel symmetrical cryptosystem based on discretized two-dimensional chaotic map. *Physics Letters. [Part A], 364*(3-4), 252–258. doi:10.1016/j.physleta.2006.12.020.

Xiong, H., Malhotra, P., Stefan, D., Wu, C., & Yao, D. (2009). User-assisted host-based detection of outbound malware traffic. In *Proceedings of the 11th International Conference on Information and Communications Security* (pp. 293-307). Berlin: Springer-Verlag.

Xu, D., & Ning, P. (2006). A flexible approach to intrusion alert anonymization and correlation. In *Proceedings of the 2nd International Conference on Security and Privacy in Communication Networks and the Workshops* (pp. 1-10). IEEE Press.

Xu, J., Ning, P., Kil, C., Zhai, Y., & Bookholt, C. (2005). Automatic diagnosis and response to memory corruption vulnerabilities. In *Proceedings of the 12th ACM Conference on Computer and Communication Security* (pp. 223-234). ACM Press.

Yang, J., Sar, C., Twohey, P., Cadar, C., & Engler, D. (2006). Automatically generating malicious disks using symbolic execution. In *Proceedings of the 2006 IEEE Symposium on Security and Privacy* (pp. 243-257). ACM Press.

Yang, J., Xiao, D., & Xiang, T. (2011). Cryptanalysis of a chaos block cipher for wireless sensor network. *Communications in Nonlinear Science and Numerical Simulation, 16*, 844–850. doi:10.1016/j.cnsns.2010.05.005.

Yen, J. C., & Guo, J. I. (2000). A new chaotic key-based design for image encryption and decryption. In *Proceedings of 2000 IEEE International Conference on Circuits and Systems* (ISACS 2000), (vol. 4, pp. 49–52). IEEE.

Yokota, H., Chowdhury, K., Koodli, R., Patil, B., & Xia, F. (2010). *Fast handovers for proxy mobile IPv6*. Internet Engineering Task Force (IETF), Request for Comments: 5949. Retrieved from http://tools.ietf.org/html/rfc5949

Yoo, H., Tolentino, R. S., Park, B., Chang, B. Y., & Kim, S.-H. (2009). ES-FHMIPv6: An efficient scheme for fast handover over HMIPv6 networks. *International Journal of Future Generation Communication and Networking, 2*(2), 11–24.

Yu, F., Alkhalaf, M., & Bultan, T. (2009). *Generating vulnerability signatures for string manipulating programs using automata-based forward and backward symbolic analyses* (Technical Report 2009-11). UCSB CS.

Zaibi, G., Peyrard, F., Kachouri, A., Fournier-Prunaret, D., & Samet, M. (2010). A new design of dynamic S-box based on two chaotic maps. In *Proceedings of the ACS/IEEE International Conference on Computer Systems and Applications - AICCSA 2010* (AICCSA '10). IEEE Computer Society.

Zaidi, F., Bayse, E., & Cavalli, A. (2009). Network protocol interoperability testing based on contextual signatures and passive testing. In *Proceedings of the 2009 ACM Symposium on Applied Computing* (pp. 2-7). ACM Press.

Zanero, S. (2004). Behavioral intrusion detection. In *Proceedings of the 19th International Symposium of Computer and Information Sciences (ISCIS)* (pp. 657-666). ISCIS.

Zaslawskiy, I., Abtisyan, A., & Gevorgyan, V. (2010). Implementation of dictionary lookup automata for UNL analysis. *International Journal Information Theories and Applications, 17*(2), 141–150.

Zetter, K. (2010). Google hackers targeted source code of more than 30 companies. *Wired Threat Level*. Retrieved from http://www.wired.com/threatlevel/2010/01/google-hack-attack/

Zha, X. (2011). Multipattern string matching on a GPU. In *Proceedings of the IEEE Symposium on Computers and Communications (ISCC)* (pp. 277-282). IEEE.

Zha, X., & Sahni, S. (2010). Fast in-place file carving for digital forensics. In *Proceedings of the e-Forensics'10* (pp. 141-158). E-Forensics.

Zhang, X., Oh, S., & Sandhu, R. (2003). PBDM: A flexible delegation model in RBAC. In *Proceedings of the Eighth ACM Symposium on Access Control Models and Technologies SACMAT 2003*, (pp. 149-157). ACM.

Zhang, F., Safavi-Naini, R., & Susilo, W. (2003). Efficient verifiably encrypted signature and partially blind signature from bilinear pairings. In *Proceedings of Progress in Cryptology - Indocrypt 2003* (Vol. 2904, pp. 191–204). Berlin: Springer. doi:10.1007/978-3-540-24582-7_14.

Zhang, Y., & Joshi, J. (2009). Access control and trust management for emerging multidomain environments. In Upadhyay, S., & Rao, R. O. (Eds.), *Annals of Emerging Research in Information Assurance, Security and Privacy Services* (pp. 421–452). Dublin, Ireland: Emerald Group Publishing.

Zha, X., & Sahni, S. (2011). Fast in-place file carving for digital forensics. In *Proceedings of Forensics in Telecommunications, Information, and Multimedia* (pp. 141–158). Berlin: Springer-Verlag. doi:10.1007/978-3-642-23602-0_13.

Zheng, Y. (1997). Digital signcryption or how to achieve cost (signature & encryption) << cost(signature) + cost(encryption). In *Proceedings of the 17th Annual International Cryptology Conference on Advances in Cryptology* (pp. 165-179). London, UK: Springer-Verlag.

Zhikui, C. (2007). *A privacy enabled service authorization based on a user-centric virtual identity management system*. Paper presented at the Communications and Networking in China, 2007. Beijing, China.

Zhou, J., Carlson, A., & Bishop, M. (2005). Verify results of network intrusion alerts using lightweight protocol analysis. In *Proceedings of the 21st Annual Computer Security Applications Conference* (pp. 117-126). ACM Press.

Zhou, J. (2004). On the security of a multi-party certified email protocol.[). Berlin: Springer.]. *Proceedings of Information and Communications Security, 3269*, 277–280.

Zhou, J., Deng, R., & Bao, F. (2000). Some remarks on a fair exchange protocol.[). Berlin: Springer.]. *Proceedings of Public Key Cryptography, 1751*, 46–57. doi:10.1007/978-3-540-46588-1_4.

Zhou, J., & Gollmann, D. (1996). Certified electronic mail. In *Proceedings of Computer Security ESORICS 96* (Vol. 1146, pp. 160–171). Berlin: Springer. doi:10.1007/3-540-61770-1_35.

Zhou, L., & Haas, Z. J. (1999). Securing ad hoc networks. *IEEE Network, 13*(6), 24–30. doi:10.1109/65.806983.

Zhou, T., Yu, M., & Ye, Y. (2006). A robust high-speed chaos-based truly random number generator for embedded cryptosystems. In *Proceeding of Circuits and Systems*. IEEE. doi:10.1109/MWSCAS.2006.381785.

Zhou, V. C., Leckie, C., & Karunasekera, S. (2010). A survey of coordinated attacks and collaborative intrusion detection. *Computers & Security, 29*(1), 124–140. doi:10.1016/j.cose.2009.06.008.

Ziminski, T. B., De la Rosa Algarín, A., Saripalle, R., Demurjian, S. A., & Jackson, E. (2012). SMARTSync: Towards patient-driven medication reconciliation using the SMART framework. In *Proceedings of 2012 International Workshop on Biomedical and Health Informatics (BHI 2012)*, (pp. 806-813). BHI.

About the Contributors

Antonio Ruiz Martínez is an assistant lecturer in the Department of Information and Communications Engineering at the University of Murcia (Spain). He also serves as ViceDean of Quality Affairs and Innovation at the Faculty of Computer Science. He received B.E., M.E., and Ph.D. degrees in Computer Sciences from the University of Murcia. His main research interests include electronic commerce, electronic payment systems, security, privacy, electronic government, and Web services, where he has participated in several research projects in the national and international areas. He has published several papers in international conferences and journals. He also serves as a technical program committee member in various conferences and is a reviewer and member of the editorial board in several international journals.

Fernando Pereñíguez-García is a post-doctoral researcher within the Department of Information and Communications Engineering at the University of Murcia. He received B.E., M.E., and Ph.D. degrees in Computer Sciences from University of Murcia in 2007, 2008, and 2011, respectively. He has participated in several projects funded by the Spanish government and the European Union such as Walkie-Talkie, ITSSv6, and INTER-TRUST. Additionally, he has been involved in standardization activities within the IETF and served as technical program committee in several international conferences. His research interests include security, privacy, and handoff management in mobile networks

Rafael Marín-López is an assistant lecturer in the Department of Information and Communications Engineering at the University of Murcia (Spain). He received B.E., M.E., and Ph.D. degrees in Computer Sciences from the University of Murcia in 1998, 2000, and 2008, respectively. He visited as intern researcher Toshiba America Research, Inc (TARI) in New Jersey (USA) for a year (2005-2006). He has collaborated actively in standardization within the IETF (PANA WG, EAP WG, HOKEY WG, ABFAB WG) and the IEEE 802.21a Task Group as co-author of the standard IEEE 802.21a-2012TM. He has also participated in several EU funded projects such as Euro6IX, Daidalos I & II, ENABLE, and GN3. He is author of several patents, as well as journals and conference papers. His main research interests include network access authentication, key distribution, and security in mobile networks.

* * *

Ahmad AlSa'deh is a PhD student at the Hasso-plattner-Institut at the University of Potsdam, Germany. His research interests include networking security, particularly IPv6 security. AlSa'deh has a MSc. in scientific computing from Birzeit University in Palestine.

About the Contributors

Tayo Arulogun is a Senior Lecturer in Computer Science and Engineering at Ladoke Akintola University of Technology (LAUTECH), Ogbomoso. He is also the Director of LAUTECH Information and Communication Technology Center. Tayo received PhD in Computer science from Ladoke Akintola University of Technology, Ogbomoso, in 2009. His research interests include networks security, mobile IPv6, wireless sensor network applications for development.

Andrea Atzeni is a postdoctoral researcher at the Politecnico di Torino. He received his doctorate in the area of risk analysis and security evaluation. His published papers address the topics of anonymity and privacy, risk analysis, security metrics, security modelisation, semi-automatic reactions to failts and usable security. He participated in a number of EU FP Projects (TESI, POSITIF, DESEREC, NEW-COM++) addressing how to model and evaluate security in complex and dependable networks, and to trigger reactions in dangerous situations, through formal description of system components and behaviour. Currently, is the technical leader for Politecnico di Torino in the EU FP7 Webinos project, where he contributed to, among the others, the security and privacy architecture and requirements, the threat analysis, the security and privacy user expectations and their impact on the Webinos security framework.

Alexandre B. Augusto got his MSc in engineering of networks and informatics systems at the Department of Computer Science on the Faculty of Science of the University of Porto, Portugal. He is currently a researcher in the field of identity and access management and also an associated member of CRACS Research Unit, a partner of INESC TEC Porto where he is responsible to research authentication, authorization and data aggregation methods related to identity and access management based on user centricity. He also has a special interesting on mobile devices, health informatics systems and computer security with a special focus on the privacy and anonymity.

Md. Abdul Based was born on 01.01.1979. In 2008, he graduated (MSc) in Information and Communication Systems Security at the Department of Computer and System Science at the Royal Institute of Technology (KTH), Stockholm, Sweden. His Master's thesis title was "Information Handling in Security Solution Decisions." This thesis was part of the VRIEND (Value-Based Security Risk Mitigation in Enterprise Networks that are Decentralized) project. He is now a Research Fellow (PhD) at the Telematics department in the Norwegian University of Science and Technology (NTNU), Trondheim, Norway. His research topic is "Security Aspects of Internet Voting." His scientific research is focusing on information security, electronic voting, cryptography, and network security.

Vít Bukač is employed as an IT Security Analyst and a member of Security Operations Center and Security Center of Excellence at Honeywell Technology Solutions, Brno, CZ, responsible for proactive threat detection and incident response. Previously, he gained experience with systems security and management in large-scale environments as an Enterprise Active Directory administrator at Institute of Computer Science, Masaryk University. He participated on numerous research projects for the Ministry of the Interior of the Czech Republic and for several private companies. He received Master's degree in IT security in 2010 at Faculty of Informatics, Masaryk University, where he currently pursues his PhD studies at the Centre for Research on Cryptography and Security under supervision of prof. Vashek Matyáš. His primary areas of research interest are intrusion detection systems, incident forensics and network security with emphasis on denial of service attacks.

About the Contributors

Manuel E. Correia got his MSc in foundations of advanced information processing technologies from the Imperial College of London in 1992 and his Phd in Computer Science from Oporto University in 2001. He is currently a lecturer at the Department of Computer Science of the Faculty of Science of Oporto University and a researcher in the field of computer security at the CRACS group of INESC TEC Porto where he is responsible for research projects related to anomaly detection and identity management and the security aspects of several industry contracts. He is also consultant for some Portuguese public agencies (Health and Education) in computer security.

Steven A. Demurjian is a Full Professor and Director of Graduate Studies in Computer Science & Engineering at the University of Connecticut, and co-Director of Research Informatics for the Biomedical Informatics Division, with research interests of: collaborative security and access control models for role-based, mandatory, and discretionary approaches with security assurance for UML, XML, and cloud computing; biomedical informatics and software architectures for health information exchange; secure software engineering with UML; and, ontology design and development models and methodologies. Dr. Steven A. Demurjian has over 140 archival publications, in the following categories: 1 book, 2 edited collections, 48 journal articles and book chapters, and 94 refereed conference/workshop articles.

Gerard Draper obtained a Telecommunications Technical Engineer degree in 2003, at the University of the Balearic Islands (UIB), and a Telecommunications Engineer degree in 2007 from the Polytechnic University of Catalonia (UPC). He has been twice ERASMUS student (2002 - KATHO, Belgium; 2006 - NTNU, Norway). Since September 2008, he is a PhD student at the department of Mathematical Sciences and Information Technology at the UIB. In 2010, he spent 5 months at the Institute for Infocomm Research (Singapore) under the supervision of Jianying Zhou, and in 2012, he spent 3 months at the Institute for Applied Information Processing and Communications (IAIK) in Graz, Austria, under the supervision of Arne Tauber. His current research interests include Web Services security, electronic contracting, fair exchange, certified e-mail security, and network and e-commerce security. Before starting his PhD, he worked at Dome-Consulting as software analyst and developer.

Shamal Faily is a post-doctoral researcher at the University of Oxford. His research explores how the design of interactive secure systems can be better supported with design techniques and software tools. This research has led to the development of the open-source CAIRIS (Computer Aided Integration of Requirements and Information Security) software tool. Shamal currently works on the EU FP7 Webinos project, where he has devised approaches for building user-expectations about security and privacy into the design of the Webinos software architecture. He has a DPhil in Computer Science from the University of Oxford, and a BSc in Business Computing Systems from City University, London.

Josep-Lluís Ferrer-Gomila received his M.S. in Telecommunications Engineering in 1991, from the Universitat Politècnica de Catalunya, and his Ph.D. in Computer Science in 1998, from the Universitat de les Illes Balears. He is an Assistant Professor at the Computer Science Department of the Universitat de les Illes Balears. His research work is centered in the area of Network Security, leading some national projects in this area. He is author of several articles published in national and international conferences and international journals.

About the Contributors

Daniele Fournier-Prunaret is a permanent professor at INSA Toulouse in France and is actually at the Laboratory for Analysis and Architecture of Systems (LAAS-CNRS). She works on analysis of nonlinear dynamical systems, mainly models using low-dimensional maps. She has several international cooperations with Tokushima University in Japan, University College Dublin in Ireland and University of Evora in Portugal, among others. She has authored or co-authored around 100 papers in International Journals and Conferences.

M. Francisca Hinarejos received her Ph.D. in Computer Science in 2010, from the Technical University of Catalonia (UPC). Since 2007, she has been an assistant professor in the Department of Mathematics and Computer Science of the University of the Balearic Islands, Spain. Her research interests include network security, electronic commerce and security in constrained environments.

Abdennaceur Kachouri was born in Kerkennah (Sfax, Tunisia) in 1954. He received the engineering diploma from National school of Engineering of Sfax in 1981, a Master degree in Measurement and Instrumentation from National school of Bordeaux (ENSERB) of France in 1981, a Doctorate in Measurement and Instrumentation from ENSERB, in 1983. He works in Wireless Sensor Networks and Biomedical Signal Processing and Control with several cooperation research groups in Tunisia and France. Currently, he is Permanent Professor at ENIS School of Engineering and member of the LETI Laboratory ENIS Sfax.

Robert Kuykendall received his B.S. in Computer Science from Texas State University. He spent his summer 2012 as a Research Experiences for Undergraduates scholar, along with Yaira K. Rivera Sánchez, at the University of Connecticut, conducting research and development on a mobile health application for medication management with a focus on patient sharing, and the security criteria of the potential scenarios. His research interests include cloud and ubiquitous computing, human-computer interaction, data mining, and the underlying security (cryptography, privacy preservation, information hiding)-access control (role-based, discretionary, mandatory) enforcement aspects of these areas, and their implications in the biomedical and health care domains.

Lam-for Kwok received his Ph.D. degree in Information Security from Queensland University of Technology, Australia. He is currently an Associate Professor of the Department of Computer Science at City University of Hong Kong. His research interests include information security and management, intrusion detection systems, and computers in education. He has extensive teaching and academic planning experience. He is the Associate Director of the AIMtech Centre (Centre for Innovative Applications of Internet and Multimedia Technologies) and the InPAC Centre (Internet Security and PKI Application Centre) at City University of Hong Kong. He actively serves the academic and professional communities and has been acting as program chairs and organising chairs of international conferences, assessors, and panel judges of various awards. He is a Fellow of Hong Kong Institution of Engineers and British Computer Society.

Martin von Löwis is a lecturer at the University of Potsdam's Hasso-Plattner-Institut in the Operating Systems and Middleware Group. His research interests include compiler construction and embedded systems, as well as IPv6 and public-key infrastructure. Löwis has a PhD in computer science from the Humboldt-University in Berlin.

About the Contributors

John Lyle is a postdoctoral researcher at the University of Oxford. He received his doctorate in the area of trustworthy computing: his thesis assessed the practicality of applying trusted computing principles to secure Web services. He is currently working on the EU FP7 Webinos project, participating in the design of the security and privacy architecture as well as in standardisation, platform implementation, and requirements engineering activities. He has been published in a range of journal, conference, and workshop proceedings on subjects including model driven security, software engineering, public key cryptography, provenance, access control, and trustworthy computing. He also holds a MEng from Imperial College London.

Václav (Vashek) Matyáš is a Professor at the Masaryk University, Brno, CZ, and Vice-Dean for Foreign Affairs and External Relations, Faculty of Informatics. His research interests relate to applied cryptography and security, where he published over a hundred peer-reviewed papers and articles, and co-authoring six books. He was a Fulbright-Masaryk Visiting Scholar with Harvard University, Center for Research on Computation and Society in 2011-12, and also worked with Microsoft Research Cambridge, University College Dublin, Ubilab at UBS AG, and was a Royal Society Postdoctoral Fellow with the Cambridge University Computer Lab. Vashek was one of the Editors-in-Chief of the *Identity in the Information Society* journal, and he also edited the *Computer and Communications Security Reviews*, and worked on the development of Common Criteria and with ISO/IEC JTC1 SC27. He received his PhD degree from Masaryk University.

Christoph Meinel is a professor and director of the Hasso-plattner-Institut at the University of Potsdam, where he leads the Internet Technologies and Systems research group. His research focuses on Future Internet Technologies, in particular Internet and Information Security, Web 3.0: Semantic, Social and Service Web, as well as innovative Internet Applications, especially in the domains of e-Learning and Telemedicine. He is author or co-author of 12 books, and editor of various conference proceedings. He has published more than 380 papers in high-level scientific journals and at international conferences. Meinel has a PhD in computer science from Humboldt University in Berlin.

Yuxin Meng received his bachelor's degree in computer science (information security) from Nanjing University of Posts and Telecommunications, China in 2009. He is currently working toward the PhD degree in the Department of Computer Science, City University of Hong Kong, Hong Kong. His research interests are information security, such as network security, intrusion detection, Web security, vulnerability, and malware detection, cloud technology in security, access control, and mobile authentication. He is also interested in cryptography, especially its use in network protocols. In addition, he is working on the application of intelligent technology in information security. He has actively served as the reviewers for many conferences and journals.

Viorel Negru (b. September 16, 1955) is a Full Professor at the Computer Science Department from the Mathematics and Computer Science Faculty, West University of Timisoara, Romania, and senior researcher at E-Austria Institute Timisoara, Romania. He has a Ph. D. in Computer Science from the 'Babes-Bolyai' University, Cluj-Napoca, Romania. He published more than 130 papers in journals or conference volumes, most of them in the topic of Artificial Intelligence. He has actively participated in more than 50 research projects and coordinated more than 15 of them. His research areas include artificial intelligence, intelligent systems, multi-agent systems, data mining, recommender systems, intelligent ambient, risk management, distributed computing and computational mathematics. He is member of the ACM, IEEE, and ARIA – Romanian Association of Artificial Intelligence.

Fabrice Peyrard was born in Tahiti (Papeete) in 1972. After university studies, he received the Ph.D. degree in computer science in 1998. He is associate professor in the Network and Telecommunication department at the Technological University Institute of Toulouse. Since 2008, he had the habilitation to supervise research at University of Toulouse in France, in IRIT-CNRS Lab in the field of wireless local network communications. He works on security and quality of service of wireless networks for embedded, industrial, and real-time systems for aerospace and healthcare applications. He is an IEEE member in both communication and computer societies.

Ciprian Pungilă (b. January 16, 1984) is a lecturer at the Computer Science Department from the Mathematics and Computer Science Faculty, West University of Timişoara, Romania and a researcher at E-Austria Institute Timişoara, Romania. He has earned a B. Sc. in Mathematics and Informatics from the same faculty (from where he also received later on a M. Sc. degree in Artificial Intelligence and Distributed Systems), a B. Sc. in Software Engineering from the "Politehnica" Technical University of Timişoara and also holds a Ph. D. in Computer Science from the same university where he is lecturing at. He has participated in multiple national and international research projects at his university or the E-Austria Institute, Timişoara, Romania. His research interests include heterogeneous systems, optimization algorithms, pattern matching, and software engineering.

Hosnieh Rafiee is a PhD student at Hasso-Plattner-Institut at the University of Potsdam. Her research interests are in network security including integration of privacy and security in IPv6 networks and the authentication problems that occur in the application layer services such as DNS and email and the deployment of SEcure Neighbor Discovery (SEND). Rafiee has a MSc in IT-Computer networks engineering from Amirkabir University of Technology in Tehran.

Alberto De la Rosa Algarín is a third year Ph.D. student of Computer Science & Engineering at the University of Connecticut, with Dr. Steven A. Demurjian as major advisor. His research interests include: security and information assurance by utilizing document-level security, privacy enforcement, security policy integration and automatic generation, security and knowledge modeling, secure information and data engineering, identity-inferred access control. His current research focuses on UML metamodel extensions for XML security and policy integration, with the end purpose of defining a software engineering process for integrated information exchange meta-systems. He received a B.S., with a major in Computer Science and a second major in Mathematics, from the University of Puerto Rico, where he had research experiences involving software engineering and reliable distributed systems.

Mounir Samet was born in Sfax, Tunisia, in 1955. He obtained an Engineering Diploma from National school of Engineering of Sfax in 1981, a Master degree in Measurement and Instrumentation from National school of Bordeaux (ENSERB) of France in 1981, a Doctorate in Measurement and Instrumentation from ENSERB in 1981, and the Habilitation Degree (Post Doctorate degree) in 1998. He works on several cooperation with medical research groups in Tunisia and France. Currently, he is Permanent Professor at ENIS School of Engineering and member of the LETI Laboratory ENIS Sfax.

About the Contributors

Yaira K. Rivera Sánchez is a first year Ph.D. student at the University of Connecticut, with Dr. Steven A. Demurjian as major advisor. She obtained a B.S. in Computer Science from the University of Puerto Rico, and spent the summer of 2012 as a Research Experiences for Undergraduates scholar at the University of Connecticut, working along with Robert Kuykendall on a mobile health application for medication management with a focus on the provider version and its security. Her research interests and undergraduate research experiences include the use of Wals-Hadamard transforms to search for high-nonlinearity Boolean functions, and architectures in biomedical and health care applications.

Jaydip Sen has 18 years of experience in the field of computer and communication networks, protocol design and development, and security and privacy issues in computing. He is currently a Professor in the Department of Computer Science and Engineering in National Institute of Science and Technology, Odisha, India. He had worked with reputed organizations like Tata Consultancy Services, India, Oil and Natural Gas Corporation Ltd., India, Oracle India Pvt. Ltd., and Akamai Technology Pvt. Ltd. His broad areas of research include security in wired and wireless networks, intrusion detection systems, secure routing protocols in wireless ad hoc and sensor networks, secure multicast and broadcast communication in next generation broadband wireless networks, trust and reputation based systems, quality of service in multimedia communication in wireless networks, privacy issues in ubiquitous computing and pervasive communication. He has more than 100 publications in reputed international books, journals, and referred conference proceedings. He is a member of ACM and IEEE and an active member of IEEE 802.16 standardization group.

Klaus Stranacher finished his MSc with distinction in Telematics at the University of Technology in the year 2006. Since 2005, he is working at the E-Government Innovation Center (EGIZ) in Graz. His main activities are in the area of E-Government and IT security especially on electronic identities, electronic documents, and interoperability. During his activities, he participates in several European research projects. He was involved the European electronic identity large-scale pilot STORK (Secure IdentTity acrOss boRders linKed) and he is the leader of work package 2 (eDocuments) in the European large scale pilot SPOCS (Simple Procedures Online for Crossborder Services) under the ICT-PSP (Policy Support Programme), co-founded by EU. Additional he is working on his PhD thesis on interoperability of electronic documents, which is also his main research interest.

Arne Tauber received his Ph.D. with distinction in Telecommunications Engineering in 2012, from the Graz University of Technology. He is currently working in the field of IT security with focus on the Austrian eGovernment initiative. Arne Tauber is the head of the eGovernment Innovation Center (EGIZ), a joint initiative of the Austrian Federal Chancellery and the Graz University of Technology. EGIZ supports the Austrian Federal Chancellery in further developing the Austrian ICT-Strategy by research and innovation. Arne Tauber participated in several European research projects. He was the leader of work package 6.4 (e-Delivery pilot) of the European eIdentity large-scale pilot STORK (Secure IdentTity acrOss boRders linKed) and was involved in the European large-scale pilot SPOCS (Simple Procedures Online for Crossborder Services) in the ICT-PSP (Policy Support Programme), co-founded by EU. He also contributed to the European project GINI-SA, which works towards the vision of a Personal Identity Management environment.

Ghada Zaibi was born in Sfax in 1982. She received the engineering diploma in Electrical Engineering in 2006 and the M.Sc. degrees in Electronics and communications in 2007 from the National Engineering School of Sfax (ENIS), Sfax University. She received the Ph.D. degree in electrical engineering and computer science in 2012 from Toulouse University and Sfax University. She is member of the LETI Laboratory at ENIS Sfax. Since 2011, she is an assistant professor at the National Engineering School of Monastir (ENIM). His current research focuses on Software engineering, security, and data encryption, wireless sensor network, chaotic dynamics, and microelectronics.

Thomas Zefferer is a researcher and PhD student at Graz University of Technology. After receiving his Master degree in 2007, he has joined the Institute for Applied Information Processing and Communications (IAIK) at Graz University of Technology. He has been participating in numerous research activities in the fields of IT security and e-government including various national and international e-government projects. For several years, he has been working for the Austrian E-Government Innovation Center (EGIZ), which is also located at Graz University of Technology. His current research focus is on smartphone and mobile security in general, and on the evaluation and development of mobile government solutions in particular.

Timoteus B. Ziminski holds the degree Diplom-Informatiker from the Technische Universität Dortmund and is a Ph.D. student at the Computer Science & Engineering department at the University of Connecticut, with Dr. Steven A. Demurjian as major advisor. His research interests include software architectures with a focus on data and system integration, emphasizing on solutions that are suitable for application in the biomedical and healthcare domains. He is also interested in software engineering, design methods, and management of computational development processes. Next to pursuing research, Mr. Ziminski is also an active software developer in industry and was the lead on the SMARTSync project.

Bernd Zwattendorfer has studied Telematics and received his master's degree from Graz University of Technology. Additionally, he holds a master's degree in International Business received from University of Graz. In 2007, he joined the eGovernment Innovation Center (EGIZ) in Graz, which supports the Austrian Federal Chancellery in further developing the Austrian ICT-Strategy by research and innovation. He is currently working on several topics related to IT security and eGovernment, focusing on electronic identity and cloud computing. During his work he participated in the following EU projects: FP6 project eGov-Bus (Cross-Border eGovernment Services), LSP project STORK (Cross-Border eID Federation), GINI-SA (Vision of Personal Identity Management Environment).

Index

A

Adaptive Learner for Alert Classification (ALAC) 221
Advanced Message Queuing Protocol (AMQP) 28, 43
Authoritative Authority (AA) 270
Boyer-Moore algorithm 240, 242

C

Certified Electronic Mail (CEM) 47, 53, 70
    Mail Transfer Agent (MTA) 63
    Mail User Agent (MUA) 49
    Non-Repudiation of Delivery (NRD) 55, 65
    Non-Repudiation of Origin (NRO) 53-54, 65
    Non-Repudiation of Receipt (NRR) 53, 55, 65
    Non-Repudiation of Submission (NRS) 55, 65
    Registered Electronic Mail (REM) 56, 62, 67
    Verifiable and Recoverable Encrypted Signatures (VRES) 57
Chaotic Key-Based Algorithm (CKBA) 108
chaotic signals 105, 123
    continuous chaotic systems 105-106
    discrete time chaotic systems 105-106
    Piecewise Linear Chaotic Map (PWLCM) 106
Clinical Document Architecture (CDA) 334-335
cloud computing 1-3, 6-10, 12-14, 16-38, 40-43, 207-208, 210, 334-335
    community cloud 2
    hybrid cloud 2, 6, 42-43
    private cloud 2, 5-6, 29, 43-44
    public cloud 2, 5-6, 10, 22-25, 44
    security threats 18
Common Attack Pattern Enumeration (CAPEC) 318
Common Vulnerabilities and Exposures dictionary (CVE) 197
Common Vulnerability Scoring System (CVSS) 197
Compute Unified Device Architecture (CUDA) 238
Continuity of Care Record (CCR) 335
Cross-Correlative Detection System (CCDS) 199
Cryptographically Generated Address (CGA) 73
Cryptographic Message Syntax(CMS) 50

D

Defense Advanced Research Projects Agency (DARPA) 48
Department of Veterans Affairs (VA) 356
    Veterans Health Information Systems and Technology Architecture (VistA) 356
Distributed Denial of Service (DDoS) 168, 170
Domain Name System (DNS) 49, 160, 162, 181-182
    Berkeley Internet Name Domain (BIND) 162
    DNS Security Extension (DNSSEC) 160-161, 168
Duplicate Address Detection (DAD) 74, 86, 174
Dynamic Host Configuration Protocol (DHCPv6) 161

E

Electronic Health Records (EHR) 336
electronic identities 288, 290, 300-301
    Austrian Citizen Card 59, 288-289, 293-297, 302, 308
    Central Register of Residents (CRR) 300
    Citizen Card Software (CCS) 295
    electronic ID (eID) 289, 293
electronic mandates 289-290, 297-298, 304-305, 307
    Mandate Issuing Service (MIS) 305
    Permission-Based Delegation Model (PBDM) 305
    Role-Based Access Control (RBAC) 305, 334, 336, 339, 359, 361, 364
European Union 290, 292, 294, 308
    EU Signature Directive 292, 294-295

e-voting 124-126, 128, 141
    coercion-resistance 124-128, 136-140, 142, 154-155, 158-159
    eligibility verifiability 125
    inalterability 125
    non-reusability 125, 142
    Polling booth-based Electronic Voting Scheme (PEVS) 124-125, 128
    remote 125
e-voting attacks
    forced-abstention attack 125, 128, 133, 142
    randomization attack 125, 142
    simulation attack 125, 142

G

General Purpose computation on Graphics Processing Units (GPGPU) 247
Genetic Information Nondiscrimination Act (GINA) 358

H

handover latency 71, 74, 76-78, 80-81, 94, 99
Health Information Exchange (HIE) 335, 353, 363
Health Information Technology (HIT) 336, 363
Health Insurance Portability and Accountability Act (HIPAA) 336
homomorphic encryption 21, 37, 43
hypervisor 9, 14, 16, 18, 23-24, 43, 200-202, 204

I

identity ecosystem 288, 290, 293, 296-298, 300-301, 307
Identity Management (IDM) 33
Image Cipher Algorithm based on Lorenz (ICAL) 111
Infrastructure as a Service (Iaas) 2, 5, 28, 30, 43
Integrity Checking and Restoring (ICAR) 192
Internet Control Message Protocol (ICMP) 165
internet e-mail
    Certificate Revocation List (CRL) 50, 181
    Delivery Status Notification (DSN) 51
    Mail eXchange (MX) 49
    Message Disposition Notification (MDN) 51
    Public Key Infrastructure Exchange (PKIX) 50
Intrusion Detection System (IDS) 184, 212
    active verification 219
    alert correlation 197, 204, 210, 220-221, 230-234, 236
    alert verification 216-217, 219-220, 224, 229-231, 236
    Cloud IDS 186, 196
    Collaborative IDS (CIDS) 195
    Host-based IDS (HIDS) 184-185, 212, 215
    Network-based IDS (NIDS) 185, 215
IP Security (IPsec) 87

M

malware
    detection 239
    Run-Time Malware Analysis System (RMAS) 243
Maxima Detection System (MDS) 199
Mobile Ad-Hoc Network (MANET) 81
Mobile Nodes (MN) 71
Mobility Access Gateway (MAG) 80
Mobility Anchor Point (MAP) 77
Multipurpose Internet Mail Extensions (MIME) 47

N

Neighbor Discovery Protocol (NDP) 74, 86, 160-161, 163-164
    SEcure Neighbor Discovery (SEND) 75, 86, 95, 172
Neighbor Unreachability Detection (NUD) 74
Network Mobility (NEMO) 81-82, 95

O

Open Federated Environment for Leveraging of Identity and Authorization (OFELIA) 266
Open Web Application Security Project (OWASP) 318

P

Parallel Failureless Aho-Corasick algorithm (PFAC) 253
Paranoid Android (PA) 201
Personal Health Assistant (PHA) 337, 344, 346, 359
Personal Health Records (PHR) 336, 363
Personal Identifiable Information (PII) 363
Platform as a Service (PaaS) 2, 5, 44
Policy Administration Point (PAP) 342

Index

Policy Decision Point (PDP) 342
Policy Enforcement Point (PEP) 342
Pseudorandom Number Generator (PRNG) 106, 110
Public Key Infrastructure (PKI) 76, 86, 181, 278

R

Regulatory Investigatory Powers Act (RIPA) 14
Return-Routability (RR) protocol 73

S

Security Assertion Markup Language (SAML) 23, 44, 287, 308
Security Information and Event Management (SIEM) system 185, 188-189
Service-Level Agreements (SLA) 3
Service-Oriented Architecture (SOA) 22, 28
Software as a Service (SaaS) 2, 4, 44
Standard Development Organization (SDO) 22
    Alliance for Telecommunications Industry Solutions (ATIS) 32
    Association for Retail Technology Standards (ARTS) 31, 36
    Cloud Security Alliance (CSA) 25, 37
    Distributed Management Task Force (DMTF) 26
    European Telecommunications Standards Institute (ETSI) 30, 56, 62
    Institute of Electrical and Electronics Engineers (IEEE) 31, 38
    International Telecommunication Union (ITU) 29
    Internet Engineering Task Force (IETF) 32, 50, 72, 95-98, 168
    Object Management Group (OMG) 30
    Open Cloud Consortium (OCC) 27
    Open Grid Forum (OGF) 27
    Organization for the Advancement of Structured Information Standards (OASIS) 28
    Storage Networking Industry Association (SNIA) 27
Stateless Address AutoConfiguration (SLAAC) 181-182
Stateless Address Auto-Configuration (SLAAC) 74
Substitutable Medical Apps, Reusable Technologies (SMART) 364

T

Timeout Detection and Recovery (TDR) 248
Transaction SIGnature (TSIG) 160-161, 171
Trusted Computing Group (TCG) 9, 40
Trusted Platform Module (TPM) 9, 44
Trusted Third Party (TTP) 47, 53, 70

U

User Datagram Protocol (UDP) 167

V

Virtual Machine (VM) 9

W

Webinos project 312
    Personal Zone Hub (PZH) 312
    Personal Zone Proxy (PZP) 312
    Web Runtime (WRT) 312
Web Services Description Language (WSDL) 34, 45
Windows Driver Model (WDM) 248
Wireless Sensor Networks (WSN) 103

X

XML Role-Slice Diagram (XRSD) 364
XML Schema Class Diagram (XSCD) 340-341, 359, 364